Government Budget Forecasting

Theory and Practice

PUBLIC ADMINISTRATION AND PUBLIC POLICY

A Comprehensive Publication Program

EDITOR-IN-CHIEF

EVAN M. BERMAN
Huey McElveen Distinguished Professor
Louisiana State University
Public Administration Institute
Baton Rouge, Louisiana

Founding Editor

JACK RABIN
Professor of Public Administration and Public Policy
The Pennsylvania State University—Harrisburg
School of Public Affairs
Middletown, Pennsylvania

1. *Public Administration as a Developing Discipline,* Robert T. Golembiewski
2. *Comparative National Policies on Health Care,* Milton I. Roemer, M.D.
3. *Exclusionary Injustice: The Problem of Illegally Obtained Evidence,* Steven R. Schlesinger
5. *Organization Development in Public Administration,* edited by Robert T. Golembiewski and William B. Eddy
7. *Approaches to Planned Change,* Robert T. Golembiewski
8. *Program Evaluation at HEW,* edited by James G. Abert
9. *The States and the Metropolis,* Patricia S. Florestano and Vincent L. Marando
11. *Changing Bureaucracies: Understanding the Organization before Selecting the Approach,* William A. Medina
12. *Handbook on Public Budgeting and Financial Management,* edited by Jack Rabin and Thomas D. Lynch
15. *Handbook on Public Personnel Administration and Labor Relations,* edited by Jack Rabin, Thomas Vocino, W. Bartley Hildreth, and Gerald J. Miller
19. *Handbook of Organization Management,* edited by William B. Eddy
22. *Politics and Administration: Woodrow Wilson and American Public Administration,* edited by Jack Rabin and James S. Bowman
23. *Making and Managing Policy: Formulation, Analysis, Evaluation,* edited by G. Ronald Gilbert
25. *Decision Making in the Public Sector,* edited by Lloyd G. Nigro
26. *Managing Administration,* edited by Jack Rabin, Samuel Humes, and Brian S. Morgan
27. *Public Personnel Update,* edited by Michael Cohen and Robert T. Golembiewski

28. *State and Local Government Administration,* edited by Jack Rabin and Don Dodd
29. *Public Administration: A Bibliographic Guide to the Literature,* Howard E. McCurdy
31. *Handbook of Information Resource Management,* edited by Jack Rabin and Edward M. Jackowski
32. *Public Administration in Developed Democracies: A Comparative Study,* edited by Donald C. Rowat
33. *The Politics of Terrorism: Third Edition,* edited by Michael Stohl
34. *Handbook on Human Services Administration,* edited by Jack Rabin and Marcia B. Steinhauer
36. *Ethics for Bureaucrats: An Essay on Law and Values, Second Edition,* John A. Rohr
37. *The Guide to the Foundations of Public Administration,* Daniel W. Martin
39. *Terrorism and Emergency Management: Policy and Administration,* William L. Waugh, Jr.
40. *Organizational Behavior and Public Management: Second Edition,* Michael L. Vasu, Debra W. Stewart, and G. David Garson
43. *Government Financial Management Theory,* Gerald J. Miller
46. *Handbook of Public Budgeting,* edited by Jack Rabin
49. *Handbook of Court Administration and Management,* edited by Steven W. Hays and Cole Blease Graham, Jr.
50. *Handbook of Comparative Public Budgeting and Financial Management,* edited by Thomas D. Lynch and Lawrence L. Martin
53. *Encyclopedia of Policy Studies: Second Edition,* edited by Stuart S. Nagel
54. *Handbook of Regulation and Administrative Law,* edited by David H. Rosenbloom and Richard D. Schwartz
55. *Handbook of Bureaucracy,* edited by Ali Farazmand
56. *Handbook of Public Sector Labor Relations,* edited by Jack Rabin, Thomas Vocino, W. Bartley Hildreth, and Gerald J. Miller
57. *Practical Public Management,* Robert T. Golembiewski
58. *Handbook of Public Personnel Administration,* edited by Jack Rabin, Thomas Vocino, W. Bartley Hildreth, and Gerald J. Miller
60. *Handbook of Debt Management,* edited by Gerald J. Miller
61. *Public Administration and Law: Second Edition,* David H. Rosenbloom and Rosemary O'Leary
62. *Handbook of Local Government Administration,* edited by John J. Gargan
63. *Handbook of Administrative Communication,* edited by James L. Garnett and Alexander Kouzmin
64. *Public Budgeting and Finance: Fourth Edition,* edited by Robert T. Golembiewski and Jack Rabin
67. *Handbook of Public Finance,* edited by Fred Thompson and Mark T. Green
68. *Organizational Behavior and Public Management: Third Edition,* Michael L. Vasu, Debra W. Stewart, and G. David Garson
69. *Handbook of Economic Development,* edited by Kuotsai Tom Liou
70. *Handbook of Health Administration and Policy,* edited by Anne Osborne Kilpatrick and James A. Johnson

72. *Handbook on Taxation,* edited by W. Bartley Hildreth and James A. Richardson
73. *Handbook of Comparative Public Administration in the Asia-Pacific Basin,* edited by Hoi-kwok Wong and Hon S. Chan
74. *Handbook of Global Environmental Policy and Administration,* edited by Dennis L. Soden and Brent S. Steel
75. *Handbook of State Government Administration,* edited by John J. Gargan
76. *Handbook of Global Legal Policy,* edited by Stuart S. Nagel
78. *Handbook of Global Economic Policy,* edited by Stuart S. Nagel
79. *Handbook of Strategic Management: Second Edition,* edited by Jack Rabin, Gerald J. Miller, and W. Bartley Hildreth
80. *Handbook of Global International Policy,* edited by Stuart S. Nagel
81. *Handbook of Organizational Consultation: Second Edition,* edited by Robert T. Golembiewski
82. *Handbook of Global Political Policy,* edited by Stuart S. Nagel
83. *Handbook of Global Technology Policy,* edited by Stuart S. Nagel
84. *Handbook of Criminal Justice Administration,* edited by M. A. DuPont-Morales, Michael K. Hooper, and Judy H. Schmidt
85. *Labor Relations in the Public Sector: Third Edition,* edited by Richard C. Kearney
86. *Handbook of Administrative Ethics: Second Edition,* edited by Terry L. Cooper
87. *Handbook of Organizational Behavior: Second Edition,* edited by Robert T. Golembiewski
88. *Handbook of Global Social Policy,* edited by Stuart S. Nagel and Amy Robb
89. *Public Administration: A Comparative Perspective, Sixth Edition,* Ferrel Heady
90. *Handbook of Public Quality Management,* edited by Ronald J. Stupak and Peter M. Leitner
91. *Handbook of Public Management Practice and Reform,* edited by Kuotsai Tom Liou
93. *Handbook of Crisis and Emergency Management,* edited by Ali Farazmand
94. *Handbook of Comparative and Development Public Administration: Second Edition,* edited by Ali Farazmand
95. *Financial Planning and Management in Public Organizations,* Alan Walter Steiss and Emeka O. Cyprian Nwagwu
96. *Handbook of International Health Care Systems,* edited by Khi V. Thai, Edward T. Wimberley, and Sharon M. McManus
97. *Handbook of Monetary Policy,* edited by Jack Rabin and Glenn L. Stevens
98. *Handbook of Fiscal Policy,* edited by Jack Rabin and Glenn L. Stevens
99. *Public Administration: An Interdisciplinary Critical Analysis,* edited by Eran Vigoda
100. *Ironies in Organizational Development: Second Edition, Revised and Expanded,* edited by Robert T. Golembiewski
101. *Science and Technology of Terrorism and Counterterrorism,* edited by Tushar K. Ghosh, Mark A. Prelas, Dabir S. Viswanath, and Sudarshan K. Loyalka

102. *Strategic Management for Public and Nonprofit Organizations,* Alan Walter Steiss
103. *Case Studies in Public Budgeting and Financial Management: Second Edition,* edited by Aman Khan and W. Bartley Hildreth
104. *Handbook of Conflict Management,* edited by William J. Pammer, Jr. and Jerri Killian
105. *Chaos Organization and Disaster Management,* Alan Kirschenbaum
106. *Handbook of Gay, Lesbian, Bisexual, and Transgender Administration and Policy,* edited by Wallace Swan
107. *Public Productivity Handbook: Second Edition,* edited by Marc Holzer
108. *Handbook of Developmental Policy Studies,* edited by Gedeon M. Mudacumura, Desta Mebratu and M. Shamsul Haque
109. *Bioterrorism in Medical and Healthcare Administration,* Laure Paquette
110. *International Public Policy and Management: Policy Learning Beyond Regional, Cultural, and Political Boundaries,* edited by David Levi-Faur and Eran Vigoda-Gadot
111. *Handbook of Public Information Systems, Second Edition,* edited by G. David Garson
112. *Handbook of Public Sector Economics,* edited by Donijo Robbins
113. *Handbook of Public Administration and Policy in the European Union,* edited by M. Peter van der Hoek
114. *Nonproliferation Issues for Weapons of Mass Destruction,* Mark A. Prelas and Michael S. Peck
115. *Common Ground, Common Future: Moral Agency in Public Administration, Professions, and Citizenship,* Charles Garofalo and Dean Geuras
116. *Handbook of Organization Theory and Management: The Philosophical Approach, Second Edition,* edited by Thomas D. Lynch and Peter L. Cruise
117. *International Development Governance,* edited by Ahmed Shafiqul Huque and Habib Zafarullah
118. *Sustainable Development Policy and Administration,* edited by Gedeon M. Mudacumura, Desta Mebratu, and M. Shamsul Haque
119. *Public Financial Management,* edited by Howard A. Frank
120. *Handbook of Juvenile Justice: Theory and Practice,* edited by Barbara Sims and Pamela Preston
121. *Emerging Infectious Diseases and the Threat to Occupational Health in the U.S. and Canada,* edited by William Charney
122. *Handbook of Technology Management in Public Administration,* edited by David Greisler and Ronald J. Stupak
123. *Handbook of Decision Making,* edited by Göktuğ Morçöl
124. *Handbook of Public Administration, Third Edition,* edited by Jack Rabin, W. Bartley Hildreth, and Gerald J. Miller
125. *Handbook of Public Policy Analysis,* edited by Frank Fischer, Gerald J. Miller, and Mara S. Sidney
126. *Elements of Effective Governance: Measurement, Accountability and Participation,* edited by Kathe Callahan
127. *American Public Service: Radical Reform and the Merit System,* edited by James S. Bowman and Jonathan P. West
128. *Handbook of Transportation Policy and Administration,* edited by Jeremy Plant

129. *The Art and Practice of Court Administration,* Alexander B. Aikman
130. *Handbook of Globalization, Governance, and Public Administration,* edited by Ali Farazmand and Jack Pinkowski
131. *Handbook of Globalization and the Environment,* edited by Khi V. Thai, Dianne Rahm, and Jerrell D. Coggburn
132. *Personnel Management in Government: Politics and Process, Sixth Edition,* Norma M. Riccucci and Katherine C. Naff
133. *Handbook of Police Administration,* edited by Jim Ruiz and Don Hummer
134. *Handbook of Research Methods in Public Administration, Second Edition,* edited by Kaifeng Yang and Gerald J. Miller
135. *Social and Economic Control of Alcohol: The 21st Amendment in the 21st Century,* edited by Carole L. Jurkiewicz and Murphy J. Painter
136. *Government Public Relations: A Reader,* edited by Mordecai Lee
137. *Handbook of Military Administration,* edited by Jeffrey A. Weber and Johan Eliasson
138. *Disaster Management Handbook,* edited by Jack Pinkowski
139. *Homeland Security Handbook,* edited by Jack Pinkowski
140. *Health Capital and Sustainable Socioeconomic Development,* edited by Patricia A. Cholewka and Mitra M. Motlagh
141. *Handbook of Administrative Reform: An International Perspective,* edited by Jerri Killian and Niklas Eklund
142. *Government Budget Forecasting: Theory and Practice,* edited by Jinping Sun and Thomas D. Lynch

Available Electronically

Principles and Practices of Public Administration, edited by Jack Rabin, Robert F. Munzenrider, and Sherrie M. Bartell

PublicADMINISTRATION*netBASE*

Government Budget Forecasting

Theory and Practice

Edited by

Jinping Sun

California State University, Bakersfield
Bakersfield, California, U.S.A.

Thomas D. Lynch

Louisiana State University
Baton Rouge, Louisiana, U.S.A.

CRC Press
Taylor & Francis Group
Boca Raton London New York

CRC Press is an imprint of the
Taylor & Francis Group, an **informa** business

Auerbach Publications
Taylor & Francis Group
6000 Broken Sound Parkway NW, Suite 300
Boca Raton, FL 33487-2742

Printed in the United States of America on acid-free paper
10 9 8 7 6 5 4 3 2 1

International Standard Book Number-13: 978-1-4200-4582-6 (Hardcover)

Library of Congress Cataloging-in-Publication Data

Government budget forecasting : theory and practice / edited by Jinping Sun and Thomas D. Lynch.
p. cm. -- (Public administration and public policy)
Includes bibliographical references and index.
ISBN-13: 978-1-4200-4582-6
ISBN-10: 1-4200-4582-2
1. Local budgets--United States--States. 2. Local finance--United States--States. I. Sun, Jinping. II. Lynch, Thomas Dexter, 1942-

HJ9147.G68 2008
336.02'730112--dc22 2007036374

Visit the Taylor & Francis Web site at
http://www.taylorandfrancis.com

and the Auerbach Web site at
http://www.auerbach-publications.com

Contents

PART 4: OTHER TOPICS IN BUDGET FORECASTING

Acknowledgments

This book is a product of the work of numerous individuals. We would like to dedicate this book to the late Jack Rabin of The Pennsylvania State University, who over the years was committed to advancing the art and science of public budgeting and was very encouraging and supportive of this project.

We would also like to acknowledge the Taylor & Francis Group's editorial and production team, particularly Richard O'Hanley, Catherine Giacari, Joette Lynch, and Jennifer Genetti for their patience, support, and assistance throughout the process. We are also grateful to the dedicated work of the staff at Macmillan India during the manuscript editing process.

This book draws on the work of more than 20 contributors (practitioners and scholars), who made this intellectual dialogue and collaboration possible. We enjoyed working with them and are grateful for the time and effort they put into this project.

We would also like to thank our colleagues at California State University, Bakersfield and Louisiana State University for their constructive comments. Special thanks to Jeffrey Marshall, a graduate student at California State University, Bakersfield, who provided fine editing and other technical services.

This book would not have been possible without the support of our families. We would like to dedicate this book to Xiaojun Ren and Cynthia E. Lynch who, with love and encouragement, have been very patient and committed to what we are doing.

Jinping Sun
Thomas D. Lynch

Editors

Dr. Jinping Sun is an assistant professor in the Department of Public Policy and Administration at California State University, Bakersfield. Her research interests are in public budgeting and finance.

Reverend Dr. Thomas D. Lynch is a professor of public administration at Louisiana State University. He has written extensively in the area of public budgeting, including the textbook *Public Budgeting in America*, which is in its fifth edition. He is best known for helping to introduce system theory to the public budgeting literature.

Contributors

Carl D. Ekstrom
Department of Political Science
The University of Nebraska
Omaha, Nebraska

Charles Garofalo
Department of Political Science
Texas State University
San Marcos, Texas

Bruce L. Gates
Atkinson Graduate School of Management
Willamette University
Salem, Oregon

Hai Guo
Department of Public Administration and Urban Studies
Andrew Young School of Policy Studies
Georgia State University
Atlanta, Georgia

Shiferaw Gurmu
Department of Economics
Andrew Young School of Policy Studies
Georgia State University
Atlanta, Georgia

Lynn Holland
New York State Division of the Budget
Albany, New York

Robert Ingenito
California Legislative Analyst's Office
Sacramento, California

Craig D. Kammholz
Office of the Comptroller
Milwaukee, Wisconsin

Hilke Kayser
New York State Division of the Budget
Albany, New York

Aman Khan
Department of Political Science
Texas Tech University
Lubbock, Texas

William Earle Klay
Reubin O'D. Askew School of Public Administration and Policy
Florida State University
Tallahassee, Florida

Jim Landers
Office of Fiscal and Management Analysis
Indiana Legislative Services Agency
Indianapolis, Indiana

Thomas D. Lynch
Public Administration Institute
E. J. Ourso College of Business Administration
Louisiana State University
Baton Rouge, Louisiana

Craig S. Maher
Masters of Public Administration Program
The University of Wisconsin
Oshkosh, Wisconsin

Patrick D. Meagher
Minnesota Department of Finance
St. Paul, Minnesota

Robert Megna
New York State Division of the Budget
Albany, New York

John L. Mikesell
School of Public and Environmental Affairs
Indiana University
Bloomington, Indiana

Ray D. Nelson
Marriott School of Management
Brigham Young University
Provo, Utah

John L. Peloquin
Minnesota Department of Finance
St. Paul, Minnesota

Rudolph G. Penner
The Urban Institute
Washington, D.C.

Yuhua Qiao
Political Science Department
Missouri State University
Springfield, Missouri

Nandhini Rangarajan
Department of Political Science
Texas State University
San Marcos, Texas

Christopher G. Reddick
Department of Public Administration
The University of Texas at San Antonio
San Antonio, Texas

James A. Richardson
E. J. Ourso College of Business Administration
Louisiana State University
Baton Rouge, Louisiana

Robert W. Smith
Department of Political Science
Clemson University
Clemson, South Carolina

William J. Smith
Department of Economics
Richards College of Business
University of West Georgia
Carrollton, Georgia

Thomas F. Stinson
Minnesota Department of Finance
St. Paul, Minnesota

Jinping Sun
Department of Public Policy and Administration
School of Business and Public Administration
California State University
Bakersfield, California

Fred Thompson
Atkinson Graduate School of Management
Willamette University
Salem, Oregon

Jon David Vasché
California Legislative Analyst's Office
Sacramento, California

Joseph A. Vonasek
Reubin O'D. Askew School of Public Administration and Policy
Florida State University
Tallahassee, Florida

Sally Wallace
Department of Economics
Andrew Young School of Policy Studies
Georgia State University
Atlanta, Georgia

Brad Williams
California Legislative
Analyst's Office
Sacramento, California

Daniel W. Williams
School of Public Affairs
Baruch College—City University of New York
New York, New York

Katherine G. Willoughby
Department of Public Administration and Urban Studies
Andrew Young School of Policy Studies
Georgia State University
Atlanta, Georgia

John D. Wong
Hugo Wall School of Urban and Public Affairs
Wichita State University
Wichita, Kansas

Qiang Xu
New York State Division of the Budget
Albany, New York

Aziza Zemrani
Public Administration Department
School of Business, Public Administration, and Information Sciences
Long Island University
New York, New York

Chapter 1

Government Budget Forecasting: Improving the State of the Art

Jinping Sun and Thomas D. Lynch

Contents

Revenue and expenditure forecasting are an integral part of government budget process and play an important role in public budgeting and financial management. Despite its significance, budget estimation is often overlooked in the literature. The focus of most public budgeting and finance books is primarily on budgetary politics, processes, or financial management, whereas revenue and expenditure forecasting are covered in certain chapters or sections in some texts (Axelrod 1995, Golembiewski and Rabin 1997, Lee et al. 2003, Lynch and Martin 1993, Mikesell 2003, Rabin 1992, Rabin et al. 1996, Steiss and Nwagwu 2001), and are "reduced to a minuscule or non-existent topic" (Frank and McCollough 1992, p. 1683) in others (Cozzetto et al. 1995, Rubin 2006, Thompson and Green 1998, Wildavsky and Caiden 2003).

Since the 1990s, the situation has improved to a certain extent, with journal articles covering different aspects of revenue or expenditure forecasting. Yet, there is a lack of comprehensive, systematic texts on the theories and practices of budget estimation in the public sector. This book intends to fill the gap by presenting the state of the art of government revenue and expenditure forecasting based on the collaboration between scholars and practitioners.

Specifically, this book has two purposes. The first is to help those interested in public budgeting and finance understand how revenue and expenditure estimation are done theoretically and practically. The second is to stimulate the dialogue and debate among practitioners and academics, so that good forecast practices can be identified and recommendations can be made to enhance revenue and expenditure estimation.

Overview of the Book

This book is divided into four parts. Part 1 covers the theories and practices of revenue and expenditure forecasting at different levels of government in the United States.

- Rudolph Penner describes the federal revenue forecasting process used by the Congressional Budget Office and speculates about the reason for its forecast errors that are serially correlated. He concludes that the uncertainty inherent in the forecasts plays a major role in budget policy debates.
- At the state level, Katherine Willoughby and Hai Guo, using data complied from the 2004 Government Performance Project survey, present an overview of revenue forecasting in U.S. state governments. They find that states using multiple methods including simple trend analysis, linear regression, or consensus forecasting tend to achieve greater accuracy in forecasting revenue, particularly for individual and corporate income taxes and general sales taxes.

  Concerning individual states, James Richardson traces the evolution of revenue forecasting in Louisiana, as a part of its political history, from the boom and bust of the oil and gas industry in the 1970s and 1980s, traditional method of funding state government in the 1990s, to the aftermath of two major hurricanes (Katrina and Rita) in 2005. In addition, the role of the Revenue Estimating Conference in the state's budget process is emphasized. Jon David Vasché et al. provide a comprehensive account of how state revenue and expenditure forecasting are done in the State of California. They examine major entities involved in the forecasting process and specific modeling used in developing estimates of different revenue sources (such as personal income tax, sales and use tax, and corporation tax) and spending areas (such as K-14 education).

  Regarding the estimation of individual revenue sources, Xu et al. and Stinson et al. explain in detail how to forecast personal income tax in

New York and Minnesota, respectively, by breaking down the components of income tax forecasts in each state and examining in depth the models used in each step. In addition to personal income tax, casino gaming has been legalized in 20 states to augment state revenues. Focusing on the State of Indiana, Jim Landers provides an overview of casino gaming activity in Indiana and discusses specific methods and issues in forecasting casino tax revenue.

On the expenditure aspect, Shiferaw Gurmu and William Smith discuss various approaches to forecasting welfare caseloads with an emphasis on Temporary Assistance for Needy Families (TANF) program, and apply them to Georgia TANF data. They also conduct short- and long-term forecasts for TANF caseloads using a dynamic model under different specification choices, and assess the accuracy of the projections.

To evaluate how states perform in budget estimation, Jinping Sun studies the revenue forecasting process and performance of three major forecasting agencies in New York. She concludes that the state's revenue forecasting process meets the majority of criteria established by national professional organizations; the three major forecasting agencies did a good job of accurately forecasting state revenues from fiscal year (FY) 1995–1996 to FY2002–2003; and the three agencies' forecasts are good by other criteria such as credibility, timeliness, and helping improve decision making.

- At the local level, John Wong develops a methodology for small and medium-sized communities to estimate the base of a new local sales tax using detailed census data. This method is applied to the City of Derby, Kansas, and is 97.7 percent accurate in forecasting taxable retail sales.

  Craig Kammholz and Craig Maher conduct a case study of revenue forecasting in the City of Milwaukee, Wisconsin, where the official revenue forecasting responsibility rests with the Comptroller's office. They find that this arrangement not only provides additional resources for revenue estimation, but also protects the city from political manipulation. Further, Milwaukee performs well when compared to nine peer cities in terms of forecast accuracy and bond ratings.

  To evaluate local government revenue forecasting, Christopher Reddick surveys city government finance directors in Texas. The results indicate that revenue forecasting is mainly an internal process and there is little participation from citizens or city council. In addition, cities have a small forecasting staff and typically use few prior years of data and expert and trend forecasting for revenue estimation.

- With a different focus, Aman Khan introduces a comprehensive model to forecast the financial condition of a government's enterprise operation based on its assets, liabilities, and net assets (fund balance) situation.

Daniel Williams looks into data preparation for forecasting with the belief that well-prepared data can help in getting reliable forecasts. Basic steps such as data editing, adjusting for inflation, and dealing with seasonality are discussed in detail in this chapter.

Consensus budget forecasting is commonly used across the states, and chapters in Part 2 pertain to this practice.

- William Earle Klay and Joseph Vonasek attempt to explore why consensus forecasting contributes to greater accuracy. They examine theories including the questioning of underlying assumptions and combining of forecasts, and present a historical study of consensus forecasting in the State of Florida—a state with more than three decades of experience in consensus revenue and expenditure forecasting.
- Yuhua Qiao, on the other hand, conducts a telephone and e-mail survey of budget offices in 27 states regarding the extent of use, implementation, and performance of consensus revenue forecasting. She finds that states vary in how to implement consensus revenue forecasting in terms of structure, legal basis, funds to cover, and binding abilities. Consistent with Klay and Vonasek's findings, consensus forecasting can improve forecast accuracy.
- The significance of consensus forecasting is further augmented in two case studies. John Mikesell's study of Indiana's consensus revenue forecasting system reveals that rather than overemphasizing sophisticated forecasting methods, a politically balanced, transparent, and trusted process can produce accurate revenue forecasts that all participants, regardless of their political affiliation, accept as the base for budget appropriations. John Wong and Carl Ekstrom present an overview of the consensus revenue estimating process in the State of Kansas, including institutional arrangements for estimating state government revenues, and specific techniques used by individual Consensus Revenue Estimating Group members in economic and revenue forecasts. They conclude that the consensus process brings professionalism and more rigorous analysis to revenue forecasting and improves forecast accuracy.

There are always uncertainty and risks involved in budget estimation. Part 3 illustrates how to reduce uncertainty and mitigate risks in budget forecasting.

- Xu et al. present methods for assessing forecast risks (including Monte Carlo simulation and fan charts), introduce symmetric and asymmetric forms for the forecaster's loss function, and discuss how to choose an optimal forecast under a given loss function and distribution of risks.
- Fred Thompson and Bruce Gates discuss risk management tools that states can use to achieve structural fiscal balance and manage cyclical fiscal imbalance, which include Monte Carlo simulation, present value cash flow analysis, target budgeting, portfolio analysis, hedging, self-insurance, and self-insurance pools

based on simple mean-variance analysis. They argue that these tools are better than shifting financial obligations to other jurisdictions, borrowing from enterprise and trust funds, and other approaches employed by state governments. They then use the case of Oregon to demonstrate how these tools can help governments manage financial risks.

- To aid budget forecasting and analysis, Ray Nelson proposes an integrated methodology that combines theories from tax policy and financial market risk management literature, and considers state sales, income, business, and other tax revenues as a portfolio. This methodology allows forecasters to better assess and predict alternative business cycle scenarios, and helps policy makers assess the implications of tax changes on base revenue levels and noncyclical and cyclical growth.

Other topics related to budget forecasting are discussed in Part 4.

- Two chapters concern ethics of budget forecasting. Robert Smith identifies ethical dilemmas in budget forecasting in the public sector, examines their relationship to ethics principles, and presents a code of ethics as guidance for budget forecasting. Charles Garofalo and Nandhini Rangarajan explore the role of transparency in the ethical environment of revenue estimation. They examine individual and institutional resistance to increased transparency and propose three approaches to increase transparency in revenue forecasting: acknowledging the moral agency of revenue forecasters, creating criteria for deciding information disclosure, and adopting a consensus forecasting.
- Different from forecast practices in the United States, budget estimation in other countries has its own contexts and characteristics. Sally Wallace develops a methodology to integrate fiscal architecture (impact of economic, demographic, and institutional changes) into budget forecasting and examines the impact of these changes on revenue forecasting and expenditure needs. She applies this methodology to India to show how it helps in improving the accuracy of budget forecasts in developing countries. Aziza Zemrani looks at the forecasting practice in Morocco and analyzes various issues, particularly transparency and accountability, in the process.

Common Themes

Although the exact budget forecasting theories and practices vary from time to time and from government to government, two themes run throughout the chapters.

- Government budget forecasting is both a science and an art; it is technical and political. As the chapters show, budget forecasting involves various participants who bring their expertise, experience, and values into the process.

It not only concerns the development and use of sophisticated forecasting methods, but it also reflects the preferences and relative power of different participants to influence the forecasts for a particular agenda. The process is highly dynamic and political, and has far-reaching policy implications.

- Budget forecasts are rarely 100 percent accurate. To narrow the range of error, forecasters can use technically sound methods and other approaches. Several chapters of this book indicate that institutional arrangements matter and contribute to greater accuracy. The institution of an independent forecasting office, the adoption of consensus forecasting, and the establishment of a transparent process can help in generating accurate forecasts and, more importantly, in bringing trust and accountability to the budget process.

Future Research

Revenue and expenditure forecasting are essential elements of the public budget process. Although chapters of this book cover a wide range of theories and practices of government budget forecasting, some topics remain untapped or are not given sufficient attention. In particular, the following areas warrant further investigation:

- Revenue and expenditure estimation are interrelated in the budget process. The attention devoted to revenue forecasting, however, far outweighs the attention given to expenditure forecasting, and there is limited research on how to balance or integrate the two. Further research can be done on expenditure forecasting and how the interplay between revenue and expenditure forecasting influences the budget process.
- As important components of government budget process, capital budgeting and long-term budgeting have their own characteristics and can have considerable future impact on the provision of public services. Therefore, special concern in the forecasting of capital budgets and long-term budgets is warranted.
- The estimation of volatile revenue sources (e.g., personal income taxes) presents unique challenges to forecasters and policy makers. In addition to the analytical tools proposed in this book (e.g., tax portfolios and risk assessment), government may restructure its revenue system. For instance, a highly unstable revenue source can be put in a special fund to help finance long-term programs such as debt and pension liability. Future studies can explore the feasibility of alternative approaches to improve budget estimation.
- Budget forecasting in other countries has its own unique contexts, processes, and results. Two chapters of this book discuss budget estimation in developing countries, one in India and the other in Morocco. Future research may look into the international context and explore budget forecasting practices in

other parts of the world. For instance, countries in the European Union share common features (e.g., having one agency to oversee their monetary policy) and in the mean time have their own distinct political, fiscal, and other attributes. Case studies or comparative studies can shed light on and enrich the literature of budget forecasting.

References

Axelrod, D. 1995. *Budgeting for Modern Government* (2nd ed.). New York: St. Martin's Press.

Cozzetto, D. A., M. G. Kweit, and R. W. Kweit. 1995. *Public Budgeting: Politics, Institutions, and Processes.* White Plains, New York: Longman.

Frank, H. A. and J. McCollough. 1992. Municipal forecasting practice: "Demand" and "supply" side perspectives. *International Journal of Public Administration* 15(9): 1669–1695.

Golembiewski, R. T. and J. Rabin (Eds.). 1997. *Public Budgeting and Finance* (4th ed.). New York: Marcel Dekker.

Lee, R. D., R. W. Johnson, and P. G. Joyce. 2003. *Public Budgeting Systems* (7th ed.). Sudbury, MA: Jones and Bartlett Publishers Inc.

Lynch, T. D. and L. L. Martin. 1993. *Handbook of Comparative Public Budgeting and Financial Management.* New York: Marcel Dekker.

Mikesell, J. L. 2003. *Fiscal Administration: Analysis and Applications for the Public Sector* (6th ed.). Belmont, CA: Wadsworth/Thomson Learning.

Rabin, J. (Ed.). 1992. *Handbook of Public Budgeting.* New York: Marcel Dekker.

Rabin, J., W. B. Hildreth, and G. J. Miller (Eds.). 1996. *Budgeting: Formulation and Execution.* Athens, Georgia: Carl Vinson Institute of Government, The University of Georgia.

Rubin, I. S. 2006. *The Politics of Public Budgeting: Getting and Spending, Borrowing and Balancing* (5th ed.). Washington: CQ Press.

Steiss, A. W. and E. O. Nwagwu. 2001. *Financial Planning and Management in Public Organizations.* New York: Marcel Dekker.

Thompson, F. and M. T. Green. 1998. *Handbook of Public Finance.* New York: Marcel Dekker.

Wildavsky, A. and N. Caiden. 2003. *The New Politics of the Budgetary Process* (5th ed.). Chicago, IL: Longman.

FORECAST PRACTICES

1

Chapter 2

Federal Revenue Forecasting

Rudolph G. Penner

Contents

Introduction

Federal revenue forecasts play an important role in shaping the national debate over future spending and tax policy. Federal revenue forecasts are often very wrong, which is not because the technicians making them are unskilled. In fact, they are generally highly talented, dedicated civil servants. The basic problem is that revenue forecasting, like hurricane forecasting or earthquake forecasting, is very difficult.

The forecasting process consists of many steps and errors that are likely to occur in each one. A series of small errors that happen to go in the same direction can make a forecast look incompetent. Large errors that offset each other—even those that could signal incompetence—can make a forecast look brilliant.

The Forecasting Process

I shall focus on the forecasting process as it exists at the Congressional Budget Office (CBO). Technically, the approach is very similar at the U.S. Treasury, but occasionally, the process in the executive branch is warped by political strategizing that differs from administration to administration. I shall return to this topic later.

The CBO and the executive branch typically provide two forecasts per year. The former usually reports to the Congress in January and August while the latter reports in January or early February and in July. CBO's January forecast is most important because the macroeconomic assumptions that it generates are used to derive the spending and revenue baseline that will be used by Congress throughout the year. Those same assumptions are often important in estimating the effect of tax policy changes on revenues or program changes on outlays. The CBO has used a time horizon of ten years for their economic and budget forecast in recent years, but the Congress most often uses a time horizon of five years for formulating their budget resolution. The administration has recently emphasized a five-year horizon, but provides some estimates for a ten-year period.

All short-run revenue forecasts must begin with an economic forecast. CBO staff carefully tracks the economy all year long, but the formal forecasting process for the January report generally begins in the fall by examining the forecasts generated by private forecasting companies, such as Macroeconomic Advisers. These forecasting companies use macroeconomic models that assume the structure of the economy to be constant. This assumption has been challenged by the so-called Lucas critique. Lucas (1976) and other rational expectations theorists argue that the structure of the economy is constantly evolving and attempts to estimate the parameters of equations that assume a constant structure can lead to a meaningless result.

But traditional macro models have one huge advantage. They contain a number of identities that must add up. For example, gross investment must equal gross domestic and foreign saving plus a statistical discrepancy. There are definitional linkages between the working age population, the labor force participation rate, and employment plus unemployment. The number of hours worked is linked to the Gross Domestic Product (GDP) through labor productivity. Such identities force the forecast to be logical.

Nonetheless, no one would blindly run a macro model and uncritically accept the result. The analysis is almost always leavened by a large dose of judgment.

For example, a housing specialist may decide that the model's forecast of residential investment is too low. The specialist can then modify the relevant equations to make it come out higher. But this change will reverberate through the model's definitional statements and may require domestic saving to be higher than that is reasonable. The analyst may then have to reexamine his or her modifications to the model.

Other statistical approaches, such as vector autoregression or other types of time series analysis, do not provide the same kind of logical check on judgmental adjustments to a forecast. Consequently, old-fashioned macro models continue to play a very important role in the forecasting process. Perhaps, one can interpret judgmental adjustments to equations as a recognition that the structure of the economy is constantly changing.

The short-run January forecast extends only to the end of the next calendar year. That is to say, the January 1990 forecast is extended through the period until the end of 1991 calendar year. CBO calls its longer run estimates as "projections." It is explicitly noted that there is no attempt to forecast the ups and downs of the business cycle in the longer run. Instead, CBO puts much effort into deriving the GDP path that the economy would be on with full employment. Defining "full employment" is no easy task, but CBO tries to estimate the level of the unemployment rate that would be neither inflationary nor deflationary. Much controversy surrounds such estimates. Having estimated the path consistent with this unemployment rate, usually called the "potential GDP" path, it is usually assumed that the economy will approach it between the end of the forecast period and five years out.

The economic forecast initially focuses on the product side of the National Income and Product Accounts (NIPA). That is to say, various types of consumption and private investment are analyzed as well as exports, imports, and purchases of the federal, state, and local government. However, the product side of the accounts is of little help when it comes to forecasting government revenue. For that, one has to forecast the different types of income generated by the production of final goods and services.

Theoretically, the income side of the NIPA should exactly equal the product side. However, no government statistician can measure either side with complete accuracy. Consequently, there is always a statistical discrepancy that jumps around from year to year. Usually, the product side exceeds the income side slightly and CBO assumes that the statistical discrepancy will revert to its average, over the period 1950–2005, or to about 1 percent of the product side (Congressional Budget Office 2006a). The assumed speed of the reversion depends on how far recent statistical discrepancies diverge from the historical mean. In 2006, the income side of the accounts grew faster than the product side and the discrepancy has been smaller than usual. Using the rule of thumb that the discrepancy will return to its historical average will imply that revenues will grow more slowly than the product side of the GDP unless there is also a change in the distribution of total income among tax brackets that raises the average tax rate.

The need to project a statistical discrepancy is just one of many difficult challenges facing revenue forecasters. It is like having to forecast a random number.

The largest share of total income goes to labor. The labor share tends to be nearly constant over time, although it can deviate from its historical average in either direction for several years in a row. The CBO assumption is that it will revert to its historical mean. The labor share is then divided into components. The most important consists of wages, salaries, and supplements. Supplements include payroll taxes and the cost of employee benefits such as health insurance. Total compensation is assumed to vary with employment, productivity, and inflation. The revenue yield per dollar of compensation clearly depends on how it is divided among wages, payroll taxes, and untaxed benefits.

The forecast of untaxed fringe benefits depends on, among other things, the rate of health cost growth and rules governing pension contributions. Aggregate wages depend on the forecast of hours worked and wage rates. The amount of income tax revenue derived from wages depends upon their distribution among various tax brackets. Withheld income taxes on wages are forecast separately from nonwithheld estimated taxes and taxes on self-employment income.

The forecast of Social Security payroll tax revenues depends on the forecast of total wages and also on their distribution because of the ceiling applying to Social Security payroll taxes. Payroll taxes for hospital insurance (Medicare) do not have a ceiling. Social insurance taxes accounted for 37 percent of total revenues in 2005.

Proprietors' income is estimated in two ways. The first method measures it as a residual. Wages, salaries, and supplements are forecast as described earlier and subtracted from the labor's overall share. It is assumed that 65 percent of proprietors' income accrues to labor; so the residual is divided by 0.65 to get total proprietors' income. As a check on this residual estimate, CBO analyzes recent trends from tax returns of farmers and professionals, but the data is of low quality. There is much tax evasion in the sole proprietor segment of the economy. The Bureau of Economic Analysis (BEA) (Congressional Budget Office 2006a) assumes that underreporting has equaled about 50 percent of nonfarm proprietors' income over the past ten years and has been as high as 70 percent. Low quality data and significant revisions of historical data are common and often conspire to make life miserable for the revenue forecaster.

After the wage share has been estimated, other income must be divided up into capital's share, the statistical discrepancy, surplus less subsidies of government enterprises, and taxes on production, such as sales taxes. Components other than the capital share are forecast independently. Numerous components of the capital share are also estimated independently. These include net income from abroad, depreciation, interest payments, proprietors' capital income, and rents and royalties. Finally, corporate profits are estimated as a residual, which is checked against private forecasts and sometimes altered. Then other components of income have to be adjusted upward or downward to be sure that everything adds up.

The concept of profits that comes from this process is known as "economic profits." CBO must also estimate "taxable profits" that are more relevant for estimating corporate tax receipts. To go from economic to taxable profits, they adjust for the difference between economic depreciation and the depreciation allowed for tax purposes and they add capital gains on inventories and other assets. Capital gains are not included in income as measured by the NIPA. Numerous other adjustments are necessary in the process of deriving taxable profits. Corporate tax receipts accounted for 13 percent of total federal revenues in 2005 and are one of the most volatile revenue sources.

Because capital gains are not counted in NIPA's definition of income, they must be estimated separately to estimate capital gains tax revenues from individual and corporate income tax returns. Capital gains are extremely volatile, but it is generally assumed that they will revert to their historical means as a ratio to GDP. The estimate of realized capital gains can be affected by changes in tax policy. For example, it is assumed that realized capital gains will rise following a rate cut. Or if rates are due to rise in the future, as they did between 1986 and 1987, it is assumed that there will be a surge in realizations just before the rate changes.

The individual income tax revenue yield per dollar of personal income depends crucially on how that income is distributed. In recent years, the very rich have become responsible for a higher share of individual income tax receipts partially because income inequality has increased and lower income groups have been taken off the tax rolls by a number of legislative actions. In 1979, the top 1 percent of the income distribution received 9.3 percent of income and paid 18.3 percent of individual tax liabilities. In 2003, their share of income had risen to 14.3 percent and their share of income tax liabilities to 34.6 percent. Because the share of the top group tends to be quite volatile, growing income inequality has added to the difficulty of forecasting individual income tax receipts. In 2000, the income share of the top 1 percent was 17.8 percent, but it was only 13.5 percent by 2002 after the stock market bubble had burst. In 2003, it again rose to 14.3 percent (Congressional Budget Office 2004).

The Forecasting Record

There can be three reasons for deviation of actual revenues from the total forecast. First, the economic forecast was wrong (it always will be in its details). Second, technical factors may distort revenues. For example, forecasters may come close with their macroeconomic forecast, but the revenue forecast may still go awry because income has been incorrectly distributed among various tax brackets. Third, the Congress may have changed the law. This analysis will focus on the sum of economic and technical errors. It is not the responsibility of CBO forecasters to predict legislative actions. The analysis will not explore the relationship between economic and technical errors. This analysis has been done by Kitchen (2003) who convincingly argues that a considerable portion of technical errors can be explained by errors in the economic forecast.

The analysis will examine forecast errors using three time horizons. The first looks at the errors in the forecast made early in the calendar year (usually January) for the fiscal year ending at the end of the following September. That is to say, the errors for forecasts are published when the fiscal year is already over three months old. The second analyzes errors in forecasts made early in the calendar year for the next fiscal year. For example, the analysis considers the error for fiscal year 1985 made in the forecast in early 1984. The third examines errors for the fiscal year five years into the future. For example, the analysis discusses the accuracy of the forecast for the fiscal year 1989 made in the forecast of early 1984.

CBO did not keep records of their errors on a consistent basis until after 1983 and as this is written, the latest year for which data is available is 2005. That implies that we must be satisfied with very small samples. The sample size is 22 for within fiscal year forecasts and for forecasts one year out. For five-year forecasts the sample size is only 17.

Errors within the Fiscal Year

Figure 2.1 illustrates the forecast errors made early in the calendar year for the fiscal year ending at the end of the following September. An error with a positive value means that actual revenues exceeded forecast revenues while a negative number means the reverse.

The average error for the 22-year period is only 0.1 percent of GDP, thus confirming Auerbach's (1999) conclusion that there is no significant positive or negative bias in CBO revenue forecasting. The average absolute error is 0.4 percent of GDP, or almost $50 billion at 2005 levels of GDP. Errors of this size can have important political significance. There are few policy changes that would have that much impact on the budget deficit over such a short period. The largest error occurred in 2002 when revenues were overestimated by 1.1 percent of GDP, or by $111 billion.

Errors for the Next Fiscal Year

The revenue forecast made in January for the fiscal year starting the following September is the most important produced by CBO for it will be used by the Congress for formulating the Budget Resolution for that fiscal year. The errors in that forecast are shown in Figure 2.2.

The average error is only −0.001 percent of GDP. Obviously, there is no significant upward or downward bias in CBO forecasting methods. The average absolute error was 0.8 percent of GDP, or $98 billion at 2005 levels of GDP. Errors of this size indicate that the Congress is often badly misled with regard to the fiscal outlook. It also implies that the deficit outlook is almost always changed more by changes in the forecast than it is by changes in policy.

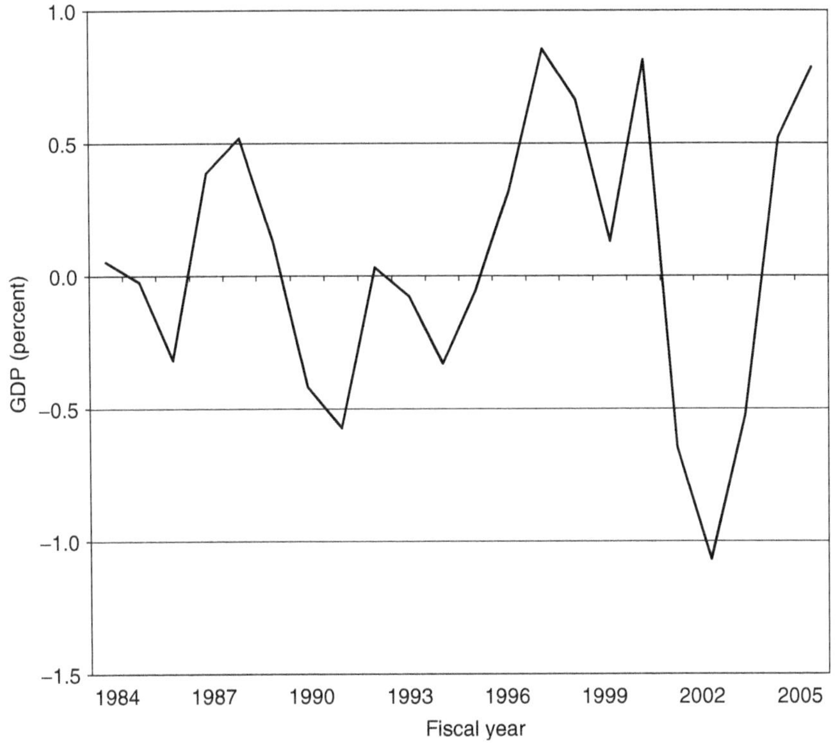

Figure 2.1 Revisions as percentage of GDP, current year projections, 1984–2005.

It is for that reason that budget plans that attempt to hit a specific deficit target in the future are almost certain to fail. Changes in policy cannot keep up with changes in the forecast. This discrepancy is the main reason for the failure of the Gramm–Rudman–Hollings legislation that tried to target deficits in the second half of the 1980s.*

The largest revenue forecasting error was made in January 2001 for fiscal year 2002. Revenues were overestimated by 3.2 percent of GDP, or by $333 billion. It is interesting to speculate whether the tax cut debate of 2001 would have been much different had legislators known that revenues were about to crash. One would think that the tax cut might have been more modest. However, a sizeable portion of the revenue shortfall was caused by the unpredicted recession of 2001 and had the recession been properly forecast it would have strengthened the case for tax cutting. The revenue and deficit forecast had become much more dismal by 2003,

* Not everyone would characterize Gramm–Rudman–Hollings as a failure (see Gramlich 1990).

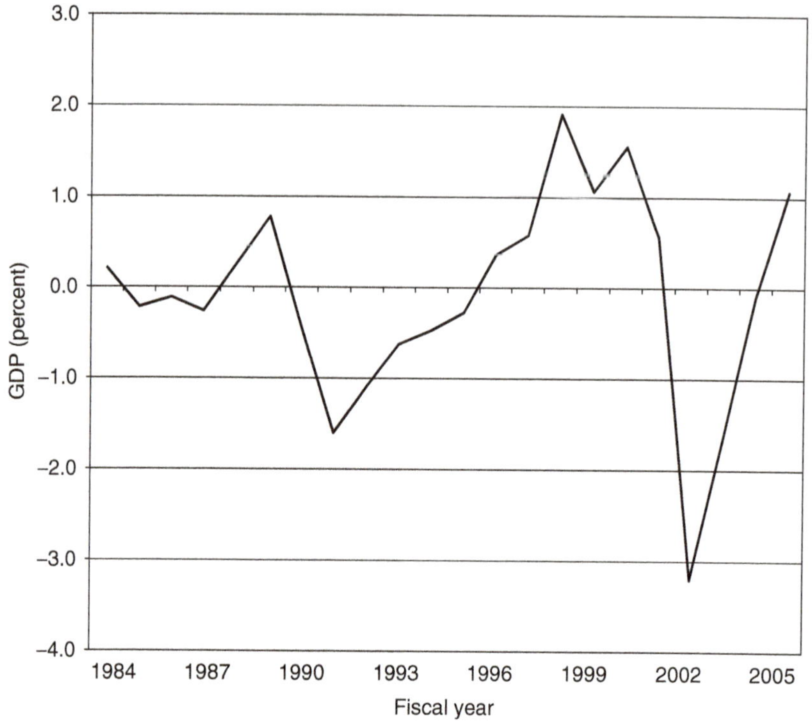

Figure 2.2 Revisions as percentage of GDP, one-year projections, 1984–2005.

but that did not deter the Congress from passing large tax cuts on dividends and capital gains.

Errors in Five-Year Forecasts

As bad as the record is for forecasts with short time horizons, it becomes much worse when one goes out for five-year forecasts. The record is revealed by Figure 2.3. There is, however, no statistically significant bias as the average error is only −0.003 percent of GDP. The average absolute error is 1.6 percent of GDP, or $196 billion at 2005 levels of GDP. The largest error occurred for the year 2000 when actual revenues exceeded the forecast made in 1995 by 3.4 percent of 2000 GDP (i.e. $330 billion).

Curiously, the five-year forecasts for the years 2002 through 2005 appear to be more accurate than the shorter run forecasts made for those years. However, one should not believe that we have suddenly become better at long-term forecasting. In 1997, when the 2002 forecast was formulated, it was recognized that revenues were coming in higher than expected. Forecasts of short-run revenues were then

Figure 2.3 Revisions as percentage of GDP, five-year projections, 1989–2005.

moved upward more than those of longer run revenues. Revenues then unexpectedly plummeted in the early years of the century. Short-term forecasts were adjusted downward, but because the long-run forecast had been kept relatively stable in the period of excess revenues, it looked pretty accurate when revenues started to fall again.

The CBO extended their forecast horizon to ten years starting in 1996. It is too early to do any statistical analysis of ten-year forecast errors because the sample is too small. But it is clear that budget projections for this time horizon have been wildly misleading. For example, the projection of the budget balance for 2007, first made in 1997, had swung through a range of $801 billion by 2000. Because policy changes had reduced the surplus in the interim, the implied economic and technical forecast error was even greater—$844 billion, or 6 percent of GDP. Future results may imply the forecast as an unusual aberration, but we do not know at this point and I would argue that ten-year forecasts are far too unreliable to serve as a basis for formulating a budget resolution that goes out that far.

That is because the Budget Resolution passed by the Congress contains very precise targets for revenues, expenditures, and deficits and ten-year forecasts are not accurate enough to support such precision. Nevertheless, I believe that CBO should continue to do ten-year forecasts because they can be useful for other purposes. For example, they are still useful for providing the economic assumptions used to evaluate the costs or gains from changes in tax and spending policies. One can examine these estimates for ten years even if the Budget Resolution only covers five years. Estimates of the effects of changes in policy are not as sensitive to errors in the economic assumptions as is the estimate of future budget deficits.

The most important reason for extending the time horizon when policy changes are considered is that their long-run effects may differ greatly from their short-run effects. If the revenue loss associated with a particular tax cut grows rapidly through time, the growing losses are likely to be revealed even if the economic assumptions used to evaluate the tax change eventually turn out to have been overly optimistic or pessimistic. That result cannot always be guaranteed, but it is true enough of the time to warrant doing long-run estimates—in some cases, even for longer than ten years. Alternatively, the present value of revenue losses or gains can be estimated for very long periods, but not many laymen understand present values, and a time profile of revenue changes may be more useful.

Serial Correlation of Forecast Errors

A superficial look at Figures 2.1 through 2.3 suggests significant serial correlation in the forecast errors. That is to say, if CBO makes an error in an overly optimistic or pessimistic direction one year, it is highly probable that it will make an error in the same direction the following year.

One indicator of serial correlation is the number of runs of positive and negative errors in a time series. A large number of runs relative to the size of the sample indicate a low serial correlation. For example, if positive and negative errors in a sample alternated year by year, there would be a large number of runs, thus indicating zero serial correlation. If all errors were positive in the first half of the sample and negative in the second half, there would be only two runs and we would say there was an extreme level of serial correlation.

In the sample of errors generated by the January forecasts for the year ending the following September, there are twelve positive errors and ten negative errors in the sample of 22. Wallis and Roberts (1958, p. 569) argue that the sampling distribution of the number of runs can be "sufficiently well approximated by a normal distribution." In this case, the mean of the sampling distribution is expected to be 11.9. The actual number of runs is eight. The probability of finding eight or fewer runs by chance is less than 7 percent, thus suggesting that it is likely that there is something in the forecasting process that generates true serial correlation.

The evidence is even stronger in the forecasts with longer time horizons. In the January forecast for the following fiscal year, there are ten positive errors, twelve negative errors, and only six runs. The probability of finding six or fewer runs by chance is less than 1 percent. In the sample of five-year forecasts, there are only three runs. Sample size of 17 is extremely small, but again the results imply the emergence of so few runs by chance to be less than 1 percent.

Why does serial correlation persist in the errors? One of the most difficult problems facing the revenue forecaster is that he or she must forecast next year's revenue before it is known why last year's forecast went wrong. Data from income tax return dribbles in over time based on samples and preliminary compilations, but the early numbers are often fraught with errors. It is roughly two years from the end of a calendar year until highly reliable income tax return data for that year becomes available.

When faced with an error, the forecaster does not know whether it is because of a temporary aberration or of a fundamental flaw in methodology. If it is the result of an aberration, his or her trusted forecasting techniques will prove much more accurate in the following year. If, however, the error occurs because of a longer-lasting change in the economy, for example, a long-lasting change in the distribution of taxable income, the old techniques will continue to produce the same kind of error. But if there is a lasting change in the economy, the forecaster does not yet have any reliable data to study its nature and therefore, there has to be a strong tendency to assume a temporary aberration. There is, in fact, little choice in the matter.

The forecaster may fudge a bit. Having made an overly optimistic forecast last year, he or she may judgmentally adjust the forecast based on traditional methods down a bit, but usually only a very little bit for reasons to be discussed later.

It was earlier noted that there are many areas in which the forecast depends on a certain variable returning to its historical norm over time. For example, that is true with the statistical discrepancy between the income and product side of the national income accounts. It is also true of the ratio of capital gains to the GDP. There are, in fact, so many areas where a regression to the historical mean is assumed that a detailed study of this assumption is not practical for this chapter, but I would conjecture that there may be a tendency to assume that a variable returns to its mean too quickly. That is to say, aberrations may generally be more persistent than assumed. That will, of course, lead to serial correlation in the errors. But if you change tactics and assume that a variable returns to its mean more slowly, you will make bigger mistakes at turning points, for example, when capital gains go quickly from being higher than usual to being lower than usual. It can be argued that it is more important not to make big errors at turning points than it is to be more accurate on a year-to-year basis. More generally, it is extremely difficult, if not impossible, for economists to predict turning points consistently and yet, that is the most important time to be accurate.

Assuming a relatively rapid return to "normality" has another advantage for the forecaster. If revenues five years out are assumed to gravitate to a normal level, the long-run end of the projected revenue path will remain fairly stable, because notions of what is normal do not change much from year to year. If the path was not anchored in this way and the whole path jumped around radically from year to year, the forecaster would probably lose the confidence of his or her client—in CBO's case, the Congress of the United States. Consequently, a wise forecaster only changes a forecast gradually until it is quite apparent that the forecast is wrong (Bachman 1996).

CBO faces another risk because of its role as a neutral adviser to both the majority and minority parties in Congress. A significant change in the methodology of forecasting might be perceived as an attempt to favor one party or the other in the partisan debate over future deficits and who caused them. But the more fundamental point was made at the beginning of this discussion. There is a long time lag between the point at which CBO knows that it made an error and the point at which it understands why it made an error. In the interim, there is little basis for changing the statistical methods and rules of thumb that go into making a forecast. Thus, if there is some long-lasting change in the way that revenues are generated, the forecast errors will become serially correlated.

The Politics of Forecasting

It has already been established that CBO revenue forecasts are not biased upward or downward in any statistically meaningful way. There would be no political gain in most circumstances of introducing a bias. CBO works for both parties. It spends much time displeasing both.

A ruling government that must prepare a budget is in a very different position. Adding a dose of optimism to the revenue forecast tends to make life easier. Fewer hard choices are necessary to promise a particular deficit target and it makes it easier to offer spending programs and tax breaks to a variety of interest groups. In poorer countries with much less borrowing power than the United States, the happiness is often short-lived because spending programs are likely to be cancelled when revenues fall short of the forecast. Nevertheless, such countries often repeat their overoptimism year after year.

Although many American administrations have leaned toward overoptimism through history—it was easier before the 1974 budget act that required the publication of long-run economic assumptions—it was the Reagan administration that garnered most criticism in its initial years for their so-called Rosy Scenario. But even that administration was not consistently overoptimistic. When Martin Feldstein became chairman of the Council of Economic Advisors in late 1982, he put out an especially pessimistic forecast, perhaps in reaction to earlier criticism.

As administrations have gained more experience with the Congressional budget process that was invented in 1974, I think it fair to say there has been a trend away from overoptimism. The new process did two important things. It required much more transparency by making economic assumptions explicit and it created CBO as a competitor in the forecasting game. During the Clinton administration, it was hard to see any bias at all in the revenue forecasts. Now, in the second Bush administration, we see a curious tendency to be highly pessimistic. I believe that it started with an honest feeling that it was wise to be conservative after the unexpected collapse in revenues at the beginning of the century. But I think that subsequently the administration felt that it gained politically when revenues came in higher than expected; and in January 2006, they put out an extremely pessimistic forecast that projected much lower revenues than CBO. As a result, they were able to proclaim a greater "improvement" in the budget picture as the year progressed. (It should be noted that CBO's early 2006 forecast, although more optimistic than the administration's, also turned out to significantly understate 2006 revenues.)

Can the Accuracy of Forecasts Be Improved?

It was noted in the beginning that revenue forecasters at CBO and the U.S. Treasury are highly capable professionals. They keep up-to-date with the literature and if new techniques are offered, they are quick to run experiments to see if any improvements in accuracy are possible. It is, therefore, unlikely that much improvement could be achieved by replacing either personnel or their techniques.

Occasionally, significant errors in the revenue forecast are the result of low quality data. For example, the historical record of corporate profits may suddenly be revised upward by the BEA and then CBO finally understands why its forecast of corporate profit tax revenues had tended to be too pessimistic over several years.

The main statistical agencies of the U.S. Government are not treated lavishly by the budget process. They must compete for funds with a great variety of programs and few lobbyists argue on their behalf. They could probably improve the quality of data if they were given somewhat bigger budgets.

Would better data greatly improve the accuracy of forecasts? It would be hard to argue that there would be a great improvement, but a better understanding of the past may lead to a marginal improvement. However, the real problem remains and that is predicting the future. A better understanding of the past may help in forecasting some variables, but it will forever remain difficult to forecast many others, like the stock market and capital gains, the income of the very rich, and short-run interest rates.

Under these circumstances, the hardest thing to do is to explain to the Congress that they must live with enormous uncertainty and that the existence of uncertainty should shape policy formulation. Congress should ask, "How will this policy appear if revenues turn out far higher than expected and how will it appear if revenues are much lower than expected?" But it is not easy to convey the degree of uncertainty to a group of nonstatisticians.

The CBO has tussled mightily with this problem and has put a lot of effort into informing the Congress of the risks to its forecasts. Every year they publish a "fan diagram" that consists of probability distributions of each year's deficit for the next five years, given their baseline forecast. It shows huge uncertainty by the fifth year out. For example, the CBO estimated in January 2006 that current policy implied a deficit of 0.7 percent of GDP, or $114 billion in 2011. However, the fan diagram indicated that there was a 5 percent chance that the deficit would be as large as 6 percent of GDP, or $1006 billion (Congressional Budget Office 2006b).

Despite CBO's best efforts, the Congress finds it extremely difficult to deal with the issue and uncertainty rarely enters the debate. Members are pretty much forced to work with point estimates. They cannot appropriate a range of funds for a specific program. They cannot promulgate ranges for their revenue, outlay, and deficit targets in a budget resolution, because they would then inevitably go to the politically easiest end of the range. So the debate typically focuses on point estimates with only occasional references to what might happen if the future does not turn out as promised. And the media is not very helpful in explaining the uncertainty to the public. Not many statisticians can be found practicing journalism or vice versa.

Conclusions

The main message of this chapter is pretty depressing. Federal revenue forecasts are highly inaccurate and there is not much that can be done to improve them significantly. But it is important to reflect on the fact that before the Budget and Impoundment Control Act of 1974, it would have been impossible to write this chapter. Budgets contained none of the relevant information. In the 1960s, a January budget would typically contain an economic forecast for that calendar year, but no economic projections. Revenue forecasts were prepared by old hands at the treasury, but they were reluctant to reveal their methods for fear of being criticized.

Now everything is laid out in excruciating detail. It may not be a pretty picture, but we can understand it and we can analyze the degree of uncertainty. The Congress may not deal well with this uncertainty; but they know about it, complain about it, and it does enter their deliberations to a small degree. They now have the information necessary to understand it and with the passage of time, they may become more and more sophisticated in introducing it into their debates.

References

Auerbach, A. J. 1999. On the performance and use of government revenue forecasts. *National Tax Journal* 52(4): 767–782.

Bachman, D. 1996. *What Economic Forecasters Really Do.* Bala Cynwyd, PA: The WEFA Group.

Congressional Budget Office. 2004. *Effective Federal Tax Rates Under Current Law, 2001 to 2014*. Washington, DC: US Government Printing Office.

Congressional Budget Office. 2006a. *How CBO Forecasts Income*. Washington, DC: US Government Printing Office.

Congressional Budget Office. 2006b. *The Budget and Economic Outlook: Fiscal Years 2007 to 2016*. Washington, DC: US Government Printing Office.

Gramlich, E. M. 1990. U.S. federal budget deficits and Gramm–Rudman–Hollings. *American Economic Review* 80(2): 75–80.

Kitchen, J. 2003. Observed relationships between economic and technical receipts revisions in federal budget projections. *National Tax Journal* 56(2): 337–353.

Lucas, R. E. 1976. Econometric policy evaluation: a critique. In *The Phillips Curve and Labor Markets*. Edited by K. Brunner and A. Meltzer. Amsterdam: Carnegie–Rochester Conference Series on Public Policy.

Wallis, W. A. and Roberts, H. V. 1958. *Statistics: A New Approach*. Glencoe, IL: The Free Press.

Chapter 3

The State of the Art: Revenue Forecasting in U.S. State Governments

Katherine G. Willoughby and Hai Guo

Contents

Introduction

Accurate, reliable forecasts of revenues and expenditures are essential to good budgeting in the public sector. Planning well for the delivery of government services and programs requires the generation of estimates of revenues needed and costs related to carrying out these activities. As witnessed over the past several years, the ability of governments to respond effectively to any number of crises is directly affected by the accuracy of information—particularly financial—that is available to government officials, policy makers, public administrators, staff, and others. It is critical that public servants have an understanding, with a reasonable degree of certainty, of both the resources and costs associated with the government activities for which they are responsible and which citizens have come to expect.

Accuracy of revenue forecasts is especially important for state governments, as these are revenue-driven entities. In other words, every state government has either an implicit or explicit requirement that revenues and expenditures must balance (Government Accountability Office 2003, National Association of State Budget Officers 2002). Unlike the federal government, state governments cannot run a deficit budget. Essentially, the revenue forecasting abilities of these governments directly affect the ability to manage well and maintain budget balance. The revenue forecast sets the stage for building the budget every fiscal year. The closer the estimate is to actual revenue, the better able a state is to plan for action regarding conduct of its regular or "general" activities as well as for any number of contingencies. Research also indicates that conservative estimates, those closer to underestimates than overestimates, can help states to deal more effectively with the uncertainties of tax collections. In particular, conservative estimates nudge states to plan for the possibility that actual revenues may not meet those revenues forecasted (Gentry 1989).

Although no one can anticipate cataclysmic natural and human disasters or the dramatic changes in federal policy that can severely test state budgets, reliable estimates of revenues and expenditures can "provide an understanding of available funding; evaluate financial risk; assess the likelihood that services can be sustained; assess the level at which capital investment can be made; identify future commitments and resource demands; and identify the key variables that cause change in the level of revenue" (National Advisory Council on State and Local Budgeting 2000). Especially during periods of fiscal decline, accurate revenue estimates can help states manage budgetary equilibrium. Finally, good forecasting improves the state's performance and increases citizens' trust (Voorhees 2004).

This chapter describes revenue forecasting in the states, focusing on methods of estimating and accuracy by source type. Using data compiled from the 2005

Government Performance Project (GPP) survey of the states,* we assess the state government's ability to provide accurate projections of general revenues, the likelihood of reestimating during budget execution, and the overall ability of states to be able to steer through crises using such knowledge.

The Complexity of Revenue Forecasting

Forecasting is a complex process. For example, a state may use a number of different analytical techniques and consult with a variety of policy makers, budgeters, finance officers, and economists to estimate individual revenue sources as well as to develop the final revenue forecast for the state. For instance, a state department of revenue may work with legislative fiscal staff and committee members responsible for the development of tax policy to determine estimates of specific tax resources. Or, the state's executive budget office may work with legislative fiscal staff to generate estimates regarding intergovernmental monies. States also engage external consultants to gain insight into the influences of regional, national, and global economies on own-source revenues. Generating efficient and accurate forecasts depends on the institutional structures that the state has established, but human relationships, judgment, and numerous analytical applications and assumptions are important as well (Kuo and Liang 2004, Penner 2002, Voorhees 2006, 2004).

* Since 1996, the GPP has generated periodic report cards of government management in the United States. Assessment of management capacity has considered a number of areas and now includes budgeting and finance, human resources, infrastructure, and information. The 2005 survey of the states was the third report card generated for this level of government. This survey involved the development of an online questionnaire and required several different data collection methods. Faculty and graduate students at four universities in the United States collected data of state management processes from electronic and hard copy materials available from the state governments as well as that provided by numerous professional and academic institutions. Each university team input data collected into the online survey. Also, journalists conducted over 1000 interviews with elected officials, administrators, staff, and citizens in the states to complement the academic data collected. The online survey was also sent to the 50 states for their response. The web-based instrument provided the states with the opportunity to answer questions as well as check data previously input by the university teams. States could provide comments regarding questions or responses, could explain the context for specific management strategies used, or could present their case for why a particular question was not applicable to them. In the end, data was collected regarding all 50 states, and state responses and comments are integral to all GPP-related analyses. The final grades generated by this survey measure the ability of states to produce results. For more information about the GPP history, the 2005 survey, research methodology, and results, visit http://www.results.gpponline.org.

Budget constraints include balanced budget requirements, tax and expenditure limitations, and supermajority voting requirements. Currently, all states except Vermont have a constitutional or statutory requirement that the state must balance its budget. Such requirements vary considerably—the governor may have to submit a balanced budget to the legislature; the legislature may be required to pass a balanced budget; the budget may need to be balanced at year-end; or a state may be bound by several other balance requirements. Whatever the case, any balanced budget requirement confines the government to spending within a determined revenue amount for a particular fiscal year.

The existence of tax or expenditure limits also constricts the use of revenue sources and expenditure categories and amounts, making forecasting accuracy even more important. Such limitations restrain rate and base changes of various revenue sources or can require a state to make certain expenditures. Somewhat similarly, supermajority requirements (i.e., when two thirds of legislators must approve a tax revenue measure) limit state flexibility in tweaking tax structures and make accurate revenue (and expenditure) estimates more significant to policy makers. Ultimately, state governments operate in a fairly constrained environment that places a premium on revenue and expenditure estimate accuracy.

Human relationships and both individual and group judgment influence the estimating process, and therefore, final forecasts. Research indicates that revenue forecasting is as much an art as an arithmetic technique (Sun 2005). The politics of forecasting encompasses the ability of external stakeholders (citizens), media, lobbyists, and others to pressure for changes to revenue forecasts. The independency and perceived strength of the forecasting group or agent influences how malleable a forecast is to such pressures (Sun 2005). Political party control influences forecasting accuracy, as one-party dominance in the government negatively influences accuracy because it permits the forecasting group or responsible agent to manipulate forecasts to the advantage of the dominant political party's policy agenda (Bretschneider et al. 1989). Further, potential bias in forecasting finds fertile ground in governments that provide one branch or one office the sole responsibility for development of the overall state revenue forecast.

Qualitative methods of forecasting that attempt to impose greater objectivity into the process include Delphi or expert judgment forecasting—the use of consultants and consensus approaches that employ human judgment. In the case of consensus methods, greater objectivity results from requiring agreement among various stakeholders to come up with a particular forecast. The GPP survey defined the following methods of forecasting that engage various stakeholders.

Delphi or expert judgment forecasting. An iterative survey process, in which a panel of experts is chosen, sent information relevant to the forecast needed, and asked to respond with a forecast(s). Experts provide their feedback to the state, their responses are summarized, and a forecast is determined by a consensus of responses. Experts may be contacted several times throughout the process to provide the feedback. Experts are not brought together and facilitated in a group setting.

Consensus forecasting. A process that requires a panel of experts brought together for the purpose of generating the requested forecast. Experts may include officials from the executive and legislative branches of the state, as well as external researchers or officials from universities, private consultants, or citizens.

Because states depend on a variety of revenue sources, not surprisingly, the process of forecasting involves many different types of quantitative and qualitative methods. Generally, forecasters need different and multiple methods of analysis for making estimates of a variety of sources of state revenue, including individual and corporate income taxes, general sales tax, motor fuel tax, tobacco product tax, alcoholic beverage tax and severance tax, current charges, tobacco settlement funds, lottery and other gambling revenue, and intergovernmental revenue.

Quantitative methods for forecasting these varied revenue sources include simple trend, time series forecasting, simulations, and regression modeling. These techniques involve the collection of numerical data and the conduct of mathematical calculations, and are often paired with qualitative approaches to generate accurate estimates and forecasts (Batchelor and Dua 1990, Bretschneider et al. 1989, Voorhees 2004).

Forecasting Methods Used

The revenue sources examined in the GPP survey include individual and corporate income taxes, general sales tax, motor fuel tax, tobacco product tax, alcoholic beverage tax and severance tax, current charges, tobacco settlement funds, lottery and other gambling revenue, and intergovernmental revenue. The forecasting methods that the GPP asked about include simple trend, time series forecasting, linear regression modeling, Delphi or expert judgment forecasting, private consultant, and consensus forecasting. States were asked to indicate which method(s) is used for each type of revenue source listed. States could indicate the use of multiple methods to forecast each revenue source.

Table 3.1 indicates the number of states using specific forecasting techniques by the type of revenue source. The top two or three methods of forecasting used by states for each revenue source appear in bold. Results show that the prevailing practice is to use simple trend analysis or linear regression, along with consensus methods to estimate the different revenue sources. Results regarding specific states yield the following:

- Three states use simple trend analysis to forecast every "tax" revenue source listed on the survey: Kansas, Utah, and West Virginia.
- Illinois, Minnesota, Mississippi, and Ohio use simple trend analysis to forecast "all" revenue sources listed on the survey.

Table 3.1 Revenue Source by Forecasting Method: Number of States Using the Method

	Personal Income Tax	*Corporate Income Tax*	*General Sales Tax*	*Motor Fuel Tax*	*Tobacco Product Tax*	*Alcoholic Beverage Tax*	*Severance Tax*	*Current Charges*	*Tobacco Settlement Funds*	*Lottery/ Other Gambling Revenue*	*Inter-governmental Revenue*
Simple trend	19	20	17	**18**	**24**	**19**	**12**	**27**	**14**	**24**	**20**
Time series	19	18	19	11	14	15	8	5	2	12	5
Linear regression	**25**	**23**	**24**	**18**	15	16	7	5	3	11	9
Delphi/ expert judgment	11	11	9	6	7	7	7	4	6	8	3
Private consultant	8	8	7	5	4	5	4	3	**11**	4	2
Consensus forecasting	**23**	**24**	**23**	**17**	**18**	**20**	**10**	9	**10**	**16**	6

- Mississippi, Pennsylvania, and Utah use linear regression modeling for all "tax" revenue sources.
- Mississippi uses linear regression modeling for "all" revenue sources.
- Five states use consensus forecasting for all the "tax" revenue sources listed: Kentucky, Louisiana, Michigan, New Mexico, and Utah.
- Illinois, Kansas, Mississippi, and South Carolina use consensus forecasting for "all" the revenue sources listed.

Measuring Accuracy in Forecasting

Forecasters can measure the accuracy of state revenue forecasting by examining the difference between estimated and actual revenues. The closer the estimate is to the actual revenue that comes into the state, the more accurate the forecast. The GPP data yields such differences for fiscal years 2002, 2003, and 2004.

Table 3.2 presents findings regarding gaps between estimated and actual general revenues in the states. Results show that during fiscal year 2002, 20 states realized actual revenues within ±5 percent of their estimated revenues. Of that set, nine states underestimated general revenues and 11 overestimated them. By 2004, however, 33 states achieved more accurate estimates of their general revenues as they were within 5 percent of estimates. And, if conservative estimates did support state efforts to reach and maintain balance, by 2004 more states were underestimating general revenues—20 states underestimated these revenues, eight overestimated, and one state indicated no difference between estimated and actual general revenues for that year. Considering all categories, in 2002, 12 of 46 states underestimated general fund revenues. In contrast, by 2004, 28 of 40 states underestimated these revenues. Figure 3.1 compares nominal to real total revenues collected by states from 1995 to 2004. After accounting for inflation, 2002 revenues just equal 1995 revenues. The precipitous drop in state revenues from 2000 to 2002 may have been the impetus for more states to underestimate revenues by 2004.

Table 3.2 Percentage Difference between General Fund Revenue Estimates and Actual Revenues for Fiscal Years 2002, 2003, and 2004 (Number of States)

	0 to <1 Percent	*1 to <5 Percent*	*5 to <10 Percent*	*10 to <20 Percent*	*≥20 Percent*	*Unknown[a]*
FY 2002	4	16	14	8	4	4
FY 2003	11	18	8	5	2	6
FY 2004[b]	9	24	7	1	0	9

[a] Data for these states is incomplete or not available for all three years.
[b] Difference between original revenue estimate and year-end estimate.

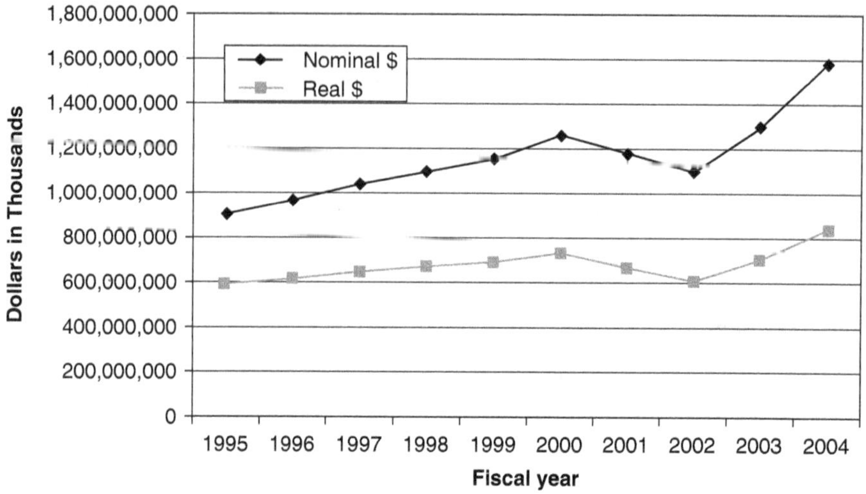

Figure 3.1 Total state revenues, 1995–2004. (From total state government revenues from U.S. Bureau of Census, State Government Finances. Total revenues in thousands at http://www.census.gov/govs/www/state.html. Summary Tables for years 1995–2004. Real dollars adjusted using average CPI-U from U.S. Bureau of Labor Statistics, 2006, base year chained, 1982–1984 = 100; available at ftp://ftp.bls.gov/pub/special.requests/cpi/cpiai.txt; accessed November 8, 2006.)

Forecasting Income Tax Revenue

Today, individual and corporate income taxes comprise about 40 percent of total taxes collected by state governments. General sales taxes collected by states comprise the second most significant tax resource for the states, totaling about 33 percent of all tax receipts (U.S. Bureau of Census, 2006). As a whole, states' estimates of revenues from individual and corporate income tax seem to be less conservative than their estimates for general sales tax revenues.

Table 3.3 indicates that in those years for which the GPP collected estimates and actuals for each of these revenue sources, most states responding indicate gaps of less than 5 percent for general sales taxes. From fiscal years 2003 to 2004, states improved their estimates of individual income tax revenues. In 2003, 16 states indicate gaps between estimates to actuals of 10 percent or greater. In 2004, just three states indicate gaps this large. Accuracy is more of a problem for states when forecasting corporate income tax revenues. In 2003, 27 states have estimates that are off by 10 percent or more, whereas in 2004, 23 states indicate such a gap. Constantly changing laws that continue the erosion of this revenue source for states may contribute to difficulties in generating accurate estimates of corporate income tax revenues.

Table 3.3 Percentage Difference between Estimates and Actuals for Fiscal Years 2003 and 2004, by Tax Type (Number of States)

		0 to <1 Percent	*1 to <5 Percent*	*5 to <10 Percent*	*10 to <20 Percent*	*≥20 Percent*	*Unknown*
FY 2003	Individual income tax	4	6	9	11	5	15
	General sales tax	12	19	6	2	0	11
	Corporate income tax	0	7	3	16	11	13
FY 2004	Individual income tax	9	20	6	2	1	12
	General sales tax	12	23	1	2	1	11
	Corporate income tax	3	6	8	13	10	10

Examining specific states, Maine and Virginia most accurately estimate revenue from individual income tax. According to the GPP survey, the percent differences between estimates and actuals in these two states were less than 1 percent in both fiscal years, 2003 and 2004. Maine employs microsimulation models using actual income tax returns for a base year, extrapolates this data to the forecast period, and then applies the tax law for that time period to estimate individual income tax revenue. Maine also relies on a consensus approach to determine the final forecast for individual income tax revenue. Virginia uses linear regression modeling to forecast individual income tax revenue and then secures the services of economic consulting firms to generate this forecast.

States use different methods to forecast general sales tax revenue. Among the states indicating a gap of less than 5 percent between estimates to actuals for this revenue source, 13 use simple trend analysis, 14 use time series analysis, 17 use linear regression modeling, 7 engage Delphi or expert judgment forecasting, whereas 4 engage private consultants. In addition, 18 use a consensus approach to provide a final forecast for this revenue source.

As noted previously, accuracy in forecasting revenue from corporate income taxes is poor compared to forecasting revenues from individual income tax or general sales tax. No state responding to the survey indicated a gap of less than 1 percent between estimates and actuals in fiscal year 2003 for corporate income taxes. However, of the three states indicating such accuracy in 2004, Minnesota realized a difference between estimates and actuals of 7 percent in 2003, reducing the gap to less than 1 percent by 2004. Minnesota uses linear regression modeling, expert judgment, a private consult, and spreadsheet analysis to forecast corporate income tax revenue.

The Comprehensive Revenue Forecast

Consensus forecasting requires agreement on a final forecast. As noted earlier, such consensus may necessitate input and agreement among officials and staff both internal and external to government. External government stakeholders may include university professors, business professionals or consultants, and others. GPP results indicate that many states incorporate a consensus format to estimate many of the individual revenue sources. For example, just half of the states use this method to estimate corporate income tax receipts.

Consistent with the National Association of State Budget Officers (NASBO) results, the GPP survey found that 24 states use a consensus forecasting method to determine the comprehensive revenue forecast, which the legislatures use for budget-making purposes (National Association of State Budget Officers 2002). States, which incorporate a consensus approach to determine any revenue forecast, use many different types of arrangements. Executive branch budgeters and state economists may work with legislators and legislative staff, or these groups may work with an outside consultant or a university research center to generate the state's final revenue forecast. The increased use of a consensus method does significantly reduce forecasting error as measured in dollars (Voorhees 2004). Use of such a method for one or several revenue sources or for the development of the comprehensive or official revenue forecast of a state advances the accuracy of the estimate.

GPP survey results suggest that states have achieved greater accuracy by using multiple methods of forecasting revenue sources. Many states apply at least two different methods to forecast individual revenue sources. This is particularly the case for estimating individual and corporate income taxes and general sales taxes. States not employing simple trend analysis tend to have the greatest differences between estimated and actual general fund revenues. Overall results imply that states using a variety of forecasting methods, including both simple trend analysis and consensus forecasting, tend to be most accurate in making estimates. Also, findings from the GPP survey show states at the tail end of a recession, realizing greater forecasting accuracy. Such results substantiate the findings of MacManus and Grothe (1989) on the local level regarding the positive relationship between fiscal stress and accuracy of revenue forecasting. Fiscal stress supports more conservative estimating.

The Frequency of Making Estimates

The frequency with which states reevaluate revenue and expenditure estimates also contributes positively to the ability of a government to maintain budget balance.

Table 3.4 Frequency of Making Estimates (Percentage of States; $n = 44$)

Frequency	Revenue Estimates (Percent)	Expenditure Estimates
Monthly	14	18
Quarterly	34	20
On ad hoc basis	45	55
No formal updates	5	2

Certainly, the earlier a forecaster can anticipate the dips in revenue or hikes in expenditures, the better it is for making informed decisions about the balancing strategies that might be necessary for a government to undertake. The GPP survey asked states about the formal processes that exist for updating revenue and expenditure estimates during a fiscal year. The survey asked states if revenue and expenditure estimates were updated, and if so, how often such updates occurred. Table 3.4 shows the likelihood of *ad hoc* approaches to reevaluating both revenue and expenditure estimates.

States are more likely to reevaluate revenue estimates quarterly rather than monthly, and close to half of the states use an *ad hoc* approach to reevaluate. However, relatively few states indicate having no formal process for reevaluating revenue or expenditure estimates.

Good Forecasting Performance

The GPP found Rhode Island, South Carolina, Michigan, and New Mexico to be good performers in forecasting revenues. These states apply a variety of forecasting methods to estimate different revenue streams, and each state uses a consensus method to generate the comprehensive revenue forecast for budget-making purposes by the legislative branch. These states apply consensus forecasting in unique ways that involve many different participants. Rhode Island, Michigan, and New Mexico also hold special conferences or meetings involving forecasting of participants who help focus attention on the factors that influence revenue growth and decline. Frequent updating of estimates helps as well. South Carolina indicates monthly updates to revenue estimates; Michigan's revenue estimates are updated at the regularly scheduled semiannual estimating conference, but can be updated more frequently if needed. In New Mexico, state economists meet three times a year leading up to and including the legislative session, once each in October, December, and mid-session (January or February). New Mexico's economists also meet every month to discuss trends in collections and estimating error. All of these states either realized fairly accurate forecasts or improved forecasting accuracy across the years examined.

Rhode Island

Rhode Island uses a consensus method to develop its comprehensive revenue forecast. By law, this is the responsibility of a Revenue Estimating Conference. This conference must meet at least semiannually, prepare quarterly estimates, and eventually reach an agreement between the state budget director and House and Senate fiscal advisors. Along with consensus, the state uses other methods to estimate individual revenue sources, including trend analysis, time series, and linear regression modeling from individual income tax, corporate income tax, general sales tax, tobacco product tax, and alcoholic beverage tax. To estimate revenue from motor fuel sales tax, the state applies trend analysis. Rhode Island also holds a caseload estimating conference that helps project expenditure figures. Typically, the revenue and caseload estimating conferences are held at least twice a year, if not more, and usually within the first ten days of May and November.

Rhode Island achieves good revenue forecast accuracy. In fiscal year 2002, the estimated total general fund revenues were 1.1 percent less than actual revenues; in fiscal 2003, estimates were 1.9 percent less than actual revenues; and in fiscal 2004, the original estimate was 1.3 percent below the projected actual.

South Carolina

South Carolina uses a consensus forecasting method to estimate all revenue sources. It has a Board of Economic Advisors (BEA) that by law provides revenue forecasts and advises the state's Budget and Control Board on revenue and expenditure estimates. The BEA also assesses and certifies amendments to appropriations that influence revenue levels. The BEA and its staff monitor revenue collections on a monthly basis and compare the revenue collections in every major area to what is called a "monitor plan." The BEA develops a schedule of when the revenue is expected to be received throughout the year. The BEA staff also prepares a five-year revenue projection, starting with the current year's forecast. The Budget and Control Board monitors agency expenditures and revenues.

The governor appoints the chair of the BEA. Both the chairman of the Senate Finance Committee and the chairman of the House Ways and Means Committee appoint one member each to the BEA. In addition, a representative of the Department of Revenue is a nonvoting member of the board.

South Carolina's total revenue forecast accuracy improved substantially across the years of study. In fiscal year 2002, total general fund revenues were overestimated by 12.3 percent; in fiscal year 2003, they were overestimated by 11.3 percent; but by fiscal year 2004, these revenues were underestimated by 1.5 percent. Overall improvements to forecast accuracy can be attributed, in part, to frequent, monthly updates to forecasts. Improvements to forecasting of specific sources also include those regarding investment income and individual income taxes. Investment income was overestimated by 77.5 percent in 2003, and then underestimated by

4.3 percent in 2004. Individual income taxes were overestimated by 24.1 percent in 2003, yet were underestimated by just 0.5 percent in 2004.

Michigan

Michigan uses a consensus method of forecasting revenues. The University of Michigan maintains and feeds into the forecast for all taxes econometric models of the United States and Michigan economies. In addition, the state uses trend analysis for all revenue sources except the motor fuel sales tax. Time series is used to forecast motor fuel sales tax. The Department of Management and Budget, the Office of Revenue and Tax Analysis in the Department of Treasury, and the state legislature contribute to a final revenue forecast used for budget development.

In Michigan, the law requires a consensus official revenue estimate. Revenue estimating conferences are a major component in the process of developing the official forecast. Each year, directors of the House and Senate fiscal agencies and the Department of Management and Budget (or a designee) hold two estimating conferences. The governor and senior officials from the Department of Treasury may also attend these conferences, which are usually held in January and May. To begin the estimating process, the first conference examines national and state economic indicators. The second conference updates the estimates and the executive and legislative members of the conference agree on a final revenue forecast.

In addition, the special conference may address unique issues. For example, in December 2004, a special conference addressed a potential revenue shortfall of more than $355 million in the subsequent fiscal year. Also, the Senate Fiscal Agency, House Fiscal Agency, and the Treasury Department held a consensus revenue estimating conference on August 17, 2005, and unanimously adopted revised revenue estimates for fiscal year 2004–2005 and the following year. Revenue estimates are updated quarterly, whereas expenditure estimates are prepared monthly.

Michigan's revenue estimating is fairly accurate, but the state has had a tendency to overestimate revenues. Total general fund revenues were overestimated by almost 3 percent in fiscal year 2002, by 2.6 percent in fiscal year 2003, and by 4.1 percent in fiscal year 2004, respectively.

New Mexico

New Mexico uses consensus forecasting to develop its revenue estimates. This process involves the departments of taxation and revenue, finance and administration, and highway and transportation, as well as the staff from the Legislative Finance Committee. The participants in this forecasting process include economists from the taxation and revenue departments, analysts from the departments of finance and administration and the highway and transportation department, and economists from the Legislative Finance Committee. Other methods of forecasting individual tax revenues include trend analysis, time series, linear regression, and use of a private consultant. The New Mexico State Board of Finance periodically posts the results from the estimating process including both estimates and their accuracy online. On an average, revenue estimates are updated three to four times every fiscal year.

The revenue estimation process in New Mexico produces accurate results. In fiscal year 2002, there was a 0.3 percent difference between estimated and actual total general fund revenues. In fiscal year 2003, the estimates were 1.3 percent less than actual revenues; and in fiscal year 2004, the estimates were 1.4 percent below the end-of-year estimates.

Conclusion: Improving Accuracy

The results presented here indicate that state governments are taking advantage of a variety of methods to estimate revenues, and many engage multiple methods to forecast individual revenues sources and the total revenue forecast. State governments improved forecast accuracy across the years examined by the GPP survey. Results indicate that states engaging multiple methods of forecasting, including simple trend analysis and some form of consensus protocol realized better accuracy. Highly complex analytical methods of forecasting do not necessarily result in greater accuracy. Rather, a mix of methods, both quantitative and qualitative, supports improved accuracy.

States did indicate difficulty in accurately forecasting certain revenue sources such as the corporate income tax. The continual erosion of this revenue source, given tax law changes and a volatile economy, undoubtedly contributes to problems with forecasting such revenue with great accuracy. However, states have made some progress forecasting both individual income and general sales tax revenues more accurately by 2004.

Fiscal climate seemed to nudge states to be more conservative with estimates across the years examined. Whereas states were more likely to overestimate general fund revenues in 2002, this was reversed by 2004, when more states underestimated these revenues. Specifically, 12 states underestimated and 34 states overestimated general fund revenues in 2002. By 2004, however, 28 states underestimated and 12 states overestimated these same revenues.

States seeking to improve forecasting accuracy might consider engaging a more formalized process for the reevaluation of estimates. Nearly half of states indicate only *ad hoc* reevaluation of revenue estimates. Each of the states, highlighted as good performers by the GPP, conducts a reevaluation of revenue estimates at least quarterly, if not monthly. In the same way that good cash management calls for continual "look backs" on cash flow and comparisons with previous periods, states would be wiser to use a more structured approach for the reevaluation of revenue forecasts. Reevaluation provides data that can help determine a propensity to overestimate or underestimate as well as to ferret out specific problems with forecasts that arise either arithmetically or through human judgment. Undoubtedly, forecasting remains as much an art as science and states can continue to improve their forecasting accuracy. States that can balance the use of each of these components in the development of revenue forecasts will be better prepared to reach and maintain budget equilibrium.

Acknowledgments

The author would like to thank the Pew Charitable Trusts for supporting this research that uses data from the 2004 GPP. The GPP is nonpartisan, independent evaluation of state management practices in the areas of money, people, infrastructure, and information. The GPP is conducted by The Pew Center on the States, a division of The Pew Charitable Trusts. The Trust and its partners examine effective policy approaches to critical issues facing government in the United States.

References

Batchelor, R., and Dua, P. 1990. Forecaster ideology, forecasting technique and the accuracy of economic forecasting. *International Journal of Forecast* 6(1): 3–10.

Bretschneider, S., Gorr, W. L., Grizzle G., and Klay, E. 1989. Political and organizational influences on the accuracy of forecasting state government revenues. *International Journal of Forecasting* 5(3): 307–319.

Gentry, W. M. 1989. Do state revenue forecasters utilize available information? *National Tax Journal* 42(4): 429–440.

Government Accountability Office. 2003. Balanced budget requirements: State experiences and implications for the federal government. Briefing Report to the Chairman, Committee on the Budget, House of Representatives. Washington (March).

Kuo, Y.-Y., and K-Y., Liang. 2004. Human judgments in New York State sales and use tax forecasting. *Journal of Forecasting* 23(4): 297–314.

MacManus, S. A., and Grothe, B. P. 1989. Fiscal stress as a stimulant to better revenue forecasting and productivity. *Public Productivity Review* 12(4): 387–400.

National Advisory Council on State and Local Budgeting. 2000. Recommended budget practices: A framework for improved state and local government budgeting. http://www.gfoa.org/services/nacslb/.

National Association of State Budget Officers. 2002. Budget processes in the states. Washington (January).

Penner, R. G. 2002. Dealing with uncertain budget forecasts. *Public Budgeting and Finance* 22(1): 1–18.

Sun, J. 2005. The dynamics of government revenue forecasting from an organizational perspective: A review of the literature. *Journal of Public Budgeting, Accounting & Financial Management* 17(4): 527–556.

U.S. Bureau of Census. 2006. State government finances. http://www.census.gov/govs/www/state.html (accessed November 8, 2006).

U.S. Bureau of Census. 2006. State government tax collections: 2005. http://www.census.gov/govs/statetax/0500usstax.html (accessed October 1, 2006).

U.S. Bureau of Labor Statistics. 2006. Average CPI-U. ftp://ftp.bls.gov/pub/special.requests/cpi/cpiai.txt (accessed November 8, 2006).

Voorhees, W. 2006. Institutional structures utilized in state revenue forecasting. *Journal of Public Budgeting, Accounting & Financial Management* 14(2): 175–195.

Voorhees, W. 2004. More is better: Consensual forecasting and state revenue forecast error. *International Journal of Public Administration* 27(8–9): 651–672.

Chapter 4

Forecasting State Revenues in Louisiana: From Dramatic Changes in the Oil and Gas Industry in the 1970s and 1980s to the Aftermath of Catastrophic Hurricanes in the 2000s

James A. Richardson

Contents

Introduction

State governments rely on revenue forecasts to establish short- and long-term budgets. Thirty states plan their budgets once every year, whereas thirteen have a biennial budget with the state legislatures meeting annually, and seven states have biennial budgets and legislative sessions.* But, in both cases, the states have made financial obligations to education, highways, public safety, and other state responsibilities based on the best revenue estimates available. Or, the states have made commitments to reduce taxes on their citizens with the belief that the revenues available, after the tax reduction, will be sufficient to fund desired public services. The bottom line is that states have to rely on some form of revenue forecasting to establish a budget for the next one or two fiscal years. Bad revenue projections can be a disaster for a state, especially if the revenue projections are too optimistic. States can usually adjust to surpluses with ease, but most states have a more difficult time adjusting to major shortfalls in incoming revenues. In other words, cutting the state budget mid-year is typically a political crisis.

The Louisiana Legislature must, according to the state constitution, submit and pass a balanced budget and maintain it throughout the course of the fiscal year. This state constitutional amendment was passed in 1990. Louisiana must not only pass a balanced budget, but if, during the fiscal year, there is a change in expected revenues, the state must also immediately take steps to eliminate the looming deficit. Before 1990, Louisiana had a relatively loose constitutional provision, which merely stated that state expenditures could not exceed "expected" state revenues with the keyword being "expected." This constitutional provision allowed the state to estimate and reestimate revenue projections until the state legislature could claim it had passed a "balanced" budget and the governor would sign it. These budgets might meet the constitutional test of passing a balanced budget, but they did not necessarily meet the more demanding test of economic reality. Most states must deal with a balanced budget because the borrowing capacity of states is much lower than the federal government's borrowing capacity. In addition, states separate their operating budgets from their capital budgets. The balanced budget rules relate to the operating budgets.

Louisiana has a rich and colorful political history. The story of state revenue forecasting in Louisiana is a part of that history. This chapter focuses on the evolution of revenue forecasting in Louisiana and, in the judgment of the author, a major

* States with annual budgets and sessions include Alabama, Alaska, California, Colorado, Delaware, Florida, Georgia, Idaho, Illinois, Iowa, Kansas, Louisiana, Maryland, Massachusetts, Michigan, Mississippi, Missouri, New Jersey, New Mexico, New York, Oklahoma, Pennsylvania, Rhode Island, South Carolina, South Dakota, Tennessee, Utah, Vermont, and West Virginia. States with annual sessions but biennial budgets include Connecticut, Hawaii, Indiana, Maine, Minnesota, Nebraska, New Hampshire, North Carolina, Ohio, Virginia, Washington, Wisconsin, and Wyoming. States with biennial sessions and budgets include Arkansas, Kentucky, Montana, Nevada, North Dakota, Oregon, and Texas.

improvement in procedure and a decidedly superior outcome. The story begins with the oil and gas boom in Louisiana in the 1970s, the bust of the oil and gas industry in the 1980s, and then a more traditional method of funding state governments in the 1990s. The story ends with the forecasting process trying to handle the revenue projections in light of the two major hurricanes in 2005—Hurricane Katrina hitting the New Orleans area and Hurricane Rita hitting southwestern Louisiana—within a gap of three weeks.

Forecasting state revenues is a necessary part of the budgeting process in relatively calm times and also in more volatile times. Louisiana has had both in the past 35 years. The story is told from the perspective of a person who was involved with this forecasting evolution: first, as one of the persons who assisted the Louisiana legislature in the 1970s to construct the first econometric model for forecasting state revenues, although these forecasts did not get drafted into the budget process; second, the person who trained the people who provided forecasts for the state legislature in the 1970s; third, the person who helped a governor in 1984 pass major tax increases to offset the fall in oil and gas revenues; fourth, the person who called attention to the developing fiscal fiasco in the 1980s by editing a book *Louisiana Fiscal Alternatives: Finding Permanent Solutions to Recurring Budget Crises*; fifth, the person who was selected in 1987 to assist in developing and using revenue forecasts based on economic parameters and not political parameters; and finally, the person who still participates in the revenue forecasting process in Louisiana (Richardson 1988).

Louisiana: The Economy and Revenue Forecasting, the 1970s and 1980s

Louisiana has always had a very strong governor. The governor and the executive branch, especially the Division of Administration, in the early 1970s provided all of the budget information to the Louisiana legislature.* At that time, the Louisiana legislature did not have a budget staff to help the members of the legislature in understanding the budget and making changes in it. The governor was in total control of the budget. This included the revenue forecasts for the state. The legislature would invite other parties from around the state to provide revenue forecasts—as many as five or six different forecasts were provided.† In the end, although, the revenue forecasts developed by the governor's office prevailed.

* The Division of Administration is the Louisiana equivalent of the Office of Management and Budgeting at the federal level. The commissioner of administration is the governor's key advisor on budget issues and will be the lead person in dealing with the state legislature.

† Groups from universities would be invited; trade associations would be asked to comment on their industry such as oil and natural gas prices; and other such groups.

In the 1970s, the legislature had a few young reformers, led by Representative Bubba Henry, who pushed for a stronger legislative role in determining state policy and establishing the state budget.* The Louisiana legislature created the Legislative Fiscal Office in 1975 to provide its members with independent information about the budget and budget alternatives. This office is similar to the U.S. Congressional Budget Office, although it does not provide the official forecast for the state budget. One of the first tasks of the Legislative Fiscal Office was to create a more independent and reliable revenue estimate for the state. The Legislative Fiscal Office commissioned Loren C. Scott, a young assistant professor in the Department of Economics at Louisiana State University (LSU), and the author, at that time an assistant professor of economics at LSU, to develop an econometric forecasting model for state revenues. We created the model; trained economists on the staff of the Legislative Fiscal Office to work with it; and provided assistance from time to time.† Econometric forecasting is still the core of the forecasting methods used by the fiscal office. Obviously, the forecasting model has been updated, enhanced, and improved. The econometric forecasts were made, but the forecasts that were combined into the Appropriations Bill, House Bill 1, were always the forecasts prepared by the office of the governor.‡

During the 1970s, the revenue forecasts were not a major issue. Substantial surpluses were typically the outcome of the budget year. The government could not anticipate how much money the oil and gas sector would generate as long as oil and gas prices were rising. This is a situation in which a major tax change in 1973 and a robust oil and gas market for producing states created a favorable state budget for Louisiana for an entire decade.

In 1973, the Louisiana legislature in an extraordinary session, in December of that year, changed the tax base for oil from a per-barrel basis to a value basis. Before this session, oil was taxed at 18–26 cents/bbl. The value of the barrel did not matter. At the 1973 extraordinary session, the Louisiana legislature, at the suggestion of the governor, changed the tax on oil from a volume tax to a value tax with the tax rate being set at 12.5 percent of value for most wells included in the Louisiana taxing

* Representative Henry was from northeast Louisiana and became speaker of the House of Representatives without the support of the governor. Typically, the governor is very involved in the selection of the speaker of the House and the president of the Senate. During the 1970s, Governor Edwards was able to convince the Senate to agree with his choice, Senator Michael O'Keefe from New Orleans, to be president of the Senate.

† The Louisiana Legislative Fiscal Office hired William Black as its first economist, a doctoral student at Louisiana State University. Black now works for the Division of Administration. The Fiscal Office then hired Greg Albrecht, a graduate of the economics program at Louisiana State University. Greg is still the forecaster for the Louisiana Legislative Fiscal Office.

‡ In the Louisiana Legislature, the Appropriations Bill is always identified as House Bill 1. The bill originates in the House of Representatives.

jurisdiction.* The Louisiana taxing jurisdiction includes the state of Louisiana and the state offshore—which is up to 3 mi offshore. The state increased the tax on natural gas but did not make it a value tax. Before 1973, the tax on natural gas was 3.3 cents/1000 ft^3. After the extraordinary session, the natural gas tax was 7 cents/1000 ft^3. Natural gas was not converted to a value tax because of the pricing provisions at the federal level. Intrastate natural gas, natural gas bought and sold within one state, did not have federal price controls over it; however, price controls were imposed on any natural gas crossing state borders. Louisiana is a major producer of natural gas, but it is also a major user of natural gas with its petrochemical industry. The petrochemical industry successfully argued that a value tax on natural gas, along with the federal price controls, would put Louisiana users of natural gas at an economic disadvantage.

At this same extraordinary session, the Louisiana legislature lowered the personal income tax by making federal taxes a deduction from adjusted gross income and taking food prepared off premises and prescriptions out of the sales tax base. Politically, a reduction in personal taxes is typically popular. The timing was extraordinary—oil prices quadrupled in 1974, and the budgetary coffers of Louisiana were overflowing and personal taxes had been reduced.

The end result was that the sources of revenues for the state were skewed toward oil and gas. By 1981, almost 40 percent of all state revenues came from oil and gas as illustrated in Figure 4.1. The state received just below 25 percent of its tax collections from sales and use taxes and about 5 percent of its revenues from the personal income tax. Oil and gas were the key to a successful budget year in Louisiana. From 1973 to 1981, the price of oil provided ample support for the Louisiana state budget.†

As illustrated in Figures 4.2 and 4.3, just as the price of oil can rise, it can also fall. In 1981, the price of oil peaked in nominal terms until much later in the 2000s; and in real terms the price of oil has never been higher than it was in 1981, even in early 2007 with the nominal price of oil being in the $60–70 range. The value of 40 percent of Louisiana tax base gradually depreciated in the early 1980s and then dramatically depreciated in 1985. The U.S. Department of Energy's Energy Information Administration forecasted in the early 1980s that oil would reach $100/bbl within a short time period. Oil prices had quadrupled in 1974 and then doubled again in 1979 due to political tensions in the Middle East. High oil prices were considered to be permanent. And, to boot, natural gas prices had been deregulated starting in 1978 with the Natural Gas Policy Act, signed by President Carter, and then in 1981, President Reagan speeded up the deregulation process.

---

* The tax on less-productive wells would be 6.125 percent and the tax on stripper well would be 3.0625 percent. A stripper well is a well that produces less than 10 bbl/day.

† The year 1977 was an exception. Oil prices were relatively stable for that one year and oil production within the Louisiana taxing jurisdiction was declining. The state decided to raise corporate income taxes to fund a teacher's pay increase.

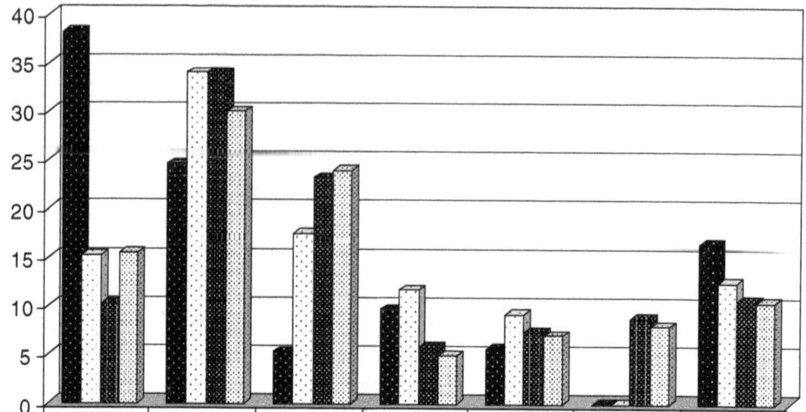

	Min	Sales	Inc	Corp	Fuels	Gam	Other
■ 1981	38.2	24.6	5.3	9.7	5.7	0	16.5
□ 1992	15.2	34	17.4	11.7	9.2	0	12.5
■ 2002	10.2	34	23.2	5.8	7.4	8.8	10.6
▫ 2006	15.5	30	24	5	7	8	10.5

Figure 4.1 Louisiana's sources of revenues for selected years (percentage of total). (Annual Financial Report, State of Louisiana for selected years.)

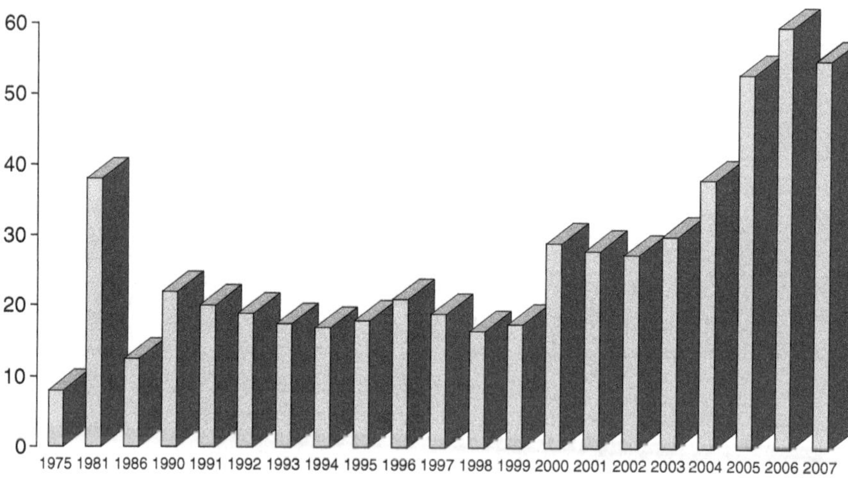

Figure 4.2 Nominal oil prices, 1975–2007. (Energy Information Administration, Annual Reports, various issues.)

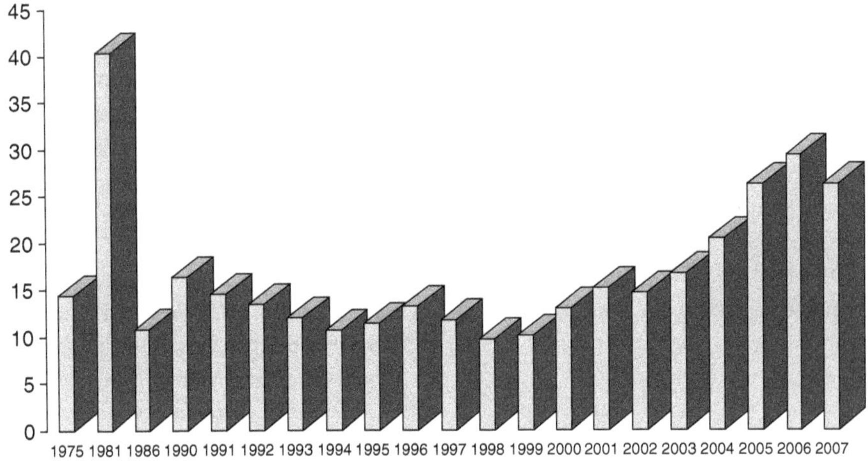

Figure 4.3 History of real oil prices, 1975–2007. (Based on nominal oil prices in Figure 4.2 and inflation index from Economic Report of the President, 2007.)

If the oil and gas tax base was the foundation of the state's revenue structure, it was also a major contributor to the overall economy. Oil and gas employment had reached over 100,000 persons in 1981, doubling over the 1970s. Exploration, development, and production had reached a frenzy because of high energy prices. Companies were reworking old reservoirs within Louisiana, typically known as a mature-producing state, because its first producing well was drilled in 1907 in Jennings—a small town in the southwestern part of the state. In addition, the Louisiana offshore in federal waters is the most productive offshore in terms of oil and gas production. Louisiana serves as the launching pad for most of this oil and gas exploration, development, and production in the federal offshore.

Edwin Edwards served as governor of Louisiana from 1971 to 1979. He was the governor who changed the tax laws in 1973. In 1979, he was succeeded by David Treen.* The budget in 1979 had a $600 million surplus. Governor Treen reduced the personal income tax as one of his first proposals in 1980. By 1983, the budget problems were beginning to be evident. The 1983 gubernatorial campaign between Treen and Edwards centered on the budget as well as the contrasting personalities—Edwards being outgoing and colorful, whereas Treen was quiet and deliberate. Edwards won in a "landslide," getting over 62 percent of the votes.

In the spring of 1984, Edwards had to call another extraordinary session of the state legislature and seek tax increases of over $1 billion—out of a budget of just about $4 billion. He was successful in getting tax increases of close to $800 million. These tax increases included increasing the sales tax a full percentage—from 3 to 4 percent;

* A governor in Louisiana can only serve for two terms of four years.

increasing fuel taxes; increasing the corporate franchise tax; increasing the tobacco tax; and a few other taxes. He and Governor Treen in 1983, before Treen's term was over, had already gone to the state legislature and repealed the Treen personal income tax reductions from 1980. The tax increases in March 1984, along with the prevailing price of oil and natural gas being in the high $20s, established the revenue forecasts for fiscal year 1984–1985 or July 1, 1984 through June 20, 1985. The governor and the state legislature believed that they had fixed the budget problems with the major tax increases of 1984.

In the late winter and early spring of 1985, the price of oil dropped quickly from the high $20s to the low teens.* What started out in July 1984 as a balanced budget suddenly became a deficit budget because of the depreciation of the price of oil. Louisiana had a deficit on its hands, not only for the fiscal year 1984–1985, but it also had to prepare a budget for 1985–1986 with a much lower revenue projection. The political process could not come to grips with how to cut state spending or raise taxes to make it in line with the new revenue projections. The executive branch then indicated that it had reworked the revenue projections and, based on its conversations with the oil industry, oil prices would rise just as rapidly as they had declined. The budget could be balanced by increasing the revenue projections due to the expectation of higher oil prices.

The governor still had control of the revenue projections. The revenue projections by the legislature were ignored. The legislature was quite willing to use the governor's revenue projections because they did not want to cut spending or raise taxes. The constitutional rule that expenditures could not exceed expected revenues was not violated. The budget for 1985–1986 as passed in the spring of 1985 met the constitutional standard.

Unfortunately, the budget for the fiscal year 1986 did not meet the economic reality standard. Louisiana incurred another deficit in the fiscal year 1986 because oil prices did not return to the high $20s. Instead, oil prices remained in the low teens. Louisiana incurred another deficit. And, the state was again faced with making a budget for the upcoming fiscal year 1986–1987. Once again, the legislature and governor could not resolve how to deal with the problem. To pass a balanced budget, the office of the governor suddenly decided the revenue projections for the fiscal year 1987 were too low. Oil prices would rise moderately, but the overall economy would grow much faster than the economists were predicting. Once more, the simple solution was to jack up the revenue projections so that it could be claimed by the governor and the legislature that the planned expenditures for the fiscal year 1987 did not exceed the projected revenues. The constitutional requirement had been satisfied.

* It was in the early spring of 1985 that I, at the encouragement of the Council for a Better Louisiana and the chancellor of Louisiana State University, put together a group of tax authorities in Louisiana to review and suggest changes in the entire Louisiana tax structure. We believed the budget crises were not temporary, but rather permanent. Hence, the name of the book was *Louisiana Fiscal Alternatives: Finding Permanent Solutions to Recurring Budget Crises.*

Once again in the fiscal year 1987, the Louisiana budget did not meet the economic realities of the day and a large deficit had been incurred. However, the large deficits that had been incurred in the previous fiscal years and the impending deficit in the fiscal year 1987 created a serious cash flow problem for the state. At some point, a state simply runs out of cash and recurring deficits will force a state into that problem. The state legislature decided that it had to find a more economically realistic way of forecasting state revenues. The politically acceptable method of establishing spending targets and then making sure the revenue projections were sufficiently high was just not working out.

The Revenue Estimating Conference in Louisiana

In 1987, the state legislature passed a law creating the Revenue Estimating Conference (REC). The REC was granted the statutory authority to establish the official revenue estimates for the state so that the proposed spending, as outlined in the Appropriations Bill, House Bill 1, would not exceed the official revenue estimates as determined by the REC. Further, the new law indicated that the REC would include four members: the governor or his representative, the speaker of the Louisiana House of Representatives, the president of the Louisiana Senate, and a private economist with expertise in economic forecasting. The private economist was to be selected by the other three members of the panel.* The legislation added one more very important provision. All decisions regarding the official revenue estimate have to be made by a unanimous vote. This simple rule gave the private economist the same power as the governor in determining the official revenue estimate.

In 1990, the state decided to make the REC a constitutional body so that it could not be undone by a simple majority vote of the state legislature. The Louisiana Constitution contains the same provisions, namely, the REC will have four members as stated in the statute and all decisions must be unanimous. In addition, the constitution added another function to the REC; namely, the REC had to determine between recurring and nonrecurring revenues and only recurring revenues could be used to fund recurring state appropriations. The private economist would still be selected by the other three members of the REC—obviously, the three members who held political positions.

One possible weakness in the structure of the REC was that the three political members could decide to get rid of the private economist if he or she would not agree with them on the revenue estimates. That has not happened in the Louisiana REC. The private economist has survived five governors, six speakers of the House, and five presidents of the Senate. The governors have been both Democrats and Republicans as have been the speakers of the House and the presidents of the Senate.

---

* The governor is typically represented by his Commissioner of Administration.

The REC hears forecasts from the Louisiana Legislative Fiscal Office and from the State Budget Office. Each office is staffed with an economist. One agency represents the legislature, the other represents the governor's office. The economists work together on getting data, making sure of any anomalies in the data, and sharing information about what might be happening at the Department of Revenue such as a major settlement being paid. They do not get together to make sure their projections are relatively close to one another.

The REC meets and can then accept one of the forecasts or pick and choose among the forecasts. The REC has almost always selected either the forecast of the Legislative Fiscal Office or the State Budget Office. The selection is based on the underlying assumptions built into the forecasts—energy prices, energy production, economic growth, interest rates, and other exogenous factors that must be built into a projection of revenues.

The meeting is open to the public and typically draws reporters from around the state as well as other interested parties. The four members of the REC cannot meet privately because of the public meetings law in Louisiana. Any analysis of the forecasts, any disagreements about the projections, and any consensus about the projections occur in the public meeting.

The REC has eliminated the practices of the 1980s—essentially making the revenue projections fit what the governor and legislature wanted to spend. Revenue projections now determine what the legislature has to spend. Bond rating companies note the nonpolitical nature of the forecasting process and the fact that it has worked for almost 20 years.

The other question, of course, is how accurate the forecasts have been. In Table 4.1, a comparison of the forecast errors is presented from the fiscal years 1989 to 2005, the fiscal year ending just before Hurricanes Katrina and Rita slammed the coast of Louisiana. The forecasting errors are based on the last meeting of the REC before the legislature adopted the Appropriations Bill. The REC typically meets in December to initiate the budget-making process for the upcoming fiscal year. The conference establishes the first official estimate for the upcoming fiscal year and the executive office starts including these estimates with the upcoming budget to be submitted by the governor to the legislature 45 days before the session begins. In Louisiana, the legislative sessions begin in late March in even number years and in late April in odd number years. The REC meets in April or May to finalize the forecasts for the upcoming fiscal year as well as revise the projections for the present fiscal year. The forecasting errors are calculated on the last official revenue projections on which the state's budget is based.

Table 4.1 shows that the REC has made projections that are under what actually happened 12 out of 17 times. To a certain extent, this is very predictable. There is a built-in caution in the revenue estimates. The state can handle an unexpected surplus much easier than it can handle an unanticipated deficit. The REC wants to be as right on the money as possible, but projections will not be 100 percent accurate—this is the nature of forecasting. Hence, the REC would rather miss by

Table 4.1 Louisiana REC: Forecasting Errors, State General Fund

Fiscal Year	*State Budget (in Billion Dollars)*	*Last Forecast Before Legislature Completes Appropriations Bill (Percent)*	*Projection (Under) or Over Actual Collections (in Million Dollars)*
1989	4.34	−3.50	(152.0)
1990	4.16	−1.34	(55.7)
1991	4.23	−0.37	(15.6)
1992	3.90	+3.16	123.2
1993	4.28	−1.79	(76.6)
1994	4.33	+0.10	4.3
1995	4.78	−2.20	(105.2)
1996	5.16	−3.87	(199.9)
1997	5.66	−1.52	(86.0)
1998	5.78	−1.80	(104.0)
1999	5.70	+1.76	100.3
2000	5.85	−0.98	(57.3)
2001	6.53	−2.93	(191.3)
2002	6.45	+0.10	6.45
2003	6.40	+0.10	6.40
2004	6.77	−0.43	(29.1)
2005	7.39	−3.08	(228.3)

Source: G. Albrecht, Legislative Fiscal Office, State of Louisiana. With permission.

being under the actual revenues that are generated as opposed to forecasting more revenues than are actually generated.

The scheduling of the REC is illustrated in Table 4.2. The REC typically meets four times per year, but can meet more frequently if needed. Most of the meetings are related to establishing and then reviewing the official revenue estimates for the state general fund. This is important because the budget process begins and ends with the official forecast made by the REC. Any downward adjustment in the revenue estimates mid-year will lead to actions by the governor and legislature to pare down state expenditures. Any upward adjustment in the official revenue estimates does not lead to any immediate increase in state spending. The legislature will deal with the pending surplus in the next regularly scheduled legislative session.

As noted in Table 4.2, an additional responsibility of maintaining a watch over the Unemployment Insurance Trust Fund has been given to the REC by statute. In 1987, this trust fund was in default and the state had to borrow over $1 billion to return it to solvency. The state reduced benefits to unemployed workers and raised contribution rates made by businesses to handle the debt service and get the trust fund solvent again. By 1995, the debt had been paid off and the trust

Table 4.2 Meeting Schedules and Responsibilities of Louisiana REC (State Fiscal Years Run from July 1 to June 30)

Typical Meeting Dates	*Responsibilities at Meetings*
September	To incorporate any changes in tax code from latest legislative session into official forecast for current and future fiscal years; REC also certifies the Unemployment Insurance Trust Fund and projects trust fund's balance as on September of the following year.
December	Review revenue projections for current fiscal year and make revisions as necessary; make official revenue projections for upcoming fiscal year.
February	Review revenue projections for current fiscal year and make revisions as necessary; review official revenue estimates for upcoming fiscal year and revise as necessary.
May	Review revenue projections for current fiscal year and make revisions as necessary; review official revenue estimates for upcoming fiscal year and revise as necessary. These are the revenue projections that are incorporated in House Bill 1, the Appropriations Bill.
As needed	Special meetings can be called at any time if any fiscal problem is becoming evident. Economists at Legislative Fiscal Office and State Budget Office monitor revenue collections on monthly basis. Commissioner of Administration and private economist follow the revenue estimates on a monthly basis. If any shortfalls are expected, a meeting can be held.

Source: Author, a member of the Revenue Estimating Conference.

fund was solvent. Businesses wanted their contribution rates to be reduced and workers were asking for increases in unemployment benefits paid to those out of work. But the state did not want to repeat the financial difficulties of the 1980s. Both the business community and the labor organizations were adamant that the state should establish a system that would maintain the long-term solvency of the Unemployment Insurance Trust Fund. The law established benchmarks for contribution rates to be reduced and unemployment benefits to be increased, if and only if the REC certified that the Unemployment Insurance Trust Fund had a sufficient balance and was projected to maintain such a balance. This law was first passed in 1995 and has been maintained since that time.

Finally, any two members of the REC can call a meeting at any time if unfavorable and unexpected economic conditions are affecting revenue collections. If the

REC meets and changes the official forecast of revenues for the fiscal year in which the state is operating, the governor and legislature have 30 days to make adjustments in the budget or call a special session of the legislature to take appropriate action, either by raising revenues or by reducing spending. Typically, the governor is given some flexibility in the Appropriations Bill to cut spending within limits if there is a budget shortfall. However, if the projected revenue decline is greater than that flexibility, then the governor has no recourse but to call a special session of the legislature to deal with the budgetary shortfall.

Forecasting Revenues in the Midst of Katrina and Rita

The Louisiana REC was created because of the volatility of revenues related to dramatic changes in the oil and gas industry. The REC in the past two years had to deal with the impact of two major hurricanes on Louisiana in August/September 2005. On August 29, 2005, Hurricane Katrina battered the Gulf Coast region causing catastrophic damage in Alabama, Mississippi, and Louisiana and, two days after the hurricane, levees protecting New Orleans were overtopped/breached causing flooding in about 80 percent of the city. Homes, businesses, public facilities, and infrastructure were destroyed. On September 23, 2005, Hurricane Rita battered the southwestern coast of Louisiana and the southeastern coast of Texas. Transmission lines were knocked down, roofs were blown off, and healthcare facilities were evacuated; in less than one month two major hurricanes came ashore in Louisiana. These two hurricanes left indelible impression on individuals, businesses, and state and local governments.

The state of Louisiana was in the first quarter of its 2005–2006 fiscal year when the hurricanes struck.* The state budget had been balanced and the expectation for the economy for 2005–2006 was moderate growth (Scott and Richardson 2004). The hurricanes suddenly changed the economic structure, altered potential revenue streams for both state and local governments, and imposed new expenditures on state and local governments.

On October 28, 2005, in a special meeting called and agreed to by all participants, the Louisiana REC met to reconsider the revenue estimates determined on May 16, 2005 for the fiscal year 2005–2006 state budget and the estimates used to determine appropriations for 2005–2006.[†,‡]

There was no direct information on actual tax collections after hurricanes Katrina and Rita because of the timing of collections and then remittance to the state. The Louisiana Department of Revenue had granted extensions to businesses in the areas affected by Katrina when taxes had to be remitted. The information

* Louisiana state fiscal year runs from July 1 to June 30.

† The Louisiana Legislature meets from late March to mid-June for its regular sessions.

‡ REC, Official Forecast, document from Fiscal Division, Louisiana House of Representatives.

available was the knowledge that a sizeable portion of the Louisiana economy had been badly damaged; over 200,000 homes were uninhabitable; the New Orleans tourist industry had been temporarily shut down; major employers such as Shell Oil Company, private and public universities, most hospitals and medical providers, and almost all law firms had seen their employees evacuate the city; the Port of New Orleans, major shipyards, and Lockheed Martin space shuttle program had been closed; and Louisiana citizens were scattered throughout the fifty states and two territories.[*,†] These are the citizens who pay personal income taxes, general sales taxes, and selective sales taxes to the state. It should be noted that the New Orleans metropolitan area accounted for over 30 percent of the Louisiana economic base—this was the potential magnitude of the disaster looking at it from the state's perspective.

Major oil and gas properties within the taxing jurisdiction of Louisiana were shut down due to damage caused by Katrina and Rita.[‡] However, due to the hurricanes and international developments, the global price of oil was reaching the \$60/bbl level and the price of natural gas in the United States was reaching in excess of \$10/1000 ft^3.[§] Louisiana gets over 12 percent of its revenues from oil and gas activities.

Finally, the state gets about 8 percent of its revenues from gaming activities—a land-based casino in New Orleans; fifteen riverboats scattered around the state, but with three located in New Orleans affected by Katrina and five located in Lake Charles affected by Rita, and video poker scattered around the state. The land-based casino and the riverboats in New Orleans were closed and two riverboats in Lake Charles were severely damaged and the others were temporarily shut down.[¶,**]

Revenue estimates were revised based on secondary information such as employment and population information, the substantial increase in the unemployment rolls, the reduction in oil and gas production, the projected loss of gaming activities, and other economic-related information. Economists in the state were concerned that Louisiana, especially because of Katrina, would not follow the same economic pattern of other states in which a natural disaster strikes. Homes, businesses, and social institutions were destroyed, and then the state quickly begins rebuilding. The rule

---

* Based on FEMA and Red Cross surveys and inspections. (Press releases of Federal Emergency Management Administration throughout the fall of 2005.)

† Federal Emergency Management Administration, January 27, 2006.

‡ Report by David Dismukes, Center for Energy Studies, Louisiana State University, Fall 2005. Professor Dismukes' estimates were based on data from the Energy Information Administration, U.S. Department of Energy.

§ Oil and natural gas prices as reported in *The Wall Street Journal* on a daily basis.

¶ The land-based casino in New Orleans has a contract with the state to pay at least \$60 million per year regardless of its business activities. The state had projected revenues of \$74.4 million from the land-based casino in 2005–2006; therefore, the loss of the casino, at the maximum, could cost the state \$14.4 million, not \$74.4 million.

** Testimony before Louisiana REC.

Table 4.3 Revenue Estimates for Louisiana for the Fiscal Year 2005–2006 (as Determined by REC in May 2005, October 2005, and Actual Collections)

Taxes	*May 16, 2005 Estimates (in Billion)*	*October 28, 2005 Estimates (in Billion)*	*Actual Collections in 2005–2006 (in Billion)*
Total ($)	9.005	8.115	10.495

Source: Official Estimates of REC, Web site of the Louisiana Division of Administration, State of Louisiana. www.doa.louisiana.gov/opb/pub/other-budget-docs.htm

of thumb is that natural disasters first create misery and then opportunity. In most natural disasters, it is not uncommon to experience an increase in revenues because of the increase in spending in the state from federal assistance to insurance payouts.

The May 16 estimates for the fiscal year 2005–2006 and the October 28 revised estimates are compared in Table 4.3. Major reductions in revenue estimates were made in personal income taxes, corporate taxes, general sales taxes, and gaming revenues. These estimates were reduced because of the loss of a large base of the Louisiana economy. Gaming revenues were reduced due to the loss of the land-based casino and the shutdown of several riverboats. Mineral revenues were increased due to the higher price of oil and natural gas than had been estimated in May 2005. The October estimates had the proportion of dollars from the general sales taxes and mineral revenues increasing and the proportion of dollars from all other revenue sources decreasing. The REC ultimately recommended a reduction in the official revenue estimate for 2005–2006 from $9.005 to 8.114 billion, a 9.9 percent reduction.

The concerns for a reduction in revenues turned out to be false. By February 2006, it was clear that the revenues were returning to and exceeding their pre-Katrina estimates. In fact, in February, the REC met and increased the revenue projections to $8.95 billion or just about the same number that had been estimated in May 2005. By the end of the year, actual revenue collections had risen to almost $10.5 billion. Revenues in Louisiana followed exactly the same pattern as revenues in other states that incurred major natural disasters. The degree of damage due to Katrina and Rita exaggerated the revenue increases instead of hampering the revenue collections.

The recovery process has accelerated the collection of sales taxes—people buying new appliances, new furniture, new clothes, and new vehicles. Individuals have also had additional money from the Federal Emergency Management Administration (FEMA) and the Red Cross. In addition, gaming revenues rose despite the fact that several gaming facilities were severely damaged. The rising gaming revenues may be the result of relief workers participating in the gaming activities—the fact that Mississippi had lost, at least temporarily, all of its gaming facilities; therefore, Mississippi customers came to Louisiana, and perhaps some people used their

FEMA money to gamble.* The average dollars lost by each participant in gaming activities increased from about $60 to almost $100 per outing.† The state's personal income tax collections rose despite the fact that over 300,000 new unemployment claims were posted just after Katrina. Oil and gas production came back and energy prices stayed high for the entire fiscal year; therefore, oil and gas revenues also rose.

During the fiscal year 2005–2006, the state's next step was to plan a budget for 2006–2007. The revenue estimates were based on judgments about the pace of recovery, the continuation of spending by consumers and businesses, the return of the state's population, and other factors for which there are no historical pattern on which the projections has to be based. The sales tax base has been ratcheted up because of the purchase of appliances, furniture, cars, clothes, and other items to get families back to normalcy. These expenditures and hence the sales tax base are not necessarily recurring. The sales tax base is in transition. Establishing the actual sales tax base is difficult because tax data is not broken down in such detail. After establishing the sales tax base, the rate of growth of a known sales tax base must be selected. This rate of growth will depend on the recovery rate of the most seriously damaged parishes. This rate of recovery is yet to be determined.

The number of persons who actually return to Louisiana as well as the types of jobs that are available for these persons will have an impact on personal income tax collections. The number of persons working in Louisiana, including relief workers, will determine taxes collected from tobacco, beer and alcoholic beverages, gaming, and general sales tax. The state is starting all over again to create a historical record by which it can project its revenues. This is especially true for the tax base for personal income taxes and general and selective sales taxes, tax collections that are paid directly by the citizens of the state and persons working in a state. Revenue estimates for 2006–2007 are illustrated in Table 4.4. The state was expected to have more money in 2006–2007 than it did in 2005–2006, but not more than it had originally expected to have for 2005–2006 based on May 2005 estimates. As it has turned out, the initial revenue estimates for 2006–2007 were much too low. Presently, it is anticipated that the state will collect $10.666 billion in 2006–2007. Again, state revenues have grown significantly because of the economic activity created by the storms.

The 2007 Regular Session of the state legislature had the following funds to appropriate: (1) a $827 million surplus left over from the fiscal year 2005–2006, (2) nonappropriated funds of almost $1.6 billion from the extra revenues being generated in 2006–2007, and (3) an additional $1.4 billion to be appropriated for the fiscal year 2007–2008—this is the difference between the revenue projection for 2007–2008 and the recurring spending obligations as defined in the 2006–2007 budget. In total, the state had over $3.8 billion to spend during the 2007 Regular Session.

---

* All of the Mississippi riverboats were shut down due to Katrina. In December, two riverboats opened up and a casino opened in January.

† Information from a report by Greg Albrecht, economist with the Louisiana Legislative Fiscal Office in the fall of 2005.

Table 4.4 Revenue Estimates for Louisiana for the Fiscal Year 2006–2007 (as Determined by REC in October 2005, May 2006, and Current Estimates)

Taxes	*October 28, 2005 Estimates for 2006–2007 (in Billion)*	*May 2006 Estimates for 2006–2007 (in Billion)*	*May 2007 Estimates for 2006–2007 (in Billion)*
Total ($)	8.644	8.722	10.666

Source: Official Estimates of REC, Web site of Louisiana Division of Administration, State of Louisiana. www.doa.louisiana.gov/opb/pub/other-budget-docs.htm

Table 4.5 Long-Term Revenue Projections by Louisiana Legislative Fiscal Office and State Budget Office

Forecasts by Agency	*2008–2009 ($)*	*2009–2010 ($)*	*2010–2011 ($)*
Legislative Fiscal Office	10.533	10.483	10.663
State Budget Office	10.271	10.111	10.104

Source: Official Estimates of REC, Web site of Louisiana Division of Administration, State of Louisiana. www.doa.louisiana.gov/opb/pub/other-budget-docs.htm

The major concern now is will the revenue growth continue; will it flatten out; or will it decline. These forecasts are important because it affects how the state spends the money. The state can put most of the money into one-time projects, thereby not creating a long-term financial obligation for the state; or it can put much of the money into recurring programs or tax cuts, thereby creating a long-term financial obligation for future governors, legislators, and the citizens of the state.

The REC also examines and approves long-term revenue projections, although these projections do not get the same attention as the revenue forecasts for the current or upcoming fiscal year. The long-term forecasts are provided in Table 4.5 for both the State Budget Office and the Legislative Fiscal Office. As is evident, there is a major gap between the long-term outlook of the Legislative Fiscal Office and the long-term outlook of the State Budget Office. This long-term difference is much greater than the differences that were projected for the fiscal years 2007 and 2008.

The REC handled the potential damage to the revenue stream in Louisiana because of Katrina and Rita very prudently. It did not want the state to incur a large shortfall after most state agencies had spent their funds for 2005–2006. In the end, the revenue projections were simply wrong. This is one of the conflicts that the REC has. The duty of the REC is to establish the official forecasts for the state, and not to set budget policy. Yet, there is a bit of budget policy in every forecast. There is no doubt that the reduction in revenue projections in October 2005 just after Katrina included a very prudent approach to handling the state finances after such a storm, but it also included a great deal of uncertainty about what might have happened to the state's economy.*

Summary and Conclusions

Louisiana's colorful political history spills over into something as mundane as revenue forecasting. The oil and gas boom and bust created the absolute need for a more economically driven forecasting process. Louisiana created its REC, a combination of political leaders and an outside economist who would have the authority to establish the official revenue forecast for the state. This combination has worked well in Louisiana since 1987. In 1987, the state had incurred three straight years of deficits due to manipulation of the revenue forecast and the state was facing a cash flow problem. Now, 20 years later, the REC is still working. From 1989 to 2005, the REC had a good record of forecast accuracy. Most of the time the REC had revenue forecasts that were lower than the actual collections. This was by design to an extent given the difficulties state government has in making mid-year budget cuts. The REC's latest challenge was to deal with the aftermath of Katrina and Rita on the state's revenue collections. The REC developed a prudent approach to forecasting state revenues. As it turned out, the revenue projections have been much too low compared to the actual collections. Now, the challenge is not to suddenly get too carefree about future growth in revenues. Forecasting is a fragile game. The REC has worked well in Louisiana.

References

Richardson, J. A. (Ed.). 1988. *Louisiana Fiscal Alternatives: Finding Permanent Solutions to Recurring Budget Crises*. Baton Rouge, LA: Louisiana State University Press.

Richardson, J. A. 2006. Natural disasters in state and local finance in Louisiana: A case study in 2005. *Municipal Finance Journal* 27(2): 53–74.

Scott, L. C. and J. A. Richardson. 2004. *Louisiana Economic Outlook, 2005–06*. Baton Rouge, LA: E. J. Ourso College of Business, Louisiana State University.

* This information was first published in Richardson (2006).

Chapter 5

Budget Forecasting for the State of California*

Jon David Vasché, Brad Williams, and Robert Ingenito

Contents

* The Legislative Analyst's Office (LAO) is the California legislature's nonpartisan fiscal and budgetary review office. The LAO is headed by Elizabeth G. Hill, California's legislative analyst. This chapter is a work product of the authors and not the LAO, and they are solely responsible for its content, including any errors or omissions.

Introduction

California is by far the largest state in the nation, virtually by any measure used; has an economy that ranks equivalent to the eighth largest country in the world; and has an over $350 billion state–local public sector. Its population and economy are also highly diverse and dynamic, making the task of accurately forecasting the state government's revenues and expenditures extremely challenging. This chapter discusses how governmental budget forecasting in California is approached; examines the specific types of modeling used; reviews the state's track record in making fiscal forecasts; and identifies the unique challenges that fiscal forecasters face in making accurate projections.

The chapter is organized as follows. First, it provides an overview of California's fiscal structure and forecasting environment. This is followed by a section that deals with forecasting California's demography and economy, which are key determinants of the state budget's main components. It then discusses the forecasting of state revenues, state expenditures, and finally, the state's bottom-line fiscal condition.

Overview of California's Fiscal Structure and Forecasting Environment

This section provides the basic background and framework necessary for thinking about governmental budget forecasting in California. It first considers the basic scope and nature of California's state budget, the constitutional framework within which the budget must be managed, and how the government sector itself is organized in the state. The latter includes the relationship between the state government and the state's approximately 7000 local governments and its implications for state fiscal forecasting. It then discusses California's recent budgetary experience, key forecasting entities, the types of forecasting products that are produced, and finally, the fundamental issue of dynamic modeling and to what extent it plays a role in making California's budgetary projections.

Scope and Nature of California's State Budget

Size and Composition

In 2006–2007, California's state budget totaled almost $130 billion and was used to fund more than 150 individual departments. In addition, another nearly $60 billion in federal funds were received by the state and allocated to state programs and local governments through the state budget process. Figure 5.1 shows the distribution of state spending by major program area. It indicates, for example, that about 40 percent of the state budget goes for education, nearly 30 percent funds health and social services programs, and the remainder funds such areas as

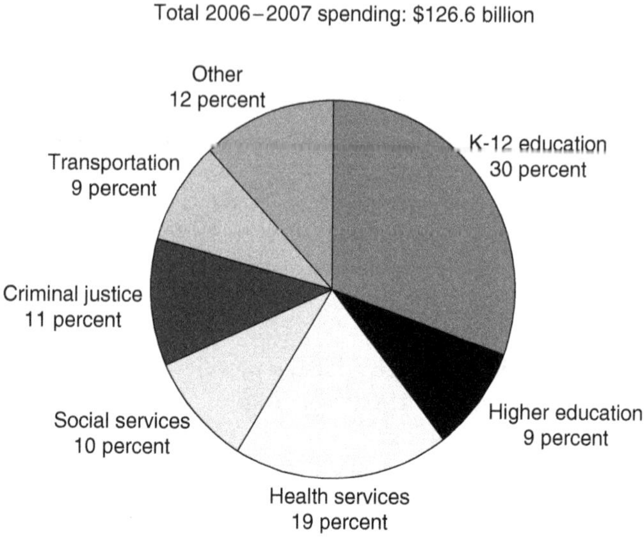

Figure 5.1 California state spending by major program area. (From Governor's Budget Summary 2007–2008, State of California, January 2007.)

corrections, transportation, general government, and resources and environment-related programs.

Trends over Time

Figure 5.2 shows the trend over approximately the past 15 years in total California state spending in both nominal dollars and real (i.e., inflation-adjusted) dollars, and real per capita dollars. It indicates that

- Nominal spending grew by over 140 percent over the entire period for an average annual growth of 6.5 percent.
- After adjusting for inflation, real spending has grown by nearly 54 percent over the entire period, or an annual average growth rate of approximately 3.1 percent.
- Real per capita spending—which adjusts for both inflation and population growth—has grown by about 27 percent over the period for an average annual growth rate of 1.7 percent. Since 2003–2004, however, the annual growth rate has approximately doubled, that is, 3.4 percent.

Each of the state's individual program areas that comprise the total requires its own forecasting approach based on the factors that combine to determine program costs such as caseloads and program-specific inflation.

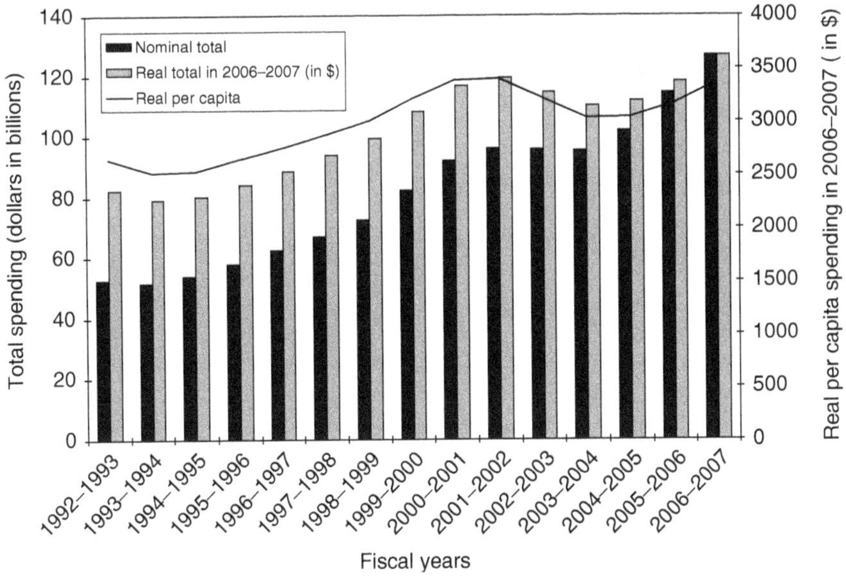

Figure 5.2 California state spending over time. (From Governor's Budget Summary 2007–2008, State of California.)

How the Budget Is Organized

California's state budget is organized according to different funds. Of these

- The largest is the General Fund, which currently accounts for about 80 percent of all budgetary spending. The General Fund is the main source of support for state programs and funds a wide variety of activities. For example, it is the major funding source for K-12 education and higher education programs, health and social services programs, youth and adult correctional programs, as well as tax relief and state debt financing.
- The remaining, approximately 20 percent of budgetary spending involves special funds. These are used to allocate certain tax revenues (such as gasoline and certain cigarette tax receipts) for specific functions or activities of government designated in law. About one-third special funds revenues come from motor vehicle–related levies, whereas one-fifth comes from sales taxes. These revenue sources are used to support transportation, resources, parks, healthcare programs, and various forms of local government assistance.
- Other categories of spending include expenditures from bond funds to support capital projects, nongovernmental cost funds (such as unemployment and disability funds), and trust funds (such as pension funds).

Although the revenues, expenditures, and balances of all of the different budget-related fund categories (General Fund and special funds) need to be forecasted individually on an annual basis, the forecasting process places special emphasis on the bottom-line situation for the General Fund.

Basic Governing Constitutional Provisions

California's basic budget process is governed by a number of provisions in the state constitution and various budget-related statutes. Some of the key constitutional provisions associated with the budget are as follows:

- *Budgetary vote requirement.* Enactment of a budget—as well as individual General Fund appropriations (other than those for public education) and all appropriations with an urgency clause—requires two-thirds vote in both houses of the legislature. California is one of the only three states to have such a supermajority vote requirement. California also requires two-thirds vote to raise taxes—one of the sixteen states that have a supermajority requirement for tax increases.
- *Balanced budget provision and borrowing.* The budget enacted into law must be balanced. The state constitution also sets forth a process for making midyear corrections in the event the governor finds that an enacted budget has fallen out of balance. However, there is no prohibition *per se* against there being a budget deficit, and the state has in fact run large deficits in a number of recent years (see section California's Recent Budgetary Environment). In addition, uncollateralized borrowing is generally prohibited without a vote of the electorate.*
- *Spending limit.* There is a state appropriations limit (SAL) that constrains the amount of spending in any one year from exceeding a base-year amount adjusted for population and inflation, as specified. However, the limit has seldom been a constraining factor on state spending.†

* To pass, general obligation bonds require a majority vote of the electorate. In terms of long-term general debt obligations, as of March 2007, California had approximately $39 billion of such outstanding debt. Of this, the vast majority is for financing capital outlay projects such as schools, prisons, and water-related delivery systems. The state also had $7.7 billion of lease-revenue bonds outstanding, which are not general debt obligations and are paid off from lease payments made for use of the facilities the bonds have financed. Finally, the state has nearly $50 billion in revenue bonds outstanding, which are paid off from project related revenue streams such as contracts for water use on water-related projects. All these borrowings constitute "long-term" debt obligations. In terms of "short term" debt obligations, these are largely used for cash flow management purposes to bridge temporary time gaps between when state expenditures must be made and state revenues are received. The amount of such short-term cash flow borrowing in recent years has been in the range $3–$6 billion.

† California's SAL was adopted as Proposition 4 in November 1979. It generally limits spending by both the state and its individual localities to prior-year amounts adjusted for population and inflation.

- *Education funding guarantee.* There is also a minimum-guaranteed annual spending amount for K-14 (kindergarten through community colleges) education that was adopted as Proposition 98 in November 1988. Under this guarantee, the amount of funding provided to education depends on which of the several "tests" are operative. These tests, in turn, depend on such factors as state per capita personal income, revenues, and school enrollments (see additional discussion on the education funding guarantee on page 96).
- *Budgetary reserves.* California has had a reserve requirement in its constitution since the late 1970s. However, until recently, there were no specific requirements or provisions regarding the size of the reserve, payments into the reserve, or withdrawals from the reserve. In 2004, though, California voters approved, as part of a deficit-financing bond package, a new reserve fund, called the budget stabilization account (BSA). A fixed percentage of revenues are required to be set aside into this fund beginning in 2006–2007. Such annual transfers, which are 1 percent in 2006–2007, 2 percent in 2007–2008, and 3 percent per year in 2008–2009 and thereafter, are required until the balance in the reserve fund reaches $8 billion or 5 percent of annual revenues, whichever is greater. The reserve can be suspended by the executive order of the governor.

Because most of these provisions (including whether the budget is projected to be in balance, the spending limit, and the education funding guarantee) ultimately depend either on state revenues, state expenditures, or demographic or economic variables, predicting each of these determinants is an important part of the fiscal forecasting process.

The State–Local Fiscal Relationship

In terms of expenditures and revenues, the size of California's combined state–local governmental sector incorporating all intergovernmental receipts measures over $350 billion. This is divided approximately 65/35 between the state government and its approximately 7000 local entities, including counties, cities, school districts, and special districts.* The state's individual localities are responsible for doing their own fiscal forecasting. However, because a substantial share of the state budget is passed forward to localities in the form of direct payments for programs, subventions and reimbursements, and grants, the budgetary projections done at the state level have important implications for the localities' own fiscal forecasts. The fiscal outlooks for the state and its localities are especially interwoven because of various ballot propositions that California's voters have enacted and various associated

* In 2003–2004, for example, according to the U.S. Census Bureau, combined own-source general revenues for the state and its localities amounted to $198 billion including $105 billion for the state and $93 billion for its localities.

statutory changes that have occurred.* Other factors relating the fiscal outlook for the two levels of government are that the property tax is not only the single most important own-source component of local revenues but also a key determinant of how much the state government contributes toward funding local schools, whereas the sales tax is the second largest own source of all-purpose revenues for both governmental levels.

Thus, the bottom line is that state budget forecasting in California has important implications for local budget forecasting as well.

California's Recent Budgetary Environment

During the late 1990s, California's state government revenues grew rapidly, driven by healthy economic growth and soaring income from stock market–related capital gains and stock option income. State-level policy makers allocated these funds to added spending on state programs and for tax relief. This boom ended in late 2000 when the stock market plunged and the subsequent economic downturn resulted in a nearly 20 percent drop in state revenues in 2001–2002. As a result of this revenue decline, ongoing projected multi-billion-dollar annual funding gaps opened up between anticipated revenues and expenditure commitments. Although budgetary actions and the resumption of strong revenue growth have since enabled the state to narrow this gap, as of mid-decade the state was still struggling with a significant and persistent structural imbalance between its General Fund revenues and expenditures.

Forecasting Entities, Products, and Timelines

In California's state government, there are two main entities involved in economic, revenue, and expenditure forecasting for budgetary purposes. These are the Department of Finance (DOF), which provides forecasts for the governor's budget, and the nonpartisan Legislative Analyst's Office (LAO), which provides forecasts for both houses of the legislature.

The DOF normally prepares three forecasts during each fiscal year. The first is an internal planning estimate, which is usually completed in early October and is used by executive branch agencies in the initial preparation of governor's proposed budget for the upcoming fiscal year. The second is prepared in November and December, and serves as the basis for the governor's budget proposal released on

* Among the key measures have been Proposition 13 (June 1978), which limits local property tax levies; Proposition 98; Proposition 1A (November 2004), which restricts the ability of the state to reduce local government revenues from the property tax, sales tax, and vehicle license fee; a local swap of vehicle license fees for property taxes (2004–2005); and a shift of property taxes between localities (2004–2005).

January 10. The third forecast is prepared in April and early May, and serves as the basis for the Governor's May Revision to the January budget proposal.

The second forecasting entity is the LAO, which is the legislature's nonpartisan fiscal and policy advisor. The LAO prepares economic and revenue forecasts for a minimum of three times every fiscal year. Its initial forecast, prepared in November, appears in an annual report entitled "California's Fiscal Outlook." This document provides the legislature with a "baseline" projection of the state's fiscal condition in the upcoming fiscal year and beyond, assuming current-law revenue and spending policies. The LAO's second forecast, presented in February, is a part of its annual review of the governor's January budget proposal. Its final forecast immediately follows the release of the Governor's May Revision. The LAO bases its February and May forecasts on the policies embedded in the governor's budget proposal. Thus, they present estimates of the consequences of the Governor's proposed policies on the state's fiscal condition in the budget year and beyond. At the request of the legislature's members or committees, the LAO also prepares projections of the state's fiscal condition under alternative budget proposals and fiscal updates at other times of the year.

Internal Dynamics of the Forecasting Process

Whether it is the LAO or DOF, a given agency's forecasts of expenditures and revenues are usually simultaneously prepared to produce that agency's "bottom-line" fiscal outlook for the budget. However, its expenditure and revenue forecasts are in most cases developed largely independent of one another.

- For example, in the case of both the DOF and LAO, those individuals who prepare the expenditure forecasts are generally different from those who prepare the revenue forecasts. For instance, both agencies have separate units staffed largely by economists who prepare their respective agency's economic and revenue forecasts. Expenditure forecasts, in contrast, tend to be prepared by individuals in other units of each agency who deal with issues associated with specific program areas of the budget, such as education, health and social services, and corrections.
- In some cases, however, there can be considerable interaction within each agency between individuals involved in the revenue and expenditure areas. An example involves projections for K-12 education, where economic and revenue assumptions play a key role in calculating the Proposition 98 funding guarantee. Another is in transportation, where projections of taxable sales on gasoline versus other items appear in formulas that play a role in determining the funding available for different programs.
- Likewise, at the LAO, the economists working in the unit preparing the economic and tax revenue forecasts also frequently work with the programmatic

staff to develop models for expenditure forecasting that utilize appropriate statistical techniques and modeling software that these economists are experts with.

- In all cases, the expenditure and revenue forecasts for each respective agency use the specific economic and demographic assumptions prepared by that particular agency. Although the LAO and DOF produce their own fiscal forecasts independent of one another, both the offices' staff communicate with their counterparts regarding program issues and developments and the basis for any forecasting differences.

Short- versus Long-Term Forecasts

For many years, fiscal projections in California focused primarily on the near-term outlook—that is, the outlook for the current year and the upcoming budget year—with relatively little attention devoted to the longer-term consequences of current or proposed fiscal policies. This projection changed beginning in the early 1990s and accelerated in the early 2000s when state policy makers, faced with large budgetary shortfalls, considered multiyear strategies to bring the budget back into balance. These involved such factors as temporary tax increases, spending deferrals, and funding shifts, all of which had varying fiscal effects over time. Today, both the DOF and LAO typically include long-term projections as part of their forecasts. The number of out-years covered and reporting format differs depending on the time of year and forecasting entity involved. For example, the LAO's November publication normally includes revenue and expenditure projections for four years beyond the budget year, and its other forecasting-related publications usually include projections extending at least one or two years into the future. Although the administration's January and May Revision budget documents typically focus on just revenues and expenditures through the budget year, the administration normally prepares longer-term projections at each of these junctures, which in most instances are available to the public.

The Use of Alternative Forecast Scenarios

In theory, alternative forecast scenarios can play an important role in state budgeting. For example, forecasters could use the projected impacts of plausible alternative scenarios relating to the economy, capital gains realizations, and other factors to calibrate the optimal size of any budgetary reserves they would include in each year's budget or for the development of contingency budget plans.*

* Under such contingency budgeting approaches, a state could, for example, adopt provisions as part of its annual budget for allocating among different program areas any unanticipated revenue increases or reductions, should they materialize.

At times, the DOF and LAO projections have incorporated such alternative scenarios. For example, in its February 2006 "Perspectives and Issues" discussion about the economy, the LAO discussed the impacts of a key risk to its economic outlook—namely, that a steeper-than-expected housing downturn would materially depress the state's economy, state tax revenues, and California's bottom-line fiscal condition (see, for example, Legislative Analyst's Office, 2006a).

Although such alternatives have been useful in providing lawmakers with perspectives about uncertainties inherent in the fiscal outlooks, policy makers have not used them explicitly in the development of the budget. Rather, California's policy makers have tended to focus on single "most likely" forecast scenarios for budgeting purposes. Decisions about how to respond to changes in the budgetary outlook have usually been made after—rather than before—their occurrence.

Dynamic Estimating

Dynamic estimating is the inclusion of the impacts into revenue and expenditure forecasts not only of various behavioral effects arising from tax and spending policies (such as reducing smoking when government raises cigarette taxes) but also their economywide impacts (such as effects on business investment and migration flows). Although California has previously experimented with dynamic estimating on the revenue side of the budget, it, like the federal government and other states, has never incorporated such calculations into its budgetary totals. This policy is largely due to the associated data, methodological, and other issues involved. California does, however, routinely incorporate the impacts of behavioral changes due to policy changes into its revenue and expenditure forecasts, when forecasters can make reliable estimates of these effects.*

Forecasting California's Demographics and Economy

Making reliable projections of California's demographics and the performance of its economy are key steps in forecasting the state's revenues, expenditures, and overall fiscal position. For example, the components of population and its changes by age group help to determine such things as school enrollments, demand for healthcare, and size of the labor force. Similarly, the amount of personal income, profits, and taxable sales generated by economic activity affect the state's income tax, corporation tax (CT), and sales and use tax (SUT) revenues that policy makers use to fund public programs. This section discusses the nature of California's demographics and economy and how forecasters develop those projections in conjunction with making fiscal forecasts.

* For a discussion of California's experience with dynamic revenue estimating and the issues involved, see Vasché (2006a). For a revised version of this paper, see Vasché (2006b).

Predicting California's Demographics

California's Basic Demographic Features

Size and growth. California's population is large, diverse, and dynamic. As of July 2007, it totaled nearly 37.9 million people, or approximately 12 percent of the nation. As shown in Figure 5.3, its annual growth has averaged about 1.6 percent over the past decade, or about 550,000 persons annually. This growth approximately equates to adding a city, which is the size of Long Beach or a state about the size of Vermont or Wyoming, to California every year. The figure also shows, however, that the pace of population growth has experienced considerable variation over time, reflecting changes in the pace of economic growth, domestic migration patterns, and birth rates.

Composition. California's population is also notable in terms of its extremely diverse age, ethnic, and racial mix. As shown in Figure 5.4, this diversity has increased over time to the point where, as of 2002, no one ethnic group has a majority.

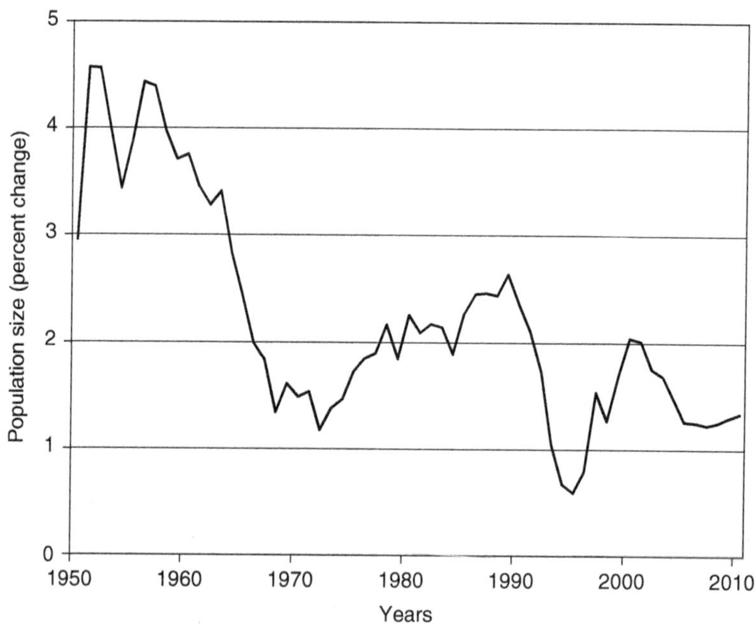

Figure 5.3 Annual growth in California's population. (From February 2007 LAO projections for 2006 and beyond.)

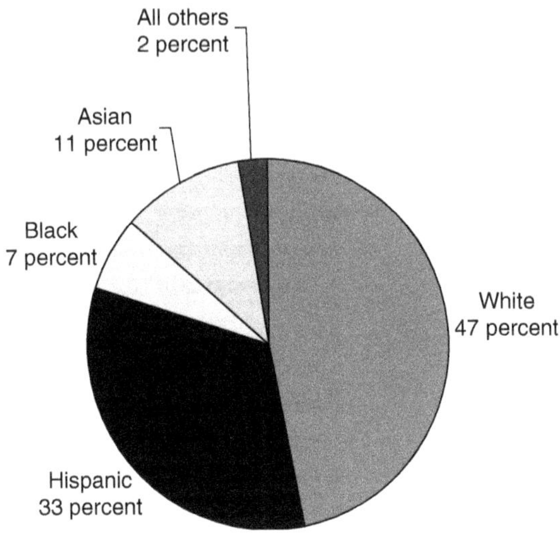

Figure 5.4 Ethnic mix of California's population. (From February 2007 LAO estimate for July 2006.)

Such diversity makes demographic forecasting especially challenging for California, given the variation in birth rates among its subcomponents and other factors that characterize it.*

Population Growth Components

For the purpose of demographic forecasting, California's population growth is best divided into two major components—"natural increase" (the excess of births over deaths) and "net in-migration" (persons moving into California from other states and countries, minus those leaving California for out-of-state destinations). In turn, net in-migration can be further classified into "domestic" net in-migration (migration between states) and "foreign" net in-migration (migration between countries).

* In the case of Hispanics, the largest and most rapidly growing ethnic group in California, recent trends involving female birth rates and fertility patterns are a good example of the demographic forecasting challenges involved. Here, due to a variety of societal and economic factors, reductions in fertility rates have been especially significant. The rate dropped from 3.4 children per woman in 1993 to only 2.6 in 2004, with some further decline still expected. This rapid drop-off had been unexpected with DOF projecting only ten years ago that it would take about 50 years for Hispanic fertility to drop even to 3.

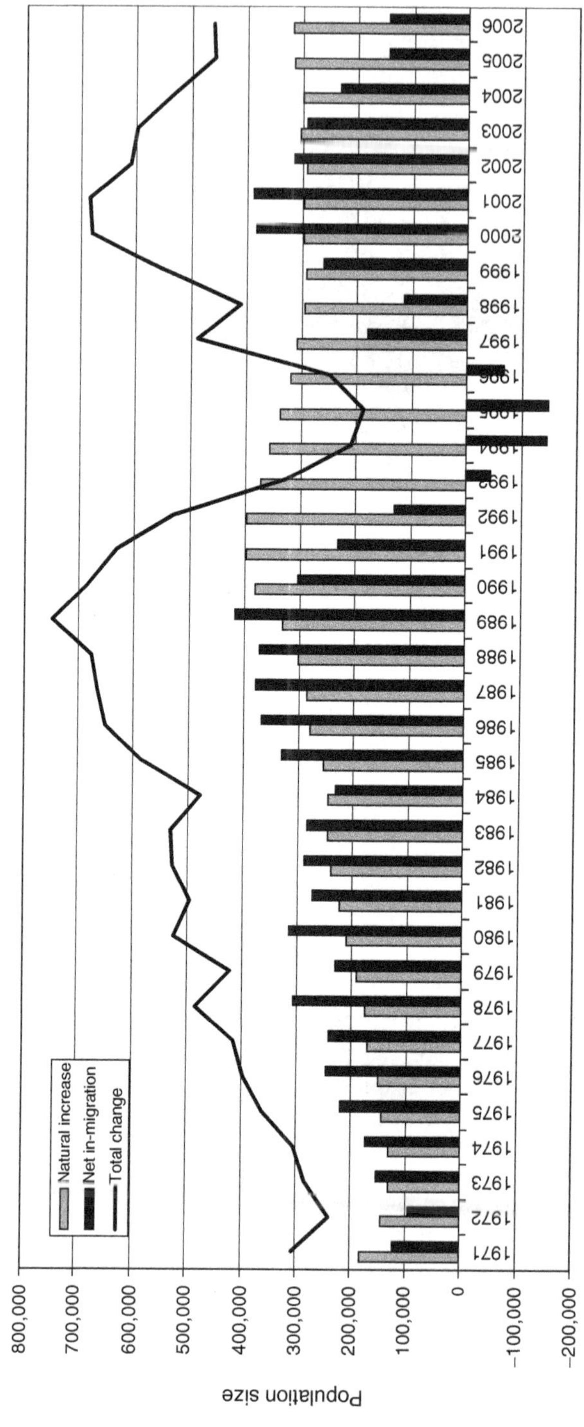

Figure 5.5 California's natural population change and net in-migration. (From LAO data as of February 2007.)

On average, the natural increase and net in-migration components have tended in the past to contribute equally to California's population growth. However, their relative shares can vary significantly from one year to the next depending largely on the strength of the domestic net in-migration component—by far the most volatile element. This is illustrated in Figure 5.5, which shows California's recent patterns of natural population change and net in-migration.

Making Demographic Projections

General Approach Used

The exact process used for making demographic projections for California varies by forecasting entity but generally follows a similar basic approach—namely, forecasts for both births and deaths are separately identified, as are domestic and foreign net in-migration. The degree to which these projections are made using an aggregate versus disaggregated approach does vary by forecasting entity. However, both the LAO and DOF generally disaggregate the totals for these components (when feasible) by age, gender, and ethnicity. The DOF also makes projections for each of California's 58 individual counties.

Forecasters use a variety of data utilized in making such projections, including information from the Department of Health Services involving birth and death records, U.S. Census data on population characteristics, data from the Immigration and Naturalization Service (INS) on foreign migration flows, driver's license information on shifts of individuals between states, and information from surveys of school attendance. Various statistical relationships also are considered, such as regression analyses relating domestic migration flows to such things as interstate differences in unemployment rates and housing prices. In terms of basic assumptions involving such things as birth rates, forecasters rely on a combination of statistical projections and subjective assumptions that are based on observed recent behavior of the population, time trends, surveys, and consensus viewpoints of demographic specialists.

Example—The Legislative Analyst's Office Process

The LAO's demographic modeling approach is highly disaggregated, incorporating a large multidimensional matrix that has specific cells of data and assumptions by age, gender, and ethnicity relating to birth rates, fertility, and migration probabilities. Figure 5.6 provides a schematic of the LAO's demographic modeling approach.

Sample Forecast Outcomes

Table 5.1 provides a recent sample of the demographic projections prepared in February 2007 by the LAO for California using the procedures discussed.

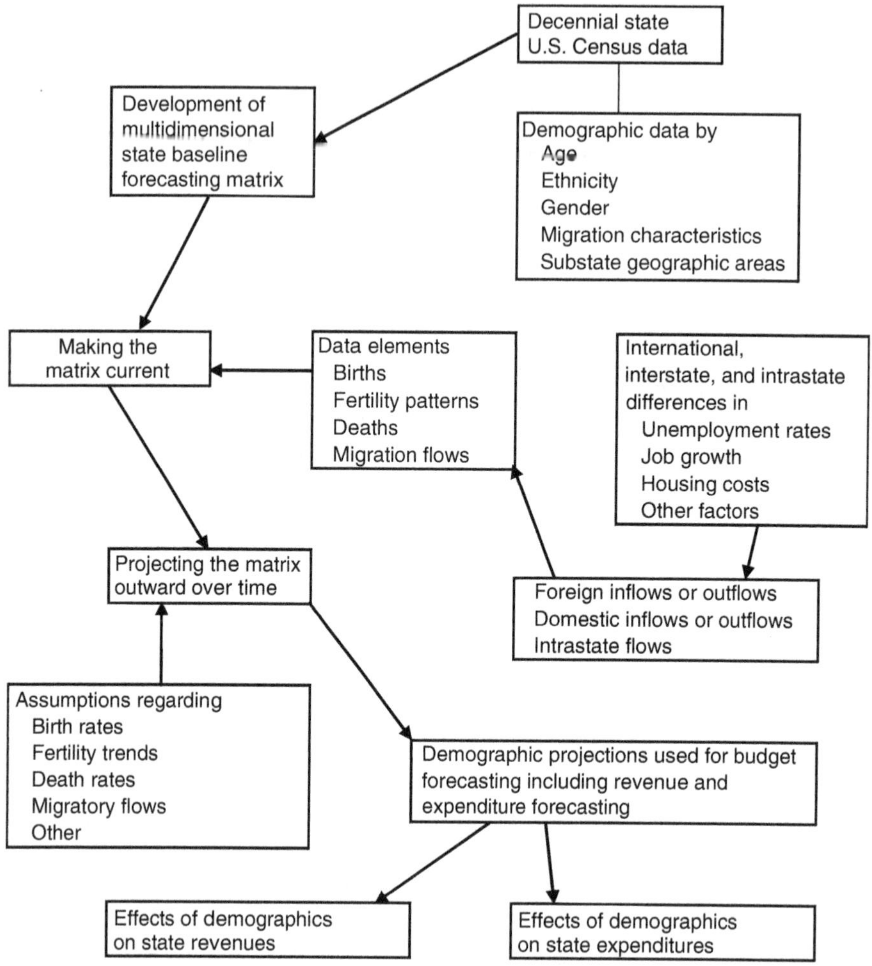

Figure 5.6 The LAO's demographic modeling approach.

It indicates that

- Total population growth is in the range of 1.3 percent annually.
- The natural population growth component is averaging approximately 315,000 persons annually, reflecting over half-a-million births partially offset by about a quarter-million deaths.*

* This forecast incorporates the well-documented trend of declining birth rates that has been occurring in essentially all ethnic groups in recent years in California. Despite these declining birth rates, however, the number of new births and the natural increase component overall were forecast to rise up a bit due to significant growth in the female population of childbearing age groups in the faster-growing segments of California's population, including Hispanic and Asian women.

Table 5.1 Sample Demographic Forecasting Outcomes

	Years						
Population Variable	*2006*	*2007*	*2008*	*2009*	*2010*	*2011*	*2012*
Total (1st July basis)	37,444,155	37,904,166	38,377,903	38,876,365	39,395,722	39,911,877	40,434,603
Absolute change	462,224	460,010	473,737	498,462	519,357	516,155	522,726
Percent change	1.25	1.23	1.25	1.30	1.34	1.31	1.31
Births	552,117	554,056	556,721	560,418	565,359	571,188	576,852
Deaths	234,893	239,046	242,984	246,955	251,002	255,033	259,126
Net domestic in-migration	–55,000	–50,000	–40,000	–20,000	0	0	5,000
Net foreign in-migration	200,000	195,000	200,000	205,000	205,000	200,000	200,000
Natural increase	317,224	315,010	313,737	313,462	314,357	316,155	317,726
Net in-migration	145,000	145,000	160,000	185,000	205,000	200,000	205,000
Total (1st January basis)	37,213,043	37,674,161	38,141,034	38,627,134	39,136,044	39,653,800	40,173,240
Percent change	1.25	1.24	1.24	1.27	1.32	1.32	1.31

Source: LAO projections as of February 2007.

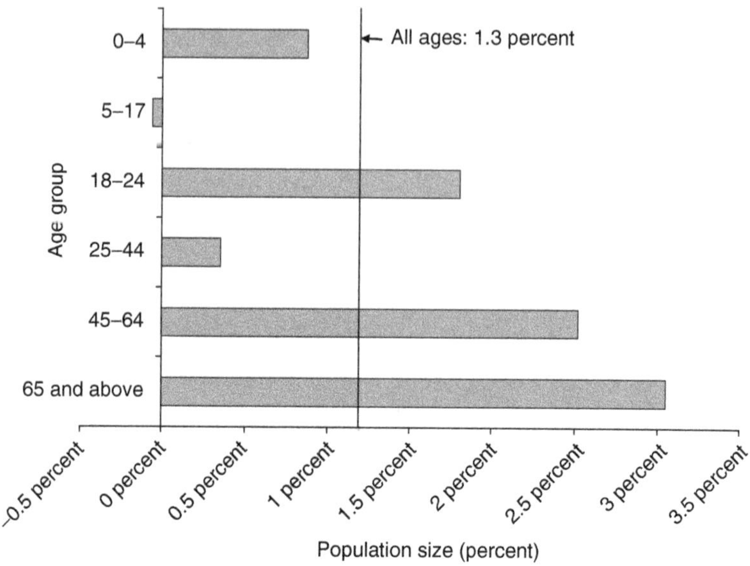

Figure 5.7 Population growth by age group. (From February 2007 LAO projections of average annual percent change, 2006–2012.)

- Combined domestic and foreign net in-migration currently averages around 145,000 persons annually. Virtually all of this figure involves "foreign" net in-migration from other nations.* Regarding "domestic" net in-migration, the figure was negative in 2005, with a return to net positive interstate population inflows by 2012 and modest increases thereafter.†
- Growth by age group is to vary significantly (see Figure 5.7) with the ranks of the baby boomers swelling, no growth for school-age population, and above-average growth for the elderly and college-age groups.‡ These various age-group demographic projections can have significant implications for the

* Net foreign in-migration has remained relatively stable over the past decade and has proved to be much less sensitive to the economy than domestic population flows between states.

† The 2005 experience, when approximately 55,000 more people left California for other states than flowed in from them, was in large part attributable to the lingering impacts of California's recent recession and factors such as its continued only-modest job market strength and high housing prices.

‡ The 45–64 age group (largely, the so-called "baby boomers") continues to be the fastest growing single segment of the population. It is projected to expand by nearly 1.4 million people over the next six years in California. Toward the other extreme, slow growth is anticipated for the K-12 school-age population due to a variety of factors including the lower rates of recent net domestic in-migration of families with school-age children, reduced birth rates during the late 1990s and early 2000s, and especially the increasing advancement of baby boomers' children into the college-age category.

state's fiscal outlook due to their impacts in such areas as school enrollments, healthcare needs, and the size and characteristics of the labor force.

Predicting California's Economy

California's Basic Economic Characteristics

Just like its demography, California's economy is large, diverse, and dynamic. For example,

- Its gross domestic product (GDP) totals over $1.6 trillion annually, ranking it eighth compared to the nations of the world, and it employs more than 17 million persons.
- It has over 120 separate nonagricultural industries operating within its boundaries and is by far the nation's largest agricultural state, with about $32 billion of total output and over 250 separate crops and livestock commodities produced annually.
- Its industry mix is heavily skewed toward new and cutting-edge technologies involving such areas as computer-related products and biotechnology. Likewise, it has a huge export–import sector equal to about $400 billion in shipments annually.

Given these factors, accurately projecting California's economic performance is both extremely challenging and important from the government finances forecasting perspective.

Key Economic Variables Affecting the State Budget

The key economic variables that affect the state budget include those that, in addition to basic demographics, help to determine both state revenues and program costs. These include statewide personal income, corporate profits, employment, unemployment, housing starts, home prices and sales rates, home construction, taxable sales, and inflation. The latter includes inflation for both the overall economy and for specific goods categories such as medical costs.

Modeling and Predicting California's Economy

General Approach Used

There are a variety of public and private entities that model and project California's economy.* Generally, forecasters use models that are structured and built around

* These currently include, among others, the LAO, the DOF, the Anderson School of Management at the University of California at Los Angeles, Chapman College, the University of the Pacific, the Center for the Continuing Study of the California Economy, and various banks, other financial entities, and private businesses.

predicting state employment and personal income. These models, in turn, are typically driven by, or integrated with, traditional expenditure-based national macroeconomic models.*

Example—The Legislative Analyst's Office Process

Structural and Econometric Specifications

Figure 5.8 provides a schematic of the LAO's economic modeling system. Forecasters link the California state economic model to a national economic model that contains approximately 40 equations. Key components of the state model include modules that forecast employment in the aggregate and by industry sector, statewide personal income in total and by type of income, housing starts, and a number of different governmental and consumer price deflators that affect the state budget.

Conceptually, the model consists of two broad categories. These are (1) the so-called export-based industries, where employment, income, and output are primarily related to "national and worldwide" demands and (2) the so-called domestic industries, where sales, employment, and income are primarily determined by conditions within California. Examples of export-based industries include manufacturing, information services (including motion picture, television, and Internet companies), professional and business services, transportation, and agriculture. By comparison, examples of domestic industries include personal services, wholesale and retail trade, state and local governments, construction, finance, insurance, and real estate.

Forecasters solve the domestic sector of the model simultaneously, reflecting the fact that increased income and sales in one sector will have ripple effects on other sectors that serve California's markets. For example, increased construction and home-buying activity have direct effects on other industries that serve the housing market directly (such as real estate brokers, mortgage finance, title companies, and insurance firms) as well as other industries that would benefit from increased

* Statewide macroeconomic models differ fundamentally in structure from national macroeconomic models due to the nature of the data that is available for them and thus the types of relationships that can be modeled. National models rely on data about the major components of aggregate demand such as consumption and investment expenditures, which in turn allow consumption functions, investment accelerator models, and other such well-established macroeconomic relationships to be estimated. In contrast, data is not regularly available in the National Income and Product Accounts for state-level expenditures. Thus, statewide models are typically built using data from the income side of the national accounts, which is available for states. As a result, state models generally focus on employment and income by detailed industry sector. Both the DOF and the LAO currently utilize the "Global Insights" national macroeconomic model to forecast national economic variables and, partially, to drive their in-house state economic models.

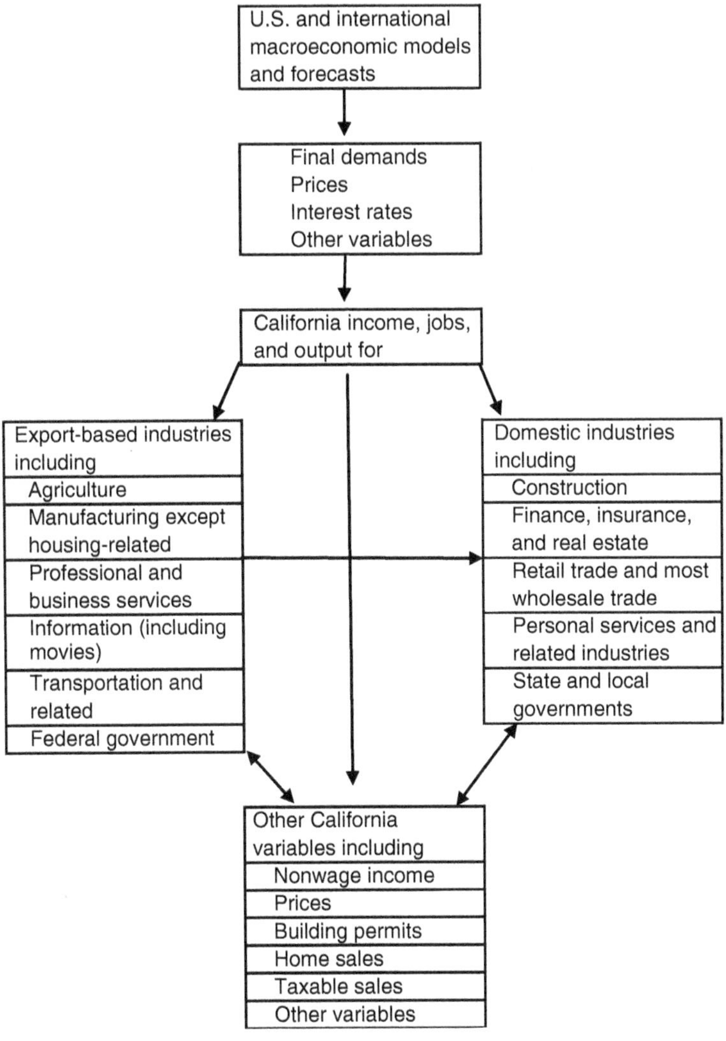

Figure 5.8 The LAO's economic modeling approach.

income accruing to construction workers along with increased spending by home owners on home furnishings and landscape services.

Sample Forecast Outcomes

As an illustration of the California's economic modeling outputs developed in conjunction with the preparation of California's fiscal forecasts, Table 5.2 shows the economic projections prepared in February 2007 by the LAO for California using the modeling approach depicted in Figure 5.8.

Table 5.2 Sample Economic Forecasting Outcomes

	Estimate	Forecast		
	2006	2007	2008	2009
U.S. forecast				
Percent change in				
Real GDP	3.4	2.5	3.1	3.4
Personal income	6.4	5.3	5.5	6.1
Wage and salary employment	1.9	1.2	1.4	1.6
Consumer Price Index	3	2.2	2.3	2.5
Unemployment rate	4.6	4.9	4.9	4.6
Housing starts (thousands)	1809	1513	1613	1712
California forecast				
Percent change in				
Personal income	6.1	5.6	5.7	6.2
Payroll employment	1.9	1.4	1.7	1.8
Taxable sales	4.8	3.5	5.2	6.2
Consumer Price Index	3.7	2.7	2.5	2.7
Unemployment rate	4.9	4.9	4.8	4.6
New housing permits (thousands)	164	138	155	170

Note: Percent change unless otherwise noted.

Source: LAO projections as of February 2007.

Forecasting State Revenues

The Nature of California's Revenue System

Forecasting California's state revenues involves predicting more than 70 of its individual revenue sources. As shown in Figures 5.9a and 5.9b, respectively, about 80 percent of total California state revenues and 95 percent of General Fund revenues are attributable to the state's "big three" taxes—the personal income tax (PIT), the SUT, and the CT. The remainder is related to a variety of other taxes (including various fuel-related levies and insurance, tobacco, alcoholic beverage, and gambling-related taxes), fees, investment earnings, and various transfers from special funds. Disability and unemployment insurance taxes also are collected, although these are placed into trust funds and do not finance other programs.*

* For a general discussion of California's basic tax system, see California Legislative Analyst's Office (2007).

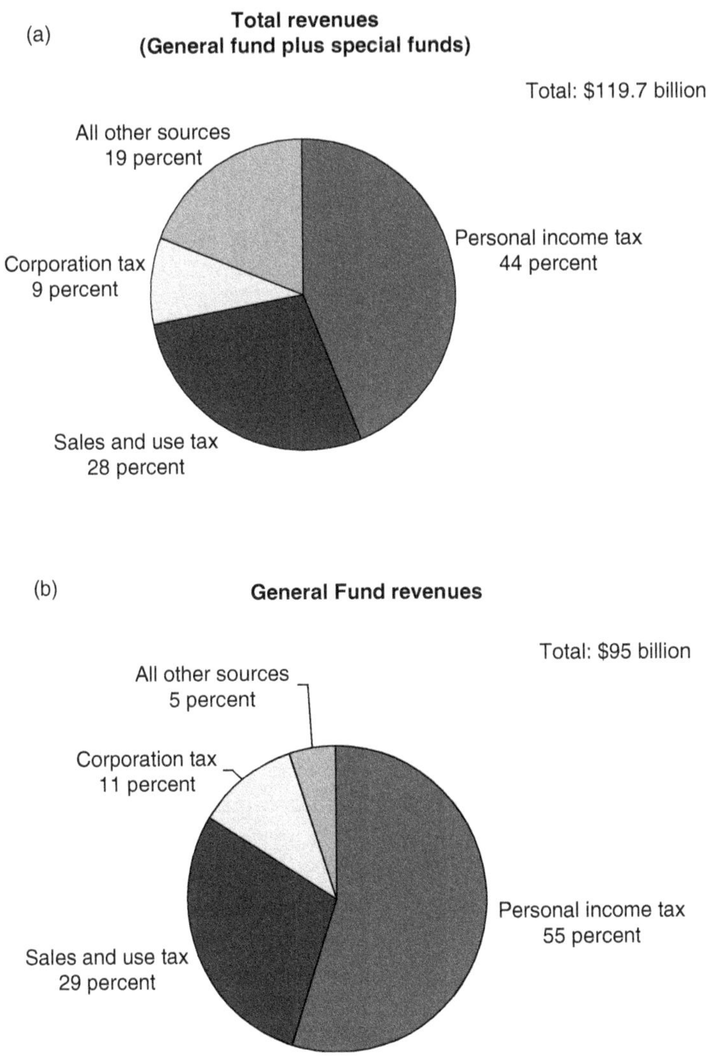

Figure 5.9 **(a) California's total revenues by source in 2006–2007 (General Fund plus special funds). (b) California's General Fund revenues by source in 2006–2007. (From 2007–2008 Governor's Budget, adjusted by LAO for BSA treatment.)**

History of Revenue Performance

Figure 5.10 shows California's General Fund revenue performance over the past several decades. It indicates that although the state's revenue base has grown at an average annual rate of approximately 9 percent over the period (largely reflecting

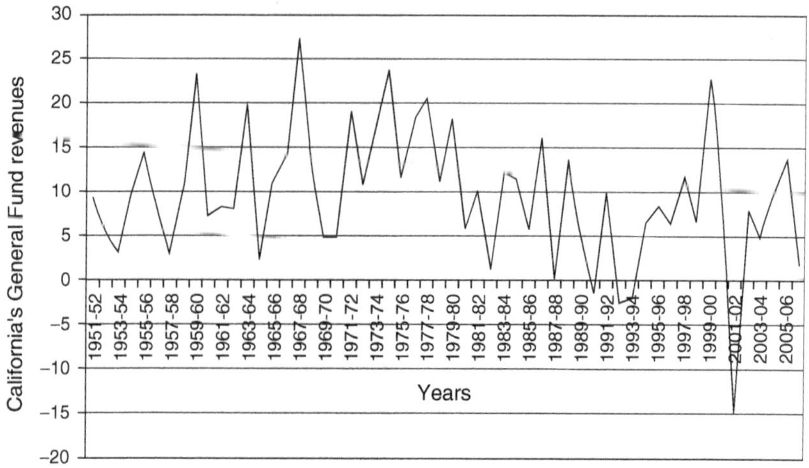

Figure 5.10 California's General Fund revenue performance over time (annual percent change in General Fund revenues). (From California State Department of Finance.)

its growing economy and population), revenues are also volatile over the course of the business cycle. This tendency for revenue growth to fluctuate considerably from one year to the next poses a special challenge to revenue forecasters because failure to anticipate such volatility can lead to a "feast or famine" budgeting environment. A good example of this fluctuation occurred in recent years, when very strong revenue growth through the mid-to-late 1990s led to program expansions and tax reductions, followed by dramatic revenue declines in the early 2000s necessitating program cutbacks and deficit-related borrowing.

Projecting State Tax Revenues Generally

Projecting the state's tax receipts, which account for most state revenues, involves predicting each of the state's dozen-plus tax bases using the economic and demographic forecasts and other factors. This is followed by applying the applicable tax rates and various credits, and finally distributing the resulting revenues by fiscal year based on payment due dates, expected audit-related collections, assumptions about taxpayer behavior, and the state's various accounting and accrual rules. Forecasters must factor the impacts that both ongoing and phasing-in tax-related law changes have in this process, including not only those that change tax bases and rates but also those dealing with such factors as periodic amnesty programs and other anomalies. Figure 5.11 shows a schematic of the LAO's revenue forecasting process.

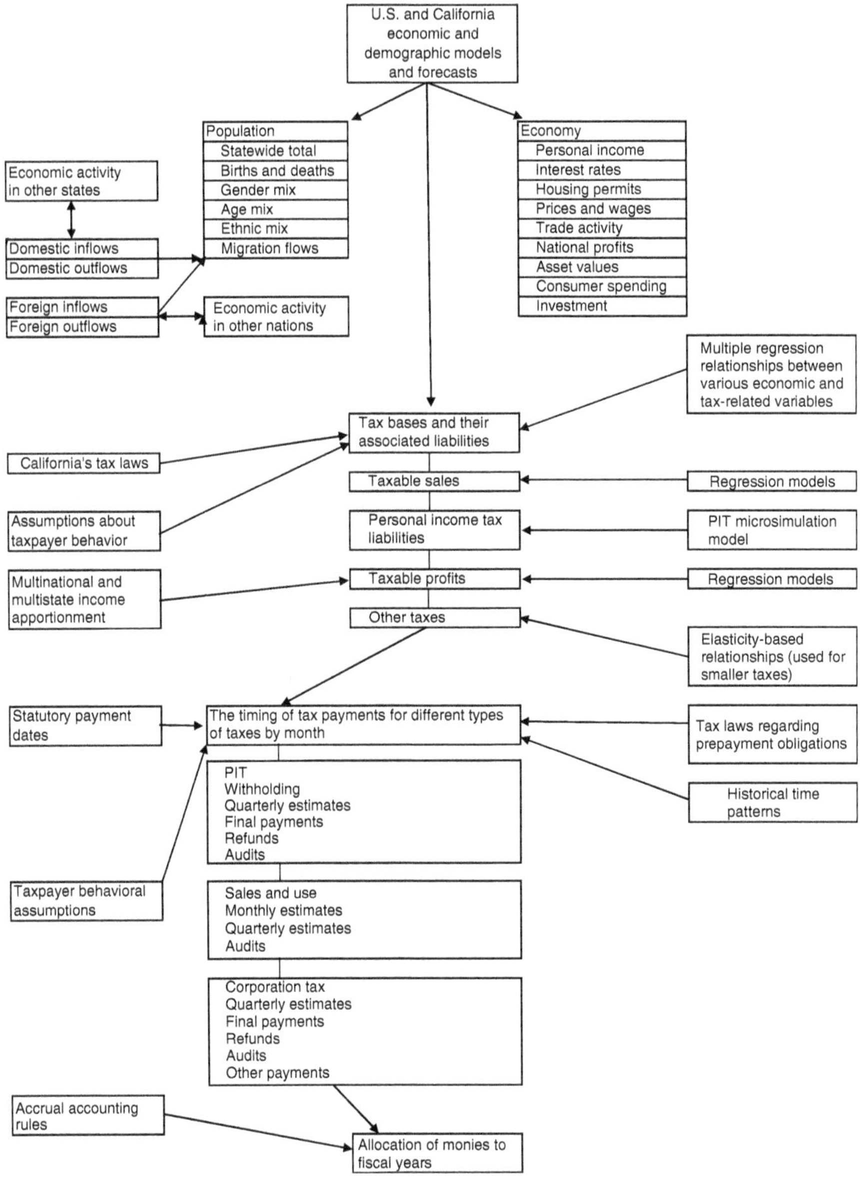

Figure 5.11 The LAO's revenue forecasting process.

Tax Expenditure Programs

An important aspect of California's tax system involves various exemptions, exclusions, deductions, credits, special tax rates, and other preferential provisions that reduce the amount of revenues that the "basic" tax system would otherwise generate.

In California, these so-called tax expenditure programs (TEPs) number in hundreds and total to approximately $40 billion annually. Forecasters must accurately project them so as not to overstate collections and thus this is an important element in the revenue forecasting process.*

Modeling Individual Revenue Sources

The Personal Income Tax

Background

The PIT is, by far, the state's single largest revenue source accounting for over half of total General Fund revenues in 2006–2007. In general, California patterned its PIT after the federal law with respect to reportable types of income, deductions, exemptions, exclusions, and credits. Under the PIT, taxable income is subject to marginal rates ranging from 1 to 9.3 percent, with the top rate applying to taxable income in excess of $86,934 for joint returns in 2006 (and one-half of that for taxpayers filing single returns). Beginning in 2005, a 1 percent additional tax was imposed on the portion of taxpayers' incomes in excess of $1 million (for a total marginal rate of 10.3 percent for affected taxpayers). California allocates the proceeds of this additional tax, which the state implemented following approval of Proposition 63 in 2004, to a special fund to support various mental health programs.

Year-to-Year Liability Changes Recently Dominated by Nonwage Income

In recent years, about two-thirds to three-quarters of adjusted gross income (AGI) declared on California's PIT returns has been due to ordinary wages and salaries of workers. However, the remainder of AGI—consisting primarily of business earnings, capital gains, stock options, and other forms of investment income—has a disproportionate effect on year-to-year changes in PIT liabilities. This is due to two main reasons:

- First, nonwage income accrues mainly to taxpayers at the top end of the income spectrum; and thus, on average the state taxes it at a higher marginal rate than wage income. For example, over 90 percent of stock options, capital gains, and business income—which combined account for the majority of nonwage income—accrued to the top 5 percent of taxpayers (those with incomes in excess of $161,000 in 2004, the most recent year for which such data is available).
- Second, nonwage income is volatile. It rises much faster than ordinary wages in good times and falls much further in bad times. This is illustrated

* For a discussion of these various TEPs, see Legislative Analyst's Office (1999).

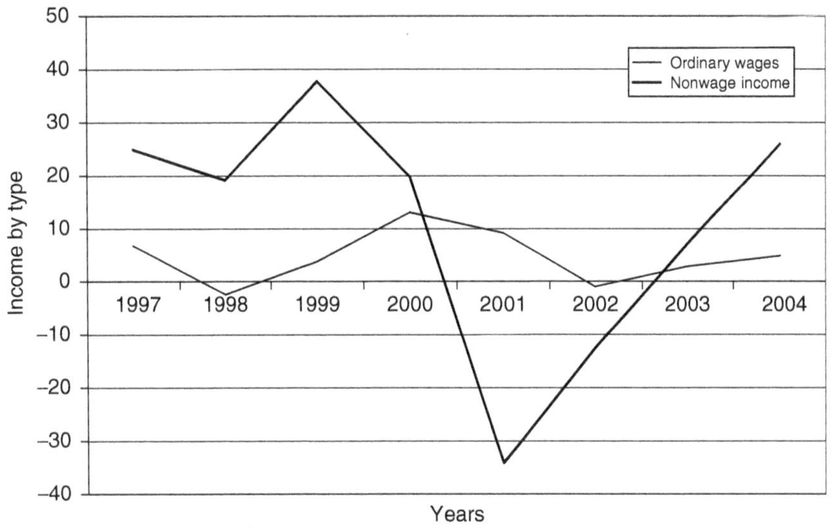

Figure 5.12 Year-to-year changes in ordinary wages versus nonwage income (annual percent change). (From Office of California Legislative Analyst.)

in Figure 5.12, which compares year-to-year changes in ordinary wages (i.e., wages excluding stock options) and nonwage income during the past 16 years. Although the extreme income changes in the late 1990s and early 2000s were the result of unprecedented swings in capital gains and stock options, the greater relative volatility in nonwage income sources has been present throughout the entire historical period shown in Figure 5.12.

In recent years, PIT revenues benefited from the boom in nonwage income. Between 2003 and 2005, for example, growth in these sources resulted in much of the more than 42 percent growth in overall PIT liabilities.

Personal Income Tax Forecasting

Given the nature of California's PIT including its many diverse income components and highly progressive marginal tax rate bracket structure, its forecasting requires a combination of (1) projecting the aggregate levels of the tax's basic income components, deductions, and credits, and then (2) distributing these aggregate amounts by income level. The former is done through the use of multiple regression relationships and various other techniques. The latter is accomplished using a microsimulation approach based on a large stratified representative random sample file constructed annually by the California Franchise Tax Board of actual California

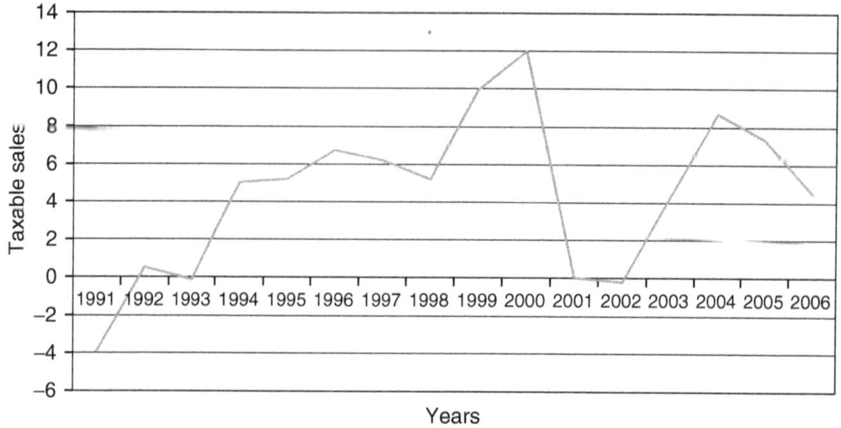

Figure 5.13 Changes in California's taxable sales (annual percent change). (From California State Department of Finance.)

taxpayers. Forecasters use the changes over time in the distribution of income, deductions, and credits, by income level, to model future distributions.*

Sales and Use Tax

Background

The SUT is the General Fund's second largest revenue source accounting for just below 30 percent of total revenues in 2006–2007. Figure 5.13 shows the past performance of taxable sales on which SUT revenues depend, including the considerable year-to-year volatility that can characterize it.

The main SUT component is the "sales" tax, which the state imposes on retail sales of tangible goods sold in California. Some examples of taxable transactions include spending on clothing, furniture, computers, electronics, appliances, automobiles, cigarettes, and motor vehicle fuel. Purchases of building materials that go into the construction of homes and buildings are also subject to sales tax, as are purchases of computers and other equipment used by businesses. Retailers remit approximately 70 percent of the SUT, whereas businesses that themselves consume or use the products being acquired directly pay the remaining 30 percent. The largest exemption from the sales tax is for most of the food items consumed at home. The great majority of services are not subject to sales tax in California.

* For additional discussion by the authors of this basic microsimulation modeling approach and its application in California, see, among others, Vasché (1980, 1981, 1982, 1987a,b); Vasché and Williams; and Williams et al. (1997a,b).

The second component of the SUT is the "use" tax, which the state imposes on products bought from out-of-state sellers by California residents and businesses for use in California. With the exception of automobile purchases, vessels, and aircraft (all of which residents must register), out-of-state purchases are difficult to monitor. Under current federal law, the state cannot require most out-of-state sellers to collect the use tax on behalf of California. As a result, the state cannot collect the majority of use taxes owed in California, and thus, those receipts account for only a small portion of total SUT revenues.

Individual SUT rates. The total SUT rate levied in California is a combination of several different individual rates imposed by the state and various local governments. In 2006, these included a state rate of 6.25 percent consisting of a 5 percent General Fund rate, two half-cent rates whose proceeds are deposited into special funds that benefit local governments, and a temporary 0.25 percent rate dedicated to the repayment of the state's deficit-financing bonds; a uniform local rate of 1.0 percent; and optional local rates that the state generally levies in 0.25 percent increments and can range from 0 to 1.5 percent.*

Combined SUT rates throughout California. The combined state–local SUT rate varies significantly across California geographically due to differences in levied local optional rates. The combined SUT rate currently ranges from 7.25 percent (for those counties with no optional rates) to 8.75 percent. The statewide average rate, weighted according to sales, is currently about 7.94 percent.

Sales and Use Tax Forecasting

SUT forecasting involves projecting taxable sales and then applying the appropriate tax rates. Depending on the forecasting entity, projecting SUT revenues is technically approached by a combination of aggregate and disaggregated multiple regression techniques relating both taxable sales and the taxable-sales-to-income ratio to the various economic and demographic variables affecting such sales. Among others, these variables include income, employment, distributed lags of permits issued for residential and nonresidential structures, consumer confidence levels, car sales, general inflation, gasoline prices, and interest rates. Forecasters make estimates

* Under the terms of Proposition 57, which was approved by California's voters in March 2004, 0.25 percent of the uniform local rate (known as the Bradley–Burns rate) is temporarily diverted to a state special fund for purposes of repayment of the deficit-financing bonds that were issued in 2004 to help deal with the state's budget problem. The purpose of this diversion was to "free up" a revenue stream that could be dedicated to repayment of the bonds. The diverted sales taxes were replaced with property taxes shifted from school districts to non-school local governments, which were in turn replaced with added General Fund payments to the schools. This arrangement has commonly been referred to as the "triple flip."

for both aggregate taxable sales and for about a half-dozen sales subcomponents. Each consists of the aggregation of various items from approximately 80 individual sectors that the Board of Equalization (the state tax agency responsible for collection of the sales tax) reports quarterly taxable sales for. The subcomponents include general merchandising, building and related materials, autos and related transportation items, fuel, and business-to-business sales.

Corporation Tax

Background

The CT is the third largest state revenue source accounting for 11 percent of the total General Fund revenues in 2006–2007. After PIT, CT is the most difficult of all taxes to accurately forecast because of its many complicated elements and the inherent volatility of corporate profits. The latter fact is demonstrated in Figure 5.14.

Basic Provisions

The state levies the CT at a general rate of 8.84 percent on California's taxable profits. Banks and other financial institutions subject to the CT pay an additional 2 percent tax, which is *in lieu* of most other state and local levies. Corporations that qualify for California's "Subchapter S" status are subject to a reduced 1.5 percent corporate rate. In exchange, however, the income and losses from these corporations are "passed through" to their shareholders where they are subject to the PIT.

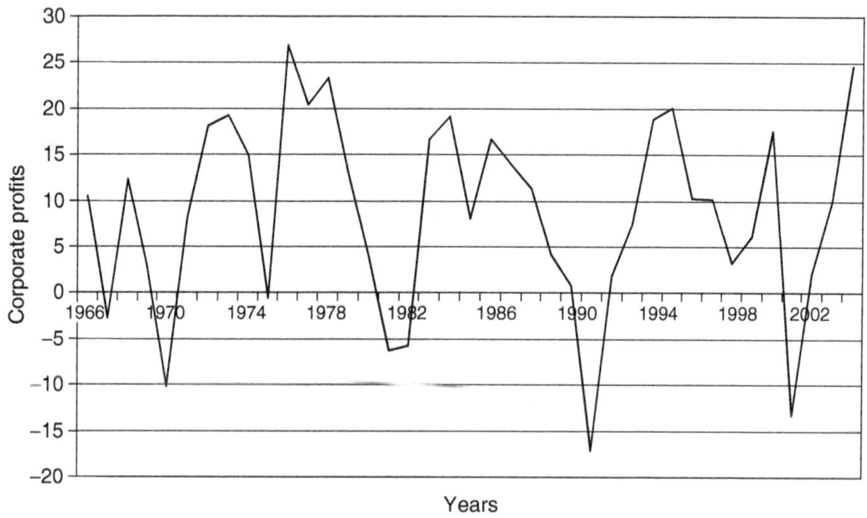

Figure 5.14 California's corporate profits over time (annual percent change). (From California State Department of Finance.)

Similarly, businesses that the state classifies as limited liability companies (LLCs) pay a separate fee at the entity level and they pass their income and losses through to their shareholders, where they are subject to the PIT.

Approximately two-thirds of all CT revenues come from multistate and multinational corporations. These companies have their consolidated U.S. income apportioned to California based on a formula involving the share of their combined property, payroll, and sales that are attributable to the state.

California's CT allows for a variety of exclusions, exemptions, deductions, and credits; many of which are similar or identical to those provided under the federal corporate profits tax. Key examples include the research and development (R&D) tax credit and net operating loss (NOL) carry-forward provisions. (Companies can use their excess operating losses incurred in one year as a deduction against earnings in subsequent years.)*

Corporation Tax Forecasting

CT forecasting for California involves a great many complications. For starters, corporate profits are extremely volatile. Beyond this, however, forecasters must identify the portion of the profits earned by multinational and multistate corporations that are taxable in California. In addition, forecasters must identify the stock of accumulated but as yet unused NOLs, which companies can apply to their future years that will, in turn, reduce their taxes. This amount currently exceeds $250 billion, with another $8.1 billion of earned, but as yet unused, R&D credits that companies also can use to directly offset their future tax liabilities. Forecasting is further complicated in that the state has periodically modified or suspended its NOL provisions in various years.

The basic approach to CT revenue forecasting involves applying regression relationships to predict taxable state corporate profits. Forecasters do this while taking into account such factors as national profits and the variables that cause California's profits to vary from the nation's, such as relative state–national differences in economic performance, especially in such key industries as construction, finance, energy, and utilities. Other key variables in the forecasts include developments involving employee compensation and productivity growth.

Other Taxes and Revenues

The approach to forecasting the remaining 5 percent of California's total General Fund revenues varies depending on the particular revenue source involved.

* In these two cases, California's law is generally similar to but not identical to federal law. For example, the state's R&D credit rate is different, and NOLs cannot be carried back and applied to prior tax years.

However, they generally rely on regression models relating the various tax bases involved to economic and demographic variables. They then apply appropriate tax rates and make adjustments for audit revenues, court litigation, law changes, and other factors. For example, insurance tax revenues involve forecasting insurance premiums; tobacco-related taxes involve forecasting cigarette consumption; and gambling-related receipts involve projecting lottery sales and horseracing-related betting. In the case of interest income, this involves projecting both investable balances and interest rates at which the state invests its available monies including the temporary cash flow balances arising throughout the year from the time gap between when the state collects its tax monies and the state expends its program funds.

Key Revenue Forecasting Challenges and Experience

The Problem of Volatility

As noted earlier, California's revenues have been quite volatile in the recent past reflecting both the dynamic changes in the overall economy and the increased reliance on high-income taxpayers, who in turn have volatile income sources such as stock options, capital gains, and business earnings. As shown in Figure 5.15, combined PIT revenues from capital gains and stock options jumped from $2 billion in 1994 to $18 billion in 2000 (to over 23 percent of General Fund revenues) before falling back to below $8 billion in 2001. The inability to accurately predict these market-related swings led to major PIT forecasting errors in the late 1990s and early 2000s (see Figure 5.16).

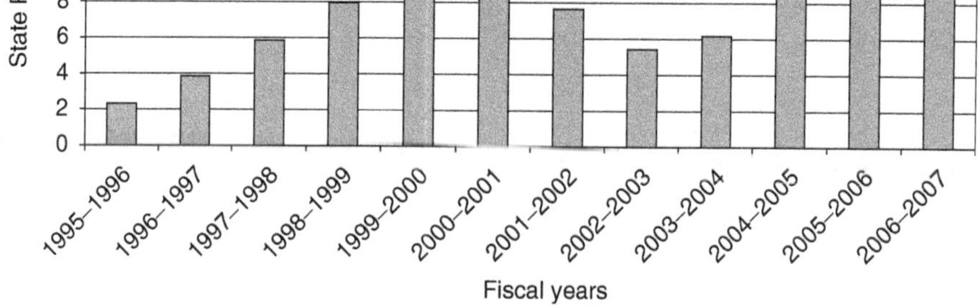

Figure 5.15 PIT revenues attributable to stock options and capital gains (dollars in billions). (From February 2007 LAO data and forecast.)

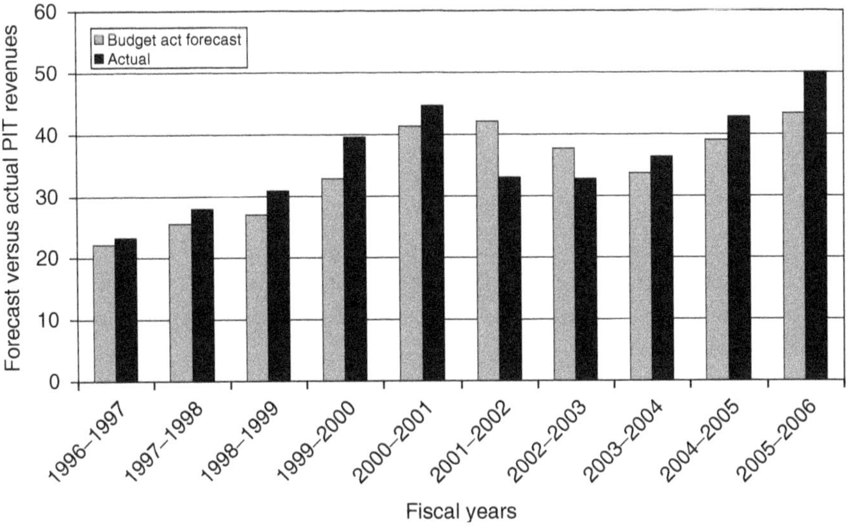

Figure 5.16 Errors in forecasting California's PIT revenues (dollars in billions). (From past governors' budgets.)

Given this history, the main challenge in revenue forecasting in California is accurately predicting future changes in inherently volatile income sources such as stock market activity, individual investor decisions, and rapidly changing levels of business profitability. The lack of timely data on the amount and composition of nonwage income hampers efforts in this area. For instance, tax return data showing sources of income are not generally available until ten months after the conclusion of the fiscal year in which the taxes are remitted.

In response to these conditions, state forecasting agencies have attempted to supplement their use of traditional economic and tax-related data with additional information from other industry sources such as company reports and filings with the U.S. Securities and Exchange Commission (SEC) regarding changes in stock ownership of major companies. Forecasters use these additional sources to identify potential stock-option income and capital gains associated with stock sales by officers, founders, board members, and others with significant holding in major companies.*

* For example, annual reports and 10-K filings with the SEC have information on companies' stock-option programs, including information about the number of shares granted at different exercise prices, the number of shares vested, and the number of shares for which options have been exercised over the recent year. Also, Form 4 filings with the SEC, which are made daily, show changes in the beneficial ownership of officers, board members, and others associated with public corporations.

However, even with these additional avenues, forecasting future changes in volatile income sources will probably remain a major challenge for revenue forecasters in California.

Amnesties and Tax Shelter Activities

Another area of major challenge that state revenue estimators currently face is to accurately estimate the revenue-related impacts of tax shelters and California's recent legislation to help curtail them, including various amnesties and voluntary compliance measures. Such measures resulted in over $5 billion of payments to the state in 2003–2004 and 2004–2005 combined. The revenue estimating challenge is to determine what portion of these funds the state will probably keep permanently versus the portion of these funds the state will probably refund in the future to taxpayers. Of the portion that is kept, estimators must also attempt to determine how much of the amnesty-related payments represent "new money" versus the mere acceleration of payments that would have eventually occurred anyway as a result of the state's normal auditing process. Estimates of the revenue impacts of new attempts to address the problem of abusive tax shelters also pose a special challenge.*

Forecasting State Expenditures

Nature of California's Expenditure Base: By Type and Amount

In 2006–2007, it was estimated that California spent about $127 billion on state-supported programs including approximately $102 billion from the General Fund and $25 billion from special funds in January 2007 (see Figure 5.1). Regarding General Fund expenditures, slightly less than one-half was for K-12 and higher education; nearly 30 percent was for health and social services; about 12 percent was for corrections; and the remainder was for a variety of other programs.

Forecasting State Expenditures Generally

For the current and budget years, the DOF's expenditure forecasts are generally based on detailed projections obtained from most of the state's major departments and programs. The governor's expenditure forecasters build up their aggregate forecasts from the individual program level. With such data, they determine

* Refunds of tax-shelter-related payments occur when, on audit, the state determines that a taxpayer's original tax sheltering claim is valid, but where that taxpayer has already made a payment to protect oneself from a penalty in the event that his claim is not ultimately upheld. For a thorough discussion of abusive tax shelters and the impact of California legislation in that area, see Legislative Analyst's Office (2006b).

departmental staffing levels, operations expenses, and equipment needs. The LAO, as noted earlier, also releases out-year expenditure forecasts as well as adjustments to the administration's current and budget-year figures, although the LAO's figures do not have the same amount of ground-up detail that characterizes the administration's figures.

Legislative Analyst's Office Sample Forecast Outcomes

Table 5.3 shows the major program areas covered by the LAO's expenditure projections made in February 2007. These estimates take into account numerous factors including statutory and constitutional funding requirements, availability of monies from federal and local government funds, the impacts of federal requirements and court decisions, inflation, and the impacts of changing levels of caseloads and workloads on state programs.

Table 5.3 Recent LAO General Fund Expenditure Forecasts by Major Program Area

	2007	*2008*	*2009*	*2010*	*2011*
Education programs					
K-14 Proposition 98	40,812	41,656	43,370	44,504	46,874
California State University	2,749	2,914	3,131	3,363	3,611
University of California	2,921	3,096	3,303	3,525	3,758
Health and social services programs					
Medi-Cal	13,649	14,642	15,389	16,247	17,234
CalWORKs	2,014	1,324	1,294	1,366	1,443
SSI/SSP	3,537	3,845	4,182	4,409	4,665
In-Home Supportive Services	1,417	1,438	1,515	1,597	1,683
Department of Developmental Services	2,562	2,600	2,950	3,218	3,520
Others	6,115	5,475	5,715	6,022	6,391
Department of Corrections and Rehabilitation	8,635	9,047	9,237	9,346	9,776
Transportation	2,643	1,561	1,638	1,732	1,829
All others	15,040	16,288	19,205	21,080	21,479
Total	102,094	103,885	110,929	116,409	122,262

Note: Dollars in millions for fiscal years ending in the years shown.

Source: LAO as of February 2007, assuming administration's January 2007 policy plans.

Because Proposition 98, as discussed earlier, largely determines K-12 education spending, the overall forecasting process is best discussed by separating the forecasting of Proposition 98 from forecasting the rest of the state budget.

Forecasting K-14 Education (Proposition 98) Expenditures

By far, the largest single component of the state budget is K-14 education. Combined state and local spending on kindergarten through community college (K-14) education totaled $55 billion in 2006–2007, of which nearly 75 percent was from the state's General Fund.

In 1988, California's voters approved Proposition 98, a constitutional measure, which sets annual minimum funding levels for K-14 education. This funding level is based on a set of formulas, or tests, that take into account General Fund revenues, local property taxes, statewide per capita personal income, and K-12 school attendance. Specifically, the Proposition 98 minimum-funding guarantee is based on the interaction of three different "tests." These include

- Test 1, in which it is guaranteed that General Fund spending on K-14 education is no less than a fixed percentage of General Fund revenues (this test has not been in effect since the late 1980s)
- Test 2, in which the prior-year's state and local funding level is increased by the growth in K-12 school attendance and statewide per capita personal income (this test is operative in normal-to-strong economic growth years)
- Test 3, in which the prior-year's state and local funding level is increased by the growth in K-12 attendance and per capita General Fund revenues (this test is normally effective in low-growth revenue years)

When funding falls below test 2 (either because of the operation of test 3 or suspension of the guarantee by two-thirds vote of the legislature), school funding is restored to the test 2 level in subsequent years through a formula that allocates above-average revenue growth to education.*

As noted earlier, the model used to forecast General Fund spending for K-14 education takes into account statutorily specified projections of K-12 attendance, local property taxes, General Fund tax revenues, and per capita personal income. These variables are, in turn, projected as part of the revenue, demographic, and economic forecasts as discussed earlier. For example, K-12 attendance uses the demographic projection of children in the 5–17 years age group, along with assumptions about the proportion of students that are in public versus private schools, and dropout rates.

* For a more complete description of Proposition 98, see Legislative Analyst's Office (2005).

Forecasting Non-Proposition 98 Spending

The non-Proposition 98 portion of California's state budget consists of the University of California system, California State University system, the Department of Corrections and Rehabilitation, major local assistance programs in the areas of health and social services, the judicial system, resources and environmental protection, general government administration, debt service, and tax relief. Although a general methodology does apply to most programs, specific methodologies can vary from one program area to another depending on program characteristics.

General Methodology for Forecasting State Programs

For individual departments and programs, forecasters project expenditures starting with a base-year spending level (usually the current year) and adjusting it for a variety of factors including caseloads, workload, prices, and other adjustments. Figure 5.17 presents the LAO process. Its key elements are discussed in detail as follows:

- *One-time costs and savings.* Forecasters must back out one-time costs and savings to arrive at a "baseline" level of program funding that they can use to project the future. Examples of one-time costs include spending for acquisition of a large information technology (IT) system and costs associated with major fires or other disasters. One-time savings can result from deferrals or one-time substitutions of special funds or federal funds to support a program.
- *Changes in caseloads or workloads.* Depending on the program involved, forecasters use a variety of techniques to forecast changes in caseloads and workloads. These can range from simple trend analysis and judgment (particularly for newly created programs with a limited historical track record) to a more structured, regression-based approach relating caseloads to demographic, societal, and economic variables. For example, the LAO projects California Work Opportunity and Responsibility to Kids (CalWORKs) caseloads using a regression model that includes the following explanatory variables: (1) the state's female population in prime fertility years; (2) the number of households with income near the poverty level; (3) lagged values of teenage birth rates; and (4) unemployment.
- *Cost per caseload or a workload factor.* Depending on the program being forecasted, forecasters use either average costs or marginal costs applicable to new caseload. They use average costs in most cash-grant programs such as CalWORKs or Supplemental Security Income/State Supplementary Payment (SSI/SSP). In comparison, they use marginal costs for state departments—such as the university and college systems or correctional system—where certain expenses for administration, facilities operations, and other overheads are fixed in the short term.

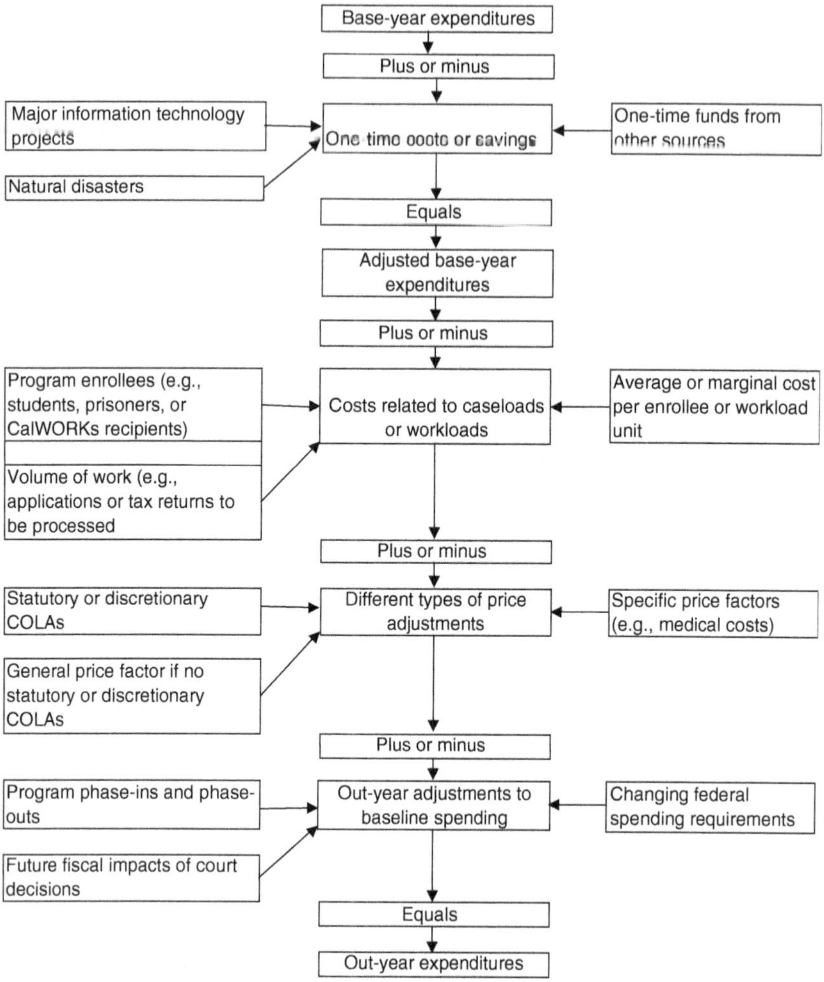

Figure 5.17 The LAO's expenditure forecasting process.

Price adjustments. Forecasters then adjust the programs for changes in prices. These adjustments fall into three general categories:

- *Cost-of-living adjustments (COLAs).* In California, COLAs influence, as directed by state law and the California Constitution, many programs. For example, the law requires forecasters to use specific subcomponents of the California Consumer Price Index (namely, food, rent, utilities, transportation, and clothing) to calculate the California Necessities Index, and the law then applies that index to adjust CalWORKs and SSI/SSP grants. As another example, state funding for the judicial branch is tied to changes in the state's spending limit adjustment factor discussed earlier. For some programs, state law provides for discretionary COLAs. In these cases, the baseline budget depends on legislative policies regarding annual adjustments.

- *General price factor.* For programs that do not have statutory price deflators, forecasters generally adjust nonwage costs with a general price deflator such as the U.S. Implicit GDP Deflator for State and Local Governments.
- *Specific price factors.* There are a number of cases where circumstances require that these be employed. For example, costs in health entitlement programs have been consistently higher than general inflation, reflecting national and state trends in this area. Projections of these costs are normally tied to economic variables that reflect both rising medical inflation and utilization of more expensive services over time. For instance, the LAO projects California's Medicaid program (Medi-Cal) cost increases using U.S. GDP per capita consumption spending on healthcare as well as industry data on regional trends in costs of medical services.

Out-year adjustments. These can include the phased effects of recently adopted program expansions or savings, future impacts of court cases or federal budget decisions, or increased operational costs associated with new college campuses or prisons.

Methodology for Employee Compensation, Debt Service, and Pension Payments

Some portions of state expenditures lend themselves to being forecast on an aggregate basis as opposed to an individual department or agency basis. In particular, employee compensation, debt service, and pension costs are normally backed out of individual departmental budgets and projected on an aggregate statewide basis.

Specifically, forecasters utilize projections for state compensation using the operative collective bargaining agreements between the state and its 20-plus employee bargaining units, taking into account the terms of each agreement, number of workers covered, and average salaries and salary distribution to which the increases apply. For periods not covered by specific employee contracts, forecasters project employee compensation using information on occupational wage trends and general inflation.

Debt-service forecasts take into account the actual amount of outstanding debt and its scheduled interest and principal repayments as well as projections of future sales of authorized or proposed bonds to meet capital outlay needs and the forecasted future level of interest rates for both general-obligation bonds and lease-revenue bonds.

Forecasters use pension fund contributions to project the number of state employees, wage levels, and actuarial assumptions about unfunded liabilities.

Expenditure Forecasting Experience in California

One of the main challenges in expenditure forecasting involves K-14 or Proposition 98 education. This challenge is due to both (1) the education's size and (2) its sensitivity to unanticipated changes in the economic and revenue factors that make up the Proposition 98 minimum funding guarantee calculation.

Outside of education, expenditure forecasts have been somewhat more accurate but unanticipated changes in caseloads or costs do significantly affect them. Other factors contributing to forecast errors include legal court rulings that have resulted in unanticipated spending. In recent years, for example, court decisions have resulted in increased spending related to healthcare and the Department of Corrections and Rehabilitation. Court decisions have also invalidated savings in the area of pension contributions. Another challenging area for forecasting is estimating the costs associated with future program expansions or savings. A key example, in recent years, was the expansion in the Healthy Families program (a federal program created in the 1990s that provided healthcare to children of low-income families not otherwise eligible for Medi-Cal services), where initial participation lagged expectations.

Forecasting California's Bottom-Line Fiscal Position

Policy makers use budget forecasts for revenues and expenditures for two main purposes. The first is to evaluate the state's "near-term" bottom-line fiscal condition under either current law or proposed law, and the second is to evaluate the relationship between revenues and expenditures "over time."

Near-Term Budget Condition

Table 5.4 (Panel A) shows the DOF's bottom-line fiscal projections included in the "2007–08 Governor's Budget" that was released in January 2007,* and compares these with the LAO's February 2007 projections (Panel B). It clearly demonstrates that California's forecasting entities provide independent projections for state policy makers to choose from. Specifically,

- Based on the governor's January 2007 policy proposals, the administration estimated that the 2007–2008 budget year would begin with a carryover balance of about $3.7 billion and 2007–2008 expenditures would exceed revenues by $841 million, resulting in a General Fund year-end balance of about $2.8 billion. After setting aside $745 million for encumbrances

* See Governor's Budget Summary (2007–2008) and accompanying Appendices and Schedules 1 through 12E.

Table 5.4 California's Estimated Near-Term General Fund Condition

	Actual 2005–2006	*Estimated 2006–2007*	*Projected 2007–2008*
A. Department of Finance, 2007–2008 Governor's Budget (January 2007)			
Prior-year fund balance ($)	8,981	10,816	3,670
Revenues and transfers	93,427	94,990	102,300
Total resources available	102,408	105,807	105,970
Expenditures	91,592	102,137	103,141
Ending fund balance	10,816	3,670	2,830
Encumbrances	745	745	745
Reserve	10,071	2,925	2,085
Budget stabilization account	0	472	1,495
Reserve for economic uncertainties	10,071	2,453	590
B. LAO (February 2007)			
Prior-year fund balance ($)	8,981	10,693	2,651
Revenues and transfers	93,427	94,052	101,253
Total resources available	102,408	104,745	103,904
Expenditures	91,715	102,094	103,885
Ending fund balance	10,693	2,651	19
Encumbrances	745	745	745
Reserve	9,948	1,906	−726
Budget stabilization account	0	472	—
Reserve for economic uncertainties	9,948	1,434	—

Note: Figures (dollars in millions) in Panels A and B assume administration's January 2007 policy proposals.

Source: Panel A: Governor's Budget Summary 2007–2008, Department of Finance, State of California, January 2007.
Panel B: Legislative Analyst's Office, February 2007.

(i.e., funds that were legally obligated but not yet spent), the reserve remaining was projected to be about $2.1 billion.

- In comparison, the LAO projected that 2007–2008 would end with a deficit of $726 million. In other words, the LAO's projected 2007–2008 year-end reserve was $2.8 billion below that of the administration. Specifically, the LAO projected that over the three years ending in 2007–2008, revenues would be $2 billion lower than the administration assumed and expenditures would be $825 million higher.

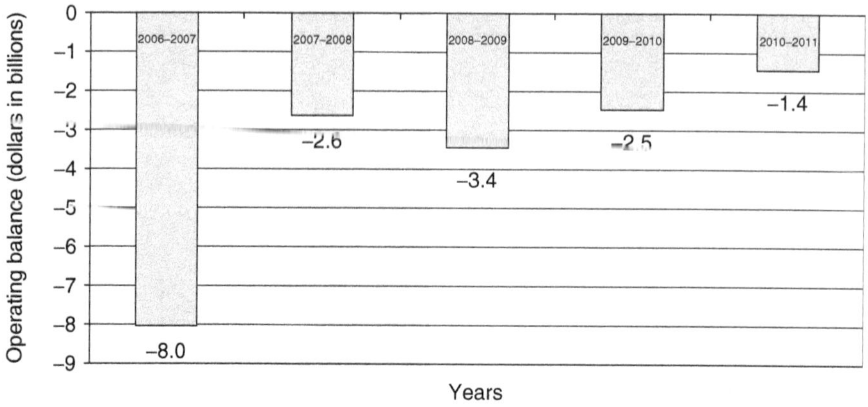

Figure 5.18 California's projected longer-term General Fund operating balance (dollars in billions). (From LAO February 2007 projections based on 2007–2008 Governor's Budget policy proposals.)

- Thus, considerable discrepancy existed between the two forecasts primarily due to differences in their revenue projections. As of early spring 2007, actual revenue collections for 2006–2007 were running more than $1 billion below the DOF's forecast. Thus, in this particular instance, the LAO's forecast was proving to be more accurate.

Longer-Term Budget Balance

The focus of the state's longer-term forecasts is the relationship between its revenues and expenditures over time. These estimates can be helpful in identifying emerging structural surpluses or deficits (i.e., a chronic mismatch between revenue and expenditure growth over time), or the multiyear effects of various state policies on the state's budget condition. Figure 5.18 shows the LAO's out-year forecasts made in February 2007 of the state's operating balance (i.e., revenues minus expenditures) under the "2007–08 Governor's Budget" policy proposals released in January 2007. It indicates projected ongoing budget shortfalls under the administration's policy proposals.

Conclusion

Budget forecasting for California is intrinsically a very complicated undertaking. Not only does it have to deal with the difficulty of accurately forecasting demographics and the economy, but projecting revenues and expenditures adds yet another layer of complexity. There are a number of excellent tools available to tackle the challenges that forecasting poses, and California attempts to utilize fairly sophisticated and state-of-the-art methodologies to address them. However, given the inherent difficulties that accompany forecasting, making accurate budget forecasts for California will undoubtedly continue to be an extremely challenging activity in the future, especially given the state's dynamic demography, economy, revenue system, and expenditure base. At the same time, meeting this challenge will be important, especially given the state's recent persistent structural budget problems and the role that good fiscal forecasts can play in helping to effectively address them.

References

California Legislative Analyst's Office (2007). *California's tax system: A primer.* April. Sacramento, CA.

Governor's Budget Summary (2007–2008). State of California, January 2007, 272pp.

Legislative Analyst's Office (1999). *California's Tax Expenditure Programs: Part One—Overview and Part Two—Compendium of Individual Programs.* February. Sacramento, CA: California Legislative Analyst's Office. 372pp.

Legislative Analyst's Office (2005). *Proposition 98 primer.* February. Sacramento, CA: Legislative Analyst's Office.

Legislative Analyst's Office (2006a). *The 2007–2008 Budget: Perspectives and issues, Part II: Perspectives on the Economy and Demographics,* February. Sacramento, CA: Legislative Analyst's Office. pp. 24–26.

Legislative Analyst's Office (2006b). *Abusive tax shelters: Impact of recent California legislation.* January 27. Sacramento, CA: Legislative Analyst's Office.

Vasché J D (1980). Income tax indexing and its revenue effects in California. *Presentations on Revenue Estimating Procedures.* National Association of Tax Administrators Conference on Revenue Estimating, 1980, Washington, DC: Federation of Tax Administrators. pp. 24–31.

Vasché, J D (1981). The fiscal implications of personal income tax indexing in California. *Western Tax Review* 2 (1): 1–29.

Vasché, J D (1982). A note on the use of elasticities versus simulation models for state income tax forecasting. *Western Tax Review* 3 (1): 15–21.

Vasché, J D and B Williams (1984). Microcomputer modeling and simulation in government tax revenue estimating. *Modeling and Simulation on Microcomputers, Part 1: Public Policy, Educational, and Economic Applications,* Society for Computer Simulation and Simulation Councils, Inc. pp. 3–9.

Vasché, J D (1987a). The California legislative analyst's PC-based revenue estimating approach. *Government Finance Review* 3 (3): 30–31.

Vasché, J D (1987b). Economic and fiscal forecasting processes used by the state of California's Legislative Analyst's Office. *The Journal of Business Forecasting Methods & Systems* 6 (2): 9–13.

Vasché, J D (2006a). Whatever happened to dynamic revenue estimating in California? Paper presented at the 2006 Federation of Tax Administrators Revenue Estimating and Tax Research Conference, September, Washington.

Vasché, J D (2006b). Whatever happened to dynamic revenue estimating in California? *State Tax Notes* 42 (8): 493–500.

Williams, B, K Szakaly, and J D Vasché (1997a). Forecasting California's personal income tax revenues in the midst of shifting income distributions. *State Tax Notes* 13 (24): 1565–1576.

Williams, B, K Szakaly, and J D Vasché (1997b). Forecasting state personal income tax revenues in the midst of shifting income distributions: The case of California. *Proceedings of the Ninetieth Annual Conference on Taxation.* National Tax Association—Tax Institute of America, pp. 335–348.

Chapter 6

Forecasting the Personal Income Tax

Qiang Xu, Robert Megna, Hilke Kayser,
and Lynn Holland

Contents

Introduction

The personal income tax (PIT) is the preeminent revenue source for many states. In New York State (NYS), the PIT accounts for almost 60 percent of all state tax receipts. This chapter presents a methodology for forecasting the PIT at the state level. Because taxpayer income is the ultimate source of PIT receipts, forecasting the components of taxable income is the first step in projecting PIT liability. Econometric models are generally used to forecast the key components of income so that forecasters can project liability into future years. This chapter discusses some specific forecasting models in detail and presents estimation results based on NYS data.

Once income component growth rates are determined, they can be incorporated into a microsimulation model that trends income forward for a weighted sample of taxpayers and determines tax liability. Because most states employ a progressive income tax structure, the distribution of a given amount of income is critical to the determination of liability. Microsimulation is the principal tool for projecting changes in the distribution of income over time, and is also useful for calculating the impact of proposed law changes on future tax liability. For the final step in the estimation of PIT receipts, forecasters require models that convert liability estimates into fiscal year tax collections, taking into account the difference in timing between when liability is incurred and taxes are actually paid by the individual taxpayer.

The chapter is organized as follows. The remainder of the introduction section outlines the nature of the problems that are unique to forecasting the PIT and provides a visual overview of the forecasting process. The section on Data Sources describes the data that the process requires. The section titled Income Component Forecasting Models provides detailed descriptions of income component forecasting models. The section Income Distribution and the Microsimulation Model describes the importance of the income distribution to liability estimation and the use of microsimulation to project the distribution of income and tax liability into future years. The section titled Cash Collections and Tax Liabilities provides an overview of the translation from liability to cash receipts. The section on Risk Assessment provides a brief discussion of the importance of providing an assessment of the risk to the forecast, and is followed by a concluding section.

The approach presented in the following sections is based primarily on the methods used by the NYS Division of the Budget. However, the models presented are similar to those employed by government agencies at the national level and can be adapted for any state that levies a PIT. The modeling structure presented in this chapter is not only useful in estimating the PIT, but also aids in explaining the critical determinants of the forecast to policy makers and other concerned parties involved in the budget process.

The Nature of the Forecasting Problem

Detailed knowledge of the composition and distribution of taxable income is critical to accurately projecting future PIT receipts. In this regard, the PIT forecasting process presents some unique challenges. One complicating factor is the complex linkage between economic activity and PIT revenue. Individual taxpayer activities generate various forms of taxable income—such as wages, noncorporate business income, capital gains realizations, dividends, and interest income—that give rise to tax liability and, in turn, their "cash" payments to the federal and state governments. There can be long lags between when the liability is incurred and when the cash payment is actually received by the taxation authority. This lag is minimal for wages and salaries due to the withholding mechanism. However, for the nonwage components, such as capital gains realizations and business income, the lag can exceed one year.

A related challenge arises from the delay in the availability of liability data, of which the primary source is individual tax returns. At the federal level and in most states, the taxation authority provides very timely information on the flow of PIT receipts throughout the tax year. Indeed, withholding data, which tracks wages and salaries closely, is compiled daily, whereas estimated payments are paid and compiled quarterly throughout the tax year. However, there is no detailed information regarding the income components that generate the underlying tax liability until the state processes the tax returns during the following year. The common practice among high-income taxpayers to request filing extensions compounds the delay. In NYS, a solid estimate of the 2005 tax liability did not become available until the end of 2006. This estimate will be further refined over the course of the first half of 2007, as the state taxation authority—the NYS Department of Taxation and Finance—closely inspects and verifies a sample of tax returns. This sample dataset, known as the PIT study file, was expected to become available during the summer of 2007 at the time of this writing.

Detailed information on both the components of taxable income and their distribution is also necessary for analyzing the impact of proposed tax law changes on PIT liability. Tax law changes that affect particular income components may have variable effects on taxpayers depending on their level of incomes. For example, a change in the tax treatment of capital gains would tend to affect higher-income taxpayers more than lower-income taxpayers, all things being equal. Therefore, it is essential to be able to project not only the total value of the components of taxable income, but also how those components are distributed across taxpayers by income.

Computing Taxable Income and Liability

The structure of the PIT for almost all states starts with the income definitions stipulated under the federal income tax law that a taxpayer uses to arrive at federal gross income. The components of federal gross income include wages, salaries, and tips; interest and dividend incomes; state and local income tax refunds; alimony received; net sole proprietorship and farm incomes; capital gain and loss realizations; IRA distributions and pensions and annuities; rents and royalties; incomes from partnerships, S corporations, estates, and trusts; unemployment compensation; and taxable Social Security benefits. The sum of federal gross income and the adjustments mandated under federal tax law is known as federal adjusted gross income (AGI). Applying various state-specific additions and subtractions to federal AGI yields a state version of AGI. A set of allowable deductions are then subtracted from state AGI producing taxable income, to which the tax rate structure is applied to arrive at tax liability before credits. Finally, the subtraction of allowable credits results in the taxpayer's state PIT liability.

For economists familiar with the U.S. Bureau of Economic Analysis (BEA) definitions of income, it will be useful to understand the differences between the various measures of income and their significance to liability estimation. As anyone who has filled out a tax form knows, income as defined for tax purposes includes gains and losses earned on the sale of financial and tangible assets known as capital gain and loss realizations. A BEA measure that is closely related to AGI is a state's personal income, which is a BEA national income and product accounts (NIPA) concept that measures income derived from value added to current production at the state level. The tie to value added precludes the inclusion of capital gains and losses in measures of personal income at either the state or federal levels. Because realizations represent a large portion of taxable income, they represent a significant difference between the BEA's measure of income and income defined for tax purposes. Moreover, the inherent volatility in asset market prices tends to make AGI much more volatile than personal income as defined under NIPA.

Figure 6.1 offers a virtual roadmap for the PIT forecasting process. In the first step, econometric models are used to forecast the components of AGI over the length of the forecast horizon, which is typically about five years. In the second step, results of these models are fed into a microsimulation model that uses tax return information for a large sample of taxpayers to convert taxable income into liability. In the final step, a set of cash collection models are used to translate

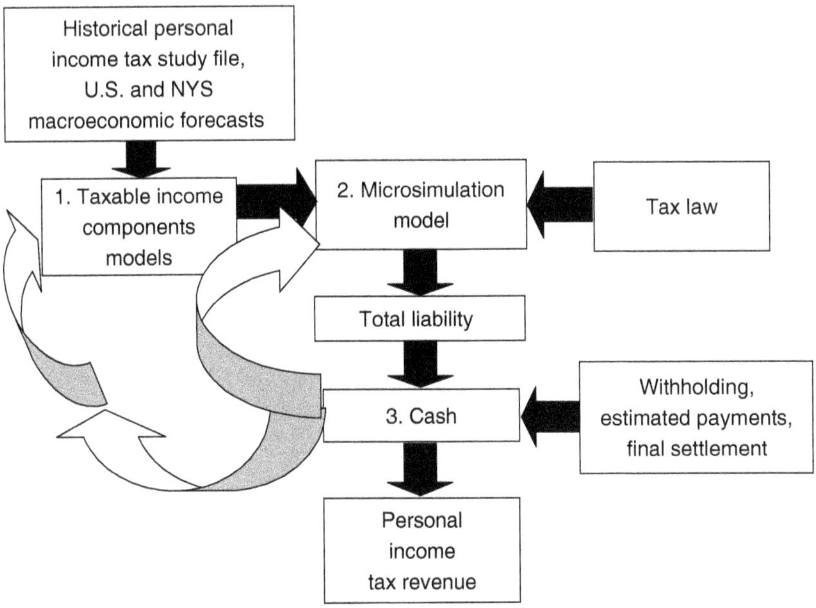

Figure 6.1 Personal income tax forecasting system. (From New York State Division of the Budget.)

liability estimates into streams of cash payments made by taxpayers over the course of the state fiscal year in the form of withholding payments, quarterly estimated payments, and a final settlement payment or refund. Although much of the discussion that follows pertains to the forecasting of PIT liability for NYS, the underlying principles can be adapted to forecasting income tax liability at any level of government that levies a PIT.

Data Sources

Tax returns are the most important data source for analyzing the PIT at the state level, but because of reporting lags, forecasters can supplement tax return data with data on cash collections, which is typically much more timely. Ancillary data is obtained from the U.S. Internal Revenue Service (IRS).

The Study File

The PIT forecast typically starts with a stratified random sample of individual income tax returns compiled annually by the taxation authority specifically for the purpose of analysis and research. Because of filing and processing lags, this weighted sample of returns, commonly referred to as the "PIT study file," does not become available until

18 months or more after the end of the pertaining tax year. In New York, 2004 was the most recent tax year for which complete tax return data was available at the time of this writing. The 2004 NYS PIT study file, which became available in August 2006, is composed of about 242,000 records, representing a universe of about 8.9 million tax returns. The study file includes detailed information such as marital and resident status, federal AGI and its components, NYS AGI (NYSAGI), deductions, exemptions, credits, and tax liability. The New York study file is stratified by income, filer type, resident status, whether the taxpayer itemizes deductions or claims the standard deduction, and whether or not the taxpayer claims at least one credit.

At the federal level, the IRS produces the national Statistics of Income (SOI) dataset, a stratified sample based on the larger of positive income or the absolute value of negative income, the size of business and farm receipts, the presence or absence of a set of specific forms or schedules, and the usefulness of returns for tax policy modeling purposes (Hollenbeck and Parisi 2006). The 2004 SOI data is based on a sample of 200,778 returns and an estimated final population of 133,189,982 returns.

Because the study file contains only a sample of the taxpayer universe, each record has a weight assigned to it. That weight corresponds to the number of returns that the record statistically represents. The weights are determined such that the weighted sums for the total number of tax filers, total NYSAGI, and total liability match the population totals. Weighted sums for the detailed components of AGI are assumed to closely approximate the population totals, although they are subject to sampling error. Because of the progressive nature of the PIT structure, it is critical that the sample data accurately reflects the actual income distribution. For a fixed level of taxable income, varying distributions of income across taxpayers will produce differing amounts of liability.

Processing Reports

In New York, the taxation authority generates daily, weekly, and monthly collection reports on withholding, estimated payments, and those components of collections that are related to the taxpayers' final settlement with the state for the previous tax year, that is, their tax returns. The Division of the Budget monitors this data closely for the purpose of both forecasting and performing monthly cash flow analysis.

Each component of receipts follows a different payment and reporting schedule. Withholding information is reported on a daily basis, whereas estimated payments approximately follow a quarterly schedule, with the largest payment months being April, June, September, and January. Final payments from taxpayers whose returns are accompanied by a remittance to the state tend to arrive during March, April, and May, and during October when returns tend to be due for taxpayers receiving extensions. Refunds on timely filed returns must be issued within 45 days of the due date or within 45 days of the filing date; whichever is later. As a result, most refunds on timely filed returns are paid out during March, April, and May.

Tax return processing reports provide year-to-date data on the number of returns filed, tax liability, and state AGI well before the study file for the same tax year becomes available. Forecasters can use this data as a reality check for the AGI component forecasting models, and adjust the model results accordingly. Where available, information on the distribution of returns, liability, and AGI by income class and resident status can be used to assess the results of the liability microsimulation model described in more detail in The Role of Microsimulation in Estimating Liability section. Of course, data availability will vary by state.

Federal Sources of Information

The SOI program makes federal data on state resident taxpayers available through electronic data files and published reports. For example, the IRS published 2004 information on some of the income components for NYS residents in late spring of 2006 in the *SOI Bulletin*. Detailed information in the form of the 2004 SOI public use datafile became available during October 2006. At the time of this writing, the IRS was planning to have 2005 tax year data available by August 2007. The SOI information is useful in that it provides valuable federal tax information that may not be available from state tax returns.

Income Component Forecasting Models

Although the PIT study file is a representative sample of taxpayers, it does not allow the analyst to track the behavior of individual taxpayers over time, that is, it is not a panel dataset. Therefore, forecasters must take additional steps to project how taxable income and tax liability will grow over the forecast horizon. The first step in this process is an aggregation of the components of AGI for every year.* The resulting historical time series are used to construct a set of single-equation econometric models used to project the rate at which the income components will grow over time in the aggregate. However, evidence suggests that the components of income do not grow at the same rate across income groups. Consequently, disaggregating growth rates by income groups can greatly improve the accuracy of the projected income distribution and, in turn, liability estimates. Thus, forecasting the components of AGI is a two-step process: (1) project aggregate growth in the income components in a manner that is consistent with the forecaster's overall economic outlook and (2) estimate income-group-specific growth rates, subject to the constraint implied by the projected aggregate component growth.

* For New York, the length of the time series available for the components of income varies. Aggregates of the major components of AGI go back to 1969, based on NYS Department of Taxation and Finance records; but some series go back only to 1985—the first year for which study files are available.

Projecting Aggregate Component Growth

At the federal level, many of the components of AGI have analogous concepts in the NIPA compiled by the BEA. For example, taxable wages, interest, and dividend income have value-added counterparts under the NIPA definition of personal income. Thus, the Congressional Budget Office (CBO) uses NIPA data, with some adjustments, as inputs in estimating values for the taxable components of income for the intervening years for which national economic data is available but SOI data are not. For future years, forecast values of the components of personal income can be used to project values for taxable income (Congressional Budget Office 2006). However, NIPA personal income data are not available at the same level of detail at the state level. In addition, the BEA's methodology for producing its initial estimates of the components of state personal income may introduce a source of error that does not exist at the national level. For example, initial quarterly state estimates are derived from the trends in the annual state estimates, and are made to sum to, or "controlled to," the NIPA national estimates (U.S. Bureau of Economic Analysis 2006). Thus, forecasters should supplement the use of state-level NIPA personal income components with additional state-specific indicators in developing forecasts for state AGI (Brown et al. 2006).

The first step in constructing econometric models should be an examination of the time series properties of the aggregate AGI component series. Where a series of sufficient length is available, the analyst should test for stationarity, and when nonstationarity is detected, the analyst should perform a transformation to make the data stationary to avoid being misled by spurious regression results. Examples from the NYS Division of the Budget's NYSAGI forecasting system are presented in the following text. In these examples, the data for which at least 20 observations are available was tested, and where found to be nonstationary, was logarithmically transformed and first-differenced.

The forecast models require explanatory variables that are available for both the historical and the forecast period. Ideally, the forecast values should be consistent with the forecaster's overall economic outlook. The Budget Division has developed detailed macroeconomic models for the U.S. and State economies. Thus, a rich set of candidate explanatory variables, including state-level NIPA personal income components, is available for capturing state-specific trends that are likely to affect future values of the components of AGI. As in any modeling effort, the data presents anomalies that can be sometimes explained by such factors as tax law changes or extraordinary events. However, at other times such anomalies remain inexplicable, possibly an artifact of sampling error. When confronted with such anomalies, forecasters can include dummy variables for the appropriate periods.

A common problem for model estimation is the relatively small number of annual observations that are typically available, particularly when viewed relative to the frequency of events that can have a large impact on AGI. For example, a long bear market in equities followed the collapse of the "dot.com" bubble in 2000, which was further exacerbated by the events of September 11 and the revelation of numerous corporate governance scandals. In New York, these events were associated with a decline in positive capital gains realizations of 50 percent in 2001 and another 27 percent in 2002. In the history of this series, which extends back to 1969, only one bear market of comparable magnitude occurred starting on January 11, 1973, when the S&P 500 fell 48.2 percent over a 21-month period. Correspondingly, positive capital gains realizations fell 20 percent in 1973 and 25 percent in 1974. Events such as a major federal law change can also have a large impact on taxpayer behavior and consequently, estimated model parameters and their associated statistics. The infrequency of such critical events adds to the uncertainty of the forecasts derived from purely statistical models of AGI. Given these limitations, forecasters cannot avoid incorporating their subjective judgments, typically through out-of-model adjustments.

For the period between the last year for which detailed taxpayer information is available and the point at which the forecast is being made, there are typically two additional sources of information that forecasters can incorporate into estimates of AGI. The first is tax return processing data, although its level of detail will depend on what the processing agency makes available. For the recent period, cash collections data can also provide guidance.

In the following sections, detailed examples of model specifications and estimation results for the number of returns and the major components of AGI based on NYS data are presented. All estimation results presented are based on tax return data from samples of NYS taxpayers through the 2004 tax year. Standard errors appear below the coefficient values. In many cases, variables enter the estimation equation in the first-differenced log form, as mentioned earlier. This transformation possesses convenience of interpretation in that it approximates percentage growth for small growth rates. However, for large rates of growth, like those that can be observed for capital gains realizations, the first-differenced log form can deviate quite dramatically from the actual growth rate. For example, for 1994, when realizations fell by 4.8 percent, the first-difference in the logs yields a very close 4.9. In contrast, for 2004, when positive capital gains realizations grew by 72.5 percent, the first-difference in the logs yields a measure of only 54.5.

Tax Returns

The number of tax returns is expected to vary with the number of households that earn any kind of income during the year that is subject to the PIT. The number of such households, in turn, should be closely associated with the number of individuals who are either self-employed, employed by others, or earn taxable income from sources other than labor. Because most taxable income is earned as wages and salaries and thus related to employment, total payroll employment is a key input to this model. Taxpayers can earn taxable income from sources other than payroll employment, such as financial assets, self-employment, or a business partnership. State proprietors' income, a component of state personal income under NIPA, is normally a good indicator of self-employment and partnership formation, after adjusting for inflation. Another source of personal income is property income, which includes interest, dividend, and rental income, again, after adjusting for inflation. Thus, the model for the number of tax returns includes these variables.

Table 6.1 summarizes the performance of the tax return forecasting model. Model results indicate that employment growth is the most important contributor to the growth in returns. A 1 percent increase in employment produces a 0.4 percent increase in the number of tax returns filed, whereas a 1 percent increase in the combined growth of real proprietors' and property income produces an increase of only about 0.1 percent. The model also includes two dummy variables that capture the impacts of two events that produced one-time changes in the growth in the number of returns. D1987 captures the impact of the Tax Reform Act of 1986 that eliminated the two-earner deduction for married couples as of the 1987 tax year, reducing the incentive for married couples to file joint tax returns and resulting in stronger growth in the number of returns than otherwise. D2000 is related to a change in the way tax returns were processed and sampled starting that year. Both variables have statistically significant effects.

For states such as New York with large commuter populations that make a significant contribution to state PIT revenues, the numbers of resident and nonresident returns are likely to follow distinct trends. Because the most accurate data available combines resident and nonresident income and employment, the NYS model contains the mentioned specification for the total number of returns, whereas a separate model is specified for nonresidents. This latter model includes total state wages, a dummy variable for the impact of the early 1990s recession, which was much more severe for New York than it was for the nation, and a dummy variable to capture unusual behavior in the series in 1988. The number of

Table 6.1 Tax Returns

$$\Delta \ln RET_t = \underset{(0.00108)}{0.00221} + \underset{(0.0741)}{0.430}\, \Delta \ln NYSEMP_t + \underset{(0.0293)}{0.0980}\, \Delta \ln((PROPNY + YENTNY)/CPINY)_t + \underset{(0.00484)}{0.0186}\, D1987_t + \underset{(0.00499)}{0.0378}\, D2000_t$$

Adjusted $R^2 = 0.897$

RET	Number of tax returns
NYSEMP	Total state employment
PROPNY	State property income
YENTNY	State proprietors' income
CPINY	Consumer price index for New York
D1987	Dummy variable for 1987 tax law change
D2000	Dummy variable for 2000 processing changes

Note: NYS Division of the Budget staff estimates.

resident returns is then the residual between the total number of returns and the number of nonresident returns.

Taxable Wages

Taxable wages are the largest and, therefore, the most important component of AGI. In New York, taxable wages have historically followed approximately the same trend as the overall state wages as measured by the data collected under the Quarterly Census of Employment and Wages (QCEW) program, the series that is used by many forecasters to produce macroeconomic projections of state employment and wages. Thus, to ensure internal consistency with the state economic forecast, forecasters may want to apply the forecast growth rate for total state wages and salaries derived from a macroeconomic model of the state economy to the wage base obtained from the taxpayer sample. This method works well for NYS and should work for most states.*

Taxable wages is the only income component for which the resident and nonresident portions are allowed to follow distinct trends in the forecast period. As for the number of returns, nonresident wages are modeled separately, with the residual between total state wages and nonresident wages allocated to residents. The model for nonresident wages includes total state wages, a dummy variable for 1988, and two additional dummy variables that presumably capture the shifting of income by taxpayers from the beginning of one tax year to the end of the prior tax year in anticipation of a tax increase. This behavior can be observed in 1992–1993 and 1996–1997.

Capital Gains Realizations

Capital gains realizations are probably the most challenging component of AGI to forecast. The large magnitude of capital gains realizations, combined with their volatility, make this component an important contributor to the overall trend in PIT revenues. However, the most important driver—financial market activity—is very volatile, and therefore, difficult to predict. Other asset prices, most notably real estate, can also be very volatile. Moreover, several significant tax law changes appear to have significantly influenced how taxpayers time the realization of their gains and losses. The capital gains realizations forecasting model incorporates those factors that are most likely to influence realization behavior: equity market activity, actual and anticipated tax law changes, and real estate market activity.

Table 6.2 summarizes the performance of the capital gains realizations forecasting model. To capture the effect of equity prices, the average price of all stocks traded on the New York Stock Exchange, the NASDAQ, and the American Stock Exchange

* The NYS Budget Division's state macroeconomic model is too large to be presented in detail in this chapter but the underlying methodology is available from the authors on request.

Table 6.2 Positive Capital Gains Realizations

$$\Delta \ln CG_t = \underset{(2.31)}{6.33}\,\Delta TRSTX_t - \underset{(0.688)}{2.65}\,\Delta PRMTX_t + \underset{(0.192)}{1.38}\,\Delta \ln EQTYP_t + \underset{(0.164)}{0.449}\,\Delta \ln RETT_t - \underset{(0.138)}{0.326}\,D1990_t$$

Adjusted $R^2 = 0.818$

CG	Positive capital gains realizations
TRSTX	Transitory tax measure
PRMTX	Permanent tax rate
EQTYP	Average price of stocks traded
RETT	Real estate transfer tax collections
D1990	Dummy variable for 1990

Note: NYS Division of the Budget staff estimates.

is incorporated into the model. This comprehensive measure has been found to be a better predictor of capital gains than any one particular stock index, such as the S&P 500. A coefficient estimate of 1.4 indicates the importance of financial asset prices in determining the direction and magnitude of capital gains. To capture the impact of real estate market activity, the model specification includes NYS real estate transfer tax collections. That the coefficient on this variable, at 0.4, is lower than the coefficient on financial market prices is not surprising. Taxpayers can exempt gains from the sale of a primary residence of up to \$250,000 for single filers and up to \$500,000 for married filers filing jointly. Capital gains realized from all other real estate transactions, such as second homes and investment properties, are completely taxable. Thus, the real estate market must be generating either very large increases in prices or a multitude of transactions involving second homes and investment—two developments that are expected to be closely related—to generate large growth in gains.

Realization behavior appears to exhibit two types of responses to changes in tax law: a transitory response to an anticipated future change in the law and a steady-state response to an actual change. For example, if the U.S. Congress enacts a tax rate increase to take effect the following tax year, taxpayers may realize additional gains during the current tax year to take advantage of today's lower rate. However, in the long run, the higher tax rate should result in a lower steady-state level of gains realizations, all things being equal. Based on Miller and Ozanne (2000), the transitory response variable is specified as the square of the difference between the rate expected to take effect next period and the current period rate, with the sign of the difference preserved. Thus, an anticipated future tax increase raises the gains in the current period. An estimated coefficient of 6.3 is consistent with that expectation. The long-term or steady-state response variable is the change in the tax rate itself for the year when the change actually occurs. Because an increase in the tax rate reduces the steady-state level of gains, a negative coefficient is obtained. Finally, a dummy variable successfully captures the large decline in gains observed in 1990 that none of the other variables in the model can explain.

Econometric analysis is limited by the information contained in the history of the data. Therefore, it is questionable whether model estimation can completely capture the impact of events that appear extraordinary in the context of that history. The 2000–2002 decline in equity prices is an example of such an event. When equity market prices fall, many taxpayers realize capital losses that can be used to offset realized gains and other forms of income in the calculation of AGI. However, state tax law typically restricts the taxpayer from declaring more than $3000 in net capital losses in any one year, although unused losses can be carried over into future years indefinitely. Because the forecaster cannot directly observe taxpayers' use of the loss carryover, it poses a significant risk to the accuracy of the model forecast. This is due to the lack of historical experience with the duration and magnitude of the bear markets experienced in the early part of the decade. Out-of-model adjustments may be deemed necessary for the years following extraordinary events to arrive at a forecast that appropriately balances the perceived risks.

Rental, Royalty, Partnership, S Corporation, and Trust Income

Another large income component is that which combines partnership, S corporation, rental, royalty, estate, and trust gains (PSG). An overwhelming proportion of PSG is accounted for by partnerships and closely held corporations organized under Subchapter S of the Internal Revenue Code known as S corporations. On the basis of national data, a large portion of partnership income appears to originate from the finance industry (IRS Statistics of Income Division 2007), whereas S corporations appear to be more representative of the broader economy (IRS Statistics of Income Division 2006).* Therefore, growth in PSG is closely related to overall economic conditions, as represented by growth in the real U.S. gross domestic product (GDP), as well as to the performance of the stock market, as represented by the S&P 500.

Selection of S corporation status allows firms to pass earnings through to a limited number of shareholders and to avoid taxation under the corporate franchise rate structure that applies to firms that choose to organize as a C corporation. Therefore, the size of the differential between the top marginal PIT rate and the corporate income tax rate should significantly affect the choice by a firm to elect S corporation status. As more firms choose S corporation status over C corporation status, income taxable under the PIT increases, all things being equal. To test this hypothesis, this differential is included in the model, where the relevant tax rates combine the federal, state, and local rates.

Table 6.3 summarizes the performance of the PSG forecasting model. As expected, these results indicate that national economic conditions as measured

---

* The finance industry's role in partnership income is probably even greater for NYS than for the nation as a whole.

Table 6.3 Positive Partnership, S Corporation, Rental, Royalty, Estate, and Trust Income

$$\Delta \ln PSG_t = \underset{(0.0817)}{0.477}\,\Delta MTR_t + \underset{(0.0637)}{0.264}\,\Delta \ln S\&P500_t + \underset{(0.453)}{2.23}\,\Delta \ln GDP_t + \underset{(0.0279)}{0.228}\,D1988\text{–}1989_t$$

Adjusted $R^2 = 0.840$

PSG	Partnership, S corporation, rent, royalty, estate, and trust income
MTR	Difference between corporate and top marginal PIT rates, divided by unity minus the corporate rate
S&P 500	Standard & Poor's 500 stock index
GDP	Real U.S. GDP
D1988–1989	Dummy variable: 1 for 1988, −1 for 1989

Note: NYS Division of the Budget staff estimates.

by growth in real U.S. GDP and equity market performance as measured by the growth in the S&P 500 contribute positively to PSG growth. The coefficient estimate for the tax variable, defined as the excess of the corporate rate over the PIT rate, divided by one minus the corporate tax rate, indicates that corporate taxpayers take tax rates into account when choosing how to organize.

Finally, changes in the tax law should account for some of the volatility in PSG. The enactment of the Tax Reform Act of 1986 (TRA86) created additional incentives to elect S corporation status. These incentives were completely implemented in 1988 and are likely to have resulted in an unusually high rate of growth in this component of income in the late 1980s. In particular, an unusually high rate of growth was observed in this component in 1988 that was followed by extremely low growth in 1989. Possible explanations are the expectation of a large tax increase after 1988, or an increase in the fee for electing S corporation status in 1989. A dummy variable that assumes a value of 1 for 1988 and −1 for 1989 captures this effect. As shown in Table 6.3, this variable has a very significant positive coefficient. This result indicates that either existing firms shifted income from 1989 to 1988 or firms that might have organized in 1989 chose to do so in 1988 to avoid a fee increase.

Dividend Income

Although dividend payouts tend to be very stable, taxable dividend income is actually quite volatile. Dividend income should rise with the fortunes of publicly held U.S. firms, which, in turn, should vary with the business cycle. In addition, dividend income is also thought to be associated with the expectations of the firms pertaining to their future profitability, which is expected to be tied to the future strength of the economy. Because interest rates incorporate inflation expectations, which in turn incorporate expectations regarding the future strength of

Table 6.4 Dividend Income

$$\Delta \ln DIV_t = \underset{(0.00965)}{0.0367}\,\Delta TRATE10_t + \underset{(0.0825)}{0.209}\,\Delta \ln S\&P500_t + \underset{(0.249)}{0.0488}\,\Delta \ln GDP_{t-1} + \underset{(0.172)}{0.457}\,\Delta \ln GDP_{t-2} + \underset{(0.434)}{1.22}\,\Delta \ln GDP_{t-3} - \underset{(0.030)}{0.127}\,DREC_t + \underset{(0.0399)}{0.121}\,D1988\text{–}1989_t$$

Adjusted $R^2 = 0.683$

DIV	Dividend income
TRATE10	Ten-year Treasury yield
S&P 500	Standard & Poor's 500 stock index
GDP	Real U.S. GDP
DREC	Recession dummy variable
D1988–1989	Dummy variable: 1 for 1988, −1 for 1989

Note: NYS Division of the Budget staff estimates.

the economy, they represent a proxy for the latter. Equity market prices are also an indicator of future profitability.

Table 6.4 summarizes the performance of dividend income–forecasting model. The indicators used as proxies for future profitability—the ten-year Treasury yield and the S&P 500—both yield positive and significant coefficients. They indicate that a 1 percent change in the S&P 500 contributes 0.2 percent change in dividend income growth, whereas an increase in the ten-year Treasury yield of ten basis points increases dividend growth by about 0.4 percentage points. The relative stability of dividend payouts is captured by the sustained impact of economic growth, as indicated by the positive and significant coefficients on the first three lagged values of the real U.S. GDP.

Historically, NYS dividend income has been much more variable than the dividend component of the U.S. personal income as defined under NIPA, ranging from a decline of 6 percent in 1991 to an increase of 22 percent in 1981. This may suggest the importance of factors affecting the way taxpayers report their income, rather than changes in the payment of dividends by firms. For example, reported dividend income grew 21.8 percent in 1988, followed by a decline of 2.6 percent the following year, presumably the impact of TRA86. A dummy variable is included in the model to capture this apparent spin-up. Another dummy variable appears to capture the extraordinary impact of recessions (1975, 1990, 1991, 1992, 2001, and 2002), beyond what is captured by fluctuations in the real U.S. GDP. Even after these adjustments, the overall fit of the model, as measured by the adjusted R^2, is low relative to other equations.

Interest Income

The interest income–forecasting model is based on the simple concept that, for a given amount of assets, an increase in interest rates will increase interest income. In addition, the volume of interest-bearing assets should increase as the economy grows.

Table 6.5 Interest Income

$$\Delta \ln INT_t = \underset{(0.202)}{0.967}\, \Delta \ln USINT_t + \underset{(0.0119)}{0.0389}\, \Delta TRATE10_t - \underset{(0.0679)}{0.204}\, D1992_t - \underset{(0.0703)}{0.214}\, D2002_t$$

Adjusted $R^2 = 0.816$

INT	Interest income
USINT	U.S. interest income (NIPA definition)
TRATE10	Interest rate on ten-year Treasury notes
D1992	Dummy variable for 1992
D2002	Dummy variable for 2002

Note: NYS Division of the Budget staff estimates.

The complete specification appears in Table 6.5. The model includes the ten-year Treasury yield and U.S. interest income, another component of the NIPA definition of U.S. personal income. Taxable interest income for New York is much more volatile than the latter measure. For the period 1976–2002, the average growth rate for U.S. interest income was 8 percent, with a standard deviation of 8.4 percentage points. In contrast, taxable interest income for NYS averaged 4.8 percent growth, with a standard deviation of over 14.7 percentage points, over the same period. The additional volatility in the New York taxable interest series may represent behavioral responses to changes in the tax law, although sampling error may also be a factor. The model includes dummy variables to capture extraordinary declines that occurred in 1992 and 2002, which changes in interest rates cannot explain.

Small Business Income

Taxable small business income includes income resulting from operating a business or practicing a profession as a sole proprietor, or from operating a farm. This component of income should vary with the overall strength of the national and state economies. These factors are captured by including real U.S. GDP growth and state proprietors' income, which is a component of the NIPA definition of personal income at the state level.

Table 6.6 summarizes the performance of the small income business–forecasting model. Both U.S. GDP growth and state proprietors' income generate positive coefficients as expected. A dummy variable captures the downward shift in reported business income growth for the period from 1989 onward. This shift is presumably a change in taxpayer behavior as new firms chose to register as S corporations rather than as sole proprietorships to take advantage of the more favorable laws pertaining to liability encompassed in TRA86. The inclusion of a lagged endogenous variable captures the dynamics of the growth path. The adjusted R^2 is relatively low compared to other estimated equations.

Table 6.6 Business Income

$$\Delta \ln BUS_t = \underset{(0.0249)}{0.0873} - \underset{(0.146)}{0.349}\,\Delta \ln BUS_{t-1} + \underset{(0.207)}{0.297}\,\Delta \ln YENTNY_t$$
$$+ \underset{(0.600)}{1.68}\,\Delta \ln GDP_t - \underset{(0.0215)}{0.102}\,D1989_t$$

Adjusted $R^2 = 0.647$

BUS	Sole proprietor and farm income
YENTNY	State proprietor income (NIPA definition)
GDP	Real U.S. GDP
D1989	Dummy variable for 1989 onward

Note: NYS Division of the Budget staff estimates.

Projecting Adjusted Gross Income Component Growth by Income Groups

The NYSAGI models forecast aggregate growth rates for all of the components of gross income. However, historical data indicates that these components do not grow at the same rate for all taxpayers. For example, when equity prices are rising briskly, capital gains realization income is likely to be growing faster for wealthy taxpayers whose assets are perhaps being managed by financial consultants than for less affluent taxpayers who cannot afford to pay high consulting fees. Indeed, rates of component income growth have been found to vary by many different factors including demographic characteristics, filing status, and so on. However, data availability may limit the level of detail at which an analysis of income growth can be conducted. The NYS Budget Division uses NYSAGI and resident status alone to disaggregate the study file sample into weighted deciles. For the purpose of creating deciles, nonresident NYSAGI is restricted to that portion of income for which the taxpayer designates NYS as the source.

For residents, projected aggregate growth rates are allowed to vary by income for the six largest components of gross income for residents—wages, positive capital gains realizations, positive partnership and S corporation gains, dividend income, interest income, and business income. For nonresidents, decile-specific growth rates are estimated only for wages. Once the deciles are created, income component shares are calculated going as far back in time as the data allow. Before estimation, the deciles whose share movements over time are highly correlated can be grouped. Estimating equations are specified for each group less one. A final equation is an identity that constrains the shares to add to unity, ensuring that the aggregate income targets are met. The share estimating equations typically include variables that are forecast within the U.S. and NYS macroeconomic models, as well as growth in the aggregate component itself.

The share estimating equations produce a "first round" of decile-specific growth rates for the major income components. Those years for which tax return processing information or cash collections data are available, the decile growth rates are typically adjusted in a second round in light of the guidance that this data provides, as described in the following section.

Income Distribution and the Microsimulation Model

When PIT rates are structured progressively, liability growth not only depends on aggregate income growth, but also on how income growth is distributed across filers. Income gains earned among wealthy filers, taxed at the top marginal tax rate, will increase liability more than the same amount of income earned among lower-income filers. In addition, as income grows over time, taxpayers move into higher-income brackets and face higher tax rates—a phenomenon commonly known as bracket creep.* Finally, certain types of income tend to be concentrated among high-income taxpayers, such as capital gains realizations and partnership income. Microsimulation models based on individual tax return data are valuable tools for accurately estimating tax liability due to their capacity to replicate shifts in the distribution of income over time.

Once the forecaster has determined the aggregate growth rates for the components of AGI and has decomposed those growth rates for the major components by decile, the income components can be trended forward at the level of the individual tax return. The decile-specific projected growth rates are applied to the major components, with the aggregate projected growth rates applied to the remaining components. The forecaster also adjusts the individual record weights so as to ensure that the aggregate forecast targets are met for both the levels of the largest income components and the total number of tax returns. As income grows and the sample weights change, the distribution of income changes in a manner that is consistent with both historical patterns of change and the macroeconomic forecast. This process is described in more detail in the following section.

The Income Distribution Is Critical

Out-year estimation of the income distribution is fraught with uncertainty because the share of income earned among the wealthiest taxpayers can fluctuate dramatically with such factors as the business cycle, the condition of financial markets, and changes in federal and state tax treatments. As incomes rise, some taxpayers move into higher-income tax brackets, increasing the effective tax rate and the amount of liability generated from a given amount of AGI. The opposite occurs as incomes fall. For example, the effective tax rate in New York fell from a high of 4.8 percent

* Although the boundaries of the income brackets are indexed to inflation at the federal level, they are not in New York.

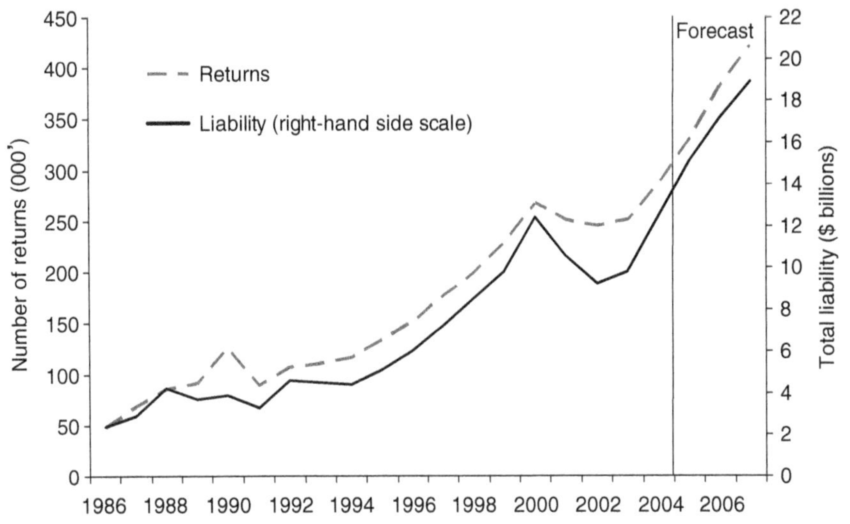

Figure 6.2 NYS high-income tax returns and liability (liability for 2003–2005 is adjusted to remove impact of a temporary surcharge). (From NYS Department of Taxation and Finance; DOB staff estimates.)

in 2000, a business cycle peak year, to a low of 4.4 percent in 2002, a recession year for the state, without any significant changes in the tax law.

"Revenue surprises" are not uncommon at the federal level. CBO recently reduced its estimate of the federal deficit by a substantial amount largely due to an underestimation of PIT revenues. As alluded to earlier, the sources of income for the wealthiest taxpayers are extremely volatile. Errors in forecasting the sources of this income can result in extremely large revenue forecast errors because wealthy taxpayers are taxed at the highest marginal tax rates. The following data from New York illustrates the problem.

The rising stock market created a substantial amount of wealth in the late 1990s, thus causing the share of total PIT liability accounted for by high-income taxpayers—those reporting NYSAGI of $200,000 or more—to grow rapidly during that period.* Figure 6.2 illustrates how the number of high-income returns and the liability accounted for by those returns have risen since 1986. Although the equity market collapse of 2000 and 2001 led to a noticeable decline in returns filed by high-income taxpayers, the 9 percent average annual growth rate in high-income returns between 1992 and 2003 far outpaced the 0.9 percent overall growth

* In 1995, 6,910 New York taxpayers had federal adjusted gross incomes of $1,000,000 or more. This number skyrocketed to 48,856 taxpayers in 2000. Between 1999 and 2000 alone, the number of millionaires almost doubled from 25,537 to 48,856.

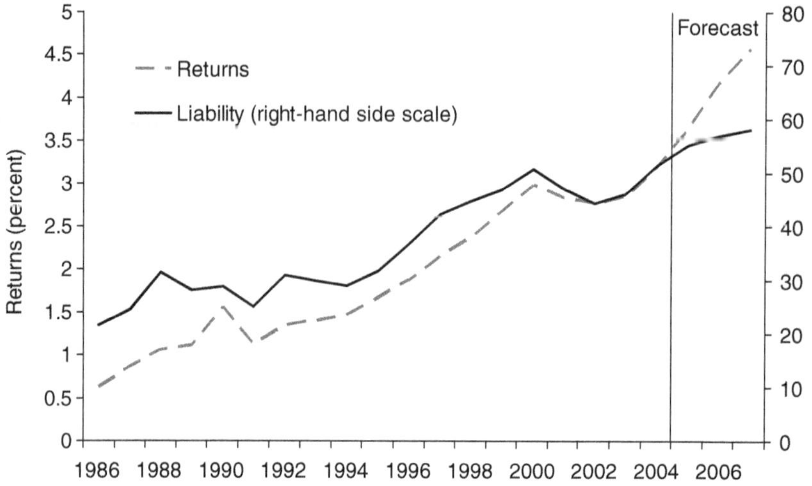

Figure 6.3 NYS high-income tax returns and liability (both capital gains and partnership and S corporation gains income are net of losses). (From NYS Department of Taxation and Finance; DOB staff estimates.)

in returns. Figure 6.3 compares the share of returns accounted for by high-income taxpayers to their share of total NYS PIT liability. In 2003, high-income taxpayers represented a mere 2.8 percent of all taxpayers but accounted for 33.5 percent of NYSAGI and 48.8 percent of PIT liability. The increasing concentration of liability among high-income taxpayers increases the elasticity of total liability with respect to both income growth and tax rate changes that affect high-income taxpayers.

Table 6.7 indicates that trends in both wage and nonwage income are responsible for the increasing concentration of liability since the early 1990s. The share of nonwage income accruing to the top 25 percent of taxpayers grew by 5.6 percentage points between 1993 and 2003, whereas that of wage income grew by 3.2 percentage points. Much of the growth in nonwage income during the 1990s was due to capital gains realizations and partnership and S corporation income, which tend to accrue primarily to high-income filers. Although wage income is more evenly distributed across taxpayers than nonwage income, the gains in wages earned since 1993 have accrued disproportionately to the top filers.

Figure 6.4 compares the composition of NYSAGI for all taxpayers for 2002, the second year of the state's recession, to that estimated for the 2007 tax year. The figure shows a substantial shift in income from wages to net capital gains realizations over the period.* For 2007, net capital gains income is projected to reach 11.6 percent of NYSAGI, up from 4.4 percent in 2002. Net capital gains realizations

* Net capital gains and partnership and S corporation income in these figures are net of the corresponding aggregate losses.

Table 6.7 Rising Concentration of State Income and Liability

1993 versus 2003	*Number of Returns*	*Gross Income*	*Wage Income*	*Nonwage Income*	*Liability*
1993					
Total (in $ millions)	7,873,667	311,033	237,972	73,061	14,981
Top 1 (percent share)	—	18.5	12.1	39.4	26.6
Top 5 (percent share)	—	33.2	26.2	56.3	45.4
Top 10 (percent share)	—	44.2	38.2	63.5	57.4
Top 25 (percent share)	—	66.1	62.7	77.0	78.8
2003					
Total (in $ millions)	8,836,584	512,628	373,313	139,315	22,465
Top 1 (percent share)	—	23.3	15.3	44.7	35.9
Top 5 (percent share)	—	38.8	30.6	60.9	56.7
Top 10 (percent share)	—	49.6	42.6	68.4	68.3
Top 25 (percent share)	—	70.4	65.9	82.6	86.9

Note: Returns are ranked on the basis of gross income and are based on weighted statistical sample of all tax returns.

Source: Reproduced from NYS Department of Taxation and Finance; NYS Division of the Budget staff estimates.

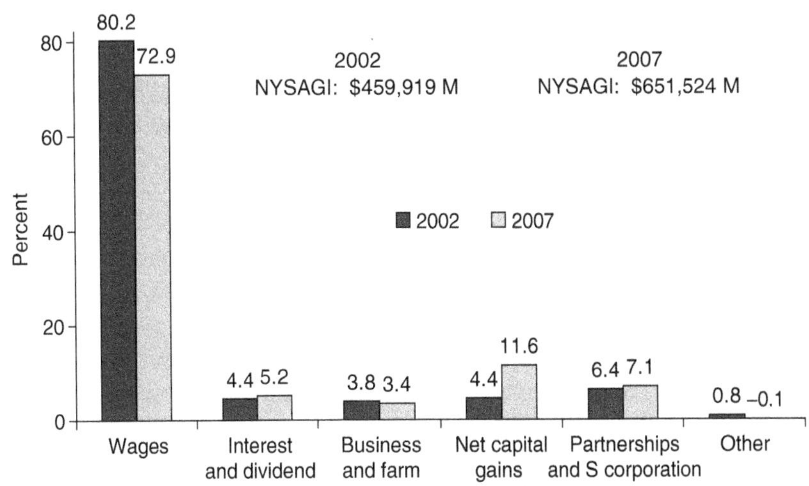

Figure 6.4 Composition of NYSAGI for all taxpayers (both capital gains and partnership and S corporation gains income are net of losses). (From NYS Department of Taxation and Finance; DOB staff estimates.)

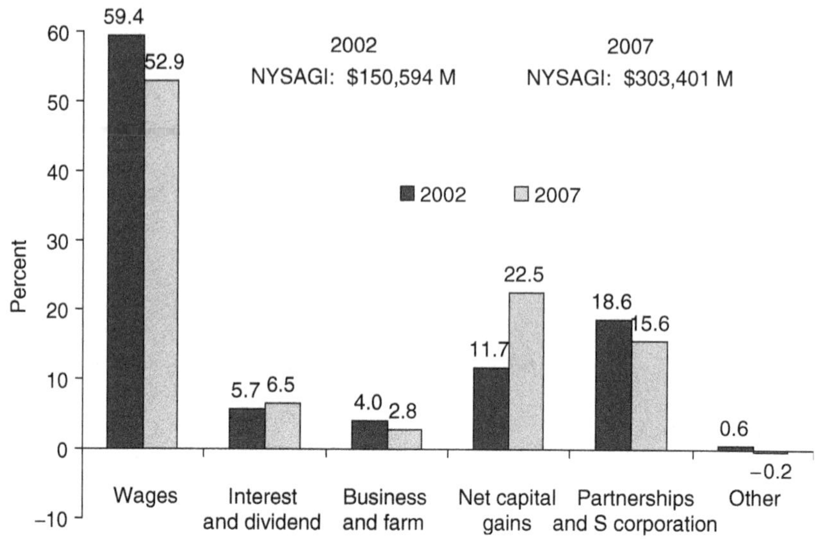

Figure 6.5 Composition of NYSAGI for high-income taxpayers (both capital gains and partnership and S corporation gains income are net of losses). (From NYS Department of Taxation and Finance; DOB staff estimates.)

peaked as a share of NYSAGI at 12.2 percent in 2000 at the height of the stock market bubble, and again in 2005 at about the same share with the estimated peaking of New York's residential real estate market boom. The wage share is projected to fall from 80.2 percent in 2002 to 72.9 percent in 2007, whereas net partnership income is projected to rise from 6.4 percent of NYSAGI to 7.1 percent over the period. The share for interest and dividend income is projected to rise over the period, whereas that for business and farm income is projected to fall.

Figure 6.5 is a recast of Figure 6.4 for high-income taxpayers only. A comparison of Figures 6.4 and 6.5 indicates that the composition of NYSAGI for high-income taxpayers differs markedly from that of all other taxpayers combined. In particular, the wage share is about 20 percentage points lower than the wage share for all taxpayers, whereas net capital gains and net partnership and S corporation income account for a much larger share of high-income taxpayer income than for taxpayers overall.* The percentage of high-income taxpayer income accounted for by net capital gains realizations is projected to double from 11.7 percent in 2002 to 22.5 percent for 2007. Meanwhile, shares accounted for by net partnership and S corporation income and wages are estimated to fall.

* Although tax return data does not differentiate bonus income from nonbonus income, it can be surmised that bonus income represents a much larger share of taxable income among high-income taxpayers than among low-income taxpayers.

The Role of Microsimulation in Estimating Liability

After aggregate AGI targets are set and decomposed into deciles for the largest components, the results can be incorporated into a microsimulation model that generates forecasts of PIT liability for future years. Forecasters can also use microsimulation to estimate the impact of tax policy proposals on overall liability and on different taxpayer groups. Examples of such proposals include changes in the standard deduction or exemption amounts, changes in the tax rate schedule, and changes in various tax credits.

The process of forecasting liability proceeds in two steps. The first step is to sequentially "advance" or "trend" the recent study file into future tax years. Thus, the 2004 study file forms the base for the 2005 trended dataset, which in turn becomes the base for creating the 2006 trended dataset, and so on. Once done for any given year, the analyst can submit the new trended dataset to the second step, which is the computation of tax liability under existing tax law for that year. This second step is essentially the application of a PIT tax liability calculator that follows the structure of the state tax form.

Trending

In New York, residents and nonresidents are trended separately. In the first step of the trending process for residents, taxpayer record weights are advanced by the projected growth in the total number of resident returns. In the second step, the major components of gross income are advanced by the projected decile-specific growth rates, discounted for the growth in the total number of returns. For New York, these resident income components include wages, positive capital gains realizations, positive PSG, dividends, interest, and business income; for nonresidents, only taxable wages are advanced by the decile-specific growth rates.

At this point, weighted sums for the major income components may not be precisely equal to the aggregate AGI targets described in the section Projecting Aggregate Component Growth. Thus, in the third step, the forecaster adjusts the individual taxpayer record weights yet again to ensure that the targets are met precisely. The method used to determine the size of these adjustments follows the U.S. Treasury department methodology (Cilke 1994). Define x_i to be the adjustment factor for weight class i. This adjustment acts as a scaling factor, such that, if $x_i = 1$, then the new weight is exactly equal to the original weight; $x_i > 1$ implies that the new weight is greater than the original weight, whereas $x_i < 1$ implies that the new weight is less than the original weight, for weight class i.

In theory, there are an infinite number of sets of adjustments that would serve the purpose. The Treasury department methodology chooses the unique set that guarantees that the targets are met with the smallest possible deviati,ons from the original weights. This is accomplished by constructing a "loss function," $\Phi(x_i)$, such that

$\Phi(1) = 0$, that is, the penalty is zero if there is no adjustment, and $\lim_{x \to \infty} \Phi(x) = \lim_{x \to \infty} \Phi(x) = \infty$, that is, upward and downward adjustments to the existing weights are equally penalized. Again, following the Treasury department, the following functional form for $\Phi(x_i)$ is chosen:

$$\Phi(x_i) = x_i^4 + x_i^{-4} - 2 \tag{6.1}$$

where x_i is the adjustment to the existing weight for the ith weight class. The analyst's goal is to choose weight adjustments that minimize the weighted sum of these "losses" subject to meeting the aggregate income targets. This goal implies a Lagrangean function of the following form:

$$L = \sum_{i=1}^{I} \left[n_i w_i \left(x_i^4 + x_i^{-4} - 2 \right) \right] + \sum_{j=1}^{J} \lambda_j \left(y_j - \sum_{i=1}^{I} x_i w_i y_{ij} \right) \tag{6.2}$$

where

I = number of weight classes
n_i = number of records in the ith weight class
w_i = existing weight for the ith weight class
J = number of major income components for which decile growth rates are estimated
λ_j = Lagrange multiplier for the jth major income component
y_j = aggregate target for the jth major income component
y_{ij} = unweighted total for the jth major income component for the ith weight class

Note that $\Phi(1) = 0$ implies that the set $\{x_i\}$ that solves the minimization problem can be expected to be close to one. Taking partial derivatives with respect to x_i and λ_j and rearranging produces the following first-order conditions:

$$4 n_i w_i \left(x_i^3 - x_i^{-5} \right) - \sum_{j=1}^{J} \lambda_j w_i y_{ij} = 0 \tag{6.3}$$

and

$$\sum_{i=1}^{I} x_i w_i y_{ij} = y_j \qquad \forall j = 1, \ldots, J \tag{6.4}$$

Equation 6.3 is nonlinear and has no analytical solution. Therefore, an iterative numerical process is employed to simultaneously solve Equations 6.3 and 6.4.

In the final step of the trending process, forecasters trend forward the remaining components of taxpayer income at the rates projected by the aggregate AGI models, discounted by the growth in the total number of returns. The entire procedure is repeated for nonresidents, except that decile-specific rates are applied only to taxable wages. Thus, $J = 1$, and the minimization of the objective function is constrained only by the need to satisfy the aggregate nonresident wage target. The final trended dataset forms the base for trending forward to the following year.

Liability Estimation

Once a trended dataset has been created, it can then be submitted to the "liability calculator." This component of the microsimulation emulates the calculations done by the tax filer in completing a state tax form by making use of all of the available information on each taxpayer's record to compute state AGI, allowable deductions and exemptions, taxable income, and all of the various allowable credits to compute that taxpayer's total tax liability under the pertaining state tax law. Total state liability is the weighted sum over all of the individual taxpayer records in the dataset, where the sum of the weights corresponds to the size of the total taxpaying population of the state.

Typically, certain tax law provisions are scheduled to change during the projection period. For example, the major provisions of the 2001 Economic Growth and Reconciliation Tax Act are scheduled to sunset at the end of 2010. Thus, the parameters used in the tax calculator portion of the microsimulation model must be consistent with the tax law in effect for the year being simulated. The analyst can simulate the impact of alternative tax regimes on liability by adjusting model parameters, such as tax rates, and repeating the tax calculating process. The capacity to alter tax law parameters makes the microsimulation model a useful tool for estimating the impact of alternative tax policy proposals, as well as the sensitivity of liability estimates to alternative economic forecast scenarios. Thus, it is important to create the capability to easily alter these parameters when constructing the microsimulation model.

Cash Collections and Tax Liabilities

Although significant risks surround any estimate of income tax liability, estimation of the level of tax liability for a particular tax year leads, with a high degree of confidence, to the approximate level of cash receipts that can be expected for the particular tax year. Figure 6.6 plots the annual level of tax receipts against the total liability for the same tax year and illustrates how consistent the relationship between the two has been. Despite the strong relationship between tax-year liability and cash receipts, estimation of cash payments is complicated by the need to apportion tax-year liability to particular state fiscal years. The tax authority tends to receive income tax prepayments—withholding tax and quarterly estimated tax payments—not long after income is earned. However, they tend to receive settlement payments—the payments that accompany taxpayer's final returns for a tax year—in April of the following year. Thus, settlement payments for the 2006 tax

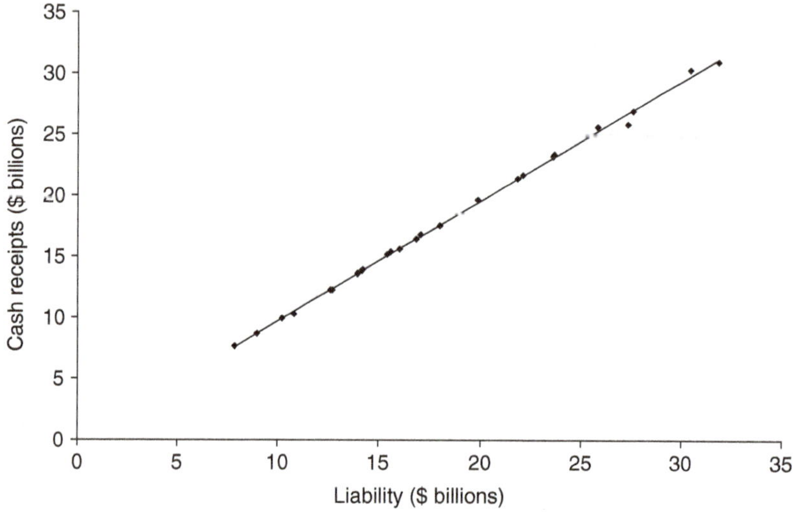

Figure 6.6 PIT liability versus PIT cash receipts, tax years 1982–2006. (From New York State Division of the Budget.)

year will be received largely in the 2006–2007 fiscal year for states whose fiscal year starts on July 1, but in 2007–2008 for New York, where the fiscal year starts on April 1.

Figure 6.7 shows net settlement payments for NYS for the 1983–2005 tax years. It is evident that the amount of liability received in the settlement can vary widely from year to year. For most years, the net settlement was quite negative, with state settlement outlays (such as refunds and offsets) far exceeding taxpayer settlement payments (such as those sent with returns and extension requests). Some notable exceptions to this pattern occurred during periods of tax reform (e.g., in 1986 and 1988), during times of rapid economic growth, and during periods characterized by large increases in nonwage income.

Settlement patterns have varied in recent years in NYS. With the rapid growth of the New York economy in the late 1990s, settlements became much less negative than they traditionally had been. This pattern resulted generally from prepayments falling short of liability, leading to the need for increased settlement payments with filed returns. This pattern reversed itself when the economy weakened in 2001 and 2002, with taxpayer prepayments now larger relative to liability, resulting in dramatically reduced settlement payments. Consequently, the total settlement became very negative again, with the net amount paid out by the state exceeding $2 billion for the 2002 tax year. Owing to the temporary tax increases enacted by the state legislature in 2003, the net settlement payout by the state remained negative but below $600 million for the 2004 tax year, and became less negative at about $380 million for tax year 2005. This net settlement increase

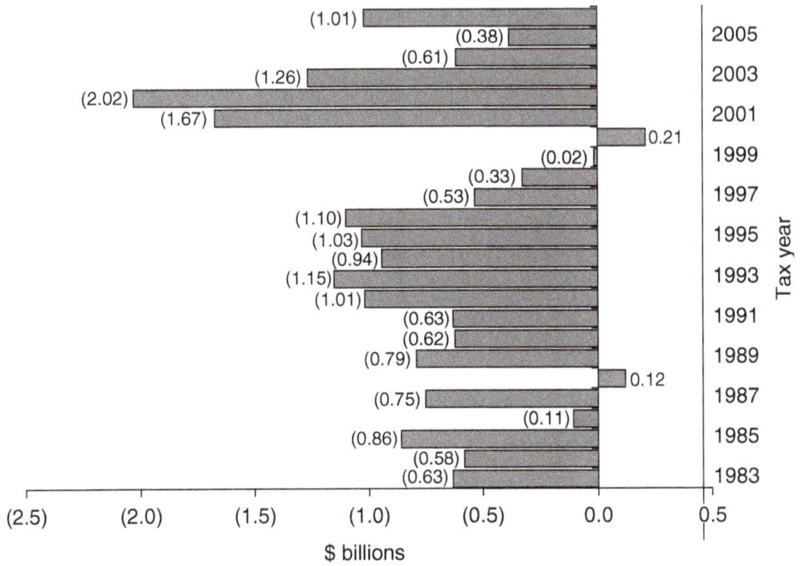

Figure 6.7 Income tax settlement, 1983–2006 (The settlement is comprised of extension payments plus final return payments minus refunds and the state–city offset). (From New York State Division of the Budget.)

reflected the need among high-income taxpayers to cover liability increases that were due to extraordinary growth in nonwage income and that the tax authority had not collected through prepayments.

Cash models should incorporate the liability forecast as a constraint on current and future fiscal year cash-collection projections. However, it is normal for cash payments to exceed liability by a relatively small amount for any given tax year. This can occur because of tax prepayments that are never followed up with a final return. This discrepancy is commonly referred to as the "bridge value" because it bridges cash and liability for a given tax year. In New York, the bridge value averaged 2.3 percent of liability over the period from 1982 to 2005, although it has fallen over time. Consequently, the cash forecasting procedure uses liability growth as a constraint on cash growth and a fixed bridge value to set total cash collections by fiscal year over the forecast period. Typically, the bridge value is set at a recent average. In years when the last actual bridge value is significantly different from the average bridge value, one can allow the bridge to gradually drift back toward the average value over the course of the forecast period.

The cash model for withholding is the starting point for cash collections. Withholding is directly related to wages, and therefore, in theory, forecasters can model it purely as a function of aggregate wages. We use a simple model that relates withholding to wages, controlling for the impact of tax law changes, and allowing for a seasonal pattern where the average tax rate is higher in the first quarter of the calendar year because of large bonus payments to high-income individuals.

Once withholding is determined, the remaining cash components can be modeled as functions of liability with the constraint that the sum of the cash components cannot exceed the total projected liability plus an amount dictated by the bridge value for any tax year. Model results can be validated by examining the unconstrained results to see if they produce bridge values that are both consistent with historical averages and roughly constant over the forecast period.

Risk Assessment

All of the forecasting models alluded to earlier presume that the historical relationships between the income components and a number of key economic indicators are useful for projecting their future behavior. The models also assume that these relationships are stable and can be estimated using standard econometric methods. Because all models are simplifications of complex relationships, they are subject to model specification error. In addition, there are risks associated with the forecasts for the exogenous economic indicators. Even if a model is well specified and the future values of the exogenous inputs can be predicted with certainty, a statistical forecast remains subject to error. There is always a component that cannot be captured by the model, which is simply ascribed to random variation. And the estimated parameters of the model are themselves random variables and, as such, subject to estimation error.

For a given model specification and a given set of exogenous inputs, one can evaluate the risk to the forecast due to the random variation in the variable one is trying to forecast, as well as the random variation in the model parameters. The tool used most commonly in econometric analysis for evaluating this risk is the Monte Carlo simulation, and a tool often used to present the results of a risk assessment is the fan chart. The chapter on risk assessment in this volume discusses in detail the development of these simulations and how they can be used to assess the risk surrounding a particular forecast.

Conclusions

This chapter summarizes a relatively sophisticated methodology for forecasting PIT collections. This methodology is currently used by the NYS Division of the Budget. Its development was motivated by the large share of total tax collections that the PIT in New York represents. A significant benefit of this methodology has been the capacity to convey forecast results to policy makers and fiscal experts. Income tax collections have been incredibly volatile over the past decade, and projections, including the division's, have often been wide off the mark. However, because of the detailed nature of our modeling approach it has been possible to quickly assess the source of errors and convey to interested parties the assumptions underlying the forecast and why they were wrong. This transparency has moved the discussion more toward an analytical appraisal of economic assumptions and away from an unproductive debate about institutional preferences.

References

Brown, R. L., A. E. Dunbar, and A. T. Pilot. 2006. The feasibility of producing personal income to adjusted gross income (PI-AGI) reconciliations by state. U.S. Bureau of Economic Analysis. http://www.bea.gov/papers/pdf/PI-AGI.pdf (accessed January 12, 2007).

Cilke, J. 1994. *The Treasury individual income tax simulation model.* U.S. Department of the Treasury, Office of Tax Analysis (April).

Congressional Budget Office. 2006. How CBO forecasts income. Background Paper (August), http://www.cbo.gov/ftpdocs/75xx/doc7507/08-25-Income.pdf (accessed May 22, 2007).

Hollenbeck, S., and M. Parisi. 2006. Individual income tax returns, 2004. *SOI Bulletin* (December 13), U.S. Internal Revenue Service. http://www.irs.gov/pub/irs-soi/04indtr.pdf (accessed May 22, 2007).

IRS Statistics of Income Division. 2006. Table 1–2003, S Corporations: Total receipts and deductions, portfolio income, rental income, and total net income. Major Industrial Group. http://www.irs.gov/taxstats/bustaxstats/article/0,,id=96405,00.html (accessed May 22, 2007).

IRS Statistics of Income Division. 2007. Table 1–2004, all partnerships: Total assets, trade or business income and deductions, portfolio income, rental income, and total net income. Selected Industrial Group. http://www.irs.gov/taxstats/bustaxstats/article/0,,id=97127,00.html (accessed May 22, 2007).

Miller, P., and L. Ozanne. 2000. Forecasting capital gains realizations. Congressional Budget Office. Technical Paper Series 2000–2005 (August).

U.S. Bureau of Economic Analysis. 2006. State personal income 2005 methodology. http://www.bea.gov/regional/pdf/spi2005/Complete_Methodology.pdf (accessed Nov 8, 2007).

Chapter 7

Income Tax Forecasting in Minnesota

Thomas F. Stinson, Patrick D. Meagher, and John L. Peloquin

Contents

Introduction

Minnesota is a biennial budget state with general fund revenues projected totaling more than $31 billion in the 2006–2007 biennium. The individual income tax provides about 43 percent of state general fund revenue. For the 2006–2007 biennium, individual income tax receipts are expected totaling more than $13.6 billion. As at the federal level and as in most other states, the income tax was the source of much of the revenue volatility over the past decade. And, as in most income tax states, the income tax estimates are the focus every time Minnesota revenues are forecast.

This chapter discusses methods used to forecast Minnesota's individual income tax. It begins with a description of the institutional background in which the income tax forecast is prepared. It then reviews particular aspects of the forecast where Minnesota practice may differ slightly from those in many other states. The following sections explain the way Minnesota economists project the growth in wages, capital gains, interest, dividends, and individual retirement accounts (IRA) distributions. The chapter concludes with a discussion of methods Minnesota economists use to allocate calendar year tax liability to fiscal year tax receipts including Minnesota's approach to forecasting withholding tax payments.

Background

Economists in the state's Department of Finance prepare Minnesota's revenue forecast twice every year. The department's budget division makes expenditure forecasts at the same time so that each state financial forecast includes projections for both current law revenues and current law spending. In even numbered years, the November forecast is the basis for the governor's biennial budget proposal. The second forecast in each budget cycle is made the following February after the legislature has convened. It updates the revenue and expenditure outlook and provides a starting point for legislative action on the state budget. Forecasts in the following November and February provide further updates on the state's financial outlook, warning when necessary of potential budget shortfalls at the end of the biennium. Minnesota's constitution prohibits borrowing across biennia to support operating expenditures.

The state's finance department prepares and issues the Minnesota financial forecast. It is the only comprehensive forecast of revenues and expenditures available to state policy makers. The state does not use a consensus approach to forecasting nor are there competing forecasts from legislative bodies.* State statutes prohibit the governor from receiving information about the forecast before its official release. The revenue and expenditure forecasts are current law forecasts. They do not reflect any tax or expenditure changes proposed by the governor.

Minnesota's Individual Income Tax

Minnesota uses federal adjusted gross income as the starting point for the computation of state income tax liability to reduce compliance burdens on taxpayers. Because the state's tax base does not perfectly conform to the federal tax base, several additions and subtractions to federal adjusted gross income are necessary to reach the Minnesota taxable income. The major additions are state income taxes claimed as an itemized deduction and municipal bond interest on bonds issued by state and local governments outside Minnesota. Important subtractions include state income tax refunds, interest on U.S. Treasury obligations, a special education expense deduction provided under state law, and military pay for active duty military and state national guardsmen serving outside the state. There is no special exemption or special tax rate for capital gains income.

As is typical in state revenue forecasts, the finance department reports expected fiscal year receipts for the income tax, not accrued tax liability. Because Minnesota operates on a July–June fiscal year, the state's fiscal year and individuals' tax years do not coincide. This means the initial tax year or calendar year forecast must be separated into fiscal years. It also means that, depending on when in the biennial budget cycle the forecast is made, as many as four years of income tax liability must be forecast. In November of even numbered years, for example, liability must be projected for the current year as well as for each of the next three years.† Separate estimates of withholding receipts, estimated tax payments, miscellaneous payments including final payments accompanying returns, and refunds are made for each fiscal year in the forecast horizon.

The House Income Tax Simulation Model

In Minnesota, as in many other states, a large microsimulation is used to compute future income tax liabilities. This model, referred to as the House Income Tax Simulation (HITS) model, calculates state tax liability for each return in a sample of more than 20,000 returns for each tax year in question. The returns used in the

* More information on Minnesota's forecast process is available in Stinson (2002).

† Minnesota's Department of Finance also provides revenue planning estimates for the following biennium. Methods used for those projections are similar to those used for the budget forecast, but only a single, general national economic growth assumption is used rather than the separate, Minnesota-specific growth rates for each type of income.

microsimulation are a stratified sample of Minnesota returns drawn annually from returns due that year.* The sum of the calculated sample filer liabilities appropriately weighted to reflect the number of filers in each of the various strata is the basis for the forecast of state income tax liability for the tax year in question. To avoid selection bias, special efforts are made to include returns from filers requesting extensions and those filing after the deadline for automatic extensions.

Responsibility for updating, maintaining, and calibrating the income tax simulation model is shared among the House Research Office, the revenue department, and the finance department. The annual programming updates necessary to ensure that the model's code reflects the current state and federal tax law are done by the legislative staff. Analysts from the Department of Revenue draw and prepare the sample of state tax returns used in the microsimulation, and finance department economists provide the growth factors needed to age sample data into the future. The HITS model is also used to prepare fiscal notes on prospective tax changes during the legislative session, ensuring that prospective changes in tax law are scored with the same assumptions about economic growth as used in the revenue forecast. Shared use of the model also reinforces the revenue forecast's credibility because growth rates used in the forecast are easily identified and the economic assumptions transparent.

The HITS microsimulation ages every sample return by applying growth factors to each separate source of income and each type of deduction on the return. The growth factors are specific to each type of income or deduction and differ for each year in the forecast horizon. Filer growth is incorporated by multiplying the sample weight attached to each observation by the projected filer growth rate between the base year and the year to be forecast. Although the microsimulation allows separate filer growth percentages for each income class, yet this feature has not been used. Instead, the number of filers in all income classes is assumed to grow at the same rate.

Choosing Parameters for the Income Tax Model

Parameters for the model and forecast growth rates for particular types of income and deductions come from several sources. Some come directly from the baseline national economic outlook provided to the Department of Finance by a large national forecasting service. For example, under Minnesota law, future tax brackets, personal exemptions, and the standard deduction are all indexed to grow at the same rate as consumer prices. The national baseline forecast of the consumer price index (CPI) is

* The lag between the end of the tax year and the availability of returns and between the availability of returns and their incorporation into the sample leaves the microsimulation typically working with data from three years earlier. For example, in February 2007, returns from tax year 2006 had yet to be filed. Preliminary data was available from sample returns from tax year 2005, but the microsimulation model used tax year 2004 returns.

used to set those tax system parameters for years for which those parameters have not yet been officially established.

Other growth rates are obtained from a model of the Minnesota economy estimated and maintained by finance department economists. The Minnesota economic model is a satellite model that translates projections for national growth into Minnesota-specific growth rates by sector. This model places special emphasis on estimates of total wage growth. Employment estimates for 38 different sectors and estimates of wage growth for 14 large aggregate sectors are prepared. The model is reestimated before each November's forecast to incorporate the most recent national and state economic data.

Determining the appropriate growth rate for particular categories of income requires special attention. In some instances, there are substantial differences between the definition of that income type as used in the national income and product accounts (NIPA) reports and the Minnesota model, and in the definition used for tax purposes. Where these definitional differences produce growth patterns that diverge substantially, finance department economists prepare separate models for projecting that type of income. Had special models for these variables not been developed, the growth rate for the variable as defined for the NIPA could be used. But, the use of the NIPA forecast could introduce potentially significant errors. And, for some types of taxable income, such as capital gains, no comparable NIPA-based measure exists.

This problem confronts all income tax forecasters. It can be illustrated using national data prepared by the U.S. Department of Commerce. Differences between NIPA estimates of income from particular sources and the income actually reported on the tax form for some key types of income are shown in Table 7.1. NIPA wages, for example, are $463 billion (9 percent) more than wages as reported on the income tax return. For dividends, the gap is substantially smaller in absolute terms, but the

Table 7.1 Comparison of Personal Income with Adjusted Gross Income by Type of Income (2003)

Item	*Personal Income (Billion $)*	*Adjusted Gross Income (Billion $)*	*Difference (Billion $)*
Personal income	9164	6207	2962
Wages and salaries	5113	4650	463
Dividends	423	115	308
Interest	914	127	787
Nonfarm proprietors income	782	340	442
Capital gains	0	296	296

Source: Bureau of Economic Analysis. 2006. *Survey of Current Business.* U.S. Department of Commerce, 06 (November), 34; Internal Revenue Service. 2003. *Statistics of Income, 2003,* Sec.1: 2.

percentage difference much larger. Dividends included in federal adjusted gross income are only 27 percent of the estimate for the national income accounts. There is also a substantial gap between the national income accounts estimate of interest income and that reported on the tax form.

Part of the gap between NIPA income and tax form income is due to differences in definitions. For example, dividends on the tax form include payments from money market funds—an item that would be considered as interest in the NIPA. Another source of differences is that a significant proportion of portfolio income goes to tax deferred accounts. Finally, because there are differences in the composition of portfolios in taxable and tax deferred accounts, and between household and business holdings, changes in the yield curve will not have the same effects on growth rates for taxable interest and dividends as on their counterparts in the NIPA.

Forecasting the Wage Growth Rate

The growth rate for wages and the filer growth rate are the two most important variables driving the microsimulation model. Wages accounted for just less than 75 percent of federal adjusted gross income for Minnesota residents in 2004, according to the state's income tax sample. Although other sources of individual income are more volatile than wage and salary income, the relative size of this component of the income tax base dictates that a major portion of forecasting resources be devoted to refining estimates of its growth.

The filer growth rate affects all sources of income and deductions. Filer growth is forecast based on the historical relationship between the number of filers and payroll employment. A simple regression equation is used to convert the forecast for Minnesota payroll employment produced by the Minnesota economic model into an expected filer growth rate. The Minnesota economic model forecasts employment using an export-base approach. Further information on the employment forecast is suppressed here in favor of more extensive discussion of our more innovative approach to forecasting compensation.

Wages

The Minnesota economic model uses data reported in the Quarterly Census of Employment and Wages (QCEW) to forecast wages.* The QCEW includes all direct

* The QCEW survey is conducted by the states under contract to the Bureau of Labor Statistics (BLS). QCEW data is based on mandatory employer reports to the unemployment insurance (UI) system. The data used in the finance department's analysis are at the individual establishment level of detail, a level of detail that is not published by BLS or the states. Employers combine all reportable income into a single total on their UI report. For details, see Bureau of Labor Statistics (2003).

payments to workers made during a quarter including hourly wages, salaries, bonuses, commissions, the cash value of meals and lodging provided by employers, severance pay, distributions from nonqualified deferred compensation plans, tips, and exercised stock options. But, the QCEW does not report the detail, only a single total.

Since the mid-1990s, performance-based compensation, here defined to include both bonuses and stock options, has increased as a proportion of total compensation. This change in the form of compensation made wage growth more volatile in the past decade. In 2001, following a significant decline in the stock market, finance department economists were concerned that the Minnesota model would overestimate the rate of wage growth in Minnesota because the portion of QCEW wages coming from the exercise of stock options was likely to fall dramatically.

A short research project was undertaken to determine the potential magnitude of the drop in wages that a decline in performance-based compensation would create. The project began by computing the average wage per job for all Minnesota firms with five or more employees. No attempt was made to differentiate between full- and part-time employees. These wage estimates, computed using firm-specific UI data, were then screened to identify firms where the average wage per job in a quarter exceeded $40/hour. Firms meeting that test were then subjected to a second screening to identify those where the average wage rate in the quarter of concern was $10 more per hour than the average wage rate in the three prior quarters. This screening separated firms that had a history of very high average wages, such as some clinics and consulting groups, from firms having a large difference in average compensation over the year.

The firms identified using the two simple screenings were assumed to be those making substantial use of options and bonuses as part of their compensation packages. The difference between wages paid in the quarter in which wages averaged more than $40/hour and the average wage in the prior three quarters was said to be the amount of performance-based compensation paid by the firm. Using the screenings described earlier, we found that 5.4 percent of all QCEW wages for Minnesota for the fourth quarter of 2000, and 6.8 percent of Minnesota QCEW wages in the first quarter of 2001 met our criteria for performance-based compensation.

Given the uncertainty about the level of bonuses in a weakened economy, and given the likelihood that the decline in the stock market would cause income from the exercise of options to be less than in prior years, revising our model to distinguish between performance-based compensation and normal wages appeared appropriate. Although confidence intervals for forecasts of the performance-based portion of wages are likely to be very wide, knowing the magnitude of the amount of bonus and option income assumed in the forecast of taxable wages would allow forecasters to better manage risk.

More formally, a decision was made to split QCEW wages into two parts at the individual establishment level of detail, separating stock options and other performance-based compensation such as large end-of-year bonuses from normal compensation. We now reserve the term "wage" for the normal compensation portion of QCEW wages agreed on in a single representative worker–employer match.

Separating wages and stock options is justified because different institutional arrangements determine the timing of payments, and the payments serve different objectives. A wage is received shortly after work is performed, whereas a stock option generates income only when exercised, and only after the firm's market value has increased sufficiently to put the option "in the money." Wages are determined by the market value of goods and services produced, whereas stock options are an incentive to increase the value of the firm. Relatively few workers receive stock options and, for those who do, normally a wage already exists when an option is granted.

In the quarterly Minnesota economic model, jobs and other variables are linked to QCEW wages for seven industries and to our subset of wages without performance-based compensation for seven additional nonfarm industries.[*,†,‡] Wages per job, stock options per job, and QCEW wages per job vary significantly across industries; therefore, the 14-industry detail allows the model to account for differences in withholding caused by changes in the composition and timing of output. In seven industries, where a filtering process indicates the presence of significant stock options, we separate the performance-based component from base wages.[§] A more formal discussion of the modeling and data development methodology used for these industries is provided in the following section, beginning with a brief review of some national models. Our review of these models is not comprehensive. It only points out elements we adapt to forecasting Minnesota wages.

---

* The jobs data comes from the Current Employment Survey (CES) conducted jointly by BLS and each state under contract. States are primarily responsible for editing and revising the data.

† In some states, a near one-to-one relationship appears to exist between state-specific CES employment growth and state-specific QCEW wages growth. This could greatly simplify forecasting QCEW wages. However, Minnesota is not one of those states (Bureau of Economic Analysis 2006).

‡ The 14 industries cover the range of activity defined by the North American Industry Classification System (NAICS) (see Office of Management and Budget [1997]). In detailed QCEW data before 2001, individual establishments are classified only according to the Standard Industrial Code (SIC) (see Office of Management and Budget [1987]). To construct quarterly time series going back to 1990, we assigned NAICS codes to Minnesota establishments based on the "dual-coded" year 2001.

§ What we consider to be significant stock options were found in the following Minnesota NAICS sectors: construction, financial activities, durables manufacturing, professional and business services, healthcare and social assistance, retail trade, and wholesale trade. Stock options are a very volatile share of QCEW wages in these industries, ranging from about 3 to 17 percent. Stock options are also a volatile share of total QCEW wages, ranging from near zero to a little more than 5 percent. There was an upward trend in the 1990s that now appears to have leveled off.

A Brief Review of Compensation in National Models

National macroeconomic models normally link aggregative output, compensation, inflation, employment, unemployment, and productivity.* In general, the models are based on the observation that rising output, employment, and productivity lead to rising compensation and lower unemployment. Traditionally, this relationship is summarized by the implied inverse relationship between changes in inflation and the unemployment rate, known as the accelerationist Phillips curve.

The Phillips model describes business cycle fluctuations regardless of region or industry. Because industry mix is often a critical factor in determining state economic conditions, the Phillips model is not suitable for state economic forecasting. However, it does offer insights useful for specifying a model for a state where impacts from national business cycles are significant.

A brief review of two national models illustrates the perspectives of practical and research economists. Both take the view that worker compensation does not adjust to allow labor markets to clear like textbook commodity markets. An accelerationist Phillips curve like Brinner's (1999) is used in large-scale commercial econometric models of the U.S. economy. It assumes that aggregate compensation consists of a nominal component driven by inflation expectations and a real component driven primarily by output and productivity. This is enough to specify an aggregate model assuming the existence of an underlying search and matching process in which a typical employer and a typical worker find one another and settle on a wage.

Hall (2005) postulates a plausible search and matching process. His is an academic effort to modify the standard microeconomic labor market model criticized by Shimer (2005) to fully account for observed fluctuations in aggregate Phillips curve variables. He assumes a typical employer has a maximum acceptable real wage, whereas a typical worker has a minimum acceptable wage, or reservation wage, below which he or she chooses to be unemployed. Consequently, in a match, the negotiated or equilibrium wage lies somewhere in between, in a region called the bargaining set, which represents the surplus created by a successful match.

Presumably, the employer and worker match reflects an agreed-on real wage based primarily on expectations concerning inflation, output, and productivity. These views do not change rapidly; therefore, in negotiations the worker has the only option of working or not, whereas the employer's options are to hire or eliminate the job (Shimer 2005). This leaves fluctuations in employment and unemployment as the labor market's principal adjustment mechanism. In comparison, the wage is much less volatile; hence this model is called a "sticky wage" model. In the presence of sticky wages, a small decline in productivity or a small increase in input prices sharply reduces the employer's surplus gained from the match, making new

* In this context, compensation is not necessarily wages as defined here. For example, Brinner (1999) uses the wage component of the BLS Employment Cost Index, a data series that is not available at the state level.

hires less likely and making layoffs more likely. Measures of labor market tightness confirm this hypothesis.

The national models are constructed to fit chosen datasets, a choice based largely on empirical observation. This approach is not without hazard. Phillips' original model was extensively revised years ago when it became obvious that earlier versions were inadequate.* And, Hall (2005) points out it is unclear why employers and workers would jointly prefer a behavior consistent with a sticky wage to other alternatives.

The Minnesota Model

There is no industry-specific detail for compensation in the national model used by the state's national forecasting service. But, clearly labor market conditions vary among states in part because of industry mix. Consequently, the Minnesota model calculates wages for separate industries. The basic identity is of the form

$$\text{Wages}_{i,t} = \text{real wages per job}_{i,t} * \text{deflator}_{i,t} * \text{jobs}_{i,t} \qquad (7.1)$$

where

i = industry
t = the current quarter†

which decomposes wages into a real component, a nominal component, and a jobs component.

Like national models, Minnesota's models are specified to fit chosen data. In it, real wages per job in each Minnesota industry are represented as a characteristic nonlinear trend with short-term deviations.‡ Trend is assumed to represent what is expected and agreed on at the time job matching takes place. But trend does not fully determine the magnitude and timing of real wages because of business cycles, a rich source of labor market shocks.§ Deviations represent unexpected impacts of

* For a brief history, see Romer (2001, pp. 247–252).

† Except for the CPI for metropolitan areas, state-specific deflators are generally unavailable; therefore, national data is used. In the Minnesota model, the services-producing sectors either use the national CPI or the personal consumption deflator from the NIPA. The manufacturing sector uses the producer price index (PPI). Ideally, it seems that the choice of an industry deflator should depend on whether decisions in a typical employer–worker match are made on the basis of the cost of living or on the price of goods or services being produced, or both.

‡ Trend is represented by output from a Hodrick–Prescott filter with a smoothing parameter of 1600 for quarterly data. This parameter is recommended in the EViews software manual. Normally, analysts make their smoothing parameter choice in an *ad hoc* manner. However, a formal estimation technique is offered by Schlicht (2005).

§ Calendar idiosyncrasies and the stochastic nature of the matching process described by Hall (2005) are additional sources of deviations from the trend not currently accounted for in the model. In the regressions, these become part of the residuals. Generally, the Durbin–Watson statistics suggest that residuals are not serially correlated.

shocks. Minnesota's experience is that the business cycle produces deviations from the trend in jobs, inflation, and productivity. These deviations, along with fluctuations in labor market tightness, have a significant impact on the level and timing of deviations from trend in real wages per job.

We assume what happens to real wages per job is determined by the real wage in a typical worker–employer match once the labor market experiences a shock. The impact of a shock in jobs seems potentially ambiguous. If the source is excess demand for labor, the real wage in a typical job should rise. However, during the past two decades, monetary policy has significantly reduced the number and duration of periods of excess demand; therefore, observed shocks are likely to be from other sources.* For example, in the slack labor market accompanying a recession or significant slowdown in real gross domestic product (GDP) growth, a typical unemployed worker might lower his or her reservation wage. As the expansion resumes, jobs rise above trend whereas real wages per job dip below trend as employers hire the now cheaper help. Also, in the early stages of an expansion, there may be new labor force participants going to work at a below-average wage. Faster-than-trend increases in jobs thus appear to be associated with below trend growth in real wages per job.

What to expect from other variables seems more obvious. An unexpected increase in inflation will leave the real wage lower than anticipated. However, an unexpected productivity gain should lead to a higher-than-expected real wage because workers normally capture the value of their marginal product. Given the other variables, increased labor market tightness should raise the real wage because it pressurizes employers to raise the wage offer. It encourages workers to raise their reservation wage and it should also increase workers' ability to capture productivity gains.

These considerations suggest an industry wage equation of the form specified in Equation 7.2, where ln indicates the natural logarithm. The *i* indicating the industry and the error term are suppressed.

$$\begin{aligned}
&\ln[\text{real wages per job}_t - \text{trend real wages per job}_{t-1}] \\
&\quad = \mathrm{a} + \mathrm{b} * \ln[\text{jobs}_t - \text{trend jobs}_{t-1}] \\
&\qquad + \mathrm{c} * \ln[\text{inflation}_t \text{ rate} - \text{trend inflation}_{t-1}] \\
&\qquad + \mathrm{d} * \ln[\text{productivity}_t - \text{trend productivity}_{t-1}] \\
&\qquad + \mathrm{e} * \ln[\text{ratio of employment to resident population}_t]^{\dagger} \qquad (7.2)
\end{aligned}$$

* Monetary policy changes are difficult to measure. However, there is some evidence that a new regime began during the Greenspan era at the Federal Reserve (Sims and Zha 2006).

† This term is a proxy for labor market tightness. It may not be the ideal choice. For a discussion, see Shimer (2005). Employment is from the CES. Population is the Bureau of the Census (Census) midyear estimate for states. Because the Census estimates are at annual frequency, a quarterly series is created by profiling from the Current Population Survey (CPS) of Minnesota population age 16 and above (Current Population Survey 2001). The CPS population series is not published, but it is available from states or BLS regional offices as an extract from the State Time Series Analysis and Review System (STARS) used to calculate state unemployment rates. In the states, STARS is operated by the Local Area Unemployment Statistics (LAUS) analyst.

In the regressions, either $a < 0$ or $a > 0$ is possible reflecting omitted variables unique to the individual industries. Evidently, $b < 0$, $c < 0$ and $d > 0$, $e > 0$. Ordinary least squares estimates satisfy these conditions in the Minnesota model.* On the right-hand side, employment and population are Minnesota-specific. The other variables are national indicators. Although national indicators may be the information firms use, the national data also serves as a proxy for unavailable or unreliable state data. State data problems and ways around them are not discussed here.

The specification used in Equation 7.2 seems appropriate when only wages are present in the data. A wage is the outcome of a match between an employer and a worker that normally reflects the value of the worker's product in the marketplace. Both parties, given expectations concerning employment, inflation, productivity, and current labor market tightness, know that outcome. A stock option, however, is an incentive to increase the financial market value of the firm. Normally, a job match and a wage already exist when a stock option is granted. Consequently, the net value of any exercised stock options must be extracted from the QCEW data before estimating the parameters of Equation 7.2.

Stock options are not directly observable in QCEW data. Employers must report the net proceeds of stock options exercised as part of their quarterly UI report, but they may simply combine the proceeds with other employee compensation on the report. We estimate stock options by filtering quarterly QCEW data. Filtering assumes that when options are exercised a shock or innovation to QCEW hourly wages is produced that is detectable at the establishment level of detail. However, a large bonus may also cause an innovation captured by the filtering. We assume a large bonus is viewed as a substitute for a stock option, whereas a small one is considered part of the wage. The distinction is built into filtering parameters qwages, B, and P; where $\text{qwages}_{i,t,x}$ is QCEW wages in industry i, quarter t, and establishment x in dollars per hour, assuming all workers work 2000 hours per year; B a threshold set to eliminate spurious increases in low wages; and P a threshold set to recognize that smaller innovations in wages may reflect bonuses, commissions, or spurious changes in labor market conditions, $0 < P_i < 1$.†

Then, again suppressing the industry i and firm x indicators, if

$$\frac{\text{qwages}_t - [\text{qwages}_{t-1} + \text{qwages}_{t+1}]}{2} > P * \text{qwages}_t \tag{7.3}$$

and

$$\frac{\text{qwages}_t - [\text{qwages}_{t-1} - \text{qwages}_{t+1}]}{2} > B \tag{7.4}$$

* Model size and time constraints preclude the use of other, possibly more appropriate estimation techniques.

† For example, a \$1 wage that rises to \$2 is an irrelevant 100 percent increase. We use $B = \$2$ as of 2001Q1 and adjust previous and subsequent quarters for inflation using the personal consumption deflator from Bureau of Economic Analysis (BEA).

then

$$\text{Stock options}_t = \frac{\text{qwages}_t - [\text{qwages}_{t-1} + \text{qwages}_{t+1}]}{2} \tag{7.5}$$

and

$$\text{Wages}_t = \frac{[\text{qwages}_{t-1} + \text{qwages}_{t+1}]}{2} \tag{7.6}$$

This decision rule splits QCEW wages into two parts, provided the criteria are met. The rule works by comparing hourly wages in three successive quarters. Equations 7.3 and 7.4 measure innovations in hourly wages in quarter t by comparison with the immediately adjacent quarters subject to conditions set by parameters B and P. Provided the inequalities in Equations 7.3 and 7.4 are satisfied, Equations 7.5 and 7.6 determine stock options and wages in quarter t.*

We have no priors about what to expect from Equation 7.5; therefore, a trial-and-error process involving Equations 7.6 and 7.2 is used to arrive at plausible estimates. First, the filter is run for all firms in all industries using alternatives $P = 0.10$, 0.15, and 0.20. Then, using ordinary least squares, the residual wages generated by Equation 7.6 are fit to Equation 7.2. Experience has shown that these alternatives for P generate a preferred choice for the parameters of Equation 7.2 for each NAICS industry, implying a reasonable estimate of stock options.† In a typical model fitting, each value of P is represented at least once in the equations of the form of Equation 7.2. Summing the resulting stock options estimates across industries gives a total, which, as a share of Minnesota BEA wages, seems generally consistent with results for the U.S. economy using SEC data reported by Jaquette et al. (2003).‡ Our estimates of the percentage of QCEW wages accounted for by performance-based compensation for 1988 through 2005 are shown in Figure 7.1.

---

* For example, if qwages$(t - 1) = 7.5$, qwages$(t) = 11.1$, qwages$(t + 1) = 10.5$, $B = 2$, and $P = 0.10$, then by Equation 7.3, $11.1 - [7.5 + 10.5]/2 > 0.10 * 11.1$ or $2.1 > 1.1$ and by Equation 7.4, $11.1 - [7.5 + 10.5]/2 > 2$ or $2.1 > 2$. Because conditions 7.3 and 7.4 are met, it is assumed that stock options are present. Therefore, using Equation 7.5, stock options$(t) = 11.1 - [7.5 + 10.5]/2 = 2.1$ and using Equation 7.6, wages$(t) = [7.5 + 10.5]/2 = 9.0$. But, if $P = 0.20$, then $2.1 < 0.20 * 11.1$; therefore, condition 7.3 is not satisfied, leading to the conclusion that qwages$(t) = 11.1$. Similarly, if $B = 3$, then $2.1 < 3$; therefore, condition 7.4 is not met, leading to the conclusion that qwages$(t) = 11.1$.

† We use a judgmental process because we are unaware of any formal guidelines. One wants the separation of wages and stock options to be as complete as possible. Therefore, we compare alternative versions of Equation 7.2 fitted with wages. The goal is to extract as much stock options as possible without destroying the significance of the estimated parameters of Equation 7.2.

‡ On its Web site, BEA posts quarterly estimates of state wage and salary disbursements by industry (bea.gov/bea/regional/sqpi/action.cfm). These estimates use the QCEW data as input. BEA enhances the QCEW data by adding, among other things, attributions for income earned by workers not eligible for UI. For details, see Bureau of Economic Analysis (2004). Industry detail on an NAICS basis is only available for first quarter 2001 onward.

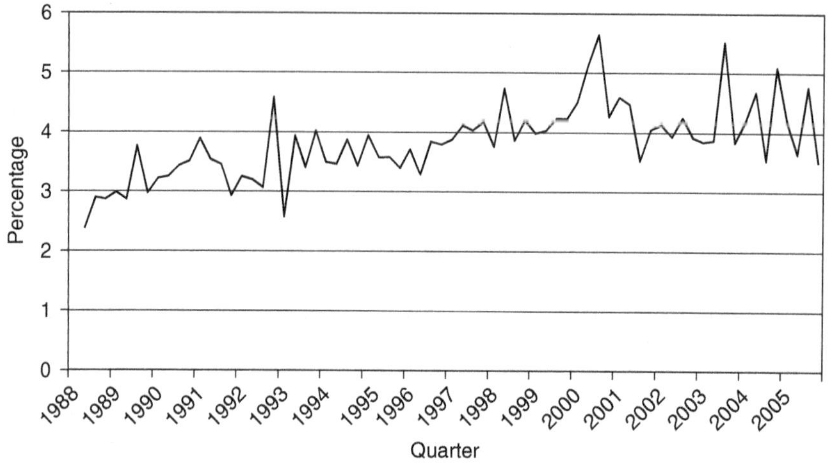

Figure 7.1 Performance-based compensation as a percentage of Minnesota total wages, quarterly, 1988–2005. (Authors' estimates.)

Once P has been decided on for a specific industry, the corresponding stock options estimates generated by Equation 7.5 are regressed on the S&P 500 index or some other stock market indicator. These regressions fit reasonably well, a further indication of the information content of the option estimates. Finally, using QCEW wages, equations of the form in Equation 7.2 are estimated for some of the remaining industries where filtering does not indicate that significant stock options are present.

Model Evaluation

As part of model evaluation, alternative versions are simulated over a history that includes the 1990–1991 and 2001 recessions. Ideally, model-generated values should not consistently under- or overestimate actual data. However, because the model has recursive and simultaneous blocks, bad equations can feed other equations bad information, making the source of bias difficult to locate. Once any reestimations are made, the model version judged to give the most satisfactory fit over the course of the business cycle is chosen as the final product.

Although simulation experiments assist in model selection and help establish validity, they do not necessarily lead to a good forecast. It is possible for bad model parameter estimates to slip through the simulation test. Also relationships among economic variables can change from those prevailing during the period to which the model is fitted.

Forecasting

Faced with such prospects, forecasters may make judgmental adjustments for likely future events. A prudent forecaster also has some means of detecting and correcting for the effects of biased parameter estimates. For example, in each Minnesota industry, and in the aggregate, real wages per job has a characteristic nonlinear trend that appears to be independent of the business cycle. This provides a check, although there may be good reasons why a particular forecast is not consistent with trend.

Another check is to compare growth rates in Minnesota's QCEW wages forecast with projected national BEA wages. This has proven to be a valuable check, provided the national forecast is credible. Implausible Minnesota results are judgmentally adjusted at the industry level of detail.

Because Minnesota's economy is assumed to be a satellite of its U.S. counterpart, a final consideration is the choice of a forecast for the national business cycle. Forecasts are available from several private sector firms. These forecasts vary greatly in detail and methodology, ranging from simple projections of real GDP to models with detailed scenarios reporting projections for dozens of categories of consumer spending, business investment, government outlays, and imports and exports, all linked to production and employment in dozens of industries. The Minnesota model is driven by a large private sector macroeconomic model with enough detail to distinguish between industries present in the state and those that are not.

Forecasting Other Sources of Income

Although wages are the largest and most important source of taxable income in Minnesota, forecasts for other sources of income must also be prepared for use in the microsimulation model. In some instances, growth rates for nonwage incomes and deductions can be taken directly from the national economic forecast. In others, average historical growth rates can be used. For some key income types, however, Minnesota forecasters use special models to provide estimates of future growth rates. These models are discussed in more detail in the following sections.

Capital Gains Income

Income from the realization of capital gains accounted for 5.1 percent of federal adjusted gross income for Minnesota filers in tax year 2004. Nationally, the taxable net gain from the sale of assets held longer than one year has been extremely volatile in the past decade, increasing by more than 40 percent in 1996 and 1997, and by 54 percent in 2004. Unlike most other major sources of taxable income, capital gains can also decline by significant amounts from year to year. In Minnesota, as in most other states, the decline in net capital gains realizations was a major

Table 7.2 Change in U.S. Net Long-Term Capital Gains Realizations (1990–2004)

Year	Amount	Percent Change
1990	124	−20
1991	112	−10
1992	127	14
1993	152	20
1994	153	0
1995	180	18
1996	261	45
1997	365	40
1998	455	25
1999	553	21
2000	644	16
2001	349	−46
2002	269	−23
2003	323	20
2004	499	54
2005	643	29

Source: Congressional Budget Office. 2007. *Budget and Economic Outlook, Fiscal Years 2008–2017*, Government Printing Office, Washington.

contributor to budget shortfalls in 2002 and 2003 (Stinson 2006). Nationally, net capital gains realizations fell 46 percent in tax year 2001 and by more than 23 percent in 2002. They also contributed to budget shortfalls in the early 1990s, dropping by 20 percent in 1990 and an additional 10 percent in 1991 (see Table 7.2).

Capital gains are largely concentrated among those with the highest incomes. In 2004, 74 percent of net gains in Minnesota came from filers with adjusted gross incomes in excess of $200,000. The state does not have a special tax rate for capital gains or a capital gains exclusion. Because capital gains are taxed at ordinary income rates, changes in net capital gains realizations have considerable leverage on the individual income tax forecast.

Revenue forecasters know they have much to be humble about in their forecasts of capital gains income. We know it is unrealistic to expect projections of the growth rate for capital gains income to match closely with what will be actually observed later. The largest portion of capital gains comes from the sale of financial assets and because no one knows how stock and bond markets will perform in any given year, all capital gains forecasts come from a very shaky foundation.

Our collective forecasting records show substantial differences between projections and actual receipts. Typically, capital gains are underforecast in good times and overestimated when times turn tough. However, using a fixed growth rate is not an attractive option. Because the range of possible growth rates for capital gains is large, and the proportion of taxable income accounted for by capital gains significant, use of a fixed growth rate could easily produce larger differences between estimated and actual receipts than would come from a forecast. Revenue losses associated with use of a fixed growth rate would be particularly large when the economy weakens and revenue growth rates decline, further compounding state budget problems.

There are a number of potential approaches to estimating capital gains realizations. The Congressional Budget Office (CBO) begins by using equations based on historical data to project realizations for the current year. Because their forecast is made near year end, it is possible to use data on that year's likely changes in the stock market, the stage of the business cycle, real output, inflation, and housing starts. The housing start variable is used as a proxy for growth in real estate values. Sales of commercial real estate make up a significant portion of capital gains realizations. Although most residential sales are exempt from capital gains taxes under current federal tax law, recent home price increases are creating situations in some housing markets where sales by long-time residents can yield a gain sufficiently large to be subject to tax.

For years beyond the current year, CBO assumes that realizations will gradually revert to their historical average relative to the size of the economy, after adjustment for differences in the current tax rate on capital gains from its historical average.*

In Minnesota a slightly different approach is followed. Minnesota's model assumes that there is an equilibrium or "normal" ratio of realizations to the stock of unrealized gains held by households in taxable accounts. This ratio is not fixed; it depends on the short-term outlook for the economy, prospective stock market performance, and prospective inflation. It is also influenced by the federal tax rate on capital gains and by other environmental variables as is shown in Equation 7.7.

$$R^{\mathrm{d}} = R(\mathrm{GDP}, S, P, T, Z) \tag{7.7}$$

where

GDP = expected real GDP growth rate
S = expected growth rate for the stock market
P = measure of expected inflation
T = federal capital gains tax rate
Z = matrix of other environmental variables
R^{d} = desired ratio of realizations to the underlying stock of capital gains

The actual ratio of realizations to the stock of unrealized gains in time t, R_t, is unlikely to exactly equal the desired realizations ratio because planned realizations depend on forecasts of economic variables that are normally not accurate. Recognizing this,

* More details about the CBO's approach can be found in Ozanne (2005).

we assume that a portion of the difference between the desired ratio of realizations and the actual level observed in the previous year will be made up during the current year.

$$R_t = a(R^d - R_{t-1}) + R^d \tag{7.8}$$

where a is the percentage of the difference between the actual and desired ratio of realizations to unrealized gains that is made up.

This expression is in the form of a standard stock adjustment model, such as is often used to estimate the demand for consumer durable goods. Substituting Equation 7.7 into Equation 7.8 leaves a regression equation of the general form:

$$R_t = (1 + a) * R(\text{GDP}_t, P_t, T_t, Z_t) - a * R_{t-1} \tag{7.9}$$

When estimating this model the tax variable, T, is entered in three separate pieces: the existing federal marginal tax rate on capital gains, any percentage increase from the prior year, and any percentage decrease from the prior year. Separate variables for an increase and decrease are used to allow for possible asymmetry in the response of capital gains realizations to tax increases and decreases. A dummy variable is used for 1986 to adjust for the huge surge in capital gains realizations in that year in anticipation of the higher capital gains tax rate that became effective in 1987.

The model is estimated using data on realizations from 1950 through the most recent year for which actual realizations are available. Because information on the stock of unrealized gains is not available, the gross value of financial assets is used as the denominator of the ratio. This data is taken from the household balance sheet in the flow of funds account data compiled by the Federal Reserve Board. The state's national forecasting service provides forecasts for all variables in their baseline forecast.

The estimated ratio is then applied to an estimate of the future level of the stock of financial assets also taken from the national baseline forecast. The regression model is reestimated every year before the November forecast to incorporate the most recent data on capital gains realizations as well as revisions to the estimates of the stock of household assets in the flow of funds report. Because forecasts for as many as four years into the future are required, projected growth rates for later years are often smoothed.

Because this model is designed to forecast changes in U.S. realizations and is not specifically designed for Minnesota capital gains, the model will underestimate state income tax receipts in years when there are mergers and acquisitions of closely held Minnesota companies. When this occurs, off-model adjustments are made to the estimated level of capital gains for the year in question. These adjustments are based on news accounts of the activity and publicly available financial filings.

Interest Income

Just under half of all Minnesota filers reported taxable interest income in 2004. For Minnesota residents, interest income totaled $2.2 billion—about 1.6 percent of adjusted gross income. Because interest income is a key component of U.S. personal income, the baseline national economic forecast provided by the state's forecasting service includes an estimate of the growth in interest income. This projected growth rate could be used to drive interest income in the microsimulation model, and initially this practice was followed in Minnesota.

But, the composition of household portfolios of taxable fixed income assets is not identical to the total level of debt outstanding. Household taxable portfolios generally are weighted more heavily in the shorter maturities. Also, taxable interest does not include interest on balances held in mutual fund money market accounts. Under current tax law, these distributions are included as dividends on the tax form. Under national income accounting rules, they are interest. These differences in definition and in portfolio composition make the growth rate for taxable interest more volatile than that for the personal interest portion of personal income.

This was most apparent in the early 1990s, when the Fed was adding to the money supply in an effort to stimulate the economy. As Figure 7.2 indicates, similar gaps in interest income occurred in 2002 and 2003 when the Federal Reserve eased monetary policy following the most recent recession. In some years, taxable interest has fallen by more than 20 percent. In 2002, taxable interest was almost 25 percent below its 2001 level. More recently, interest rate hikes have produced very rapid

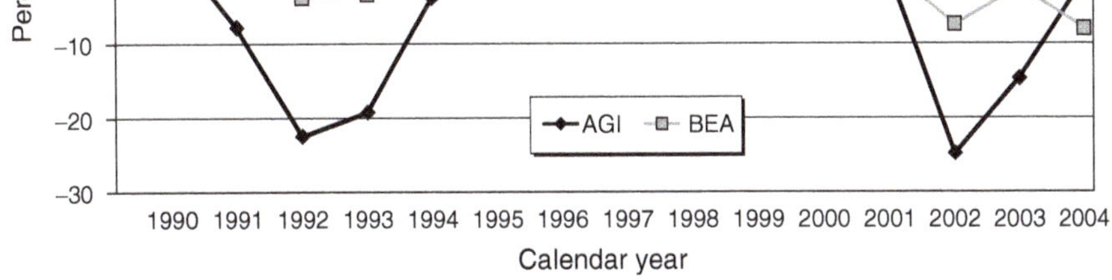

Figure 7.2 Annual growth rates for interest in U.S. personal income and interest reported on individual income tax returns, 1990–2004. (Computed from Bureau of Economic Analysis, 2006 Annual U.S. Personal Income Estimates, U.S. Department of Commerce; Internal Revenue Service, *Statistics of Income*.)

growth in interest income. In 2005, preliminary data shows taxable interest grew by more than 25 percent nationally as a policy of tighter monetary policy began to affect the interest rates typically received on household savings.

Finance Department economists have long recognized that although much of the time the growth rate for interest in personal income may be a satisfactory proxy for growth in taxable interest, under some conditions it could significantly over- or understate growth rates and contribute significantly to forecast error. Originally, when these conditions emerged, *ad hoc* adjustments were made to the growth rate used for the interest income forecast in the microsimulation.

In recent years, a more systematic approach has been followed. The interest income growth rate is estimated using a side model of household interest income. That model's estimates are not Minnesota-specific because the data used to calibrate the model is available only at the national level. But, this model's forecasts for growth in taxable interest income have outperformed the national forecast of interest in personal income as a predictor of taxable interest.

In the interest income model, taxable interest is disaggregated into six categories: Treasury instruments, bank deposits, corporate bonds, commercial paper, mortgages, and agency credits such as Government National Mortgage Act (GNMA) pass-throughs and Farm Credit bonds. The base level of household holdings in each of these asset classes is taken from the flow of funds household balance sheet. Estimates of future levels of household holdings for each category are then produced using growth rates taken from the baseline national economic forecast that are appropriate for that class of asset.

For example, a forecast for interest income from bank deposits for the next year is made by multiplying the level of time deposits reported in the most recent flow of funds report by the projected growth rate for household holdings of money and close substitutes to obtain a projected level of time deposits for the year of interest. This stock of deposits is then multiplied by the projected interest rate on time deposits for that year. In this model a ten-quarter moving average of the federal funds rate is used as a proxy for the expected interest rate on time deposits.* Interest payments to households in each of the separate categories are then summed for each year in the forecast horizon, and the percentage growth rates of this estimate of total taxable interest received is used in the microsimulation model.

Dividend Income

Taxable dividend income for Minnesota residents totaled $2.4 billion in 2004, about $200 million more than taxable interest income. Taxable dividends include dividends paid directly to individual taxpayers by corporations, dividends paid to mutual funds that are passed forward to taxpayers and interest on money market

* Typically, the federal funds rate exceeds the rate on interest-bearing deposits; therefore, an adjustment is made for this gap.

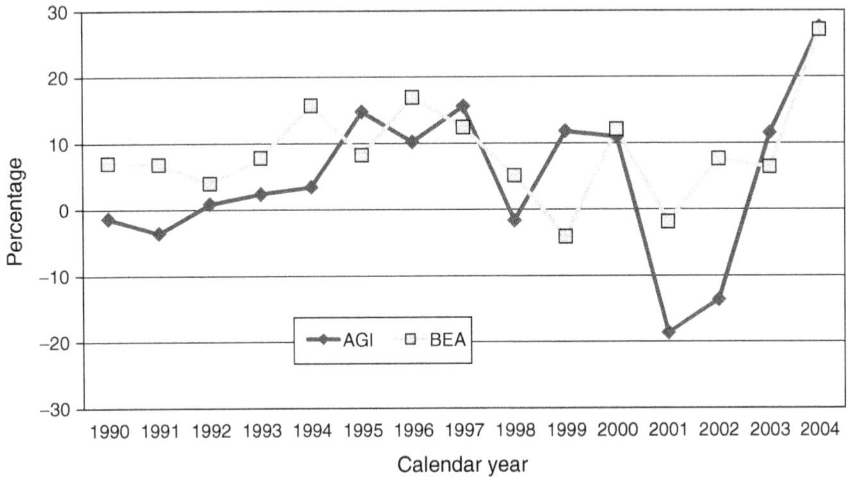

Figure 7.3 Annual growth rates for dividends in U.S. personal income and dividends reported on individual income tax returns, 1990–2004. (Computed from Bureau of Economic Analysis, 2006 Annual U.S. Personal Income Estimates, U.S. Department of Commerce; Internal Revenue Service, Statistics of Income.)

mutual fund accounts. As with interest income, in recent years taxable dividend income has become more volatile than its counterpart in the national income accounts. There have been years when the growth rate for dividends subject to tax (IRS dividends) and that for dividends in the NIPA have diverged substantially. For example, in the early 1990s, IRS dividends declined whereas NIPA dividends increased. In 1999, the opposite occurred, with taxable dividends growing by more than 10 percent and NIPA dividends declining. There also have been substantial absolute differences in the growth rates for the two series. The largest coming in 2002 when the difference in growth rates for the two measures of dividend income exceeded 20 percentage points (see Figure 7.3).

As with interest income, an attempt was made to produce a better forecast for future dividends than would come from using the forecast for dividends in the national income accounts provided to the state by its forecast service. There are two major reasons for the difference in growth rates between taxable dividend income and dividend income in the NIPA. First, NIPA dividends include the earnings of S corporations.* These earnings are not considered to be dividends for tax purposes. IRS dividends also include interest income from mutual funds, which is treated

* The earnings of S corporations are reported as "Schedule E" income on Federal Form 1040, where they are commingled with rents, royalties, partnerships, estates, trusts, and real estate mortgage investment conduits.

as interest in the NIPA. For Minnesota income tax purposes dividend income is forecast using a simple regression where dividend income is a function of the S&P 500 dividend index and a proxy for mutual fund interest.*

Several alternative specifications of this regression are possible. The most satisfactory has been to regress IRS dividends on S&P 500 dividends and a variable representing the amount of money market fund interest received by taxpayers. Because this variable cannot be observed directly, a proxy, the product of household holdings of money market funds taken from the household balance sheet in the flow of funds report and the annual average of the three-month Treasury bill rate, is used. The dependent variable and the independent variables are all expressed in logs. Forecast data for the three key variables from the national baseline forecast are then used to produce the growth rate used for dividends in the microsimulation.

Individual Retirement Accounts Distributions

Distributions from IRAs are a small but rapidly growing portion of the individual income tax base. Nationally, IRA distributions accounted for less than 0.8 percent of federal adjusted gross income in 1994. In 2004, their share of adjusted gross income had grown to 1.5 percent. The importance of this income source is likely to continue to increase because the number of taxpayers with IRAs who have reached age 70.5 (when compulsory distributions are required) is expected to grow substantially over the next decade. IRA distributions are also expected to be much more volatile than most sources of income because federal law requires a minimum distribution of a fraction of the value of the portfolio every year with the fraction increasing with the age of the taxpayer. This means that changes in the portfolio values can have a significant impact on the size of the distribution a recipient is required to take in any year.

Minnesota uses a spreadsheet model to provide a crude measure of potential growth in IRA distributions. A portfolio containing an S&P 500 index mutual fund and fixed income investments in three-month Treasury bills; one-, two-, five-, and ten-year bonds; and mortgage-backed security mutual funds is used. The return on all of these investments is computed every year including unrealized capital gains. IRA assets are assumed to be allocated 50 percent to the S&P 500 mutual fund and 50 percent to fixed income; and the fixed income investments are distributed equally across the various fixed income securities. The portfolio is assumed to be rebalanced at the end of every year. All bonds are purchased at par and sold at prices consistent with the prevailing interest rate one year later. The return on the mortgage-backed

* IRS dividends include interest from all mutual funds. We believe that the largest source of taxable mutual fund interest is from money market mutual funds. The interest from bond funds is more likely to come from nontaxable accounts than that of money market funds. Ideally a proxy that included interest from other bond funds would be used, but there is little information on the maturity structure of bonds in taxable accounts.

security is inferred by looking at the historical relationship between a widely held mortgage-backed security mutual fund and the 30-year mortgage interest rate.

The return on this hypothetical portfolio is then applied to the IRS's minimum IRA distribution tables for a 78 year old, and the percentage difference between the distribution that would have been required at age 77 and the distribution required at age 78 is computed. This percent change is the IRA growth (decline) rate assumed per return. Additional adjustments are made to the aggregate IRA growth factor to take into account the fact that returns with IRAs have been growing faster than returns in general.

Forecasting Withholding Tax Receipts

Cash flow is an important constraint on state budget decisions; therefore, revenue forecasts must project actual receipts for the fiscal year, not simply accrued liability. For taxes paid on a current basis, such as the sales tax, differences between the time the liability is incurred and receipt of the payment are less and typically do not extend across fiscal years; therefore, the liability forecast also can serve as the receipts forecast. For the individual income tax, however, many taxpayers remit substantial settle-up payments when they file their return on April 15, more than three months after the close of the tax year in which the income creating that liability was earned. Others receive significant sums in refunds in the period after the liability was accrued because they were over withheld or made excessive quarterly estimated payments.

To accurately reflect the state's financial position, the forecast of projected final tax year liability must be disaggregated into a forecast of actual receipts by type of receipts for each month of the tax year in which the income was earned and for each month of the following tax year when refunds and settle-up payments are made. Withholding receipts are the single largest source of these receipts, totaling $5.228 billion or about 82 percent of net Minnesota income tax receipts in the 2005 fiscal year.

Although historical receipt patterns could be used to project monthly income tax receipts and allocate the forecast of total liability to the various receipt categories, Minnesota follows a more structured approach. A separate microsimulation has been created specifically to estimate withholding tax receipts. The difference between estimated liability and projected withholding is then allocated to refunds, estimated payments, and final payments based primarily on historical patterns. Use of a separate model to independently calculate withholding receipts improves forecast accuracy on a receipts basis by allowing the ratio of withholding collections to other receipts to vary inversely with the proportion of taxable income coming from nonwithheld sources such as capital gains, portfolio income, and farm and nonfarm proprietors' income.

Finance Department economists created the withholding microsimulation and they update it before each forecast. The model is populated with data from the same sample of Minnesota income tax returns provided by the Department of Revenue for use in the income tax simulation. The withholding model, however, requires only information on wages, state withholding, number of dependents claimed, and filing status. The wage and withholding data are taken from the W-2 forms so that wages and withholding for dual income households and those holding multiple jobs can be more accurately represented.

Wages for each earner in the sample are converted to quarterly values for the sample base year. The conversion is based on annual average wages for the base year and quarterly values of average QCEW wages in that year. These four quarterly data points become the basis for the creation of both a history of wages for each filer and a forecast of future wages. Estimated wages in quarters of prior years are created by decreasing the actual wages earned in the tax year covered by the sample using the average annual growth rate for average QCEW wage and salary income in Minnesota between the sample year and the year in question. Future wages for sample filers are projected based on the average quarterly wage forecast provided by the Minnesota economic model.

The withholding microsimulation contains Minnesota withholding tables for all previous tax years beginning in 1995, as well as projected tables for the years in the forecast horizon. Withholding payment requirements changed in 1995, thus receipt patterns for earlier years are not comparable with current patterns.

Estimated withholding payments are calculated by the microsimulation for each tax filer in the sample for all quarters between the third quarter of 1995 and the present. The microsimulation also provides a forecast for withholding receipts for each quarter of the forecast horizon. As with the HITS model, these filer estimates are multiplied by their sample weights and by projected employment growth between the quarter year forecast and the baseline quarter. For quarters before the most recent quarter for which data is available, the model produces a time series of simulated, or synthetic quarterly estimates of past state withholding receipts. Lottery winnings, withholding on partnership returns, and the withholding from the state's large pension plans are all netted out of the historical withholding receipt data. This time series is used to calibrate forecast estimates.

Future withholding receipts are forecast using the same procedure. Quarterly growth rates in Minnesota employment and wages, taken from the Finance Department's forecast of the Minnesota economy, are used to age filers' incomes into the future. Then, as with the historical data, the sums of the weighted quarterly withholding payments are used to produce a quarterly time series of projected withholding receipts through the end of the forecast horizon. The baseline withholding forecast is obtained by inserting projected withholding receipts into a calibration equation that reflects the historical relationship between past projections and actual withholding receipts. This estimate is then adjusted for withholding on large lottery winnings, withholding on partnership income, and withholding on pensions.

If income tax liability is fixed at the level established by the HITS model and withholding tax receipts are held at the level computed by the withholding model, the difference between them must be equal to the combination of estimated payments, final payments, and refunds. Estimates for each of these revenue sources are produced in a less rigorous manner and ultimately involve judgments made by Finance Department economists. As a starting point, quarterly estimated tax payments are assumed to grow over prior year levels at the rate at which liability grows, and final payments are assumed to remain at the same absolute level as in the prior years. The refund forecast is then used to bring the sum of the various sources of revenues equal to projected tax year liability. These results are then examined to see if they appear reasonable, given past refund and final payment patterns and given what is known about the sources of recent income growth. Often receipts are shifted from one category to another based on forecasters' judgments.

Conclusion

Revenue forecasters know that their forecasts will always be wrong. They recognize their forecasts rely on national economic projections coming from economic models that do not fully incorporate all the complexities of modern state and national economies. These models and forecasts are not always able to anticipate short-term economic fluctuations. In addition, there are often random shocks that are unanticipated in the scenario used in the national projections. Sometimes, these shocks can make a forecast obsolete only a few days after it is completed.

There are, however, ways the accuracy of forecasts can be improved. Focusing on the methods used to estimate the growth rates of the components of taxable income is an approach that offers particular promise. It is important to recognize that growth rates for types of income in the national income accounts will not always be similar to the growth rates for taxable income categories having the same name. Side models that translate projected growth rates provided by national forecasting services into projected growth rates for particular types of taxable income are important, as are models that disaggregate variables into components so that they can be better forecast. The use of these models should reduce average forecast error. It should also reduce the dispersion of these errors because it appears that the divergences between growth rates for incomes as defined in the national income accounts and those for taxable income differ the most when the economy is weakening or growing very strongly.

References

Brinner, R. E. 1999. Is inflation dead? *New England Economic Review* (January–February): 37–49.

Bureau of Economic Analysis. 2004. *State Personal Income Methodology*, www.bea.gov/bea/regional/docs/spi2004/ (accessed May 21, 2007).

Bureau of Economic Analysis. 2006. *Survey of Current Business.* U.S. Department of Commerce 86(10): 117.

Bureau of Labor Statistics. 2003. *BLS Handbook of Methods.* U.S. Department of Labor, www.bls.gov/opub/hom/home.htm (accessed May 21, 2007).

Current Population Survey. 2001. *A Joint Project of the Bureau of Labor Statistics and the Bureau of the Census,* www.census.gov/cps/ (accessed May 21, 2007).

Hall, R. E. 2005. Employment fluctuations with equilibrium wage stickiness. *American Economic Review* 95(1): 50–65.

Jaquette, S., M. Knittel, and K. Russo. 2003. Recent trends in stock options. OTA Working Paper 89, United States Treasury.

Office of Management and Budget. 1987. *Standard Industrial Classification Manual.* Washington: GPO.

Office of Management and Budget. 1997. *North American Industry Classification System.* Washington: GPO.

Ozanne, L. 2005. Testing alternative methods for forecasting capital gains. Working Paper 2005-03, 81, Congressional Budget Office.

Romer, D. 2001. *Advanced Macroeconomics,* 2nd ed. Boston, MA: McGraw-Hill/Irwin.

Schlicht, E. 2005. Estimating the smoothing parameter in the so-called Hodrick–Prescott filter. *Journal of the Japan Statistical Society* 35(1): 99–119.

Shimer, R. 2005. The cyclical behavior of equilibrium unemployment and vacancies. *American Economic Review* 95(1): 25–49.

Sims, C. A. and T. Zha. 2006. Were there regime switches in U.S. monetary policy? *American Economic Review* 96(1): 54–81.

Stinson, T. F. 2002. State revenue forecasting: an institutional framework. *Government Finance Review* (June)18: 12–15.

Stinson, T. F. 2006. Sources of error in state revenue forecasts. *Public Budgeting, Accounting, & Financial Management* 18(1): 100–125.

Chapter 8

Methods and Issues in Forecasting Casino Tax Revenue

Jim Landers

Contents

Introduction

Since 2002, estimating the determinants of adjusted gross wagering revenue (AGR) generated by Indiana's riverboat casinos and forecasting AGR has become an annual task for state revenue forecasters. AGR is the amount of wagering dollars retained by casinos after pay out of winnings to gamblers and forms the base for Indiana's wagering tax. Beginning in FY 2003, a substantial share of wagering tax revenue has annually been directed to property tax relief. In FY 2003, the tax generated $294.7 million for property tax relief forming about 17.9 percent of total state funding for property tax relief. In FY 2006, $459 million of wagering tax revenue was directed to property tax relief. The FY 2006 revenue represented about 23.3 percent of the total state funding for property tax relief (Indiana Legislative Services Agency 2003, 2006).

This chapter examines modeling issues relating to forecasting casino AGR for casino tax projections. It reviews pertinent empirical literature informing the forecast model specifications and examines adjustments of the forecast time series to account for casino start-up effects and seasonal variation. The chapter also compares and contrasts a base linear forecast model with the curvilinear specification currently utilized for the state revenue forecast. The model comparisons are performed by examining summary measures of model fit and prediction error and *ex ante* error analysis. Ultimately, the chapter presents a linear model with a truncated data series that performs better than the current forecast model. The remainder of this chapter (1) reports on casino gaming activity nationally and in Indiana; (2) describes the revenue forecasting process in Indiana focusing on how it influences forecast model specification; (3) reviews existing empirical evidence regarding the important determinants of casino gaming revenue; (4) compares and contrasts model specifications and varying estimation series; and (5) discusses future modeling possibilities.

U. S. Casino Gaming Activity

Legalization of casino gaming by states for the purpose of revenue generation and economic development has surged in the United States over the past 15 years. Since 1989, when Iowa legalized riverboat casinos, 18 states have legalized casino gaming in land-based, riverboat, and racetrack casino venues operated by either corporate casino companies or state lottery agencies.* Annual AGR generated by casinos in these states currently ranges from something less than $100 million in

* In 2005, 28 states contained tribal casinos, which are not authorized by state action or regulated by state gaming regulators. Eleven of the states with tribal casinos also have commercial casinos. The casino gaming totals reported in this chapter do not include tribal casino revenue.

Maine, Oklahoma, and South Dakota to over $2 billion in Indiana, Louisiana, and Mississippi. Nevertheless, activity in the two traditional gambling states of Nevada and New Jersey still tends to dwarf the activity in these new gaming states. Current annual AGR generated by casinos in Nevada and New Jersey totals about $11.8 billion and $5.2 billion, respectively. Total AGR generated in all the casino gaming states, including Nevada and New Jersey, currently exceeds $33 billion. Table 8.1 summarizes the annual AGR and gaming tax totals, along with venue type, for 18 casino gaming states during the period July 1, 2005–June 30, 2006. In addition to the states identified in Table 8.1, Florida and Pennsylvania have also legalized racetrack casinos, however, gaming operations have not yet commenced.

Annual gaming taxes from casino operations currently total over $6.4 billion. The state casino taxes represent about 19.3 percent of casino AGR, with this rate ranging from a low of about 8.5 percent in Nevada to a high of about 61.6 percent in Rhode Island.* The most prevalent gaming tax levied in the states is the wagering tax. The wagering tax is imposed on the casino owner as a percentage of the AGR generated by the casino. Other gaming taxes include admissions taxes imposed on the casino owner at a fixed dollar rate per casino patron and machine taxes imposed at a fixed dollar rate per gaming device installed in a casino. Admissions and machine taxes are imposed only in a limited number of gaming states. In contrast to states where casino gaming is entirely private with state taxes imposed on casino owners, gaming at racetrack facilities in Delaware, New York, Rhode Island, and West Virginia is operated as video lottery by the state lottery agency. The racetrack owners actually operate as retail agents of the state lotteries with the video lottery machines actually installed and maintained at the racetrack casinos by the state lottery agency. In these cases, a percentage of the casino AGR is paid to racetrack owner as a retailer's commission. The remainder that is not directed to the racetrack owner for the owner's general use is equivalent to a wagering tax, although these states impose no explicit gaming tax.

Casino Gaming in Indiana

Riverboat casinos were legalized in Indiana in 1993. The riverboat gambling law authorized a total of 11 casinos—five operating on Lake Michigan, five operating on the Ohio River, and one casino to operate on Patoka Lake in southern Indiana.† The first casino began operating in Evansville in December 1995, and five more

* The Rhode Island rate is based on the proportion of AGR generated by video lottery terminals at racetrack facilities that is retained by the state.

† The Patoka Lake license was never issued and was ultimately eliminated by legislation enacted in 2003. The legislation replaced the Patoka Lake license with a license for a casino to be located in the French Lick–West Baden Springs area. The casino began operating in October 2006.

Table 8.1 AGR, Gaming Taxes, and Gaming Venues by State (Dollar Amounts in Millions)

State	*AGR*	*Gaming Taxes*	*Land-Based Casinos*	*Riverboat Casinos*	*Racetrack Casinos*
Colorado	765.4	106.1	X		
Delaware[a]	603.5	316			X
Illinois	1,870.30	762.2		X	
Indiana	2,483.90	803.2		X	
Iowa	1,149.10	260.7		X	X
Louisiana	2,383.90	570.4	X	X	X
Maine[b,c]	21.3	10.2			X
Michigan	1,261.50	302.7	X		
Mississippi	2,239.20	273.6		X	
Missouri	1,570.30	421.8		X	
Nevada	11,803.80	1,003.10	X		
New Jersey	5,160.50	477.3	X		
New Mexico	229.6	59.7			X
New York[a]	315.7	193.6			X
Oklahoma[b,c]	45.1	17.5			X
Rhode Island[a]	416.5	256.6			X
South Dakota	85.4	13.3	X		
West Virginia[a]	942.3	433.9			X

[a] Racetrack gaming facilities operate as lottery retailers. Tax amount is computed as the AGR minus the lottery retailer commission paid to racetrack owner.

[b] Maine financials for November 2005–June 2006. Oklahoma financials for October 2005–June 2006.

[c] Tax amount is equal to the AGR minus amounts retained by racetrack owner for general purpose use.

Note: Data was obtained from Colorado Department of Revenue (2006); Delaware Lottery (2006); Illinois Gaming Board (2007); Indiana Gaming Commission (2006); Iowa Racing and Gaming Commission (2006a, b); Louisiana State Police (2006a,b,c); Maine Gambling Control Board (2005, 2006a, b); Michigan Gaming Control Board (2005, 2006); Mississippi State Tax Commission (2006); Mississippi State Tax Commission (2006); Missouri Gaming Commission (2006); Nevada Gaming Commission (2006); New Jersey Casino Control Commission (2005, 2006); New Mexico Gaming Control Board (2006); New York State Lottery (2006); Oklahoma State Auditor (2006a, b); Rhode Island Lottery (2006); South Dakota Commission on Gaming (2006); West Virginia Lottery (2006).

began operating in 1996. Currently, there are eleven casinos operating, with the last opening in October 2006. Since FY 1997 (the first full year of riverboat gaming), annual AGR has increased by about 236 percent from approximately $738.2 million in FY 1997 to about $2483.9 million in FY 2006. Even more striking,

Table 8.2 Annual Gaming Performance in Indiana (Dollar Amounts in Millions)

		Wagering Tax			*Admissions Tax*		
Fiscal Year	*AGR*	*State*	*Local*	*Total*	*State*	*Local*	*Total*
1996	73.2	7.1	2.4	9.5	0.6	1.3	1.9
1997	738.2	100.1	32.9	133.0	12.4	28.9	41.3
1998	1164.7	171.5	56.6	228.1	25.2	58.7	83.8
1999	1465.4	215.2	71.2	286.4	32.0	74.7	106.8
2000	1645.1	247.6	82.0	329.7	34.8	81.2	116.1
2001	1754.1	262.5	86.7	349.2	35.2	82.2	117.4
2002	1926.4	286.4	95.0	381.5	37.7	87.9	125.6
2003	2160.7	433.0	95.0	528.1	28.4	66.2	94.5
2004	2312.8	603.7	128.0	731.8	23.8	55.6	79.4
2005	2405.1	587.0	128.0	715.1	24.1	56.3	80.5
2006	2483.9	592.3	128.0	720.4	24.4	56.9	81.3

Note: Data was obtained from the Indiana Auditor of State (1996, 1997, 1998, 1999, 2000, 2001, 2002, 2003, 2004, 2005, 2006).

gaming tax revenue increased during this period by about 360 percent from about \$174.3 million in FY 1997 to about \$801.7 million in FY 2006. Table 8.2 provides a history of annual AGR and gaming tax totals through FY 2006.

Until August 2002, the riverboat casinos were required to leave the dock and cruise while gambling was conducted onboard. Typically, the riverboats conducted two-hour gaming excursions. Casino owners were subject to both an admissions tax and a wagering tax. The admissions tax was \$3 per person admitted to a gaming excursion and the wagering tax was imposed at a flat rate of 20 percent on a casino's AGR.* From FY 1996 to FY 2002, the admissions tax and wagering tax generated approximately \$2.3 billion in revenue for state and local governments.† Under this regulatory and tax regime, 70 percent of the admissions tax revenue and 25 percent of the wagering tax revenue was distributed to local governments where the riverboat casinos were docked. Meanwhile, 30 percent of the admissions tax revenue was distributed to the state for horse racing, state fair, and mental health uses. In addition, 75 percent of the wagering tax revenue was used by the state to replace local motor vehicle excise taxes and to fund state and local government capital projects.

The regulatory and tax regime for Indiana's casino gambling industry changed markedly in August 2002 when the excursion requirement was eliminated (the

* The wagering tax rate was increased to 22.5 percent beginning in July 2002 for riverboats that conducted gambling excursions.

† Indiana state fiscal year runs from July 1 to June 30.

Table 8.3 Current Indiana Wagering Tax

Annual AGR (Dollar Amounts in Millions)	*Wagering Tax Rate (Percent)*
Less than 25	15
25–50	20
50–75	25
75–150	30
Over 150	35

riverboat casinos were allowed to remain dockside while conducting gambling operations). This regulatory change was implemented solely to increase the number of patrons that could gamble at a riverboat casino each day. Thus, although the average amount wagered by patrons was not expected to increase due to the change, the aggregate amount wagered was, as more patrons cycled through the casinos on a daily basis. Along with the elimination of the excursion requirement, the admissions tax and wagering tax were altered. Under the dockside regime, the admissions tax is imposed only on the number of patrons entering the riverboat casino and not on the number of patrons admitted to a two-hour gaming excursion.* More importantly, the wagering tax is imposed under a five-tier graduated rate structure specified in Table 8.3, where incremental AGR generated by a casino during the fiscal year is taxed at an increasing rate. Under the graduated rate structure, the first $25 million in AGR generated by a casino is taxed at the rate of 15 percent and AGR generated in excess of $150 million during the year is taxed at the rate of 35 percent. During FY 2006, seven of the ten casinos in Indiana paid a top marginal wagering rate of 35 percent, with the remaining three paying a top marginal rate of 30 percent.

Corresponding to the regulatory and tax changes, the local share of wagering tax revenue was frozen at the FY 2002 level (approximately $95.1 million per year) to ensure that the revenue effects of the regulatory and tax structure changes accrued to the state. Beginning in FY 2003, much of the state's share of wagering tax revenue was directed to continuing expenses relating to property tax relief. The state pays for reductions in property taxes levied by local governments and school districts under the property tax replacement credit and homestead credit. These credits are financed from the state's property tax replacement fund. The state's consensus revenue forecast consists of estimates of the revenue sources that are

* The admissions tax based on a head count for each excursion and a 22.5 percent flat-rate wagering tax would be imposed in the future on riverboats that choose to discontinue dockside gaming operations and operate under the excursion regime.

deposited in the property tax replacement fund as well as the state's general fund. Consequently, for the first time a forecast of wagering tax revenue was required in FY 2003.

Indiana's Consensus Revenue Forecasting Process

Indiana employs a consensus revenue forecasting process to generate annual revenue projections for the state's general fund and property tax replacement fund. In conjunction with the structural changes to the wagering tax enacted in June 2002, the revenue forecasting process has influenced the specifications of the AGR forecast model. The consensus process involves officials of both the executive and legislative branches. The forecast is generated annually in December before the legislative session, and every other year it is updated in April before the legislature enacts a new biennial budget. The forecast before the budget session covers the remainder of the fiscal year in progress and the immediately following two fiscal years for which the legislature is budgeting. The update generated in December before the nonbudget session covers the remainder of the first fiscal year of the biennium and the second year of the biennium.

The revenue forecast is generated by two independent forecasting committees: the Revenue Technical Committee (RTC) and the Economic Forecast Committee (EFC). The RTC consists of six members: two members appointed by the governor and four members representing each party caucus in the House of Representatives and the Senate. The RTC selects the forecasting models for the various taxes that provide revenue for the general fund and the property tax replacement fund. The focus of the RTC's work falls on the three primary revenue sources—the individual income tax, the corporate income tax, and the sales tax—for these two funds. In addition, the RTC selects forecast models for the state's cigarette tax and alcoholic beverage taxes and develops forecasts, although without formal models, for the state's insurance premium tax and inheritance tax. Owing to the tax distribution changes discussed earlier, beginning in FY 2003, the riverboat wagering tax was added to the RTC's forecasting tasks in December 2002.

The EFC is a panel of five private economists who operate independent of the RTC. The EFC projects four economic measures that are reviewed and utilized by the RTC in the revenue forecasting process. The measures projected by the EFC are U.S. Personal Income, Non-Farm Indiana Personal Income (NFIPI), U. S. Gross Domestic Product (GDP), and the GDP Price Deflator. Quarterly and annual measures are projected on a nominal and real basis. Historically, the EFC's work product has carried great weight with policy makers. Consequently, the model specification work of the RTC focuses on the EFC's forecast of economic measures and, to some extent, constrains the modeling that is conducted by the RTC.

The RTC typically employs causal regression models that estimate the determinants of a tax revenue source or its tax base. The models tend to be very parsimonious, with the primary driver variable being one of the economic measures forecast by the EFC. The forecast models for the individual income tax, the corporate income tax, and sales tax project these revenue streams directly. The primary driver variable in the individual income tax and sales tax models is NFIPI, with the primary driver variable in the corporate income tax model being U. S. GDP. Meanwhile, the cigarette tax and alcohol beverage tax models utilize NFIPI as one of the driver variables but provide forecasts of the tax base—cigarette sales and alcohol beverage sales—instead of the revenue stream itself.

Likewise, the forecast model for the wagering tax reflects the various influences of this process. Although the model specification lends itself to prior empirical research on gambling taxes and gambling expenditures, the model also has been inextricably influenced by the consensus forecasting process. In addition, the structural changes to the wagering tax beginning in July 2002 required forecasters to specify a regression model to project the wagering tax base (AGR) instead of wagering tax revenue. Because the wagering tax was changed from a flat-rate tax to a graduated rate structure, the revenue series was interrupted in August 2002. In addition, the graduated tax rate structure commencing in August 2002 could not be easily specified in a forecast model nor could the potential average effective wagering tax rate be reasonably projected. Thus, the wagering tax forecast is developed from a forecast model of the wagering tax base (AGR) and not from a model of wagering tax collections. The wagering tax base—aggregate AGR—is forecast utilizing a causal regression model. However, the aggregate wagering tax is computed by dividing the aggregate AGR (in a simulation) between the ten riverboat casinos based on the prior year's distribution of actual AGR among the casinos. The forecast wagering tax for each casino is then computed and aggregated to produce a state wagering tax forecast.

Potential Determinants of Wagering Expenditures

Empirical research on determinants of casino, *pari-mutuel*, and lottery spending inform the specifications of the wagering tax forecast model. The literature suggests a number of potential determinants for casino wagering expenditures including income, unemployment, population, competing forms of gambling, seasonal effects, government regulatory constraints, and the potential life cycle of the casino product. The literature suggests that personal income, by far, is the most important determinant of gambling expenditures. In addition, personal income, seasonal effects, and regulatory constraints were the most feasible measures for use in constructing a single state forecast model, given the economic measures projected by the EFC.

Both econometric and survey research suggest that income is likely the most influential determinant of gaming participation and expenditures. Econometric analyses suggest that income has a direct and statistically significant effect on gaming expenditures such as lottery ticket sales (Ashley et al. 1999, Cook and Clotfelter 1993, Layton and Worthington 1999, Mikesell 1994, Mikesell and Zorn 1987); spending on poker machines and casino games such as black jack or roulette (Layton and Worthington 1999); spending on video lottery machines (Potiowsky and Parker 2000); wagering at casinos (Nichols 1998a, Rivenbark 1998); and *pari-mutuel* betting (Gulley and Scott 1989). These analyses suggest that the income elasticity of spending on gambling activities can be quite large and extremely varied. The estimated income elasticities of wagering on these different gambling forms ranged from 0.11–3.9 for lottery ticket sales, 0.2 to 1.05 for *pari-mutuel* betting, and 0.4 to 1.7 for wagering on video lottery terminals, poker machines, and casino type games.

Survey research by Gazel and Thompson (1996) and Harrah's Entertainment, Inc. (2002, 2003, 2004, 2006) confirms the income effects estimated in the econometric literature.* The survey research suggests that participation and spending by gamblers is increasing with personal income. Gazel and Thompson (1996) estimated that the mean gaming losses incurred by Illinois casino patrons in 1995 increased from about $28 per visit for patrons earning $10,000 or less annually to about $54 per visit for patrons earning over $30,000 annually. Participation rate estimates from the Harrah's Entertainment, Inc. (2002, 2003, 2004, 2006) surveys indicate that about 20–22 percent of adults earning less than $35,000 annually participate in gambling activities. Meanwhile, the estimated participation rate increases to about 31–35 percent for adults earning over $95,000 annually.

Because quarterly economic series could potentially be utilized to forecast AGR from Indiana casinos, seasonal variation in the flow of AGR may be an important and confounding factor, which would require some seasonal adjustment. Cargill and Eadington (1978) analyzed the seasonal movements underlying the upward trend in quarterly AGR generated by Nevada casinos from 1955 to 1975. Moreover, they demonstrated quite clearly that the seasonal variation is, in particular, related to varying winter weather patterns. Cargill and Eadington (1978) compared performance in the Las Vegas market to other more weather-affected markets in Nevada. Although the Las Vegas market (with mild winters) exhibits an average variation from the best to the worst quarter of only about 10 percent, the average variation in the Reno and Lake Tahoe markets (which experience harsh winters) was 50 and 90 percent, respectively, best quarter over worst quarter. Given the potential for inclement weather in the Midwest during the November–March period, seasonal fluctuation in the quarterly AGR from Indiana casinos is likely. Therefore, this

* Gazel and Thompson (1996) conducted interviews of randomly selected patrons (n = 785) visiting five Illinois riverboat casinos during July–August 1995. Harrah's Entertainment, Inc. (2002, 2003, 2004, 2006) annually conducts interviews of a random national sample (n = 2000) of men and women 18 years of age and older; and mails survey questionnaires to a randomly selected panel (n = 100,000) of men and women 21 years of age and older.

seasonal pattern is worthy of investigation. The data series could potentially require seasonal adjustment as well.

Variation in AGR over time could also result from different regulatory regimes. Beginning in 1994, the casino gaming states in the Midwest have considered and implemented various deregulatory policies as a means to facilitate market expansion and competitive advantage of local casinos (Atkinson et al. 2000). Primarily, these deregulatory efforts focused on eliminating betting and loss limits, excursion requirements for riverboat casinos, and allowing 24-hour gaming operations. Available econometric research suggests that eliminating excursion requirements leads to a significant upward shift in casino AGR as more patrons are admitted to casinos per day.

Nichols (1998a, 1998b) and Thalheimer and Ali (2003) generated estimates of the impact of regulatory restrictions. Nichols (1998a) estimated that monthly AGR generated at Iowa riverboat casinos experienced a permanent upward shift of about $825,000 per month beginning in 1994 due to the elimination of betting and loss limits, an excursion requirement, and a limit on casino size. On the basis of the average monthly AGR in Iowa from 1991 to 1997, this translated into a 5 percent increase in monthly AGR. Nichols (1998b) also estimated the impact of deregulatory efforts in New Jersey implemented in 1991. The data analysis was inconclusive as to the impact of allowing casinos to operate 24-hours per day. However, the model estimates suggested that increasing the limit on floor space devoted to slot machines was positive. It was estimated that annual growth in slot machine AGR was increased by about 14.25 percent in the first year after deregulation, and by more than 100 percent by the third year of deregulation.

Thalheimer and Ali (2003) also estimated that betting limits and riverboat casino excursion requirements had a significant negative effect on slot machine AGR at casinos and racinos in Illinois, Iowa, and Missouri during the period 1991–1998. It was estimated that betting limits lowered AGR by about 36 percent and excursion requirements lowered AGR by an average of 35 percent. Confirming the latter, empirical analysis of the impact of dockside gaming in Illinois by Indiana Legislative Services Agency (2001) suggested that the change led to an average increase of about 30 percent in casino AGR.

Research by various sources—Gazel and Thompson (1996), Illinois Gaming Board (1997, p. 6), Przybylski et al. (1998), and Thalheimer and Ali (2003)—also suggests that the vast majority of casino patrons live in proximity to the casinos. About 83 percent of Illinois casino visitors interviewed by Gazel and Thompson (1996) resided in Illinois.* In terms of distance, 50 percent of the interview subjects resided within 25 mi of the casino. An additional 35.1 percent of the interview subjects resided between 25 and 50 mi of the casino. Only 4.6 percent of the

* Based on interviews of 785 patrons randomly selected at five riverboat casinos in July and August 1995.

interview subjects traveled more than 100 mi to visit the casino. Illinois Gaming Board (1997, p. 6) survey research suggests that about 62 percent of Illinois casino patrons travel 50 mi or less to visit a casino.* More than half of these casino patrons travel 25 mi or less. In addition, according to the survey responses, over 62 percent of Illinois casino patrons are Illinois residents. Przybylski et al. (1998) find that almost 88 percent of patrons at the northwest Indiana casinos are from other states with about 46 percent of patrons from other states at the southern Indiana casinos.† Nevertheless, this research tends to confirm the previous findings with only about 4 percent of patrons at southern Indiana casinos traveling more than 120 mi, and only about 3 percent of patrons at northwestern Indiana casinos traveling more than 60 mi. These proximity findings are important in terms of specifying the forecast model. Although a large percentage of Indiana casino patrons are not from Indiana, they reside in surrounding states in proximity to Indiana. This suggests that Indiana's income likely serves as an effective proxy for income of casino patrons coming from cross-border areas of Illinois, Kentucky, Michigan, and Ohio. Therefore, the forecast model likely will not suffer from specification problems if income measures specific to the surrounding states are omitted from the model.

Recently, research by Moss et al. (2003) suggests that casino gaming revenue exhibits a growth pattern over time consistent with Butler's S-shaped product life cycle. Prior literature on state lotteries by DeBoer (1986) and Mikesell and Zorn (1987) touch on the potential for growth in state lottery revenue to slow or flatten out over time. However, no prior research focuses on the product life cycle characteristics of casino gaming revenue as Moss et al. (2003) do. They modeled gaming revenue growth from 1992 to 1999 in the Mississippi casino industry, finding a third-order polynomial model as the best fitting model for estimating industry trend in gross gaming revenue. Moss et al. (2003) indicated that this model form was superior to the other trend equations tested, including log and exponential forms. The analysis suggests that gaming revenue growth by the late 1990s had leveled off, and this coincided with industry consolidation and casino closings. In addition, the authors found that the industry's response to the slowing growth was to increase the scale of casino operations providing more amenities to attract and keep the gamblers.

Other determinants of wagering expenditures investigated in the literature include unemployment rate (Mikesell 1994), population differences (Ashley et al. 1999, Cook and Clotfelter 1993, Mikesell 1994), and competing forms of gambling (Ashley et al. 1999, Gulley and Scott 1989). However, these measures were deemed

---

* Based on a survey of 13,000 randomly selected casino patrons at ten casino sites in Illinois. Surveys completed over four days in June 1997.

† Based on casino patron socioeconomic and zip code location data supplied by Indiana casinos.

to be less practical and effective for modeling a single state over a short time span. Mikesell (1994) estimated the unemployment elasticity of lottery sales in the range 0.05–0.17 as compared to the estimated income elasticity ranging from 3.5 to 3.9. An important reason for sidestepping unemployment rate is that the EFC does not project unemployment for the RTC. Modeling the potential displacement effects of lottery spending, *pari-mutuel* betting, and spending on charity gaming was not considered because annual lottery sales in Indiana have shown only a nominal upward trend since the mid-1990s, and *pari-mutuel* wagering and charity gaming receipts have mostly experienced declining annual performance. This suggests that lottery, *pari-mutuel* wagering, and charity gaming have likely had little or no significant long-term impact on spending at casinos in Indiana. Finally, the significant effects of population differences on lottery sales were derived by comparative state studies using pooled state-level lottery data or cross-sectional state lottery data. Although these studies suggest that lottery sales are increasing with population, we are forecasting AGR for one state over a relatively short time span so that population change and its effects are very minimal.

Seasonal Variation of AGR and Casino Start-Up Effects

Figure 8.1 illustrates quarterly AGR and casino patron totals from the inception of riverboat casino operations in Indiana in the fourth quarter of 1995 to the second quarter of 2006. The quarterly totals are indexed to the first quarter of the series. The graph illustrates several important components of each quarterly series: (1) trend, (2) seasonal variation, (3) the effects of casino start-ups at the beginning of the series, (4) the effects of dockside gaming in Indiana beginning in 2002, and (5) potential product life cycle attributes throughout the series. The graph suggests that the AGR series contains a distinct quarterly seasonal pattern. After the initial 18–24 months of casino operations, second and fourth quarter performance is consistently below performance during the first and third quarters. The first quarter contains the historically high performance month of March and the third quarter contains typically high performance summer months. In the case of the fourth quarter performance, it appears to be well below the remainder of the year. The graph also indicates that casino start-ups during 1996 substantially mask the quarterly pattern over the initial 18–24 months of operations. After the first casino start-up in December 1995, three casinos began operating in the second quarter of 1996 and two began operating in the fourth quarter of 1996. Despite casino start-ups in 1997 and 1998, the base AGR by then was sufficiently large that the incremental AGR increases no longer obscure the quarterly pattern.

To better test for the impact of seasonal variation and casino start-ups, two trend models are estimated with the parameter estimates presented in Table 8.4. Model 1 controls for quarterly seasonal variation and Model 2 controls for both seasonal variation and start-ups of casinos from 1996 to 2000. The coefficients

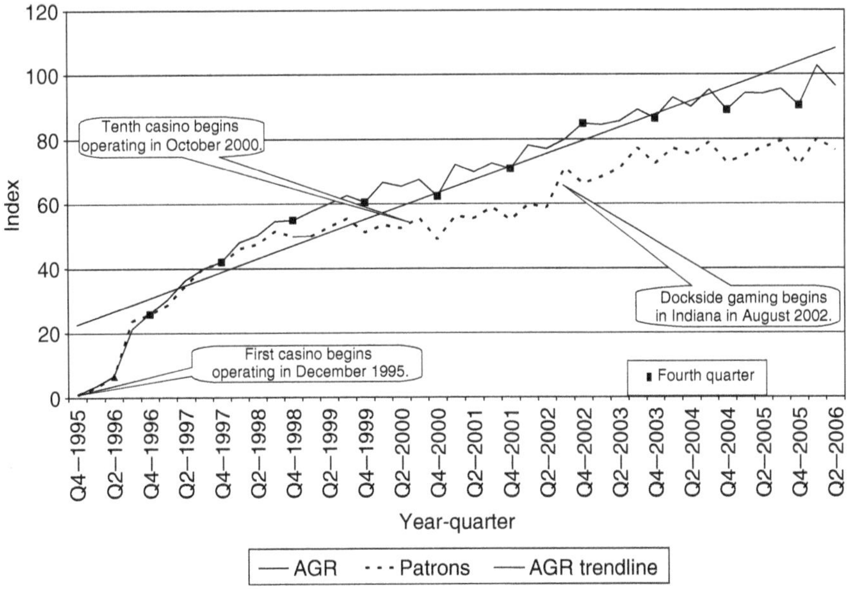

Figure 8.1 Quarterly AGR and patron history. (Data was obtained from the Indiana Gaming Commission, *Monthly Summary of Wagering and Admission Tax*, 1995–2006.)

Table 8.4 Analysis of Quarterly Variation and Casino Start-Up Effects

Determinant	*Coefficient* Model 1	*Coefficient* Model 2	*Impact (Percent)*
Constant	127,406.45*	788.83	
Trend	13,137.20*	9,424.54*	
Q2	−137.44	18,092.95**	−4.29
Q3	21,331.82	−634.89	−0.15
Q4	1,185.35	−28,964.64*	−6.87
Three casino starts Q2—1996		65,885.52*	15.63
Two casino starts Q4—1996		78,726.84*	18.67
One casino starts Q2—1997		42,134.05***	9.99
One casino starts Q3—1997		31,231.25	7.41
One casino starts Q4—1998		36,891.29*	8.75
One casino starts Q4—2000		3,341.20	0.79

Note: $^{*}p < .01$; $^{**}p < .05$; $^{***}p < .10$; $^{****}p < .15$.

on the second and fourth quarter dummies in Model 2 are statistically significant after controlling for casino start-ups. These parameter estimates suggest that second quarter performance is, on average, about 4.3 percent below first quarter performance; and fourth quarter performance is, on average, about 6.9 percent below first quarter performance. The Model 2 parameter estimates also suggest that there is no statistical difference between the average first and third quarter performance, with the percent impact computed on the third quarter coefficient amounting to only 0.15 percent. The trend model results also suggest that casino start-ups have resulted in significant upward shifts in the AGR series. The initial impact of the successive casino start-ups, however, declines as the base AGR increases. Three casino starts in the second quarter of 1996 resulted in an upward shift in AGR of about 15.6 percent on the average and two casino starts in the fourth quarter of 1996 resulted in an upward shift in AGR of about 18.7 percent on the average. Subsequent casino starts in the second quarter of 1997 and the fourth quarter of 1998 also had statistically significant impacts on AGR, averaging 10 and 8.8 percent, respectively. Other subsequent casino starts in the third quarter of 1997 and the fourth quarter of 2000 did not result in statistically significant shifts.

Two adjustments are made to the series to minimize the potential confounding effects of seasonal variation and casino start-ups. The AGR series is smoothed utilizing a centered four-quarter moving average. To control for the effects of initial casino starts, the first five quarters of casino gaming activity (the fourth quarter of 1995 to the fourth quarter of 1996) are eliminated from the AGR series. This step eliminates a significant portion of the initial ramping up of gaming activity that could potentially bias parameter estimates. In particular, the series is truncated to avoid inflating the income elasticity of AGR due to the correspondence between (1) the extremely high growth rates in AGR from 1996 to 2000 due to significant supply expansion and (2) relatively high growth in personal income occurring during the same period. Nevertheless, two significant start-ups were left in the series (the third quarter of 1997 and the fourth quarter of 1998) to avoid truncating the series too severely (limiting the regression degrees of freedom) and thus restricting the forecasters' ability to add variables to the model if necessary.

The Base AGR Forecast Model: Estimating the Income Elasticity and Dockside Gaming Impact

The base forecast model estimates the determinants of quarterly AGR with the following specification

$$\text{AGR} = f(Y, X) \tag{8.1}$$

where the primary driver variable *Y* is quarterly NFIPI generated by the U.S. Bureau of Economic Analysis and *X* represents other control variables. Projections of the quarterly income series by the EFC are utilized to generate forecasts of quarterly AGR. The models summarized in Table 8.5 are estimated with AGR and income series spanning the first quarter of 1997 to the second quarter of 2004. Income is specified in each of the models. In addition, an intercept dummy is specified in two models corresponding to the period since the third quarter of 2002 when dockside gaming on Indiana's riverboat casinos began.

Beyond the explanatory variables specified in the models, different functional forms also were tested for the forecast model based on the "bulging rule" proposed by Mosteller and Tukey (1977). The functional forms tested included linear models (Models 1.1 and 1.2) and curvilinear functional forms with AGR^2 (Models 2.1 and 2.2), as well as specifications with AGR^2 and either LN(Y) or $Y^{1/2}$. Generally, the linear models performed poorly in comparison to the curvilinear functional forms, generating the largest prediction errors above actual AGR at the end of the series. A review of the quarterly AGR history in Figure 8.1 suggests that AGR is somewhat concave rather than linear. The hashed linear trend line in Figure 8.1 suggests that a linear forecast model will result in an overforecast of AGR and will do so with increasing error provided the quarterly year-over-year growth rate in AGR continues to decline. Consequently, the curvilinear functional forms were tested as a means of improving the fit of the model to the series, in particular, at the end of the series. The functional form containing AGR^2 with no transformations of the explanatory variables performed better than the other curvilinear functional forms as the series was extended. Table 8.5 reports parameter estimates, model fit and prediction error statistics, and results of *ex ante* error analysis.

As expected, the parameter estimates suggest that personal income has an overwhelming impact on wagering levels. The models suggest that the income elasticity of wagering is between 2.1 and 2.8 on average. Thus, a 1 percent increase in personal income is estimated to result in a 2.1–2.8 percent average increase in wagering. Models 1.2 and 2.2 also suggest that the shift to dockside gaming in Indiana in August 2002 has, on average, had a positive effect on wagering in Indiana. The parameter estimates suggest that the average percentage impact of the shift to dockside gaming is in the range of 5.8–12.7 percent. On the basis of the series average, this is an impact on the scale of about $25–54 million in AGR per quarter. Assuming an average effective wagering tax rate of about 29 percent, this finding suggests a quarterly tax impact of $7.2–15.8 million per quarter.* The parameter estimates in Model 2.2 are more consistent with 2002–2003 year-over-year growth figures

* The FY 2006 average effective wagering tax rate for Indiana casinos was 29.08 percent.

Table 8.5 Base Forecast Model and Forecast Model with Dockside Gaming Control

	Model 1.1		*Model 1.2*		*Model 2.1*		*Model 2.2*	
Determinant	*b*	e	*b*	e	*b*	e	*b*	e
Constant	−790,534.54*		−708,789.80*		−8.04E+11*	2.56	−6.42E+11*	
Income	0.01*	2.84	0.01*	2.64	6,172.61*		5,088.02*	2.11
Indiana dockside			24,961.54**	5.82			4.96E+10*	12.70
R^2	0.9686		0.9734		0.9461		0.9781	
Durbin–Watson	0.7838		0.9925		0.5698		1.7967	
MAE	14,450.23		13,066.83		18,613.64		11,210.75	
RMSE	18,556.84		16,851.99		23,352.68		14,086.94	
Forecast error (percent)	−8.15		−8.33		−2.08		−2.43	
Attributable to model error (percent)	−8.94		−9.06		−2.65		−2.89	
Attributable to exogenous variable error (percent)	0.79		0.73		0.57		0.46	

Note: Models 1.1 and 1.2 Dependent variable = AGR (in thousands); Models 2.1 and 2.2 Dependent variable = AGR^2 (in thousands); estimating series from Q1–1997 to Q2–2004, $n = 30$; forecast period from Q3–2004 to Q1–2006; *$p < .01$; **$p < .05$; ***$p < .10$; ****$p < .15$; b = Coefficient; e = Elasticity.

indicating that quarterly AGR grew by an average of 12.2 percent from the third quarter of 2002 to the third quarter of 2003.*

Overall, Model 2.2 performs better than the other three models. Model 2.2 exhibits the best fit ($R^2 = 0.978$) and exhibits no first-order autocorrelation ($1.57 < \text{DW} < 2.43$). In contrast, the remaining models exhibit slightly lower measures of fit ($0.945 < R^2 < 0.974$) and statistically significant positive first-order autocorrelation ($\text{DW} < 1.28$). This indicates that the errors in successive quarters tend to be similar or positively correlated. Consequently, Models 1.1, 1.2, and 2.1 could potentially generate large errors (positive or negative) in consecutive quarters. More importantly, Model 2.2 exhibits the lowest prediction error based on both the mean absolute error (MAE) and the root mean squared error (RMSE). Although all of the models tend to overforecast AGR consistently, the average prediction error generated by Model 2.2 is above 20 percent less than Models 1.1 and 2.1 prediction errors, and about 15 percent less than the prediction error generated by Model 1.2. Model 2.2 is superior on RMSE measure that emphasizes the largest errors.

The *ex ante* error analysis also tends to confirm the performance of Model 2.2. The *ex ante* error analysis measures the forecast error (the difference between actual AGR and forecast AGR) and the portion of this error attributable to the regression model and to the projected exogenous variables in the model. The *ex ante* error analysis is based on the AGR forecast over seven quarters (the third quarter of 2004 to the first quarter of 2006). Quarterly income projections generated by the EFC are utilized with the estimated forecast models to generate AGR projections over these seven quarters. Model error is based on the difference between actual AGR and AGR simulated over the seven quarter forecast period utilizing actual income instead of projected income in the forecast model. The exogenous variable error is the residual. During the seven quarter forecast period, Models 1.1 and 1.2 resulted in an overforecast of AGR in the range 8.2–8.3 percent. The overforecast totals about $378–387 million in AGR, and assuming an average effective wagering tax rate of about 29 percent, this estimate translates to an overforecast of tax revenue during the seven quarter period in the range of $110–112 million. In contrast, Models 2.1 and 2.2 overforecast AGR by about $90–106 million (an excess of

---

* Although year-over-year growth during the preceding four quarters averaged 9.9 percent, the 2002–2003 AGR growth was fairly robust because of the behavior in consumption expenditures nationally, employment in Indiana, and AGR of Illinois riverboat casinos during the same period. From the first quarter of 2002 to third quarter of 2003, personal consumption expenditures grew by only about 0.8 percent per quarter nationally; and consumption expenditures on recreation services were even more anemic growing at about 0.4 percent per quarter nationally. During the same period, employment in Indiana increased by about 0.3 percent per quarter, and the unemployment rate remained well within the range of 4.9 to 5.2 percent. Moreover, Illinois casinos experienced decreasing year-over-year growth in AGR from July 2002 to September 2002, and then, from October 2002 to October 2003, Illinois casinos experienced year-over-year decline in AGR for 13 consecutive months. On average, monthly AGR in Illinois was down by an average of 5 percent per month during this period.

about 2–2.4 percent) during the forecast period, with the tax impact ranging from about $26 to 31 million. Each of the forecast models overforecasts AGR, with the projected exogenous variables resulting in slight underforecast of AGR.

Model estimates and forecast results utilizing the updated AGR and Income series spanning the first quarter of 1997 to the second quarter of 2005 are consistent with the results derived from the 1997–2004 series. The *ex ante* error analysis is based on the AGR forecast over three quarters (the third quarter of 2005 to the first quarter of 2006). Updated quarterly income projections published by the EFC in 2005 are utilized to generate AGR projections over the three-quarter period. Model 2.2 remains the superior model showing a slight improvement in model fit ($R^2 = 0.981$) and exhibiting no first-order autocorrelation ($1.58 < DW < 2.42$). The estimated impacts of income and dockside gaming are slightly lower. The estimated income elasticity suggests a 1 percent increase in income resulting in a 1.9 percent increase in AGR. The estimated impact of dockside gaming suggests that the regulatory change has resulted in a 10.94 percent upward shift in AGR. Finally, the *ex ante* error analysis indicates that the forecast error and model error are reduced apparently with the longer series. Over the three-quarter forecast period, the model error is reduced from about 3.55 percent of forecast, using the older 1997–2004 series, to 2.48 percent of forecast using the newer 1997–2005 series.

Accounting for Potential Capacity Restrictions or Market Maturation in the AGR Forecast Model

The curvilinear forecast models specified in Table 8.5 generate predicted AGR that tends to flatten out at the end of the series more so than the AGR levels predicted by the linear forecast models. This is consistent with the analysis of the Mississippi casino industry by Moss et al. (2003) suggesting that industry revenue exhibits an S-shaped growth curve. Still, the curvilinear models tend to overforecast AGR and fail to match the declining year-over-year growth rates exhibited by AGR in recent years. Figure 8.1 highlights the noticeable slowing in growth that has occurred in both the AGR and patron total series since 2000. It appears that Indiana casino AGR and patron totals may be in a period of nominal year-over-year growth. Whether this trend is due to market maturation or capacity restrictions on some of the riverboat casinos is uncertain. Gambling participation rates estimated by Harrah's Entertainment, Inc. (2002, 2003, 2004) for Illinois, Indiana, Kentucky, Michigan, and Ohio suggest that the Indiana market may have stabilized in recent years.* Also, casino expansions are being undertaken in Indiana to upgrade facilities and increase capacity. One casino expansion was completed in 2005 and two others

* Participation estimates from 2002, 2003, and 2004 suggest that annual casino trips by adults in Illinois, Indiana, Kentucky, Michigan, and Ohio declined by about 11.7 percent from 2002 to 2004. For the same period, annual casino trips by adults in the United States increased by about 2.2 percent.

are currently planned for the 2007–2008 period. This expansion period may be transitory to the extent that capacity restrictions are the cause of lower growth in AGR and patrons, and casino expansions are undertaken to alleviate these restrictions. To proxy for the potential market maturation or capacity restriction effects, the quarterly patron count variable is specified in the forecast model as an additional control. As with the AGR series, the patron count series exhibits seasonal variation and, as a result, is adjusted using a centered four-quarter moving average. Table 8.6 reports estimation results for the curvilinear models using income, AGR, and patron count series spanning the first quarter of 1997 to the second quarter of 2004, and the second quarter of 2005.

Change in the model specification again improves the model fit and forecast performance. Model 2.3 results in income elasticity estimates considerably smaller than the prior models ranging from 1.35 to 1.55 depending on the estimation series. Thus, the specification is an important step in reducing the income elasticity and,

Table 8.6 Forecast Model Controlling for Market Maturation and Capacity Restrictions

	Model 2.3			
	1997–2004 Series[a]		*1997–2005 Series*[b]	
Determinant	b	e	b	e
Constant	−5.42E+11*		−5.19E+11*	
Income	3,742.11*	1.55	3,496.82*	1.35
Patrons	2.50E+07**	0.32	2.84E+07*	0.34
Indiana dockside	3.06E+10*	7.85	2.67E+10**	6.22
R^2	0.9826		0.9860	
Durbin–Watson	1.8812		1.9346	
MAE	10,923.83		10,798.67	
RMSE	13,515.40		13,342.10	
Forecast error (percent)	−0.87		−1.26	
Attributable to model error (percent)	−1.22		−0.53	
Attributable to exogenous variable error (percent)	0.35		−0.74	

[a] Estimating series from Q1–1997 to Q2–2004, $n = 30$; forecast period from Q3–2004 to Q1–2006.

[b] Estimating series from Q1–1997 to Q2–2005, $n = 34$; forecast period from Q3–2005 to Q1–2006.

Note: Dep. variable = AGR^2 (in thousands); *$p < .01$; **$p < .05$; ***$p < .10$; ****$p < .15$; b = Coefficient; e = Elasticity.

consequently, overforecast of AGR. Model 2.3 also shows improved model fit ($0.9825 < R^2 < 0.9861$) and does not exhibit first-order autocorrelation ($1.65 <$ DW < 2.35). The specification also continues to decrease the AGR prediction error ($13{,}342 <$ RMSE $< 13{,}516$). The *ex ante* error analysis suggests that the Model 2.3 specification further reduces both the forecast error and model error components to about 1 percent of forecast as well.

An alternative to model specification changes and curvilinear model forms is to further truncate the estimating series to eliminate the effects of casino start-ups from the forecast. Comparing the quarterly AGR series to the hashed linear trend line in Figure 8.1, it appears that eliminating the quarters before 1999 or 2000 would isolate the more recent slower growth periods and would provide a better representation of current industry performance. In addition, using the series since the first quarter of 2000 or first quarter of 2001 would still provide sufficient observations (18–22) and degrees of freedom, and may permit the use of a more simplified linear form. Model 3.0, summarized in Table 8.7, is estimated using the

Table 8.7 Forecast Model Controlling for Market Maturation and Capacity Restrictions by Series Truncation

	Model 3.0			
	2000–2005 Series[a]		*2001–2005 Series*[b]	
	b	*e*	*b*	*e*
Constant	−9.72E+04		−9.23E+04	
Income	0.00***	0.49	0.00**	0.57
Patrons	6.33E+01*	0.70	5.38E+01*	0.60
R^2	0.97		0.96	
Durbin–Watson	2.1219		2.7728	
MAE	8,904.27		7,906.13	
RMSE	11,224.42		10,429.80	
Forecast error (percent)	0.01		0.01	
Attributable to model error (percent)	0.93		0.88	
Attributable to exogenous variable error (percent)	0.38		0.10	

[a] Estimating series from Q1–2000 to Q2–2005, $n = 22$; forecast period from Q3–2005 to Q1–2006.

[b] Estimating series from Q1–2001 to Q2–2005, $n = 18$; forecast period from Q3–2005 to Q1–2006.

Note: Dep. variable = AGR (in thousands); $*p < .01$; $**.01 < p < .05$; $***.05 < p < .10$; $****.10 < p < .15$; b = Coefficient; e = Elasticity.

truncated first quarter of 2000 to second quarter of 2005 series and the truncated first quarter of 2001 to second quarter of 2005 series.

With the truncated series, the linear model was superior to the curvilinear models in terms of both model fit and prediction error. Model 3.0 diverges from prior estimation results as the dockside gaming dummy fails to be statistically significant. The truncated series also reduces the income elasticity to a range well below the results of the prior models, ranging from 0.49 to 0.57 depending on the estimation series. The specification and truncated series also continue to decrease the AGR prediction error (10,429 $<$ RMSE $<$ 11,225). Model 3.0 also exhibits no first-order autocorrelation with the 2000–2005 series (1.05 $<$ DW $<$ 2.47), whereas the result of the Durbin–Watson test is inconclusive when using the 2001–2005 series (2.46 $<$ DW $<$ 2.85).

The most important result of truncating the series is evident in the *ex ante* error analysis. The truncated series and linear estimating model result in a marked shift in the forecast error. Although the forecast error in absolute terms is not much different, the model error component of the overall forecast error is reduced to less than 1 percent. More importantly, the forecast error changes from a slight overforecast in Model 2.3 to a slight underforecast in Model 3.0. Model 2.3 estimated with the first quarter of 1997 to second quarter of 2005 series results in an overforecast of 1.26 percent, or about $37.5 million in AGR for the forecast period from the third quarter of 2005 to first quarter of 2006. This translates into an overforecast of about $10.9 million in wagering tax assuming an average effective tax rate of 29 percent. In comparison, Model 3.0 estimated with the truncated series results in an underforecast for the third quarter of 2005 to first quarter of 2006 forecast period ranging from 0.98 to 1.31 percent, or about $18.1–24 million in AGR. This translates into an underforecast of wagering tax ranging from only about $5.2 to 7 million.

Conclusion

This chapter highlights several aspects of the development of models to forecast the wagering tax base in Indiana. Changes to the state law for regulating and taxing the riverboat casinos in Indiana initiated the distribution of a significant portion of the state wagering tax to the state's property tax relief programs. As a result, state revenue forecasters were required to project wagering tax revenue beginning in FY 2003. Owing to the structural wagering tax changes enacted in 2002, the forecast is based on model estimates of the wagering tax base (AGR) and not wagering tax collections. The development of the forecast model has been influenced substantially by empirical literature examining the determinants of consumer spending on various forms of gambling, including lottery, *pari-mutuel*, and casino gambling. In addition, the model has been strongly influenced by the consensus revenue forecasting process. In particular, the scope of the economic variables projected by the EFC has served to focus model selection and selection of explanatory variables. Finally, the chapter demonstrates the trial and error process of developing a reasonably effective forecast model. This involves examining the parameter estimates for stability and rationality as well as comparing model fit and prediction error statistics. This process also involves *ex ante* analysis of forecast error to determine the error attributable to the regression model and to estimate the impact that any error in forecasting the explanatory variables has on the main forecast error.

Analysis of the AGR series and parameter estimates in the various forecast models are consistent with several findings in the empirical literature that was reviewed to guide the model-building process. Analysis of the AGR series reveals a seasonal pattern. The parameter estimates relating to income in all of the forecast models suggest that income is the dominant factor affecting casino AGR. The parameter estimates suggest that the income elasticity of AGR ranges from about 0.5 to 2.8, which is within the range found in the empirical literature. The parameter estimates relating to the impact of dockside gaming are somewhat varied and insignificant in the final modeling efforts. However, given the year-over-year growth exhibited after the regulatory change, the estimation results still appear to be reasonable. The addition of the patron count variable and the truncation of the estimating series reduce the estimated income elasticity to more conservative levels. Both the model and series changes also further reduce the forecast error generated by the models. The trial and error with model specifications and series length presented in this chapter appears to suggest that additional model specifications and time series should be examined. Additional model specifications potentially include the addition of a casino space (in square feet) variable or single-quarter dummies for quarters with unusually high AGR levels. The latter would remove the influence of such quarters on the average prediction and would be based on analysis of influence statistics such as DFFITS or Cook's D. Also, further testing of models with varying series lengths may be useful in deriving a forecast model and procedure that continues to isolate the forecast from past industry performance (not likely to reoccur) and that better reflects current industry performance.

References

Ashley, T., Liu, Y., and Chang, S. 1999. Estimating net lottery revenue for states. *American Economic Journal* 27: 170–178.

Atkinson, G., Nichols, M., and Oleson, T. 2000. The menace of competition and gambling regulation. *Journal of Economic Issues* 34: 621–634.

Cargill, T. F. and Eadington, W. R. 1978. Nevada's gaming revenues: Time characteristics and forecasting. *Management Science* 24: 1221–1230.

Colorado Department of Revenue. 2006. *FY2006 Gaming Statistics*. Denver, CL: Colorado Department of Revenue.

Cook, P. and Clotfelter, C. T. 1993. The peculiar scale of economies of lotto. *American Economic Review* 83: 634–643.

DeBoer, L. 1986. When will state lottery sales growth slow? *Growth and Change* 17: 28–36.

Delaware Lottery. 2006. *The Delaware Lottery 2006 Annual Report: For the Fiscal Year Ending June, 30, 2006.* Dover, DE: Delaware Lottery.

Gazel, R. C. and Thompson, W. N. 1996. *Casino Gamblers in Illinois: Who Are They? A Demographic and Economic Study.* Chicago, IL: Better Government Association.

Gulley, O. D. and Scott, F. A. Jr. 1989. Lottery effects on pari-mutuel tax revenues. *National Tax Journal* 42: 89–93.

Harrah's Entertainment, Inc. 2002. *Harrah's Survey 2002: Profile of the American Casino Gambler.* Las Vegas, NV: Harrah's Entertainment, Inc.

Harrah's Entertainment, Inc. 2003. *Harrah's Survey 2003: Profile of the American Casino Gambler.* Las Vegas, NV: Harrah's Entertainment, Inc.

Harrah's Entertainment, Inc. 2004. *Harrah's Survey 2004: Profile of the American Casino Gambler.* Las Vegas, NV: Harrah's Entertainment, Inc.

Harrah's Entertainment, Inc. 2006. *Harrah's Survey 2006: Profile of the American Casino Gambler.* Las Vegas, NV: Harrah's Entertainment, Inc.

Illinois Gaming Board. 1997. *1997 Annual Report.* Springfield, IL: Illinois Gaming Board.

Illinois Gaming Board. 2007. *Gaming Board 2006 Annual Report.* Springfield, IL: Illinois Gaming Board.

Indiana Auditor of State. 1996. *Budget Revenue Trial Balance as of 6/30/1996.* Indianapolis, IN: Indiana Auditor of State.

Indiana Auditor of State. 1997. *Budget Revenue Trial Balance as of 6/30/1997.* Indianapolis, IN: Indiana Auditor of State.

Indiana Auditor of State. 1998. *Budget Revenue Trial Balance as of 6/30/1998.* Indianapolis, IN: Indiana Auditor of State.

Indiana Auditor of State. 1999. *Budget Revenue Trial Balance as of 6/30/1999.* Indianapolis, IN: Indiana Auditor of State.

Indiana Auditor of State. 2000. *Budget Revenue Trial Balance as of 6/30/2000.* Indianapolis, IN: Indiana Auditor of State.

Indiana Auditor of State. 2001. *Budget Revenue Trial Balance as of 6/30/2001.* Indianapolis, IN: Indiana Auditor of State.

Indiana Auditor of State. 2002. *Budget Revenue Trial Balance as of 6/30/2002.* Indianapolis, IN: Indiana Auditor of State.

Indiana Auditor of State. 2003. *Budget Revenue Trial Balance as of 6/30/2003.* Indianapolis, IN: Indiana Auditor of State.

Indiana Auditor of State. 2004. *Budget Revenue Trial Balance as of 6/30/2004.* Indianapolis, IN: Indiana Auditor of State.

Indiana Auditor of State. 2005. *Budget Revenue Trial Balance as of 6/30/2005.* Indianapolis, IN: Indiana Auditor of State.

Indiana Auditor of State. 2006. *Budget Revenue Trial Balance as of 6/30/2006.* Indianapolis, IN: Indiana Auditor of State.

Indiana Gaming Commission. 2006. *2006 Indiana Gaming Commission Annual Report.* Indianapolis, IN: Indiana Gaming Commission.

Indiana Legislative Services Agency. 2001. *Fiscal Impact Statement—SB 255-2002.* December 18. Indianapolis, IN: Indiana Legislative Services Agency.

Indiana Legislative Services Agency. 2003. *Indiana Handbook of Taxes, Revenues, and Appropriations: FY 2003*. Indianapolis, IN: Indiana Legislative Services Agency.

Indiana Legislative Services Agency. 2006. *Indiana Handbook of Taxes, Revenues, and Appropriations: FY 2006*. Indianapolis, IN: Indiana Legislative Services Agency.

Iowa Racing and Gaming Commission. 2006a. *Riverboat Revenue Report, YTD FY 2006*. Des Moines: Iowa Racing and Gaming Commission.

Iowa Racing and Gaming Commission. 2006b. *Track Gaming Report, YTD FY 2006*. Des Moines, IA: Iowa Racing and Gaming Commission.

Layton, A. and Worthington, A. 1999. The impact of socio-economic factors on gambling expenditure. *International Journal of Social Economics* 25: 430–439.

Louisiana State Police. 2006a. *Monthly Activity Summary—Landbased: June 2006*. Baton Rouge, LA: Louisiana State Police.

Louisiana State Police. 2006b. *Monthly Activity Summary—Riverboats: June 2006*. Baton Rouge, LA: Louisiana State Police.

Louisiana State Police. 2006c. *Monthly Activity Summary—Slots at Racetracks: June 2006*. Baton Rouge, LA: Louisiana State Police.

Maine Gambling Control Board. 2005. *State Revenue from Racino Operation—Bangor*. Bangor, ME: Maine Gambling Control Board.

Maine Gambling Control Board. 2006. *State Revenue from Racino Operation—Bangor*. Bangor, ME: Maine Gambling Control Board.

Michigan Gaming Control Board. 2005. *Detroit Casino Revenues and Wagering Taxes—2005*. Lansing, MI: Michigan Gaming Control Board.

Michigan Gaming Control Board. 2006. *Detroit Casino Revenues and Wagering Taxes—2006*. Lansing, MI: Michigan Gaming Control Board.

Mikesell, J. L. 1994. State lottery sales and economic activity. *National Tax Journal* 47: 165–171.

Mikesell, J. L. and Zorn, C. K. 1987. State lottery sales: Separating the influence of markets and game structure. *Growth and Change* 18: 10–19.

Mississippi State Tax Commission. 2006. *Casino Gross Gaming Revenues*. Jackson, MS: Mississippi State Tax Commission.

Mississippi State Tax Commission. 2006. *Tax Revenues from Gaming*. Jackson, MS: Mississippi State Tax Commission.

Missouri Gaming Commission. 2006. *Annual Report to the General Assembly: Fiscal Year 2006*. Jefferson City, MO: Missouri Gaming Commission.

Moss, S. E., Ryan, C., and Wagoner, C. B. 2003. An empirical test of Butler's resort product life cycle: Forecasting casino winnings. *Journal of Travel Research* 41: 393–399.

Mosteller, F. and Tukey, J. W. 1977. *Data Analysis and Regression: A Second Course in Statistics*. Reading, MA: Addison–Wesley.

Nevada Gaming Commission. 2006. *Quarterly Report for the Quarter Ended June 30, 2006*. Carson City, NV: Nevada Gaming Commission.

New Jersey Casino Control Commission. 2005. *Monthly Press Release and Statistical Summary*. Trenton, NJ: New Jersey Casino Control Commission.

New Jersey Casino Control Commission. 2006. *Monthly Press Release and Statistical Summary*. Trenton, NJ: New Jersey Casino Control Commission.

New Mexico Gaming Control Board. 2006. *Quarterly Licensee Quick Facts: FY 2006*. Las Cruces, NM: New Mexico Gaming Control Board.

New York State Lottery. 2006. *Basic Financial Statements: March 31, 2006 and 2005.* Albany, NY: New York State Lottery.
Nichols, M. W. 1998a. Deregulation and cross-border substitution in Iowa's riverboat gambling industry. *Journal of Gambling Studies* 14: 151–172.
Nichols, M. W. 1998b. The impact of deregulation on casino win in Atlantic City. *Review of Industrial Organization* 13: 713–726.
Oklahoma Office of the State Auditor and Inspector. 2006a. *Oklahoma Horse Racing Commission Statistical Audit Report of Gaming Operations: Calendar Year 2005.* Oklahoma City, OK: Office of the State Auditor and Inspector.
Oklahoma Office of the State Auditor and Inspector. 2006b. *Oklahoma Horse Racing Commission Statistical Audit Report of Gaming Operations: June 2006.* Oklahoma City, OK: Office of the State Auditor and Inspector.
Potiowsky, T. and Parker, C. 2000. Oregon's lottery revenue forecast. Paper presented at the Federation of Tax Administrators Annual Revenue Estimating and Tax Research Conference, September 24–27, Waterville Valley, NH.
Przybylski, M., Felenstein, D., Freeman, D., and Littlepage, L. 1998. Does gambling complement the tourist industry? Some empirical evidence of import substitution and demand displacement. *Tourism Economics* 4: 213–232.
Rhode Island Lottery. 2006. *Comprehensive Annual Financial Report: For the Fiscal Year Ended June 30, 2006.* Cranston, RI: Rhode Island Lottery.
Rivenbark, W. C. 1998. The tax incidence of casino gaming in Mississippi. *Public Finance Review* 26: 583–598.
South Dakota Commission on Gaming. 2006. *Annual Report: FY 06.* Pierre, SD: South Dakota Commission on Gaming.
Thalheimer, R. and Ali, M. M. 2003. The demand for casino gaming. *Applied Economics* 35: 907–918.
West Virginia Lottery. 2006. *Comprehensive Annual Financial Report for the Fiscal Year Ended June 30, 2006.* Charleston, WV: West Virginia Lottery.

Chapter 9

Estimating and Forecasting Welfare Caseloads

Shiferaw Gurmu and William J. Smith

Contents

Introduction

Since the passage of the Personal Responsibility and Work Opportunity Reconciliation Act (PRWORA) of 1996, renewed interest in examining all aspects of the welfare programs and the population receiving government assistance has been observed. This chapter focuses on presenting an overview of modeling welfare caseloads and on developing forecasting methods for welfare caseloads, with an emphasis on Temporary Assistance for Needy Families (TANF) program. The purpose of the chapter is threefold. First, an overview of the caseload literature, with a focus on the impact of the business cycle and welfare reform on TANF caseloads and its predecessor program—Aid to Families with Dependent Children (AFDC)—is provided. Special attention is paid to studies that develop models that can reasonably forecast changes in welfare caseloads over time using state-level (in some cases city-level) administrative data. Second, various approaches to forecasting welfare caseloads are examined. These include simple time trend approaches, more complex time series models, panel data econometric models, and dynamic models of welfare caseloads, whereby changes in welfare caseloads are explained by past values of caseloads, economic conditions as well as policy environment, and a Markov forecasting method that exploits the dynamics in caseload entries and exits (Grogger 2005, Gurmu and Smith 2005a,b). Third, an application using Georgia TANF administrative data is provided. Using a dynamic model of TANF caseloads under different specification choices, short- (up to 12 months ahead) and long-term (up to 29 months ahead) caseload forecasts are provided and the accuracy of the projections are assessed. The forecasts are driven from a sluggish adjustment of current caseloads to past caseloads, lags in economic conditions (e.g., national and state unemployment rates), and nonstationarities in caseloads, particularly, at monthly frequencies. Other potential applications are also considered, including food stamp caseloads and Medicaid enrollments. Finally, overarching considerations in modeling welfare caseloads at the state level are provided.

Discussions of the interactions between block grant funding, growth in welfare caseloads, changes in different programs, and states evolving policies on welfare eligibility and benefits are presented on a number of occasions in the chapter.

The section on The Need for Accurate Forecasts sets the stage by focusing on the question: Why are accurate welfare caseload forecasts needed? The section titled Overview of the Caseload Literature provides a review of the caseload literature, with a focus on modeling and forecasting aggregate welfare caseloads followed by the section on Estimation and Forecasting Methods. The section titled Application: Estimating Welfare Caseloads describes the data and presents estimation results. The section on Application: Forecasting Welfare Caseloads presents TANF projection results. Other potential applications are also considered. The last section concludes.

The Need for Accurate Forecasts

Changes in the federal welfare grant formula from an entitlement program under the AFDC to a block grant under PRWORA has increased the uncertainty faced by states looking for future funding assurance and overall funding adequacy for welfare programs.* The recent state budget shortfalls brought on by the 2001 recession exacerbated the lack of security in funding. Many states trying to balance their budgets have made cuts to welfare programs or made the requirements for receiving welfare benefits more stringent. However, even during the 2001 recession, TANF caseloads continued to decline.

There remains a considerable debate as to the source of the decline. Some cite the decline in welfare roles as clear evidence that policy changes under welfare reform have directly reduced welfare participation. Increased work requirements, lifetime benefit limitations, and the imposition of harsh sanctions for participants who did not meet the new TANF program requirements, are identified as the incentives necessary to push welfare participants in the direction of economic self-sufficiency.† Others credit the unusually strong economic conditions of the mid- and late 1990s as the source of the reduction in participation. During this period of economic expansion, many adult welfare participants found employment and gained work experience that they were lacking before that point. It is likely that both changes made the welfare system under PRWORA, and the prevailing economic conditions that occurred at the same time played a role in the precipitous decline in caseloads. However, the determination of which was the major and

* King and Mueser (2005), in Chapters 1–2, discuss the structure of welfare reform and trends in caseloads and employment, with a focus on six cities: Atlanta, Baltimore, Chicago, Fort Lauderdale, Houston, and Kansas City.

† Using a dynamic discrete choice model, Gurmu et al. (2007) study the employment experiences of TANF recipients living in Atlanta.

minor cause could provide valuable information that might be used to improve the effectiveness of program requirements and provide states with insight into how to predict their future caseloads. Under the current welfare system, policy makers can limit access to control state welfare. Nevertheless, the question remains as to how to continue to effectively provide a social safety net for those who are truly in need when economic conditions change dramatically in the negative direction. The current uncertain consequences of a severe economic downturn and the potential for future changes in the federal funding of welfare programs have provided strong incentives for state welfare administrators across the country to find ways to accurately predict and reduce their welfare caseloads. In 1997, the state of Washington even passed legislation (43.88C.010) creating a caseload forecast council, whose job is to prepare and submit an official forecast of state caseloads to be used for budgetary purposes.

AFDC—TANF's predecessor—began as an entitlement program. An entitlement program is one that must serve any eligible person who signs up for the program. Under AFDC, states were free to be more generous with welfare benefits than required by federal law; however, they were not free to be less generous than the law allowed. PRWORA, the legislation establishing TANF, made substantial changes to the way welfare was administered. First, it placed strict limitations on the length of time individuals could continue receiving welfare and required able-bodied recipients to obtain work within a two-year period. Coupled with the new time limitations was a change in the way federal welfare grants were distributed. Rather than money being distributed based on the number of individuals receiving welfare, states now receive a block grant. More control over the eligibility requirements was also shifted from the federal government to the states. TANF set limits on maximum rather than minimum benefits.

The federal programmatic changes meant that welfare administrators had to substantially rethink their approach to providing welfare services. Before TANF, states and the federal government shared the cost of AFDC, and therefore, federal funding depended somewhat on state expenditures. Because the federal funding now comes in the form of a block grant, substantial growth in state-level TANF eligibility could force adjustments to state eligibility requirements to stay within federal funding allotments. Potential alternatives to eligibility adjustments include increasing taxes to support a state's TANF commitments, reducing TANF benefits for all currently eligible recipients, changing the internal structure of TANF benefits, or reducing spending on other state programs to offset increased spending on welfare.

Current federal funding levels and recent trends in state-level TANF caseloads have not yet led any state legislators to face these difficult choices. Given the reduction in welfare cases since the late 1990s, some recent federal legislative initiatives propose to reduce the size of the federal block grants. If the block grants were to be substantially reduced or if TANF caseloads were to make a dramatic rebound, or both, states may be forced to make some difficult decisions about how to allocate TANF dollars among its eligible population or be forced to reallocate state tax revenues differently among important programs within the state. For this reason, accurate prediction of state-level caseloads and turning points in caseload trends becomes crucial in developing proactive funding policies related to the welfare-eligible population.

Overview of the Caseload Literature

Modeling Aggregate Caseloads and Recent Trends

There are a variety of studies that have estimated the effects of economic conditions, participants' characteristics, changing policies, past welfare participation, past caseloads, and seasonal fluctuations on the state-level TANF caseloads. In the process of developing estimates of caseloads, some researchers have also tried to evaluate the effectiveness of competing econometric models in forecasting caseloads. A central debate within the recent caseload modeling literature is over the relative size of the effect from economic conditions versus policy changes subsequent to the passage of PRWORA.*

Ziliak et al. (2000) used state-level monthly panel data to measure the relative effects of different macroeconomic conditions along with welfare reform policies to account for the decline in AFDC caseloads over the period 1993–1996. Because their monthly measures of these variables were not seasonally adjusted, they used month-of-year dummies to capture seasonal fluctuations in both caseloads and employment. They estimated a simple static model. A first-difference (FD) model was used to remove any linear time trend in caseloads and to capture individual and state-level heterogeneity. The dynamic FD model was used to account for the possibility that the past level of caseloads may directly impact the future caseload levels. Their results suggested that the decline in per capita AFDC caseloads (caseloads over population) is primarily due to overall economic conditions, and not due to changes in welfare policies such as the extension of waivers from federal policies. They estimated that approximately two-thirds of the national caseload decline is due to fluctuations in economic activity.

Looking within a state for determinants of welfare usage, Brady et al. (2000) examined the factors that affect the duration of welfare spells and exits at the individual level and caseloads at the county level. Using a monthly panel for California spanning the years 1985–1997, they estimated a model of duration, controlling for residential location (urban versus rural). For California, a larger share of the

* See, for example, Bartik and Elberts (1999), Blank (2001), Figlio and Ziliak (1999), Figlio et al. (2000), Wallace and Blank (1999), and Ziliak et al. (2000, 2003).

population receiving aid is in rural counties. Furthermore, rural aid recipients are more likely to move into and out of assistance programs. As a result, rural welfare participants have both more increased and shorter welfare spells than their urban counterparts. The authors concluded, however, that the entry–exit patterns of rural welfare participants is probably caused by the more cyclical nature of the agricultural employment patterns in these rural California counties, as compared with employment fluctuations in urban counties.

In a similar study, Figlio and Ziliak (2000) looked at the differences between rural and urban TANF and AFDC and food stamp caseloads and how these caseloads are affected by changes in both welfare policies and changes in the economic climate of each region. They speculated that it is possible that economic events and changes in welfare policy may have different impacts in urban versus rural areas in a state. They used caseload data from Oregon and Wisconsin because of these states' proactive history of welfare reform. For example, in February 1993, Oregon requested and was allowed a waiver that required more clients to participate in the Job Opportunities and Basic Skills (JOBS) education and training program. Welfare recipients, who did not comply with state rules, faced program sanctions. Using a two-state panel, they estimated caseloads controlling for local economic conditions. Rather than looking at state-level caseloads, they examined county-level caseloads. Using data on unemployment rates, population characteristics, the number of welfare waivers approved, and other county-level administrative welfare data, they estimated the effects on county-level caseloads. In the static models for both states, they found substantial differences in the impact of local macroeconomic variables by geographic location, which extend to both the AFDC and TANF caseloads and the food stamp caseloads. However, once they accounted for the business cycle and caseload dynamics, the effect of geographic location is substantially diminished. This suggests that much of the difference in urban and rural welfare usage can be attributed to differences in local economic conditions. This supports the conclusions of Brady et al. (2000).

Many of the recent studies (e.g., Wallace and Blank 1999, Ziliak et al. 2000) of welfare enrollment concluded that the lion's share of the fluctuation in welfare caseloads is not due to welfare policies or welfare reform efforts, but rather due to local economic conditions. However, the 2001 recession did not result in large-scale welfare reenrollment, as expected. Despite conventional wisdom, national welfare rolls continued a slow decline during that period. Rising unemployment during the recession did not produce the expected large-scale increase in TANF enrollment. In fact, some state time limits had already led to the expelling of families from the rolls. The question then became, "When would the turning point in welfare rolls occur?" Most standard forecasting models tend to make relatively large errors as turning points approach; therefore, accurate prediction of turning points would lead to substantial improvements in forecasting. Given that eligibility is now primarily determined by the state, turning points present logistical problems for administrators who are charged with developing eligibility requirements. Therefore, accurate prediction of turning points would be of particular interest to welfare administrators because they have typically faced budgets that shrank (or remained constant) as eligibility for the programs they administer increased.

Figure 9.1 shows March 2003 TANF rolls as a percent of August 1996 rolls. As of 2003, welfare rolls for the United States were at 46.3 percent of what they

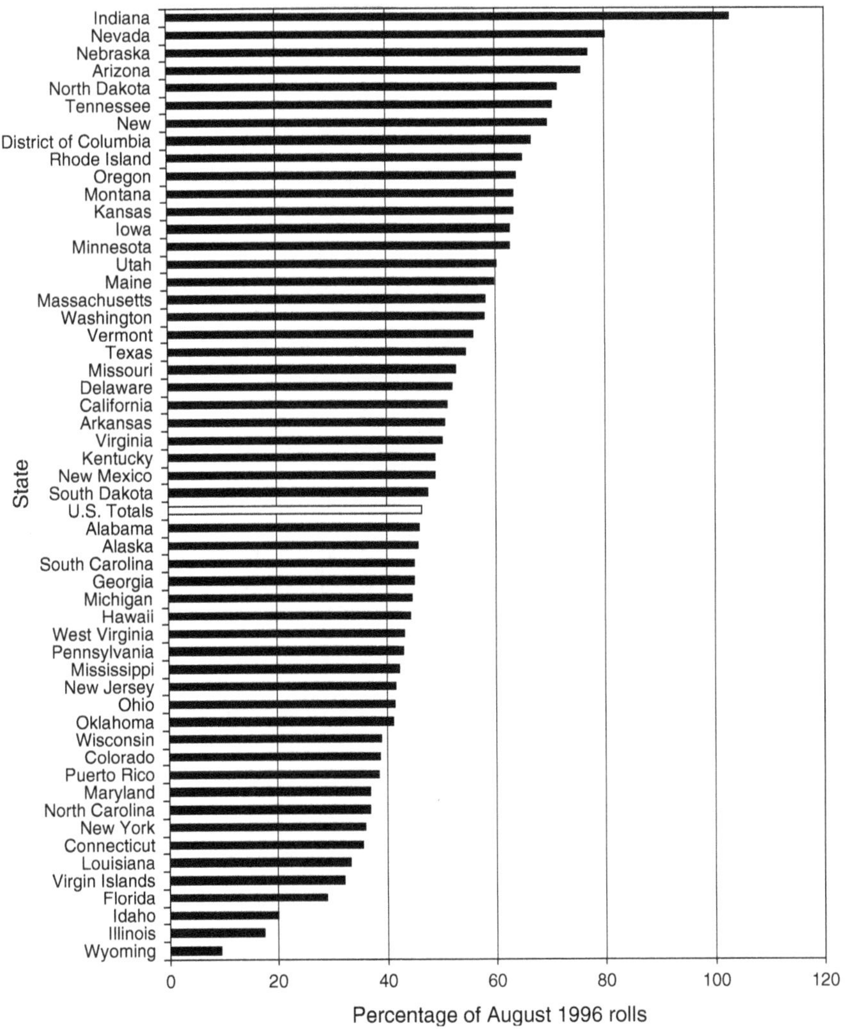

Figure 9.1 March 2003 TANF rolls as a percentage of August 1996 rolls. (Calculations from welfare rolls data from the U.S. Department of Health and Human Services, Administration of Children and Families at http://www.acf.hhs.gov, accessed March 2006.)

were in 1996. Furthermore, 29 states had maintained TANF caseload levels at or below 50 percent of what they were in 1996. However, some states have recently experienced a noticeable rebound in TANF cases. Indiana, Nevada, Nebraska, and Arizona have seen their welfare rolls creep upward toward prereform levels. As of March 2003, Indiana exceeded its number of families on its prereform rolls. For these states, the turning point may have already occurred.*

Forecasting Practices

Practitioners versus Academic Studies

There are primarily two major groups interested in producing forecasts of welfare caseloads: state welfare administrators and academic researchers, with some interaction between them. State agencies charged with administering TANF are the organizations most interested in the accuracy of caseload prediction, primarily for budgeting purposes. Typically, officials in these agencies prepare multiple alternative forecasts using different methodologies and then select a final technique based on (in-sample) accuracy and institutional knowledge. Over time, they compare these estimates against new caseload data as it becomes available to aid in the future method selection. The second group comes from a more academic environment, which has the development of an appropriate methodology set of determinants for estimating caseloads as its goal. Some of these studies are reviewed in the previous section.

In our review of the caseload literature and forecasting practices, we have examples of reports that state welfare agencies produced for planning and budgeting purposes. We also provide examples of forecasts that are more academic in nature and intended to explore more fundamental issues related to the forecasting process.

We group most of the past studies aimed at predicting caseloads into two broad methodologies: time series and econometric forecasting. The former uses past history of caseloads to predict future caseloads. In contrast, econometric forecasting methods model causal relationships between caseloads and (nondeterministic) explanatory variables, including own-variable dynamics. Forecasters base time series forecasts on either simple trend forecasting or complex models incorporating regime switching.

* Hotchkiss et al. (2005) consider the role of changes in policy regimes and socioeconomic factors in explaining welfare exit and employment rates of welfare recipients during the 1990s in six metropolitan areas. For the same set of six sites, Gurmu et al. (2005a,b) provide analysis of job stability and earnings of welfare caretakers, including the role played by personal and job characteristics. Using county-level data, Black et al. (2005) examine the effect of long-term changes in local economic opportunities for low-skilled workers on welfare expenditures.

Trend Forecasting

Trend forecasting uses history of caseloads to predict future caseload levels and is relatively straightforward to implement. Modeling the trend can also produce a reasonably good short-term forecast with a minimum of observations. Unlike the econometric model, time series methods do not require additional explanatory variables. Thus, they are not encumbered by problems associated with the trade off between additional regressors and the associated loss in degrees of freedom. Typically, the forecaster's main consideration in developing these types of purely time series models is describing the behavior of the data over time. The presence of seasonality, long-term trends, or some other recurring pattern in the series generally necessitates choosing between alternative weighting schemes to maintain accuracy in the forecast.

A major disadvantage of this technique is closely tied to one of its advantages. Because it does not include explanatory variables, it does not provide much, if any, information about why caseloads change. Forecasters assume only past caseload variation to explain future fluctuations. A second disadvantage is that forecasting a trend model does not incorporate changes in program policies. The passage of PRWORA increased the flexibility with which states can administer their own welfare systems as it allows each state to determine its eligibility requirements for TANF participation. Although time series models that are based solely on historical data can forecast regular or recurring fluctuations in caseload levels, these models are not able to anticipate caseload changes caused by program policy changes. Funding changes, more restrictive time limitations, or redefining who is eligible within the state's population are all policy changes that are allowed under the current federal law, and each would affect caseloads. However, each change would require some *post hoc* adjustment to the final forecasted caseloads if forecasters only use trend models. The lack of prior information about how similar policy measures affect caseloads seriously limits the usefulness of strictly time series models for forecasting caseloads. Typically, historical caseload data are not available in the presence of such policy changes. Thus, forecasters are forced to "adjust" the estimates to reflect their best guess as to the impact of the policy change.

In some cases, time trend methods may be both effective and appropriate. Oregon's Department of Human Services (DHS), as the following quote illustrates, relies heavily on time trend methodologies to forecast a variety of welfare-related program caseloads, such as food stamps, TANF, and Temporary Assistance for Domestic Violence Survivors (TA-DVS), and other employment and day care–related programs.

> DHS determines how many clients it *has* served in the past and applies mathematical models to project how many it *will* serve in the future.

> There are counts of clients for each month and the forecast predicts a number of clients for each future month of the forecast. (Oregon Department of Human Services 2006)

Since 2000, Oregon's TANF caseloads followed almost a linear trend, and thus, future caseloads may be more easily and effectively estimated with trend-based models. Many other states use time trend forecasts as part of their arsenal aimed at caseload prediction, but seldom are these methods the only ones they use.

Econometric Methods

The standard alternative approach to time trend forecasting is econometric forecasting. However, the choice of a forecasting method is rarely a mutually exclusive selection process. Forecasters use time trend and econometric forecasting methods in conjunction with one another. Econometric forecasting techniques attempt to directly model caseloads as a function of societal and individual demographic characteristics along with prevailing local economic conditions as well as policy changes that are expected to influence enrollment. Because these models are based on some hypothesized connection between caseload levels and a set of explanatory variables, forecasters interpret the results as evidence of a causal relationship. Then by using expectations or predictions of important explanatory variables, analysts can develop a forecast of caseloads (e.g., rising unemployment might signal an increase in TANF cases). The primary advantage of using an econometric approach is that it allows the researcher to explain not only how, but why caseloads are expected to change. Knowing the impact of policy changes on caseloads also permits administrators to conduct policy simulations and gauge the impact of future policy changes.

Several states produce their own welfare caseload forecasts. Common to all state forecasts included here is the incorporation of state- and national-level economic factors (e.g., unemployment rate). The Georgia Department of Human Resources (Gurmu and Smith 2005b), the Texas Health and Human Services (2002a), the Nevada State Welfare Division (2004), and the Tennessee DHS (Center for Business and Economic Research 2003) use econometrically based methods to model and forecast their state caseloads. In the Tennessee results that apply to all states, the independent variables are grouped into four types: economic and demographic factors that increase caseloads, policy factors that increase caseloads, economic and demographic factors that reduce caseloads, and policy factors that reduce caseloads. This categorization provides policy makers with direct information on the factors that are under their control and their potential impacts along with factors that are not under their control. Some of these states also produce, not one, but multiple forecasts, including time trend forecasts, for comparison. Ultimately, each state evaluates its forecast accuracy and in doing so they prefer the forecasting method or methods that consistently perform well (see, e.g., Center for Business and Economic Research 2003, Texas Health and Human Services 2002a).

Because an econometric model of TANF caseloads provides information about the causes of caseload fluctuations, they also provide a list of potential policy levers that forecasters can use to change the caseload levels. The techniques used to produce an appropriate forecast range from simple to fairly complex. Any independent variables that are under the control of a policy maker and have a significant impact on the level of caseloads potentially can influence future caseload levels. This is important all by itself because often welfare administrators not only wish to forecast costs, but are also looking for avenues of controlling cost. The main disadvantage of the econometric approach is its cost of implementation. Often these models are composed of a large number of independent variables, and data collection can be both difficult and time-consuming. Forecasters must find or forecast values of the independent variables to produce the caseload estimates.

Markov Methods

Forecasters use the Markov chain forecasting technique in more recent studies of welfare participation because of its ability to forecast turning points (Grogger 2005). Previously mentioned studies of welfare largely ignored the potential effects of time limitations, entries, and exits in their model specification. Because of time limits, past participation influences future eligibility for TANF case heads. Strict time limitations force cases off the rolls and forecasters should account for these changes in their modeling process as explained in the following quote:

> Markov forecasting is based on a model of caseload evolution. In the simplest terms, today's caseload depends on yesterday's caseload plus entries and exits. Because today's caseload depends in part on yesterday's caseload, the caseload exhibits inertia. Markov forecasting exploits that inertia to base forecasts of the future caseload on current entries and exits. (Grogger 2005, p. 3)

Grogger (2005) used a Markov chain in forecasting welfare caseloads for the state of California. He used a sample of monthly welfare caseloads from July 1985 to March 2005 to estimate the dynamic nature of TANF eligibility under time limits. He found that turning points in entry and exit rates tended to precede turning points in the overall caseload. Therefore, he was able to accurately predict directional changes in welfare caseloads throughout the span of his data. Grogger's model provides evidence that caseload changes lag behind changes in poverty rates. This implies that caseloads will begin to rise after an increase in the rate of poverty.

Forecasting versus Managing Caseloads

Now that states have additional control over their eligibility under TANF, they should be able to more accurately predict their enrollment. If they can anticipate changes in the economy or in demographics or in the entry and exit behavior that might lead to a shift in eligible applicants, they could change their policies in advance and keep costs from rising too quickly; the process has become an endogenous one by its design.

According to Texas Health and Human Services (2002b), the proportion of the TANF caseloads that are "payee" cases (child-only cases) is growing. In fiscal year (FY)2002, the monthly average reached 35 percent of the total caseload. The growth is attributed to cases in which the parent(s) "do not meet citizen requirement" or have "timed out" of the system. In families that reach the state time limit of benefits, the adult(s) become ineligible, but the children remain on TANF with a cash grant. There is no work requirement in law for the caretaker adults in either of these cases. This trend is also occurring nationally, with the U.S. proportion being around 30 percent child-only cases in 2002.

There continues to be a problem with families cycling on and off TANF. Although the proportion of the TANF caseloads, which are former TANF recipients, has dropped slightly in the past two years, it is about 50 percent for FY2002. Many factors are associated with recidivism. According to *Texas families in transition: surviving without TANF* (Texas Health and Human Services 2002b), a study commissioned by the Texas DHS, many of the adults who leave TANF reapply within 18 months. They also leave without transitional benefits, and in many cases without food stamps. There is some general confusion among the adults interviewed in the study as to their eligible benefits after they leave TANF.

Through a childcare program called Choices, Texas has significantly increased childcare funding in recent years and in the process serving thousands of additional children. However, as more TANF families participate in Choices and enter the workforce, Texas uses more childcare funding to meet Choices and transitional childcare demands, both of which are priority categories. Under current funding methods, this leaves fewer funds available for "at-risk" childcare for low-income working families.

The following section presents estimation and forecasting methods. We focus on the specifications of models that forecasters employ in the empirical sections of this chapter.

Estimation and Forecasting Methods

We specify basic time series and econometrics models for empirical analysis and forecasting of welfare caseloads. These models go beyond trend analysis of historical caseload data. Taken together, caseload forecasts from these models allow for changes in economic conditions, welfare reform policies, and own dynamics in caseloads. As noted, the Markov method is particularly useful in predicting turning points in welfare rolls.

Static and Dynamic Specifications

We start with the specification of the static model of welfare caseloads, in which the variables for any observation is from the same time period. Because estimating and forecasting welfare caseloads (such as TANF) at a state level is important to policy makers, we focus on the analysis of caseloads for a given state over time in, for example, months t ($t = 1, \ldots, T$). Unlike state-panel data models where welfare reform policies and implementation affect states at different times, in state-specific caseload analysis such as ours, forecasters can identify the impact of changes in welfare policies only through time series variation in caseloads. Because AFDC and TANF caseloads are likely to be nonstationary, but could be difference stationary; this chapter considers first difference (FD) models. The FD regression model is

$$\Delta \log C_t = \Delta A_t \alpha + W_t \beta + X_t \gamma + \varepsilon_{1t} \tag{9.1}$$

where

C_t = caseload in month t
A_t = measure of economic activity in log or level forms (possibly a vector of measures of economic activity)
W_t = vector of measures of welfare policies
X_t = vector of other control variables, including monthly effects
ε = error terms.

As argued by Ziliak et al. (2000), for example, the static framework is restrictive in that it ignores the possibility that caseloads may sluggishly adjust to changing economic and political conditions. Further, lagged economic indicators (e.g., local unemployment rate) may be important because welfare recipients are less likely to instantaneously move from welfare to work. We specify a dynamic model of welfare caseloads, whereby lagged values of caseloads as well as lagged values of unemployment rates (or employment) and other controls are added to the right-hand side of the caseloads equation. The dynamic FD regression model can be specified as

$$\Delta \log C_t = \sum_{i=1}^{I} \rho_i \Delta \log C_{t-i} + \sum_{j=1}^{J} \Delta A_{t-j} \alpha_j + W_t \beta + X_t \gamma + \varepsilon_{2t} \tag{9.2}$$

where variables are as defined in Equation 9.1 and elements of W_t and X_t can be in logarithmic or FD form. Generally, the lag lengths for caseload dynamics (I) and for distributed lag effects of the business cycle (J) need not be restricted to be the same.

In the empirical section, we also consider the level form of Equations 9.1 and 9.2, where ΔC_t is the dependent variable, and control variables are also in level form. Forecasting caseloads using econometric models generally requires predicting future values of explanatory variables such as business cycle factors, which introduces additional source of forecast error in caseloads. To minimize problems that may arise due to forecasting the right-hand side variables, one can use a dynamic model in log FD of the form:

$$\Delta \log C_t = \sum_{i=1}^{I} \rho_i \, \Delta \log C_{t-i} + Z_t\gamma + \varepsilon_{3t} \tag{9.3}$$

where Z_t is now a vector of deterministic regressors such as seasonal components, where future values are known. Dynamic forecasting from model 3 can generate forecasts of future caseloads using recursively computed forecast of the past values of welfare caseloads. Alternatively, we can capture the dynamics in FD of log of caseloads by using a time series model with autoregressive moving average (ARMA) disturbances. A simple model is

$$\Delta \log C_t = Z_t \gamma + v_t \tag{9.4}$$

where v_t are ARMA disturbances.

Markov Forecasting Method

Models with regime switching, including threshold models, have long been used in business cycle analysis and forecasting turning points in economic activity, including where forecasters can define turning points in terms of times separating expansions and contractions (Diebold 2004, Chapter 7, Hamilton 1994, Chapter 22). In such a setup, switches between, for example, good and bad states, are governed by the Markov process.

In the context of welfare caseload analysis, Grogger (2005) developed forecasts based on Markov chain method. The basic Markov framework relates the current month caseload to past caseload and current entries and exits:

$$C_t = C_{t-1} + \text{entry}_t - \text{exit}_t \tag{9.5}$$

where

C_t = caseload during the current month
C_{t-1} = caseload for the last month
Entries and exits = caseloads for this month.

Equation 9.5 is basically a first-order Markov chain process with an observable threshold, as opposed to traditional latent state models, because it depends on last month caseloads and the current entries and exits.

The Markov forecasting approach uses a broadly defined notion of implied steady state (ISS), which generally displays volatility over time but provides a leading indicator of the caseload that forecasters can use as a basis of caseload forecasting. Grogger (2005) proposed using smoothing techniques to adjust the ISS, and then using the smoothed ISS series for forecasting caseloads. Alternatively, forecasters can obtain the adjusted ISS series from smoothed entries and exits. During the implementation, Grogger adopted Lowess smoother. The forecasts for welfare caseloads are then generated from the regression of caseloads on lagged smoothed ISS.

Application: Estimating Welfare Caseloads

Data

The data on state-level monthly AFDC and TANF rolls come from the Georgia Department of Human Resources (DHR). These include all cases that are enrolled and are currently eligible to receive benefits. The monthly caseloads sample runs from January 1985 to November 2005, but the sample for our analysis is restricted to post-1990 period: January 1990–November 2005. Consequently, for the post-1990 period, we are able to use data on employment series for the state and by industry classified according to the North American Industry Classification System (NAIC). As of December 2000, the data also consist of the number of TANF closures due to the time limit.

Employment-related explanatory variables include the U.S. employment rate, U.S. total employment, Georgia's unemployment rate, labor force, total employment, and total unemployment. This data set is from the Bureau of Labor Statistics and is available on a monthly basis. State population is from the Bureau of the Census; however, it is available on an annual basis. Georgia's per capita income is from the Bureau of Economic Analysis on an annual basis, and is similarly spread over the corresponding year. In addition to total employment, we obtain industrial employment to control for differences in the effect of individual industrial categories of jobs. This data set also comes from the Bureau of Labor Statistics.

Summary statistics and definition of variables are given in Table 9.1. The plot of monthly caseloads in Georgia during the period January 1985–November 2005 is shown in Figure 9.2. After moderate growth in the 1980s, the AFDC caseloads reached 100,000 cases by 1990. Between 1990 and 1994, the caseloads reached a peak of 141,200 cases, and then started to decline, largely paralleling the national trend. By June 2000, Georgia TANF roll declined to about 50,000 cases. Researchers credit welfare reform with the rapid and sustained reduction in welfare cases (e.g., see King and Mueser 2005, Chapter 1). In the next four years, caseloads grew moderately, followed by a generally declining trend in 2004 and 2005, and reaching a minimum of about 37,000 by the end of 2005.

Table 9.1 Definition of Variables and Summary Statistics for Georgia, January 1990–November 2005

Variable	*Definition*	*Mean*	*Standard Deviation*	*Minimum*	*Maximum*
Caseloads	Total AFDC and TANF caseloads	90,935	37,554	36,560	141,153
Unemployment rate	Unemployment rate	4.8	0.9	3.0	7.5
Employment	Total employment	3,730,986	397,327	3,090,488	4,339,203
National unemployment rate	U.S. unemployment rate	5.5	1.0	3.6	8.2
National employment	U.S. total employment (1000s)	129,522	8,085	115,837	143,340
Population	Population size	7,762,421	786,833	6,512,602	9,111,497
Closures	Number of TANF closures due to time limit	73	113	0	355
Construction	Employment in construction	171	30	116	209
Finance	Employment in finance	189	24	153	224
Government	Employment in government	585	37	522	658
Manufacturing	Employment in manufacturing	505	37	436	551
Retail	Employment in retail	767	75	636	889
Service	Employment in services	416	43	336	492
Transportation	Employment in transportation and utilities	2,862	352	2,276	3,329
Wholesale	Employment in wholesale	188	20	157	213

Note: All employment figures by industry for Georgia are in thousands. The employment numbers for Georgia are based on NAIC system. The empirical analysis includes indicators for welfare policies and seasonal patterns.

Source: Calculation from the datasets obtained from the Georgia Department of Human Resources at http://domestic.gsu.edu/gadp/index.html (accessed March 2006); Bureau of Labor Statistics at http://www.bls.gov (accessed March 2006); Bureau of Census at http://www.census.gov (accessed March 2006); and Bureau of Economics Analysis at http://www.bea.gov (accessed March 2006).

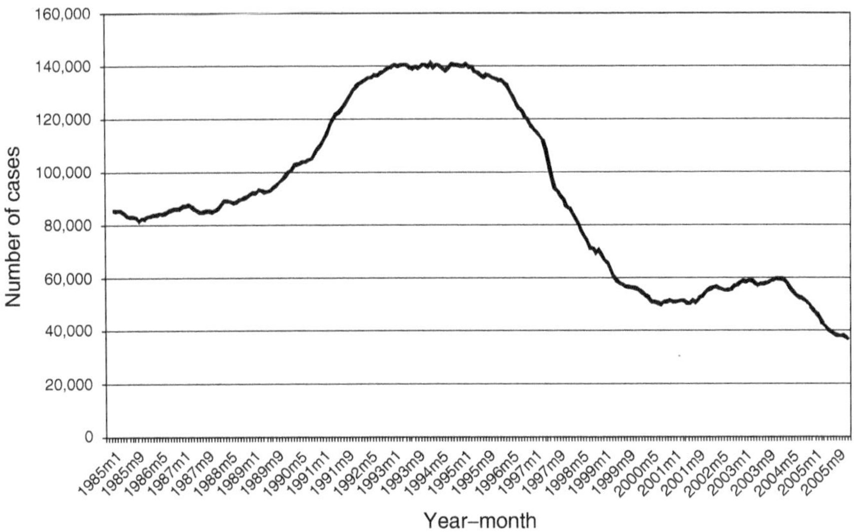

Figure 9.2 AFDC and TANF caseloads for Georgia (January 1985–November 2005). (Caseloads data obtained from the Georgia Department of Human Resources, http://domestic.gsu.edu/gadp/index.html.)

Estimation Results

We use monthly AFDC and TANF caseloads from Georgia to investigate the responsiveness of caseloads to changes in economic conditions, such as local and national unemployment rates, welfare programs, and seasonal patterns. For the purpose of estimation, we focus on the period January 1990–November 2004, called period 1. First, we conducted both the augmented Dickey–Fuller (ADF) and the Phillips–Perron unit root tests to assess the stationarity of the monthly caseload and logarithm of caseload variables. We did not reject the null hypothesis of a unit root for the caseload series or its log using conventional levels of significance. There is strong evidence that TANF caseload (or log caseload) series is nonstationary. The result is similar to that found by Ziliak et al. (2000) using state-level monthly panel AFDC caseload data for the United States. However, when we focused on FD of these variables, we rejected the null hypothesis of a unit root at a 1 percent level of significance using the Phillips–Perron test and we rejected it at only 10 percent using the ADF unit root test. The results suggest that the TANF caseload, particularly in log form, is FD stationary. Consequently, we focused on estimation of welfare caseloads in FD form.

To assess the sensitivity of the results to choice of specification, we estimated various models, including static versus dynamic specification, level versus log form, time series versus econometric models, state versus local cyclical indicators, and specifications for short- versus long-term forecasting. We estimated variants of models specified in Equations 9.1 through 9.4 with least squares, where C_t in these equations is represented by caseloads (t) in the result tables. Because data on entries and exits are not available to us, we were unable to estimate the Markov chain model.

Table 9.2 reports estimation results for FD of AFDC and TANF caseloads from six specifications. Specification 1 is a time series model with an autoregressive error term, whereas model 2 is a dynamic model without measures of economic activity. Specifications 3 through 6 are dynamic models that differ by which measure of economic activity is included on the right-hand side: local (Georgia) versus national unemployment rate or the total employment. Table 9.3 also gives estimation results for a set of six specifications, but using FD of logarithms of caseloads as well as logs of most of the explanatory variables. Although we experimented with higher-order lags, the reported results are based on three lags for own-variable effects and distributed lag effects of economic and related variables.

We focus on the results from the preferred log specifications reported in Table 9.3. The results show that there is a strong own-variable (state-dependence) effect and significant lagged responses to changes in unemployment and employment rates. This is particularly true at the national level. Indeed, it seems that, as compared to local measures such as unemployment rate in Georgia, national measures of economic activity are strong predictors of changes in the state TANF caseloads, at least for in-sample predictions. By adding the unemployment rate coefficients, we observe that a one percentage point increase in local unemployment rate leads to a 1.4 percent increase in caseloads and a one percentage point increase in U.S. unemployment rate results in a 5.1 percent increase in the state caseloads. Likewise, a one percent decrease in local (national) employment lasting a quarter leads to 2.1 percent (2.4 percent) increase in caseloads, all things being equal.

The coefficient associated with the post-1996 dummy variable is always negative, and is significant in most specifications. TANF closures variable is marginally significant. Estimation results also show that there is significant seasonality in caseloads.

Specification 7 (not reported) considers employment (or log employment) in Georgia by eight major industries, listed in Table 9.1, taken together as a measure of economic activity. The results from this specification also reveal that there is strong positive state dependence. The employment coefficients are generally not tightly estimated, conceivably due to the high correlation among the employment series. However, employment in the construction industry has a significant impact on caseloads. A 1 percent decrease in employment in the construction industry lasting two months leads to a 0.3 percent increase in TANF caseloads.

To evaluate the model's forecasting performance, we varied the forecasting horizon. We used estimate models for caseloads for two additional time periods: period 2 spanning January 1990–March 2004 and period 3 covering January 1990–June 2003. We reported selected results in Tables 9A.1 through 9A.3 in the appendix. Although the numbers of observations are different, the results are largely consistent

Table 9.2 Estimates from FD Models, January 1990–November 2004 (Dependent Variable: FD of Welfare Caseloads)

Variable	Model 1	Model 2	Model 3 Unemployment Rate	Model 4 Employment	Model 5 National Unemployment Rate	Model 6 National Employment
FD caseloads ($t-1$)		0.4482*** (5.63)	0.4407*** (5.45)	0.3791*** (4.69)	0.3671*** (4.58)	0.3746*** (4.66)
FD caseloads ($t-2$)		0.3012*** (3.61)	0.3030*** (3.59)	0.2752*** (3.61)	0.2723*** (3.36)	0.2838*** (3.49)
FD caseloads ($t-3$)		0.0745 (0.93)	0.0625 (0.77)	0.0688** (0.88)	0.0687 (0.89)	0.0948 (1.22)
FD cyclical indicator (t)			179.0930 (0.73)	−0.0100** (−1.98)	925.1814** (2.41)	−0.4351*** (−2.81)
FD cyclical indicator ($t-1$)			171.2489 (0.70)	−0.0079 (−1.55)	848.9378** (2.20)	−0.3280* (−2.10)
FD cyclical indicator ($t-2$)			289.9280 (1.19)	−0.0130*** (−2.53)	867.559** (2.21)	−0.3165** (−1.98)
FD cyclical indicator ($t-3$)			294.8968 (1.21)	−0.0054*** (−1.05)	712.0119* (1.79)	−0.1716 (−1.09)
FD closures			2.0608 (1.06)	2.4783 (1.32)	2.5045 (1.35)	2.6586 (1.43)
FD population	No	No	Yes	Yes	Yes	Yes
1994 Quarter 2 dummy	Yes	Yes	Yes	Yes	Yes	Yes
1996 Quarter 2 dummy	Yes	Yes	Yes	Yes	Yes	Yes
Monthly dummies	Yes	Yes	Yes	Yes	Yes	Yes
AR(1)	0.7065*** (12.32)					
Akaike information criterion	16.29	16.17	16.21	16.15	16.12	16.12
Schwartz criterion	16.56	16.48	16.63	16.57	16.54	16.54

Note: t Ratios are within parentheses. Statistical significance at 10, 5, and 1 percent levels are denoted by *, **, and ***, respectively. Estimation models allow for endpoint adjustments due to differencing and lagging of variables. AR(1) denotes autoregressive process of order 1.

Source: Calculation from the datasets obtained from the Georgia Department of Human Resources at http://domestic.gsu.edu/gadp/index.html (accessed March 2006); Bureau of Labor Statistics at http://www.bls.gov (accessed March 2006); Bureau of Census at http://www.census.gov (accessed March 2006); and Bureau of Economics Analysis at http://www.bea.gov (accessed March 2006).

Table 9.3 Estimates from FD Log Models, January 1990–November 2004 (Dependent Variable: FD of Log of Welfare Caseloads)

			Model 3	Model 4	Model 5	Model 6
Variable	*Model 1*	*Model 2*	*Unemployment Rate*	*Log Employment*	*National Unemployment Rate*	*Log National Employment*
FD log caseloads ($t-1$)		0.3976*** (5.01)	0.3851*** (4.80)	0.3155*** (3.99)	0.2886*** (3.66)	0.3055*** (3.93)
FD log caseloads ($t-2$)		0.2926*** (3.57)	0.2863*** (3.49)	0.2428*** (3.10)	0.2366*** (3.03)	0.2502*** (3.21)
FD log caseloads ($t-3$)		0.1304 (1.63)	0.1228 (1.53)	0.1379* (1.82)	0.1364* (1.81)	0.1790** (2.36)
FD cyclical indicator (t)			0.0024 (0.80)	−0.4835** (−2.17)	0.0110** (2.37)	−0.6417*** (−2.80)
FD cyclical indicator ($t-1$)			0.0022 (0.74)	−0.2480 (−1.11)	0.0118** (2.53)	−0.4206* (−1.83)
FD cyclical indicator ($t-2$)			0.0055 (1.81)*	−0.8610*** (−3.85)	0.0156*** (3.25)	−0.680*** (−2.90)
FD cyclical indicator ($t-3$)			0.0041 (1.36)	−0.5080** (−2.22)	0.0122** (2.50)	−0.665*** (−2.88)
FD closures			0.0000 (1.42)	0.00004* (1.76)	0.00004* (1.86)	0.00004* (1.86)
FD population	No	No	Yes	Yes	Yes	Yes
1994 Quarter 2 dummy	Yes	Yes	Yes	Yes	Yes	Yes
1996 Quarter 2 dummy	Yes	Yes	Yes	Yes	Yes	Yes
Monthly dummies	Yes	Yes	Yes	Yes	Yes	Yes
AR(1)	0.6574*** (10.79)					
Akaike information criterion	−6.29	−6.41	−6.39	−6.51	−6.52	−6.54
Schwartz criterion	−6.02	−6.11	−5.98	−6.09	−6.10	−6.12

Note: t Ratios are within parentheses. Statistical significance at 10, 5, and 1 percent levels are denoted by *, **, and ***, respectively. Estimation models allow for endpoint adjustments due to differencing and lagging of variables.

Source: Calculation from the datasets obtained from the Georgia Department of Human Resources at http://domestic.gsu.edu/gadp/index.html (accessed March 2006); Bureau of Labor Statistics at http://www.bls.gov (accessed March 2006); Bureau of Census at http://www.census.gov (accessed March 2006); and Bureau of Economics Analysis at http://www.bea.gov (accessed March 2006).

with those reported in Tables 9.2 and 9.3 for period 1, January 1990–November 2004. For more details, compare Table 9.2 with Table 9A.1 and Table 9.3 with Tables 9A.2 and 9A.3. We focus on forecasting welfare caseloads in the following section.

Application: Forecasting Welfare Caseloads

Measuring Forecast Accuracy

The projection results are evaluated in terms of some accuracy measures that are commonly used in forecast evaluation. Suppose we have $T + S$ months of observed (or actual) TANF caseloads, and we use T observations in estimation, then the forecast sample is $s = 1, 2, \ldots, S$. For month s, the forecast error (E) is defined as the difference between the actual or observed TANF caseload (O) and its forecast (F) for month s is $E_s = O_s - F_s$. The projection performance measures are defined as

$$\text{AE}_s = |E_s|\text{: absolute error (cases for month } s\text{)}$$

$$\text{APE}_s = \left|\frac{E_s}{O}\right|\text{: absolute percentage error (percent for month } s\text{)}$$

$$\text{RMSE} = \sqrt{\frac{1}{S}\sum_{s=1}^{S} E_s^2}\text{: root mean square error (cases per month)}$$

$$\text{MAE} = \frac{1}{S}\sum_{s=1}^{S}\text{AE}_s\text{: mean absolute error (cases per month)}$$

$$\text{MAPE} = \frac{1}{S}\sum_{s=1}^{S}\text{APE}_s\text{: mean absolute percentage error (percent)}$$

$$\text{Theil IC} = \frac{\text{RMSE}}{\left[\sqrt{\frac{1}{S}\sum_{s=1}^{S} F_s^2} + \sqrt{\frac{1}{S}\sum_{s=1}^{S} O_s^2}\right]}\text{, Theil inequality coefficient (IC)}$$

Both MAPE and Theil IC are scale-invariant. Theil inequality lies between zero and unity, where zero indicates a perfect projection.

Short-Term Forecasting

The goal is to assess the forecasting performance of methods presented in the preceding sections, with focus on the dynamic models. We used a subset of the sample spanning January 1990–November 2004 for estimation. This leaves 12 observations, December 2004–November 2005 for forecast evaluation.

Future values of the regressors are predicted using simple time series models in FD of the form

$$\Delta X_t = Z_t\gamma + v_t$$

where

X_t = any of the measures of economic activity or TANF closures in level or log form
Z_t = vector of deterministic variables such as seasonal dummies
v_t = ARMA errors

Because the actual values of the explanatory variables are observed during the forecasting period, we can evaluate forecast accuracy using actual versus predicted independent variables.

We focused on forecasts generated from the estimates of the FD log models reported in Table 9.3. Figure 9.3 gives a comparison of the fitted and observed values of the FD log caseloads as well as the ensuing residuals from one of the models, model 2. The model fits the data reasonably well.

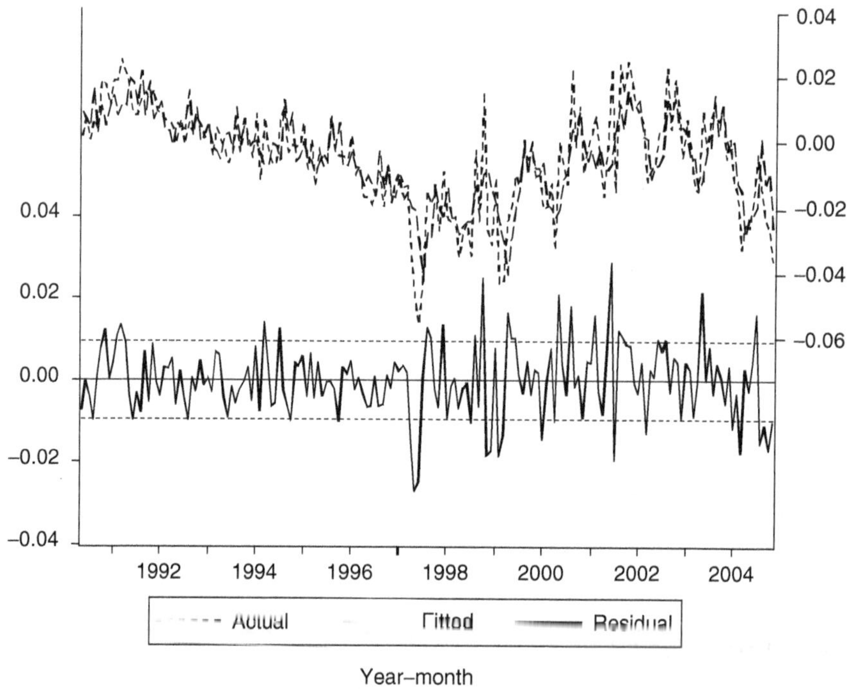

Figure 9.3 Actual versus fitted first-difference log caseload series (right-hand side scale) and residuals (left-hand side scale) from model 2, 1990:01–2004:11. (Calculations and analysis from the data obtained from the Georgia Department of Human Resources, http://domestic.gsu.edu/gadp/index.html.)

Table 9.4 Comparison of Six Forecasting Models for Caseloads (Forecast Period 2004:12–2005:11)

Model	*RMSE*	*MAE*	*MAPE*	*Theil IC*
1	2435	2267	5.830	0.030
2	668	582	1.471	0.008
3	646	815	2.042	0.012
4	1380	1280	3.258	0.017
5	2791	2590	6.694	0.034
6	1338	1240	3.177	0.016

Note: Estimation based on FD of log models with estimation period January 1990–November 2004.

Source: Calculation from the datasets obtained from the Georgia Department of Human Resources at http://domestic.gsu.edu/gadp/index.html (accessed March 2006); Bureau of Labor Statistics at http://www.bls.gov (accessed March 2006); Bureau of Census at http://www.census.gov (accessed March 2006); and Bureau of Economics Analysis at http://www.bea.gov (accessed March 2006).

Table 9.4 shows four measures of forecast accuracy for forecasting TANF caseloads 12 months out or ahead. Generally, model 2 (dynamic model without other regressors) dominates the remaining specification in terms of forecasting accuracy because the mean absolute percentage error of 1.47 percent and Theil's IC of 0.008 are much smaller than those of the rest of the models. The second best specification is model 3, a dynamic model with lagged local unemployment rate. Models 1 (time series model) and 5 perform worst. In some of these models, the forecast accuracy may have been affected adversely due to uncertainty in predicting explanatory variables. Indeed, this seems to be the case with model 5, which requires predicting the national unemployment rate. In fact, models with predicted regressors potentially have higher prediction errors because the reported results are based on conventional standard errors, and consequently ignore the additional source of error due to the predicted regressor. To shed further light on the prediction performance of the six models, Figure 9.4 provides plots of caseload forecasts for December 2004–November 2005. Models 2 and 3 generally produce better forecasts, whereas specifications 1 and 5 produce relatively high forecast errors, largely overpredicting the actual caseloads, particularly as the forecast horizon increases.

Out-of-sample point and interval forecasts for caseloads obtained from the preferred model (model 2) appear in Figure 9.5 and Table 9.5. The out-of-sample 95 percent predictions for caseloads are given in Figure 9A.1. The forecasts from this model seem quite accurate, with point forecasts closely following the observed caseloads throughout the forecasting period: December 2004–November 2005.

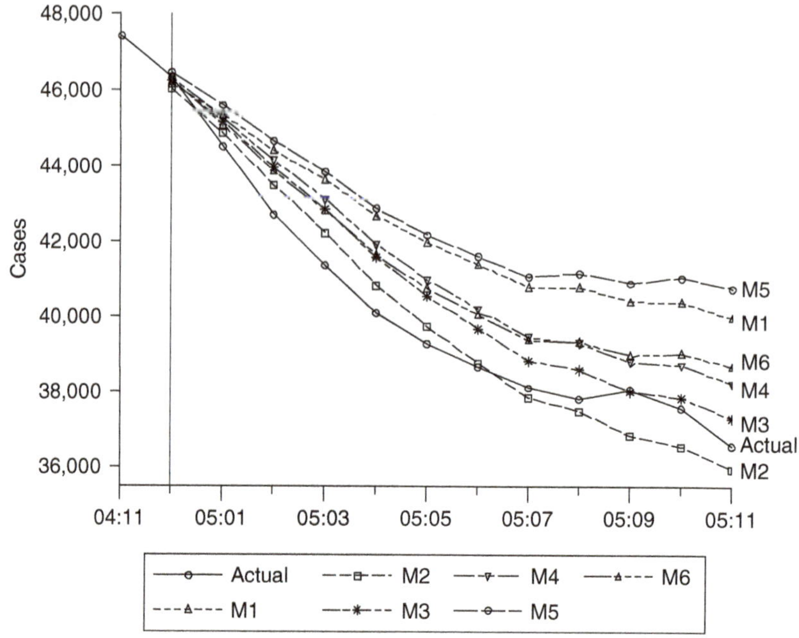

Figure 9.4 Comparison of six models for forecasting welfare caseloads (forecast period: December 2004–November 2005). (Calculations and analysis from the datasets obtained from the Georgia Department of Human Resources, http://domestic.gsu.edu/gadp/index.html; Bureau of Labor Statistics, http://www.bls.gov; Bureau of the Census, http://www.census.gov; and Bureau of Economic Analysis, http://www.bea.gov.)

The forecast error varies from a low of underprediction of 88 caseloads in June 2005 to a high of 1208 cases of overprediction for September 2005. The actual caseload numbers are always well within the upper and lower 95 percent forecast intervals. This is true for the other models, except for models 1 and 5, where the actual cases fall below the lower end of the 95 forecast interval for some of the months toward the end of the forecasting period.

In the context of econometrics models, if future values of measures of economic activity and other regressors can be predicted accurately, then the accuracy of caseload forecast would improve. Table 9A.4 in the appendix shows forecast performance of models 3 through 6 when forecasts are generated using actual values of explanatory variables. As expected, compared to the corresponding measures based on predicted regressors reported in Table 9.4, the magnitudes in Table 9A.4 are substantially lower in all cases, except for RMSE from model 3. Table 9A.5 provides point and interval forecasts from model 5 when actual values of regressors, including the national unemployment rate, are employed in generating the caseload

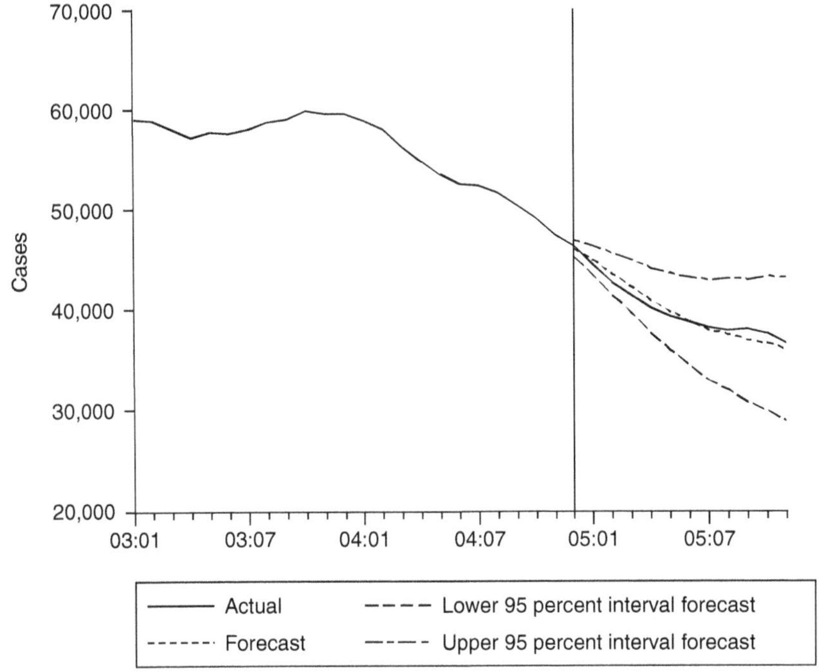

Figure 9.5 Acutal and interval forecasts for welfare caseloads from model 2 (forecast period: December 2004–November 2005). (Calculations and analysis from the data obtained from the Georgia Department of Human Resources, http://domestic.gsu.edu/gadp/index.html.)

projections. The forecasts are now fairly accurate, with absolute forecast error as low as 25 cases and a high of 1182 TANF cases. In contrast, when regressors are predicted, the range of the absolute forecast error from model 5 is between 438 and 4804 cases. These results suggest that dynamic models without regressors, but possibly incorporating deterministic covariates, are potentially useful for accurately forecasting welfare caseloads in the short run.

Long-Term Forecasting

We now consider the forecasting performance of various models when forecasts are made over a longer horizon, one-month-ahead to more than twelve-month-ahead forecasts. The following three forecast periods are considered:

- *Forecast period 1.* 2004:12–2005:11 (12 months) with estimation period, 1990:01–2004:11

Table 9.5 Short-Term Point and Interval Forecasts of Welfare Caseloads up to One Year Out from End of Estimation Period, November 2004

Month	*Actual*	*Lower 95 Percent Forecast Interval*	*Point Forecast*	*Upper 95 Percent Forecast Interval*	*Forecast Error*
December 2004	46,337	45,173	46,035	46,897	302
January 2005	44,510	43,409	44,852	46,295	−342
February 2005	42,695	41,421	43,476	45,530	−781
March 2005	41,350	39,533	42,218	44,903	−868
April 2005	40,078	37,547	40,830	44,113	−752
May 2005	39,269	35,851	39,726	43,602	−457
June 2005	38,669	34,305	38,757	43,209	−88
July 2005	38,104	32,834	37,835	42,836	269
August 2005	37,808	31,892	37,494	43,097	314
September 2005	38,053	30,710	36,845	42,981	1208
October 2005	37,560	29,852	36,556	43,260	1004
November 2005	36,560	28,764	35,957	43,149	603

Note: Forecasts are generated from dynamic estimates of Model 2 reported in Table 9.3.

Source: Calculation from the datasets obtained from the Georgia Department of Human Resources at http://domestic.gsu.edu/gadp/index.html (accessed March 2006); Bureau of Labor Statistics at http://www.bls.gov (accessed March 2006); Bureau of Census at http://www.census.gov (accessed March 2006); and Bureau of Economics Analysis at http://www.bea.gov (accessed March 2006).

- *Forecast period 2.* 2004:04–2005:11 (20 months) with estimation period: 1990:01–2004:03
- *Forecast period 3.* 2003:07–2005:11 (29 months) with estimation period: 1990:01–2003:07

The estimation and projection results for period 1 are discussed in the preceding subsections. We see from Figure 9.2 that period 3 covers the turning point that occurred at the end of 2003, which was followed by gradual and continuous decline in caseloads.

Table 9.6 provides the measures of forecast accuracy for forecast periods 2 and 3. The corresponding values for period 1 are given in Table 9.4. Generally, the forecast error increases as forecast horizon increases. For example, the mean absolute forecast errors from model 2 are 1.5, 8.2, and 16.2 percent for forecasting periods 1, 2, and 3, respectively. Model 2 is still the best for period 2 forecasts, whereas projections for period 3 produced from model 1 dominates the remaining

Table 9.6 Comparison of Six Forecasting Models for Caseloads by Forecasting Horizon

	Forecast Period 2: 2004:04–2005:11				*Forecast Period 3: 2003:07–2005:11*			
Model	*RMSE*	*MAE*	*MAPE*	*Theil IC*	*RMSE*	*MAE*	*MAPE*	*Theil IC*
1	5689	5652	11.6163	0.060372	5463	4290	10.17842	0.053689
2	4001	3282	8.180198	0.043101	8628	6765	16.19532	0.082051
3	4461	3644	9.096739	0.047871	8533	6698	16.02889	0.081164
4	6209	5179	12.85729	0.065389	7172	5570	13.37244	0.068898
5	7798	6344	15.87902	0.081199	13190	10411	24.88289	0.121016
6	8616	6947	17.43313	0.089166	14897	11830	28.21693	0.134877

Note: Estimation period for forecast period 2 (3) is January 1990–March 2004 (January 1990–June 2003). Forecast performance measures for period 1: December 2004–November 2005 are reported in Table 9.4.

Source: Calculation from the datasets obtained from the Georgia Department of Human Resources at http://domestic.gsu.edu/gadp/index.html (accessed March 2006); Bureau of Labor Statistics at http://www.bls.gov (accessed March 2006); Bureau of Census at http://www.census.gov (accessed March 2006); and Bureau of Economics Analysis at http://www.bea.gov (accessed March 2006).

five competitors in terms of all reported measures of forecast accuracy. The next best is model 3, closely followed by model 2. Forecasts from these preferred models are shown in Figure 9.6. Period 3 forecasts from model 1, and to some extent, second period forecasts from model 2, appear to be high as we approach the end of the forecasting period.

Other Potential Applications

The forecasting methods considered in the preceding sections could in principle be applied to other caseloads, including food stamp, Medicaid, and foster care caseloads. In developing the particulars of the underlying models, and in addition to the methods examined earlier for TANF caseloads, one could use estimation techniques similar to those used in modeling food stamp caseloads (Figlio and Ziliak 2000, Figlio et al. 2000, Wallace and Blank 1999, Zedlewski and Rader 2004, Ziliak et al. 2003), growth in foster care cases (Swan and Sylvester 2005), and growth in Medicaid participation (Holahan and Bruen 2003, Ku and Garret 2001). Most of these studies use state-level longitudinal data; therefore, variations in observed state characteristics as well as state-fixed effects play an important role in understanding the growth in caseloads. In contrast, state-specific caseload modeling can

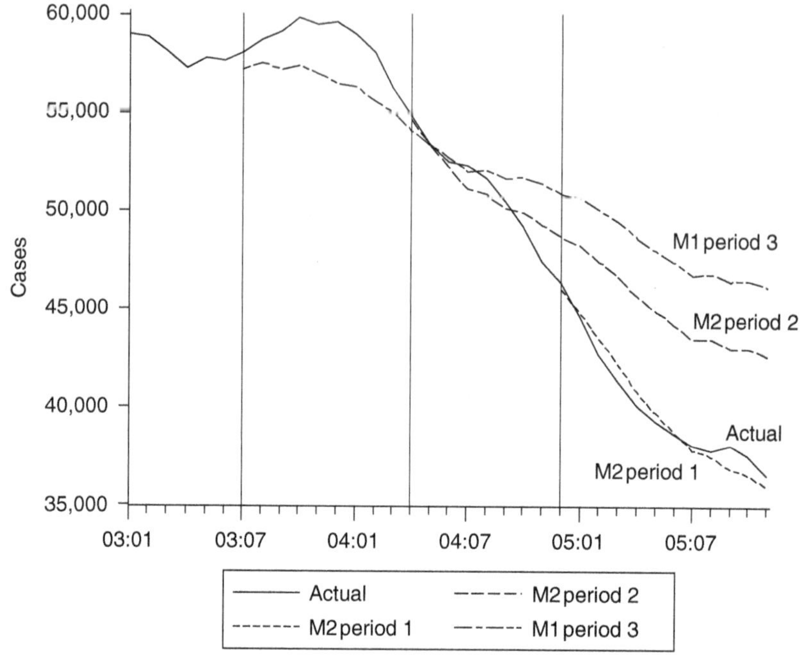

Figure 9.6 Short- and long-term forecasting of welfare caseloads (Period 1: 2004:12–2005:11; Period 2: 2004:04–2005:11; Period 3: 2003:07–2005:11).(Calculations and analysis from the datasets obtained from the Georgia Department of Human Resources, http://domestic.gsu.edu/gadp/index.html; Bureau of Labor Statistics, http://www.bls.gov; Bureau of the Census, http://www.census.gov; and Bureau of Economic Analysis, http://www.bea.gov.)

only exploit the time series variations in relevant state characteristics and national factors.

Using dynamic models and monthly time series data from July 1994 to December 2005, Gurmu and Smith (2005a) provide forecasts of Medicaid enrollments for the state of Georgia by major aid categories. The aid categories include the aged, blind and disabled, low income Medicaid (adult and child groups), Medicare, peachcare, right from the start Medicaid (mother and child groups), and others. Lagged values of enrollment numbers as well as current and lagged values of local and national unemployment rate (or employment) are included on the right-hand side of each equation. Additional regressors are included for some of the aid categories: population size by age group, number of uninsured individuals adjusted for population size, and TANF caseloads. Their estimation and forecasting results show that it is important to incorporate dynamics, major changes in Medicaid policies (particularly eligibility requirements), and structural breaks in modeling Medicaid enrollments.

Conclusion

Looking across multiple states, there is considerable evidence to date that the overall strength of the economy of the late 1990s as well as changes to the welfare system brought about by the transition from AFDC to TANF both affected welfare rolls. However, the primary cause of the declines in caseloads remains a point of considerable debate. For Georgia, peak enrollment occurred in January 1994, before the passage of PRWORA, but Georgia's most pronounced caseload declines began near its 1996 PROWRA's adoption, when economic activity in the state was also in full swing (this also coincides with Atlanta's hosting of the 1996 Olympic Games). In forecasting caseloads based on data from this period, there are inherent difficulties in disentangling the effects of the economy and the policy decisions that occurred after the implementation of TANF.

The changes in the federal welfare grant formula from an entitlement program under the AFDC to a block grant under PRWORA has increased the uncertainty faced by states looking for future funding assurance and overall funding adequacy for welfare programs. More control over the eligibility requirements was also shifted from the federal government to the states. The lack of security in funding has been exacerbated by recent state budget shortfalls brought on by the 2001 recession. Consequently, it has become increasingly important to have accurate forecasts of state-level caseloads and to predict turning points in caseloads.

In this chapter, we have focused on estimation and forecasting welfare caseloads at the state level. We reviewed the caseload literature, with a focus on caseload forecasting practices at the state or local level. Our data on TANF caseloads from Georgia allowed us to estimate static and dynamic models, generate short- and long-term forecasts, and evaluate forecast accuracy of various model specifications. The dynamic model of welfare caseloads provides reasonably accurate short-term caseload forecasts. Markov chain and threshold models are potentially useful in forecasting turning points in caseloads.

Acknowledgments

We thank the Georgia Department of Human Resources for providing the welfare caseloads data; David Sjoquist for his helpful suggestions; and Thomas D. Lynch, Jinping Sun, and seminar participants at the 2006 South Eastern Conference for Public Administration for their useful comments. The views expressed herein are those of the authors and do not necessarily represent the views of DHR. Any errors are our own.

Appendix

Table 9A.1 Estimates from FD Models, January 1990–March 2004 (Dependent Variable: FD of Welfare Caseloads)

			Model 3	Model 4	Model 5	Model 6
Variable	*Model 1*	*Model 2*	*Unemployment Rate*	*Employment*	*National Unemployment*	*National Employment*
FD caseloads ($t-1$)		0.4485*** (5.47)	0.4448*** (5.34)	0.3795*** (4.55)	0.3724*** (4.51)	0.3819*** (4.60)
FD caseloads ($t-2$)		0.2933*** (3.39)	0.2889*** (3.30)	0.2621*** (3.09)	0.2573*** (3.05)	0.2631*** (3.17)
FD caseloads ($t-3$)		0.0866 (1.06)	0.0768 (0.92)	0.0855 (1.07)	0.0848 (1.07)	0.1102 (1.38)
FD cyclical indicator (t)			209.4599 (0.84)	−0.0099* (−1.94)	958.3304*** (2.47)	−0.4436*** (−2.84)
FD cyclical indicator ($t-1$)			126.0242 (0.51)	−0.0076 (−1.48)	761.8528* (1.94)	−0.2947* (−1.86)
FD cyclical indicator ($t-2$)			323.5902 (1.30)	−0.0131*** (−2.51)	890.8561** (2.24)	−0.3105* (−1.92)
FD cyclical indicator ($t-3$)			309.4394 (1.25)	−0.0056 (−1.07)	696.2833* (1.73)	−0.1653 (−1.05)
FD closures			2.6450 (1.25)	3.12545 (1.52)	3.0955 (1.53)	3.3982* (1.67)
FD population	No	No	Yes	Yes	Yes	Yes
1994 Quarter 2 dummy	Yes	Yes	Yes	Yes	Yes	Yes
1996 Quarter 2 dummy	Yes	Yes	Yes	Yes	Yes	Yes
Monthly dummies	Yes	Yes	Yes	Yes	Yes	Yes
AR(1)	0.7177*** (−12.347)					
Akaike information criterion	16.30	16.18	16.22	16.16	16.13	16.14
Schwartz criterion	16.58	16.50	16.65	16.59	16.56	16.56

Note: t Ratios are within parentheses. Statistical significance at 10, 5, and 1 percent levels are denoted by *, **, and ***, respectively. Estimation models allow for endpoint adjustments due to differencing and lagging of variables.

Source: Calculation from the datasets obtained from the Georgia Department of Human Resources at http://domestic.gsu.edu/gadp/index.html (accessed March 2006); Bureau of Labor Statistics at http://www.bls.gov (accessed March 2006); Bureau of Census at http://www.census.gov (accessed March 2006); and Bureau of Economics Analysis at http://www.bea.gov (accessed March 2006).

Table 9A.2 Estimates from FD Log Models, January 1990–March 2004 (Dependent Variable: FD of Log of Welfare Caseloads)

			Model 3	*Model 4*	*Model 5*	*Model 6*
Variable	*Model 1*	*Model 2*	*Unemployment Rate*	*Log Employment*	*National Unemployment*	*Log National Employment*
FD log caseload ($t-1$)		0.3757*** (4.595)	0.3663*** (4.431)	0.2784*** (3.45)	0.2663*** (3.29)	0.2858*** (3.58)
FD log caseload ($t-2$)		0.2886*** (3.44)	0.2721*** (3.237)	0.2236*** (2.82)	0.2209*** (2.77)	0.2314*** (2.89)
FD log caseload ($t-3$)		0.1467* (1.799)	0.1425* (1.753)	0.1648** (2.18)	0.1636** (2.15)	0.2041*** (2.67)
FD cyclical indicator (t)			0.0031 (1.026)	−0.4917** (−2.27)	0.0116*** (2.53)	−0.6420*** (−2.85)
FD cyclical indicator ($t-1$)			0.0020 (0.66)	−0.2625 (−1.20)	0.0110*** (2.36)	−0.3631 (−1.60)
FD cyclical indicator ($t-2$)			0.0059** (1.982)	−0.9053*** (−4.12)	0.0160*** (3.40)	−0.6944*** (−3.01)
FD cyclical indicator ($t-3$)			0.0044 (1.454)	−0.5819*** (−2.58)	0.0122*** (2.54)	−0.6965*** (−3.07)
FD closures			0.0000 (1.589)	0.00005* (1.95)	0.00005** (2.00)	0.00005** (2.06)
FD population	No	No	Yes	Yes	Yes	Yes
1994 Quarter 2 dummy	Yes	Yes	Yes	Yes	Yes	Yes
1996 Quarter 2 dummy	Yes	Yes	Yes	Yes	Yes	Yes
Monthly dummies	Yes	Yes	Yes	Yes	Yes	Yes
AR(1)	0.6516*** −10.434					
Akaike information criterion	−6.31	−6.44	−6.43	−6.57	−6.57	−6.59
Schwartz criterion	−6.03	−6.12	−6.00	−6.14	−6.14	−6.16

Note: t Ratios are within parentheses. Statistical significance at 10, 5, and 1 percent levels are denoted by *, **, and ***, respectively. Estimation models allow for endpoint adjustments due to differencing and lagging of variables.

Source: Calculation from the datasets obtained from the Georgia Department of Human Resources at http://domestic.gsu.edu/gadp/index.html (accessed March 2006); Bureau of Labor Statistics at http://www.bls.gov (accessed March 2006); Bureau of Census at http://www.census.gov (accessed March 2006); and Bureau of Economics Analysis at http://www.bea.gov (accessed March 2006).

Table 9A.3 Estimates from FD Log Models, January 1990–June 2003 (Dependent Variable: FD of Log of Welfare Caseloads)

			Model 3	*Model 4*	*Model 5*	*Model 6*
Variable	*Model 1*	*Model 2*	*Unemployment Rate*	*Log Employment*	*National Unemployment Rate*	*National Log Employment*
FD log caseloads ($t-1$)		0.3804*** (6.60)	0.3794*** (2.49)	0.2762*** (3.37)	0.2878*** (3.46)	0.2870*** (3.55)
FD log caseloads ($t-2$)		0.2505*** (2.87)	0.2302*** (2.60)	0.1976** (2.40)	0.1689** (1.99)	0.1987** (2.40)
FD log caseloads ($t-3$)		0.1862** (2.22)	0.1784** (2.11)	0.1979** (2.53)	0.1943** (2.44)	0.2416*** (3.07)
FD cyclical indicator (t)			0.0035** (1.14)	−0.4985** (−2.24)	0.0139*** (2.92)	−0.6553*** (−2.88)
FD cyclical indicator ($t-1$)			0.0005 (0.18)	−0.2921 (−1.31)	0.0090* (1.84)	−0.3829* (−1.66)
FD cyclical indicator ($t-2$)			0.0060* (1.94)	−0.8457*** (−3.75)	0.0164*** (3.33)	−0.6918*** (−2.94)
FD cyclical indicator ($t-3$)			0.0033 (1.08)	−0.6200*** (−2.69)	0.0102** (2.01)	−0.7163*** (−3.10)
FD closures			0.00003 (1.13)	0.00004 (1.59)	0.00004 (1.45)	0.00004* (1.69)
FD population	No	No	Yes	Yes	Yes	Yes
1994 Quarter 2 dummy	Yes	Yes	Yes	Yes	Yes	Yes
1996 Quarter 2 dummy	Yes	Yes	Yes	Yes	Yes	Yes
Monthly dummies	Yes	Yes	Yes	Yes	Yes	Yes
AR(1)	0.6485*** (10.14)					
Akaike information criterion	−6.31	−6.43	−6.41	−6.55	−6.55	−6.58
Schwartz criterion	−6.02	−6.10	−5.96	−6.10	−6.10	−6.13

Note: t Ratios are within parentheses. Statistical significance at 10, 5, and 1 percent levels are denoted by *, **, and ***, respectively. Estimation models allow for endpoint adjustments due to differencing and lagging of variables.

Source: Calculation from the datasets obtained from the Georgia Department of Human Resources at http://domestic.gsu.edu/gadp/index.html (accessed March 2006); Bureau of Labor Statistics at http://www.bls.gov (accessed March 2006); Bureau of Census at http://www.census.gov (accessed March 2006); and Bureau of Economics Analysis at http://www.bea.gov (accessed March 2006).

Table 9A.4 Comparison of Four Forecasting Models for Caseloads using Actual Values of Explanatory Variables (Forecast Period: 2004:12–2005:11)

Model	*RMSE*	*MAE*	*MAPE*	*Theil IC*
3	837	745	1.875	0.010
4	1361	1240	3.151	0.017
5	673	572	1.452	0.008
6	639	551	1.375	0.008

Note: The corresponding measures from models using forecasted values of explanatory variables are given in Table 9.4.

Source: Calculation from the datasets obtained from the Georgia Department of Human Resources at http://domestic.gsu.edu/gadp/index.html (accessed March 2006); Bureau of Labor Statistics at http://www.bls.gov (accessed March 2006); Bureau of Census at http://www.census.gov (accessed March 2006); and Bureau of Economics Analysis at http://www.bea.gov (accessed March 2006).

Table 9A.5 Short-Term Point and Interval Forecasts of Welfare Caseloads up to One Year Out from End of Estimation Period, November 2004

Month	*Actual*	*Lower 95 Percent Forecast Interval*	*Point Forecast*	*Upper 95 Percent Forecast Interval*	*Forecast Error*
December 2004	46,337	45,503	46,312	47,121	25
January 2005	44,510	43,847	45,133	46,419	−623
February 2005	42,695	41,942	43,691	45,440	−996
March 2005	41,350	40,317	42,532	44,746	−1182
April 2005	40,078	38,485	41,105	43,726	−1027
May 2005	39,269	37,120	40,136	43,153	−867
June 2005	38,669	35,806	39,184	42,561	−515
July 2005	38,104	34,664	38,380	42,096	−276
August 2005	37,808	34,050	38,131	42,212	−323
September 2005	38,053	33,199	37,591	41,982	462
October 2005	37,560	32,686	37,408	42,129	152
November 2005	36,560	31,975	36,976	41,977	−416

Note: Forecasts are generated from dynamic estimates of Model 5, but using actual values of explanatory variables during the forecasting period. Model 5 with predicted covariates produce relatively large forecast errors ranging from −438 for January to −4804 for November.

Source: Calculation from the datasets obtained from the Georgia Department of Human Resources at http://domestic.gsu.edu/gadp/index.html (accessed March 2006); Bureau of Labor Statistics at http://www.bls.gov (accessed March 2006); Bureau of Census at http://www.census.gov (accessed March 2006); and Bureau of Economics Analysis at http://www.bea.gov (accessed March 2006).

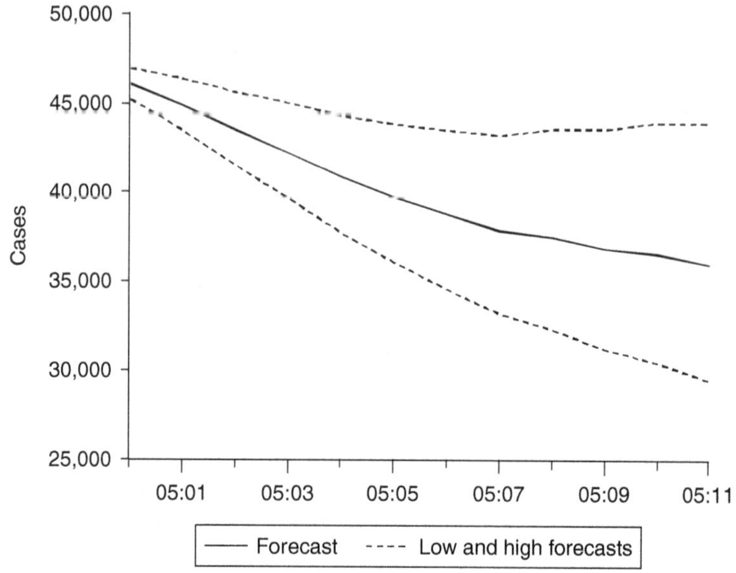

Figure 9A.1 Ninety-five percent interval forecasts for welfare caseloads from model 2 (forecast period: December 2004–November 2005). (Calculations and analysis from the data obtained from the Georgia Department of Human Resources, http://domestic.gsu.edu/gadp/index.html.)

References

Bartik, T. J. and R. W. Elberts. 1999. Examining the effect of industry trends and structure on welfare caseloads. In S. H. Danziger (Ed.) *Economic Conditions and Welfare Reform*, Kalamazoo, MI: W.E. Upjohn Institute for Employment Research, pp. 119–157.

Black, D., T. McKinnish, and S. Sanders. 2005. The economic impact of the coal boom and bust. *Economic Journal* 115: 444–471.

Blank, R. 2001. What causes public assistance caseloads to grow? *Journal of Human Resources* 36: 85–118.

Brady, H., M. H. Sprague, F. C. Gey, and M. L. Wiseman. 2000. *The interaction of welfare-use and employment dynamics in rural and agricultural California counties*. Working Paper, Department of Political Science, University of California, Berkeley.

Bureau of Census at http://www.census.gov (accessed March 2006).

Bureau of Economics Analysis at http://www.bea.gov (accessed March 2006).

Bureau of Labor Statistics at http://www.bls.gov (accessed March 2006).

Center for Business and Economic Research. 2003. *Assessment of Tennessee's Families First caseload trends*. Knoxville, TN: University of Tennessee. http://cber.bus.utk.edu/TDHS/ffnov03.pdf. (May 2006).

Diebold, F. X. 2004. *Elements of Forecasting*, 3rd ed. Cincinnati, OH: South-Western College Publishing.

Figlio, D. and J. Ziliak. 1999. Welfare reform, the business cycle, and the decline in AFDC caseloads. In S. H. Danziger (Ed.) *Economic Conditions and Welfare Reform*, Kalamazoo, MI: W.E. Upjohn Institute for Employment Research, pp. 19–48.

Figlio, D. and J. P. Ziliak. 2000. *Geographic differences in AFDC and food stamp caseloads in the welfare reform era.* Working Paper, University of Oregon.

Figlio, D., C. G. Gundersen, and J. P. Ziliak. 2000. The effects of the macroeconomy and welfare reform on food stamp caseloads. *American Journal of Agricultural Economics* 82(3): 635–641.

Georgia Department of Human Resources at http://domestic.gsu.edu/gadp/index.html (accessed March 2006).

Grogger, J. 2005. *Markov forecasting methods for welfare caseloads.* Working Paper #11682, National Bureau of Economic Research.

Gurmu, S., C. T. King, and P. R. Mueser. 2005a. Job stability for welfare recipients: A comparison of matched job spells. In C. T. King and P. R. Mueser (Eds.) *Welfare and Work: Experiences in Six Cities*, Chapter 4. Kalamazoo, MI: W.E. Upjohn Institute for Employment Research.

Gurmu, S., C. T. King, and P. R. Mueser. 2005b. Explaining job stability for welfare recipients. In C. T. King and P. R. Mueser (Eds.) *Welfare and Work: Experiences in Six Cities*, Chapter 5. Kalamazoo, MI: W.E. Upjohn Institute for Employment Research.

Gurmu, S., K. R. Ihlanfeldt, and W. J. Smith. 2007. Does residential location matter to the employment of TANF recipients? Evidence from a dynamic discrete choice model with unobserved effects. *Journal of Urban Economics* (In press, doi: 10.1016/j.jue.2007.02.002).

Gurmu, S. and W. J. Smith. 2005a. *Projections of Medicaid enrollments for the state of Georgia.* Report prepared for Georgia Department of Community Health, Andrew Young School of Policy Studies, Fiscal Research Center, Georgia State University.

Gurmu, S. and W. J. Smith. 2005b. *Forecasting welfare caseloads for Georgia.* Report prepared for Georgia Department of Human Resources, Andrew Young School of Policy Studies, Fiscal Research Center, Georgia State University.

Hamilton, J. D. 1994. *Time Series Analysis.* Princeton, NJ: Princeton University Press.

Holahan, J. and B. Bruen. 2003. *Medicaid spending: What factors contributed to the growth between 2000 and 2002?* Report, The Kaiser Commission on Medicaid and the Uninsured.

Hotchkiss, J., C. T. King, and P. R. Mueser. The determinants of welfare exits and employment. In C. T. King and P. R. Mueser (Eds.) *Welfare and Work: Experiences in Six Cities*, Chapter 3. Kalamazoo, MI: W.E. Upjohn Institute for Employment Research.

King, C. T. and P. R. Mueser. 2005. *Welfare and Work: Experiences in Six Cities.* Kalamazoo, MI: W.E. Upjohn Institute for Employment Research.

Ku, L. and B. Garret. 2001. *How welfare-reform and economic factors affected Medicaid participation.* Assessing the New Federalism Working Paper #00-01, Urban Institute.

Nevada State Welfare Division. 2004. *Caseload projections state fiscal year 2004 and 2005.* http://www.welfare.state.nv.us/budget/caseload_proj_synopsis-fy04-05.pdf. Accessed April 2006.

Oregon Department of Human Services. 2006. *Finance and policy analysis client caseload forecasting, Spring 2006 forecast.* http://www.oregon.gov/DHS/data/forecasts/2006/spring_06.pdf. Accessed June 2006.

Swan, C. A. and M. S. Sylvester. 2005. The foster care crisis: what caused caseloads to grow. *Demography* 43(2): 309–335.

Texas Health and Human Services. 2002a. *Consolidated budget for fiscal years 2004–2005.* http://www.hhsc.state.tx.us/about_hhsc/finance/reports/cbud0405_toc.html. Accessed April 2006.

Texas Health and Human Services. 2002b. *Texas families in transition: Surviving without TANF.* http://www.utexas.edu/research/cswr/projects/pj0163.pdf. Accessed April 2006.

U.S. Department of Health and Human Services, Administration of Children and Families. http://www.acf.hhs.gov. Accessed March 2006.

Wallace, G. and R. Blank. 1999. What goes up must come down? Explaining recent changes in public assistance caseloads. In S. H. Danziger (Ed.) *Economic Conditions and Welfare Reform*, Kalamazoo, MI: W.E. Upjohn Institute for Employment Research, pp. 49–89.

Zedlewski, S. R. and K. Rader. 2004. *Recent trends in food stamp participation: Have new policies made a difference?* Report, Urban Institute.

Ziliak, J. P., D. N. Figlio, E. E. Davis, and L. S. Connolly. 2000. Accounting for the decline in AFDC caseloads: Welfare reform or the economy? *Journal of Human Resources* 35(3): 570–586.

Ziliak, J. P., C. Gundersen, and D. Figlio. 2003. Food stamp caseloads over the business cycle. *Southern Economic Journal* 69: 903–913.

Chapter 10

Forecast Evaluation: A Case Study

Jinping Sun

Contents

Introduction

As an important practice in the forecasting literature, forecast evaluation helps identify problems in the estimation process and sets the stage for forecast improvement (Armstrong 1985, Shkurti 1990, Shkurti and Winefordner 1989). Most prior research in government budget forecasting focuses on forecast accuracy and investigates what factors affect forecast error (Bretschneider and Gorr 1987, Jonas et al. 1992, Rubin et al. 1999, Shkurti 1990). This chapter intends to assess the performance of revenue estimation in state governments using New York as a case study. In particular, this study aims to address the following two questions:

1. Is New York state revenue forecasting process sound?
2. How well do the major forecasting agencies perform?

This chapter consists of three sections. The first section introduces major forecasting agencies in New York and the political environment in which revenue estimation is conducted. The second section identifies professional standards used in forecast evaluation in the public sector and examines whether New York meets these criteria. The third section assesses the three agencies' forecast accuracy and attempts to find out if additional criteria are used in forecast evaluation.

State Revenue Forecasting in New York

New York is a politically charged state with political power unequally distributed among the Governor, the Assembly, and the Senate—the so-called Albany Triad (Benjamin 2003). The governor has broad formal and informal power, among which budgeting power and appointment power are prominent examples. The legislature "has enormous *potential* power, although it seldom exercises that power fully" (Ward 2002, p. 90). The authority vested in the legislature ranges from initiating laws and setting public policies to sharing the budgeting role with the governor.* Although executive influence has become constrained to a certain degree since the late 1970s due to an increasingly assertive legislature, New York has the tradition of a strong chief executive and the governor is regarded as "the most powerful actor in the triad" as a result of "a long chain of constitutional changes and fundamental transformations in the social, economic and political environment" (Benjamin 2003, p. 6).

In New York, divided control characterizes political life for the past three decades. In the legislature, the Democrats have controlled the Assembly since 1975 and the Republicans have controlled the Senate since 1965. Regarding the governorship, the Democrats held the governor's office from 1975 to 1994 when

* For a detailed description of the powers of the governor and the legislature, see New York State Constitution, Articles VI and III, respectively.

George Pataki, a Republican, was elected. Twelve years later in November 2006, Eliot Spitzer (a Democrat) captured New York governorship by a landslide margin over the Republican candidate John Faso. Such partisan control of the executive and the legislature makes the cooperation between the two branches difficult, results in tensions and even conflicts, and stalls government decision process (Forsythe and Boyd 2004). An example of this dysfunctional relationship between the governor and the legislature is the state's persistently late budgets.

In the state's revenue forecasting process, both the executive and the legislature play an active role. Historically, the Division of the Budget (DOB) was solely responsible for forecasting state revenues. Since the 1980s, legislative fiscal committees have built up their capacity to develop independent revenue forecasts. The majorities of the Senate Finance Committee (SFC) and Assembly Ways and Means Committee (AWAM) started to prepare revenue estimates in the 1980s, whereas the minorities began to get involved in the 1990s. The three major players, however, are the DOB, SFC, and AWAM, whereas the minority legislative fiscal committees have a relatively short history of revenue estimation and have little influence on the state budget process. The independent legislative forecasts provide the basis for the Senate and Assembly to reshape the budget and lay the foundation for budget negotiations among the Big Three—the Governor, Senate majority leader, and Assembly speaker.

Under the political environment, not surprisingly, the DOB, SFC, and AWAM produce different revenue forecasts. To help resolve the differences, an annual economic and revenue consensus forecasting conference was enacted in 1996 by the State Finance Law, which requires the executive and the legislature to reconcile the differences and release a consensus economic and revenue report by March 10 of every year. Since 1996, however, it has been a rather difficult task for the state leaders to reach an agreement on revenue estimates in a timely manner.

Using professional guidelines in forecast evaluation, this chapter assesses how New York state revenue estimation performs by examining its forecasting process and the three agencies' forecasts. To do this, this research draws on modified general fund (GF) tax revenues—all fund taxes are used for personal income and sales taxes, whereas GF taxes are used for business and other taxes. Data on the three agencies' revenue forecasts was assembled from their first set of publicly released official forecasts from fiscal year (FY)1995–1996 to FY2002–2003. In addition, a mail survey of the forecasting staff in the DOB, SFC, and AWAM was conducted in 2004. The survey included questions on forecasters' personal background, their forecasting activities, and perception of various aspects of the state's revenue forecasting process. At the time of the survey, there were twenty-four forecasters in the DOB, two in the SFC, and twelve in the AWAM. A total of thirty completed surveys were returned with nineteen from the DOB, two from the SFC, and nine from the AWAM, yielding a response rate of 79 percent. Survey findings are incorporated and discussed in the following sections.

Evaluating New York State Revenue Forecasting Process

To evaluate New York state revenue forecasting process, this study locates professional guidelines established by national organizations that are well recognized in the area of public budgeting and financial management.

Professional Guidelines in Evaluating Revenue Forecasting Process

There are two sets of professional criteria in forecast evaluation in the public sector. Developed by the National Association of State Budget Officers and the Federation of Tax Administrators, the first set contains ten criteria from the perspective of the executive branch (Howard 1989). Basically, these guidelines place revenue estimation responsibility in the executive and in the meantime, encourage ongoing involvement of the legislature, businesses, and other stakeholders.

The second set of professional guidelines was issued by the National Advisory Council on State and Local Budgeting (1998) (Element 9 Develop and Evaluate Financial Options). It puts revenue forecasting in the context of financial planning and recommends six budget practices related to revenue estimation. In addition to what is mentioned in the first set of criteria, the second publication suggests that the government prepare multiyear revenue and expenditure projections, document revenue sources and factors relevant to estimation, and consider revenue and expenditure options together before making budget decisions.*

Because certain overlap exists between the two sets of criteria, this study combines them to form the following eight standards to evaluate New York's revenue forecasting process. The case study is done in a similar manner as Jonas et al. (1992).

Involving the Executive and the Legislature and Achieving Consensus Forecasts

The executive and the legislature should both engage in the forecasting process and reach consensus on their forecasts. New York has an executive budget system and the legislature has been participating in economic and revenue forecasting since the 1980s. The DOB, SFC, and AWAM all employ professional staff to produce independent economic and revenue forecasts, and the consensus conference provides an opportunity for them to reach an agreement on the estimates. Since the institution of the consensus conference in 1996, however, agreement was reached only in 2003 when there were minor differences between executive and legislative forecasts and the three parties agreed to use executive revenue estimates.

* This section is based on Sun (2005).

A number of factors account for the lack of agreement on revenue estimates. First, the three major players may not be able to agree on the core assumptions for revenue estimation on economy, policy, and other conditions. In particular, economic outlook drives revenue receipts, and differences in national and state economic forecasts may lead to different state revenue estimates. For instance, the legislative fiscal committees had confidence in a stronger national and New York state economic growth for FY2000–2001 (as reflected in optimistic forecasts of such major economic indicators as gross domestic product [GDP], personal income, and inflation), which translated into higher revenue forecasts than the DOB. A second contributing factor is the three parties have divergent interests, political agendas, and spending needs. They produce various versions of revenue forecasts in an effort to serve their respective purposes as revenue estimation sets limits on spending forecasts and gives them an edge in budget negotiations. Third, the consensus process has no binding power. The state's leaders may ignore the statutory deadline, and disagreement on revenue forecast still exists to impede further budget talks.

Considering Revenue and Expenditure Options Together

Revenue and expenditure are two sides to a state's budget. The process for considering revenue and expenditure options together can help improve a state's financial position by taking necessary actions in case any problem occurs. One component of the process is developing revenue and expenditure projections.

The DOB, SFC, and AWAM conduct revenue estimation and budget analysis. Expenditure forecasting is normally done simultaneously with or after revenue forecasting. Within the DOB, the Expenditure and Debt Unit prepares and updates state expenditure estimates and monitors state cash flow and financial commitments, whereas the Economic and Revenue Unit performs economic and revenue forecasts. In the legislative fiscal committees, the staff dealing with tax studies is responsible for revenue estimates and tax analysis and the staff on budget studies is responsible for spending analysis.

Although all three agencies prepare spending forecasts, New York does not have a strong spending estimation record. According to New York State Office of the State Comptroller (2000, p. 2), reductions in spending estimates were more significant than the revisions to revenue estimates during FY1995–1996 budget negotiations, and "nearly 20 percent of the total year-end unanticipated surplus was attributable to errors in spending projections" from FY1996–1997 to FY1999–2000.

Preparing Multiyear Projections

Preparing multiyear revenue and expenditure projections is a key component of a state's overall financial planning. To better understand future funding, it is recommended that government project revenues and expenditures at least three years into the future. New York is not particularly good at multiyear projections. The DOB prepares three-year revenue and expenditure forecasts in conjunction with the submission of the governor's proposed *Executive Budget* and in its 30-day amendments to the *Executive Budget*. The AWAM and SFC also prepare out-year forecasts. The adopted budget, however, is not accompanied by multiyear revenue and expenditure forecasts, and the projections are not required to be updated to reflect the changes in the economy and other conditions later during the year (New York State Office of the State Comptroller 1996). States with top credit ratings such as Delaware, Utah, and Maryland are better at multiyear planning and there is much for New York to learn from these states (Citizens Budget Commission 2003).

Using Experts in the Forecasting Process

The successful use of experts in the forecasting process can provide independent feedback on government forecasts, and government should use outside expertise in the estimation process. In New York, all three agencies consult outside experts and incorporate their comments in the forecasts. The DOB and AWAM have a board of economic advisors from the academia, businesses, and other fields, whereas the SFC has a long-term working relationship with Global Insight, a private, lead consulting firm that produces economic and tax revenue forecasts and serves in an advisory capacity to the committee. These outside economists meet with the three agencies on a regular basis and provide expert opinions on the state of economy and revenue outlook.

Understanding the Risks to the Forecasts

Uncertainties are inherent in revenue estimation and there is a myriad of risks in the forecasting process including political decisions, taxpayer behavior, and other factors such as oil price changes, unexpected weather changes, and international events. Government should identify major assumptions and produce single or range projections for different scenarios. In New York, all three agencies prepare point revenue forecasts and include risk assessment in their reports to minimize the impact of potential risks.

To deal with uncertainties in revenue estimation, most forecasting staff surveyed stated the best solution was to use caution given that a conservative forecast could reduce risks. This preference for underestimation is consistent with the literature (Rodgers and Joyce 1996) and is evident in the three agencies' forecasts (see Figure 10.4). In addition, they developed and utilized sophisticated models to account for uncertainties. Table 10.1 summarizes the techniques used

Table 10.1 Forecasting Techniques in New York

	DOB	*SFC*	*AWAM*
Expert	*		*
Time series	*	*	*
Econometric	*	*	*
Microsimulation	*		*

by the DOB, SFC, and AWAM in forecasting state revenues and it shows they all employ time series and econometric analysis in their forecasting process. When technical modeling was not adequate, they applied a variety of other methods including making subjective adjustment, using historical average as a guide, staying abreast of current data, and performing range forecasts to capture and gauge the impact of unanticipated events. Particularly, the staff emphasized that technical modeling should be tempered with judgment. There is "some judgment in all forecasts" (Fischhoff 1988, p. 337), and the value of judgment is especially crucial in times of change when informed judgment is needed to incorporate additional information, make adjustments, and detect changes (O'Connor et al. 1993).

Maintaining Flexibility in Revising the Forecasts

Revenue estimation is subject to changes in the economy, federal and state tax legislation, taxpayer behavior, and other factors, and government must respond to these changes and revise its forecasts. In New York, all three agencies revise their forecasts regularly. The DOB prepares quarterly updates in addition to forecasts contained in the *Executive Budget* and 30-Day Amendments. The legislative fiscal committees review the executive financial plan updates, monitor the estimates, and issue their own revenue forecasts.

Ensuring Proper Documentation of Revenues and Expenditures

Government should keep proper documentation of revenues and expenditures, including reports on revenue sources and collections, funding level and spending areas, revenue and expenditure projections, and assumptions made for projections. In New York, the DOB and AWAM maintain their own in-house databases, and the SFC relies on Global Insight to analyze existing revenues and programs and publish economic and revenue projections. The three agencies' reports have limitations in that each agency merely compares its forecasts with the other two agencies.

No comparison is made between their estimates and actual results, and no track record of their forecasting performance is provided.

Keeping the Process Open and Sharing Information with the Public

Government should keep the forecasting process open and make relevant budget information available to all interested parties. In New York, the consensus conference is open to the public, and the Freedom of Information Law requires government agencies to provide information that is not specifically exempted from disclosure.

Despite the procedures and policies, the current New York state revenue forecasting process has room for improvement, especially in enhancing meaningful public participation and full disclosure of relevant budget documents. The public is generally excluded from the state's forecasting process as they neither know how the three agencies conduct their forecasts, nor are they aware of the budget negotiations that often take place behind closed doors among the governor, Senate majority leader, and Assembly speaker. Legislative conference committees were experimented in 1998 to open up the process. Unfortunately, the legislators were not given sufficient authority and major budget decisions were still made privately by the three leaders. Further, the public is not provided with adequate information on government forecasts. None of the three agencies share their expenditure forecasting methodology with the public, and spending estimation is often believed to be driven by political agendas and subject to manipulation.* Making public the expenditure forecasting process could contribute to the practice and study of expenditure forecasting as there has been little literature "arguing a systematic, analytic approach to expenditure forecasting" (Bahl 1980, p. 126).

In summary, New York state revenue forecasting process could be improved. Ideally, the process should conform to professional guidelines, especially in reaching consensus on revenue estimates and enhancing transparency through public participation and accessibility of budget information. The failure of state leaders to resolve dispute and agree on revenue estimates holds up further budget negotiations and is linked to the state's persistently late budgets (New York Office of the State Comptroller 2006). Experience from other states suggests that opening up the process by fostering public participation could make revenue estimation less like a black box, encourage cooperation between the executive and legislative branches, bring discipline into the process, enhance credibility of the forecasts, and improve accountability (Stinson 2002). Having an effective procedure in place is

* Although there is limited literature on state expenditure forecasting, the little research that exists suggests that judgmental and naïve approaches are generally used in forecasting state spending, and complex quantitative methods such as econometrics are seldom employed (Frank 1992).

instrumental in improving revenue forecasting practice in New York, but it would require strong and continuing commitment from state leaders.

Evaluating New York State Revenue Forecasts

Accuracy is the primary criterion in evaluating revenue forecasts. The degree of accuracy is found to vary dramatically depending on the level of government and source of revenue (Lynch 1995, pp. 146–147). Accuracy is essential because forecast errors can cause nightmares for government officials and have considerable fiscal and political costs (Rodgers and Joyce 1996).

In a review of forecasting practices in private industries, accuracy is found to be the most important criterion. Other criteria—such as cost, timeliness, and consistency with the purpose of management—are highly rated as well (Yokum and Armstrong 1995). In the context of government forecasting, there has also been a constant search for additional criteria in forecast evaluation (Agostini 1991, Bretschneider and Gorr 1999, Shkurti 1990). According to Agostini (1991), accuracy, being informative, being relatively inexpensive, and easy to use are the standards used to evaluate revenue projections in San Francisco.

The following sections analyze the forecast accuracy of the DOB, SFC, and AWAM using survey findings and examine whether other standards, besides improved accuracy, are considered in evaluating revenue forecasts in New York.

Accuracy of New York State Executive and Legislative Forecasts

The literature mentions various means to measure forecast error including absolute percent error and mean absolute error.* This chapter uses percentage forecast error (PFE), which is computed as

$$\text{PFE} = 100 \times \frac{(\text{forecasted revenues} - \text{actual revenues})}{\text{actual revenues}}$$

A positive PFE means more revenues are projected than actual receipts, corresponding to an overforecast, and a negative PFE implies a conservative forecast or underforecast.

In addition to PFE, this research reports the three agencies' average revenue forecast error, which is measured by mean absolute percent error (MAPE) and is calculated by dividing the sum of the absolute value of PFEs by the number of years. MAPE is used to compute average forecast error as it indicates more clearly

* For details on measures of forecast error, see Voorhees (2000).

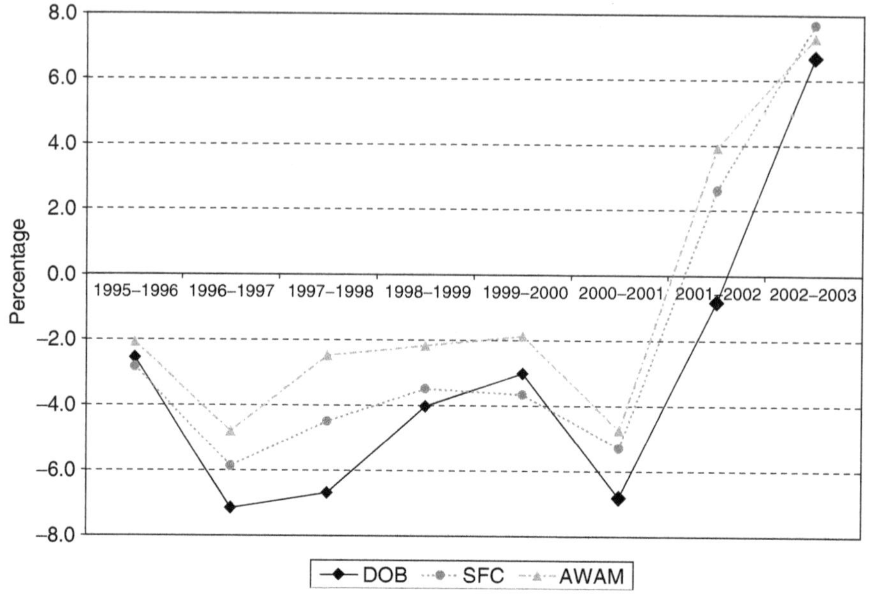

Figure 10.1 Accuracy of PIT forecasts.

the discrepancy between the forecasts and actual receipts regardless of arithmetic signs. Thus, under- and overestimates do not offset one another in this measure.

Figures 10.1 through 10.3 compare the accuracy of the DOB, SFC, and AWAM in forecasting three major New York state taxes: personal income tax (PIT), sales and use tax (SUT), and corporation franchise tax (CFT). Major findings are as follows:

- Average forecast errors vary significantly across the taxes. MAPE is lowest for SUT and highest for CFT. Errors are large for CFT because CFT forecasting involves managing risks from its many complicated elements and volatile corporate profits and accounting for a number of tax law changes in recent years that have had a substantial impact on tax collections. The rates are especially high for FY2001–2002 and FY2002–2003, when the state suffered from recession and the September 11 tragedy. The PIT forecast is also subject to considerable uncertainties in the economy, firm productivity, consumer spending, performance of the stock market and financial services, and volatility of capital gains realizations and other income components.
- Average forecast errors also differ across the agencies. The AWAM is most accurate in forecasting PIT with an MAPE of 3.7 percent, and the SFC is most accurate in forecasting CFT with an MAPE of 7 percent. All three agencies demonstrate smaller errors in estimating SUT.

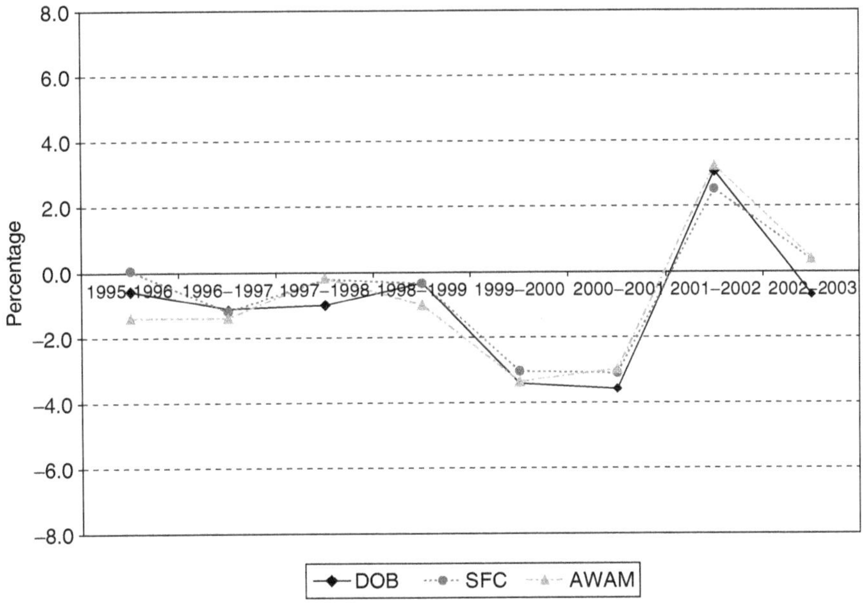

Figure 10.2 Accuracy of SUT forecasts.

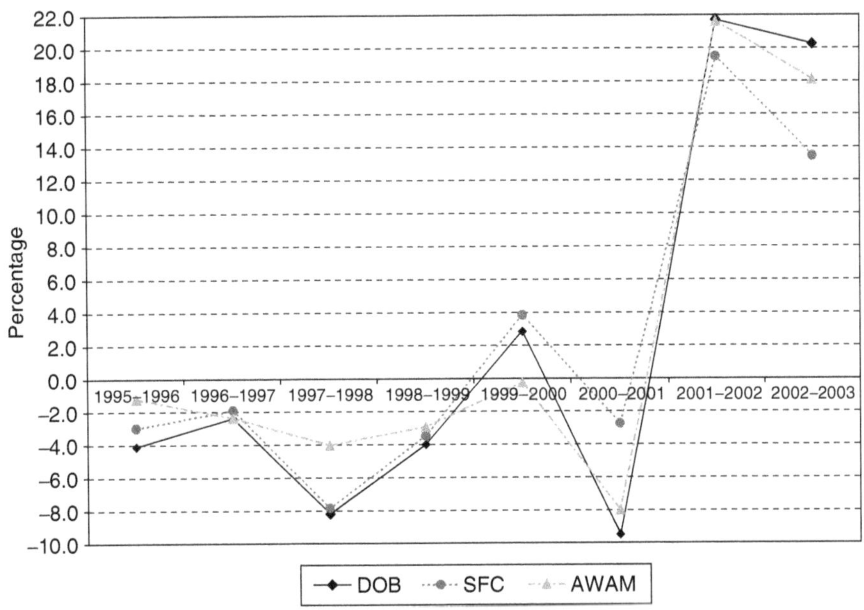

Figure 10.3 Accuracy of CFT forecasts.

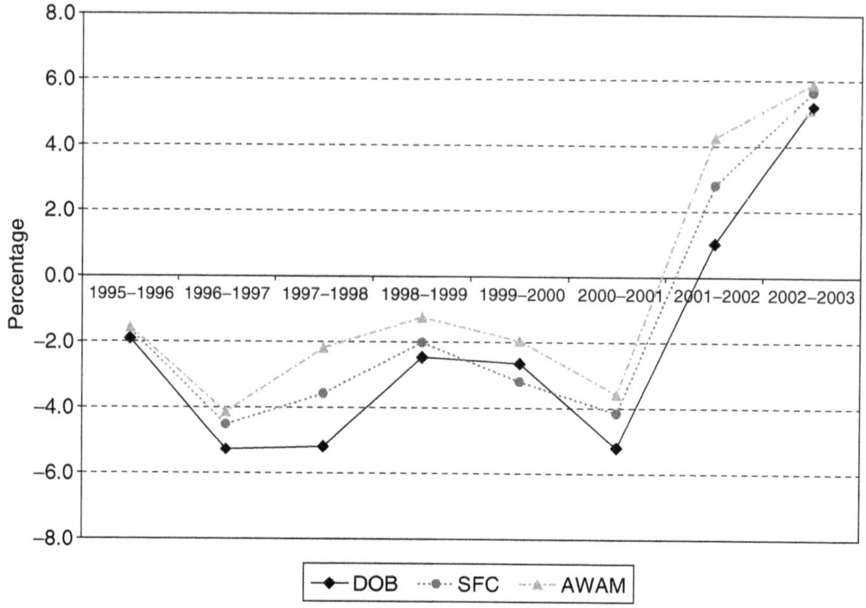

Figure 10.4 Accuracy of total modified GF tax revenue forecasts.

Small and large errors in individual tax revenue forecasts cancel one another and result in a total estimate that is reasonably good. Figure 10.4 provides a comparison of the three agencies' forecast accuracy of total modified GF tax revenues from FY1995–1996 to FY2002–2003. The total forecast is significant in that it provides the context for budget deliberations and sets budget constraints. Figure 10.4 shows the following:

- Overall, the three agencies' errors are within 6 percent and are negative except for the past two years, implying the three agencies have the tendency to underestimate revenues. Survey results reveal that the DOB, SFC, and AWAM have strong incentives to project revenues downward to accommodate risk preferences, balanced budget requirement, and other concerns, and underestimation is often regarded as a standard operating procedure (Rodgers and Joyce 1996). Consistent with the literature, the three agencies tend to be conservative as underforecasting revenues is less risky than overforecasting revenues, which necessitates cutting programs, raising taxes, and public hostility, and costs more politically and fiscally (Bretschneider and Schroeder 1988, Rodgers and Joyce 1996).
- PFEs vary from year to year and from agency to agency. The three agencies' forecast errors are within 2 percent for FY1995–1996, whereas the deviations are much larger for FY2002–2003 (in the range 5–6 percent of actual revenue

collections). Agencywise, the AWAM is most accurate from FY1995–1996 to FY2000–2001 and the DOB is most accurate during FY2001–2002 and FY2002–2003. Large and small errors balance out one another in MAPE, resulting in smaller average forecast errors: 3.6, 3.5, and 3.1 percent for the AWAM, SFC, and DOB, respectively.

Overall, the DOB, SFC, and AWAM did a decent job in forecasting state revenues during the past eight years. The existence of competing forecasts, professionalism among forecasters, and oversight of outside advisors contribute to the three agencies' forecast accuracy.

Other Criteria in Evaluating Revenue Forecasts in New York

Accuracy is the top priority in assessing revenue forecasts. Nonetheless, the performance of estimation cannot be judged by accuracy alone. Other standards, such as the ability to minimize uncertainty and improve decision making within the government (Mahmoud 1984), are also essential. This is because revenue forecasts "are much less an assertion of what will happen in the future than they are guides for policymakers and the electorate in devising more effective public management" (Schroeder 1982, p. 126) and "accuracy may be only a desired, but not necessarily imperative, by product" (Mahmoud et al. 1992, p. 259).

Focusing on the perceptions of professional staff, Table 10.2 summarizes what forecasters in the DOB, SFC, and AWAM consider to be important criteria in forecast evaluation.

- Consistent with the existing literature, accuracy was the most commonly cited standard in evaluating revenue forecasts. All 30 forecasters across the three agencies reported accuracy as an important criterion, and the previous section shows the three agencies' forecasts are within a reasonable range.
- Helping improve decision making was the second most frequently cited criterion after accuracy. Twenty-six of the thirty forecasters (86.7 percent) said

Table 10.2 Forecast Evaluation Criteria in New York

Criteria	*Frequency*	*Percentage*
Accuracy	30	100.0
Help improve decision making	26	86.7
Credibility	25	83.3
Speed	25	83.3
Ease of interpretation	21	70.0
Ease of use	18	60.0
Cost	12	40.0

their forecasts were used not only for internal analysis to ensure that state revenues were sufficient to meet spending obligations, but also to serve as the basis for political leaders to make budget decisions.

- Next, 25 respondents (83.3 percent) confirmed that credibility and timeliness of the forecasts were desirable. To achieve credibility, they employed sophisticated methods and developed complex models—thanks to the advancement of computer technology—and had a consistent forecasting record over time. As Figure 10.4 illustrates, except for FY1999–2000, the DOB is always conservative in forecasting state revenues, whereas the AWAM is optimistic and the SFC is in the middle. Since the 1980s, the three agencies have released their annual revenue forecast reports to gain credibility. The DOB took a step further by publishing its revenue estimation methodology in 2004 to help the public better understand the theory and methodology underlying its forecasts. Concerning timeliness of the forecasts, all three agencies completed their estimates by the constitutional or statutory deadline.
- Finally, ease of use and ease of interpretation were regarded as important by 21 forecasters (70 percent) and 18 forecasters (60 percent), respectively. The least well-rated criterion was cost of developing and updating forecasts, and 12 forecasters (40 percent) viewed it as important.

In summary, New York state revenue forecasts were good from the forecasting staff's point of view. Note that standards of forecast evaluation may differ depending on the occupations of respondents and the nature and purpose of the forecasts (Winklhofer et al. 1996). Forecasters and political leaders may select different criteria or rate them differently. Future research can extend the study to other stakeholders with divergent preferences and interests and compare whether and how they choose criteria in evaluating revenue forecasts. In addition, accuracy is important for both the forecasting staff and politicians. Nevertheless, they may have different attitude toward the level of accuracy needed. The staff strives for professionalism and attempts to make the best use of information and project revenues as well as they possibly can. Political leaders are more concerned with what lies behind the numbers—policy initiatives, programs, power, and other considerations. As a result, accuracy may not be as important as it appears to be. Future study can compare how forecasters and politicians look at forecast accuracy and how different points of view affect the size of forecast error.

Conclusions and Implications

This study evaluates New York state revenue forecasting process and the three agencies' forecasts for the past eight years. The analysis reveals problematic areas in New York state revenue forecasting process, among which lack of meaningful public participation and effective consensus process are prominent examples.

Regarding forecast accuracy, the three agencies' forecasts are generally within acceptable margin of error except few large errors for certain taxes or certain years. Beyond accuracy, the study finds that forecasters consider credibility, helping improve decision making, timeliness, and ease of use and interpretation as important criteria in their forecasting activities.

The evaluation of New York state revenue estimation has significant implications for budget reform in New York. New York has been well known for its persistently late budgets and budget fights among the Big Three. Improving revenue estimation is part of the state's comprehensive budget reform package and can make a step forward on its overall budget process. The study shows politics is a major reason for the lack of a truly effective consensus process in New York. The consensus conference could work, as it has worked well in many other states including the State of Michigan, where the consensus estimates are accurate and the process "focuses the legislative debate onto *how* to spend a fixed amount of revenue rather than simply 'adjusting' revenue estimates to 'fund' new or expanded programs that exceed budget targets" (Haas and Knittel 1998, p. 314). Political concerns also underlie other problems in the state's revenue estimation such as inadequate disclosure of revenue forecasting documents. Therefore, to improve New York state revenue estimation and reform the state budget process requires changing the political dynamics and inviting genuine commitment and cooperation from all parties involved. As New York State Office of the State Comptroller (1996) says, the "foremost concern must be fixing the process and tangential issues, driven by institutional or partisan ideology, should be put aside" (the Comptroller's Letter). In this regard, New York can learn from other states where consensus revenue forecasting has been successful. For instance, William Earle Klay and Joseph A. Vonasek in Chapter 16 of this book document how consensus revenue forecasting helps in reducing political conflicts and improving forecast accuracy in the State of Florida.

State revenue forecasting is technical and political. Following are the several points that should be stressed:

- Forecasters in the DOB, SFC, and AWAM serve their political leaders by providing information and analysis. They strive for professionalism and with the assistance of outside advisors have strong incentives to forecast as well as possible. Political leaders give due respect and trust to their staff in each agency, especially concerning the diligence and credibility of their staff's work. This, however, does not exclude the possibility that political leaders do whatever is politically beneficial and make decisions independent of relevant data on economic and revenue realities furnished by the staff. For instance, in March 1995, Governor Pataki was criticized for increasing his previous revenue projections by $300 million without presenting a sound justification and the purpose was to be simply "raising revenue estimates to accommodate spending desires" (Sack 1995).

- Virtually every forecasting staff surveyed believed that the leaders of their agency were influenced by the economic or revenue forecasts in the decision process, and the staff attributed the influence to their expertise. Although the staff see themselves as having influence, their influence should not be overestimated as their role is to process and supply information to the leaders. Political leaders make the final decision about how much revenue the state is likely to have in the upcoming FY and which number will appear in their official reports.
- Several norms of staff behavior, as identified by Balutis (1975a,b),* still exist. In particular, the staff in each agency tended to adopt the norms of loyalty, deference, anonymity, and specialization, which were expressed explicitly or implicitly in the survey. For instance, they were ready to defend their forecasts and their agency by asserting that their forecasts were better than others and they had better information, methodology, and more advanced technology.

Although this study sheds light on the New York experience, there are limitations associated with the research. This is a case study of New York state revenue forecasting, and the forecasting staff surveyed may not be representative of their counterparts in other states. In addition, their perceptions and understandings of state revenue estimation may not represent those of other states due to differences in institutional, political, fiscal, and other environment. In addition, the author collected eight years of forecast data. Future research may use a larger dataset and study more states with similar or different institutional arrangements to enrich the literature on state revenue forecasting.

References

Agostini, S. J. 1991. Searching for a better forecast: San Francisco's revenue forecasting model. *Government Finance Review* 7(6): 13–16.

Armstrong, J. S. 1985. *Long-Range Forecasting*, 2nd ed. New York: Wiley.

Bahl, R. W. 1980. Revenue and expenditure forecasting by state and local governments. In J. E. Petersen, C. L. Spain, and M. F. Laffey (eds.), *State and Local Government Finance and Financial Management*, pp. 120–126. Washington: Government Finance Research Center.

Balutis, A. P. 1975a. The budgetary process in New York state: the role of the legislative staff. In A. P. Balutis and D. K. Butler (eds.), *The Political Pursestrings: The Role of the Legislature in the Budgetary Process*, pp. 139–171. New York: Sage.

* Alan Balutis (1975a,b) studied state legislative staffing movement in New York in the 1960s and 1970s and concluded that there are certain behavioral norms among legislative staff members, which include limited advocacy, loyalty, deference, anonymity, specialization, partisanship, apprenticeship, institutional patronage, and legislative work.

Balutis, A. P. 1975b. Legislative staffing: a view from the states. In J. J. Heaphey and A. P. Balutis (eds.), *Legislative Staffing: A Comparative Perspective*, pp. 106–137. New York: Sage.

Benjamin, G. 2003. Reform in New York: the budget, the legislature and the governance process. A background paper prepared for a Citizens Budget Commission Conference November 13–14, 2003.

Bretschneider, S. I. and W. L. Gorr. 1987. State and local government revenue forecasting. In S. G. Makridakis and S. C. Wheelwright (eds.), *The Handbook of Forecasting: A Manager's Guide*, 2nd ed., pp. 118–134. New York: Wiley.

Bretschneider, S. I. and W. L. Gorr. 1999. Practical methods for projecting revenues. In R. T. Meyers (ed.), *Handbook of Government Budgeting*, pp. 308–331. San Francisco, CA: Jossey-Bass.

Bretschneider, S. I. and L. Schroeder. 1988. Evaluation of commercial economic forecasts for use in local government budgeting. *International Journal of Forecasting* 4: 33–43.

Citizens Budget Commission. 2003. *Fixing New York State's Fiscal Practices*. New York: Citizens Budget Commission.

Fischhoff, B. 1988. Judgment aspects of forecasting: needs and possible trends. *International Journal of Forecasting* 4: 331–339.

Forsythe, D. and D. Boyd. 2004. Budgeting in New York state: the growth and waning of executive power. Unpublished manuscript.

Frank, H. A. 1992. Expenditure forecasting. In J. Rabin (ed.), *Handbook of Public Budgeting*, pp. 167–209. New York: Marcel Dekker.

Hass, M. P. and M. J. Knittel. 1998. Revenue forecasting in Michigan. *Proceedings: Ninetieth Annual Conference on Taxation and Minutes of the Annual Meeting of the National Tax Association*, Washington, D.C.: The National Tax Association, pp. 313–318.

Howard, M. A. 1989. *Good Practices in Revenue Estimating*. Washington: National Association of State Budget Officers and the Federation of Tax Administrators.

Jonas, K., G. J. Rest, and T. Atkinson. 1992. Virginia's revenue forecasting process and models. *Public Budgeting & Finance* 12(2): 70–81.

Lynch, T. D. 1995. *Public Budgeting in America*, 4th ed. Englewood Cliffs, NJ: Prentice-Hall.

Mahmoud, E. 1984. Accuracy in forecasting: a survey. *Journal of Forecasting* 3: 139–159.

Mahmoud, E., R. DeRoeck, R. Brown, and G. Rice. 1992. Bridging the gap between theory and practice in forecasting. *International Journal of Forecasting* 8: 251–267.

National Advisory Council on State and Local Budgeting. 1998. Recommended budget practices: A framework for improved state and local government budgeting, http://gfoa.org/services/nacslb/ (accessed September 5, 2006).

New York State Office of the State Comptroller. 1996. *Budget Reform: Review of Issues and Proposals*. Albany, NY: New York State Office of the State Comptroller.

New York State Office of the State Comptroller. 2000. *2000–01 Budget Analysis: Review of Economic and Revenue Forecasts*. Albany, NY: New York State Office of the State Comptroller.

New York State Office of the State Comptroller. 2006. *Fiscal Reform for New York State: Improving Accountability, Transparency and Fiscal Responsibility*. Albany, NY: New York State Office of the State Comptroller.

O'Connor, M., W. Remus, and K. Griggs. 1993. Judgmental forecasting in times of change. *International Journal of Forecasting* 9: 163–172.

Rodgers, R. and P. Joyce. 1996. The effect of underforecasting on the accuracy of revenue forecasts by state government. *Public Administration Review* 56: 48–56.

Rubin, M. M., N. Mantell, and J. L. Peters. 1999. Revenue forecasting and estimation. In W. B. Hildreth and J. A. Richardson (eds.), *Handbook on Taxation*, pp. 769–799. New York: Marcel Dekker.

Sack, K. 1995. State leaders agree on revenue estimate. *New York Times*, March 16.

Schroeder, L. 1982. Local government multi-year budgetary forecasting: some administrative and political issues. *Public Administration Review* 42: 121–127.

Shkurti, W. J. 1990. A user's guide to state revenue forecasting. *Public Budgeting & Finance* 10(1): 79–94.

Shkurti, W. J. and D. Winefordner. 1989. The politics of state revenue forecasting in Ohio, 1984–1987: a case study and research implications. *International Journal of Forecasting* 5: 361–371.

Stinson, T. F. 2002. State revenue forecasting: an institutional framework. *Government Finance Review* 18(3): 12–15.

Sun, J. 2005. The dynamics of government revenue forecasting from an organizational perspective: a review of the literature. *Journal of Public Budgeting, Accounting & Financial Management* 17(4): 527–556.

Voorhees, W. 2000. The impact of political, institutional, methodological, and economic factors on forecast error. PhD Dissertation, Indiana University. Bloomington, Indiana: Indiana University.

Ward, R. B. 2002. *New York State Government: What It Does, How It Works*. Albany, NY: The Rockefeller Institute Press.

Winklhofer, H., A. Diamantopoulos, and S. F. Witt. 1996. Forecasting practice: a review of the empirical literature and an agenda for future research. *International Journal of Forecasting* 12: 193–221.

Yokum, J. T. and J. S. Armstrong. 1995. Beyond accuracy: comparison of criteria used to select forecasting methods. *International Journal of Forecasting* 11: 591–597.

Chapter 11

Using Census Data to Forecast New Local Sales Taxes

John D. Wong

Contents

Introduction

Revenue forecasts are integral components of the fiscal planning process. Because they are the fundamental building blocks of the budget, revenue forecasts are often highly political. According to Stinson (2002, p. 5), "[r]evenue projections provide the starting point for dealing with the challenges that accompany each new budget. By quantifying the size of the gap between spending and expected revenues, forecasts help focus the budget discussion, providing necessary discipline for negotiations between the executive and legislative branches of government." The importance of revenue forecasts in politically charged decisions increases the need for clear communication on how the forecasts are generated, why errors occur, how forecasts are to be interpreted, and potential risks to current projections.

Recent revenue shortfalls have increased the importance of financial forecasting at all levels of government. Beckett-Camarata (2006) concludes that fiscal stress has forced local governments to pay increasing attention to the importance of revenue forecasting. According to MacManus (1992, p. 7), "[p]ressures for revenue and expenditure forecasting accuracy are never greater than during periods of recession." Consistent with this, Rodgers and Joyce (1996) found that during recessions, revenue forecasts were much more accurate than during economic expansions. During the robust growth experienced in much of the 1990s, policy makers, responding to the perceived mood of the public, placed tax cuts and limitations at the top of their priorities. However, there has been no commensurate decrease in the public's desire for government services. Taxpayers wanted more and more public services, yet were not willing to pay increased taxes. Because of this, all levels of government must now look at objective projections of available resources and toward the management of revenues with the same intensity with which expenditures are monitored. Both the National Advisory Council on State and Local Budgeting (NACSLB) and the Government Finance Officers Association (GFOA) recommend continuous monitoring of revenue forecasts. Specifically, the NACSLB Practice 9.2 recommends that (National Advisory Council on State and Local Budgeting and Government Finance Officers Association 1998, pp. 44–45)

- A government should prepare multiyear projections of revenue and other sources.

- A government should maintain an in-depth understanding of its major revenues.
- A government should evaluate and understand the effect of potential changes to revenue sources and bases.

O'Toole et al. (1996) found that 98 percent of local government jurisdictions surveyed monitored expenditures, whereas 96 percent monitored revenues. This combination of increased public fiscal conservatism and local fiscal stress has prompted various governments to investigate the use of revenue forecasting models (Frank 1990).

Both overly optimistic and overly pessimistic revenue estimates can have undesirable consequences. Overly optimistic revenue projections can lead to fiscally unsustainable budgets, whereas overly pessimistic revenue projections can lead to unnecessary budget cuts. Because revenue estimates establish the fiscal parameters for expenditure decisions, increased fiscal stress accentuates the importance of accurate revenue forecasts. According to Agostini (1991, p. 13), "in public-sector budgeting, the availability of resources circumscribes discussions about expenditures. As these discussions intensify in the face of mounting fiscal stress, reliable and informative revenue forecasts become critical elements of the budgetary process." Growing revenue constraints have also increased the importance of debt financing in local government. An important consideration in this respect is that "the more meticulous a jurisdiction is in documenting and projecting its revenue trends, the more favorably the rating service will view the riskiness of the bond issue supported by the revenue" (Wong 1995, p. 65).

There are numerous methods of generating forecasts, and these vary in conceptual sophistication and resource requirements. The range of local government financial forecasting techniques runs from very rudimentary best guess estimates of future trends to very sophisticated statistical models. According to Frank (1990), one major obstacle to the use of quantitative methods to forecast local government revenues is the lack of adequate data. Moreover, as local governments continue to reduce their reliance on property taxes and shift more toward less stable revenue sources such as sales taxes and user charges, the establishment of a systematic revenue forecasting system will become even more important. According to MacManus (1992, p. 8), "[c]ities have more difficulty forecasting accurately than either counties or school districts, most likely because they rely on more revenue sources."

Unfortunately, most systematic revenue forecasting techniques require detailed information concerning the base underlying the revenue source to be estimated. According to McCullough (1990, p. 39), "[t]raditional approaches, trend-line and judgmental techniques, are more predominant in municipal forecasting and for the most part only larger cities indicate the use of more sophisticated methods." Although the federal government, state governments, and large metropolitan areas tend to have a wide array of data at their disposal concerning their respective jurisdictions, the same cannot be said for small- and medium-sized communities.

According to McCullough (1990, p. 39), many small local governments "have only a small staff and are plagued with missing data making statistical applications beyond their current capabilities." Although most states track state sales tax receipts down to the county level, the same cannot be said of collections at the municipal level. Because city boundaries tend to change with time, most state revenue departments do not track sales tax revenues down to the city level unless a municipal tax is already in place. Therefore, smaller municipalities contemplating to adopt a local sales tax do not have a reliable benchmark against which to gauge the potential yield of the new tax. MacManus (1992, p. 8) concludes that "[s]maller jurisdictions, mostly municipalities, have a more difficult time forecasting revenues than larger jurisdictions." Reddick (2004a, p. 598) indicates that "past research has shown that local officials are generally deficient in knowledge of revenue forecasting techniques." Reddick (2004b, p. 33) goes on to conclude that "Past research indicates that local government revenue forecasting technology tends to be methodologically unsophisticated relative to its state and federal counterparts."

This chapter develops and documents a local sales tax forecasting methodology that small- and medium-sized communities can use to estimate the base of a new local sales tax. The methodology revolves around using data from the U.S. Census Bureau's *County Business Patterns*; *Economic Census, Retail Trade, Geographic Area Series*; and *Annual Benchmark Report for Retail Trade and Food Services*. Because data in *County Business Patterns* is reported all the way down to the zip code level, detailed information on retail activities may be very closely matched to municipal boundaries. The *Economic Census* contains detailed information on industry sales sectorwise. The *Annual Benchmark Report* contains up-to-date information on industry growth trends by sector. Combining information from the three sources allows forecasters to impute and estimate the potential base for the new sales tax. Specifically, this chapter illustrates the use of this methodology to estimate the potential receipts from a newly adopted local sales tax to support a local bond issue in a medium-sized suburban community.

Data

County Business Patterns

County Business Patterns is an annual series that provides subnational economic data by industry. The series is useful for studying the economic activity of small areas; analyzing economic changes over time; and as a benchmark for statistical series, surveys, and databases between economic censuses. Businesses use the data for analyzing market potential, measuring the effectiveness of sales and advertising programs, setting sales quotas, and developing budgets. Government agencies use the data for administration and planning.

County Business Patterns covers most of the country's economic activity. The series excludes data on self-employed individuals, employees of private households, railroad employees, agricultural production employees, and most government employees. Beginning in 1998, data is tabulated by industry as defined in the North American Industry Classification System (NAICS), United States, 1997. Data for 1997 and earlier years is based on the Standard Industrial Classification (SIC) system.

ZIP Code Business Patterns (ZBP) presents data on the total number of establishments, employment, and payroll for more than 40,000 ZIP Code areas nationwide. In addition, the number of establishments for nine employment-size categories is provided by detailed industry for each zip code.

ZBP provides counts of establishments of industry by employment size for a broader range of industries that are included in the Economic Census ZIP Code statistics. ZBP is published generally two to three years after the end of the reference year, starting with 1994. Starting in 1998, the data is classified by NAICS. SIC classified data for 1994–1997.

Most ZIP Codes are derived from the physical location address reported in Census Bureau programs. The Internal Revenue Service provides supplemental address information. Those employers without a fixed location or with an unknown zip code are included under an "Unclassified" category indicated by ZIP Code 99999.

Economic Census

The Economic Census is the systematic measurement of the following:

- Almost all economic activity in the United States.
- Major business activity in Puerto Rico, the Virgin Islands of the United States, Guam, and the Commonwealth of the Northern Mariana Islands.
- Business activity within the scope of special programs including the Survey of Minority-Owned Businesses, Survey of Women-Owned Businesses, Business Expenditures Survey, Vehicle Inventory and Use Survey, and Commodity Flow Survey.

The Economic Census is the major economic statistical program of the United States. It constitutes the chief source of data about the structure and functioning of the nation's economy and provides the foundation and framework for a host of other statistical endeavors by public and private sector alike. Title 13 of the U.S. Code (Sections 131, 191, and 224) directs the Census Bureau to take the economic census every five years, covering years ending in 2 and 7.

Since 1997, data from the Economic Census has been published primarily on the basis of the NAICS, unlike earlier censuses, which were published according to the SIC system. NAICS is in the process of being adopted in the United States, Canada, and Mexico.

Most economic census reports cover one of the following NAICS sectors:

- 21 Mining
- 22 Utilities
- 23 Construction
- 31–33 Manufacturing
- 42 Wholesale trade
- 44–45 Retail trade
- 48–49 Transportation and warehousing
- 51 Information
- 52 Finance and insurance
- 53 Real estate and rental and leasing
- 54 Professional, scientific, and technical services
- 55 Management of companies and enterprises
- 56 Administrative and support and waste management and remediation services
- 61 Educational services
- 62 Health care and social assistance
- 71 Arts, entertainment, and recreation
- 72 Accommodation and foodservices
- 81 Other services (except public administration)

The agriculture, forestry, fishing, and hunting sector (NAICS 11) are not listed as they are partially covered by the census of agriculture conducted by the U.S. Department of Agriculture, Public Administration sector (NAICS 92), and census of governments conducted by the Census Bureau. The 20 NAICS sectors are subdivided into 96 subsectors (three-digit codes), 313 industry groups (four-digit codes), and, as implemented in the United States, 1170 industries (five- and six-digit codes).

The retail trade sector (sector 44–45) consists of establishments engaged in retailing merchandise, generally without transformation, and rendering services incidental to the sale of merchandise. The retailing process is the final step in the distribution of merchandise; retailers are, therefore, organized to sell merchandise in small quantities to the general public. This sector consists of two main types of retailers—store and nonstore retailers.

Store retailers operate fixed point-of-sale locations, located and designed to attract a high number of walk-in customers. In general, retail stores have extensive displays of merchandise and use mass-media advertising to attract customers. They typically sell merchandise to the general public for personal or household consumption, but some also serve business and institutional clients. In addition to retailing merchandise, some types of store retailers are also engaged in the provision of after-sales services such as repair and installation. As a general rule, establishments engaged in retailing merchandise and providing after-sales services are classified here.

Nonstore retailers, like store retailers, are organized to serve the general public but their retailing methods differ. The establishments of this subsector reach customers and market merchandise with methods such as the broadcasting of "infomercials," the broadcasting and publishing of direct-response advertising, the publishing of paper and electronic catalogs, door-to-door solicitation, in-home demonstration, selling from portable stalls (street vendors, except food), and distribution through vending machines. Establishments engaged in the direct sale (nonstore) of products, such as home heating oil dealers and home delivery newspaper routes, are classified here.

Excluded from this sector are governmental organizations classified in the covered industries except for liquor stores operated by state and local governments. Data for direct sellers with no paid employees and post exchanges, ship stores, and similar establishments operated on military posts by agencies of the federal government is not included.

Data is reported according to geographic area, merchandise line sales, establishment and firm size, and zip code. The basic tabulations in this report do not include data for establishments, which are auxiliary (primary function is providing a service, such as warehouses) to retail establishments within the same organization.

Annual Benchmark Report for Retail Trade and Food Services

The U.S. Census Bureau produces the *Annual Benchmark Report for Retail Trade and Food Services* to provide national estimates by kind of business of annual and monthly sales for establishments classified in the retail trade and food services industries. Estimates of end-of-month inventories, inventory-to-sales ratios, annual purchases, gross margin, gross margin as a percent of sales, end-of-year accounts receivable, and per capita sales are also provided, but only for retail establishments.

The U.S. Census Bureau develops these estimates using data from the *Monthly Retail Trade Survey (MRTS), Annual Retail Trade Survey (ARTS)*, and administrative records. For each survey, questionnaires are mailed to a probability sample of firms located in the United States and having paid employees. The samples are updated regularly and periodically reselected. These samples include firms of all sizes. Administrative records data is used to account for firms without paid employees.

The estimates in this publication are summarized by kind-of-business classification based on the 1997 NAICS. NAICS groups establishments into industries based on the activities in which they are primarily engaged. The joint efforts of statistical agencies in Canada, Mexico, and the United States developed this system. The common industry definitions allow for statistics to be compared by business activity across North America.

Retail trade, as defined by NAICS sectors 44–45, includes establishments engaged in selling merchandise in small quantities to the general public, without transformation, and rendering services incidental to the sale of merchandise. Two principal types of establishments classified in retail trade can be distinguished as follows:

- Store retailers operate fixed point-of-sale locations, located and designed to attract a high number of walk-in customers. They have extensive displays of merchandise, use mass-media advertising to attract customers and typically sell merchandise to the general public for personal or household use. Some store retailers also provide after-sales services such as repair and installation, for example, new automobile dealers.
- Nonstore retailers also serve the general public, but their retailing methods differ. Such methods include paper and electronic catalogs, door-to-door solicitation, in-home demonstration, "infomercials," and selling from portable stalls or through vending machines.

Food services, as defined by NAICS subsector 722, include establishments that prepare meals, snacks, and beverages to customer order for immediate on- and off-premises consumption.

New samples were introduced with the *1999 Annual Retail Trade Survey and with the March 2001 Monthly Retail Trade Survey*. The new samples were designed to produce NAICS estimates and replace the samples designed to produce SIC estimates.

Methodology

Sales per Establishment by Location

The number of establishments and total sales were obtained from the *Economic Census—Establishment and Firm Size Report* and the *Economic Census—Geographic Area Report* for the various NAICS sectors that include taxable retail sales. The NAICS sectors that include taxable retail sales were obtained from the state department of revenue. From these data, sales per establishment were computed by dividing sales in each sector by the number of establishments in each sector at the national level, the state level, the metropolitan statistical area (MSA) level, and the county level.

$$\frac{\text{Sales}}{\text{Establishment}} = \frac{\text{retail sales}}{\text{number of establishments}}$$

A composite measure of sales per establishment was also computed based on the average of state, MSA, and county sales per establishment. Five measures of sales per establishment were instituted to serve as alternative benchmarks on which retail sales tax projections will be based. Alternative benchmarks are presented to examine differences in sales per establishment based on differences in economies of scale, market areas, and other factors based on the area under consideration. Table 11.1 shows sales per establishment by location based on the five benchmarks.

Table 11.1 Sales per Establishment by Location

Industry Code	*Industry Code Description*	*Sedgwick County*	*Wichita MSA*	*Kansas*	*Composite*	*United States*
22	Utilities	—	26,108,889	14,910,790	26,108,889	27,404,458
221310	Water supply and irrigation systems	—	—	—	1,166,222	1,166,222
44	Retail trade	2,364,427	2,229,105	1,839,452	2,364,427	2,424,933
441110	New car dealers	23,262,889	21,177,489	13,902,525	23,262,889	21,091,453
441120	Used car dealers	—	1,884,750	1,460,638	1,884,750	1,694,281
441310	Automotive parts, accessories, and tire store	907,294	848,059	714,246	907,294	1,072,188
441320	Tire dealers	894,581	816,541	—	894,581	1,195,124
442210	Floor covering stores	1,283,579	1,081,731	912,306	1,283,579	1,089,724
443112	Radio, television, and other electronics stores	2,609,256	2,317,367	1,508,539	2,609,256	1,925,836
443120	Computer and software stores	1,306,826	1,183,259	1,560,695	1,306,826	2,461,500
444130	Hardware stores	797,760	752,781	—	797,760	922,272
444190	Other building material dealers	3,333,463	3,225,102	2,067,516	3,333,463	2,959,424
444210	Outdoor power equipment stores	686,429	—	702,567	686,429	936,815
444220	Nursery and garden centers	1,480,353	1,498,654	—	1,480,353	1,870,467
445110	Grocery (except convenience) stores	10,700,475	9,599,649	5,225,596	10,700,475	5,768,148
445310	Beer, wine, and liquor stores	785,102	748,010	531,588	785,102	843,530
446110	Pharmacies and drug stores	2,251,797	2,147,254	1,642,436	2,251,797	2,364,136
446120	Cosmetics, beauty supplies, and perfume store	—	412,381	417,474	412,381	527,277
446130	Optical goods stores	—	435,033	340,087	435,033	441,368
447110	Gasoline stations with convenience stores	2,186,262	2,011,543	1,459,739	2,186,262	1,634,535

(continued)

Table 11.1 (continued)

Industry Code	*Industry Code Description*	*Sedgwick County*	*Wichita MSA*	*Kansas*	*Composite*	*United States*
447190	Other gasoline stations	1,038,162	1,066,836	1,187,881	1,038,162	1,707,911
448110	Men's clothing stores	—	664,522	541,379	664,522	858,247
448120	Women's clothing stores	641,982	637,935	498,869	641,982	739,238
448140	Family clothing stores	1,834,677	1,660,000	1,219,561	1,834,677	2,353,465
448210	Shoe stores	685,860	656,053	624,838	685,860	672,216
451211	Book stores	—	—	—	1,091,213	1,091,213
452910	Warehouse clubs and superstores	—	—	—	53,787,711	53,787,711
452990	All other general merchandise stores	—	—	—	260,694	260,694
453110	Florists	287,316	287,347	202,151	287,316	231,189
453220	Gift, novelty, and souvenir stores	391,478	365,136	316,897	391,478	444,783
453910	Pet and pet supplies stores	—	486,619	593,279	486,619	813,432
453930	Manufactured (mobile) home dealers	—	3,868,933	—	3,868,933	2,635,827
453998	All other misc store retailers (except tobacco)	—	—	—	581,951	581,951
454110	Electronic shopping and mail-order houses	—	—	—	9,102,286	9,102,286
454390	Other direct selling establishments	453,976	413,383	—	453,976	1,137,750
713940	Fitness and recreational sports centers	466,583	428,893	348,276	466,583	584,811
713950	Bowling centers	1,191,818	923,933	391,192	1,191,818	562,951
713990	All other amusement and recreation industries	—	—	269,818	269,818	495,494

722110	Full-service restaurants	—	582,476	466,125	582,476	693,848
722211	Limited-service restaurants	—	552,899	533,880	552,899	600,758
722213	Snack and nonalcoholic beverage bars	—	366,000	—	366,000	344,937
722410	Drinking places (alcoholic beverages)	—	194,390	166,602	194,390	260,638
811111	General automotive repair	401,817	396,465	306,122	401,817	367,621
811112	Automotive exhaust system repair	—	348,667	341,083	348,667	405,684
811121	Automotive body, paint and interior R&M	554,382	524,128	409,925	554,382	558,050
811122	Automotive glass replacement shops	479,500	395,125	358,853	479,500	607,268
811191	Automotive oil change and lubrication shops	—	484,167	408,692	484,167	409,567
811192	Car washes	—	237,771	210,000	237,771	333,983
811310	Commercial equipment (except automotive and electronic) R&M	997,438	896,128	656,331	997,438	974,408
811490	Other personal and household goods R&M	—	150,800	199,117	150,800	354,911
812111	Barber shops	—	132,167	179,442	132,167	110,146
812112	Beauty salons	—	152,529	130,576	152,529	167,622
812191	Diet and weight reducing centers	216,909	216,909	186,326	216,909	360,928
812199	Other personal care services	114,350	105,043	119,250	114,350	162,806
812210	Funeral homes	—	568,821	425,180	568,821	617,381
812320	Drycleaning and laundry services (except coin-op)	—	205,439	248,039	205,439	279,905

Note: Author's own computations based on data from the U.S. Census Bureau, *1997 Economic Census—Geographic Area Report.*

Sales per Establishment by Employment Class Size

The level of sales per establishment is, however, likely to vary based on the size of the establishment. As such, the number of establishments by employment-size class and sales by employment-size class were obtained from the *Economic Census—Establishment and Firm Size Report* for the various NAICS sectors that include taxable retail sales. From these data, sales per establishment were computed by dividing sales in each sector by employment-size class by the number of establishments in each sector by employment-size class. Unfortunately, data based on employment class size is available only at the national level. From this data, a ratio was computed comparing average sales per establishment based on employment class size to the overall average sales per establishment in each sector. This adjustment was made to account for the fact that retail establishments in smaller communities may be somewhat smaller than the national average. Table 11.2 shows sales per establishment ratios by employment class size.

Number of Establishments by Employment-Size Class for Forecast Area

The number of establishments by employment-size class for the forecast area was obtained from ZBP for the various NAICS sectors that include taxable retail sales. The boundaries for the municipality correspond very closely to the boundaries of the zip code that includes the municipality. Table 11.3 shows the number of establishments by employment-size class.

Total Sales by Benchmark Location

Total sales were computed by multiplying the number of establishments in each sector in the forecast area by sales per establishment in each sector at the national, state, MSA, county, and composite benchmark levels.

$$\text{Retail sales} = \text{number of establishments} \times \frac{\text{sales}}{\text{establishment}}$$

Again, five measures of total sales were established to serve as alternative benchmarks on which retail sales tax projections will be based. The five measures include Sedgwick County (the county that includes the city of Derby); the Wichita MSA (the MSA that includes the city of Derby); the state of Kansas; a composite measure of the county, the MSA, and the state; and the United States as a whole. Table 11.4 shows total sales by benchmark location.

Total Sales by Employment Class Size

Total sales by employment class size were computed by multiplication of average total sales by benchmark location with the sales per establishment by employment

Table 11.2 Sales per Establishment Ratio by Employment Class Size

Industry Code	Industry Code Description	1–4 (Percent)	5–9 (Percent)	10–19 (Percent)	20–49 (Percent)	50–99 (Percent)	100–249 (Percent)	250–499 (Percent)	500–999 (Percent)	1000 or More (Percent)
22	Utilities	6.2	14.9	38.7	65.3	155.2	458.5	642.4	1884.4	—
221310	Water supply and irrigation systems	14.8	59.2	180.5	543.1	1516.8	0	0	0	—
44	Retail trade	15.7	37.1	70.3	158.3	285.1	267.3	174.3	129.7	186.2
441110	New car dealers	4.1	13.2	29.6	73.4	150.7	258.8	245.5	265.9	237.9
441120	Used car dealers	51.5	118.6	230.6	408	742.6	457	0	0	—
441310	Automotive parts, accessories and tire store	29.4	68.2	119.4	171.3	203.4	218.5	172.3	138.5	133.6
441320	Tire dealers	25.9	63.5	115.6	164.6	192.8	161.9	155.2	0	0
442210	Floor covering stores	41.8	96.2	164.9	236.9	340.6	272.5	443.2	0	0
443112	Radio, television, and other electronics stores	15	37.4	68	98.7	97	138.4	234.8	0	0
443120	Computer and software stores	21.6	51	102	221.8	328.1	351.1	0	0	0
444130	Hardware stores	30	66.3	121.6	216.2	254.9	202.1	0	0	0
444190	Other building material dealers	16	41.8	84.1	152	208.5	242.4	232	199	206.4
444210	Outdoor power equipment stores	36.9	94.6	202.3	374.9	703.2	0	—	0	—
444220	Nursery and garden centers	24.1	63.2	117.9	177.5	265.8	250	174.3	204.8	184.6
445110	Grocery (except convenience) stores	5.9	13.8	26.4	55.7	101.2	132.6	153.8	164.9	243

(continued)

Table 11.2 (continued)

Industry Code	*Industry Code Description*	*1–4 (Percent)*	*5–9 (Percent)*	*10–19 (Percent)*	*20–49 (Percent)*	*50–99 (Percent)*	*100–249 (Percent)*	*250–499 (Percent)*	*500–999 (Percent)*	*1000 or More (Percent)*
445310	Beer, wine, and liquor stores	55.5	106.1	172.1	272	253	166.8	143	245.8	132
446110	Pharmacies and drug stores	24	46.6	72.2	100.3	120.4	123.1	105.1	143.6	157.8
446120	Cosmetics, beauty supplies, and perfume store	38.2	82.6	124.7	132.6	189.3	155.4	0	0	0
446130	Optical goods stores	51	108.8	140.8	128.1	95.7	103.4	148.3	117.7	118.6
447110	Gasoline stations with convenience stores	42.9	84	117	115.7	104.7	107.3	109.1	109.3	122.1
447190	Other gasoline stations	39.4	84.6	125.9	171.5	183.7	182.5	152.2	221.4	226.9
448110	Men's clothing stores	34.3	76.7	125.4	157.9	136.9	131.9	125.9	276	121.9
448120	Women's clothing stores	30	65.5	112.4	142.7	131.6	124.8	134.2	135.3	132.5
448140	Family clothing stores	10.3	24.3	41.7	56.5	72.6	80.5	103.2	68.9	156.9
448210	Shoe stores	40.4	88.3	129.4	145.1	126.9	143.9	132	79	105.1
451211	Book stores	18.8	41.2	73.1	111.7	117.9	0	157.7	0	176.1
452910	Warehouse clubs and superstores	—	0	0	0	—	0	0	100	100
452990	All other general merchandise stores	100	0	0	0	861.2	827	0	0	594.5
453110	Florists	54.8	106.5	183	276.4	386.7	307.3	336.2	—	—
453220	Gift, novelty, and souvenir stores	42.7	86.4	146.2	187.4	236.1	0	0	367.2	151.2

453910	Pet and pet supplies stores	27.4	56.2	92.7	128.8	155.9	177.8	0	0	312.3
453930	Manufactured (mobile) home dealers	38.3	80.6	117.4	164.6	195.5	147.6	0	—	0
453998	All other misc store retailers (except tobacco)	46.7	100	165.7	257.3	245	0	0	166	0
454110	Electronic shopping and mail-order houses	4.5	13.3	27.9	58.3	186.2	394.9	497.6	570.2	1024.4
454390	Other direct selling establishments	26.4	69.3	112.9	201.1	473.4	636.5	0	0	209
713940	Fitness and recreational sports centers	22	40.5	64.3	117.7	226.1	350.5	360.1	0	0
713950	Bowling centers	25.5	42.8	76.5	149.8	229.3	183.6	206.3	0	0
713990	All other amusement and recreation industries	41.6	90.1	155.3	267.4	349.2	486.5	530.9	270.3	—
722110	Full-service restaurants	18.1	35.6	61.4	121	238.8	273	229.4	219.8	240.2
722211	Limited-service restaurants	20.8	41.3	68.2	117.2	148.1	158.5	157.3	142.3	152.2
722213	Snack and nonalcoholic beverage bars	35.5	66.3	106.2	164.6	185.3	180.4	167.6	160.2	158.7
722410	Drinking places (alcoholic beverages)	51.1	95	167.3	322.3	587.5	999.2	971.3	0	0
811111	General automotive repair	58.1	135.5	262.6	438.3	618.6	448.2	572.1	0	0
811112	Automotive exhaust system repair	56.7	120.4	160.1	156.9	149.3	161.1	0	—	0
811121	Automotive body, paint, and interior R&M	37.8	97.6	195.6	367.3	491.7	764.9	0	—	0

(continued)

Table 11.2 (continued)

Industry Code	Industry Code Description	1–4 (Percent)	5–9 (Percent)	10–19 (Percent)	20–49 (Percent)	50–99 (Percent)	100–249 (Percent)	250–499 (Percent)	500–999 (Percent)	1000 or More (Percent)
811122	Automotive glass replacement shops	39.3	90.3	159	185.8	191.9	120.9	0	—	0
811191	Automotive oil change and lubrication shops	42.9	91	129	139.1	147.5	110.9	111.6	0	0
811192	Car washes	40.1	73.7	111.3	195.8	248.8	311.7	602.1	0	0
811310	Commercial equipment (except automotive and electronic) R&M	22.6	62	132.3	260.7	421.2	521	404	397.3	504.9
811490	Other personal and household goods R&M	42.9	115.9	233.8	505.5	665.5	0	0	—	0
812111	Barber shops	63.5	149.2	242.5	467	0	0	—	—	0
812112	Beauty salons	43.6	101.9	196.9	0	274.6	0	205.4	0	0
812191	Diet and weight reducing centers	34.7	67.2	122	239.8	97	0	1456.2	0	126.2
812199	Other personal care services	56.7	98.6	185.5	244.2	534.1	0	—	0	—
812210	Funeral homes	52.9	87.9	121.2	161.1	190.4	295.2	—	164.7	157.9
812320	Drycleaning and laundry services (except coin-op)	44.7	81.4	126.8	178.1	243.3	267.4	273.6	0	0

Note: Author's own computations based on data from the U.S. Census Bureau, *1997 Economic Census—Employment and Firm Size Report.*

Table 11.3 Number of Establishments by Employment Class Size

Industry Code	*Industry Code Description*	*Total*	*1–4*	*5–9*	*10–19*	*20–49*	*50–99*	*100–249*	*250–499*	*500–999*	*1000 or More*
22	Utilities	1	—	1	—	—	—	—	—	—	—
221310	Water supply and irrigation systems	1	—	1	—	—	—	—	—	—	—
44	Retail trade	55	27	11	12	2	1	1	0	1	0
441110	New car dealers	1	1	0	0	0	0	0	0	0	0
441120	Used car dealers	2	2	0	0	0	0	0	0	0	0
441310	Automotive parts, accessories and tire store	4	2	1	1	0	0	0	0	0	0
441320	Tire dealers	1	1	0	0	0	0	0	0	0	0
442210	Floor covering stores	1	1	0	0	0	0	0	0	0	0
443112	Radio, television, and other electronics stores	2	1	1	0	0	0	0	0	0	0
443120	Computer and software stores	1	1	0	0	0	0	0	0	0	0
444130	Hardware stores	2	1	1	0	0	0	0	0	0	0
444190	Other building material dealers	1	0	0	1	0	0	0	0	0	0
444210	Outdoor power equipment stores	1	1	0	0	0	0	0	0	0	0
444220	Nursery and garden centers	1	1	0	0	0	0	0	0	0	0
445110	Grocery (except convenience) stores	2	0	0	0	0	1	1	0	0	0
445310	Beer, wine, and liquor stores	3	2	0	1	0	0	0	0	0	0
446110	Pharmacies and drug stores	4	1	1	1	1	0	0	0	0	0
446120	Cosmetics, beauty supplies, and perfume store	1	0	1	0	0	0	0	0	0	0
446130	Optical goods stores	1	1	0	0	0	0	0	0	0	0
447110	Gasoline stations with convenience stores	4	0	1	3	0	0	0	0	0	0

(continued)

Table 11.3 (continued)

Industry Code	*Industry Code Description*	*Total*	*1–4*	*5–9*	*10–19*	*20–49*	*50–99*	*100–249*	*250–499*	*500–999*	*1000 or More*
447190	Other gasoline stations	2	0	1	1	0	0	0	0	0	0
448110	Men's clothing stores	1	0	0	1	0	0	0	0	0	0
448120	Women's clothing stores	1	1	0	0	0	0	0	0	0	0
448140	Family clothing stores	1	0	0	1	0	0	0	0	0	0
448210	Shoe stores	1	1	0	0	0	0	0	0	0	0
451211	Book stores	1	1	0	0	0	0	0	0	0	0
452910	Warehouse clubs and superstores	1	0	0	0	0	0	0	0	1	0
452990	All other general merchandise stores	3	2	1	0	0	0	0	0	0	0
453110	Florists	2	1	1	0	0	0	0	0	0	0
453220	Gift, novelty, and souvenir stores	3	1	1	1	0	0	0	0	0	0
453910	Pet and pet supplies stores	1	1	0	0	0	0	0	0	0	0
453930	Manufactured (mobile) home dealers	1	0	0	0	1	0	0	0	0	0
453998	All other misc store retailers (except tobacco)	1	0	1	0	0	0	0	0	0	0
454110	Electronic shopping and mail-order houses	2	1	0	1	0	0	0	0	0	0
454390	Other direct selling establishments	2	2	0	0	0	0	0	0	0	0
713940	Fitness and recreational sports centers	1	1	0	0	0	0	0	0	0	0
713950	Bowling centers	1	0	0	0	1	0	0	0	0	0
713990	All other amusement and recreation industries	2	1	1	0	0	0	0	0	0	0

722110	Full-service restaurants	11	4	2	2	3	0	0	0	0	0
722211	Limited-service restaurants	15	2	1	3	8	1	0	0	0	0
722213	Snack and nonalcoholic beverage bars	2	0	0	1	1	0	0	0	0	0
722410	Drinking places (alcoholic beverages)	2	1	0	1	0	0	0	0	0	0
811111	General automotive repair	5	4	1	0	0	0	0	0	0	0
811112	Automotive exhaust system repair	1	1	0	0	0	0	0	0	0	0
811121	Automotive body, paint and interior R&M	5	3	1	0	1	0	0	0	0	0
811122	Automotive glass replacement shops	1	1	0	0	0	0	0	0	0	0
811191	Automotive oil change and lubrication shops	2	1	0	1	0	0	0	0	0	0
811192	Car washes	2	1	0	0	1	0	0	0	0	0
811310	Commercial equipment (except automotive and electronic) R&M	1	1	0	0	0	0	0	0	0	0
811490	Other personal and household goods R&M	1	1	0	0	0	0	0	0	0	0
812111	Barber shops	3	3	0	0	0	0	0	0	0	0
812112	Beauty salons	8	4	4	0	0	0	0	0	0	0
812191	Diet and weight reducing centers	1	1	0	0	0	0	0	0	0	0
812199	Other personal care services	1	0	0	1	0	0	0	0	0	0
812210	Funeral homes	1	0	0	1	0	0	0	0	0	0
812320	Drycleaning and laundry services (except coin-op)	3	1	2	0	0	0	0	0	0	0

Note: Author's own computations based on data from the U.S. Census Bureau, *2000 Zip Code Business Patterns*.

Table 11.4 Total Sales by Benchmark Location

Industry Code	*Industry Code Description*	*Sedgwick County*	*Wichita MSA*	*Kansas*	*United States*
22	Utilities	—	26,108,889	14,910,790	26,108,889
221310	Water supply and irrigation systems	—	—	—	1,166,222
44	Retail trade	130,043,476	122,600,771	101,169,871	130,043,476
441110	New car dealers	23,262,889	21,177,489	13,902,525	23,262,889
441120	Used car dealers	—	3,769,500	2,921,275	3,769,500
441310	Automotive parts, accessories, and tire store	3,629,176	3,392,238	2,856,986	3,629,176
441320	Tire dealers	894,581	816,541	—	894,581
442210	Floor covering stores	1,283,579	1,081,731	912,306	1,283,579
443112	Radio, television, and other electronics stores	5,218,512	4,634,735	3,017,078	5,218,512
443120	Computer and software stores	1,306,826	1,183,259	1,560,695	1,306,826
444130	Hardware stores	1,595,520	1,505,563	—	1,595,520
444190	Other building material dealers	3,333,463	3,225,102	2,067,516	3,333,463
444210	Outdoor power equipment stores	686,429	—	702,567	686,429
444220	Nursery and garden centers	1,480,353	1,498,654	—	1,480,353
445110	Grocery (except convenience) stores	21,400,949	19,199,299	10,451,191	21,400,949
445310	Beer, wine, and liquor stores	2,355,307	2,244,029	1,594,764	2,355,307
446110	Pharmacies and drug stores	9,007,186	8,589,015	6,569,744	9,007,186
446120	Cosmetics, beauty supplies, and perfume store	—	412,381	417,474	412,381
446130	Optical goods stores	—	435,033	340,087	435,033
447110	Gasoline stations with convenience stores	8,745,050	8,046,174	5,838,957	8,745,050
447190	Other gasoline stations	2,076,324	2,133,672	2,375,762	2,076,324

448110	Men's clothing stores	—	664,522	541,379	664,522
448120	Women's clothing stores	641,982	637,935	498,869	641,982
448140	Family clothing stores	1,834,677	1,660,000	1,219,561	1,834,677
448210	Shoe stores	685,860	656,053	624,838	685,860
451211	Book stores	—	—	—	1,091,213
452910	Warehouse clubs and superstores	—	—	—	53,787,711
452990	All other general merchandise stores	—	—	—	782,081
453110	Florists	574,632	574,694	404,301	574,632
453220	Gift, novelty, and souvenir stores	1,174,435	1,095,407	950,692	1,174,435
453910	Pet and pet supplies stores	—	486,619	593,279	486,619
453930	Manufactured (mobile) home dealers	—	3,868,933	—	3,868,933
453998	All other misc store retailers (except tobacco)	—	—	—	581,951
454110	Electronic shopping and mail-order houses	—	—	—	18,204,573
454390	Other direct selling establishments	907,951	826,766	—	907,951
713940	Fitness and recreational sports centers	466,583	428,893	348,276	466,583
713950	Bowling centers	1,191,818	923,933	391,192	1,191,818
713990	All other amusement and recreation industries	—	—	539,636	539,636
722110	Full-service restaurants	—	6,407,240	5,127,375	6,407,240
722211	Limited-service restaurants	—	8,293,486	8,008,207	8,293,486
722213	Snack and nonalcoholic beverage bars	—	732,000	—	732,000
722410	Drinking places (alcoholic beverages)	—	388,781	333,204	388,781
811111	General automotive repair	2,009,085	1,982,326	1,530,609	2,009,085
811112	Automotive exhaust system repair	—	348,667	341,083	348,667
811121	Automotive body, paint, and interior R&M	2,771,912	2,620,641	2,049,626	2,771,912

(continued)

Table 11.4 (continued)

Industry Code	*Industry Code Description*	*Sedgwick County*	*Wichita MSA*	*Kansas*	*United States*
811122	Automotive glass replacement shops	479,500	395,125	358,853	479,500
811191	Automotive oil change and lubrication shops	—	968,333	817,385	968,333
811192	Car washes	—	475,543	420,000	475,543
811310	Commercial equipment (except automotive and electronic) R&M	997,438	896,128	656,331	997,438
811490	Other personal and household goods R&M	—	150,800	199,117	150,800
812111	Barber shops	—	396,500	538,326	396,500
812112	Beauty salons	—	1,220,229	1,044,609	1,220,229
812191	Diet and weight reducing centers	216,909	216,909	186,326	216,909
812199	Other personal care services	114,350	105,043	119,250	114,350
812210	Funeral homes	—	568,821	425,180	568,821
812320	Drycleaning and laundry services (except coin-op)	—	616,318	744,118	616,318

Note: Author's own computations based on data from the U.S. Census Bureau, *1997 Economic Census—Geographic Area Report and 2000 County and Zip Code Business Patterns*.

class size ratio. Again, this adjustment was made to account for the fact that retail establishments in smaller communities maybe somewhat smaller than the national average. Table 11.5 shows total sales by employment class size.

Percentage of Sales to the General Public

All sales are, however, not taxable. The percentage of sales to the general public, that is, household consumers and individuals was obtained from the *Economic Census—Miscellaneous Subjects Report*. Generally, wholesale transactions are not subject to retail sales tax. Table 11.6 shows the percentage of sales to the general public.

Total Taxable Retail Sales

Total taxable retail sales were computed by multiplication of total sales by employment class size with the percentage of sales to the general public size for each sector. Total projected taxable retail sales may be obtained by summing taxable retail sales across all sectors. Total taxable retail sales were projected to the forecast year using sales growth rates computed based on data from the *Annual Benchmark Report for Retail Trade and Food Services*. Table 11.7 shows potential taxable retail sales within the city of Derby. From this, anticipated retail sales tax receipts were projected. On the basis of this computation, projected retail sales tax receipts accounted for 97.7 percent of the actual sales tax receipts received over this period.

General Demographic Data and Trends

The city of Derby, Kansas, is located in southeast Sedgwick County bordered by the Arkansas River on the west, smaller towns on the east and south, and Wichita, the state's largest city approximately 5 mi to the north. The Wichita metropolitan area has a population of approximately 600,000. The area is served by four major highways: Interstate 35 (the Kansas Turnpike), Interstate 135, U.S. Highway 54, and Kansas Highway 15. The city of Derby encompasses approximately 6.6 mi^2 and has a population of about 20,000. Although Derby started in 1869 as a farming community, stage and freight stop, it is now primarily residential. The surrounding farm area is devoted principally to the production of wheat, corn, sorghum, soybeans, maize, and cattle.

Economic Base and Core Industries

The city is home to numerous employees of many national corporations such as Boeing, Cessna, Coleman, Learjet, and Raytheon. In addition, the city counts many McConnell Air Force families among its residents. Derby has almost doubled its size in the past 20 years. The city is in proximity to large industries including the Boeing Company as well as the entire Wichita area industrial base.

Table 11.5 Total Sales by Employment Class Size

Industry Code	*Industry Code Description*	*1–4*	*5–9*	*10–19*	*20–49*	*50–99*	*100–249*	*250–499*	*500–999*	*1000 or More*	*Total*
22	Utilities	—	3,879,979	—	—	—	—	—	—		3,879,979
221310	Water supply and Irrigation systems	—	690,894	—	—	—	—	—	—		690,894
44	Retail trade	10,013,241	9,651,110	19,943,259	7,484,697	6,739,982	6,321,224	—	3,067,348	—	63,220,860
441110	New car dealers	948,721	—	—	—	—	—	—	—	—	948,721
441120	Used car dealers	1,942,426	—	—	—	—	—	—	—	—	1,942,426
441310	Automotive parts, accessories, and tire store	532,805	618,935	1,083,717	—	—	—	—	—	—	2,235,457
441320	Tire dealers	231,863	—	—	—	—	—	—	—	—	231,863
442210	Floor covering stores	536,280	—	—	—	—	—	—	—	—	536,280
443112	Radio, television, and other electronics stores	390,415	974,563	—	—	—	—	—	—	—	1,364,977
443120	Computer and software stores	281,780	—	—	—	—	—	—	—	—	281,780
444130	Hardware stores	239,379	529,265	—	—	—	—	—	—	—	768,644
444190	Other building material dealers	—	—	2,802,845	—	—	—	—	—	—	2,802,845
444210	Outdoor power equipment stores	253,160	—	—	—	—	—		—		253,160
444220	Nursery and garden centers	356,950	—	—	—	—	—	—	—	—	356,950
445110	Grocery (except convenience) stores	—	—	—	—	10,825,515	14,191,231	—	—	—	25,016,746

445310	Beer, wine, and liquor stores	871,526	—	1,351,451	—	—	—	—	—	—	2,222,977
446110	Pharmacies and drug stores	540,924	1,048,686	1,625,167	2,257,649	—	—	—	—	—	5,472,426
446120	Cosmetics, beauty supplies, and perfume store	—	340,687	—	—	—	—	—	—	—	340,687
446130	Optical goods stores	221,867	—	—	—	—	—	—	—	—	221,867
447110	Gasoline stations with convenience stores	—	1,835,568	7,672,181	—	—	—	—	—	—	9,507,749
447190	Other gasoline stations	—	878,281	1,307,479	—	—	—	—	—	—	2,185,760
448110	Men's clothing stores	—	—	833,189	—	—	—	—	—	—	833,189
448120	Women's clothing stores	192,778	—	—	—	—	—	—	—	—	192,778
448140	Family clothing stores	—	—	765,321	—	—	—	—	—	—	765,321
448210	Shoe stores	277,242	—	—	—	—	—	—	—	—	277,242
451211	Book stores	205,202	—	—	—	—	—	—	—	—	205,202
452910	Warehouse clubs and superstores		—	—	—	—	—	—	53,787,711	—	53,787,711
452990	All other general merchandise stores	521,388	—	—	—		—	—	—	—	521,388
453110	Florists	157,495	305,886	—	—	—	—	—			463,382
453220	Gift, novelty, and souvenir stores	167,304	338,287	572,357	—	—	—	—	—	—	1,077,947
453910	Pet and pet supplies stores	133,342	—	—	—	—	—	—	—	—	133,342
453930	Manufactured (mobile) home dealers	—	—	—	6,368,988	—	—	—		—	6,368,988

(continued)

Table 11.5 (continued)

Industry Code	*Industry Code Description*	*1–4*	*5–9*	*10–19*	*20–49*	*50–99*	*100–249*	*250–499*	*500–999*	*1000 or More*	*Total*
453998	All other misc store retailers (except tobacco)	—	581,748	—	—	—	—	—	—	—	581,748
454110	Electronic shopping and mail-order houses	408,002	—	2,543,616	—	—	—	—	—	—	2,951,618
454390	Other direct selling establishments	239,476	—	—	—	—	—	—	—	—	239,476
713940	Fitness and recreational sports centers	102,689	—	—	—	—	—	—	—	—	102,689
713950	Bowling centers	—	—	—	1,785,135	—	—	—			1,785,135
713990	All other amusement and recreation industries	112,299	243,066	—	—	—	—	—	—		355,365
722110	Full-service restaurants	421,053	414,804	714,726	2,114,630	—	—	—	—	—	3,665,213
722211	Limited-service restaurants	230,357	228,397	1,130,759	5,185,390	818,642	—	—	—	—	7,593,545
722213	Snack and nonalcoholic beverage bars	—	—	388,700	602,304	—	—	—	—	—	991,004
722410	Drinking places (alcoholic beverages)	99,306	—	325,295	—	—	—	—	—	—	424,600
811111	General automotive repair	934,422	544,537	—	—	—	—	—	—	—	1,478,959
811112	Automotive exhaust system repair	197,816	—	—	—	—	—	—		—	197,816

811121	Automotive body, paint, and interior R&M	628,431	541,224	—	2,036,110	—	—	—		—	3,205,765
811122	Automotive glass replacement shops	188,412	—	—	—	—	—	—		—	188,412
811191	Automotive oil change and lubrication shops	207,937	—	624,730	—	—	—	—	—	—	832,667
811192	Car washes	95,288	—	—	465,524	—	—	—	—	—	560,813
811310	Commercial equipment (except automotive and electronic) R&M	225,398	—	—	—	—	—	—	—	—	225,398
811490	Other personal and household goods R&M	64,696	—	—	—	—	—	—		—	64,696
812111	Barber shops	251,855	—	—	—	—	—			—	251,855
812112	Beauty salons	265,938	621,986	—	—	—	—	—	—	—	887,924
812191	Diet and weight reducing centers	75,171	—	—	—	—	—	—	—	—	75,171
812199	Other personal care services	—	—	212,164	—	—	—		—		212,164
812210	Funeral homes	—	—	689,481	—	—	—		—	—	689,481
812220	Drycleaning and laundry services (except coin-op)	91,758	334,411	—	—	—	—	—	—	—	426,169

Note: Author's own computations based on data from the U.S. Census Bureau, *1997 Economic Census—Establishment and Firm Size Report and 2000 Zip Code Business Patterns.*

Table 11.6 Percentage of Sales to General Public

Industry Code	*Industry Code Description*	*Total (Percent)*
22	Utilities	100
221310	Water supply and Irrigation systems	100
44	Retail trade	84.2
441110	New car dealers	84.2
441120	Used car dealers	77.1
441310	Automotive parts, accessories, and tire store	33.2
441320	Tire dealers	60.4
442210	Floor covering stores	59.9
443112	Radio, television, and other electronics stores	94.8
443120	Computer and software stores	58.7
444130	Hardware stores	69.7
444190	Other building material dealers	14.4
444210	Outdoor power equipment stores	52.6
444220	Nursery and garden centers	27.6
445110	Grocery (except convenience) stores	99.2
445310	Beer, wine, and liquor stores	94.2
446110	Pharmacies and drug stores	98.5
446120	Cosmetics, beauty supplies, and perfume store	83.7
446130	Optical goods stores	97.4
447110	Gasoline stations with convenience stores	97
447190	Other gasoline stations	84.4
448110	Men's clothing stores	97.8
448120	Women's clothing stores	99.1
448140	Family clothing stores	99.7
448210	Shoe stores	98.9
451211	Book stores	96.8
452910	Warehouse clubs and superstores	73.1
452990	All other general merchandise stores	96.3
453110	Florists	86.9
453220	Gift, novelty, and souvenir stores	96.2
453910	Pet and pet supplies stores	97.4
453930	Manufactured (mobile) home dealers	98.7
453998	All other misc store retailers (except tobacco)	81.7
454110	Electronic shopping and mail-order houses	76.8
454390	Other direct selling establishments	73.8
713940	Fitness and recreational sports centers	100
713950	Bowling centers	100
713990	All other amusement and recreation industries	100
722110	Full-service restaurants	100
722211	Limited-service restaurants	100
722213	Snack and nonalcoholic beverage bars	100

(*continued*)

Table 11.6 (continued)

Industry Code	*Industry Code Description*	*Total (Percent)*
722410	Drinking places (alcoholic beverages)	100
811111	General automotive repair	100
811112	Automotive exhaust system repair	100
811121	Automotive body, paint, and interior R&M	100
811122	Automotive glass replacement shops	100
811191	Automotive oil change and lubrication shops	100
811192	Car washes	100
811310	Commercial equipment (except automotive and electronic) R&M	100
811490	Other personal and household goods R&M	100
812111	Barber shops	100
812112	Beauty salons	100
812191	Diet and weight reducing centers	100
812199	Other personal care services	100
812210	Funeral homes	100
812320	Drycleaning and laundry services (except coin-op)	100

Source: U.S. Census Bureau, *1997 Economic Census, Miscellaneous Subjects Report.*

Local Retail Sales Tax Projections

Kansas Local Retail Sales Taxes

Authority for Kansas cities and counties to levy local sales tax was enacted in 1970 (K.S.A. 12-187, *et seq*.). Cities and counties may levy a tax up to a normal maximum of 2 percent. Sales taxes of up to 1 percent may be used for general purposes, but the additional authority normally must be used only for the financing of "healthcare services." A city may impose a tax earmarked for healthcare only if the county has no such tax. Moreover, any such city tax expires immediately on the imposition of a county healthcare sales tax. Elections normally are required to be held before the imposition of or increase in any local sales tax, and a statement describing the purposes for which the taxes will be used must be part of the ballot proposition.

City of Derby Local Sales Tax

Pursuant to its authority under K.S.A. 12-187 *et seq*., on August 27, 2002, the governing body of the city of Derby, Kansas, decided to submit to the voters of the city the question of imposing a citywide retailers' sales tax to finance the acquisition of

Table 11.7 Retail Trade (Total Sales)

Industry Code	Industry Code Description	1–4	5–9	10–19	20–49	50–99	100–249	250–499	500–999	1000 or More	1997 Sales	2001 Index (Percent)	2001 Sales	2001 Tax
220000	Utilities	—	3,87,9979	—	—	—	—	—	—	—	3,879,979	126.2	4,898,151	24,491
441110	New car dealers	798,823	—	—	—	—	—	—	—	—	798,823	129	1,030,683	5,153
441120	Used car dealers	1,497,610	—	—	—	—	—	—	—	—	1,497,610	140.6	2,105,510	10,528
441310	Automotive parts, accessories and tire store	176,891	205,486	359,794	—	—	—	—	—	—	742,172	112.8	837,155	4,186
441320	Tire dealers	140,045	—	—	—	—	—	—	—	—	140,045	112.8	157,968	790
442210	Floor covering stores	321,232	—	—	—	—	—	—	—	—	321,232	128	411,325	2,057
443112	Radio, television, and other electronics store	370,113	923,885	—	—	—	—	—	—	—	1,293,998	142.9	1,849,412	9,247
443120	Computer and software stores	165,405	—	—	—	—	—	—	—	—	165,405	102.4	169,346	847
444130	Hardware stores	166,847	368,898	—	—	—	—	—	—	—	535,745	117.8	631,274	3,156
444190	Other building material dealers	—	—	403,610	—	—	—	—	—	—	403,610	129.9	524,362	2,622
444210	Outdoor power equipment stores	133,162	—	—	—	—	—	—	—	—	133,162	129.7	172,756	864
444220	Nursery and garden centers	98,518	—	—	—	—	—	—	—	—	98,518	129.7	127,812	639

445110	Grocery (except convenience) stores	—	—	—	—	10,738,911	14,077,701	—	—	—	24,816,612	114.0	28,296,720	141,484
445310	Beer, wine, and liquor stores	820,977	—	1,273,067	—	—	—	—	—	—	2,094,044	126.4	2,647,684	13,238
446110	Pharmacies and drug stores	532,810	1,032,956	1,600,790	2,223,784	—	—	—	—	—	5,390,340	144.7	7,801,820	39,009
446120	Cosmetics, beauty supplies, and perfume store	—	285,155	—	—	—	—	—	—	—	285,155	143	407,873	2,039
446130	Optical goods stores	216,098	—	—	—	—	—	—	—	—	216,098	143	309,097	1,545
447110	Gasoline stations with convenience stores	—	1,780,501	7,442,016	—	—	—	—	—	—	9,222,517	118.9	10,966,736	54,834
447190	Other gasoline stations	—	741,269	1,103,512	—	—	—	—	—	—	1,844,781	118.9	2,193,678	10,968
448110	Men's clothing stores	—	—	814,859	—	—	—	—	—	—	814,859	105.7	861,032	4,305
448120	Women's clothing stores	191,043	—	—	—	—	—	—	—	—	191,043	117.9	225,231	1,126
448140	Family clothing stores	—	—	763,025	—	—	—	—	—	—	763,025	126.6	966,160	4,831
448210	Shoe stores	274,193	—	—	—	—	—	—	—	—	274,193	104.2	285,589	1,428
451211	Book stores	198,636	—	—	—	—	—	—	—	—	198,636	131.3	260,804	1,304
452910	Warehouse clubs and superstores	—	—	—	—	—	—	—	39,318,817	—	39,318,817	200.9	78,975,054	394,875

(continued)

Table 11.7 (continued)

Industry Code	Industry Code Description	1–4	5–9	10–19	20–49	50–99	100–249	250–499	500–999	1000 or More	1997 Sales	2001 Index (Percent)	2001 Sales	2001 Tax
452990	All other general merchandise stores	502,096	—	—	—	—	—	—	—	—	502,096	121.7	611,108	3,056
453110	Florists	136,863	265,815	—	—	—	—	—	—	—	402,679	122.2	492,062	2,460
453220	Gift, novelty, and souvenir stores	160,946	325,432	550,607	—	—	—	—	—	—	1,036,985	122.2	1,267,168	6,336
453910	Pet and pet supplies stores	129,875	—	—	—	—	—	—	—	—	129,875	122.2	158,703	794
453930	Manufactured (mobile) home dealers	—	—	—	6,286,191	—	—	—	—	—	6,286,191	122.2	7,681,553	38,408
453998	All other misc store retailers (except tobacco)	—	475,288	—	—	—	—	—	—	—	475,288	122.2	580,789	2,904
454110	Electronic shopping and mail-order houses	313,345	—	1,953,497	—	—	—	—	—	—	2,266,842	151.9	3,443,185	17,216
454390	Other direct selling establishments	176,733	—	—	—	—	—	—	—	—	176,733	134.4	237,453	1,187
713940	Fitness and recreational sports centers	102,689	—	—	—	—	—	—	—	—	102,689	126.2	129,636	648

713950	Bowling centers	—	—	—	1,785,135	—	—	—	—	—	1,785,135	126.2	2,253,585	11,268
713990	All other amusement and recreation industries	112,299	243,066	—	—	—	—	—	—	—	355,365	126.2	448,619	2,243
722110	Full-service restaurants	421,053	414,804	714,726	2,114,630	—	—	—	—	—	3,665,213	120.1	4,401,799	22,009
722211	Limited-service restaurants	230,357	228,397	1,130,759	5,185,390	818,642	—	—	—	—	7,593,545	126.5	9,604,100	48,020
722213	Snack and nonalcoholic beverage bars	—	—	388,700	602,304	—	—	—	—	—	991,004	124.3	1,231,688	6,158
722410	Drinking places (alcoholic beverages)	99,306	—	325,295	—	—	—	—	—	—	424,600	124.7	529,479	2,647
811111	General automotive repair	934,422	544,537	—	—	—	—	—	—	—	1,478,959	126.2	1,867,063	9,335
811112	Automotive exhaust system repair	197,816	—	—	—	—	—	—	—	—	197,816	126.2	249,726	1,249
811121	Automotive body, paint, and interior R&M	628,431	541,224	—	2,036,110	—	—	—	—	—	3,205,765	126.2	4,047,012	20,235
811122	Automotive glass replacement shops	188,412	—	—	—	—	—	—	—	—	188,412	126.2	237,854	1,189

(continued)

Table 11.7 (continued)

Industry Code	*Industry Code Description*	*1–4*	*5–9*	*10–19*	*20–49*	*50–99*	*100–249*	*250–499*	*500–999*	*1000 or More*	*1997 Sales*	*2001 Index (Percent)*	*2001 Sales*	*2001 Tax*
811191	Automotive oil change and lubrication shops	207,937	—	624,730	—	—	—	—	—	—	832,667	126.2	1,051,173	5,256
811192	Car washes	95,288	—	—	465,524	—	—	—	—	—	560,813	126.2	707,979	3,540
811310	Commercial equipment (except automotive and electronic) R&M	225,398	—	—	—	—	—	—	—	—	225,398	126.2	284,546	1,423
811490	Other personal and household goods R&M	64,696	—	—	—	—	—	—	—	—	64,696	126.2	81,673	408
812111	Barber shops	251,855	—	—	—	—	—	—	—	—	251,855	126.2	317,946	1,590
812112	Beauty salons	265,938	621,986	—	—	—	—	—	—	—	887,924	126.2	1,120,931	5,605
812191	Diet and weight reducing centers	75,171	—	—	—	—	—	—	—	—	75,171	126.2	94,897	474

812199	Other personal care services	—	—	212,164	—	—	—	—	—	—	212,164	126.2	267,839	1,339
812210	Funeral homes	—	—	689,481	—	—	—	—	—	—	689,481	126.2	870,412	4,352
812320	Drycleaning and laundry services (except coin-op)	91,758	334,411	—	—	—	—	—	—	—	426,169	126.2	538,003	2,690
	Total core retail sales	11,715,087	13,213,090	20,350,631	20,699,069	11,557,553	14,077,701	—	39,318,817	—	130,931,948	127	191,921,215	959,606
	Other taxable sales												4,563,585	22,818
	Total taxable sales												196,484,800	982,424
	Ratio of core retail sales to total taxable sales (percent)													97.7

Note: Author's own computations based on data from the U.S. Census Bureau, *Annual Benchmark Report for Retail Trade and Food Services: January 1992 Through March 2002.*

a site and the construction of a municipal aquatic park facility and related appurtenances and the payment of operating and maintenance costs.

The question would also authorize the city to issue bonds to finance these public improvements with bonds payable from and secured by the proceeds of the sales tax or the sales tax with general obligation backing if the city receives a comprehensive feasibility study that indicates that the revenues received from such sales tax will be sufficient to retire such bonds. The proposition was passed by a 3182–3107 margin on November 5, 2002 (Graham 2002).

City of Derby Sales Tax Estimates

Three sets of sales tax estimates were derived for Derby. As discussed earlier, because consumers will respond to changes in the tax rate much as they would respond to a price change, changes in the overall sales tax rate will have an impact on consumption behavior. Consumers will react to the overall tax rate and most will not distinguish to whom the tax will be going. The recent increase in the state sales tax rate combined with the imposition of the Derby local sales tax will reduce retail sales initially. However, as the state tax is phased down over the next couple of years, this will tend to have a modest stimulative effect on retail sales. On the basis of the past behavior of Kansas and Sedgwick County tax collections, forecasters assumed that local sales taxes will have an elasticity rate of −0.5 percent. In other words, for each 1 percent increase in the overall sales tax rate, retail sales would decrease by 0.5 percent. The Derby forecasters also assumed that retail sales in 2002 would be relatively flat because of the lingering aftermath of the 2001 recession and the September 11 terrorist attacks.

For each of the alternatives, a recession and no recession alternative was given. The "no recession" alternative assumes that there will be no recession between the baseline year of 2000 and 2016. This is highly unlikely given that the longest sustained period without a recession just ended in 2001 after a little more than ten years. More likely, there will be one or more recessions over this period. Historically, there has been a recession every five years on average. If history holds true, it would be expected that the economy will pass through three recessions between 2000 and 2016. However, it is impossible to estimate when and if these recessions will in fact occur. As such, under the "recession" scenario, it was assumed that a recession will occur every five years, namely, in 2006, 2011, and 2016. For each recession it was assumed that retail sales will fall by 5 percent.

The "realistic" scenario is based on the assumption that sales tax will continue to grow at a moderate 5 percent rate. This assumes that the real rate of retail sales growth will be approximately 2–3 percent per year. This also assumes that the accelerated growth that has persisted over the past 50 years will abate somewhat.

The "optimistic" scenario is premised on the assumption that sales taxes will grow at a more robust 7 percent rate. This alternative assumes that real retail sales

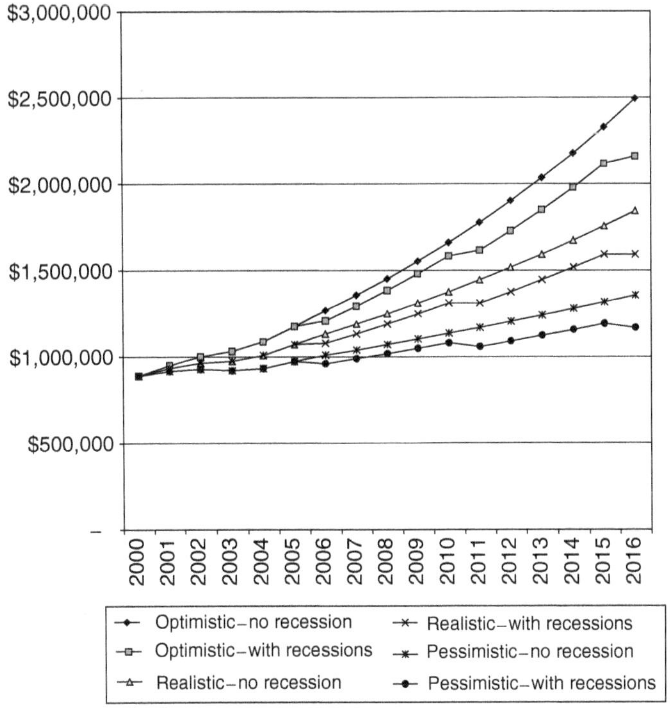

Figure 11.1 Derby sales tax projections. (From Wong, J. D., *Review of The City of Derby, Kansas Retail Sales and Local Sales Tax Trends*, City of Derby, Derby, KS, 2003, p. 53. With permission.)

will grow approximately 4–5 percent per year. This would be consistent with growth in the Derby area continuing much as it has been in recent years.

The "pessimistic" scenario assumes that local sales will only increase 3 percent per year. This alternative assumes that, adjusted for inflation, retail sales will essentially remain constant. This would be consistent with growth in the Derby area largely abating. Figure 11.1 shows sales tax projections for the city of Derby from 2000 through 2016.

Conclusion

Revenue forecasts are an integral component of the fiscal planning process. Recent revenue shortfalls have increased the importance of financial forecasting at all levels of government. All levels of governments must now look at monitoring and managing revenues with the same intensity with which expenditures are monitored. Because revenue estimates define the fiscal parameters for budgetary decisions, fiscal stress magnifies the importance of accurate revenue forecasts. Growing revenue constraints have also increased the importance of debt financing in local government and further accentuated the need for reliable revenue forecasts.

Unfortunately, most systematic revenue forecasting techniques require detailed data concerning the base underlying the revenue source to be estimated. Although the federal government, state governments, and large metropolitan areas tend to have a wide array of data at their disposal concerning their respective jurisdictions, the same cannot be said for small- and medium-sized communities. Although most states track sales tax receipts down to the county level, the same cannot be said of collections at the municipal level. This finding is especially true of medium-sized and smaller communities. Therefore, smaller municipalities contemplating to adopt a local sales tax have a difficult task in establishing a reliable benchmark against which to gauge the revenue potential of the new tax.

This chapter developed and documented a local sales tax forecasting methodology that may be used by small- and medium-sized communities to estimate the base of a new local sales tax. Combining information from various publicly available data sources allows the potential base for the new sales tax to be imputed and estimated. Specifically, this chapter illustrated how this methodology can be used to estimate revenues from a newly adopted local sales tax to support a local bond issue in a medium-sized suburban community. When compared to actual local sales tax collections in the city of Derby, Kansas, in the baseline year, the methodology described earlier identified 97.7 percent of actual taxable retail sales occurring in the city during that year. Because this methodology exclusively employs data that is publicly available down to the zip code level, it is a technique that could reasonably be employed by most small- to medium-sized communities looking to estimate the potential revenues from a proposed or newly enacted local sales tax. The methodology would be applicable to either a general use tax or as in this case a dedicated use sales tax. In addition, the methodology could be used for a general sales tax or a selective sales tax.

References

Agostini, S. J. 1991. Searching for a better forecast: San Francisco's revenue forecasting model. *Government Finance Review* 7(December): 13–16.

Beckett-Camarata, J. 2006. Revenue forecasting accuracy in Ohio local governments. *Journal of Public Budgeting, Accounting & Financial Management* 18(Spring): 77–99.

Frank, H. A. 1990. Municipal revenue forecasting with time-series models: A Florida case study. *American Review of Public Administration* 20(March): 45–59.

Graham, S. 2002. Derby moves on $7M water park. *Wichita Business Journal* 17(November 22), http://www.bizjournals.com/wichita/stories/2002/11/25/story4.html (May 31, 2007).

MacManus, S. A. 1992. Forecasting frustrations: Factors limiting accuracy. *Government Finance Review* 8(June): 7–11.

McCullough, J. 1990. Municipal revenue and expenditure forecasting: Current status and future prospects. *Government Finance Review* 6(October): 38–40.

National Advisory Council on State and Local Budgeting and Government Finance Officers Association. 1998. *Recommended Budget Practices: A Framework for Improved State and Local Government Budgeting.* Chicago, IL: National Advisory Council on State and Local Budgeting and Government Finance Officers Association. pp. 44–45.

O'Toole, D. E., Marshall, J., and Grewe, T. 1996. Current local government budgeting practices. *Government Finance Review* 12(December): 25–29.

Reddick, C. G. 2004a. Assessing local government revenue forecasting techniques. *International Journal of Public Administration* 27(8, 9): 597–613.

Reddick, C. G. 2004b. An empirical examination of revenue forecasting techniques in local governments. *Municipal Finance Journal* 24(Winter): 25–48.

Rodgers, R. and Joyce, P. 1996. The effect of underforecasting on the accuracy of revenue forecasts by state governments. *Public Administration Review* 56(January–February): 48–56.

Stinson, T. F. 2002. State revenue forecasting: An institutional framework. *Government Finance Review* 18(June): 12–15.

Wong, J. D. 1995. Options, challenges, and incentives for implementing systematic revenue forecasting in local government. *Municipal Finance Journal* 16(Spring): 63–79.

Wong, J. D. 2003. *Review of the City of Derby, Kansas Retail Sales and Local Sales Tax Trends.* Derby, KS: City of Derby.

Chapter 12

Does Revenue Forecasting Responsibility Matter: The Case of Milwaukee, Wisconsin

Craig D. Kammholz and Craig S. Maher

Contents

Introduction

Bahl (1978) in reference to state and local governments wrote "... the state of the art in revenue and expenditure forecasting is primitive" (p. 120). In most respects, this is no longer the case, particularly at the state level, where a growing body of literature describing and analyzing various facets of forecasting techniques and processes exists (Cassidy et al. 1989, Federation of Tax Administrators 1993, Gentry 1989, Klay and Grizzle 1992, Rodgers and Joyce 1996, Shkurti and Winefordner 1989, Voorhees 2002, 2006). Perhaps because of its growing importance, research on local government forecasting has expanded considerably in recent years (Agostini 1991, Beckett-Camarata 2004, 2006, Betschneider and Gorr 1992, Cirincione and van de Sande 1999, Giannakis and Frank 1993, Wong 1995).

Although the body of literature on state and local revenue forecasting has grown over the past 25 years, in most of the work the emphasis has been on techniques and their accuracy and little attention has been given to process(es) (Beckett-Camarata 2006, Bretschneider and Gorr 1987, Sun 2005). This is unfortunate, as the few studies on the organizational influences on revenue forecasting have raised some important questions including the role of political influences (Cassidy et al. 1989, Feenberg et al. 1989, Jones et al. 1997, MacManus 1992, Rubin 1987, Stinson 2002) and managerial influences (Forrester 1993, Klay 1992, Lee 1991).

This research, which includes a case study, adds to the body of work on organizational influences on revenue forecasting processes using the city of Milwaukee, Wisconsin. Like most other municipalities, the fiscal pressures, both in terms of politics dictating limited levy growth and the overall economic environment, have placed a premium on the need for accurate revenue forecasting models. Unlike most other large municipalities, the city of Milwaukee has an independently elected comptroller, the municipality's chief financial officer, who is responsible for estimating and budgeting all city revenues. As a result, the official revenue estimation responsibility does not lie in the city's budget office. In Milwaukee, the responsibility for revenue estimation rests with the comptroller's office. Although the budget office staff may also estimate revenue, the official scoring or estimates used for budgeting are the comptroller's estimates. One of the benefits of this arrangement is that it provides additional resources for revenue estimation that might not otherwise be available. Perhaps more importantly, this structural arrangement provides an internal balance that protects the city from the risks of revenue estimation based on political objectives. Comparing Milwaukee to nine peer cities on the bases of forecasting accuracy and bond rating agency evaluations, we demonstrate that Milwaukee fares quite well on both counts, despite having a less favorable economic picture.

Importance of Forecasting for Local Governments

Having worked at the federal, state, and now local levels, we believe that the need for accurate and precise forecasting is generally greater for municipal and county governments than for state and federal governments. This is due to the nature of the services provided by local governments and the fiscal constraints they face. Local governments are primarily responsible for providing direct services to citizens, such as police, fire, emergency medical services, and sanitation collection. In addition, the basic infrastructure constructed and maintained by local governments, such as bridges, roads, and sewers are, in essence, direct services to those citizens who utilize them. If a negative fiscal event were to occur, its effects would be more immediate, simply because of the direct nature of the local government service provision. In other words, funding reductions to local government services tend to have a more direct and immediate impact on citizens.

In comparison, state governments generally provide fewer direct services than local governments. In Wisconsin, for example, court administration and most social service programs are administered by counties but are supported by the state. Similarly, as a means of indirectly providing services, states administer general or categorical aid programs to assist in the provision of local government services. In Wisconsin, the predominant examples are the Shared Revenue Program, modeled after the defunct federal revenue sharing program of the 1970s, and the School Aid Program. Through these programs, the state provides general unrestricted aid to all municipalities, counties, and school districts on a formula basis. An example of a categorical aid program in Wisconsin is the General Transportation Aid program, whereby counties and municipalities receive assistance for transportation-related infrastructure projects (Wisconsin Legislative Fiscal Bureau 2007b).

In addition to the direct nature of service provision, local governments also have significantly less fiscal flexibility relative to states and the federal government. For this reason, it is even more important for local governments to have a systematic and thorough revenue estimation process. For instance, unlike many comparable municipalities, state law prohibits Milwaukee from imposing a sales or income tax. The city's principal revenues have historically been property taxes (34 percent of total revenues in 1990) and shared revenues (39 percent of total revenues in 1990). Since 1990, the city's reliance on these relatively stable revenue sources has declined to 27 percent for property taxes (2004 data) and 34 percent for shared revenues. In their place, charges for services have grown from 4 percent of total revenues in 1990 to 8 percent in 2004, and intergovernmental charges have risen from 1 percent of the total in 1990 to 5.4 percent in 2004 (City of Milwaukee Comptroller's Office 2006b). Such a shift from more stable revenue sources to less stable revenue sources puts a premium on forecasting accuracy.

Another factor resulting in more limited fiscal flexibility is the stringent budgetary environment of local governments. All states, with the exception of Vermont, require local governments to adopt balanced budgets every year, both on budgetary and accounting bases (National Conference of State Legislators 1999). If revenues do not materialize as estimated, reserve fund balances will be impacted by the amount of the shortfall; and in the event that fund balance is insufficient to cover the shortfall, a mid-year budget adjustment would be required. At the state level, there is a greater flexibility as revenue shortfalls may be rolled into the subsequent budget cycle, unless so severe that state statute requires a budget adjustment (Wisconsin Legislative Fiscal Bureau 2007a).

In Wisconsin, mid-budget period adjustments are required if it is anticipated that expenditures exceed revenues by more than 1.5 percent. Also, state governments have additional flexibility because many of their expenditures are to other governments. Payment deferrals can help states "get through" an otherwise unbalanced budget period, albeit such measures create a generally accepted accounting principles (GAAP) deficit. For example, the Wisconsin legislature passed a "balanced" fiscal year (FY) 2005 budget as part of its 2003–2005 biennial budget using a cash basis of accounting (Wisconsin Department of Administration 2006). According to its FY 2005 Comprehensive Annual Financial Review, Wisconsin had a General Fund deficit of $2.5 billion. Thus, the ability of the state to ignore GAAP requirements enabled it to pass a "balanced" budget. The federal government has even greater flexibility, as deficit spending is permitted because a balanced budget is not required (U.S. General Accounting Office 1993).

Local Forecasting Constraints

Despite the greater need for accurate forecasting at the local level, counties and municipalities face a number of constraints that make it more difficult to generate forecasts that accurately predict revenues and expenditures. State and federal governments are more likely than counties and municipalities to have teams of economists and other professionals dedicated to forecasting various revenue streams and expenditure obligations (Frank 1993). Our experience at the local level has been that estimation is often left up to one or two individuals, and typically, for smaller local governments it is a function left up to a single administrator such as a finance director or his or her assistant. Given the multitude of other assignments, these individuals typically have limited time to dedicate to forecasting. Consequently, revenue estimation can fall by the wayside as more pressing or immediate concerns consume the time of limited staff. Oftentimes, revenue estimation can become nothing more than a series of best guesses and they often are *apriori* actual revenue figures with modest adjustments.

It has been our experience that the three interrelated constraints impeding revenue estimation at the local level are money, time, and data. Not having the financial resources means that there is no staff support dedicated to a comprehensive revenue estimation process. This results in subjective "eyeballing" of estimates or the perfunctory "back of the envelope" estimates that lack accuracy and precision. These approaches leave much to be desired because the quality of the estimates is often poor.

Oftentimes, the justification for these less than ideal approaches is due to the limited time available to thoroughly estimate revenues, particularly given the other demands and deadlines of the budget process. These justifications may explain why "eyeballing" or "back of the envelope" approaches are used; however, the result is poor-quality estimates.

Although constraints such as limited financial resources and limited staff time may impede the development of an accurate and precise revenue estimation process, a third constraint is data limitation. A lack of data or an abundant amount of unorganized data can be a constraint, as limited or poor data leads to poor conclusions. As data development and organization typically follows an organization's need for information, organizations lacking an adequate revenue estimation process will tend to have greater data constraints than an organization with a well-established revenue estimating process. In other words, data limitations can have a compounding effect as additional staff time and resources are required for the revenue estimating process.

Milwaukee and its similar-sized counterparts are large enough to overcome these constraints. For instance, Milwaukee Comptroller's Office had a FY 2006 budget in excess of $6.4 million (City of Milwaukee Comptroller's Office 2006a). Within its office is a Financial Advisory Division that has two full-time employees, with additional administrative staff. This, of course, does not include staff in the mayor's budget office. One of the outcomes of such organizational capacity is a formalized estimation process that includes a detailed format and requirements of departments as well as an oversight and a review by both the comptroller's office and mayor's budget office, with the formal estimation and official scoring of estimates by the comptroller's office.

Risks of Overestimation

As indicated earlier, the risks associated with overestimating revenues are greater than underestimation. If estimated revenues fail to materialize, normally, the city will reduce its fund balance or the rainy day reserve by that amount. If a rainy day reserve does not exist or is insufficient to cover the revenue shortfall, a mid-year budget adjustment or correction must be made to address the shortfall. Irrespective of the need for any mid-year budget adjustment, a reduction in fund balance or rainy day reserve is a destabilizing factor as reductions in fund balance reduce the amount available for potential draws for future years. In addition, the continuation of such patterns runs the risk of bond rating downgrades. This is precisely what happened to the state of Wisconsin in the early 2000s. In response to recent bond rating downgrades from Moody's and Standard & Poor's, the Wisconsin Department of Administration (2001) issued a press release that included the statement, "they (the bond rating agencies) have cited the inadequate level of reserves designated in the budget bill and the fact that the budget includes $800 million of stop-gap measures ..." (p. 1).

Risks of Underestimation

Although the risks of overestimating revenues may be more severe, the risks of excessive underestimation cannot be ignored as it also creates its problems for policy makers and administrators. Typically, an underestimation of revenues results in increasing the fund balance or a rainy day reserve, which may be drawn on in subsequent budgets. Thus, the problem is not as serious as not having enough money in an FY than what was planned. At a first glance, there appears to be little or no risk to underestimating revenues, as fund balance would continually build over time. Under this scenario, revenues would be consistently underestimated and the planned draws from reserves would be less than the amount contributed due to underestimation of revenues.

However, consistently underestimating revenues results in two or three possible situations: (1) citizens are overtaxed, (2) new and old programs are less funded than policy makers wish, or (3) a combination of (1) and (2). In other words, the result of underestimating revenues is a levying of property taxes for reserves, which may not be warranted if reserves are adequately funded; the generally accepted measure is 5 percent of general fund expenditures according to the National Advisory Council on State and Local Budgeting Government Finance Officers Association (1999). To summarize, the risk of consistently underestimating revenues is often excessive taxation in a scenario where reserves are adequately funded.

Revenue estimation for budgeting at the local level requires point estimates, that is, a specific dollar estimate for each specific revenue account (each permit, fine, and fee), which, with rare occurrence, is never achieved with absolute precision. In other words, there will always be variances, both positive and negative, from the estimates. Reasons for inaccurate estimates are numerous, including fluctuations in the weather, unanticipated personnel changes, natural disasters, etc. Given this and the numerous revenue sources to estimate (the city of Milwaukee has over 200), the objective is not to achieve absolute precision with each and every revenue source, but to strive for a series of estimates that are accurate in aggregate.

However, given the greater financial risk to local governments associated with overestimation than underestimation, a certain degree of conservatism should be built into the estimation process to hedge against risk. One benchmark used by the city of Milwaukee is to ensure that actual revenues are within 2.5 percent of estimated revenues to generate an overall positive revenue variance with the hopes of avoiding fund balance reductions or mid-year budget adjustments (City of Milwaukee 2006). In other words, a risk-based approach toward revenue estimation requires a certain degree of conservatism to ensure that aggregated actual revenues exceed estimates, but only to a limited extent (for Milwaukee, 2.5 percent of nonproperty tax revenues).

It has been our experience that irrespective of a risk-based approach to revenue estimation, there is a tendency in local government to overestimate revenues, as the pressure to maintain low taxes exceeds the desire to maintain adequate reserve levels. One indication of these ordinal pressures is the lack of reserves maintained by local units of government. Despite the recommendation by the Government Finance Officers Association (GFOA) (1990) to maintain reserves of at least 5 percent of general fund expenditures, most local governments do not meet this recommendation.

However, a balance can be struck between tax and service provision objectives on the one hand and risk avoidance and reserve objectives on the other. Critical to this balance is a revenue estimation process that is both accurate and precise and that reasonably accounts for the risk associated with overestimation of revenues. Although imperfect, the city of Milwaukee, Wisconsin, has a revenue estimation process that attempts to strike this balance.

Figure 12.1 compares Milwaukee's general fund revenue estimates to actuals for FY 1991–2005. The graph shows that only in three of the fifteen years revenue estimates were greater than actual collections (1991, 1998, and 1999); conversely, in twelve of the fifteen years, Milwaukee's actual revenues exceeded estimates. Thus, in 12 of the 15 years, the city had excess revenues that added to its reserve. In addition, the general fund budget estimates have met the city's objective of being within 2.5 percent of actuals in each of the 15 years, except 2003 and 2004 when collections were underestimated by 3.1 percent in each of the two years.

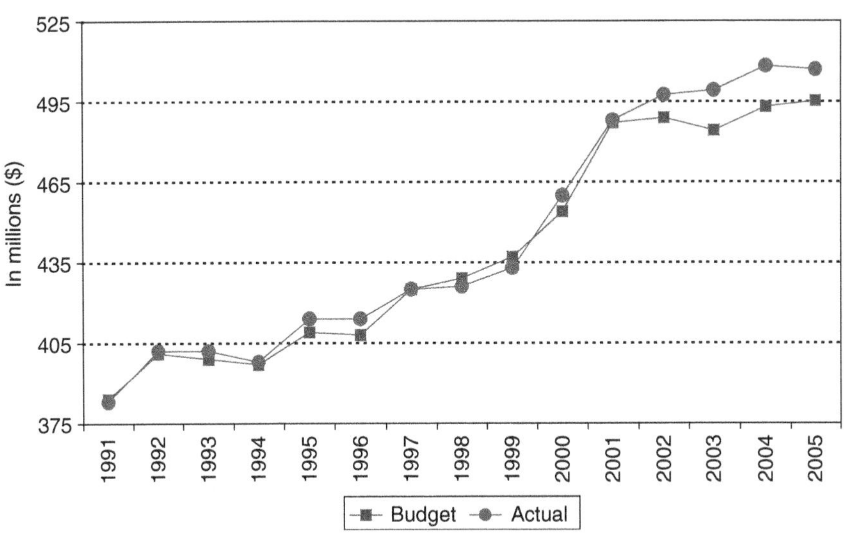

Figure 12.1 Comparison of Milwaukee's actual general city revenue to budgeted general city revenue. (From City of Milwaukee Budget Office, 2006b.)

The Structure of Revenue Estimation in Milwaukee

As stated earlier, revenue estimation in the city of Milwaukee resides with the comptroller's office. The city of Milwaukee's comptroller is an independently elected citywide official who is the chief financial officer of the city. The primary mission of the city comptroller is to maintain and enhance the city's financial condition and implement and advance measures that are in the best financial interest of the city. The office carries out several finance functions for the city, such as general accounting, financial system technical support, payroll processing, grant and aid administration, internal audit, debt issuance, financial analysis and advisement, and revenue estimation (see Figure 12.2) (City of Milwaukee Charter 2002).

When it comes to revenue estimation, the comptroller has the sole discretion and responsibility with respect to "recognizing" or scoring revenues. This authority, which effectively allows the comptroller to establish the revenue component of the annual city budget, is established in the city's charter. This unique arrangement originated in the early 1850s through a charter provision creating the elected office. This provision was one of the "checks and balances" established in the city charter as part of an overall effort to reform city government (City of Milwaukee Legislative Reference Bureau 2001).

The charter provision requires that the annual budget contains only those revenues estimated by the comptroller's office. In addition, the charter gives the

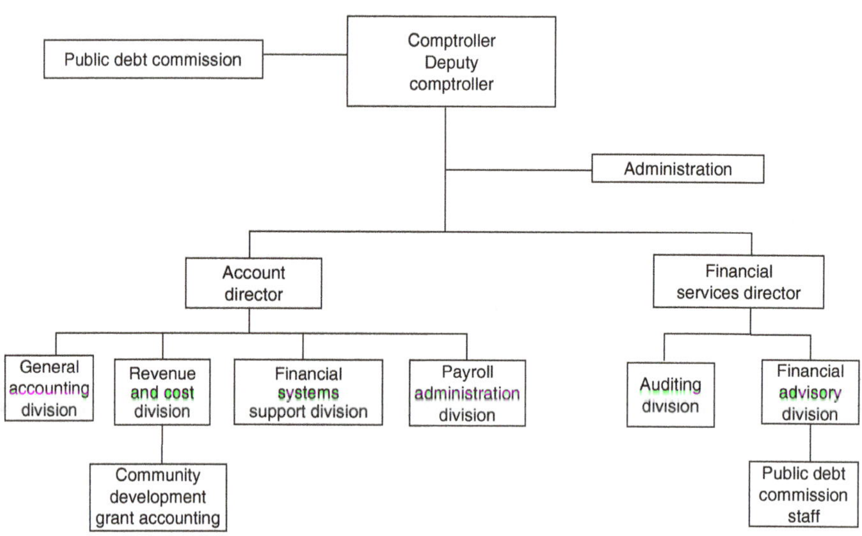

Figure 12.2 Organizational structure of city of Milwaukee's Comptroller. (From City of Milwaukee, Department of Employee Relations, 2007, http://www.city.milwaukee.gov/router.asp?docid=18253.)

comptroller the authority to certify the tax levy every year. Because the city is required to adopt a balanced budget every year, expenditures cannot exceed the revenues recognized and the levy certified by the comptroller. If the budgeted expenditures exceeded estimated revenues and levy, the comptroller would notify the mayor and City Council of the imbalance. Ultimately, these elected officials would have to approve a levy amount sufficient to bring the budget into balance before the comptroller would certify the levy—a step required before the assessor places the levy onto the tax rolls (City of Milwaukee Charter 2002).

Relationship between Comptroller's Office and Mayor's Budget Office

There exists a natural but positive tension between the comptroller's office and the budget office in the revenue estimation process, which relates directly to each entity's agency mission. Although the comptroller's office ultimately has the legal authority over revenue recognition, the budget office does have some influence over revenue estimates, as budget office staff conduct their own estimates. Although estimates conducted by the budget office often results in a confirmation of the comptroller's estimates, they sometimes indicate differences. Where differences exist, some agreement or disagreement regarding the estimate is ultimately arrived. To better understand the roles of these two offices, it is important to understand their competing interests, which are embedded in the mission of each office.

The comptroller, as the chief financial officer of the city, has the primary mission to act in accordance with what is in the best financial interest of the city. As such, estimates are neither overly optimistic nor overly pessimistic, but are, in total, accurate within a reasonable standard as explained earlier. Because overestimation carries with it the risks of reduction to reserves and budget adjustments, and because underestimation can, if ongoing, result in a loss of credibility, the agency bias of the comptroller's office is to develop accurate, albeit slightly conservative, estimates. In other words, the comptroller's office strives to issue estimates that are attainable and at minimum 97.5 percent accurate.

In contrast to the comptroller's office, the primary mission of the budget office is to develop a balanced budget every year (City of Milwaukee Charter 2002). Balanced budgets result from a combination of expenditure cuts and revenue increases. Because the most politically sensitive revenue increase involves the property tax, a more refined statement of the mission of the budget office is to develop a balanced budget every year with the lowest possible property tax increase. This, in effect, means that budget office must pursue the recognition of sufficient nonproperty tax revenues to achieve its annual target goals with respect to the property tax. Because shared state revenues, the city's second largest revenue source, has been frozen since the mid-1990s, there is tremendous pressure to seek the recognition of substantial amounts of own-source nonproperty tax revenues

(revenues other than intergovernmental aids and property taxes).* This bias is mitigated to a certain extent by the realization that overestimation may result in a mid-year budget correction.

Given these differing agency objectives, there is a tension that occurs in developing the city's annual revenue budget. As the budget season progresses, both agencies continually update estimates and develop data sources that support the estimates. Ongoing discussions occur between the two agencies, with both agencies eventually coming to a consensus. In those rare situations when consensus cannot be reached, the comptroller office estimates are budgeted (City of Milwaukee Charter 2002). These are professional, noncontentious discussions focusing on issues regarding data, estimation techniques, and in some instances, revenue administration.

Revenue Estimation Process

As a result of city charter and government culture, the process of establishing the comptroller's revenue estimates begins in March every year, when all departments in the city receive estimation forms for revenues for which each department is responsible. This is done to query departments about what they believe is attainable in terms of revenue for the subsequent year and to see if the departmental estimates concur with the comptroller's preliminary estimates. This process also allows the comptroller's office staff to obtain qualitative information from the departments on environmental or exogenous factors impacting the amount of revenues that may be collected as well as any management issues relating to the collection of revenues. An example of an exogenous variable that may be discussed is the interest rate environment and its potential impact on building permits issued for new construction and home improvements. Administrative issues bring to light administrative factors that may result in an apparent change in revenue collection or accruals of revenue. The process of surveying the departments also provides the comptroller's office staff with an indication of management strength and the degree of importance a department places on revenue collection and monitoring. Once these survey forms are completed by the department, they are signed by the preparer and department head and returned to the comptroller's office in mid-April.

As the departmental responses are advisory, there is nothing that compels the comptroller to recognize the amounts estimated by the departments. Ideally, departments submit estimates with supporting data, identifying factors used in estimating the revenue, which positively or negatively impacts the estimates, and

* This program is modeled after the now defunct federal revenue-sharing program of the 1970s. The basis for aid is, essentially, property taxes. Those communities with lower tax bases receive more aid and vice versa.

discuss any administrative issues that may affect the amount of revenue collected. Ultimately, it is hoped that the departmental estimates concur with the comptroller's estimates that were prepared before the receipt of the departmental responses. In reality, however, this rarely happens. Departmental estimates range from the fairly well reasoned to the barely considered. Also, the fact that both the preparer and the department head must sign the estimates places a degree of ownership or responsibility for the departmental estimates with those individuals. In cases where the departmental estimates are well developed, supported by underlying data, and where exogenous and management issues are disclosed, great weight is given to departmental estimates that diverge from the comptroller's preliminary April estimates. However, less consideration is given to departmental estimates that contain calculation errors, little or no qualitative discussion of exogenous or management issues is provided, or simply the prior year's actual revenues as estimates are reported. The best information received from the departments typically pertains to contextual information or comments from management regarding issues that may affect estimates based exclusively on trends.

Once the departmental surveys are returned, the comptroller's office uses this information to prepare the revenue budget for submission to the mayor's budget office in May. Departmental estimates are compared to initial estimates prepared by the comptroller staff to see if there is concurrence between the departmental estimates and comptroller preliminary estimates. Estimates where the comptroller and department agree are set aside and analyzed last.

In developing the revenue budget for the May submission, the focus is on the largest revenue sources to the smallest. Most of the large nonproperty tax revenue sources are general revenues, which are revenues that are not tied to any specific department and are centrally administered. Intergovernmental revenue is the primary revenue source aside from the property tax. Intergovernmental revenue consists of shared revenue, expenditure restraint, general transportation aid, payment for municipal services, and swing lift and bridge aid. Other general revenues include interest earnings and payments *in lieu* of taxes from the city's water and parking enterprises. On completing these estimates, the focus is on those estimates with the greatest variation between the comptroller's preliminary estimates and the departmental estimates in terms of dollars (not in terms of percent). The objective is to identify, review, and analyze variances from the largest to the smallest to reduce estimation risk. In other words, to identify revenues with potential variability that could also have large dollar impacts on the city and to provide time and care in estimating these revenues. This is not a step taken to compromise or "split" estimates between the comptroller and the departmental estimates. Small dollar revenue sources and small variances follow.

Overall, the comptroller's office staff covers all revenue sources between mid-April and mid-May. As indicated earlier, the amount of time spent on any specific revenue source largely depends on the size of the revenue source and potential variability or beta, if you will. Additional time on estimates relates to everything from developing multiple estimation techniques, reviewed and cleaning data, research on additional data sources, and interviewing departmental staff.

After the May cutoff, the comptroller's office works with the budget office on any revisions due to new information that may arise. This lasts till mid-September when the mayor proposes his budget. After the mayor's recommended budget is proposed, the Common Council members may ask for additional revenue recognition as the budget is under the control of the Common Council until passage in November. Although revenue changes are less frequent than during the May–September period, revenue changes during the Common Council's period of control can have a material impact on the budget. The entire revenue estimation and recognition process by the comptroller concludes with a final budget adoption in November.

Evaluation of Forecast Accuracy in Milwaukee, Wisconsin

There are a variety of means by which forecasting accuracy can be evaluated. Here, we focus on the relationship between annual budget estimates and end-of-year actual collections using several techniques, including time series (discussed previously) and cross-sectional analysis. The City of Milwaukee Comptroller's Office (2006a) published a report comparing its revenues and expenditures to nine comparable cities. The selection process, described in the report's appendix (Appendix IV), was principally based on population, location (central cities), and government functions. These same municipalities are included in this analysis; however, our analysis is separate from that conducted by the city. Available electronic versions of audited annual financial statements were collected for each of the ten cities for the years 2001–2005 (see Table 12.1).

One of the striking features from the comparison of general fund revenues is Milwaukee's reliance on intergovernmental funds (see Table 12.1). In FY 2005, intergovernmental revenues accounted for 55 percent of Milwaukee's general fund. In comparison, Cleveland was the closest to Milwaukee at 20 percent, whereas Pittsburgh and Oklahoma city received no state or federal aid. Conversely, Milwaukee has limited taxing authority beyond property taxes; "other taxes" account for 1 percent of Milwaukee's general fund revenues. Cleveland, Oklahoma City, and Toledo exceed 50 percent and Pittsburgh's reliance on nonproperty general fund tax revenues is 48 percent.

Revenue structures play an important role on the forecasting process (Beckett-Camarata 2006). Property taxes, for instance, are less difficult to estimate than sales or income taxes. Similarly, license and permit revenues and intergovernmental revenues are a challenge to predict because of enforcement efforts and state and federal fiscal decisions (Beckett-Camarata 2006). Therefore, given Milwaukee's revenue structure, it should be in a better position to estimate revenues than its

Table 12.1 Budgetary Comparison Schedule (General Fund Only)

		2002		2003		2004		2005	
	Revenues	Budget($)	Variance (Percent)	Budget($)	Variance (Percent)	Budget($)	Variance (Percent)	Budget($)	Variance (Percent)
Milwaukee	Property taxes	118,875	–4.0	131,672	–3.7	133,542	–3.3	$139,930	–3.1
	Other taxes	2,212	33.1	3,473	24.3	2,754	29.4	$2,915	27.2
	Intergovernmental	282,750	0.1	284,218	0.1	273,548	0.1	$272,544	0.1
	Charges	50,986	13.3	47,900	16.3	53,954	12.7	$56,523	12.2
	All other	23,341	6.0	21,310	16.4	21,902	15.4	23,473	34.0
	Total revenues	478,164	0.9	488,573	1.6	485,700	1.4	$495,385	2.4
Cincinnati	Property taxes	221,109	–2.8	218,701	0.5	227,141	–1.7	$226,245	6.2
	Other taxes	13,695	6.6	11,020	24.2	11,625	–11.2	$12,965	–20.7
	Intergovernmental	51,907	3.1	53,638	1.3	51,239	9.2	$51,367	3.7
	Charges	14,270	4.7	15,246	–13.4	13,773	13.8	$15,966	9.0
	All other	7,998	–0.9	9,010	16.1	10,171	–0.4	$11,462	12.2
	Total revenues	308,979	–1.0	307,615	1.2	313,949	0.5	$318,005	5.0
Pittsburgh	Property taxes	127,700	–3.8	126,971	–1.9	130,650	–4.9	$135,166	–7.3
	Other taxes	170,768	–0.9	171,081	–2.3	184,860	–4.7	$199,775	6.2
	Intergovernmental	NA		NA		NA		NA	
	Charges	NA		NA		NA		NA	
	All other	60,560	1.2	88,344	–34.9	73,321	–26.0	$82,635	–7.0
	Total revenues	359,028	–1.6	386,396	–9.6	388,831	–8.8	$417,576	–0.7
Cleveland	Property taxes	47,295	1.3	41,214	–02	43,700	2.3	$42,021	3.4
	Other taxes	249,909	–1.4	250,617	–0.4	251,500	0.0	$261,770	0.4

(continued)

Table 12.1 (continued)

		2002		2003		2004		2005	
	Revenues	*Budget($)*	*Variance (Percent)*	*Budget($)*	*Variance (Percent)*	*Budget($)*	*Variance (Percent)*	*Budget($)*	*Variance (Percent)*
	Intergovernmental	87,911	−0.2	95,205	−1.3	94,260	−0.5	$94,591	0.4
	Charges	15,495	5.6	16,122	−3.6	16,729	2.8	$19,658	−1.2
	All other	63,210	−2.3	59,883	−7.5	58,266	−10.3	$52,767	−3.2
	Total revenues	463,820	−0.8	463,041	−1.6	464,455	−1.1	$470,807	0.2
Charlotte	Property taxes	185,366	2.1	193,622	−0.8	212,855	1.1	$223,007	−1.1
	Other taxes	41,565	−10.2	60,633	−2.4	74,766	0.8	$76,756	5.9
	Intergovernmental	52,098	−16.7	23,339	−3.0	24,887	−1.1	$25,221	1.5
	Charges	22,220	−20.6	27,806	−3.8	27,032	0.0	$27,497	1.5
	All other	39,668	4.9	58,087	4.6	40,200	−2.0	$39,033	3.2
	Total revenues	340,917	−3.4	363,487	−0.6	379,740	0.5	$391,514	1.1
Columbus	Property taxes	329,200	−0.3	331,500	−0.7	340,800	−0.1	$352,300	0.2
	Other taxes	41,450	−0.2	45,396	−0.1	45,793	0.6	$45,900	0.8
	Intergovernmental	56,646	0.1	56,666	0.9	55,307	1.1	$56,371	1.9
	Charges	29,112	1.5	32,300	1.5	37,415	1.4	$38,583	2.6
	All other	43,190	5.4	31,151	4.9	91,806	1.5	$45,326	0.4
	Total revenues	499,598	0.3	497,013	0.1	571,121	0.4	$538,480	0.6

Oklahoma city	Property taxes	NA		NA		NA		NA	
	Other taxes	167,616	–3.0	171,272	–6.1	165,002	2.8	170,326	3.8
	Intergovernmental	NA		NA		NA		NA	
	Charges	5,926	–1.7	6,691	–5.3	8,189	1.6	8,180	10.5
	All other	68,439	–1.0	65,042	6.0	71,644	–2.8	73,558	–2.4
	Total revenues	241,981	–2.4	243,005	–2.9	244,835	1.1	252,064	2.2
Sacramento	Property taxes	177,987	0.4	179,936	4.8	193,932	7.2	211,680	6.0
	Other taxes	NA		NA		NA		NA	
	Intergovernmental	35,563	3.3	36,735	–0.6	30,114	7.9	38,027	26.9
	Charges	26,383	13.1	28,111	17.7	32,786	18.5	45,490	7.9
	All other	9,161	15.8	8,326	11.8	9,855	–13.3	10,064	4.0
	Total revenues	249,094	2.7	253,108	5.7	266,687	7.9	305,261	8.8
Toledo	Property taxes	15,728	–1.9	15,615	–2.5	17,228	–0.1	17,488	–1.5
	Other taxes	153,750	0.1	158,377	–2.1	159,322	–2.6	156,092	2.9
	Intergovernmental	23,829	1.4	23,597	–2.4	22,849	1.2	23,770	–2.1
	Charges	12,151	3.7	13,043	–1.9	12,735	1.4	13,515	–5.2
	All other	10,093	–6.2	8,054	1.6	10,146	–10.1	12,768	–13.5
	Total revenues	215,551	0.0	218,686	–2.0	222,280	–2.1	223,633	0.6
Portland	Property taxes	156,751,364	–0.1	158,463,624	–0.4	159,878,589	0.7	163,178,883	1.6
	Other taxes	NA		NA		NA		NA	
	Intergovernmental	18,382,964	8.5	18,739,545	2.5	24,011,381	1.8	24,415,707	–7.1
	Charges	97,550,680	–87.9	12,590,440	0.9	13,098,347	2.7	13,182,597	5.4
	All other	40,130,758	211.7	127,231,540	–3.0	134,800,782	2.1	145,664,811	4.9
	Total revenues	312,815,766	0.2	317,025,149	–1.3	331,789,099	1.4	346,441,998	2.5

Source: Electronic versions of selected audited annual financial reports. Data compiled by City of Milwaukee Comptroller's Office, *City of Milwaukee Comparative Revenue and Expenditure Report*, Milwaukee, 2006a.

comparables because it has limited taxing authority, yet be in a more difficult fiscal position than its peers due to its greater reliance on intergovernmental revenues.

Forecasting Responsibilities

Our argument is that an elected comptroller, independent of either a council or mayor, with responsibility for estimating budgeted revenues, removes the pressure of overestimation for either tax levy or programmatic considerations. With the sole responsibility of estimating budgeted revenues comes the pressure of estimation and this will result in more conservative estimates, given that overestimation carries with it a higher penalty than underestimation. Reading these two sentences together: in the absence of the pressure to overestimate, the effect of an independently elected comptroller's office that is responsible for estimating revenues should be a higher probability that actual revenues will meet or surpass the estimates, and as previously noted it does.

Another benefit of the identified cities is that they represent a mix of revenue estimation responsibilities. Table 12.2 shows that of the ten cities, only two—Milwaukee and Columbus—have a separately elected official responsible for the general fund revenue estimates included in their budgets. The remaining cities delegate general fund revenue estimation to finance departments or offices of management and budget.

Does Structure Matter?

As described earlier, in general, underestimation of revenues has greater consequences than overestimation. Interestingly, between the FYs 2002 and 2005, only three of the ten cities included in this analysis—Milwaukee, Columbus, and

Table 12.2 Budgeted Revenue Forecasting Responsibility

City	*Office or Department*
Sacramento	Finance department
Charlotte	Finance department
Cincinnati	Finance department
Cleveland	Finance department
Columbus	Auditor (nonpartisan election)
Milwaukee	Comptroller (nonpartisan election)
Oklahoma City	Finance department
Pittsburgh	Office of Management and Budget
Portland	Office of Management and Finance
Toledo	Finance department

Note: Telephone interviews conducted by authors, March 2007.

Sacramento—did not have negative revenue estimates in any of the four FYs. Thus, of the cities in which revenue estimation is the executive's responsibility, only Sacramento met this forecasting benchmark. Where the adopted general fund revenue estimates are under the jurisdiction of a separately elected body (Milwaukee and Columbus), revenue estimates were below actuals in each of the four FYs.

In addition to ascertaining whether or not a city under- or overestimated revenues, accuracy of the estimates should also be considered. Once again, the general fund revenue estimates for Columbus and Milwaukee were some of the most accurate estimates. Over the four FYs analyzed, Milwaukee averaged 1.6 percent below actuals. Columbus fared even better, averaging 0.4 percent below actual general fund revenues. Sacramento, the only other city in the analysis to have positive revenue estimates in each of the four years, averaged 6.4 percent below actual revenues. On the basis of underestimation and accuracy, at least during the FYs 2002–2005, the two cities that fared the best were Columbus and Milwaukee—the only cities in the group with revenue estimation in the hands of a separately elected officer. Thus, the facts affirm the argument made in this chapter.

Bond Ratings

Another benefit of revenue underestimation is that it should result in the building of reserves and, therefore, positive credit quality. The extent to which reserves affect bond ratings varies. For instance, according to a recent Standard & Poor's (2006b) report, "... economic variables have the closest correlation with bond rating categories" (p. 2). This, of course, suggests that reserves play a limited overall role in ratings. This should be bad news for Milwaukee as its economic picture has not been painted well by Standard & Poor's. According to the U.S. Bureau of Census (2000) data, Milwaukee experienced a 5 percent decline in its population between 1990 and 2000, its poverty rate is greater than 20 percent, and median household income lags well behind the national average (75.7 percent of the U.S. average). According to Standard & Poor's (2004), the city's future prospects does not look much brighter, "The worst prospects are for Detroit and Milwaukee, which ranks near the bottom of the U.S. metropolitan areas in terms of future job growth prospects" (p. 2).

Yet, despite this bleak economic picture, Milwaukee's current bond rating is Aa2. According to WM Financial Strategies (2007), "Issuers or issues rated Aa demonstrate very strong creditworthiness relative to other US municipal or tax-exempt issuers or issues." One of the principal reasons for the rating is its financial management. At the end of the year 2004, Milwaukee's general fund balance as a percentage of revenues was 15.9 percent, its unreserved general fund balance as a percentage of revenues was 6.2 percent, and its unreserved undesignated general fund balance as a percentage of revenues was 6.2 percent. When compared to similar-sized midwestern cities, Milwaukee fares favorably (Tables 12.3 and 12.4).

Table 12.3 consists of financial and demographic information for 12 comparable cities. It shows that between June 2004 and December 2005, six cities had

TABLE 12.3 Comparative City Financial and Demographic Information

	City of Chicago, Illinois	*City of Cincinnati, Ohio*	*City of Cleveland, Ohio*	*City of Columbus, Ohio*	*City of Des Moines, Iowa*	*City of Detroit, Michigan*	*City of Indianapolis, Indiana*	*City of Kansas, Missouri*	*City of Louisville, Kentucky*	*City of Milwaukee, Wisconsin*	*City of Minneapolis, Minnesota*	*City of Omaha, Nebraska*	*City of Saint Louis, Missouri*
Rating (Moody's /S&P/Fitch	*Aa3/A+ /NA*	*Aa1/AA+ /AA*	*A2/A /A+*	*Aaa/AAA /AAA*	*Aa2/ AA+ /NA*	*Baa2/ BBB–/BBB*	*Aaa/AAA /NA*	*Aa3/AA /AAA*	*Aa2/AA /NA*	*"Aa2" /"AA"/*	*Aa1/AAA /NA*	*Aaa/AAA /NA*	*A3/A– /A–*
Statement date	*12/05*	*12/05*	*12/05*	*12/05*	*6/05*	*6/04*	*12/04*	*4/05*	*6/04*	*12/04*	*12/05*	*12/04*	*6/05*
Demographic statistics													
Population (2000 census)	2,896.016	331,285	478,403	711,470	198,682	951,270	791,926	441,545	256,231	596,974	382,618	390,007	348,189
Population change 1990–2000 (percent)	4.00	–9.00	–5.40	12.40	2.80	–7.50	8.30	1.50	–4.80	–5.00	3.90	16.10	–12.20
Poverty rate (percent) (2000 census)	19.60	21.90	26.30	14.80	11.40	26.10	11.90	14.30	21.60	21.40	16.90	11.30	24.60
Unemployment rate (percent) (2006 MSA)	4.50	5.20	5.50	4.80	2.90	7.00	4.60	5.10	5.40	4.80	3.30	3.3.0	5.30
Per capita income ($; 2000 census)	20,175	19,962	14,291	20,450	19,467	14,717	21,640	20,753	18,193	16,181	22,685	21,758	16,109
Median family income as percentage of state (2000 census)	76.90	75.00	60.50	94.70	97.10	63.30	97.00	99.90	89.60	71.60	85.50	105.80	70.80

Median family income as percentage of United States (2000 census)	85.40	75.00	60.50	94.70	93.10	67.60	97.40	91.90	73.30	75.70	97.10	101.50	65.10
Financial statistics													
General fund balance as percentage of revenues	3.05	21.20	7.57	17.20	10.10	4.10	52.00	7.70	18.30	15.90	18.00	13.10	17.90
Unreserved general fund balance as percentage of revenues	1.76	16.80	5.10	15.50	7.70	–5.70	30.00	4.30	17.50	6.20	17.10	12.00	11.70
Unreserved undesignated general fund balance as percentage of revenues	1.76	16.80	5.10	3.77	7.70	–5.70	0.00	4.30	17.50	6.20	17.10	12.00	0.00
Debt statistics													
Direct net debt as percentage of full value	2.40	1.41	2.44	1.43	5.20	6.30	1.30	7.80	0.40	2.60	3.10	3.10	3.00
Direct net debt per capita ($)	2,242	590	728	941	2,528	1,792	649	4,224	1,039	1,148	3,234	1,517	1,307
Debt burden (overall net debt as percentage of full value)	4.81	6.61	3.32	1.43	6.10	12.40	5.00	10.20	1.00	4.70	4.40	5.40	4.10

(continued)

TABLE 12.3 (continued)

	City of Chicago, Illinois	*City of Cincinnati, Ohio*	*City of Cleveland, Ohio*	*City of Columbus, Ohio*	*City of Des Moines, Iowa*	*City of Detroit, Michigan*	*City of Indianapolis, Indiana*	*City of Kansas, Missouri*	*City of Louisville, Kentucky*	*City of Milwaukee, Wisconsin*	*City of Minneapolis, Minnesota*	*City of Omaha, Nebraska*	*City of Saint Louis, Missouri*
Tax base statistics													
Full value per capita ($)	90,981	41,572	37,421	65,695	48,994	28,246	49,307	54,490	263,157	44,989	103,378	49,073	43,696
Top ten taxpayers as percentage of total, most recent value	4.90	10.50	9.80	11.00	14.40	21.90	7.50	8.00	NA	4.30	10.80	3.00	2.20

Note: 1. Use only as guide. Information obtained from various sources (Moody's, S&P, and CAFRs).
2. Unemployment information obtained from the U.S. Bureau of Labor Statistics.

Source: City of Milwaukee Comptroller's Office, *1990 through 2004 City Revenue Data*, Financial Services Division, Milwaukee, 2006b.

Table 12.4 Excerpts from Bond Rating Agencies about Milwaukee, Wisconsin

Fitch

"The 'AA+' rating on the city's general obligation (GO) notes and bonds reflects the City of Milwaukee's conservative financial management, which contributes to sizable long-term reserves and fiscal flexibility" (Fitch Ratings Ltd. 2006, p. 1).

Standard & Poor's

"The 'AA' ratings reflect: Strong property tax base growth in recent years; Diverse, manufacturing-focused employment base with continuing diversification in the service sector; Sound financial operations with adequate reserves and fully funded pensions; High overall net debt offset by rapid amortization; and Manageable capital needs. Offsetting credit factors include: High unemployment and below-average income levels, and Vulnerability to economic downturns affecting manufacturing ... The stable outlook reflects Standard & Poor's Ratings Services' expectation that Milwaukee will maintain sound financial operations and adequate reserves in spite of the state-imposed levy cap and flat state-shared revenues through careful budgeting and fiscal management" (Standard & Poor's 2006a, p. 9).

general fund balances as a percent of revenues less than Milwaukee, and seven cities had an unreserved undesignated general fund balance as a percentage of revenues less than Milwaukee. Similarly, Milwaukee's debt burden, measured as overall net debt as a percentage of full value, was 4.7 percent, which was less than seven of the other twelve cities.

Finally, Table 12.4 provides recent excerpts from two bond rating agencies, Fitch and Standard & Poor's, that help make the connection between Milwaukee's bond rating and its financial management. Important to this presentation is the acknowledgment that despite Milwaukee's economic picture, the city has retained positive financial management reviews, which reflect directly its bond ratings.

Conclusion

State and local government revenue estimation techniques and assessment of their accuracy have come a long way within the past 20 years. The amount of published research on the subject has grown significantly since Bahl's call in 1978. This chapter adds to the field by emphasizing the role of institutional structure on revenue estimation. Despite the acknowledgment of political influences on revenue estimation, the amount of research is limited (Cassidy et al. 1989, Feenberg et al. 1989, Jones et al. 1997, MacManus 1992, Rubin 1987, Stinson 2002).

Using the city of Milwaukee, Wisconsin, as a case study, we assert that revenue estimation is improved when the official responsibility lies with a separately elected official (comptroller or auditor). As described, there is an inherent difference in goals when comparing that of the executive's office and the comptroller's office, which has a direct impact on revenue estimation. In addition, given the fact that there are different objectives between the two offices, a positive tension exists that improves the estimation outcome.

Our hypothesis was supported by analyzing the general fund forecast accuracy of Milwaukee over time (fifteen years) and compared to nine cities between FYs 2002 and 2005. We demonstrated that of the nine, three cities (Milwaukee, Sacramento, and Columbus) underestimated their revenues in each of the four years. Given the political consequences and the benefit of building reserves, underestimation is clearly more favorable than overestimation. Of the three cities that consistently underestimated general fund revenues, two—Milwaukee and Columbus—have separately elected officials responsible for estimation. Just as importantly, Milwaukee and Columbus' estimates were within two percentage points of actuals over the four years. Sacramento's revenue estimates averaged more than six percentage points below actuals between 2002 and 2005.

Finally, we attempted to make the case that Milwaukee's favorable bond rating was largely the result of sound fiscal management, which can be at least partially attributed to the role of the comptroller's office. According to a recent Standard & Poor's report, economic conditions play a key role in determining municipal bond ratings. Milwaukee's economic picture has been and is estimated to be "bleak" in the near future. Key indices for Milwaukee include population decline, relatively high poverty and unemployment rates, and lower than average household income. Despite these facts, Milwaukee maintains a positive bond rating according to Fitch, Standard & Poor's, and Moody's, largely due to its sound financial management.

References

Agostini, S. J. 1991. Searching for a better forecast: San Francisco's revenue forecasting model. *Government Finance Review* 7(6): 13–16.

Bahl, R. W. 1978. Revenue and expenditure forecasting by state and local governments. In *Essays in Public Finance and Financial Management: State and Local Perspectives*, Eds. J. E. Petersen and C. L. Spain. Chatham, NJ: Chatman House, pp. 120–126.

Beckett-Camarata, J. 2004. Identifying and coping with fiscal emergencies in Ohio local governments. *International Journal of Public Administration* 27: 615–630.

Beckett-Camarata, J. 2006. Revenue forecasting accuracy in Ohio local governments. *Journal of Public Budgeting, Accounting and Financial Management* 18: 77–99.

Bretschneider, S. I. and Gorr, W. L. 1987. State and local government revenue forecasting. In *The Handbook of Forecasting: A Manger's Guide*, 2nd ed, Eds. S. G. Makridakis and S. C. Wheelwright. New York: Wiley, pp. 118–134.

Betschneider, S. I. and Gorr, W. L. 1992. Revenue forecasting errors in Pennsylvania Local government budgeting: Sources and remedies. *Public Budgeting and Financial Management* 4: 721–743.

Cassidy, G., Kamlet, M. S., and Nagin, D. L. 1989. An empirical examination of bias in revenue forecasts by state governments. *International Journal of Forecasting* 5: 321–331.

Cirincione, C. and van de Sande, B. 1999. Municipal government revenue forecasting: Issues of methods and data. *Public Budgeting and Financial Management* 19: 230–261.

City of Milwaukee Budget Office 2006b.

City of Milwaukee Charter. 2002. *City Charter and Code of Ordinances.* http://www.city.milwaukee.gov/TableofContents1179.htm.

City of Milwaukee. 2006. *2006 Plan and Budget Summary.* Milwaukee, WI: City of Milwaukee, Department of Administration.

City of Milwaukee Comptroller's Office. 2006a. *City of Milwaukee Comparative Revenue and Expenditure Report.* Milwaukee, WI

City of Milwaukee Comptroller's Office. 2006b. *1990 through 2004 City Revenue Data.* Milwaukee, WI: Financial Services Division.

City of Milwaukee, Department of Employee Relations, 2007. http://www.city.milwaukee.gov/router.asp?docid=18253.

City of Milwaukee Legislative Reference Bureau. 2001. Interdepartmental correspondence to Ald. Michael Murphy, from Barry Zalben, Manager Legislative Reference Bureau, dated June 21.

Federation of Tax Administrators. 1993. *State Revenue Forecasting and Estimation Practices.* Washington.

Feenberg, D. R., Gentry, W., Gilroy, D., and Rosen, H. S. 1989. Testing the rationality of state revenue forecasts. *The Review of Economics and Statistics* 71: 300–308.

Fitch Ratings Ltd. 2006. Fitch rates Milwaukee WI's $109 Million G.O.s 'AA+'; $66 Million Notes 'F1+'. *City of Milwaukee Credit Rating Report of March 2006 Debt Issuance.* Chicago, Il: Press Release Issued March 13.

Forrester, J. P. 1993. Use of revenue forecasting techniques. In *Handbook of Comparative Public Budgeting and Financial Management*, Eds. T. D. Lynch and L. L. Martin. New York: Marcel Dekker, pp. 149–167.

Frank, H. 1993. *Budgetary Forecasting in Local Government: New Tools and Techniques.* Westport, CT: Quorum Books.

Gentry, W. 1989. Do state revenue forecasts utilize available information? *National Tax Journal* 42: 429–439.

Giannakis, G. A. and Frank, H. 1993. Implementing time series forecasting models: Considerations for local governments. *State and Local Government Review* 25(2): 130–144.

Government Finance Officers Association. 1990. Unreserved fund balance and local government finance. *Research Bulletin: Research and Analysis on Current Issues* (September): 1–13.

Jones, V. D., Bretschneider, S. I., and Gorr, W. L. 1997. Organizational pressures on forecasting evaluation: Managerial, political and procedural influences. *Journal of Forecasting* 16: 241–254.

Klay, W. E. 1992. Revenue forecasting: Learning perspective. In *Handbook of Public Budgeting*, Ed. J. Rabin. New York: Marcel Dekker, pp. 211–239.

Klay, W. E. and Grizzle, G. 1992. Forecasting state revenues: Expanding the dimensions of budgetary forecasting research. *Public Budgeting and Financial Management* 4: 381–405.

Lee, R. D. 1991. Educational characteristics of budget office personnel and state budgetary processes. *Public Budgeting and Finance* 11: 69–79.

MacManus, S. A. 1992. Forecasting frustration: Factors limiting accuracy. *Government Finance Review* 8: 7–11.

National Advisory Council on State and Local Budgeting Government Finance Officers Association. 1999. *Recommended Budget Practices: A Framework for Improved State and Local Government Budgeting.* Chicago, IL, June.

National Conference of State Legislators. 1999. *State Balance Budget Requirements.* Denver, CO, April.

Rodgers, R. and Joyce, P. 1996. The effect of underforecasting on the accuracy of Revenue forecasts by state governments. *Public Administration Review* 56: 48–56.

Rubin, I. S. 1987. Estimated and actual urban revenues: Exploring the gap. *Public Budgeting and Finance* 7(4): 83–94.

Shkurti, W. and Winefordner, D. 1989. The politics of state revenue forecasting in Ohio, 1984–1987: A case study and research implications. *International Journal of Forecasting* 5: 361–371.

Standard & Poor's. 2004. *Essentiality and Recovering Economies Help Keep U.S. Midwestern Cities' ratings Steady.* Chicago, IL, June.

Standard & Poor's. 2006a. Milwaukee, WI credit profile. *City of Milwaukee Credit Rating Report of March 2006 Debt Issuance.* Chicago, IL: Press Release Issued March 15.

Standard & Poor's. 2006b. *U.S. GO Rating Distributions and Summary Ratios.* Chicago, IL, November.

Stinson, T. F. 2002. State revenue forecasting: An institutional framework. *Government Finance Review* 18(3): 12–15.

Sun, J. 2005. The dynamics of government revenue forecasting from an organizational perspective: A review of the literature. *Journal of Public Budgeting, Accounting and Financial Management* 17: 527–556.

U.S. Bureau of Census. 2000. http://quickfacts.census.gov/qfd/states/55/55079.html.

U.S. General Accounting Office. 1993. Balanced budget requirements, state experiences and implications for the Federal Government. Briefing Report presented to the Chairman, Committee on the Budget, House of Representatives, Washington, March.

Voorhees, W. 2002. Institutional structures utilized in state revenue forecasting. *Journal of Public Budgeting, Accounting and Financial Management* 14: 175–196.

Voorhees, W. 2006. Consistent underestimation bias, the asymmetrical loss function, and homogeneous sources of bias in state revenue forecasts. *Journal of Public Budgeting, Accounting and Financial Management* 18(1): 61–76.

Wisconsin Department of Administration. 2001. http://www.doa.state.wi.us/press_releases_detail.asp?prid=67&locid=12. *Lightbourn Stresses Need to Strengthen State Government Finances.* Office of the Secretary, Press Release, August 21.

Wisconsin Department of Administration. 2006. *Comprehensive Annual Financial Report for the Fiscal Year Ended June 30, 2005.* Madison, WI: State Controller's Office.

Wisconsin Legislative Fiscal Bureau. 2007a. *State Budget Process.* Informational Paper #70.

Wisconsin Legislative Fiscal Bureau. 2007b. *Transportation Aid (General Transportation and Connecting Highway Aid).* Informational Paper #22.

WM Financial Strategies. 2007. Municipal Bond Ratings. http://www.munibondadvisor.com/rating.htm.

Wong, J. D. 1995. Local government revenue forecasting: Using regression and econometric revenue forecasting in a medium-sized city. *Public Budgeting and Financial Management* 7: 315–335.

Chapter 13

Evaluating Revenue Forecasting in City Governments: A Survey of Texas Finance Directors

Christopher G. Reddick

Contents

Introduction

This chapter examines revenue forecasting in city governments using Texas as a case study. The focus of this study is on evaluating the effectiveness of revenue forecasting as it pertains to its impact on the budgetary process of cities. A survey of Texas city government finance directors was conducted to evaluate this important part of the budgetary process. There is also an examination of the revenue forecasting techniques that are used by city governments and the perception of their effectiveness. This chapter outlines the opinions of finance directors on revenue forecasting accuracy. Finally, this study provides information on the impact of participation in the revenue forecasting process. Particularly, this research examines how open and transparent the forecasting process is in Texas city governments.

This chapter is divided into several sections. The following section outlines the literature that is used in this study on the investigation of local government revenue forecasting. This is followed by a discussion of the research methods and the results of the survey of Texas finance directors. Finally, there is a summary of the most important information covered in the chapter.

Literature on Revenue Forecasting in Local Governments

The literature on local government revenue forecasting has tended to concentrate on the evaluation of different forecasting techniques through competitions of their predictive abilities. There is also ample literature that deals with the underestimating of revenue forecasts. This study is different because it focuses on evaluating the revenue forecasting institutions and processes in city governments, with Texas used as a case study, which has been relatively unexplored (Jonas et al. 1992, Shkurti 1990).

There are four important themes that are discussed in the local government revenue forecasting literature. Specifically, they are revenue forecasting and the budgetary process, revenue forecasting techniques used, revenue forecasting accuracy, and participation in the revenue forecasting process; each of these is discussed.

Revenue Forecasting and the Budgetary Process

Government revenue forecasting is the starting point of the budget process by setting the level of future spending; therefore, playing a significant role in the budget cycle (Klay 1983, Sun 2005). The implementation of a sound revenue forecasting program should be the objective of professional public managers (Frank and Gianakis 1990). Revenue forecasting decisions on the allocation of scarce resources are more informed when the mayor and staff of cities are more knowledgeable about the extent of these resources (Agostini 1991). Empirical evidence shows that local government budgetary actors see forecasts as pertinent to the budgetary process (Forrester 1993).

Given the uncertainty in economic behavior, a systematic approach to monitoring, revision, and evaluation is essential to any revenue forecast (Shkurti 1990). There are a few studies that evaluate forecasting institutions and processes (Jonas et al. 1992). This is especially the case for local government revenue forecasting. Internal managerial and procedural influences tend to have a dominant and positive effect on revenue forecasting evaluation (Jones et al. 1997).

Revenue forecasting is not simply a managerial activity, but it serves political and policy ends as well (Bretschneider and Gorr 1992). In a review of government revenue forecasting from an organizational perspective, Sun (2005) found that there should be more attention to managerial influences. In particular, internal managerial influences deserve more attention, and issues such as performance, evaluating, and monitoring the forecast should be researched.

Revenue Forecasting Techniques Used and Evaluated

Many local governments use quantitative methods, with some even using econometric models; but they rely much more often on judgmental approaches. The literature shows that simpler, more readily communicated revenue forecasting models generally perform at least as well as more complex methods (Cirincione et al. 1999). Research also shows that local governments do a reasonable job at forecasting tax revenues, but a poor job of forecasting intergovernmental and other revenues (Bretschneider et al. 1992). Empirical evidence indicates that the greater the fiscal stress, the more likely the jurisdiction is to utilize complex predictive forecasting models (MacManus and Grothe 1989).

One factor that might explain the underutilization of more advanced forecasting techniques is that the individuals doing the forecasting are not getting training on more advanced techniques from public administration programs, but from workshops and seminars on forecasting (Reddick 2004). Therefore, most local governments have neither the data nor the expertise to perform causal analysis (Beckett-Camarata 2006). The literature shows that larger organizations that make use of more sophisticated techniques of forecasting are more likely to establish formal forecast accuracy evaluation processes than smaller units using less sophisticated techniques (Jones et al. 1997).

Empirical evidence indicates that municipalities use a range of qualitative and quantitative techniques to forecast tax revenues with larger cities being more likely to use multiple techniques than smaller cities; the primary method employed depends on the tax being forecast (Rubin and Mantell 2000). A national survey of local governments, in 1999, in the United States of revenue forecasting indicated that expert forecasting was the most common method for estimating property tax and state and federal aid (Reddick 2004). Trend forecasting was most commonly used for sales tax, income tax, and other fees. Deterministic forecasting was most often used to forecast revenues from sales taxes and other fees. Relatively few cities used econometric forecasting, but of those that did, it was most often used to forecast sales taxes and other fees (Reddick 2004).

Revenue Forecasting Accuracy

City governments generally need to bring budgets into balance; therefore, the process of estimating revenues low increases the likelihood of a surplus, which protects against running out of funds (Caiden and Wildavsky 1974). One study has noted that since the passage of Proposition 13, the property tax limitation in California in 1978, there has been more bias in the underestimation of revenues for city government because of fiscal stress (Chapman 1982). Research shows that the greater the cities' overall fiscal stress, the greater the likelihood of underestimating revenue (Rubin 1987). An analysis of government revenue forecasting indicated that there was an underforecast between 2 and 5 percent (Rodgers and Joyce 1996).

The greater the level of information in the revenue forecast, the less likely that forecasters will experience "assumption drag" because the organization will base its forecasts on accurate and up-to-date assumptions (Voorhees 2002). Assumption drag, which is one of the most significant sources of forecasting error, is the tendency of forecasters to cling to assumptions that are no longer valid (Wong 1995).

There is risk aversion in municipal revenue underestimation, and a reliance on judgmental techniques could place cities at increased risk in planning over the long term (Frank 1990, Frank et al. 2005). Indeed, the risk is that budgetary shortfalls can be seized upon by political opponents as evidence of "gross mismanagement" of a city (Schroeder 1982).

Having a finance director with an advanced degree makes the city government more likely to pursue forecasting accuracy more vigorously (Frank and McCollough 1992). In addition, forecasting accuracy increases when there are independent forecasts from competing agencies (Bretschneider et al. 1989). Therefore, a level of participation in the revenue forecasting process should increase forecast accuracy.

Participation in Revenue Forecasting Process

One of the most innovative issues discussed in the revenue forecasting literature is participation in the forecasting process. Voorhees (2004) stresses the importance of broad-based participation in the forecasting process for two reasons. First, the broader the consensus and diversity of people involved in the forecasting process, the less likely that political bias will affect the forecast. Second, the diversity of the participants and increased competition between perspectives can help reduce "assumption drag." Voorhees study concluded that the degree of consensus in the forecast formulation significantly reduced forecast error.

Research shows that the creation of an independent agency and establishment of technical workgroups depoliticize the forecast and improve communication between those involved in the forecast (Deschamps 2004). However, there is a general view that budgeters and planners are quite isolated from elected officials when it comes to revenue forecasting (Rubin et al. 1999). The actual impact of forecasting on budgetary decisions is often limited because the results tend to be used more for internal analysis rather than as information to be analyzed by the city council (Forrester 1993). According to a national survey of cities, nearly 80 percent reported forecasting results to the city council at least "sometimes" (Forrester 1991). The following section provides the research questions that delve into these four important issues of the impact of revenue forecasting on the budget process, techniques used, accuracy, and participation in the process.

Research Questions

There are four research questions that have been derived from the existing literature on revenue forecasting in local governments; they are examined in this study using survey data from Texas City governments.

1. What is the relationship between revenue forecasting and the budgetary process?
2. What are the typical revenue forecasting techniques used?
3. What is the level of revenue forecasting accuracy in city governments?
4. What is the extent of participation in the revenue forecasting process in city governments?

Before this chapter attempts to shed some light on these four questions, the following section outlines the research methods of this study.

Survey Data Collection and Research Methods

The data for this study was collected by a mail survey conducted during the summer of 2006. A comprehensive mailing list of finance directors was provided by the Texas Municipal League. City governments serving populations of 10,000 residents or greater were sent a copy of the survey, which is a reasonable cutoff point for examining revenue forecasting processes and techniques. The survey protocols involved sending a cover letter introducing the project to finance directors and a copy of the survey to be completed was also enclosed. To get greater candor in responses, the finance directors were assured that their responses would be anonymous. A second mailing occurred one month after the initial mailing. Out of the 158 finance directors in Texas who were sent a survey, 66 responded, which is a response rate of 42 percent. This response rate is similar to other surveys of local government officials administered by the International City/County Management Association (ICMA).

This chapter uses descriptive statistics to demonstrate characteristics of revenue forecasting in local governments. For many of the questions, Likert scales are used with a coding of "2" for strongly agree, "1" for agree, "0" for neutral, "−1" for disagree, and "−2" for strongly disagree. Because this study uses ordinal data, an appropriate summary statistic is the median. The following section discusses some of the characteristics of the cities that responded to the survey to determine how representative the results are to the larger population.

Descriptive Characteristics of Finance Directors and Their Cities

A descriptive profile of the finance directors in Texas who responded to the survey and their city governments is provided in Table 13.1. The typical city size reflected in full-time equivalent (FTE) employment is around 100–499 employees. One very large city that employs 5000 or more workers responded to the survey. Ten small cities responded with 99 or fewer FTE. Therefore, the results for this study are most generalizable to medium-sized cities in Texas.

The survey also asked questions about the fiscal capacity of the city governments. This is defined as the government's ability to raise taxes or fees, given political and legal limitations (Table 13.1). A large percentage of finance directors, 56 percent, believe that the fiscal capacity of their city is favorable. In addition, the economic development climate of the city government examines job growth and unemployment for the municipality. There was a strong majority of respondents who believed that their economic development climate was favorable for their city (81.8 percent). Finally, the political climate of the city government, which measures the political relationship with the city council and its citizens, was also examined. According to finance directors, there is a very optimistic political climate in the cities surveyed, with 78.8 percent believing this as favorable.

Table 13.1 also provides information on the demographic characteristics of the finance directors who responded to the survey. The survey results indicate that almost half of the city managers were 45 and 54 years old (47 percent). Only 38 percent of finance directors have a graduate degree as an academic qualification.

Table 13.1 Descriptive Characteristics from This Survey of Finance Directors and Their Cities

	Frequency	*Percentage*
FTE employment		
99 or less	10	15.2
100–499	46	69.7
500–999	5	7.6
1000–4999	4	6.1
5000 or more	1	1.5
How would you characterize your city government's fiscal capacity?		
Very favorable	9	13.6
Favorable	28	42.4
Neither favorable nor unfavorable	15	22.7
Unfavorable	12	18.2
Very unfavorable	2	3.0
How would you characterize your city government's economic development climate?		
Very favorable	13	19.7
Favorable	41	62.1
Neither favorable nor unfavorable	9	13.6
Unfavorable	3	4.5
Very unfavorable	0	0.0
How would you characterize your city government's political climate?		
Very favorable	11	16.7
Favorable	41	62.1
Neither favorable or unfavorable	9	13.6
Unfavorable	5	7.6
Very unfavorable	0	0.0
Gender		
Male	40	60.6
Female	26	39.4
Age range (years)		
25–34	3	4.5
35–44	14	21.2
45–54	31	47.0
55–64	16	24.2
65 or above	2	3.0
Graduate degree		
Yes	25	37.9
No	41	62.1

The descriptive results of finance directors and their cities indicated that the survey is more representative of medium-sized cities, which have favorable fiscal, economic, and political climates. Respondents are more likely to be male, middle-aged, and not have an advanced degree. The following section discusses some key characteristics of the revenue forecasting function in city governments.

Revenue Forecasting Function

Table 13.2 provides information on the approximate number of years of prior data used in producing the revenue forecast for the upcoming fiscal year. Only one city in Texas used more than ten years of prior data for the revenue forecast. The majority of cities used less than five years of data for the forecast (56.1 percent). The small amount of prior data employed to produce the revenue estimate is consistent with research on local government forecasting (Forrester 1993, Frank 1990, Reddick 2004).

The cities in Texas also have very few staff members participating in the revenue forecasting process (Table 13.2). Only 13.6 percent of cities have five or more staff working on the forecast. The vast majority of cities have four or fewer staff working on the forecast. Therefore, most of the forecasting is done with limited amount of staff, which is also consistent with the existing literature (Forrester 1993).

Revenue Forecasting and the Budgetary Process

Table 13.3 provides information on the influence that revenue forecasting has on the budgetary process in Texas cities. The last column of this table shows the median responses, which indicate that forecasting is viewed as the most important stage of the budgetary process. In addition, finance directors are in strong

Table 13.2 Information from This Survey on the City Government Revenue Forecasting Function

	Frequency	*Percentage*
Approximately how many years of prior data is used in producing the revenue forecast for the upcoming fiscal year?		
<5	37	56.1
5–10	28	42.4
>10	1	1.5
How many staff members participate in the revenue forecasting process?		
2 or less	28	42.4
3–4	29	43.9
5 or more	9	13.6

Table 13.3 Revenue Forecasting and the Budgetary Process

In Our City Government	*Strongly Agree (Percent)*	*Agree (Percent)*	*Neutral (Percent)*	*Disagree (Percent)*	*Strongly Disagree (Percent)*	*Median Response*
The availability of revenues as a result of the revenue forecast determines expenditure for the upcoming budget	56.1	39.4	1.5	3.0	0.0	2
Revenue forecasting is the most important stage in our budgetary process	31.8	37.9	24.2	6.1	0.0	1
As a result of the revenue forecasting methods used, decisions on the allocation of scarce resources are more informed	31.8	54.5	13.6	0.0	0.0	1
The balanced budget required or other budget constraints have a substantial influence on the revenue forecast	10.6	40.9	25.8	21.2	1.5	1
The revenue forecast is primarily used as an internal document	7.6	66.7	6.1	18.2	1.5	1
Our revenue forecasting process is very structured and formalized	6.1	28.8	42.4	22.7	0.0	0
We revise our revenue forecasts regularly, rather than once a year	6.1	42.4	15.2	31.8	4.5	0
We have enough administrative resources to carry out revenue forecasting	4.5	34.8	36.4	19.7	4.5	0

Note: Strongly agree = 2, agree = 1, neutral = 0, disagree = −1, and strongly disagree = −2.

agreement that, as a result of the revenue forecasting methods used, decisions on the allocation of scarce resources are more informed. Revenue predictions based on the forecast determines how much is going to be spent in the upcoming budget cycle. The balanced budget and other budget constraints have an influence on the revenue forecast. There was less agreement that the revenue forecast is revised regularly, rather than once a year. However, the most interesting response in Table 13.3 is that the revenue forecast is viewed by finance directors as primarily an internal document. This study discusses this important issue of openness and transparency in the forecasting process later in the chapter, after dealing with what techniques are actually used by city governments.

Revenue Forecasting Techniques Used

Table 13.4 provides information on the revenue forecasting techniques that are currently used by city governments in Texas. Definitions of the major revenue forecasting techniques were provided to finance directors before they answered this question on the survey. Expert forecasting predicts a revenue source made by a person who is very familiar with the particular source of revenue. Consensus forecasting uses information from several forecasts to arrive at a final determination of future revenues. Trend forecasting predicts revenue from a specified source based on prior changes in the revenue from that source. Deterministic forecasting predicts revenue from a source based on a percentage change in social, economic, or other variables that directly affects the revenue from that source. Finally, econometric forecasting predicts revenue from a source based on statistically estimated coefficients of one or more economic predictor variables.

Table 13.4 Revenue Forecasting Technique(s) Used According to Revenue Source

Source of Revenue	*Expert Forecasting (Percent)*	*Consensus Forecasting (Percent)*	*Trend Forecasting (Percent)*	*Deterministic Forecasting (Percent)*	*Econometric Forecasting (Percent)*
Property tax	54.5	6.1	36.4	24.2	7.6
Sales tax	16.7	22.7	78.8	19.7	15.2
License fees	30.3*	15.2	62.1	15.2	6.1
User charges	22.7*	16.7	68.2	13.6	6.1
Federal or state grants	43.9*	12.1	12.1	7.6	3.0

Note: *χ^2 *p*-Value is significant at the 0.05 level for employee size.

Table 13.4 shows that the forecasting technique(s) used depend(s) on the revenue source that is being forecast.* In terms of property tax, the most important tax for Texas local governments, expert forecasting is commonly conducted by 54.5 percent of cities. Trend forecasting is being done by 36.4 percent of cities for property taxes. For sales taxes trend forecasting was employed by 78.8 percent of cities, which is far above any other method used. Trend forecasting is also commonly used to forecast license fees, with 62.1 percent of cities using this method. Expert forecasting was used by 30.3 percent of cities to forecast license fees. Existing literature argues that the size of city government will have an impact on revenue forecasting techniques used (Reddick 2004). The χ^2 statistic indicates that smaller-sized cities, in terms of FTE employment, are more likely to use expert forecasting to estimate license fees. Forecasting user charges was done most commonly with trend forecasting, with 68.2 percent of cities using this method. Finally, expert forecasting was the most common method for forecasting federal and state grants with 43.9 percent of cities using this technique. In addition, the χ^2 statistics indicated that the smaller-sized cities were more likely to use expert forecasting for user charges, federal, and state grants.

Overall, the results in Table 13.4 indicate that trend forecasting is the most commonly used technique for the revenue sources of sales taxes, license fees, and user charges. Expert forecasting is done most frequently to predict property taxes, federal, and state grants. Not surprisingly, the least commonly used forecasting techniques were econometric, deterministic, and consensus forecasting with typically less than 10 percent of cities using these methods. The overall higher use of expert and trend forecasting is consistent with existing research on revenue forecasting in local governments. The following section takes this analysis a step further by evaluating the effectiveness of revenue forecasting methods that cities in Texas currently use.

Evaluating Revenue Forecasting Processes and Techniques

Table 13.5 provides summary information on the level of agreement and disagreement in the evaluation of revenue forecasting processes and techniques. The median responses show that cities tend to rely on a combination of revenue forecasting techniques rather than just one, with 80.3 percent agreeing that this is the case. In addition, 77.2 percent of respondents indicate that they use many assumptions in their revenue forecasting models. The remaining questions did not show as much agreement, but the results are equally interesting.

First, there is some agreement that quantitative techniques of revenue forecasting are superior, with 45.4 percent of cities agreeing to this statement (Table 13.5). There was much less agreement that qualitative techniques such as expert forecasting are superior, with only 25.7 percent of finance directors agreeing to this. Only 36.3 percent of cities used a consensus approach for producing the revenue forecast.

* There is no state income tax in Texas; therefore, this revenue source was not examined.

Table 13.5 Revenue Forecasting Processes and Techniques

In Our City Government	*Strongly Agree (Percent)*	*Agree (Percent)*	*Neutral (Percent)*	*Disagree (Percent)*	*Strongly Disagree (Percent)*	*Median Response*
We tend to rely on a combination of revenue forecasting techniques, rather than one method	24.2	56.1	13.6	6.1	0.0	1
We do not use more sophisticated forecasting techniques because of the lack of resources for staff training	15.2	25.8	25.8	33.3	0.0	0
We use many assumptions in our revenue forecasting models	9.1	68.2	15.2	7.6	0.0	1
The costs in terms of time, effort, and resources of estimating revenues have increased over the past five years	7.6	31.8	45.5	13.6	1.5	0
Qualitative techniques of revenue forecasting (e.g., expert) are superior at producing more accurate revenue forecasts	3.0	22.7	53.0	21.2	0.0	0
Quantitative techniques of revenue forecasting (e.g., trend) are superior at producing more accurate revenue forecasts	1.5	43.9	40.9	13.6	0.0	0
We use a consensus approach when producing the revenue forecasts	1.5	34.8	37.9	24.2	1.5	0
There is a risk involved with implementing a new revenue forecasting technique(s); therefore, we have chosen not to adopt any new techniques	0.0	12.1	48.5	36.4	3.0	0

Note: Strongly agree = 2, agree = 1, neutral = 0, disagree = −1, and strongly disagree = −2.

Overall, in terms of evaluating revenue forecasting, the results indicate that there is agreement that cities use multiple techniques to forecast revenues (also shown in Table 13.4) and make many assumptions in their models.

Revenue Forecasting Accuracy

Table 13.6 provides information on revenue forecasting accuracy, one of the most commonly debated issues in the forecasting research. On the question of whether revenue forecasts are underestimated, 54.6 percent of respondents agree that this is the case in their city governments. This is further explored in Figure 13.1, which shows that cities typically underestimate revenues in the range 2–5 percent, which is consistent with the existing time series analysis. The majority of finance directors (60.6 percent) believe that they have enough information to produce accurate revenue forecasts. In addition, 89.4 percent of respondents believe that more accurate and informed revenue forecasts greatly enhance decision making in the budgetary process. There is a general consensus with 68.2 percent of respondents believing that when revenues are overestimated, program cuts or revenue increases are necessary. There was less agreement that information technology (IT) produces more accurate revenue forecasts (39.4 percent). The consensus-based forecasting approach, according to finance directors, is a method that produces more accurate revenue forecasts (27.3 percent).

Overall, the results in Table 13.6 and Figure 13.1 support the literature on underestimating revenues in local government revenue forecasting (Beckett-Camarata 2006). This is further supported by the open-ended question in this survey that asked finance directors to comment on the overall effectiveness of revenue forecasting in their city governments. The most common response by finance directors was to be very conservative in their revenue forecast. Finance directors have enough information to produce the revenue forecast; they believe forecast accuracy enhances the budget process, and program cuts are a consequence of not having accurate revenue forecasts. The following section delves into a related issue to forecast accuracy, rating the current revenue forecasting practices that cities use in Texas.

Rating the Current Revenue Forecasting Practices

Table 13.7 provides information on how finance directors rate their current forecasting practices used in their cities. The survey findings indicate high ratings for revenue forecasting practices used by city governments in Texas. The results from these questions indicated that the quality of economic assumptions and estimating techniques were viewed as good according to 80.3 and 87.9 percent of cities, respectively. The system for monitoring revenue forecasts, revision, evaluation, and presentation indicated very high ratings as well with 77.3 percent rated good for these questions. The least well-rated practice was the use of alternative revenue forecasts, with 46.9 percent believing that this was good.

Table 13.6 Revenue Forecasting Accuracy

In Our City Government	*Strongly Agree (Percent)*	*Agree (Percent)*	*Neutral (Percent)*	*Disagree (Percent)*	*Strongly Disagree (Percent)*	*Median Response*
More accurate and informed revenue forecasts greatly enhance decision making in the budget process	28.8	60.6	9.1	1.5	0.0	1
When revenues are overestimated, program cuts or revenue increases are necessary	9.1	59.1	19.7	10.6	1.5	1
There is a tendency to underestimate revenues	9.1	45.5	25.8	18.2	1.5	1
We have enough information to produce accurate revenue forecasts	3.0	57.6	27.3	10.6	1.5	1
IT helps to produce more accurate revenue forecasts	3.0	36.4	25.8	28.8	6.1	0
More individuals involved in the production of the forecast will produce a more accurate forecast	3.0	27.3	36.4	27.3	6.1	0
During economic slowdowns, revenue forecasts are much more accurate than during economic expansions	3.0	19.7	54.5	21.2	1.5	0
A forecast that uses a consensus approach will have greater accuracy than one that does not	0.0	27.3	40.9	28.8	3.0	0

Note: Strongly agree = 2, agree = 1, neutral = 0, disagree = −1, and strongly disagree = −2.

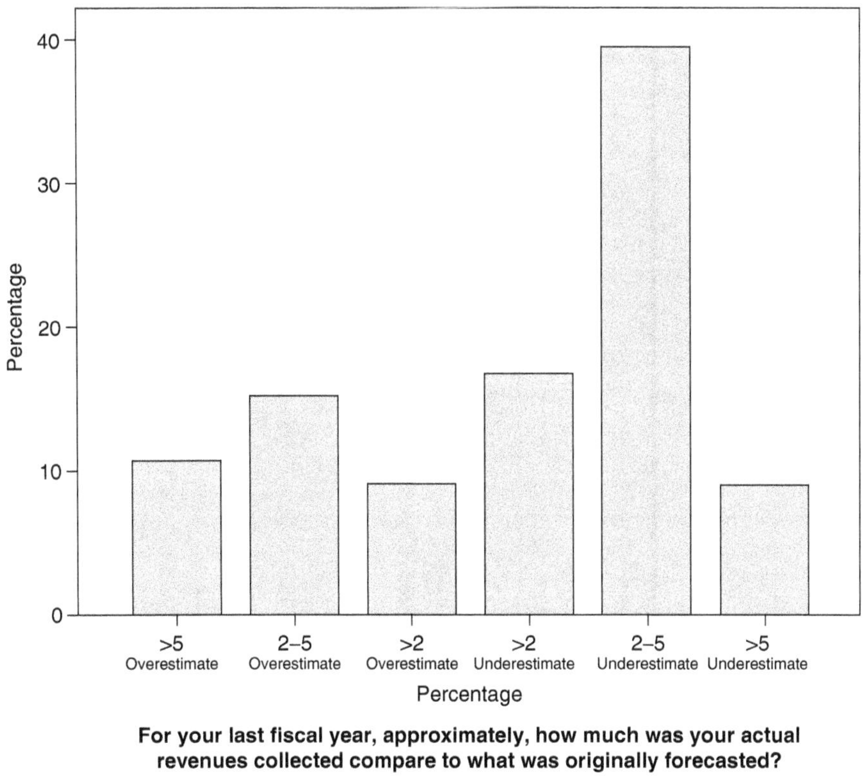

Figure 13.1 Percentage of over- and underestimating of revenue.

Although the techniques, assumptions, presentation, monitoring, and evaluation of forecasts are highly rated, there is not much use of alternative techniques challenging the status quo of forecasting methodologies. The following section discusses the degree of participation in the revenue forecasting process. Existing research indicates that more openness and transparency in the forecast should lead to more accurate revenue forecasts (Voorhees 2004).

Participation in the Revenue Forecasting Process

Table 13.8 shows some very mixed responses to the degree of participation in the revenue forecasting processes of city governments in Texas. Input from citizens and businesses were typically not included in the revenue forecasting process. A large proportion of respondents (92.3 percent) agree that the city council is accepting the revenue forecasting approach that is currently in place. There is a disagreement (62.2 percent) that the city council takes an active role in revenue forecasting. There is also a disagreement (66.6 percent) that the city council has substantial

Table 13.7 Rating of Current Revenue Forecasting Practices

How Would You Rate the Current Revenue Forecasting Practices That Your City Has in Terms of	*Very Good (Percent)*	*Good (Percent)*	*Neither Good Nor Poor (Percent)*	*Poor (Percent)*	*Very Poor (Percent)*	*Median Response*
Presentation of the revenue forecasts	10.6	66.7	19.7	3.0	0.0	1
Quality of estimating techniques	9.1	78.8	12.1	0.0	0.0	1
System of monitoring revenue forecasts	9.1	68.2	18.2	4.5	0.0	1
Revision and evaluation of revenue forecasts	7.6	69.7	18.2	4.5	0.0	1
Quality of economic assumptions	4.5	75.8	16.7	3.0	0.0	1
Use of alternative revenue forecasts	3.0	43.9	43.9	9.1	0.0	0

Note: Very good = 2, good = 1, neither = 0, poor = −1, and very poor = −2.

Table 13.8 Participation in the Revenue Forecasting Process

In Our City Government	*Strongly Agree (Percent)*	*Agree (Percent)*	*Neutral (Percent)*	*Disagree (Percent)*	*Strongly Disagree (Percent)*	*Median Response*
The working revenue forecast is discussed with some or all of the council members before the budget is formally presented to the city council	15.2	36.4	12.1	27.3	9.1	1
The city council accepts the revenue forecasting approach that we currently use	9.1	83.3	7.6	0.0	0.0	1
Our revenue forecasting process is open and transparent	6.1	40.9	36.4	10.6	6.1	0
If the city council disagrees with, or has serious concerns about the revenue forecast, it is likely to see that the estimate is changed	4.5	33.3	28.8	27.3	6.1	0
Our city council takes an active role in the revenue forecasting process	4.5	12.1	21.2	45.5	16.7	−1
Political considerations influence revenue forecasting	3.0	13.6	19.7	48.5	15.2	−1
The city council has substantial involvement in adjusting the revenue forecast for use in the actual budget document	1.5	13.6	18.2	53.0	13.6	−1
The input from citizens and businesses is included in the revenue forecasting process	1.5	7.6	21.2	59.1	10.6	−1

Note: Strongly agree = 2, agree = 1, neutral = 0, disagree = −1, and strongly disagree = −2.

involvement in adjusting the revenue forecast for use in the budget document. Political considerations, according to finance directors, influence the revenue forecast (16.6 percent). There is some discussion with the city council on the working revenue forecast, with 52.6 percent agreeing that this takes place.

The results on participation in the revenue forecasting process do not indicate that this is very common among city governments. It is not evident from the data that revenue forecasting is a very participatory process. Indeed, it seems to be well insulated from the stakeholders. This insulation is both positive and negative. It is positive with less partisan influences on forecasting, which should make the revenue forecast more accurate. The downside is that because there is little active participation in the process, there is less impetus for change that could also affect accuracy as well. This important point is discussed in the conclusion of this study.

Summary and Conclusion

This chapter has evaluated revenue forecasting in local governments through a case study of city governments in Texas. Because there is no state income tax, revenue forecasting in Texas cities is limited in the sources of revenue forecasted. Cities in Texas tend to rely on revenues from sales and property taxes to finance their governments. This lack of diversity in revenue sources makes revenue forecasting critically important. Some of the most interesting findings from the survey of finance directors were that cities typically use very few prior years of data for the revenue estimate and have a small forecasting staff. However, there is agreement that the revenue forecast is an important component of the overall budgetary process.

In terms of the forecasting techniques used, the most common were expert and trend forecasting for estimating different sources of revenues. The results of this study are consistent with other survey researches showing that the impact of causal-oriented forecasting techniques is limited in cities, which has a bearing on forecasting accuracy (Reddick 2004). The more accurate causal techniques of consensus, deterministic, and econometric forecasting techniques were used by only around 10 percent of cities in Texas. The reasons for not using more advanced techniques could be explained by several factors found in this study such as lack of graduate education, forecasting staff, and prior years of data used to produce the forecast. Many of the more causal techniques such as econometric forecasting would require these factors. There is an agreement that cities tend to rely on a combination of revenue forecasting techniques and make many assumptions in their revenue forecasting models.

In revenue forecasting accuracy, there is a majority of cities in Texas that agree that they tend to underestimate revenues. City governments tend to underestimate revenues between 2 and 5 percent, which is consistent with the literature (Rodgers and Joyce 1996). There was only a small amount of agreement that consensus forecasting will produce more accurate forecasts. This may be attributed to only a minority of cities actually using this method.

In rating the current revenue forecasting practices of cities there are high marks for the presentation, quality of techniques, monitoring, revision, and economic assumptions. However, there is less use of alternative revenue forecasts that may support the tendency of cities to rely on certain revenue forecasting models, thereby creating an "assumption drag" in these models.

Finally, the most interesting results of this study indicate that the revenue forecasting is mainly an internal process. There is not much participation from either citizens or the city council in the revenue forecasting process. This lack of participation is also consistent with only a minority of cities using consensus-based forecasting. This finding is problematic because it shows the extent to which revenue forecasting is not a very open and participatory process in city governments, going against the trend for this in public sector management. The revenue forecasting literature argues that being a more open process would promote greater forecasting accuracy and indeed most importantly accountability for the governing institutions of the city.

References

Agostini, S. J. 1991. Searching for a better forecast: San Francisco's revenue forecasting model. *Government Finance Review* 7(6): 13–16.

Beckett-Camarata, J. 2006. Revenue forecasting accuracy in Ohio local governments. *Journal of Public Budgeting, Accounting, & Financial Management* 18(1): 77–99.

Bretschneider, S., B. Bunch, and W. Gorr. 1992. Revenue forecast errors in Pennsylvania local government budgeting: sources and remedies. *Public Budgeting and Financial Management* 4(3): 721–743.

Bretschneider, S. and W. Gorr. 1992. Economic, organizational, and political influences on biases in forecasting state sales tax receipts. *International Journal of Forecasting* 7(4): 457–466.

Bretschneider, S., W. Gorr, G. Grizzle, and E. Klay. 1989. Political and organizational influences on the accuracy of forecasting state government revenues. *International Journal of Forecasting* 5(3): 307–319.

Caiden, N. and A. Wildavsky. 1974. *Planning and Budgeting in Poor Countries*. New York: Wiley.

Chapman, J. I. 1982. Fiscal stress and budgetary activity. *Public Budgeting & Finance* 2(1): 83–87.

Cirincione, C., G. Gurrieri, and B. Van De Sande. 1999. Municipal government revenue forecasting: issues of method and data. *Public Budgeting & Finance* 19(1): 26–46.

Deschamps, E. 2004. The impact of institutional change on forecast accuracy: a case study of budget forecasting in Washington State. *International Journal of Forecasting* 20(4): 647–657.

Forrester, J. P. 1991. Multi-year forecasting and municipal budgeting. *Public Budgeting & Finance* 11(2): 47–61.

Forrester, J. P. 1993. Use of revenue forecasting techniques. In T. D. Lynch and L. L. Martin (eds), *Handbook of Comparative Public Budgeting and Financial Management*. New York: Marcel Dekker, pp. 149–167.

Frank, H. A. 1990. Municipal revenue forecasting with time-series models: a Florida case study. *American Review of Public Administration* 20(1): 45–59.

Frank, H. A. and G. A. Gianakis. 1990. Raising the bridge using time series forecasting models. *Public Productivity & Management Review* 14(2): 171–188.

Frank, H. A., G. A. Gianakis, and C. P. McCue. 2005. Will GASB 34 induce changes in local government forecasting practice? A preliminary investigation. *Journal of Public Budgeting, Accounting, & Financial Management* 17(4): 557–573.

Frank, H. A. and J. McCollough. 1992. Municipal forecasting practice: "demand" and "supply" side perspectives. *International Journal of Public Administration* 15(9): 1669–1695.

Jonas, K., G. Rest, and T. Atkinson. 1992. Virginia's revenue forecasting process and models. *Public Budgeting & Finance* 12(2): 70–81.

Jones, V. D., S. Bretschneider, and W. L. Gorr. 1997. Organizational pressures on forecast evaluation: managerial, political, and procedural influences. *International Journal of Forecasting* 16(4): 241–254.

Klay, W. E. 1983. Revenue forecasting: an administrative perspective. In J. Rabin and T. Lynch (eds), *Handbook of Public Budgeting and Financial Management*. New York: Marcel Dekker, pp. 287–314.

MacManus, S. A. and B. P. Grothe. 1989. Fiscal stress as a stimulant to better revenue forecasting and productivity. *Public Productivity Review* 12(4): 387–400.

Reddick, C. G. 2004. Assessing local government revenue forecasting techniques. *International Journal of Public Administration* 27(8,9): 597–613.

Rodgers, R. and P. Joyce. 1996. The effect of underforecasting on the accuracy of revenue forecasts by state governments. *Public Administration Review* 56(1): 48–56.

Rubin, I. S. 1987. Estimating and actual urban revenues: exploring the gap. *Public Budgeting & Finance* 7(4): 83–94.

Rubin, M. M. and N. H. Mantell. 2000. Municipal government revenue forecasting methodologies. Paper presented at the Association of Budgeting and Financial Management Conference, October 5–7, Kansas City, MO.

Rubin, M. M., J. L. Peters, and N. Mantell. 1999. Revenue forecasting and estimation. In W. B. Hildreth and J. A. Richardson (eds), *Handbook of Taxation*. New York: Marcel Dekker, pp. 769–800.

Schroeder, L. 1982. Local government multi-year budgetary forecasting: some administrative and political issues. *Public Administration Review* 42(2): 121–127.

Shkurti, W. J. 1990. A user's guide to state revenue forecasting. *Public Budgeting & Finance* 10(4): 79–94.

Sun, J. 2005. The dynamics of government revenue forecasting from an organizational perspective: a review of the literature. *Journal of Public Budgeting, Accounting, & Financial Management* 17(4): 527–556.

Voorhees, W. R. 2002. Institutional structures utilized in state revenue forecasting. *Journal of Public Budgeting, Accounting, & Financial Management* 14(2): 175–195.

Voorhees, W. R. 2004. More is better: consensual forecasting and state revenue forecast error. *International Journal of Public Administration* 27(8,9): 651–671.

Wong, J. D. 1995. Options, challenges, and incentives for implementing systematic revenue forecasting in local government. *Municipal Finance Journal* 16(1): 63–79.

Chapter 14

Pro Forma Forecasting for Determining the Financial Position of Enterprise Operations in Government

Aman Khan

Contents

Introduction

Forecasting is an integral part of financial decision making in government, yet conventional literature on forecasting has predominantly focused on the General Fund to the neglect of enterprise funds, even though they make up a sizeable portion of governmental activities (Boswell and Carpenter 1986, Bretschneider and Gore 1987, Forrester 1991, Frank 1990, Goldberg and Scott 1985, Khan 1989, 2003, Scott 1972). This provides a one-dimensional approach to forecasting. The objective of this chapter is to introduce a simple forecasting approach to predict the financial position of an enterprise operation based on three essential components of a balance sheet that are frequently used to measure the financial condition of an organization – assets, liabilities, and net assets. The forecasting model suggested here offers a comprehensive rather than an ad hoc approach that neatly ties these components together to provide a fuller explanation of the future financial condition of a government enterprise.

Enterprise operations have become extremely important in government in recent years. Three factors have contributed to this remarkable growth: (1) a declining revenue base as governments at all levels compete for limited resources to meet the increasing needs of their citizens; (2) growing unwillingness on the part of the taxpayers to pay more in taxes to support the rising costs of public services; and (3) increasing reliance on enterprise operations to compensate for revenue shortfalls that otherwise would have to be raised through taxes, user fees, and charges. The critical role that enterprises play in government has been extensively discussed in the literature on public finance by DeHoog and Swansen (1988), Dilorenzo (1982), Lynch (1987), Strauss and Wertz (1976), Tyer (1989), Vogt (1978), and recently by Khan and Stumm (1993) among others.

The Basic Model and Assumptions

This chapter starts with a simple notion that all financial activities of an organization go through a cyclical process with a beginning position, activities throughout the year, and an ending position. This is consistent with the fund balance statements one would find in most annual financial reports. However, from a forecasting point of view, what is important and should be of considerable interest to the decision makers is the ending position that reflects the changes that have taken place in an enterprise from its initial position as a result of the activities throughout the year. The objective then is to focus on the ending position, which in essence becomes the beginning position for the next cycle. To do so, it is necessary to start with the beginning position, a set of behavioral conditions, and other related assumptions. The conditions, beginning position, and the assumptions that underlie these conditions serve as important inputs for the forecasting process. Although no attempt has been made here to simulate the development of these inputs, they will be considered using hypothetical data as the chapter progresses. Figure 14.1 shows the basic structure of the model.

Figure 14.1 shows that enterprise operations, like any other operation in government, have four basic elements that serve as the foundation for service provision or delivery: (1) the service needs of the population the enterprises serve, (2) the input requirements for the services and their costs, (3) the administrative expenses independent of input costs, and (4) the nature of cash collection and disbursement. Information obtained on these conditions and the manner in which it is obtained has a significant effect on how one would assess the financial condition of an enterprise, in particular its cash position, income situation, and ending position.

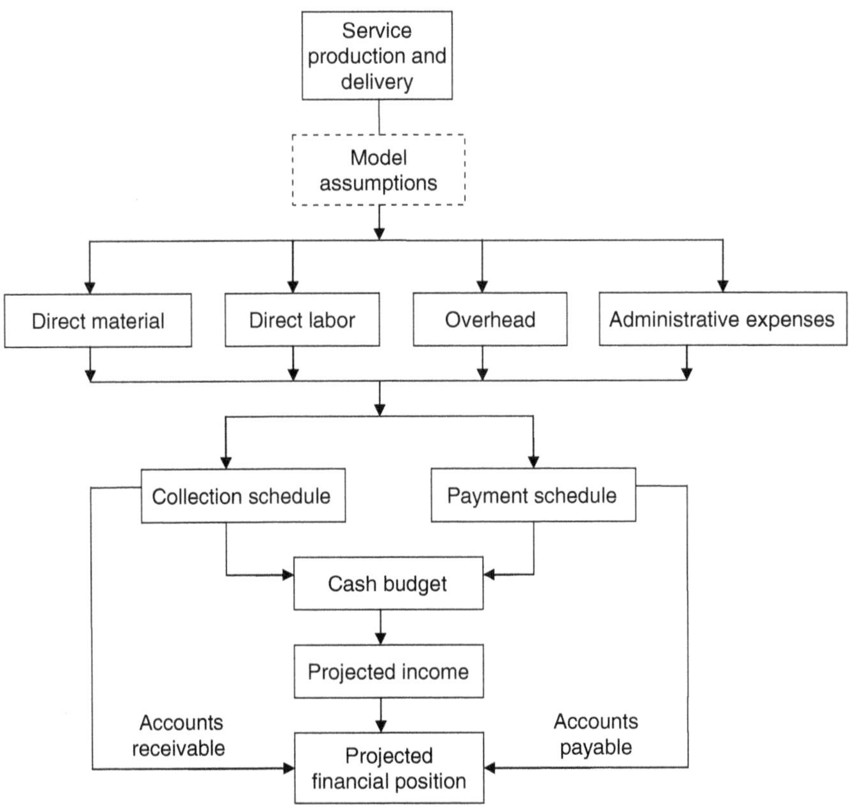

Figure 14.1 The basic model.

Determining Demand for Service

For a government to be able to efficiently deliver services, it must first determine the service needs of its population. But determining the service needs for government, that is, its population is often difficult because of the difficulty in determining the exact nature of demand for public goods and services, as well as the difficulty in determining the price that would reflect this demand. The problem, however, is much less for enterprise operations because of the business-like manner in which they operate and the nature of services they provide. For the present purpose, it is assumed that the demand for a service is directly related to the characteristics of the population being served, their willingness to consume, as well as their ability to pay. This relationship can be easily shown with the help of a simple linear model of the form:

$$Y = a + \sum_{i=1}^{n} b_i X_i + e$$

where

Y = demand for service Y
X = set of explanatory variables (such as population characteristics, and willingness or ability to consume as determined by median household income, past consumption behavior, and price of the good service being consumed, etc.)
a, b = parameters of the model
e = stochastic term

Determining Input Requirements and Costs

Once we know the amount of service the enterprise needs to provide, the next step in the process is to determine the input requirements for the service and their costs. Three sets of inputs are generally used when producing or delivering a service: direct material, direct labor, and overhead. Direct materials are items used in the production or delivery of a good or service that can be directly attributed to it. Direct labor includes labor or wages paid to those who are directly involved in that process, and overhead includes costs that are neither direct material nor direct labor. The effectiveness of service provision depends on how efficiently the operation utilizes these inputs and the costs they will incur. The model assumes that input costs are a direct function of the quantity of inputs used. Because these costs depend on input quantity, we can use the standard cost function for this purpose.

$$C_Y = pI$$

where

C_Y = input cost for service Y
I = input quantity
P = price per unit of input

Determining Administrative Expenses

In addition to determining the input costs, it is also assumed that an enterprise will incur administrative costs or expenses independent of the input costs. Let us assume that this expense is a function of the amount of service the enterprise will provide and that this relationship can be expressed by a model similar to the one suggested earlier for determining service needs

$$C_Y = a + \sum_{i=1}^{n} b_i Q_i + e$$

where

C_Y = administrative cost for service Y
Q = quantity of service
a, b = parameters of the model
e = stochastic term

Other Related Conditions

Two additional conditions are included in this section to complete the model—"accounts receivable" to keep track of funds the enterprise will receive for the services it provides, and "accounts payable" to keep track of the payments it must make for the input factors. To keep the model simple, it is assumed that the collection and disbursement rates are fixed during the accounting cycle.

The end product of the process will be a series of quarterly statements, called *pro forma* statements, consistent with the basic model presented in Figure 14.1. If properly structured, *pro forma* statements are effective tools for analyzing the results of an organization's planned activities on financial performance. In addition, *pro forma* statements can serve as a benchmark or standard against actual operating results. In addition, they can also serve as an important instrument for controlling and monitoring financial changes throughout the forecasting period.

Model Application

To illustrate the model, consider the beginning financial position of an enterprise operation for a hypothetical city that offers two different services—A and B. The beginning financial position represents the typical balance sheet or statement of financial position at the beginning of the month with assets, liabilities, and net assets. Assets include both current assets (cash, investments, accounts receivable, due from other funds, and inventories) and fixed assets (land, buildings, and equipment), liabilities include current liabilities (accounts payable, debt payable, due to other funds, and short-term loan payment) and noncurrent liabilities (claims and judgment, long-term debt payables), and net assets are the residual. The model assumes that part of the net assets is invested in capital assets and part is divided between restricted and unrestricted accounts. Table 14.1 presents the statement of financial position for the hypothetical city at the beginning of the month.

Table 14.2 provides information on the model conditions, including the levels of services that would be required for the next quarter, the standard costs for the inputs, and information on accounts receivable and payable. For instance, to meet the service needs for A, assume that the enterprise must produce 10,000 units in January, 12,000 in February, and 15,000 in March; and for B it must produce 7,500, 8,700, and 10,000 units, respectively. Also, assume that to produce one unit of service A, it will need two units of materials, three units of labor, and two units of overhead at a cost of $31. Similarly, it will need two units of materials, two units of labor, and four units of overhead to produce a unit of service B at a cost of $28. For accounts receivable and payable, assume further that they will be collected and disbursed at a fixed rate based on prior knowledge.

Production Budget

Our next objective is to prepare the "service requirements budget." As noted earlier, the purpose of this budget is to produce an estimate of service needs for the enterprise operation. For convenience, we will call it a "production budget," because most government enterprises produce as well as deliver goods and services. The budget consists of three basic elements: (1) service needs for the forecasting period, which are assumed to have been obtained by estimating the regression equation discussed earlier under model assumptions; (2) the beginning inventory, which is known *a priori*; and (3) a desired ending inventory at the end of each month to avoid stock-out and other costs. The desired ending inventory can be determined using models such as Baumol's (1952) well-known Economic Order Quantity, but, for the present purpose, it is assumed to be a fixed percentage of service needs.

Given this background information, the service requirement for any given month can be obtained by adding the estimated needs for the month to the desired ending inventory. However, the portion of these needs must be adjusted by the amount of beginning inventory to determine the production requirements for the month. Thus to obtain the service requirements for all the three months, one would simply add the estimated requirements for the individual months. For instance, if we would add the estimated requirements of 10,000 units for service A for January to the desired inventory of 1,000 units and subtract the total from the beginning inventory of 1,200 units, it will give us the production requirements for the month

Table 14.1 Hypothetical Fund: Statement of Financial Position (January 1, 2XXX)

Assets	
Current assets ($)	
Cash	250,000
Investments	75,000
Accounts receivable	125,000
Due from other funds	100,000
Inventories	325,000
Total current assets	875,000
Noncurrent assets ($)	
Land	100,000
Buildings	400,000
Accumulated depreciation	(50,000)
Equipment	650,000
Accumulated depreciation	(150,000)
Total noncurrent assets	950,000
Total assets	1,825,000
Liabilities	
Current liabilities ($)	
Accounts payable	350,000
Debt payable (P&I)	270,000
Due to other funds	150,000
Short-term loan payment	–
Total current liabilities	770,000
Noncurrent liabilities ($)	
Claims and judgments	25,000
Debt payable (P&I)	–
Total noncurrent liabilities	25,000
Total liabilities	795,500
Net assets ($)	
Investments in capital assets	485,500
Restricted for debt retirement	–
Unrestricted	545,000
Total net assets	1,030,000
Total liabilities and net assets	1,825,000

of January. The process can be repeated for February and March to produce the total requirements for the forecasting period. The results are shown in Table 14.3.

It should be pointed out that the production budget can further be made complicated, depending on how the production is scheduled during a given period and by including other requirements, but, for convenience, they will not be considered here.

Table 14.2 Hypothetical Fund: Model Assumptions (First Quarter: 2XXX)

	Selling Price ($)	*January*	*February*	*March*	*Total*
Service type					
S-A	40.00 per unit	10,000	12,000	15,000	37,000
S-B	45.00 per unit	7,500	8,700	10,000	26,200
	Service A	Service B			
Standard costs					
Material					
S-A (2@$2.00)	4.00	—			
S-B (2@$3.00)	—	6.00			
Direct labor					
S-A (3@$8.00)	24.00	—			
S-B (2@$8.00)	—	16.00			
Overhead					
S-A (2@$1.50)	3.00	—			
S-B (4@$1.50)	—	6.00			
	31.00	28.00			

Collection and payment pattern

Accounts receivable

50 percent collected in the month of sale
30 percent collected in the month following sale
15 percent collected in the second month following sale
3 percent collected after the second month following sale
2 percent uncollectible

Accounts payable

60 percent payable in the first month
35 percent payable in the second month
05 percent payable after the second month

Administrative expense equation (estimated)

$\hat{Y} = 15{,}000 + \$3Q_A + \$4Q_B$

Direct Material, Labor, Overhead, and Administrative Expense Budgets

Once the production budget has been prepared, the next step in the process is to project the costs of inputs for services, that is, the costs of direct material, direct labor, overhead, and administration. The material budget can be prepared in the same fashion as the production budget. To keep it simple, assume that each service utilizes the same type of materials. The standard material allowances are shown under budget assumptions in Table 14.2. Now to obtain the direct materials required, simply multiply the standards by the scheduled requirements in Table 14.3 and adjust them

Table 14.3 Hypothetical Fund: Production Budget (Units) (First Quarter: 2XXX)

	January	*February*	*March*	*Total*
Service A				
Service needs	10,000	12,000	15,000	37,000
Desired ending inventory[a]	1,000	1,200	1,500	1,500
	11,000	13,200	16,500	38,500
Beginning inventory	1,200	1,400	1,500	1,200
Production requirements	9,800	11,800	15,000	37,300
Service B				
Service needs	7,500	8,700	10,000	26,200
Desired ending inventory[a]	750	870	1,000	1,000
	8,250	9,570	11,000	27,200
Beginning inventory	700	800	1,000	700
Production requirements	7,550	8,770	10,000	26,500

[a] Assumed to be a fixed percentage of service needs.

for the desired ending and beginning inventories. Multiplying these further by per unit cost will produce the total cost of materials as shown in Table 14.4.

The direct labor budget, the second component in input requirements, is shown in Table 14.5 and should be self-explanatory in that it follows the same format as the material budget—determine the total labor requirements, then calculate the total cost of labor for each service. Let us assume that the budgeted production of service A for January is 10,000 units and the labor requirement is three units for each unit of service, whereas the cost of labor is $8.00 an hour. Now to obtain the total cost of labor for service A, all one has to do is multiply the total labor hours by cost per unit of labor, and repeat the process for February and March. Similarly, repeat the steps to obtain the cost of direct labor for service B, then add it to the cost of service A to obtain the total cost of direct labor for both services. The results of this process are presented in Table 14.5.

Table 14.6 presents the overhead budget for the enterprise. As can be seen from Table 14.6, the budget has two components: (1) a variable component, which includes standard items such as supplies, indirect labor, overtime, vacation pay, etc.; and (2) a fixed component, which, for convenience, is assumed to be a fixed percentage (say 25 percent) of expected direct labor. To obtain the overhead cost for a given month, the individual items are then multiplied by the expected labor for that month. From this, it is easy to obtain the total cost of overhead for the entire forecasting period by simply adding the overhead for each of the three months. Assume that the expected labor hours required for service A for January were 30,000. When this is multiplied by the rate for each item under variable costs and added together, it will produce the overhead budget for the month. The process is repeated for all

Table 14.4 Hypothetical Fund: Material Budget (First Quarter: 2XXX)

	January	*February*	*March*	*Total*
Service A				
Estimated production needs (production × 2)	20,000	24,000	30,000	74,000
Desired ending inventory	1,000	1,200	1,500	1,500
Total (units)	21,000	25,200	31,500	75,500
Beginning inventory	1,200	1,400	1,500	1,200
Total material needs	19,800	23,800	30,000	74,300
Per unit cost ($)	2.00	2.00	2.00	2.00
Total cost of materials ($)	39,600	47,600	60,000	148,600
Service B				
Estimated production needs (production × 2)	15,000	17,400	20,000	52,400
Desired ending inventory	750	870	1,000	1,000
Total (units)	15,750	18,270	21,000	53,400
Beginning inventory	700	800	1,000	700
Total material needs	15,050	17,470	20,000	52,700
Per unit cost ($)	3.00	3.00	3.00	3.00
Total cost of materials ($)	45,150	52,410	60,000	158,100

Table 14.5 Hypothetical Fund: Direct Labor Budget (First Quarter: 2XXX)

	January	*February*	*March*	*Total*
Service A				
Budgeted production	10,000	12,000	15,000	37,000
Labor requirement per unit	3	3	3	3
Total labor required (hours)	30,000	36,000	45,000	111,000
Labor cost per hour ($)	8.00	8.00	8.00	8.00
Total labor cost for A ($)	240,000	288,000	360,000	888,000
Service B				
Budgeted production	7,500	8,700	10,000	26,000
Labor requirement per unit	2	2	2	2
Total labor required (hours)	15,000	17,400	20,000	52,400
Labor cost per hour ($)	8.00	8.00	8.00	8.00
Total labor cost for B ($)	120,000	139,200	160,000	419,200
Total labor cost ($)	360,000	427,200	520,000	1,307,200

Table 14.6 Hypothetical Fund: Overhead Budget (First Quarter: 2XXX)

	Rate	*January*	*February*	*March*	*Total*
Service A					
Expected direct labor (hours)	—	30,000	36,000	45,000	111,000
Variable cost					
Supplies	0.25	$7,500	$9,000	$11,250	$27,750
Indirect	0.15	4,500	5,400	6,750	16,650
Overtime	0.25	7,500	9,000	11,250	27,750
Vacation pay	0.10	3,000	3,600	4,500	11,100
Repair	0.30	9,000	10,800	13,500	33,300
Miscellaneous	0.20	6,000	7,200	9,000	22,200
Total variable overhead ($)	1.25	37,500	45,000	56,250	138,750
Fixed cost	0.25	$7,500	$9,000	$11,250	$27,750
Total overhead for A ($)	1.50	45,000	54,000	67,500	166,500
Service B					
Expected direct labor (hours)	—	15,000	17,400	20,000	52,400
Variable cost					
Supplies	0.25	$3,750	$4,350	$5,000	$13,100
Indirect	0.15	2,250	2,610	3,000	7,860
Overtime	0.25	3,750	4,350	5,000	13,100
Vacation pay	0.10	1,500	1,740	2,000	5,240
Repair	0.30	4,500	5,220	6,000	15,720
Miscellaneous	0.20	3,000	3,480	4,000	10,480
Total variable overhead ($)	1.25	18,750	21,750	25,000	65,500
Fixed cost	0.25	$3,750	$4,350	$5,000	$13,100
Total overhead for B ($)	1.50	22,500	26,100	30,000	78,600
Total overhead ($)		67,500	80,100	97,500	245,100

the three months to produce the total overhead budget for service A. The process is identical for service B and, as before, the two are added to obtain the total overhead budget for both services. The results are shown in Table 14.6. It should be pointed out that the model assumes the variable rates to be the same for both services, but, in reality, they will be different.

To complete the computation of costs of input requirements for the two services, the next obvious step is to obtain the administrative expense budget. This is done by estimating the parameters of the regression equation discussed under model assumption for input requirements. Assume that the model has been estimated and that it has produced the following results: $\hat{P}$ = \$15,000 + \$3 (sale of service A) + \$4 (sale of service B), where the constant term represents "fixed expense" and the regression coefficients the "variable rates." Therefore, to obtain the administrative expense for January, one would simply insert the projected sales figures for the month (assumed to be 10,000 for service A and 7,500 for service B) in the estimated equation so that $\hat{Y} = \$15{,}000 + \$3(10{,}000_A) + \$4(7{,}500_B)$. The result would produce the expense budget for January as shown in Table 14.7. The process is repeated for February and March, and added together to obtain the total administrative expense for the entire forecasting period.

Schedule of Collection

A good cash collection system lies at the heart of a good financial management system. In fact, the efficiency of an organization's financial activities can be greatly enhanced by knowledge of its cash collection procedure. The collection schedule, as suggested in this section, is achieved in two steps. First, we calculate the collection for each month by multiplying the expected sale of service by unit price, which will produce the total revenue from the sale of service. Next, we multiply this total revenue by the collection rates in Table 14.2 to obtain the cash inflow for the month. Assume that the collection rate is 50 percent in the month of sale, 30 percent in the month following sale, 15 percent in the second month following sale, etc. Assume further that the revenue from the expected sale of service for January is $737,500,

Table 14.7 Hypothetical Fund: Administrative Expense Budget (First Quarter: 2XXX)

	January	*February*	*March*	*Total*
Service A				
Sales (Units)	10,000	12,000	15,000	37,000
Variable rate (from Table 14.2 administrative expense equation) ($)	3.00	3.00	3.00	3.00
Total variable expense for A ($)	30,000	36,000	45,000	111,000
Service B				
Sales (Units)	7,500	8,700	10,000	26,200
Variable rate (from Table 14.2 administrative expense equation) ($)	4.00	4.00	4.00	4.00
Total variable expense for B ($)	30,000	34,800	40,000	104,800
Total variable expense ($)	60,000	70,800	85,000	215,800
Fixed expense (from Table 14.2 administrative expense equation) ($)	15,000	15,000	15,000	45,000
Total administrative expense ($)	75,000	85,800	100,000	260,800

which is obtained by multiplying the total amount of service units for the month by its selling price (10,000 × \$40 + 7,500 × \$45). Therefore, to obtain the total collection for the month, one would simply multiply this total by 50 percent for the first month and add the portion of amount due from the previous months. As before, the process is repeated for the remaining months to obtain the schedule of collection for all the three months. The results of this process are shown in Table 14.8.

Because the collection pattern is critical in determining the projected inflows, we could have used formal models such as time-series regression to determine the rates instead of using a fixed percentage. For instance, assume that the collection for a month C_i depends on the amount of sale for the month i plus all other previous months, then cash flow from the operation could be written as

$$C_i = a + bS_i + cS_{i-1} + dS_{i-2} + \cdots + zS_{i-n}$$

where

C = collection
S = sales data
a, b, c, d, z = parameters of the model

Furthermore, if we assume that the collection depends on factors other than or in addition to sales, we could easily define a different regression model-one that would also explain most of the variation in the model.

Table 14.8 Hypothetical Fund: Schedule of Collection (First Quarter: 2XXX)

	Total (\$)	*Collected in January*[a] *(\$)*	*Collected in February*[a] *(\$)*	*Collected in March*[a] *(\$)*	*Collectible after March 31 (\$)*	*Un-collectible (\$)*
Beginning accounts receivable (\$)	125,000	73,200	51,800	0	0	0
January (\$40 × 10,000 + \$45 × 7,500)	737,500	368,750	221,250	110,625	22,125	14,750
February (\$40 × 12,000 + \$45 × 8,700)	871,500	0	435,750	261,450	156,870	17,430
March (\$40 × 15,000 + \$45 × 10,000)	450,000	0	0	225,000	216,00	9,000
Total (\$)	2,184,000	441,950	708,800	597,075	394,995	41,180

[a] At a pre-specified rate

Occasionally government enterprises, like private organizations, offer cash discounts for early payments. If so, it is possible to forecast the amounts received within the discount period, with one provision—the discounts earned in each month must be subtracted from the gross accounts collected to project the correct inflow of cash.

Schedule of Payments

Like cash collection, a good disbursement policy is critical to an effective cash management system. Timing, more than anything else, should be an important consideration of this policy. Let us assume that the payment schedule is determined by analyzing the timing of cash disbursements. Assume further that the payment structure follows the pattern suggested in Table 14.2. Payments are computed for each month by the individual input category and added together to obtain the total cash payments for all the three months. For instance, assume the payment for materials used in January was $84,750, of which 60 percent or $50,400 would be paid in January, $29,400 in February, and the remaining $4,950 in March. The process is repeated for both direct labor and overhead, and then added to obtain the total cash payment for the entire forecasting period. Table 14.9 shows the payment schedule.

Cash Budget

Once we have constructed the schedules of collection and payment, it becomes relatively easy to prepare the cash budget. A cash budget serves three important purposes: (1) it provides a detailed plan of future cash flows, (2) it provides a basis for taking corrective measures in the event if budgeted figures do not match actual or realized figures, and (3) it can provide an important benchmark for evaluating financial performance. Table 14.10 provides the cash budget for the current example. As can be seen from Table 14.10, the cash budget consists of four major elements: beginning balance, cash receipts, cash disbursements, and ending balance. For instance, assume that the cash receipts from operation for January were $441,950 and another $275,000 due from other funds. The two are then added together to the beginning balance, say, of $250,000, which will give us the total cash inflow for the month. By the same token, add the hypothetical operating expenses of $656,840 for January to $100,000 due to other funds and $270,000 in debt payable. The result will produce the total disbursement for the month. Finally, take the difference between the two to produce the ending balance for January. As before, the process is repeated for the remaining months to obtain the ending balance for all the three months.

Table 14.9 Hypothetical Fund: Schedule of Payment (First Quarter: 2XXX)

	Total ($)	*Payment in January ($)*	*Payment in February ($)*	*Payment in March ($)*	*Payable after March 31, 2XXX ($)*
Accounts payable January 1, 2XXX	350,000	350,000	—	—	—
Materials					
January	84,750	50,400	29,400	4,950	0
February	100,010	0	62,886	36,684	440
March	120,000	0	0	75,600	44,400
Total	304,760	50,400	92,286	117,234	44,840
Direct labor					
January	360,000	216,000	126,000	18,000	0
February	427,200	0	256,000	149,520	21,680
March	520,000	0	0	313,000	207,000
Total	1,307,200	216,000	382,000	480,520	228,680
Overhead					
January	67,500	40,440	23,590	3,470	0
February	80,100	0	48,060	28,035	4,005
March	97,500	0	0	58,500	39,000
Total	245,100	40,440	71,650	90,005	43,005
Total cash payment	2,207,060	656,840	545,936	687,759	316,525

Table 14.10 Hypothetical Fund: Cash Budget (First Quarter: 2XXX)

	January	*February*	*March*	*Total*
Beginning balance ($)	250,000	(59,890)	(47,026)	250,000
Operating receipts (from Table 14.8) ($)	441,950	708,800	597,075	1,747,825
Due from other funds ($)	275,000	285,000	325,000	885,000
Total cash receipts ($)	966,950	933,910	875,049	2,882,825
Disbursements				
Operating expense (from Table 14.9) ($)	656,840	545,936	687,759	1,890,535
Due to other funds ($)	100,000	165,000	125,000	390,000
Debt payable ($) (P&I)	270,000	270,000	270,000	810,000
Total disbursements ($)	1,026,840	980,936	1,082,759	3,090,535
Cash balance ($)	(59,890)	(47,026)	(207,710)	(207,710)
Short-term borrowing ($)	—	—	235,000	235,000
Ending balance ($)	(59,890)	(47,026)	27,290	27,290

Income Statement

Because the study is dealing with enterprise operations, it is important to look at the income statement to determine the projected income for the enterprise. Income statements are necessary to provide information on financial viability of an organization such as those given by gross margins from operations after adjusting for all expenses, costs of services, etc. Costs of services are usually calculated at standard costs for income statements. Table 14.11 presents the projected statement of income. According to Table 14.11, the projected income for the enterprise does not appear to be encouraging as it comes out to be negative, which is understandable given the negative balances obtained for two of the three months for the cash budget.

Statement of Financial Position

The forecasting process ends with the projected statement of financial position. Table 14.12 presents the projected financial statement for the enterprise. Looking at the statement, it does not appear that there has been any significant improvement in performance. The enterprise's overall asset position seems to have improved marginally from the initial position, whereas its liabilities have increased considerably for the same period producing a smaller gain in net assets. In the same vein, its cash position has declined significantly from the initial level, but the good news is that the unrestricted portion of net assets has increased somewhat, which will give some flexibility in spending (if need be) although not very much. Nothing else has significantly changed from the initial position.

This finding should not be taken, however, as an indication of poor performance on the part of the enterprise because the results are based on forecasts for a single quarter. As all practitioners of public finance know, governments spend more

Table 14.11 Hypothetical Fund: Projected Statement of Income (First Quarter: 2XXX)

Sales (from Table 14.8)		*Amount in Dollar*
$737,500 + $871,500 + $450,000		2,059,000
Less uncollectible (from Table 14.8)		41,180
Net sales		2,017,820
Cost of services sold (at standard)		
Service A: 37,000 × $31 (from Table 14.2)	1,147,000	
Service B: 26,200 × $28 (from Table 14.2)	733,600	1,880,600
Gross margin		137,220
Administrative expense (from Table 14.7)	260,800	260,800
Projected net income		(123,580)

Table 14.12 Hypothetical Fund: Projected Statement of Financial Position (March 31, 2XXX)

Assets	
Current assets ($)	
Cash (from Table 14.10)	27,290
Investments (no change)	75,000
Accounts receivable (from Table 14.8)	394,995
Due from other funds (from Table 14.10)	325,000
Inventories	375,000
Total current assets	1,197,285
Noncurrent assets ($)	
Land	200,000
Appreciation	5,000
Buildings	400,000
Accumulated depreciation	(55,000)
Equipment	650,000
Accumulated depreciation	(165,000)
Total noncurrent assets	1,035,000
Total assets	2,232,285
Liabilities	
Current liabilities ($)	
Accounts payable (from Table 14.9)	687,759
Debt payable (P&I) (from Table 14.10)	270,000
Due to other funds (from Table 14.10)	125,000
Short-term loan payment	235,000
Total current liabilities	1,317,759
Noncurrent liabilities ($)	
Claims and judgments	25,000
Debt payable (P&I)	—
Total noncurrent liabilities	25,000
Total liabilities	1,342,759
Net assets ($)	
Investments in capital assets	225,000
Restricted for debt retirement	—
Unrestricted	664,526
Total net assets	889,526
Total liabilities and net assets	2,232,285

money during certain times of the year than they collect in revenues and collect more than they spend at other times. To get a complete assessment of the financial position of the enterprise, one would therefore need to expand the forecasting period to the entire year and beyond, if possible, but *pro forma* forecasts are usually limited to a quarter or so as they are used mostly for short-term planning, monitoring, and performance evaluation.

Conclusion

This chapter has presented a simple example of how one would prepare *pro forma* statements (forecasts) for enterprise operations in government. Although it is not necessary for these statements to be as detailed as they have been shown in this chapter, detailed statements provide a more comprehensive scenario of projected financial condition than fractional statements. Also, most financial forecasts are done on a piecemeal basis that fails to show the internal workings of an enterprise and how that eventually produces information on financial position. The approach presented in this chapter has been an attempt to fill that gap. Additionally, conventional *pro forma* statements are prepared using simple measures such as percentage changes; but, in reality, there should not be any difficulty in using more complex forecasting techniques such as causal models with multiple equations as opposed to single equations as well as time-series models such as those used in transfer functions, or any combination of them, to prepare these statements. Finally, although the example used in this chapter refers to local government, the general approach suggested here can be used for any level of government as long as it has enterprise operations.

References

Baumol, W. J. 1952. Transaction demand for cash: An inventory theoretic approach. *Quarterly Journal of Economics* 66: 545–556.

Boswell, C. and M. J. Carpenter. 1986. Long-range forecasting in Fort Worth. *Government Finance Review* 6: 7–10.

Bretschneider, S. and W. Gore. 1987. State and local government revenue forecasting. In *The Handbook of Forecasting: A Managerial Perspective*, S. Makridakis and S. Wheelright (eds). New York: Wiley, pp. 118–134.

DeHoog, R. H. and B. E. Swanson. 1988. Tax and expenditure effects of municipal enterprises. *Public Budgeting & Finance* 8: 48–57.

Dilorenzo, T. J. 1982. Utility profits, fiscal illusions, and local public expenditures. *Public Choice* 8: 242–252.

Forrester, J. 1991. Multiyear forecasting and municipal budgeting. *Public Budgeting & Finance* 11: 47–61.

Frank, H. A. 1990. Municipal forecasting with time-series models: A Florida case study. *The American Review of Public Administration* 20: 45–59.

Goldberg, K. and R. Scott. 1985. City sales and property tax restructuring: Household and business incidence effects. *Public Budgeting & Finance* 5: 89–98.

Khan, A. 1989. Forecasting a local government budget with time-series analysis. *State and Local Government Review* 21: 123–129.

Khan, A. 2003. Forecasting the general fund budget of a local government: The case study of Pleasantville. In *Case Studies in Public Budgeting and Financial Management*, 2nd edition, A. Khan and W. B. Hildreth (eds). New York: Marcel Dekker, pp. 253–276.

Khan, A. and T. J. Stumm. 1993. Enterprise fund operation in a West Texas City. In *Case Studies in Public Budgeting and Financial Management*, 2nd edition, A. Khan and W. B. Hildreth (eds). New York: Marcel Dekker, pp. 253–276.

Lynch, T. D. 1987. Local government budget strategy: A case study of South Florida. *Public Administration Quarterly* 11: 361–378.

Scott, C. 1972. *Forecasting Local Government Spending.* Washington: The Urban Institute Press.

Strauss, R. P. and K. L. Wertz. 1976. The impact of municipal electric profits on local public finance. *National Tax Journal* 29: 22–30.

Tyer, C. B. 1989. Municipal enterprises and taxing and spending policies: Public avoidance and fiscal illusions. *Public Administration Review* 49: 249–256.

Vogt, J. A. 1978. Operating revenue of North Carolina municipal governments: Overview and comparison of electric and nonelectric cities. *Popular Government* 44: 11–20.

Chapter 15

Preparing Data for Forecasting

Daniel W. Williams

Contents

Introduction

Forecasting, at its core, refers to procedures used to estimate unknown values of interest. These are either the anticipated actual future values of some data series, or they are the possible values associated with a scenario that may be contemplated for the future. On rare occasions, the values are not associated with a data series, that is, they are some unique future event of interest. However, this chapter focuses on forecasts of data series—sets of values that are reported periodically over time. Much of forecasting is about data that occurs in series.

In the budget world, there is a lot of talk about "revenue" and "expenditure" forecasting. However, in the forecasting world there are simply data series. Excluding the issue of the budget maker's somewhat more discretionary control on the expenditure side, there is not much interesting difference between revenue and expenditure data series.* This chapter focuses on things that should be carried out to get the data series ready to be forecast. The intended forecast is technical, not exercise of discretion. Thus, these techniques apply to revenue data series such as income from sales tax or to expenditure data series such as the population of school children, but they do not (necessarily) apply to revenue discretionary decisions such as the decision to give a special one weekend sales tax abatement to a distressed district or to discretionary expenditure decisions such as to pay for exactly 500 additional units of homeless shelter service in the coming year (however, they may use such information to retrospectively understand data series).

An important consideration with time series forecasting and other forecasting methods based on data is the preparation of the data. In this chapter, content and

* There is one important way in which revenue and expenditure data series differ for forecasting, and that has to do with what forecasters call "loss function," or what is more commonly known as risk. That is, risk-averse budget directors prefer to underestimate the benefit of data series that will produce revenue. These same risk-averse budget directors prefer to overestimate the effect of data series that will produce costs. Subjective, and potentially objective, loss functions (methods for evaluating forecast error) are, therefore, asymmetrical (lopsided) in the opposite directions; or in other words, budget directors punish overestimation of revenue and underestimation of data series that force spending.

methods issues are secondary. The primary issue is whether the data are in good condition for forecasting.

Let us stop for a minute and think about what forecast in the public sector is. Two standard types of forecasts focus on revenue and major categories of expenditure, such as personnel expenditure. However, there are also many other types of forecasts such as population forecasts, school enrollment, or prison populations; matters related to health such as teen pregnancy, infant mortality, and epidemics; weather; traffic; policy effects; the productivity of enterprise activities; and so on.

Where do the forecasters for all these activities get their data? The most obvious place is the accounting system. This is where records are made of revenue and expenditures. Expanding a little, other standard systems such as the personnel and enrollment systems are likely to record other critical data such as personnel pay rates, student enrollment by grade level, or the number of births to teens in the current recording period. Occasionally, the data are collected through a special survey or observational technique, but most often the data are the by-product, or the principal product, of administrative records.

The forecaster should become familiar with how the data are collected and summarized, if possible. Such familiarity can provide insight into some of the topics that are discussed in this chapter. It may also provide the forecaster the opportunity to influence how data are summarized, which may be beneficial.

Time Intervals

Forecasting is much more robust if the forecaster summarizes data over equal, or nearly equal, and consistent time intervals. Consistent means that protocols should exist to consistently link the origin, or other key event, of the data to the interval into which it is recorded. For example, revenue received on one day may be attributed to the next, but then this should be the consistent practice. It should not be attributed to the same day sometimes and to the next day at other times. In this way, when data are summarized for a longer time period, there is no confusion about the number of time units contained.

Ideally, forecasters should summarize data over shorter (monthly) as compared with longer (annual) time periods. Data can be forecast at the weekly, daily, or even shorter level, but the effort is likely to be enormous. The monthly level is not especially difficult and offers particular advantages over annual data. First, it provides the opportunity for tracking forecast success within budgetary cycles. This tracking allows for corrective decisions before the advent of disastrous outcomes. Second, it provides forecasters the opportunity to know short-term changes at the time of the forecast. Many forecast methods are able to take advantage of information about short-term changes.

Months and, for some purposes weeks, are not always equal time periods. Depending on the type of service you provide, February has 18–28 business days some years and 19–29 days in others, whereas August has 23–31 business days some years and 21–31 days in others. A 23-day business month is more than 25 percent longer than an 18-day business month. Sometimes these inequalities matter and sometimes they do not. If you have any reason to suspect that there is a relation between the business days of the month or week and the data-generating process, then you can adjust your data by dividing them by the number of business days in the summarizing period.

You should record all adjustments, as many of them must be processed in reverse at the end of your forecast. In this case, the reverse process is simply to multiply your forecast by the number of business days in the forecast period.

How Much Data?

Use as much data as may be available. This principle, which is widely held in the forecasting community, is commonly disbelieved by others. It is, however, strongly advised by the two most prominent names in forecasting, Spyros Makridakis and J. Scott Armstrong. Their message is "do not discard data unless they are clearly irrelevant or defective; use them."

Plotting Data

Plot the data to look for patterns and peculiarities. Plot data in an *x–y* scatter plot using the *y*-axis as the values of the data and the *x*-axis as the time index. Older data are on the left-hand side and more current data are on the right-hand side as shown in Figure 15.1. We will call Figure 15.1 a "time plot." The time index on this plot is an ordered series of numbers. Frequently, dates are used.

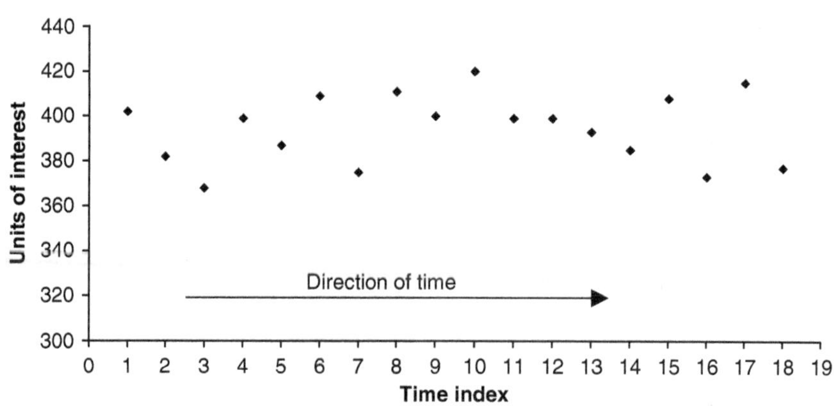

Figure 15.1 *x–y* Time plot.

Data Editing

The first thing to do after plotting the data is to look for obvious instances of erroneous or problem data. Three are cited here.

Outlier

First is the outlier. The outlier is shown in Figure 15.2. It is an observation that is extreme in value compared with the other observations. The most likely explanation of an outlier is a data entry error. Two common sources of data entry error are reversal of numbers (e.g., entering 27 as 72) and decimal error (e.g., entering 27.19 as 271.9). Also, when entering several columns of data, the analyst may copy from the wrong column.

Other explanations might be as follows:

1. Is the data subject to occasional large disturbances? If so, leave the data as it is. If this is a typical, but infrequent observation, it is probably important that the forecasting equations have the information available.
2. Is there an undiscoverable recording error (because it is impossible, but the source data is unavailable)? If so, correct the error with the best information available, by substituting a corrected ("interpolated") observation for the erroneous one. To interpolate a value, calculate the average of the surrounding

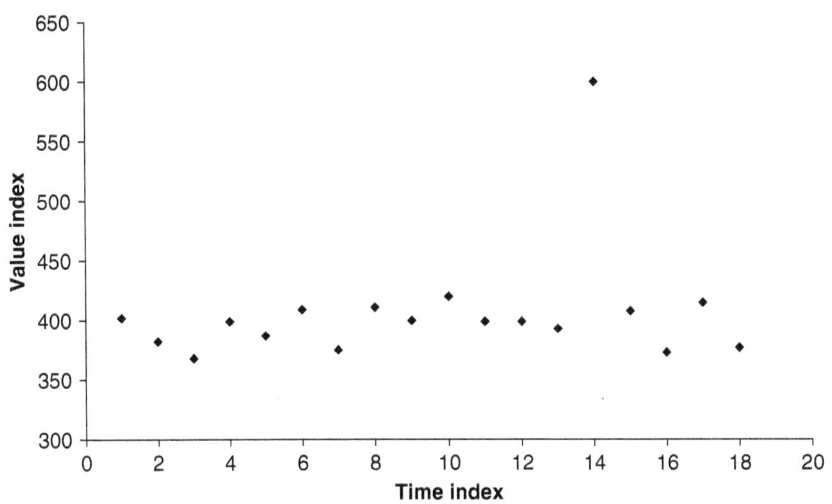

Figure 15.2 Example outlier.

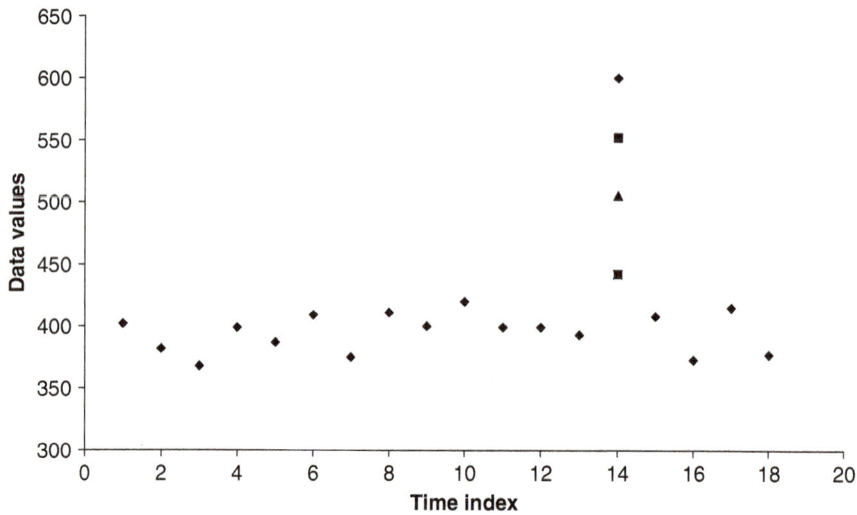

Figure 15.3 Adjusting the outlier.

data, or if the data are seasonal, calculate the average of the two observations from the same period in surrounding seasonal cycles (years).

3. In the past, there was an unusual disturbance, but is it unlikely to recur? Or, is it probably a recording error, but it might not be? In this case, windsorize the observation (Armstrong 1985). This practice consists of reducing the outlier to the most extreme value that is likely to occur. For example, if nearby observations take values from 360 to 420, and the extreme observation is 600, the analyst might choose to reduce the extreme observation to 440. This adjustment is shown in Figure 15.3. Be very cautious with the use of windsorizing. Do not repeatedly windsorize the same series.

Suppose that the analyst is not sure what the most extreme likely value is and the data are not following a particularly large trend. Then, an option is to calculate the standard deviation (excluding the outlier) of the immediately surrounding data and place the observation at three standard deviations from the average of those data in the direction of the outlier. If the resulting observation is more extreme than the original outlier, the original value should be retained. This technique will not work, however, with rapidly trending data, or data that is very seasonal. In these cases, the data may be windsorized using a judgmental estimate of the most extreme likely value.

In Table 15.1, observation 14 is windsorized by calculating the average plus three standard deviations using the equation, $O' = \mu' + 3 * \sigma'$, where O' is the windsorized observation, and μ' and σ' the mean and standard deviation, respectively, of the series excluding the extreme observation.

Table 15.1 Windsorizing Data

Period	Original X	X′	E = X−Average	E^2	Revised X
1	402	402	6.9	47.4	402
2	382	382	−13.1	172.1	382
3	368	368	−27.1	735.4	368
4	399	399	3.9	15.1	399
5	387	387	−8.1	65.9	387
6	409	409	13.9	192.7	409
7	375	375	−20.1	404.7	375
8	411	411	15.9	252.2	411
9	400	400	4.9	23.8	400
10	420	420	24.9	619.1	420
11	399	399	3.9	15.1	399
12	399	399	3.9	15.1	399
13	393	393	−2.1	4.5	393
14	600				442.2
15	408	408	12.9	166.0	408
16	373	373	−22.1	489.2	373
17	415	415	19.9	395.3	415
18	377	377	−18.1	328.2	377
	Total	6717	SSQ	3941.8	
	Count	17	DF	16	
	μ'	395.1	VAR	246.4	
			σ'	15.7	
			$\sigma' \times 3$	47.1	
			$\mu' + 3\sigma'$	442.2	

Note: Additions and subtractions may not be exact because they have been rounded off.

Paired Opposite Outliers

A frequent pattern is the paired opposite outlier pattern. This pattern usually emerges because of the violation of one of the recording guidelines mentioned earlier, although the violation may be inadvertent or unavoidable. The violation is the carrying forward of data from its typical period to the next period, or recording the data earlier than usual. In Figure 15.4, the data would be recorded early. This violation can arise for such simple reasons as trying to pay bills in one fiscal year rather than another; workers trying to clean out their work before going on vacation; or—for the reverse order—postal delays. If possible, the erroneous amount should

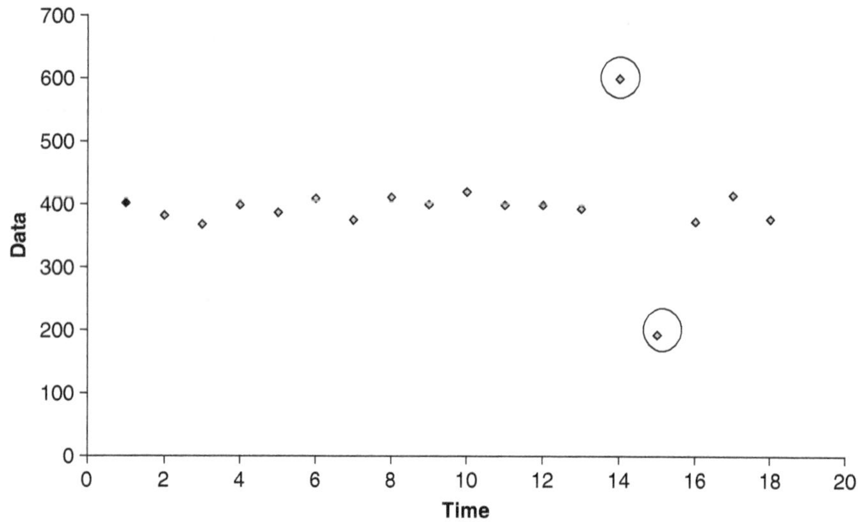

Figure 15.4 Opposite outliers.

be reassigned to the correct period. Alternatively, the two observations might be averaged. Averaging should be avoided if the two periods normally have substantially different seasonal factors.

Shifts and Ramps

Shifts and ramps can be upward as shown in Figures 15.5 and 15.6, or they can be downwards. Sometimes they carry forward through a period of time, then shift back away. They may signal policy events, changes in causal forces, or redefinitions of the data. Typical forecasting advice is to know the data-generating process well enough to be able to discover what causes these shifts and ramps. Unexplained shifts and ramps are well known to be a substantial source of forecasting error (Williams and Miller 1999). The following section examines how to adjust for some of the more common sources of shifts and ramps.

Other Patterns

Figures 15.7 and 15.8 demonstrate other typical patterns that can be found in data. What gives rise to these patterns is that the phenomena measured are strongly related to recording periods. In Figure 15.7, data accumulates over the whole month. In longer months more data accumulates. In Figure 15.8, data accumulates over a week but is recorded on one specific day of the week, perhaps on Fridays. If the forecaster accumulates the data to months, there will be a

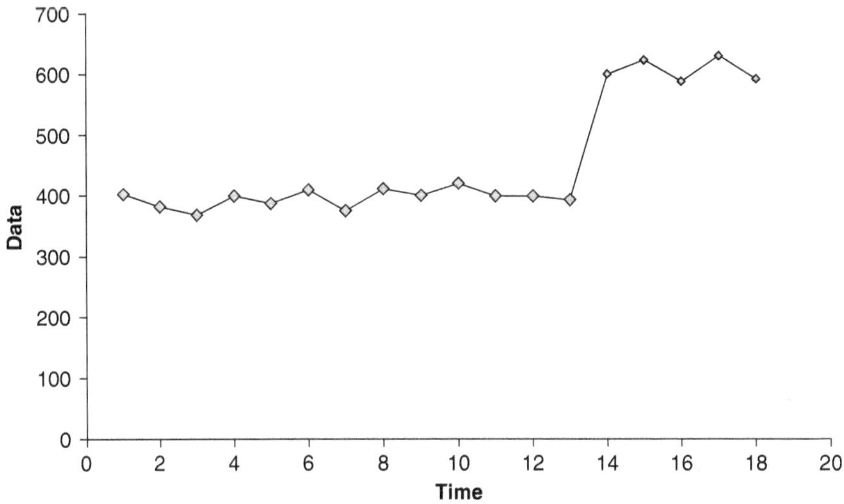

Figure 15.5 Upshift.

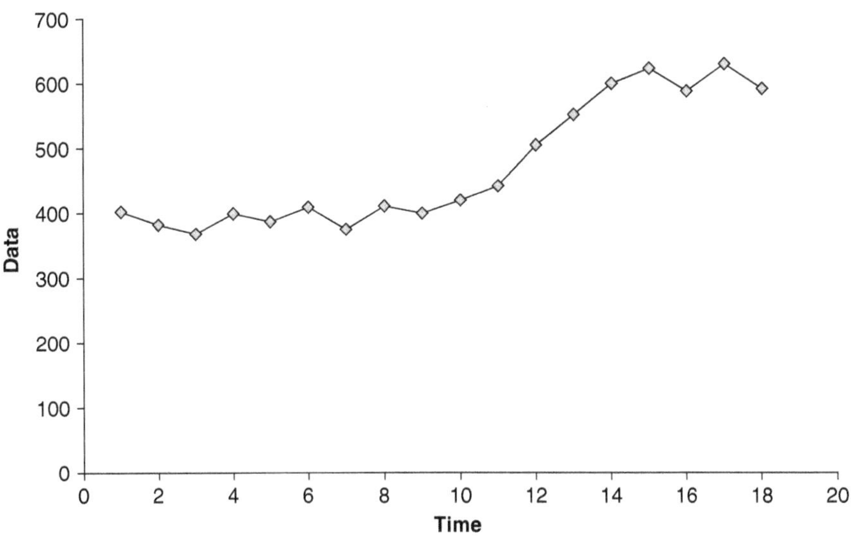

Figure 15.6 Ramp.

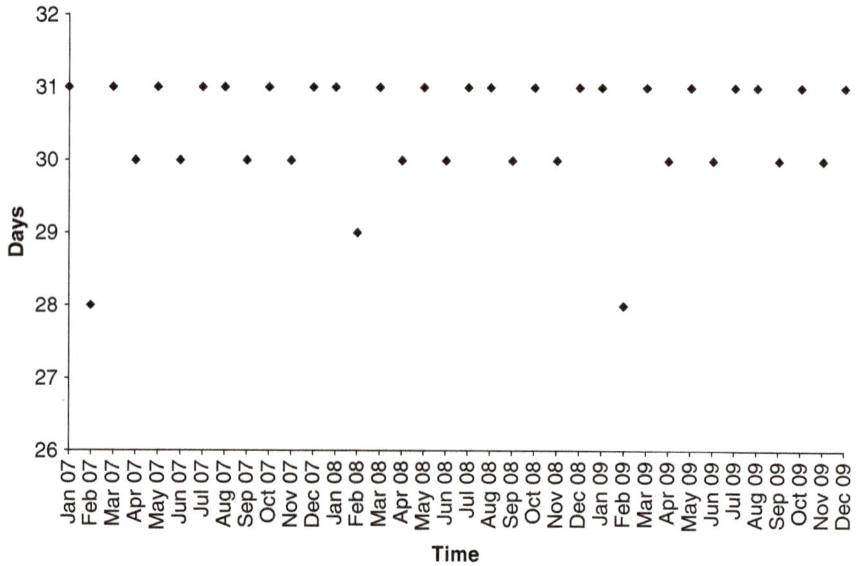

Figure 15.7 Days in the month.

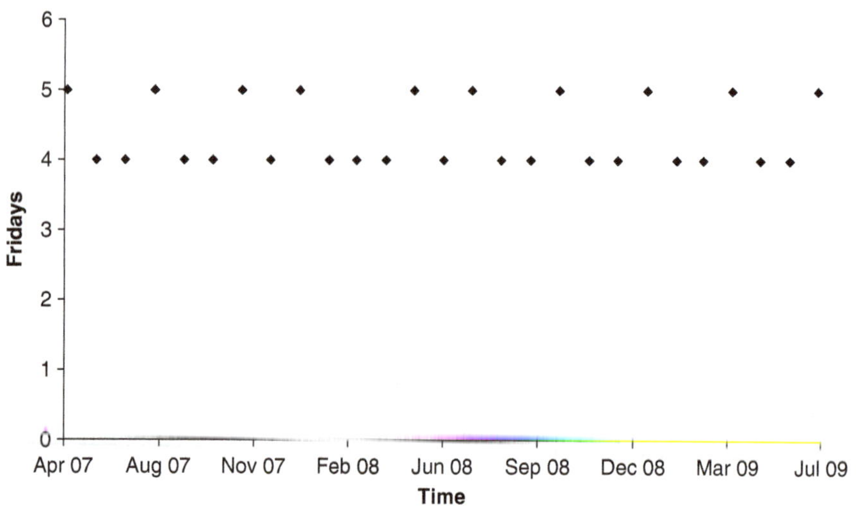

Figure 15.8 Fridays.

natural fluctuation because some months contain four Fridays and others contain five.

In preparing to forecast data that exhibits such patterns, forecasters should first account for this completely predictable variation. The best way to account for these predictable phenomena is to "normalize" it, that is, divide the data by the factor that causes it to fluctuate. For example, when forecasting data that is affected by a Friday recording factor, divide it by the number of Fridays. Forecast the normalized data series. To complete the forecast, reverse the normalization, that is, multiply the forecast by the future month's normalizing factor. For example, if you divide the data by the number of Fridays before forecasting, you should multiply the forecast by the number of Fridays in the future period to get the whole forecast.

There are many other possibilities. For example, if employees are paid "weekly" and the payday happens to be the "first day of the year," it will also be the "last day of the year." That year will contain "53 paychecks," which has the effect of "increasing the payroll cost by roughly 2 percent." By plotting the data, analysts can discover patterns, and by examining the process that generates the data, they can determine what the patterns mean. This examination of patterns and data-generating process is part of the use of causal information in time series forecasting.

Decomposing Complex Data

The procedure of taking sources of variation, such as the days-of-the-month or recording-day-of-the-week, into account is sometimes called decomposition. With decomposition, a complex data series is broken into several component series (Armstrong 1985). The simpler data series should be easier to forecast and, where relevant, "different methods can be used to forecast different component series." In the examples from the previous section, the systematic variation (days-of-the-month, etc.) can be known without error; therefore, forecasting it can only introduce error. Once this variation is removed from the data series, the task of the mathematical forecasting model is simpler.

Although plotting data reveals patterns that arise across the time index, it may not help with other complexities. Consider the problem of forecasting teen pregnancy. Two components of this series are the number of female teens and the rate at which they become pregnant. It is ineffective to confuse these issues. Predicting the number of teens over the next few years may be relatively easy, because they are already around as preteens, assuming no important net migration issues. The forecasting challenge involves pregnancy rate. The best way to find these components is to examine the process that generates the series of interest.

Often data can be simplified through decomposition. Sometimes decomposition eliminates the need to forecast some of the variation, as with days-in-the-month variation. Other times, component forecasts can be obtained from outside sources.

Yet other times, the chief gain through decomposition is the opportunity to forecast more meaningful homogeneous data series.

In the examples, the decomposition—also called disaggregation—is relatively simple, following a few easy steps; however, when working with real-world data, you may need to go through a series of steps to decompose your data sufficiently to make forecasts. Avoid decomposing your data so far that they have extremely small numbers; it is difficult to forecast a data series that has zero values for some observations or one that has a large variation relative to the average observation.

Completeness

Another important consideration when decomposing data is whether the resulting series is complete. Decomposition not only provides the opportunity of discovering information left out of the combined data, but it also increases the risk of losing something that is included in the gross data. For example, when forecasting income from licenses, what happens to fines for late applications? Also, if the licensee moves out of the locality, does he or she receive a refund? What source of money pays the refund? When working with financial data, obtain the organization's annual financial reports and reconcile the data sources with these reports. Find out what is missing and assure that it is accounted for. With other data, look for annual reports or other periodic reports with which to reconcile. Imagine how the data could be incomplete and look to see what happens with such data. An excellent forecast of the wrong data can be useless or worse.

When decomposing complex data to make a forecast, decomposition must be reversed to complete the forecast. Combine the data by precisely reversing the steps followed when decomposing them.

Adjusting for Inflation

An important form of decomposition for public decision making is the removal of inflation from revenues and expenditures (Ammons 1991, 2001). The impact of inflation can be estimated from indexes known as deflators, which, in the United States, are available from the Bureau of Labor Statistics of the Department of Commerce. There are many deflators depending on the sorts of things a government agency usually purchases. Analysts must choose a deflator that relates to the data forecasted.

To apply the deflator, the following equation is used:

$$\mathrm{CD}_t = \frac{\mathrm{ND}_t \times \mathrm{DF}_b}{\mathrm{DF}_t}$$

where for year t

ND_t = nominal dollars, funds expressed in dollars before adjusting for inflation

CD_t = constant dollars, funds expressed in dollars after adjusting for inflation

DF_t = deflator index
DF_b = deflator index value for a chosen constant year b

As an example, the analyst may be interested in forecasting sales tax revenue. First, sort out the components of this revenue. If there is no data on total sales within the locality, reason backward from taxes received to tax base. If there is a constant tax rate, simply divide the tax income by the rate. If there is more than one rate, or if the rate changed during the period of time over which there is data, divide each amount by its related rate. Table 15.2 demonstrates working through the process from revenue and rate information, backward to tax base and from tax base to the expenditures on which that tax base developed. This is artificial data intended to demonstrate the necessity to work with the underlying real-dollar information, not the net tax information. Reconstructing the base is shown in columns 2 through 4 of Table 15.2 (the revenue data are artificial). Choose an index; for sales tax revenue the analyst might choose the consumer price index (CPI) for all urban consumers, and convert nominal dollars to constant dollars, using the equation above, as shown in columns 4 through 7 of Table 15.2, using the average CPI for all urban consumers based in 1982–1984 (U.S. Department of Labor Statistics, 2006). The last column of Table 15.2 shows what the trend in revenue would have been with the historical trend in the tax base and the current tax rate.

Figure 15.9 demonstrates the effect of these calculations. The tax revenue (indexed against the right-hand side, y-axis) grows faster than the nominal base (left-hand side y-axis), because the rate has several incremental increases. More significantly, although the nominal base is growing, the constant base (left-hand side y-axis) is shrinking. Forecasting the tax revenue or the nominal tax base without adjusting for these factors could lead to significant error. As shown with the adjusted revenue trend, the revenue is actually declining. This, however, is not the optimum series to forecast. The tax base should be forecast. Revenue can then be determined by applying the tax rate.

Adjusting for Changes in the Base

As the earlier example has shown, another problem that might arise with public data is that the basis on which the data is derived may change from time to time. In this case, the data derives in part from tax rates that change from time to time. The example is somewhat artificial because most effective government organizations will have a record of their revenue basis as well as their gross take, but this practice will not be universal.

Another way in which matters similar to this change from time to time is that revenue bases may change. For example, at present there is a substantial trend in breaking up urbanized counties into incorporated communities in some states. The counties see revenue decline because their tax base is shrinking. This effect is not

Table 15.2 Constant Dollars (in Thousands)

	Finding the Base			*Conversion to Constant Dollars*			
Year	*Revenue (R)*	*Tax Rate (T)*	*Nominal \$ (ND; R/T)*	*CPI (82–84) (DF)*[a]	*DF_{2004}/DF Factor (DF_b/DF_t)*	*Constant \$ (CD; Factor×ND)*	*Reconstructed Revenue*
1980	584.9	0.05	11,698	82.4	0.4362	26,817	1,944
1981	605.1	0.05	12,102	90.9	0.4812	25,149	1,823
1982	605.1	0.05	12,102	96.5	0.5109	23,690	1,718
1983	615.2	0.05	12,304	99.6	0.5273	23,336	1,692
1984	625.2	0.05	12,504	103.9	0.5500	22,733	1,648
1985	698.9	0.055	12,707	107.6	0.5696	22,309	1,617
1986	710	0.055	12,909	109.6	0.5802	22,249	1,613
1987	732.2	0.055	13,313	113.6	0.6014	22,137	1,605
1988	754.3	0.055	13,715	118.3	0.6263	21,899	1,588
1989	776.5	0.055	14,118	124	0.6564	21,507	1,559
1990	871.3	0.06	14,522	130.7	0.6919	20,988	1,522
1991	895.5	0.06	14,925	136.2	0.7210	20,700	1,501
1992	919.7	0.06	15,328	140.3	0.7427	20,638	1,496
1993	1035.7	0.065	15,934	144.5	0.7650	20,830	1,510
1994	1048.8	0.065	16,135	148.2	0.7845	20,567	1,491
1995	1101.2	0.065	16,942	152.4	0.8068	20,999	1,522
1996	1195.6	0.0675	17,713	156.9	0.8306	21,325	1,546
1997	1203	0.0675	17,822	160.5	0.8497	20,976	1,521
1998	1213	0.0675	17,970	163	0.8629	20,826	1,510
1999	1223	0.0675	18,119	166.6	0.8819	20,544	1,489
2000	1263.4	0.07	18,049	172.2	0.9116	19,799	1,435
2001	1319.1	0.07	18,844	177.1	0.9375	20,100	1,457
2002	1325	0.07	18,929	179.9	0.9524	19,876	1,441
2003	1363.6	0.07	19,480	184	0.9741	19,999	1,450
2004	1435.5	0.0725	19,800	188.9	1.0000	19,800	1,436

Note: Additions and subtractions may not be exact because they have been rounded off.

[a] Taken from BLS.

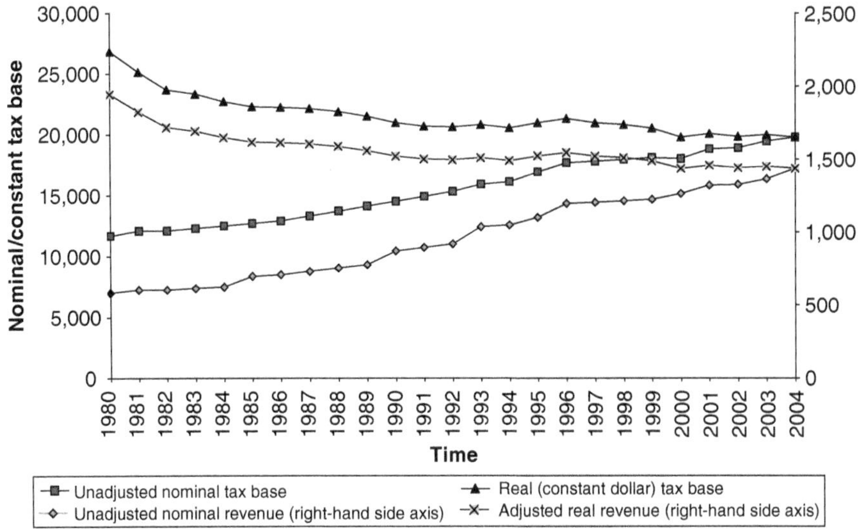

Figure 15.9 Compare trends in dollars.

because of decline in economic activity, but because there is a literal removal of taxable units as they are attributed to other jurisdictions. Forecasting future economic activities in the remaining jurisdiction is best accomplished by removing the data for the now irrelevant units from the historical record. Where the historical record is no longer relevant and there are data for correction, correction should be made. Correction can also be made in the opposite direction, where two municipalities merge; historical records should be brought together in the most reasonable way possible for forecasting.

Adjustments for Changes in Data Definitions

Data definition changes are not limited to changes in the revenue base. The No Child Left Behind Act may have changed the way your local school district counts pupil enrollment. A court decision might change the way you count overtime hours for your employees. Or, poor documentation and a change of personnel might be all it takes to change the definition of any data element appearing in your information system.

When data are redefined, the best remedial action is to redefine the historical series as well. "Do not destroy" the original historical series! You may find that your redefinition is incorrect. However, it is best to forecast using a consistent series. If you cannot actually redefine the series, an estimate is suitable, provided it is reasonable. If there are multiple segments of the series that require redefinition in different ways, or if your confidence in the method of redefinition is weak for older data, you may encounter a situation where it is reasonable to discard (not from your records, but from your current use) older data. Reasonable people will differ on what is old enough to be "older." I suggest five or more years for monthly data and ten or more (preferably many more) for annual data.

Transformations

Sometimes data exhibits one of the two problematic behaviors. Either, as in Figure 15.10a, they exponentiate over part or all of their length, or the variance in the data exponentiates over their length, as in Figure 15.10b. Exponentiating variance is often easier to see in seasonal data, where the peaks and troughs of the seasons push further and further away from one another, yet this is also a natural effect of multiplicative seasonality, as discussed in the following section. Exponentiating of a series generally consists of a looping up or down effect.

Often forecasters advocate that such data be transformed before it is forecast. "Transform" generally means to process through a mathematical function that linearizes a nonlinear series (Makridakis et al. 1998). The same sort of procedures tend to reduce exponentiating variance. Common transformations include the logarithm, the square root, and the cube root, as shown in Figures 15.10c through 15.10e, respectively, for the data found in 15.10a. Figure 15.10a comes closest to a line with the cube root (Figure 15.10e). The log produces a series that is as nonlinear as the original series. Linearizing a nonlinear series may be helpful with all the techniques discussed in this book, but it is of special importance if you choose a technique that involves regression. There is further description of transformation in Makridakis et al. (1998).

Seasonality

Seasonal patterns repeat over a fixed period of time, usually a year (Makridakis et al. 1998). In Figure 15.11, we observe peaks in July and troughs in December. Seasonality may be easier to observe if the *x*-axis of the plot is limited to the length of the suspected season and sequential cycles are plotted separately as shown in Figure 15.12. Figure 15.12 is a "seasonality plot." Data that tends toward the same ups and downs over each segment is seasonal. If the overlapping series appear random or have conflicting peaks and troughs, the data are not seasonal.

Although seasonality is commonly thought to be an annual phenomenon, it is also possible to have seasonality within other time segments. Figure 15.13 demonstrates seasonality within weeks. This data reflects daily traffic in British Columbia. Traffic may also reflect a within-day pattern. Figure 15.14, which reflects financial data found at a regional Federal Reserve Bank, demonstrates seasonality within quarters. Seasonality within quarters may reflect business practice patterns.

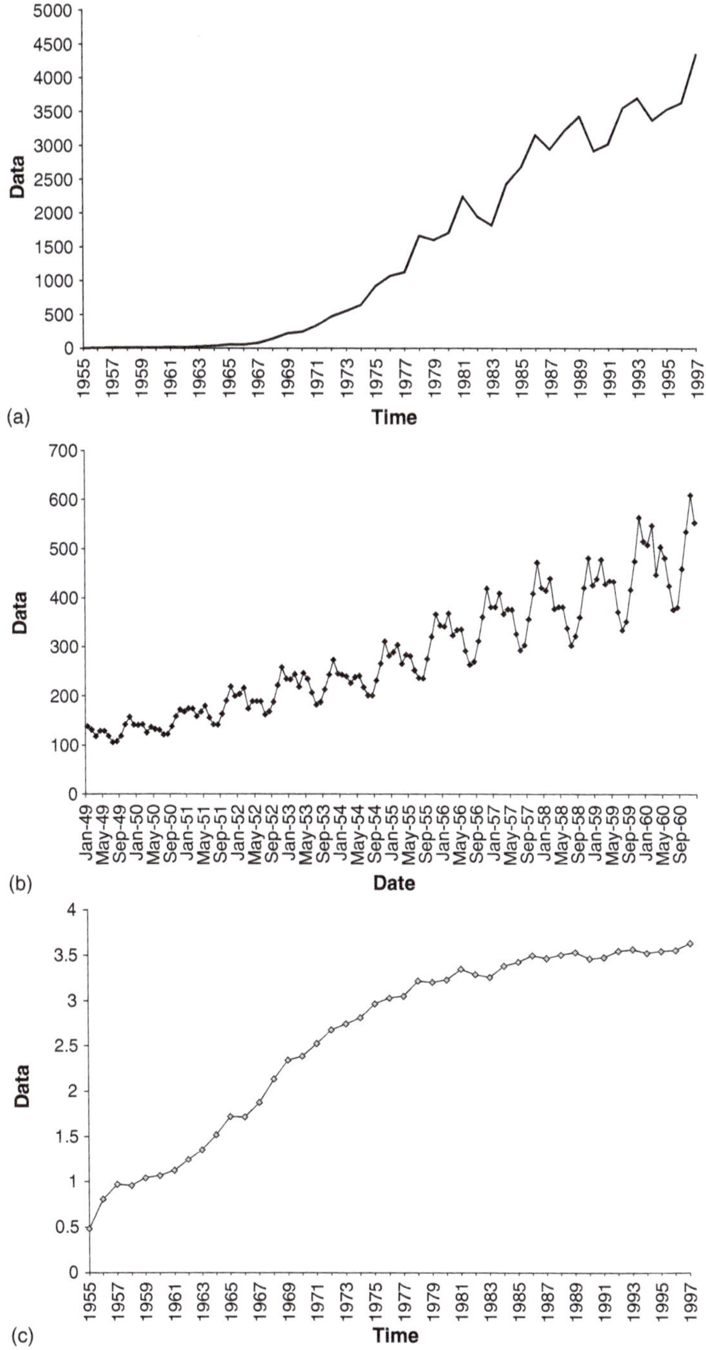

Figure 15.10 (a) Exponentiating; (b) exponentiating variance; (c) log;

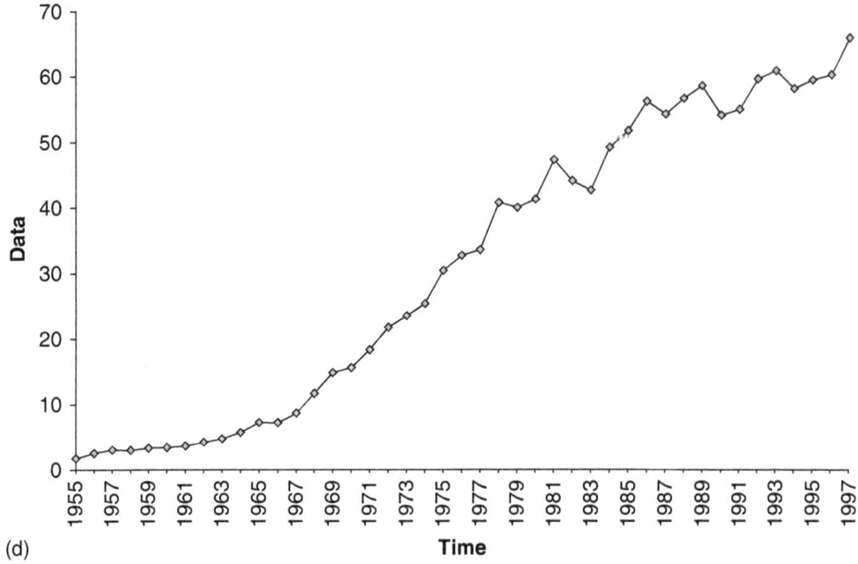

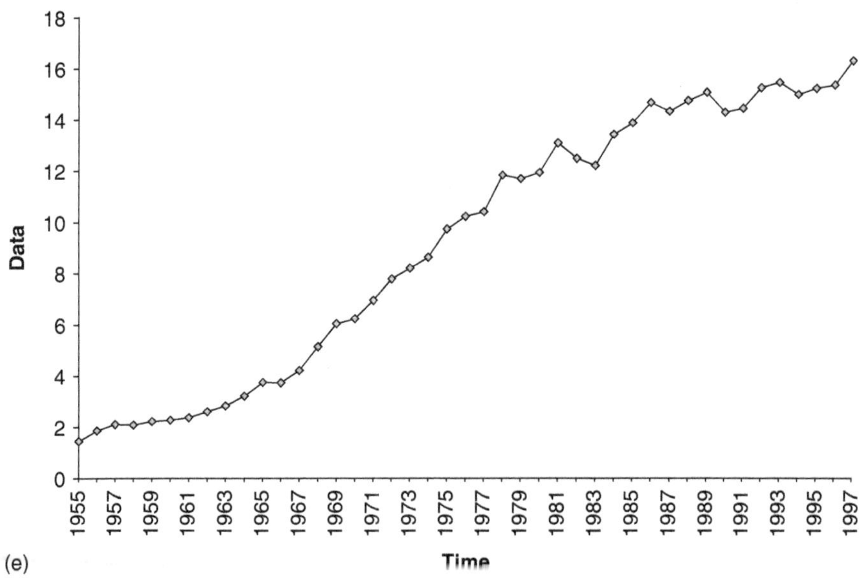

Figure 15.10 (d) square root; (e) cube root.

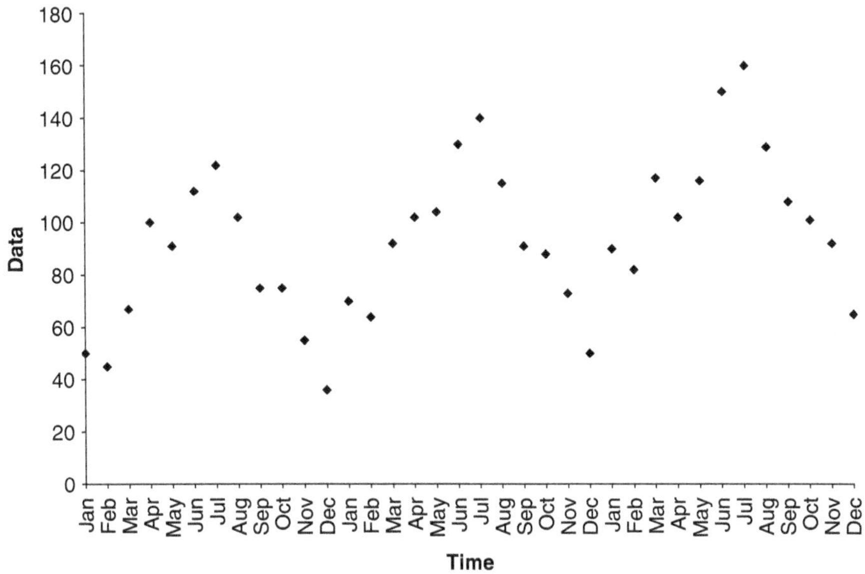

Figure 15.11 Seasonal data.

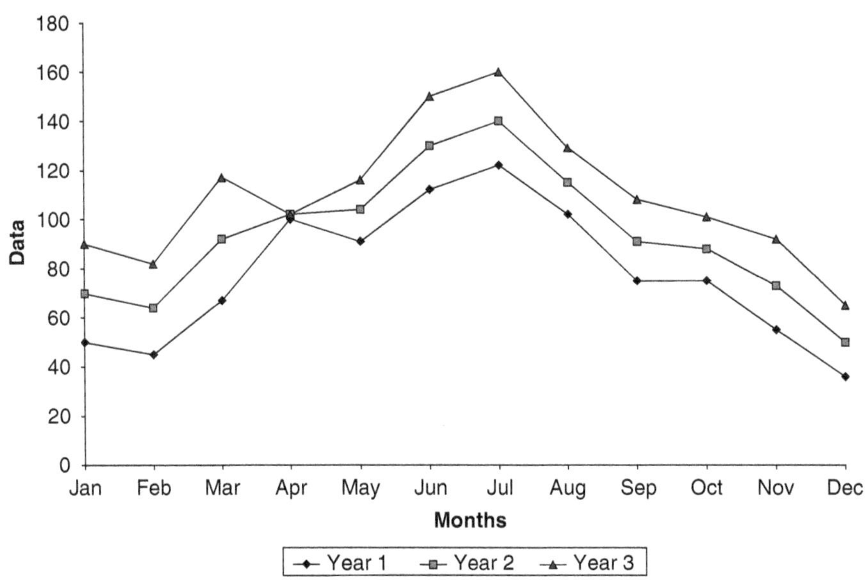

Figure 15.12 Overlapping years.

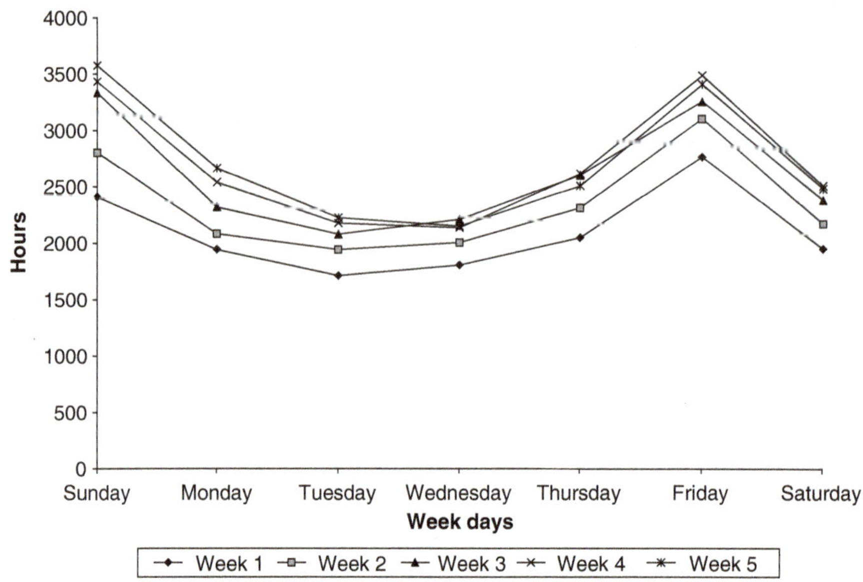

Figure 15.13 Seasonality within weeks daily traffic in British Columbia (http://www.th.gov.bc.ca/trafficData/tradas/tradas.asp?loc=P-17-6EW, traffic data for Nicolum - P-17-6EW - N; accessed December 4, 2006).

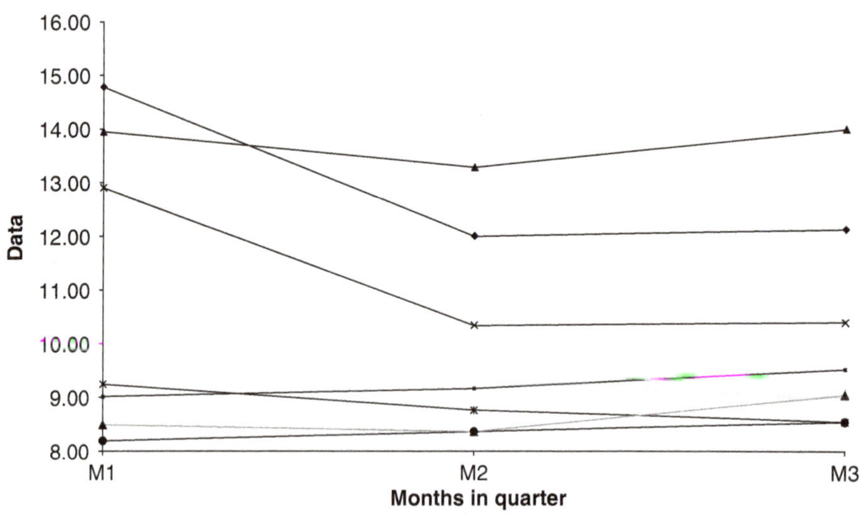

Figure 15.14 Within quarter seasonality (lines represent exemplar quarterly data; points represent exemplar months).

A procedure called "seasonal adjustment" is recommended here. The seasonal adjustment techniques discussed here rest on the assumption that data are systematically collected over at least two seasonal cycles, preferably three or more. This chapter only introduces the simplest techniques. Some directions are given for exploring more sophisticated techniques.

Sometimes seasonality depends on the current mean of the series at the time of the season. Other times seasonality is unrelated to the level. Judge this by asking whether the seasonal difference is additive (more like "50 units more in December") or multiplicative (more like "15 percent more in December"). Figure 15.15 shows multiplicative seasonality around linear growth of ten units per month. With larger values of the level, the seasonal peaks and troughs get farther away from the line. Figure 15.16 shows additive seasonality around the same ten units per month growth, and the size of the peaks and troughs is unrelated to level.

Calculating a Simple Seasonal Index Using "Classical Decomposition"

Deseasonalizing means adjusting a series to remove seasonal impact. The following shows the calculation of a simple annual seasonal index for monthly data for both multiplicative and additive techniques. This technique requires a minimum of two

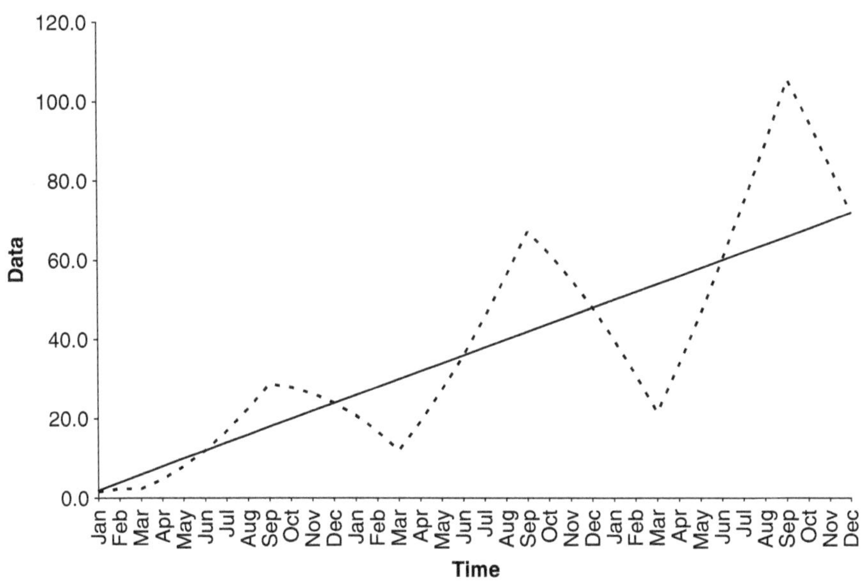

Figure 15.15 Multiplicative seasonality.

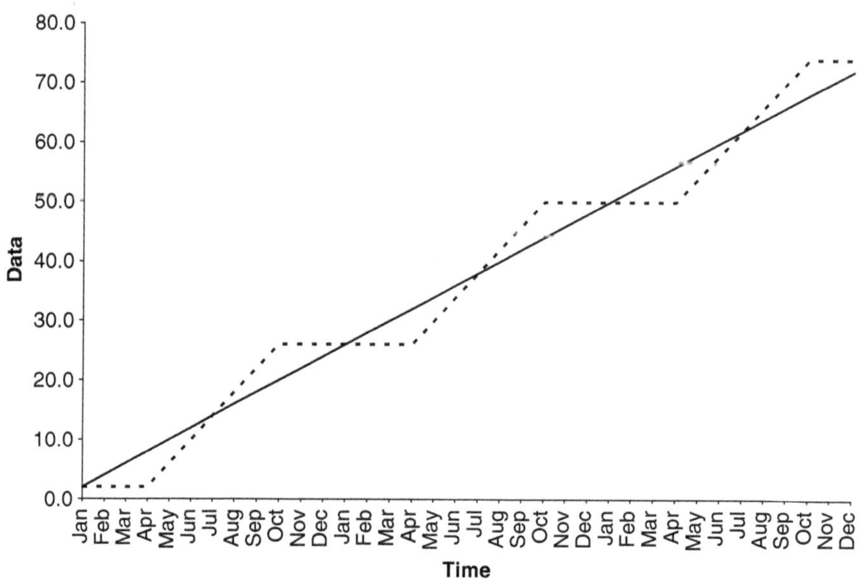

Figure 15.16 Additive seasonality.

seasonal cycles, but works better with three or more seasonal cycles. You may refer to Table 15.3 while following this discussion.

First, calculate a 12-period moving average as follows:

$$\text{MA}_t = \frac{(X_t + X_t - 1 + \cdots + X_t - (L - 1))}{L}$$

where L is 12.

Next, calculate a two-period moving average ($L = 2$) of the twelve-period moving average. This new moving average is a 12×2 "double moving average." For seasonal periods other than monthly, calculate an $L \times 2$ moving average, where L is the number of periods for one seasonal cycle. For the rest of this explanation, the 12×2 moving average is labeled $\text{MA}^{12\times2}$.

The "center" of a moving average is found by the expression $(L + 1)/2$. For example, the center of the moving average for data over January–December (points 1–12) occurs at the end of June and the beginning of July. Because June is point number 6 and July is number 7, the midway point is 6.5. The next moving average covers February through the next January, points 2–13, and by the same reasoning as before, the midway point is 7.5. The first double moving average value represents the center points 6.5 and 7.5, so its center is at 7, which is July in this example.

To prepare to calculate a seasonal index, first enter the result of the $\text{MA}^{12\times2}$ on the same row as the actual observation for its centered period (July for years starting in January). There are twelve fewer moving average values than original (raw) values

Table 15.3 Seasonality, Classical Decomposition with Normalization

				Multiplicative Seasonality				Additive Seasonality			
Month	Date	MA 12	MA 12 × 2	Approximate Index	Average Index	Index	Multiplicative Deseasonalization	Approximate Factor	Average Factor	Factor	Additive Deseasonalization
Jan	50					0.848	59.0			−14.0	64.0
Feb	45				11,979	0.763	59.0		−2.2	−22.3	67.3
Mar	62				12	1.078	62.1		12	2.9	59.1
Apr	100					1.050	95.3			4.2	95.8
May	91					1.112	81.8			10.9	80.1
Jun	112					1.394	80.4			39.5	22.5
Jul	122	27.5	38.3	1.557	1.523	1.525	80.0	43.7	44.8	45.0	27.0
Aug	102	29.2	80.0	1.236	1.239	1.241	82.2	22.0	22.0	20.9	81.1
Sep	75	80.8	81.8	0.912	0.925	0.927	80.9	−6.8	−6.6	−6.4	81.4
Oct	75	82.8	82.9	0.925	0.899	0.901	83.3	−7.9	−9.2	−9.0	84.0
Nov	55	83.0	83.5	0.658	0.608	0.699	78.7	−28.5	−27.3	−27.1	82.1
Dec	36	84.1	84.8	0.424	0.461	0.462	77.9	−48.8	−49.6	−49.4	85.4
Jan	90	85.6	86.3	0.811	0.847	0.848	82.5	−16.3	−14.2	−14.0	84.0
Feb	64	82.1	87.6	0.730	0.362	0.363	83.9	−23.6	−22.5	−22.3	86.3
Mar	92	88.2	88.8	1.036	1.077	1.078	85.3	3.2	3.3	7.9	84.1
Apr	102	89.5	90.0	1.133	1.048	1.050	97.2	12.0	4.0	4.2	97.8
May	104	90.6	91.3	1.139	1.110	1.112	93.5	12.7	10.7	10.9	93.1
Jun	130	92.1	92.7	1.403	1.391	1.394	93.3	37.3	39.3	39.5	90.5
Jul	140	93.3	94.1	1.438		1.525	91.8	45.9		45.0	95.0

(continued)

Table 15.3 (continued)

				Multiplicative Seasonality				Additive Seasonality			
Month	*Date*	*MA 12*	*MA 12 × 2*	*Approximate Index*	*Average Index*	*Index*	*Multiplicative Deseasonalization*	*Approximate Factor*	*Average Factor*	*Factor*	*Additive Deseasonalization*
Aug	115	94.9	95.7	1.202		1.241	92.7	19.3		20.9	94.1
Sep	91	96.4	97.5	0.934		0.927	98.2	−6.5		−6.4	97.4
Oct	88	98.5	98.5	0.893		0.901	97.7	−10.5		−9.0	97.0
Nov	73	98.5	99.0	0.737		0.699	104.4	−26.0		−27.1	100.1
Dec	50	99.5	100.3	0.498		0.462	108.2	−50.3		−49.4	99.4
Jan	90	101.2	102.0	0.882		0.848	106.1	−12.0		−14.0	104.0
Feb	82	102.3	103.4	0.793		0.763	107.5	−21.4		−22.3	104.3
Mar	117	104.0	104.7	1.117		1.078	108.5	12.3		7.9	109.1
Apr	102	105.4	106.0	0.963		1.050	97.2	−4.0		4.2	97.8
May	116	106.5	107.3	1.081		1.112	104.3	8.7		10.9	105.1
Jun	150	108.1	108.7	1.330		1.394	107.6	41.3		39.5	110.5
Jul	160	109.3				1.525	104.9			45.0	115.0
Aug	129					1.241	103.9			20.9	108.1
Sep	108					0.927	116.5			−6.4	114.4
Oct	100					0.901	112.2			−9.0	110.0
Nov	92					0.699	131.6			−27.1	119.1
Dec	65					0.462	140.6			−49.4	114.4

Note: Additions and subtractions may not be exact because they have been rounded off.

(the six observations at the beginning and the six at the end do not have enough observations for a 12 × 2 period moving average to be centered beside them).

These calculations produce an estimate of the trend cycle in the data as shown by the solid line in Figure 15.17. The seasonal data are shown with the scatter plot. The centered trend-cycle estimate extends from the seventh period through the $n-6$th period (7 periods before the end of the series).

To calculate a multiplicative seasonal index, proceed as follows:

Calculate an approximate index (I') by dividing each actual value by the $MA^{12\times2}$ value.

$$I'_7 = \frac{X_7}{MA_7^{12\times12}}, I'_8 = \frac{X_8}{MA_8^{12\times12}}, \ldots, I'_{n-6} = \frac{X_{n-6}}{MA_{n-6}^{12\times12}}$$

Average the index estimates for each month to get a smoother index (I). This produces twelve values, one for each month:

$$\frac{I''_{\text{Jul}} = (I'_7 + I'_{19} + I'_{31} + \cdots)}{\text{count of Julys}}$$

$$\frac{I''_{\text{Aug}} = (I'_8 + I'_{20} + I'_{32} + \cdots)}{\text{count of Augusts}}$$

Normalize the index. Sum the 12 seasonal factors. Use this sum as the denominator in a fraction where the numerator is 12. The resulting value is an adjusting value, P,

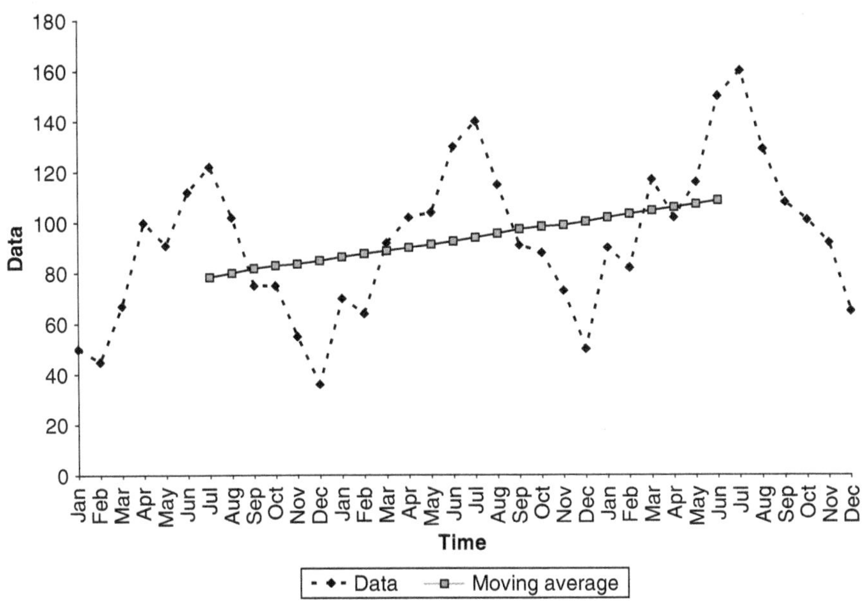

Figure 15.17 Trend cycle.

that is multiplied by each value I''_t to produce an index that sums to 12. When periods are not months, adjust the summing value to reflect the number of periods in the index.

$$P = \frac{12}{\sum_{i=1}^{12} I''}$$

$$I_{\text{Jul}} = I''_{\text{Jul}} * P$$

$$I_{\text{Aug}} = I''_{\text{Aug}} * P, \ldots$$

Divide the actual data by the index to obtain deseasonalized (DESEAS) data:

$$\text{DESEAS}_t = \frac{X_t}{I_t}$$

For additive seasonality, the steps mirror those for multiplicative seasonality, but substituting addition and subtraction for multiplication and division, is as follows.

Calculate an approximate factor (I') by subtracting each $\text{MA}^{12\times2}$ from the actual observation:

$$I'_7 = X_7 - \text{MA}_7^{12\times2},\ I'_8 = X_8 - \text{MA}_8^{12\times2},\ \ldots,\ I'_{n-6} = X_{n-6} - \text{MA}_{n-6}^{12\times2}$$

If $\text{MA}^{12\times2}$ is greater than X, the approximate factor will be negative.

Average the factor estimates for each month to get a smoother factor (I):

$$\frac{I''_{\text{Jul}} = (I'_7 + I'_{19} + I'_{31} + \cdots)}{\text{count of Julys}}$$

$$\frac{I''_{\text{Aug}} = (I'_8 + I'_{20} + I'_{32} + \cdots)}{\text{count of Augusts}}$$

Normalize the index. Sum the 12 seasonal factors. Divide this sum by 12. The resulting value is an adjusting value, P, that is subtracted from each value I''_t to produce an index that sums to zero. When periods are not months, adjust the denominator to the number of periods in the index.

$$P = \frac{\sum_{i=1}^{12} I''}{12}$$

$$I_{\text{Jul}} = I''_{\text{Jul}} - P$$

$$I_{\text{Aug}} = I''_{\text{Aug}} - P, \ldots$$

Subtract the factor from the actual data to obtain DESEAS data:

$$\text{DESEAS}_t = X_t - I_t$$

The use of these equations is demonstrated in Table 15.3. In the column labeled Index and the column labeled Factor, the average of I' is calculated in the boxed area, the values shown above and below that area repeat the values from the same months in the calculation area.

Figures 15.18 and 15.19 show the results of multiplicative and additive deseasonalization. The DESEAS series is marked with triangles.

After forecasting, reseasonalize the data to know what to expect for various months. Reseasonalize the multiplicative series by multiplying it by the seasonal factor, or reseasonalize additive data by adding back the same additive factor. Sometimes it may seem that reseasonlizing is not needed because you only want reports at the annual level. However, there can be many reasons why it is useful to have the data at the monthly level. If you have decomposed the data into units and cost per unit, seasonality may ultimately affect how these data combine to make the total. Similarly, seasonality will affect your ability to track your forecast success over the year.

This discussion has focused on annual seasonality of monthly data with the year beginning in January, but the actual data may begin in any month, be it quarterly data, or have seasonality over some period other than a year. If appropriate adjustments are made, this method can be used with data cumulated over any interval and with any seasonal cycle.

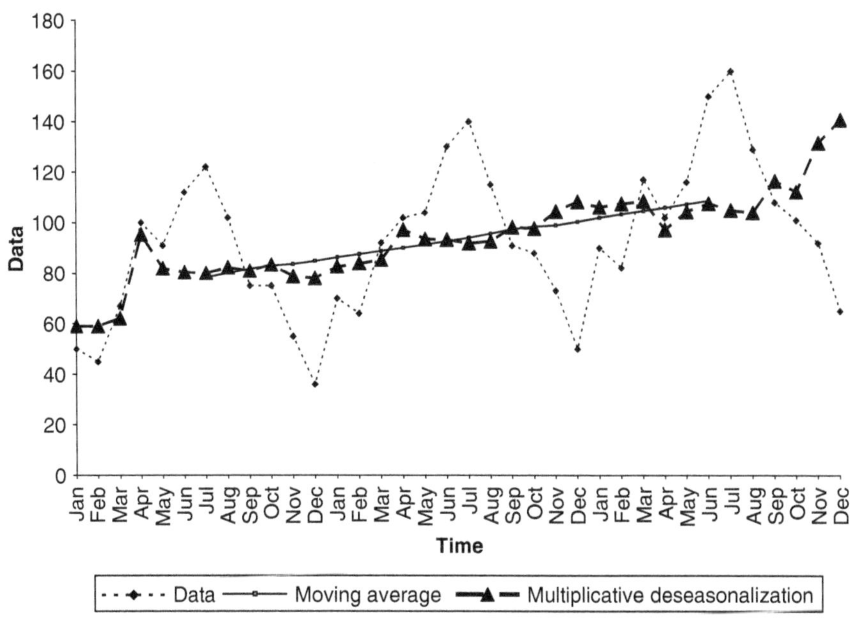

Figure 15.18 Multiplicative deseasonlization.

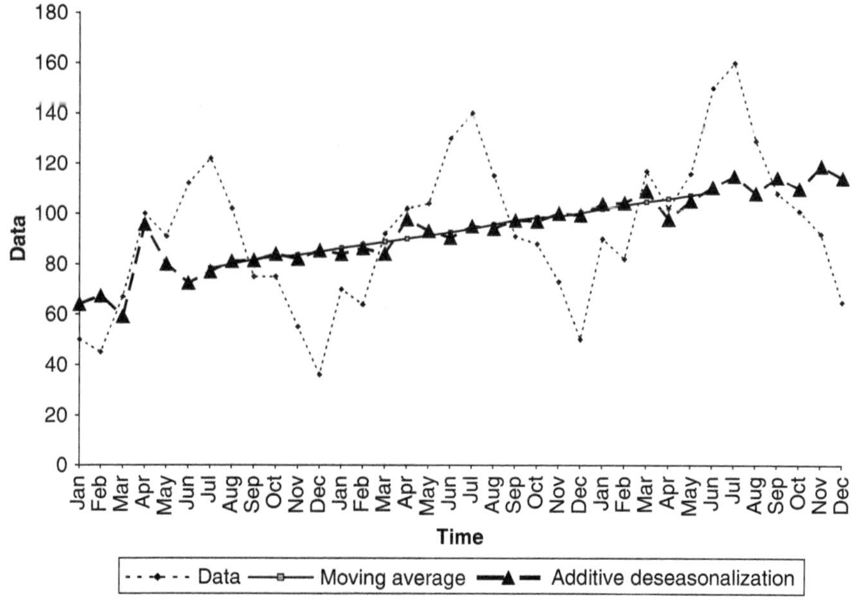

Figure 15.19 Additive deseasonlization.

There is a more advanced version of this procedure known as Census-X12. It is documented on the Census Bureau Web site at http://www.census.gov/srd/www/x12a/. This procedure is not recommended for the novice.

Cumulating Data

An alternative for working with seasonal data is to cumulate them across the season and forecast the cumulated data. For example, if the season is monthly within quarters, cumulate the data to quarters (four observations a year, each accumulated across three months). There are two important restrictions on cumulating data across seasons. First, the forecast need not be updated more frequently than allowed by the level chosen. For example, a forecast cannot be updated every month if the data are cumulated to quarters. Second, the analyst need not know about units of data smaller than the cumulated level. If data has been cumulated to quarters, the analyst cannot speak about monthly data.

Sometimes analysts cumulate data to the annual level for reporting purposes. This can lead to the temptation to cumulate data to the annual level for forecasting purposes, thereby eliminating seasonal variation. This temptation may be a bad idea. First, there is a serious loss of information at the annual level. What happened over the year may not be what was happening at the end of the year, or during the last half of the year. Bunching up the data into one large chunk loses this information. In addition, annual forecasts cannot be checked against reality until the year is over. This may be too late to take remedial action or plan for shortfalls. This chapter has focused on monthly level data. Where circumstances do not clearly call for other levels of data, this level is likely to be the most meaningful.

Differencing

An alternative to seasonal adjustment before forecasting is to calculate the first differences of the seasonal period. That is, the difference between observations that occur at the same point in two sequential seasons. For example, if monthly data follows annual seasonality, as with the previous discussion, calculate differences across years by subtracting the observation in January of first year from the observation in January of second year. For the third year, subtract the second year data from the third year data, continuing until the data runs out. The resulting data are no longer seasonal. Observations have been differenced (subtracted one from another) at the same point in the season; between them there was no seasonality. All the new observations are without seasonality. These differenced data will also reflect the same impact on trend as occurred when the first differences of the first period (that is, the sequential differences) were calculated. Then the differencing must be reversed to produce the full forecast.

After Deseasonalization

The inexperienced forecaster may not realize that all the issues raised before the seasonality may not appear until "after" deseasonalization. So, once again, make an x–y plot and inspect for outliers, paired opposite outliers, shifts, ramps, and the other matters discussed before the discussion of seasonality. Take corrective action as may be appropriate.

Differencing of Trending Data

A procedure of particular importance with trending data, if you choose to use regression methods, is differencing. Differencing is quite easy. Beginning with the second observation of the series, subtract the first observation. This leaves the first "differenced" observation. The third observation subtracts the second. Continue the process until the end of the series. In general, if you difference the dependent variable (the one you are interested in), you should also difference the other variables.

The reason to difference the data is to associate that part of the data you are interested in with regression diagnostics. The part you are interested in is the change from one period to the next. This is the information you collect by differencing the data. If you do not difference the data and if both the dependent and independent data contain trends, then in general, the regression statistics that are usually used to estimate whether the regression is of any benefit will be confused by the association of trends, which is likely to be strong regardless of whether there is any actual relationship in the data.

Means of Reaggregating Data

There are, in principle, two ways to reaggregate decomposed or disaggregated data. The first is straightforward. The second uses regression. There is no special reason to believe one is more effective than the other, although each has its appeal.

The first method is simply to reverse the decomposition math. Suppose the analyst has made two forecastable series by dividing units into total dollars to get a units series and a cost per units series. The analyst can then multiply future cost per unit times future units to get future total dollar value. The appeal of this method is that it is simple and intuitive.

The other possible way to use the forecasts is to construct a "regression model" of the ultimate variable using the component variables as the predictor variables; continuing with the example of the previous paragraph, the total dollar value is the ultimate variable and the predictor variables are units and cost per unit. This model would require autocorrelation correction because of the nature of the variables, and will also suffer the risk of other sources of collinearity as well as misleading diagnostics. Thus, it is not recommended, especially for the novice. Nevertheless, it offers the opportunity for finding subtle marginal relationships between the variables that may not exist with the straightforward accounting style recombination.

Conclusion

This chapter focuses on specific steps taken to make data ready for forecasting. These steps are summarized in the checklist as shown in Table 15.4. Armstrong (1985; 2001a,b) has emphasized the need to examine the empirical evidence for advice such as that given in this chapter. Limited empirical evidence supporting some of these techniques is provided in Armstrong (1985). However, most forecast researchers prefer to examine new, innovative, and sometimes complex techniques. The methods discussed here are well established and relatively simple. The consequences of failing to follow these recommendations can range from slight errors to dramatic forecast failure or simply to excess uncertainty at the wrong time of the year. For example, failure to deal with seasonality where it exists or ineffective solutions for seasonality are well known to be a substantial source of forecast error.

Table 15.4 Checklist for Suggested Data Preparation before Forecasting

	Yes or No	*Remediate?*	*Comment*
Equal time period			
Adjust for business cycle			
Using all available data?			
Time plot made?			
Outliers found?			
Paired outliers found?			
Shifts or ramps?			
"Friday" pattern?			
Days of month pattern?			
Other patterns?			
Other decomposition?			
All components?			
Adjusting for inflation			
Changes in the base			
Changes in data definition			
Exponentiating data			
Exponentiating variance			
Multiplicative seasonality			
Additive seasonality			
Repeat time plot steps after deseasonalization			
Differencing of trending data for regression			
Reaggregation			

The purpose of this chapter is to provide a reference in one place that will get you started in your forecasting effort. Errors may be avoided by taking these simple steps before applying more sophisticated techniques. Preparing well is the first step to getting reliable results.

Further Resources

Several times during this discussion, I have cited Makridakis et al. (1998) as a source of information. Other sources the reader may consult are Armstrong (2001a) and Williams (1999). Equations are consistent with Williams (1999).

References

Ammons, D. N. 1991. *Administrative Analysis for Local Government: Practical Application of Selected Techniques*. Athens, Georgia: Carl Vinson Institute of Government.

Ammons, D. N. 2001. *Tools for Decision Making: A Practical Guide for Local Government*. Washington: CQ Press.

Armstrong, J. S. 1985. *Long-Range Forecasting: From Crystal Ball to Computer*, 2nd ed. New York: Wiley.

Armstrong, J. S. 2001a. Extrapolation for time-series and cross-sectional data. In *Principles of Forecasting a Handbook for Researchers and Practitioners*, ed: J. S. Armstrong. Norwell, MA: Kluwer Academic, pp. 217–243.

Armstrong, J. S. 2001b. *Principles of Forecasting a Handbook for Researchers and Practitioners*. Norwell, MA: Kluwer Academic.

Makridakis, S. G., S. C. Wheelwright, and R. J. Hyndman. 1998. *Forecasting: Methods and Applications*, 3rd ed. New York: Wiley.

Williams, D. W. 1999. Forecasting methods for serial data. In *Handbook of Research Methods in Public Administration*, eds: G. J. Miller and M. L. Whicker. New York: Marcel Dekker, pp. 301–352.

Williams, D. W. and D. Miller. 1999. Level-adjusted exponential smoothing for modeling planned discontinuities. *International Journal of Forecasting* 15(3): 273–289.

U.S. Department of Labor Statistics. 2006. Consumer Price Index, http://www.bls.gov/cpi/home.htm and ftp://ftp.bls.gov/pub/special.requests/cpi/cpiai.txt (accessed December 3, 2006).

CONSENSUS FORECASTING

2

Chapter 16

Consensus Forecasting for Budgeting in Theory and Practice

William Earle Klay and Joseph A. Vonasek

Contents

Introduction

A budget is a plan for the future. Good budgeting requires good forecasting. Most of the literature related to budgetary forecasting—both revenue forecasting and expenditure forecasting—is devoted to the methodologies involved. Seldom is any attention given to the social and organizational dimensions of budget forecasting. Yet these dimensions are often of great importance.

Budget forecasting can become highly politicized. Nowhere is this more evident than in larger governments that operate under the concept of separation of powers. Even where the same political party controls the executive and legislative branches, policy goals often differ and personalities can clash. In the theater of political conflict, the budgeting process can become the front line of political jousting. One group wants a favorable revenue forecast to justify a tax cut, others to increase spending on favored programs, and so forth. It is not surprising, then, that budget forecasting can become a focal point of political conflict.

Some legislatures have rejected forecasts put forth by chief executives due to the political implications of the forecasts, rather than on their technical merits. For example, if a chief executive's revenue forecasts are lower than legislative leaders would prefer, they might choose to adopt a rival, more optimistic, forecast. Adopting a higher forecast as official, one would free the legislature to either reduce tax rates or spend more. Consequently, legislators have been known to spend time on the floors of their chambers debating revenue forecasts. Although they bring a vast array of educational and life experiences to their jobs, few legislators are educated in budgetary forecasting. The authors of this chapter are former practitioners who have worked in executive budget offices, and for legislative bodies, in states and local governments. We have seen that legislators are very busy people, particularly during session, and their time is very limited. We believe that legislators' time is best spent learning about policy needs and opportunities, and deliberating about substantive policy. We do not think that legislators should spend their limited time debating the technical merits of forecasts—something that legislators are not well prepared to do—when, in truth, what they often really seek is political advantage. A few budgetary practices can help budgeters, including the legislators themselves, to more effectively utilize their available time. Consensus forecasting is one of these. This chapter discusses how it has been successfully used to curtail debate over forecasts.

Consensus budget forecasting involves the development of forecasts of revenues, and sometimes expenditures, through the input of information from multiple persons and sources. In a consensus forecasting process, input is sought from persons from different agencies or organizations that might have different perspectives regarding the future of a state's economy, revenues, or costs. Consensus forecasting can be highly formalized, even constitutionally or statutorily mandated, or be rather informal. It is usually done through conferences or committees. The individuals involved usually come from the executive and legislative branches, but might also come from operating agencies, universities, or private companies such as banks or economic forecasting firms. Although the level of influence each participant has on the forecasting process can vary, the resulting forecast(s) from a consensus process will be a joint product of the participants. Often, officials of both the executive and legislative branches accept and use the resulting common forecasts in their budget preparations and deliberations. It is this acceptance of consensus forecasts that prompts a reduction in legislative debate over the merits of competing forecasts.

In addition to its potential to reduce political strife over budgetary forecasts, consensus forecasting also seems to enhance accuracy. Despite the fact that consensus forecasting seems to lessen strife over forecasting, although contributing to accuracy, surprisingly little research attention has been given to the consensus processes themselves. What might account for these likely favorable effects on both accuracy and the political process? Exploring possible answers to this question is the purpose of this chapter.

In Chapter 17 of this volume, Yuhua Qiao presents an extensive review of the literature that has linked consensus forecasting to accuracy in governmental revenue forecasting. This finding of enhanced accuracy for consensus approaches has also generally been found in business settings. The present chapter focuses, instead, on explorations as to why consensus forecasting seems to contribute to greater accuracy. We explore some underlying theory relevant to consensus forecasting. Specifically, theory related to the questioning of underlying assumptions, and to the combining of forecasts, as possible contributors to forecast accuracy, is reviewed. Some theory that seems relevant to developing a sense of ownership toward forecasts is also briefly discussed. It concludes with information about some of the ways in which consensus forecasting can be done. Of particular importance here is a brief historical case study of consensus forecasting in the state of Florida, a state with more than three decades of experience in consensus forecasting of both revenues and expenditures.

Consensus Processes Seem to Enhance Accuracy

Studies of the relationship between the use of consensus forecasting and state governments' revenue forecast accuracy have repeatedly found that consensus forecasting seems to improve accuracy. The reader should refer to the review of this literature in Chapter 17 of this volume by Qiao. Qiao's empirical research is based on information gathered for the 2004 Government Performance Project (GPP) ratings of the 50 states. This data is also being studied by Willoughby and Guo (2006) who concur with Qiao in that consensus forecasting processes are associated with better revenue forecasting accuracy. The GPP data indicates that the states that used multiple methods for forecasting—especially simple trend analysis and consensus forecasting—were more accurate. All four of the highest-performing states utilized consensus forecasting. In fact, as will be seen, the GPP data suggests that states might be getting better at doing consensus forecasting.

The strength of the associations found in recent studies of consensus forecasting and accuracy raise an intriguing question, "Are the states getting better at doing consensus forecasting?" This does seem a possibility as consensus forecasting is a group process and groups are capable of collective learning and improvement. To answer this question, although, researchers will need to do qualitatively oriented longitudinal studies of groups engaged in consensus forecasting.

State governments are not alone in embracing consensus forecasting processes. Researchers of business forecasting find that the literature of that field also suggests that consensus methods can enhance forecasting accuracy. Weltman (1995–1996, p. 16), for example, conducted a literature review of economic forecasting for business uses and concluded that "overall, the results of numerous academic studies undertaken in this area have supported the consensus approach." The Institute of Business Forecasting conducted a survey in 2000 of companies that used its training sessions and conferences and found that about 78 percent of these companies hold consensus-seeking meetings (Jain 2001, p. 3). Chaman L. Jain, editor in chief of the *Journal of Business Forecasting*, described how such meetings typically occur in businesses that are effective at forecasting. He indicated that collaboration, especially in a monthly consensus-seeking meeting, is very important. "In this meeting, members of different functions such as Marketing, Production, Finance and Sales get together, review the statistically generated forecasts, and, if necessary, *overlay judgment on them (emphasis added)* to arrive at the final forecasts" (Jain 2001, p. 15).

What might be occurring within the interpersonal relationships that are requisite to consensus forecasting to enhance forecast accuracy? Jain's (2001, p. 15) use of the phrase "overlay judgment on them" is suggestive of some of what might be happening. We now turn to some possible theoretical explanations.

Theoretical Underpinnings of Consensus Forecasting

Questioning Underlying Assumptions

One of the most important studies of forecasting accuracy ever is that by William Ascher. His findings help to understand how the dynamics of consensus forecasting processes can contribute to greater forecasting accuracy. Ascher's contribution was to study past forecasting in several distinct subject areas—demographic, economic, energy, transportation, and technology forecasting—to learn if there might be common causes of some of the inaccuracies observed in each area of forecasting. He concluded that there was a common root, "The core assumptions underlying a forecast, which represent the forecaster's basic outlook on the context within which the specific forecasted trend develops, are the major determinants of forecast accuracy" (Ascher 1978, p. 199).

Ascher described how demographers, following World War II (WWII), failed to recognize the phenomenon now known as the "baby boom." They assumed that the upswing in births in the late 1940s was a temporary phenomenon, a response to the disruptions of the war years. Demographers shared the assumption that the "demographic transition," the long-term fertility decline that had been observed in the United States and northern Europe from the earliest days of the Industrial Revolution, would prevail. It was widely assumed that American women would quickly return to the "replacement rate" (2.1 children per woman of childbearing age), which the United States had reached in the 1930s.

What the demographers failed to see was that family formation conditions for young adults had radically changed. Young men returning from the war took advantage of government programs for veterans, making them considerably more educated, and more employable, than preceding generations had been. America's economy was rapidly expanding; government housing and transportation policies ignited a housing boom. Surveys revealed that women wanted, on average, slightly more than three children. Family formation conditions were so favorable that couples ended up having almost exactly that number of children. Demographers, clinging to their cherished demographic transition theory, failed to recognize the many clues that conditions had changed. It was not until several years into the boom that their faulty underlying assumptions finally began to be rejected.

Forecasters in other subject areas were also found to make similar errors. Energy forecasters following WWII, for example, tended to doubt that the postwar period's rapid economic expansion and concomitant energy use could continue as long as it had. Consequently, for a period of time, nonjudgmental methods outperformed judgmental ones in energy forecasting. The tendency to cling to outdated assumptions was what Ascher (1978, p. 202) termed "the problem of assumption drag." The essential characteristic of consensus forecasting, bringing together persons who work for different bosses and possibly bringing different perspectives to the table, seems likely to stimulate questioning of one another's assumptions.

Questioning Can Stimulate Learning by Forecasters

The propensities of budget forecasters to question their underlying assumptions have rarely been studied. Klay (1985) conducted a survey of forecasters in state governments, in which items that inquired about the inclination of elected officials to question the underlying assumptions of the forecasts submitted to them were included. Where survey respondents (state forecasting officials) said that elected officials were more likely to question the forecasters regarding the assumptions made about the national economy, the respondents indicated that the forecasters themselves had learned more about the workings of the state's economy. Similarly, the forecasters themselves seemed to be learning more when elected officials questioned the forecasters about their level of confidence for the overall forecasts. Respondents also indicated that they thought elected officials learned more about the workings of their state's economy when they actively questioned the forecasters. As any teacher knows, learning is facilitated when questioning occurs. This seems to happen in budget forecasting too.

Unfortunately, no systematic longitudinal survey data exists regarding the propensity of budget actors to raise questions about forecasts, much less whether that propensity increases when consensus forecasting is adopted. There is reason to suspect that it might because the questioning of one another's assumptions is inherent to consensus forecasting. Participants are unlikely to "sign on" to forecast outcomes until they have reached an acceptable level of comfort regarding the resolution of differences, for example, resolving differences between outputs of different forecasting models, over values of exogenous variables, and over the likelihood of specific future events occurring.

Klay's finding that the propensity of elected officials to question budgetary forecasters was related to the learning that occurred among forecasters is suggestive. Questioning is a stimulant for learning. Consensus forecasting inherently promotes questioning between and among participants. It seems likely, therefore, that these same processes of questioning and learning are related to the positive relationships between consensus forecasting and accuracy reported by Qiao and others.

Combining Forecasts Can Enhance Accuracy

A large body of research exists on the topic of combining forecasts. Combining forecasts is not the same thing as consensus forecasting (as we use that term here). Consensus forecasting is a group process. A single individual can conduct multiple forecasts, using different methods, and then mathematically combine them to get a single forecast. Similarly, one individual can combine the forecasts of others to arrive at a single "combining" forecast. Methods for combining forecasts range from simply calculating the means of multiple forecasts to more complex methods that differentially weigh the forecasts being combined. In mathematically combining forecasts, no mutual questioning among group participants occurs, as it does with consensus forecasting. A preponderance of evidence indicates that combining forecasts, absent any interpersonal interactions and questioning, does generally enhance accuracy.

An impressive review of the literature on combining forecasts, encompassing more than 200 articles, was conducted by Clemen. He noted that the amount of literature on the topic is quite large. From his review, he concluded that there is a broad consensus of findings that combining multiple individual forecasts can substantially improve forecast accuracy (Clemen 1989, p. 559). These studies also indicated that relatively simple combining methods often perform as well as more complex methods for combining forecasts.

Clemen (1989, p. 559) recommended that "combining forecasts should become part of the mainstream of forecasting practice." Spyros Makridakis, a well-known scholar of forecasting in many contexts, offered some explanations as to why combining forecasts generally enhances accuracy in contexts as varied as weather forecasting, energy consumption forecasting, and revenue forecasting. He pointed out that simple methods of combining forecasts, such as calculating a simple mathematical mean, are as accurate as complex combining methods (Makridakis 1989, p. 601). When multiple methods are used to forecast something, the resulting errors are, to some extent, independent and often somewhat offsetting. Combining forecasts takes advantage of this. Makridakis cautioned that forecasters should not blindly cling to forecast methods that repeatedly perform poorly and should drop those from the ones being combined.

Makridakis (1989, p. 601) recommended that forecasters "use combining to elicit judgmental inputs." In many governments where consensus forecasting occurs, two or more forecasts are often combined, or, if not completely combined then elements of one forecast are deliberated and perhaps included in another forecast that is subsequently adopted. In doing this, governments that practice some combining within the context of consensus forecasting are heeding Makridakis' (1989, p. 601) advice to "elicit judgmental inputs."

Legitimating Forecasting through Participation

To this point, this chapter has reviewed literature that indicates consensus forecasting is likely to enhance accuracy, and it has explored some theory that points to why greater accuracy might occur. But consensus forecasting has been adopted in some places for reasons other than accuracy. In the state of Florida, for example, consensus forecasting was initiated to reduce legislative debating over contending forecasts. Early proponents of consensus forecasting in Florida felt that it was a waste of legislators' valuable time to debate the merits of competing forecasts, something they were not trained to do, and that they should focus more on debating the merits of substantive policy. It was believed that consensus processes could lead to single forecasts that would be accepted and used by the governor and by both houses of the legislature. This belief proved correct. Why would legislators end their practice of debating competing forecasts? In purely political terms, it would seem that a consensus estimating process comprises a surrender of some of the political power of the appropriations process to others.

Consensus forecasting involves processes of legitimation, and possibly of co-optation. If the intent is to provide legitimacy, or for co-optation to occur, the participants in the consensus process must all have reasonable expectations of positive benefits from participating in the process. Actual use of the results of consensus forecasting is essential; otherwise, the processes would probably become shallow rituals, pointless exercises for those who participate. From the perspective of legitimating, the greatest value of the consensus forecasting process appears to be that it promotes both dialogue and the forging of a basis of agreement among its participants.

The contribution of consensus forecasting to gaining acceptance of its outcomes is rooted in its deliberative processes. Afterward, participants seem to have a "sense of ownership" of the outcomes. Research has shown that involving persons in deliberative processes gives them a stake in accepting outcomes. Involvement in the requisite deliberative processes becomes a source of self-discipline over the process' members, which does not depend on a command-and-control structure to have an effect (Anderson 1999, p. 191).

Consensus forecasting processes may be either formal or informal. Formal processes are based either in statutes or formal rule making. Informal systems may encompass elaborate decision-making procedures, adopted over time and through mutual agreement, but they remain outside the purview of formal statutes or rules. Whether formally or informally established, consensus forecasting groups typically evolve organizational norms and customary procedures.

Dachler and Wilpert's (1978) review of the early decades of the literature on participation in organizations is useful in understanding the effects of the participatory processes of consensus forecasting. They observed that whether informal organizational participation becomes formal is a product of the organization's objectives for using a participatory process and the context of participation within the social structure of the organization. That is, it is dependent on what the system's designers intend to accomplish. When informal processes undergo strains that might be relieved by formalization of a process, a formal status might become imposed on the existing informal process.

Consensus forecasting requires genuine, not merely symbolic, participation. Gellar (1985, p. 25) observed that, to be effective, participatory processes must be reasonably employed through an effective legitimation process that empowers all participants including those who might find themselves in a minority position. Negotiation necessarily replaces top-down management of the forecasting process. The idea that participation in deliberations is likely to enhance a "sense of ownership" of resulting decisions is not a new one. Morrell (1999, p. 293) traces this idea as far back as the concepts of Aristotle, Marsiglio of Padua (a fourteenth-century Italian political philosopher who argued that the rights of rulers originated in popular consent), Rousseau, and J. S. Mill. A considerable amount of modern empirical literature from the field of organization development indicates that participation in deliberative processes is conducive to gaining participants' subsequent support for resulting decisions. Consequently, the Organization and Human Systems Development Credo, adopted in 1996, emphasizes the importance of "meaningful participation" in enhancing organizational efficacy (Organization Development Network).

Consensus decision making differs in important ways from majority decision making. In the latter, minority positions can be opposed and subordinated. In a consensus process, however, the subsequent support of all participants is needed. Consequently, the majority members must deliberate with minority members until the latter feel that their views have been sufficiently included to a point that they are willing to accept decision outputs. Resolving inevitable disagreements requires mutual recognition of the positions of others and the incorporation of their concerns into policy. As a participatory process, consensus forecasting requires addressing and resolving the things that hinder mutual agreement. Consensus forecasting enables its parties to engage in open dialogue, making their concerns known, and generating an avenue for "reasoning toward" a rational collective decision (Dryzek 1989, p. 97). In this, the consensus forecasting process has the potential, in one limited technical context, to alleviate some of the political gamesmanship that exists in the legislative process.

The legislative process is often resistant to the use of systematic inquiry in the formation of policy. Within the framework of consensus budgetary forecasting, and its participatory mechanisms for building a sense of ownership for its outputs, complex and often normative issues can be addressed within the context of microeconomic analysis and demographic models. Thus, the general organization of the consensus forecasting process takes a shape similar to Lasswell's (1960, p. 213) "decision seminar." Consensus forecasting is generally done by a small group of knowledgeable and committed individuals who engage in extended discourse on an object of study that has ongoing continuity. Lessons from previous rounds of forecasting can be learned and applied. Participants typically have extensive data for their use and they can regularly criticize and counter one another's positions and arguments. Briefly, one of the merits of consensus forecasting is that it requires active, not passive, participation and, thus, is likely to engender a stronger sense of ownership of forecasts.

Case Study: Consensus Forecasting in Florida

There are many ways of organizing to do consensus forecasting. The specific organizational arrangements employed by a government are a result of historical precedents, existing legal frameworks, current political realities, and the personalities and positions of the persons who promote the process. Generally, though, several basic questions, such as the following, need to be resolved when organizing to do consensus forecasting:

1. Where will the responsibility for conducting the process lie?
2. Who are the parties to be included in the consensus forecasting process and what is their relative level of authority to be (e.g., voting or nonvoting participant)?
3. Is the process to be implemented through a formal or an informal method?
4. Is the process to be restricted to certain revenue sources or to specific programs or governmental funds?
5. Is use of the resulting forecasts by the various branches and agencies of government to be advisory or mandatory?

6. If one or more participants feel that they can no longer support a consensus forecast, is there a mechanism for resolving the tension and establishing a new consensus?

The State of Florida has been doing consensus forecasting since 1970. The ways in which it organizes to do forecasting illustrate how the foregoing questions might be addressed. Consensus forecasting began in Florida when a senior career budget official in the executive branch became bothered by observing legislators spending time to debate competing forecasts on the House and Senate floors. He believed their time would be better spent debating policy. Consequently, he invited senior staff members from both houses, specifically the staff directors of the two revenue committees, to join with the governor's budget director to begin a consensus forecasting process.

A basic decision rule was established at the outset. To assure that the governor, the House, and the Senate would use the forecasts, it was decided that each forecast had to be approved by the designated representatives of all the three. Deliberations continue until a consensus is reached. If subsequent events cause any one of the three to become no longer able to support a consensus forecast, any of the three can call a new meeting to discuss and amend the forecast until a new consensus is reached.

For more than a decade, Florida's process was based on mutual agreement but it was not formalized in law. In the early 1980s, however, tension emerged between the legislature and the governor's Office of Planning and Budgeting (OPB) over several aspects of budgeting. The legislature responded to these tensions by weakening the governor's role in budgeting. It did so by thereafter requiring state agencies to submit their budget requests to each house at the same time that they submit them to the governor's OPB. The legislature also enacted a change to the budget statute (Chapter 216, Florida Statutes) that formalized the consensus process. What was written into law was essentially the very process that had already emerged informally. Florida's experience suggests that governments should probably develop their own consensus processes informally before formalizing them into law. Florida's participants had over a decade to work out their respective roles and decision procedures. They were comfortable with these to the point that no substantive alteration was needed to formalize the process in statute. Adopting a statute prematurely, before letting participants evolve their own understandings and procedures, might inhibit needed experimentation and evolution of the process.

Consensus forecasting in Florida was begun solely to generate forecasts for the state's General Revenue Fund. The basic framework for consensus forecasting has evolved to where it is now applied to all major revenue sources and to major areas of expenditures as well. The budget statute defines the term "consensus" as unanimous consent of each of the "principals." The law names 12 specific topics to be forecasted by a "consensus estimating conference." When consensus forecasting began in Florida, the expertise for formal econometric modeling resided in the executive office of the governor (specifically in the OPB), and the legislature utilized the governor's staff. Over the years, however, the legislature also developed its own forecasting office with expert staff, which has taken the leading role in modeling.

The duties and membership of each of the 12 estimating conferences is stipulated in the statute. Membership in the estimating conferences is divided between two classes of members: "principals" and "participants." Principals include the staff members designated by the governor, the president of the Senate, and the speaker of the House of Representatives, as well as the coordinator of the legislature's Office of Economic and Demographic Research (or the coordinator's designee). Consensus must be attained among the principals. In contrast, any principal can invite other people to become involved as "participants." These people may, at a principal's request, supply information, perform analysis, and even provide alternative forecasts. Principals may be members of a state agency involved in the activities of a specific estimating conference, an outside expert, or a member of an academic institution.

Estimating conferences can be convened at any time of the year by principals from either the executive or legislative branches. Regularly scheduled conferences are held each fall for budget development and then again shortly before the legislature convenes annually in the spring. Critical to Florida's process is that each principal effectively has a veto power. Once any new estimating conference is convened, no official estimate exists until a new consensus is reached. All involved, therefore, are under pressure to reach consensus.

Florida's initial successes in forecasting general fund revenues encouraged its members to expand consensus forecasting to include other revenue sources as well as the major categories of expenditures. Estimating conferences now include the following:

1. Economic Estimating Conference
2. Demographic Estimating Conference
3. Revenue Estimating Conference
4. Education Estimating Conference
5. Criminal Justice Estimating Conference
6. Social Services Estimating Conference
7. Child Welfare Estimating Conference
8. Juvenile Justice Estimating Conference
9. Workforce Estimating Conference
10. School Readiness Program Estimating Conference
11. Self-Insurance Estimating Conference
12. Florida Retirement System Actuarial Assumptions Estimating Conference

All other conferences must use the outputs of the Economic Estimating Conference and the Demographic Estimating Conference. This establishes a common basis for the estimating conferences. When conferences must deal with long-range multiyear projections—as with transportation infrastructure or the retirement system—the common assumption is that current law and administrative practices will remain in effect for the entire forecast period.

To summarize, Florida's consensus estimating process measures up very well according to the criteria set by Lasswell (1960) for his "decision seminars." In Florida, consensus forecasting is done by overlapping small groups of persons with substantial formal expertise in the subject areas being forecasted. The process is continuous; extended discourse has been sustained for more than three decades. Discussions in conference meetings often begin with recaps of how well the previous forecast anticipated events and what the causes of observed errors were. Improvements in data gathering have been ongoing and participants do not hesitate to criticize one another's arguments. Accuracy has been impressive; an internal study done by the legislature's forecasting office, provided to the authors, revealed that the average annual percentage error for the general revenue tax collection estimates was 4.4 percent for a thirty-two-year period beginning in fiscal year (FY) 1972 and 2.2 percent for the final ten years of the study. The largest errors by far were in the volatile 1970s; a 10 percent shortfall happened in FY1975 when tourism collapsed during the Organization of Petroleum Exporting Countries (OPEC) oil boycott, and unexpectedly high inflation caused sizeable underestimates earlier in that decade.

States rarely stop doing consensus forecasting once it is begun. Florida's experience is illustrative as to why consensus forecasting has staying power. Consensus forecasting has succeeded in accomplishing its original purpose in Florida—to stop legislators from debating alternative forecasts. These kinds of debates have not happened yet. Budgeting is inherently political, yet Florida's consensus forecasting process has allowed systematic analysis to become more influential. In addition to revenue analysis, Florida's policy makers now have better information about major cost drivers (e.g., school populations, offender populations, and number of unemployed persons) on the expenditure side. Political gamesmanship continues, to be sure, but it is better informed than before and the budget gamesmanship has not interfered with the consensus forecasting processes.

Conclusion

Consensus forecasting can be done in varied kinds of organizations. As discussed earlier, consensus forecasting is a widespread practice in business corporations. Data from the GPP indicates that various states can do consensus forecasting and that doing so is likely to enhance accuracy. The finding that all four of the highest-performing states utilized consensus forecasting clearly points to the wisdom of adopting consensus processes in states and other governments. But consensus forecasting, like any other reform, is dependent on continuing sponsorship. When the initiators of reforms depart from an organization, the reforms often fail to take root. Florida's experience, however, reveals that consensus forecasting can be successfully institutionalized to the point that it successfully weathers major structural turmoil. In the year 2000, strict term limits (eight years maximum) took effect for all state-elected officials, including legislators. Leadership turnover in the legislature, among both elected officials and staff directors, has been unprecedented in the state's history. None of the original initiators of consensus forecasting in Florida are still participants in its estimating conferences. Nevertheless, Florida's estimating conferences continue to function without intrusion or serious threat, indicating that their value to the institution has become well established.

The popularity of consensus forecasting is not difficult to explain. Empirical research indicates that it enhances forecast accuracy. Our review of related theory shows that consensus forecasting is sound from two perspectives. It can enhance the questioning of underlying assumptions. It can also benefit from the accuracy-enhancing effects of combining forecasts. Additionally, consensus forecasting can help in reducing political conflict over contending forecasts while increasing opportunities to do analysis that is used by political leaders. The dual potential of consensus forecasting—to improve accuracy while better informing the political process—makes it attractive indeed.

References

Anderson, G. L. 1999. The politics of participatory reforms in education. *Theory into Practice* 38: 191–195.

Ascher, W. 1978. *Forecasting: An Appraisal for Policy-Makers and Planners*. Baltimore, MD: The Johns Hopkins University Press.

Clemen, R. T. 1989. Combining forecasts: a review and annotated bibliography. *International Journal of Forecasting* 5: 559–587.

Dachler, P. H. and B. Wilpert. 1978. Conceptual dimensions and boundaries of participation in organizations: a critical evaluation. *Administrative Science Quarterly* 23: 1–39.

Dryzek, J. S. 1989. Policy sciences of democracy. *Polity* 22: 97–118.

Gellar, S. 1985. The Ratched-McMurphy model revisited: a critique of participatory development models, strategies, and projects. *Issue: A Journal of Opinion* 14: 25–28.

Jain, C. L. 2001. Forecasting practices in corporate America. *Journal of Business Forecasting* 20: 2–3.

Klay, W. E. 1985. The organizational dimension of budgetary forecasting: suggestions from revenue forecasting in the states. *International Journal of Public Administration* 7: 241–265.

Lasswell, H. D. 1960. The technique of decision seminars. *Midwest Journal of Political Science* 4: 213–236.

Makridakis, S. 1989. Why combining works? *International Journal of Forecasting* 5: 601–603.

Morrell, M. E. 1999. Citizens' evaluations of participatory democratic procedures: normative theory meets empirical science. *Political Research Quarterly* 52: 293–322.

Organization Development Network. Organization and human systems development network credo, http://www.odnet.org (accessed October 25, 2006).

Weltman, J. C. 1995–1996. Using consensus forecasting in business planning. *Journal of Business Forecasting* 14: 13–16.

Willoughby, K. and H. Guo. 2006. The state of the art: revenue forecasting in U.S. state governments. Paper presented at the 18th Annual Conference of the Association for Budgeting and Financial Management, October 21, Atlanta, GA.

Chapter 17

Use of Consensus Revenue Forecasting in U.S. State Governments

Yuhua Qiao

Contents

Introduction

In the last three decades, 27 U.S. states have come to use consensus revenue forecasts in the hope of improving revenue forecast accuracy and providing the executive and legislative branches a common ground about the amount of revenue available for the budget. Although the consensus process has assumed a great importance in state budgeting process, research on this topic is extremely limited. This chapter seeks to fill this gap by investigating the use of consensus revenue forecasting from the following aspects: (1) the extent of its use (e.g., which states use it and what funds it covers); (2) how it is implemented; and (3) its performance (e.g., whether it improves accuracy of revenue forecasting).

Data used in this chapter is from several sources. In addition to the review of the very limited literature, the author gathered data from state government Web sites, government reports, online reports, and an e-mail and telephone survey of state budget officers, or revenue forecast staff. The e-mail and telephone survey was conducted during September 2006 and March 2007. The survey was sent to the 27 states that the Government Performance Project (2005) identified as those that use consensus revenue forecasts. The author obtained contact information of state revenue forecasters from state government Web sites. The author contacted revenue forecast agencies to locate the people involved in consensus revenue forecasting and then sent them the written survey. Twenty-one states responded to the survey. In the survey, the author asked respondents when their states started to use consensus revenue forecasting, reasons for using it, what funds it covers, whether it is required in statute or by informal arrangement, whether it is legally binding, what issues and challenges it has, and to what extent consensus revenue forecasts have improved forecast accuracy.

The Use of Consensus Revenue Forecast and Its Advantages

Revenue forecasts play a critical role in the public budgeting process. They are essential planning tools, providing critical data underlying fiscal policies. Projecting how much revenue is available for governments restrains their spending levels. This is particularly true for state and local governments that have to balance their operating budgets.

However, the accuracy of revenue forecasts "is generally assumed inversely proportional to their importance" (Wallack 2005, p. 2). Revenue forecasts are well known for their inaccuracy. According to Stinson (2002) and Penner (2002), the only thing certain about the forecasts is that they will be wrong and they are often very wrong.

Because of human bias, political pressures, and economic unpredictability, revenue forecasts will never be perfectly accurate. But revenue forecasts are not hopeless and dependent on luck either. Among various efforts to improve the process in the past several decades were changes in the institutional arrangements within which the revenue forecasts take place. For example, many states have established Governor's Council of Economic Advisors in order to make the process more objective (Niederjohn 2004). Another important institutional arrangement is to use consensus revenue forecasts. Although no scholar has ever defined this term, it applies an agreement about the forecast from a wide range of participants. In the context of state revenue forecasts, consensus revenue forecasts require, at least, the engagement of participants from the executive and legislative branches.

Florida was the first to use consensus revenue forecasts. It held its first consensus revenue forecast conference in 1970. At the beginning, the procedure was informal and not rigorous. In 1980, the state legislature created the Division of Economic and Demographic Research under the Joint Legislative Management Committee and formalized the process through a memorandum of agreement among the parties involved. In 1982, the process was legally required by statute (Office of Economic & Demographic Research, the Florida Legislature).

Over the years, more states adopted consensus revenue forecasts. The 1970s saw three more states, in addition to Florida, using it, and the 1980s saw seven more. The biggest jump was in the 1990s when nine more states came to use the process. By 2005 when the Government Performance Project (GPP) was issued, there were 27* states identified as using consensus revenue forecasts (see Table 17.1). The most recent state, New Hampshire, adopted it in 2003. As of March 2007, New Hampshire has not implemented it yet. The Alabama legislature proposed a bill in its 2004 legislative session to create a Revenue Consensus Forecasting Panel like the one in Florida (Ciamarra 2004).

Consensus revenue forecasts are well grounded in their logic. They incorporate the elements of good practices in revenue estimating recommended by the National Association of State Budget Officers (NASBO) (Howard 1989). According to Howard (1989, p. 4), the first good practice suggests that "governors should understand and participate directly in the development of a state economic forecast

* National Conference of State Legislature (1997, pp. 1–5) identified 22 states using consensus revenue forecasts. National Association of State Budget Officers (Jan. 2002, p. 19, Table G) listed 24 states. According to the Government Performance Project (2005), 27 states used consensus revenue forecasts. Three states including Alabama, South Dakota, and Arizona, were listed as consensus revenue forecast users in the earlier two reports, but not in the GPP report. Because GPP is more recent, the three states are removed from user list in this study.

Table 17.1 Use of Consensus Revenue Forecast in the States

States Using Consensus Revenue Forecast (Total = 27)	*Adopting Year*	*Funds To Be Covered*	*Required in Law*	*Legally Binding*
Delaware	NA	General fund	NA	Yes
Florida	Early 1970s	General funds, lottery, transportation fund, Gross Receipt Tax, and more	Yes	Yes
Indiana	Early 1980s	General fund	No	Yes
Iowa	1986	General fund	Yes; Iowa Code 8.22A	Yes
Kansas	1974	General fund	No	Yes
Kentucky	1996	General fund and road fund	Yes; Kentucky Revised Statute (KRS) 48.115	Yes
Louisiana	1987	General fund, fuel tax, sales tax, and mineral taxes	Yes; Revised Statute (RS) 39:21.1–26	Yes
Maine	Early 1990s	General fund, highway fund, fund for a healthy Maine	Yes; Maine Revised Statute Annotated (MRSA), Chapter 151-B, Sec 1710	Yes
Maryland	1993	General fund, transportation trust fund, transfer tax forecast	Yes; State Gov 6-102	No, but always accepted
Massachusetts	NA	NA	NA	Yes
Michigan	1991	General fund, school aid fund, and more[a]	Yes; Michigan Compile Laws (MCL) 18.1367a–f.	Yes
Mississippi	Mid-1980s	General fund	Yes	No, but almost always accepted
Missouri	Early 1990s	General fund	No	Yes
Nebraska	1985	General fund	Yes; Sec 77-27, 156-27, 159	Yes
New Hampshire	2003	NA	Yes	NA

New Mexico	Late 1970s	Formally only general fund, informally state road fund and expenditure	Yes; New Mexico Statute Annotated (NMSA) 1978, Chapter 6-3	Yes
New York	1996	Tax receipts for all funds, lottery receipts, and miscellaneous receipts for general fund	Yes; Sec 23 of State Finance Law	No
North Carolina	1975	General fund	No; informal arrangement	No
North Dakota	NA	NA	NA	Yes
Rhode Island	Early 1990s	General fund	Yes; Title 35 Chapter 16	Yes
South Carolina	Early 1990s	General fund, lotteries, and education improvement fund	Yes; Section 11-9-810	Yes
Tennessee	NA	NA	NA	No
Utah	NA	NA	NA	Yes
Vermont	1996	General fund, transportation, education, and health access trust fund	Yes; 32 Vermont Statute Annotated (V.S.A) Sec 305a	No
Virginia	NA	Also for prison population and Medicaid population	NA	Yes
Washington	1984	General fund	Yes; Chapter 82.33	Yes
Wyoming	1983	All types of funds	No	Yes

[a] It also includes an estimate of the number of pupils in Michigan's K-12 schools. The process includes a national and state economic forecast. The process is fairly successful, so it is often repeated informally in other areas including expenditure.

Source: From National Association of State Budget Officers, 2002, http://www.nasbo.org/publications.php and National Conference of State Legislatures, 1997, http://www.ncsl.org/programs/fiscal/lbp98sum.htm.

that has broad acceptance." Second, the process "should utilize the expertise of academic and business economists in developing the state economic forecasts." Third, the legislative branch should be included in the development of the economic forecast, at least to certain degree. With its wide range of participants from both branches of government, academic circles and the business world, consensus revenue forecasts are applications of what NASBO recommended.

There are two main reasons behind the adoption of consensus revenue forecasts. The first one is at a practical level. In many states, both the governor and the legislature have their own budget staff that develops their own revenue forecasts. When the budget process starts, lawmakers usually debate which revenue forecast is more accurate and reliable instead of debating the substance policy issues. A consensus process, including all the major stakeholders into the process, will eliminate or minimize this unnecessary argument and turn their attention to policy.

Secondly, consensus revenue forecasts are believed to lead to more accurate forecasts. The process taps the intelligence gathered from the most knowledgeable people in the state and makes the best use of the available data (Howard 1989). At the same time, when a wide range of experts get involved, they generate a greater diversity of information and provide better checks on the rationality of the model estimates. This, in turn, provides better decision-making capacity (Voorhees 2004). Additionally, consensual structures usually use multiple forecasts based on differing perspectives, and the forecasting literature has found that multiple forecasts usually enhance forecast accuracy (Voorhees 2004). Consensual forecasts may also reduce political pressures in skewing revenue forecasts by providing checks from various participants, some of whom are independent.

The survey results confirm the two rationales behind the use of consensus revenue forecast. Respondents from nine out of the twenty-one states indicate that they started using consensus revenue forecasts to improve their revenue accuracy. A good example of this is Louisiana. During the several years before its adoption of consensus revenue forecasting in 1987, its revenue forecasts were optimistic, which led to budget deficits. Consensus revenue forecast was expected to avoid this problem. In addition, they state that the consensus process is implemented to produce a single consensus revenue forecast or to take politics out of the revenue forecasting process. Three out of these nine respondents declared that improving revenue forecast accuracy is just the side effect, if it does. A respondent from North Carolina states that the process is also intended to provide a more independent role for the legislature in budgets. Other reasons for the adoption of the consensus revenue process, according to the respondents, are to use the intellectual resources from economists who work for the governor and legislature, enhance communication about revenue developments and forecasts, give legislators more influence in revenue forecasts, increase the credibility of revenue forecasts, increase revenue forecasting transparency, and overcome the distrust on the part of the legislature and the public that the administration was inflating the revenue forecasts to make the situation look better.

Implementation of Consensus Revenue Forecast

The consensus revenue forecast is a blanket term that covers a wide range of different arrangements. States have adopted different formats and processes. Even the term "consensus" has different meanings. In general, it means that the participants will discuss and come to a unanimous agreement about the economic and revenue forecasts, but this agreement can differ from state to state. The author finds that in North Carolina like in many other states, consensus means 100 percent agreement, but in Rhode Island, the consensus is sometimes reached through negotiation by splitting the difference. Appendix provides a detailed description of the consensus revenue forecasting processes in several states. This section highlights several implementation aspects—its legal basis, who participates, what to forecast, and its binding ability.

Louisiana has constitutional amendment to require the consensus process. Fifteen out of twenty-one states passed statutes specifying the structure and use of consensus revenue forecasting (see Table 17.1). It is common that a consensus revenue forecast conference is held at least twice a year, one in winter for governors to prepare their proposed budgets and one in spring for legislative appropriations. The conferences are open to the public. Conference principals (voting members) usually include one or more representative(s) from the governor's office, the House of Representative, and the Senate. Although the conference principals are responsible for the final estimate of the state economic outlooks, which are used to project revenues, they get inputs from a wide range of conference presenters, including relevant revenue departments and agencies and their economists, economists from universities and private businesses, personnel from the key local industries, and even the Federal Reserve offices. The number of principals varies from state to state (see Table 17.2). Delaware has thirty-five principals, whereas Iowa has only three.

In Missouri, Wyoming, Indiana, and North Carolina, there are no legal provisions to require the use of consensus revenue forecasts. The practice is less formal, usually based on an informal agreement between the governor's office and the legislature. North Carolina has worked under an informal consensus process since 1975. Wyoming started to use it in 1983 with a mutual agreement signed by the governor and the legislature. It is well structured at present. Missouri started to use the process in the early 1990s, and there were no written guidelines specifying when to reach an agreement and how to develop the forecast. In the past few years, Missouri has established the current tradition of holding a series of meetings in late fall to develop a consensus forecast.

Survey results indicate that the final consensus revenue forecasts are binding in 20 states. They are the official forecasts. Governors and legislatures have to use them as the basis for their budget proposals and fund appropriations. For example, in Florida, if the conference principals cannot come to a unanimous agreement, there will not be any official revenue forecasts. Consensus revenue forecasts are not binding in six states. For example, New York uses consensus revenue forecasts.

Table 17.2 Participants in Consensus Revenue Forecasting Conference

States	*Participating Members*
Delaware	Delaware Economic & Financial Advisory Council: 35 members appointed by the governor including members of the House, Senate, and cabinet; Office of the Controller General; private sector and university representatives
Florida	General REC: one representative from the staffs of the governor's office, House, Senate, and joint Legislative Management Committee
Indiana	Revenue Forecast Technical Committee: fiscal analysts of the four caucuses, governor's designee, and the chief revenue forecaster from the State Budget Agency; Economic Forecast Committee: economists from Ball State University and Indiana University and from private industry
Iowa	The REC: legislative fiscal director, governor or designee and a nonstate employee (agreed by the other two members)
Kansas	CREG: Department of Revenue, governor's Division of the Budget, Legislative Research Department, and three consulting economists from three different state universities
Kentucky	Consensus Revenue Group (six to seven members chaired by the Secretary of Finance): four university economists, appropriations and revenue staff administrator, Executive Financial Management and Economic Analysts, and staff member (revenue estimating)
Louisiana	REC: governor or designee, Senate president or designee, speaker of the House or designee, faculty member of a Louisiana university or college
Maine	Revenue Forecasting Committee: state budget officer, state tax assessor, state economist, university economist, director of Fiscal and Program Review Office
Maryland	Board of Revenue Estimates: state comptroller, state treasurer, secretary of budget and planning
Massachusetts	State Department of Revenue, House, and Senate committees on Ways and Means
Michigan	Consensus Revenue Estimating Committee: director of HFA, director of SFA, director of the Department of Management and Budget, or state treasurer
Mississippi	Tax Commission, University Research Center, state treasurer, Department of Finance and Administration, Legislative Budget Office
Missouri	House and Senate appropriations staffs, Division of Budget and Planning (and governor), and staff from University of Missouri
Nebraska	Economic Forecasting Advisory Board: five legislative appointees and four gubernatorial appointees
New Hampshire	Conference Committee: four representatives from the legislature, three from the executive branch, two from academia, and three from business

Table 17.2 (continued)

States	*Participating Members*
New Mexico	Taxation and Revenue Department economists, Department of Finance and Administration economists, legislative Finance Committee economists, and Highway and Transportation Department economists
New York	Division of the Budget, Office of Fiscal Planning, Assembly Ways and Means Committee, and Senate Finance Committee
North Carolina	Legislative fiscal office, State Budget Office and Management
North Dakota	Tax and finance legislators, legislative fiscal officer, director of Office of Management and Budget (OMB), and analysts
Rhode Island	Consensus Revenue Estimating Conference: House Fiscal Advisor, Senate Fiscal Advisor, and State Budget Director
South Carolina	Board of Economic Advisors: one appointment by governor to serve as chair, one appointment by the chair of the Senate Finance Committee, one by the House Ways and Means Committee, and the designated representative of the Department of Revenue and Taxation
Tennessee	State Funding Board: Executive—governor, commissioner of finance and administration; legislative—comptroller, treasurer, and secretary of state
Utah	The Revenue Assumptions Committee: members from governor's office, the Legislative Fiscal Agency, the Tax Commission, and economists from the university and business sector
Vermont	Emergency Board: governor and four chairs of money committees in the legislature
Virginia	Governor's Advisory Council on Revenue Estimates; Advisory Board of Economics
Washington	Economic and Revenue Forecast Council (six members): two appointed by the governor and two each appointed by the legislature from caucus of the Senate and House
Wyoming	CREG: legislature—Legislative Service Office budget or fiscal manager; Executive—Economic Analysis Administration; representatives from state auditor and state treasurer; superintendent of public education, director of Department of Revenue, state geologist, oil and gas commissioner; economics professor from University of Wyoming and representatives from state auditor's office, Department of Revenue, Department of Education, and the state treasurer's office

Source: From Survey conducted by the author during September 2006–March 2007 among the revenue forecasting personnel in the twenty-seven consensus revenue forecasting user states; National Conference of State Legislatures, 1997, http:// www.ncsl.org/programs/fiscal/lbp98sum.htm. (accessed August 29, 2006); Government Performance Project, 2005, http://results.gpponline.org/ (accessed October 1, 2006); and state government Web sites.

Various offices from both legislative and executive branches participate in the process. If the two sides—the governor and the legislature—cannot come to an agreement, the governor's forecast is used as the official revenue forecast (Government Performance Project 2005). Tennessee uses a modified consensus revenue forecast. The State Funding Board presents the governor with a range of estimates (usually within ±0.25 percent) for the governor and legislators to choose (Government Performance Project 2005). Even if the consensus revenue forecasts are not binding, they may well be accepted in states like Maryland and Mississippi.

Consensus forecasts usually include forecasting the national economy, state economy, and state revenue. Several states such as Florida and New Mexico also use it to project expenditures in certain areas. In Michigan, the process is informally applied to the estimate of the number of pupils in the state's K-12 schools. Florida also uses it for demography, state employee health insurance, Medicaid, actuarial assumptions, and state casualty self-insurance. On the revenue side, almost all the states use it to project general fund revenues. At least nine states, including Florida, Louisiana, Maryland, Michigan, New York, South Carolina, and Vermont, also use it for other funds. For example, New York uses it to estimate tax receipts for all funds and lottery receipts. South Carolina uses it for lotteries and educational improvement funds. Vermont uses it for transportation, education, and health access trust funds. Wyoming uses it for all funds. Table 17.1 presents the funds that the consensus revenue forecasts cover in each state.

The Accuracy of Consensus Revenue Forecasts

As stated earlier, there are two major reasons for the 27 states to adopt consensus revenue forecasts—to provide a single consensus revenue estimate to aid in the budgeting process and to improve revenue forecast accuracy. In general, survey respondents state that consensus revenue forecasts achieve the first purpose reasonably well. It takes the politics out of the revenue forecast process. Governors and legislatures have accepted and are pleased with the process. However, occasionally, disagreements cannot be removed. A good example is Missouri's fiscal year (FY) 2004 budget. Owing to ideological differences, in the 2003 legislative session, the Republican-controlled General Assembly used original revenue forecast, which was more "optimistic" than the revised January forecast, to defeat the Democratic governor's revenue measures. Overall, consensus revenue forecasts eliminate the disagreement about how much is available to spend and allow the lawmakers to focus on policy issues.

In the remaining of this section, the author will explore whether consensus revenue forecasts have improved forecast accuracy from three angles. In addition to reviewing the limited existing literatures, the author will examine the survey results from state revenue forecasting personnel and compare forecast errors of the states that adopt consensus revenue forecast to those that do not use the process using the data from FY 2002 to FY 2004.

Table 17.3 Accuracy of Consensus Revenue Forecasts: Revenue Forecasters' Perspective

Ratings	1	2	3	4	5	Others[a]	Missing
Frequency	1	1	6	6	2	2	3

[a] This includes answers such as consensus revenue forecast is not to improve revenue accuracy but to take politics out of the process.

Note: The question asks, "To what extent has the consensus revenue forecasts have improved forecast accuracy?" Marked on a 1–5 scale, where 1 means "not at all" and 5 means "greatly."

Perspective of Revenue Forecast Personnel

In the survey, the author asked the respondents the following question—To what degree has the consensus revenue forecasts improved the forecast accuracy? Marked on a 1–5 scale, where 1 means "not at all" and 5 means "greatly." The results are reported in Table 17.3. As shown, six of the nineteen respondents agreed that the process had improved revenue forecast accuracy; two agreed that the process had greatly improved accuracy; and six remained neutral. Only two respondents stated that the process had not improved revenue accuracy, but one of the two stated that the process in theory could improve the process, although the way it has been implemented has not. Overall, the results revealed that more state revenue forecasters believed consensus revenue forecasts had improved revenue forecast accuracy in their states.

The findings may contain subjective judgment because it basically shows the perception of the revenue forecasters. The fact that they are familiar with the performance of the consensus revenue forecasts in their states can reduce this concern. To further address this concern, the author compared the actual forecast errors of the states that employ consensus revenue forecast to the actual forecast errors of those that do not use consensus process (the author will refer to them as users and nonusers in the following discussion).

Comparing the Actual Forecast Errors

The author used data from the Government Performance Project (2005) report. GPP rated each state in terms of "money," "people," "infrastructure," "information," and "agencies." Under "long-term outlook," there is the "money" section where GPP provides the actual forecast errors for each state during FY 2002–2004. The author recorded the forecast errors for all the states for the three fiscal years FY 2002–2004 in Table 17.4 columns III–V, respectively. Because revenue forecast errors less than 5 percent are common (Smith and Lynch 2004), the author uses 5 percent forecast error as a threshold to evaluate forecast accuracy. The author calculated the number

Table 17.4 Comparing Actual Revenue Forecast Errors: Consensus Revenue Forecast Users versus Nonusers

		Revenue Forecast Errors (FY 2002–2004)			
States	*User or Nonuser*	*FY 2002*	*FY 2003*	*FY 2004*	*Number of Years with Errors Greater Than 5 Percent*
I	II	III	IV	V	VI
Alabama	No	NA	NA	NA	NA
Alaska	No	NA	−12.5 percent	NA	1/1
Arizona	No	11.5	0.7	6	2/3
Arkansas	No	NA	NA	NA	NA
California	No	Erratic[a]			Erratic[a]
Colorado	No	Erratic[a]		4.7 percent	1/2
Connecticut	No	5	3	2	13
Delaware	Yes	−2.6	On target[a]	8.3 percent	1/3
Florida	Yes	2 percent since 1993			0/3
Georgia	No	2	8.9	0.8	1/3
Hawaii	No	5	0.95	On target[a]	0/3
Idaho	No	17.6	9.2	13.6	3/3
Illinois	No	NA	NA	NA[b]	NA
Indiana	Yes	−8.8	0.9	0.7	1/3
Iowa	Yes	−7.5	−1	0.9	1/3
Kansas	Yes	11	8	3	2/3
Kentucky	Yes	9	15	3.7	2/3
Louisiana	Yes	0.8	1.5	−4.4	0/3
Maine	Yes	5	2.8	2.4	0/3
Maryland	Yes	1.9	2.1	2.65	0/3
Massachusetts	Yes	Erratic[a]			Erratic[a]
Michigan	Yes	3	2.5	4.3	0/3
Minnesota	No	−8.5	2	1.2	1/3
Mississippi	Yes	−3	−15	6	2/3
Missouri	Yes	10	NA	4	1/2
Montana	No	5.6	3	NA	1/2
Nebraska	Yes	−10	4	NA	1/2
Nevada	No	−9	−10	NA	2/2
New Hampshire	Yes	3	0.2	−2.4	0/3
New Jersey	No[c]	10	5	2.9	1/3
New Mexico	Yes	0.3	1.3	1.4	0/3
New York	Yes	0.9	6.2	1.4	1/3
North Carolina	Yes	5.7	3.7	NA	1/2
North Dakota	Yes	NA[d]	NA	NA	NA
Ohio	No	2.1	0.05	On target[a]	0/3
Oklahoma	No	8.6	11.4	−4.9	2/3
Oregon	No	17.1	5.4	2.7	2/3

Table 17.4 (continued)

		Revenue Forecast Errors (FY 2002–2004)			
States	*User or Nonuser*	*FY 2002*	*FY 2003*	*FY 2004*	*Number of Years with Errors Greater Than 5 Percent*
Pennsylvania	No	4.8	2.2	1.2	0/3
Rhode Island	Yes	1.1	1.9	1.3	0/3
South Carolina	Yes	10.9	10.1	1.5	2/3
South Dakota	No	1.9	1.6	1.6	0/3
Tennessee	Yes	−2	0.9	2.4	0/3
Texas	No	NA	Over 15 percent[e]		1/1
Utah	Yes	−3.3	7.2	7.2	2/3
Vermont	Yes	8.4	1.9	−7.9	2/3
Virginia	Yes	Fair accurate[a]	NA	NA	0/1
Washington	Yes	3.8	0.7	3.1	0/3
West Virginia	No	−0.85	0.45	−4.1	0/3
Wisconsin	No	1.8	1.8	1.4	0/3
Wyoming	Yes	−5.9	−1.6	−9.1	2/3
		All less than 5 percent[f]	Greater than 5 percent in one year[g]	Greater than 5 percent in two years[h]	All greater than 5 percent[i]
Summary	Number of users	11	7	7	1
	Number of nonusers	6	6	3	5

[a] GPP (2005) report does not give the specific forecasting errors. It used the words—erratic, on target, or fairly accurate—for these states.

[b] According to GPP's report (2005), Illinois has improved the accuracy of estimating revenue in the past three years although no specific data is provided.

[c] According to Government Performance Project (2005), New Jersey applies some principle of consensus revenue forecasting although it does not use consensus revenue forecasting.

[d] North Dakota has a biennial budget. Legislators meet only once in alternate years, which makes the estimate accuracy difficult. Government Performance Project (2005) did not specify the errors.

[e] Texas had a total revenue shortfall of $9.9 billion for the biennium of FY 2004–2005. According to NASBO's State Fiscal Condition of 2005, Texas' General Revenue for that biennium was $29,659 million.

[f] This includes those states whose value in column VI is 0/3 and 0/1

[g] This includes those states whose value in column VI is 1/2 and 1/3.

[h] This includes those states whose value in column VI is 2/3.

[i] This includes those states whose value in column VI is 3/3, 2/2, 1/1, and "erratic."

Source: Data for each state is from the section entitled "Long-term Outlook" in Government Performance Project, 2005, http://results.gpponline.org/.

of years (out of the three) in which states made forecast errors greater than 5 percent and presented this ratio in Table 17.4 column VI. If a state had forecast errors greater than 5 percent in two of the three years, the author assigned a value of 2/3 to that state. If a state had forecast errors greater than 5 percent in three years, then the author assigned a value of 3/3 to that state. Then the author compared the number of years that consensus revenue forecast user states had forecast errors greater than 5 percent with the number of years of nonusers that had forecast errors greater than 5 percent. The summary results are reported at the bottom of Table 17.4.

As expected, 11 out of the 27 states, which used consensus revenue forecasts, made errors lesser than 5 percent in all the three years under examination. Only one of the user states made errors greater than 5 percent in all the three years. By contrast, five out of the twenty-three nonuser states made errors greater than 5 percent in all the three years, and forecast errors were lesser than 5 percent in all the three years in six states. This analysis indicates that the consensus process does contribute to the revenue forecast accuracy, although some nonusers such as West Virginia, Ohio, and South Dakota have achieved remarkable accuracy.

Readers may ask why West Virginia, Ohio, and South Dakota do so well even if they do not use consensus revenue forecasts? The reason is that many other variables influence revenue forecast accuracy, which the current analysis is not able to take into consideration. Examples are revenue structure and the duration of time between the development of revenue forecasts and its implementation. For instance, stable revenue structure in South Dakota helps improve revenue forecast accuracy, whereas erratic revenue forecasts in Alaska are due to the state's heavy reliance on oil-related industry whose market price changes dramatically. Although consensus revenue forecast is used in North Dakota, its biennial budget and the fact that its legislature is in session once in alternate years makes its revenue forecast accuracy difficult.

The existing literature has also identified other variables that have a statistically significant impact on revenue forecast accuracy. The number one factor is economic stability. Political pressures can also skew the revenue forecasting process. Political ideology is another factor (Wallack 2005). In conservative states, there is a tendency to lower revenue forecasts to lower government spending. Other factors influencing forecast accuracy include forecast frequency, the use of economic advisors, and the use of university consultation (Voorhees 2004).*

* The existing literature has found that the increase in the frequency of revenue forecasting is negatively related to revenue forecasting accuracy. There are two explanations. First, too frequent revenue forecast provides too much information. Second, revenue forecast frequency "may be an indicator of economic stability/instability with forecasters forecasting more frequently under conditions of economic instability" (Voorhees 2004, p. 666). The use of university personnel is associated with reduction in forecast accuracy. This may be due to the fact that states that use academic personnel have considerably less experienced revenue forecast staff. Those that have highly qualified staff do not have to use academic personnel and their staff outperform university faculty (Voorhees 2004).

Another way to test the effect of consensus revenue forecasts on forecast accuracy is to use a time-series analysis for each user state and compare the revenue forecast errors made before the adoption of the process with those after the adoption. The advantage of this approach is the elimination of other controlling variables. If data is available, future researchers might consider this inquiry.

Evidence from the Existing Literature

The inability to control other variables in this current analysis does not negate the findings. This analysis is consistent with the existing literature, which has concluded that when economic and political variables are controlled, the effect of consensus forecasting in improving accuracy stands out clearly. Bretschneider et al. (1989) found that like the balance of power, consensus between different branches is negatively related to forecast errors. Mocan and Azad (1995) found smaller revenue forecasting errors in states that use consensus forecasts and duplicate forecasts than those that do not use them.

Voorhees (2004) tested the effect of consensus revenue forecasts on revenue forecast accuracy using data from *The Fiscal Survey of States* (1989–1997) controlling other variables. His results show that the increase in the consensus variables leads to decrease in the forecast error. Wallack (2005) came to a similar conclusion. The degree of consensus between governors and legislatures in developing forecasts "has statistically and economically significant effect on estimates' accuracy and bias" (Wallack 2005, p. 3). According to Wallack (2005), the accuracy is partially due to the groups' superior ability to project economic changes that affect revenues, and the fact that consensus groups may have a balanced political view does not seem to contribute to the improvement of its accuracy. To conclude, consensus revenue forecasting in general has improved forecast accuracy.

Conclusion

This chapter provides a general description of the use of consensus revenue forecasts in the states. The implementation of consensus revenue forecasts varies from state to state in terms of its structure, legal basis, what to cover, and its binding abilities. The chapter also explores whether consensus revenue forecasting has improved the accuracy of revenue forecasts.

Consensus revenue forecasts have become the norm in the states. This is due to its advantages over nonconsensus revenue forecasts. It provides a common ground for state legislators and governors to budget their limited resources so that they can focus on policy issues. By using experts from both branches of government and from the academic and business world, the process usually produces more accurate forecasts. This, in turn, will give the public more confidence in government. The author will not be surprised if more states will adopt it in years to come.

The federal government also needs to consider incorporating consensus elements into its budget forecasting.

At the same time we should realize that consensus revenue forecast is not a panacea for forecast errors. Consensus revenue forecast has not and will not eliminate the inaccuracy of revenue forecast. The economic unpredictability, the politics of budgeting, and human bias and error will always remain.

What issues and challenges do consensus revenue forecasts face? The survey identified several of them. First, the process is time-consuming. Finding time within everyone's busy schedule to discuss models adequately is a big problem. It adds one more task to their calendar of events that must be completed to pass an on-time budget. This may delay the serious discussion of the budget in the legislative session.

Another issue is related to the different philosophies of committee members. Some want the best estimate, and some want the conservative estimate. One respondent states that the process, by its very nature, introduces a conservative bias. Above-average growth rates are rarely forecasted, even if the available economic data make such a forecast defensible.

Third, it is a challenge to find a way to reach consensus when there are genuine differences among the parties. To reach a genuine consensus, respecting others, willingness to compromise, thorough discussion and documentation of the models, and leadership are all essential. A commitment to leave political agendas outside the discussion is equally important.

Further, there is a small number of staff that prepare all the relevant information and have a difficult time to effectively pass the information to all the principals. Lastly, several respondents make it very clear that consensus revenue forecasts face the same challenges any other revenue forecasts face—how to handle the changing economy and how to predict it as close as possible.

Although it is not possible to address every challenge and issue, some fine-tuning can be made. For instance, state government can provide an adequate working staff. Efforts can be made to generate genuine discussions of the data and models by eliminating political influence, encouraging compromise, and providing leadership to the process. Learning can also take place through experience, including bad experience. Even if the consensus revenue forecasts go wrong, the forecasters can learn from the experience and do a better job next time.

Appendix: Descriptions of Consensus Revenue Forecast Process in the U.S. State Governments

The section "Implementation of Revenue Consensus Forecast" provides a general description of consensus revenue forecasting process. Because its implementation differs from state to state, the appendix attempts to provide detailed descriptions of how the process works in some states so that readers can have a better grasp of this approach. The following states are chosen because either they represent one approach of the implementation or they are unique in certain aspects. Three chapters in this book examine consensus revenue forecasting in Florida, Indiana, and Kansas, respectively. These three states do not appear in this appendix to avoid overlap.

Iowa

Iowa's consensus revenue forecasting is a model in the nation. The Revenue Estimating Conference (REC) convenes four times every year in July, October, December, and April. The conference consists of the governor's designee, the director of the Legislative Services Agency, and a third member agreed by the other two members. The state's Department of Management contracts with the Institute for Economic Research at the University of Iowa to develop economic and revenue forecasts. These forecasts are shared with the conference and used in determining the state's general fund estimates. The governor and the legislature are bound to prepare the state budget on the basis of REC estimates (Government Performance Project 2005).

Michigan

In Michigan, The Management and Budget Act of 1991 defines the state's consensus revenue forecasting process. The Consensus Revenue Estimating Conference is held twice a year in the second week of January and in the last week of May. Any of the three conference principals (e.g., the voting member) can request additional conference if the need arises. The conference is open to the public. The presenters include economists from the House Fiscal Agency (HFA), Senate Fiscal Agency (SFA), and Department of Treasury; experts from universities and business (e.g., analysts from automotive companies); and Federal Reserve members. Economists from the agencies will present their own independent economic and state revenue forecasts for the year and for the upcoming year. Others will present their economic forecasts. Five major components determined at the consensus conference include national and state economic forecasts; major state revenue and total General Fund/General Purpose and School Aid Fund revenue; compliance with the revenue limit; required pay-outs or pay-ins to Budget Stabilization Fund; and annual percentage growth in the basic foundation allowance.

The three consensus conference principals are the State Budget Director or State Treasurer, director of the HFA, and director of the SFA or their respective designees. They will review forecasts and all inputs from the conference presenters and work to reach a unanimous agreement. The governor uses the January forecast to propose his or her budget. The May forecast serves as the base for the appropriations. The legislative and executive branches are constantly kept informed of the available revenue through various ways including an HFA quarterly report (Ross 2001).

Missouri

In Missouri, the consensus revenue forecasting process started in the early 1990s. It is an informal process. There are no written guidelines mandating when an agreement must be reached or how the forecast must be developed. However, the tradition has been established in the past several years. Late in autumn, a series of meetings are held to develop a consensus forecast. Currently, the staff of the Division of Budget & Planning, the appropriations staff of the House of Representatives and Senate, and staff from the University of Missouri independently develop revenue forecasts based on the current economic outlook. The forecasts include a revision of the forecast of the current fiscal year (which ends June 30) and the following fiscal year, so forecasts are completed over an 18-month time frame (Missouri's response to author's survey conducted during September 2006–March 2007 among the revenue forecasting personnel in the twenty-seven consensus revenue forecasting user states).

New York

The consensus revenue forecasting in New York is not binding. Various agencies are involved in the process, including the Division of the Budget, Office of Fiscal Planning, legislative Ways and Means, and Finance Committee. The governor prepares an estimate. The Assembly and Senate prepare their forecasts. Then a joint executive–legislative consensus forecast is conducted by March 10 every year. If they cannot reach a consensus, the governor's forecast is used as the official revenue forecast (Government Performance Project 2005).

Rhode Island

The REC convenes at least twice a year in May and November. It can meet any other time if a principal feels the need. There are three conference principals: the Budget Office director, the House Fiscal Advisor, and the Senate Fiscal Advisor. Within the Budget Office, its director and the economist are responsible for the development of revenue estimates for the REC. The other budget analysts provide valuable information and make projections for departmental receipts.

The Budget Office also works closely with the Rhode Island Division of Taxation and the Rhode Island Lottery (RIL) throughout the year. The Budget Office employs the use of economic forecasts and econometric data from Economy.com, a leading international economic forecasting company. The Rhode Island General Assembly employs Global Insight for similar purposes. The Budget Office uses no other outside organizations to assist in the economic forecasting or revenue forecasting processes.

The annual revenue estimating process begins at the REC in November of every year for the next fiscal year's budget. The REC is an open public meeting that lasts for a few days. The first day of the REC consists of testimony from the state's two economic consulting firms, Economy.com and Global Insight, and the Rhode Island Department of Labor and Training (DLT). The economic consultants provide the

REC principals and their staff with an overview and forecast of the U.S. economy and Rhode Island economy. DLT provides information on the Rhode Island labor market and its performance over the previous 12 months.

At the conclusion of the testimony and after all questions from the members of the REC have been answered, the REC's principals adopt the consensus economic forecast (CEF). The CEF consists of annual growth in Rhode Island nonfarm employment, personal income, wage and salary income, farm income, nonfarm business income, dividends, interest and rent, and total transfer payments. In addition, the CEF includes forecasts rates for Rhode Island unemployment, U.S. Consumer Price Index (CPI), the three-month U.S. Treasury bill, and the ten-year U.S. Treasury note. These forecasts are conducted on both a calendar and fiscal year basis and cover the immediate past fiscal and calendar years as well as ten years into the future. Typically, the REC adjourns the day after the adoption of the CEF. All principals must agree to the revenue estimates and each is bound to the conference recommendation about revenue estimates.

At the next open public meetings of the REC, testimony is received from the RIL, the Office of the General Treasurer's Unclaimed Property program, and the Rhode Island Division of Taxation to provide input about revenue in these areas. The REC adopts the official estimates for each general revenue source based on current law. These estimates form the basis for the governor's proposed budget and can only be altered (either raised or lowered) by changing current law. After the General Assembly receives the governor's budget, it holds hearings on all budget articles including those that involve changes in the adopted revenue estimates. In May, the REC convenes again to revise the revenue estimates adopted at the November REC based on current collections, revised economic forecast, and current law. Once the May REC adopts the consensus revenue estimates, the General Assembly cannot alter them without changing current law (Survey).

Tennessee

Tennessee consensus revenue forecast is a modified process conducted by its State Funding Board. The members are the state comptroller, the state treasurer, the secretary of state, and the finance and administration commissioner. The Board holds at least two meetings a year to forecast revenue. In December, the board presents the governor with a range of growth estimates (usually only ±0.25 percent). The governor and the legislature can then choose from the range to base their budget (Government Performance Project 2005).

Vermont

In Vermont, the ultimate official revenue estimate rest in the Board of Emergency consisting of the governor and four chairs of the money committees. Before the

Board can reach the consensus forecast, there are two major steps in the process. First, the executive and legislative branches each contract with private economists who help to model revenue in the general fund and transportation fund. The economists make detailed estimate for a twenty four month period and a general estimate for the coming eight-year period. They first work independently and then consider their differences and come to a consensus, which will be presented to the Board of Emergency. With economists' support, the executive (e.g., the Department of Finance and Management) and legislative branches will prepare their own revenue forecast and present it to the Board. The Board merges all the estimates into the state's official revenue forecast (Government Performance Project 2005).

Wyoming

Wyoming's Consensus Revenue Estimating Group (CREG) was created by a mutual informal agreement between the executive and legislative branches in the fall of 1983 as an effort to eliminate the divergent forecasts from the governor and the legislature. The process starts in August every year when the members of mineral subgroup of CREG meet preparing estimates of mineral valuations. The subgroup is made up of the director of the Wyoming Oil and Gas Commission, director of the Wyoming Geological Survey, supervisor of the Mineral Tax Valuation Division of the Department of Revenue, and CREG cochairmen. The minerals subgroup meets and finalizes the estimates of mineral valuation in late September. The entire CREG group meets in early October to review the minerals subgroup's valuation estimates and to forecast the balance of the revenue categories.

After the projections are completed, the State Legislative Office and the Economic Analysis Division compile the information into the annual CREG report. The CREG forecast is then used by the governor and the legislature as the official revenue estimates for preparing and adopting state agency budgets. The report is revised in January if necessary and then issued as the official revenue forecast (Consensus Revenue Estimating Group).

Acknowledgments

The author would like to express her sincere thanks to the survey respondents whose input and comments are critical for the completion of this chapter and for enhancing the quality of this chapter. The author would also like to express her thanks to the book editors, Dr. Thomas D. Lynch and Dr. Jinping Sun for their comments.

References

Bretschneider, S., W. Gorr, G. Grizzle, and W. E. Klay. 1989. Political and organizational influences on the accuracy of forecasting state government revenues. *International Journal of Forecast* 5(3): 307–319.

Ciamarra, M. 2004. Revenue consensus forecasting panel: A solution to conflicting revenue estimates. Alabama Policy Institute. http://www.alabamapolicy.org/press-2004-3-15.html (accessed October 2, 2006).

Consensus Revenue Estimating Group. 2006. A brief description of CREG. Department of Administration & Information. http://eadiv.state.wy.us/CREG/CREG.asp (accessed September 30, 2006).

Government Performance Project. 2005. http://results.gpponline.org/ (accessed October 1, 2006).

Howard, M. A. 1989. Good practices in revenue estimating. National Association of State Budget Officers. http://www.nasbo.org/publications.php (accessed June 2, 2006).

Mocan, H. N. and S. Azad. 1995. Accuracy and rationality of state general fund revenue forecast: evidence from panel data. *International Journal of Forecast* 11(3): 417–427.

National Association of State Budget Officers. 2002. Budget process in the states. http://www.nasbo.org/publications.php (accessed August 29, 2006).

National Conference of State Legislatures. 1997. Legislative budget procedures: Budget framework. http://www.ncsl.org/programs/fiscal/lbp98sum.htm (accessed August 29, 2006).

Niederjohn, S. 2004. State revenue forecasting in Wisconsin: A critical examination. Wisconsin Policy Research Institute Report 17(3). http://www.wpri.org/Reports/Volume17/Vol17no3.pdf (accessed September 20, 2006).

Office of Economic & Demographic Research, the Florida Legislature. No date. Florida's revenue estimating process. http://edr.state.fl.us/conferences/confprocess.pdf (accessed June 1, 2006).

Penner R. G. 2002. Dealing with uncertain budget forecasts. *Public Budgeting & Finance* 22(1): 1–18.

Ross, R. 2001. Consensus revenue estimating: The process. Fiscal forum: A legislative briefing. http://house.michigan.gov/hfa/PDFs/consens.pdf (accessed May 25, 2006).

Smith, R. W. and T. D. Lynch. 2004. *Public Budgeting in America.* 6th ed. Upper Saddle River, NJ: Pearson Prentice Hall.

Stinson, T. F. 2002. State revenue forecasting: an institutional framework. *Government Finance Review* 18(3): 12–15.

Voorhees, W. R. 2004. More is better: consensual forecasting and state revenue forecast error. *International Journal of Public Administration* 27(8,9): 651–671.

Wallack, J. S. 2005. Politics, institutions, and data quality: The highs and lows of revenue estimating. http://irpshome.ucsd.edu/faculty/jwallack/revest0805.pdf (accessed May 20, 2006).

Chapter 18

State Revenue Forecasting in the State of Indiana: A Consensus System in a Politically Divided State

John L. Mikesell

Contents

Introduction

Economist John Kenneth Galbraith did not have great regard for economic forecasts; this is proved by the following statement he is reputed to have made: "The only function of economic forecasting is to make astrology look respectable." Because of the accuracy problem, revenue forecasters in Indiana and elsewhere do face an uphill struggle as they make their contribution to the development of government budgets. And their task is a critical and necessary one, in spite of its difficulty. The revenue forecast process provides a fiscal baseline that will serve as a hard budget constraint for use in preparing and adopting the expenditure plan that will guide government operations in the forthcoming fiscal year, or indicate the possible need for an increase in tax rates when appropriate spending cannot be accommodated within available revenue.* A forecast that is too high leaves the government with an expenditure budget that cannot be executed without entering into debt or drawing down on state reserves (should they exist). A forecast that is too low causes taxpayers to pay more taxes than necessary for the delivery of state services. And without a forecast to provide a budget constraint, there is no guide to preparing the state budget. Therefore, the revenue forecast, despite any accuracy issues, provides a vital building block in developing a financial program that contributes to long-term state fiscal sustainability. What matters for budgeting is not so much whether the annual forecasts are right or wrong, because they will be wrong. What matters most is whether budget participants trust the forecasts because trust creates the hard budget constraint that is necessary for the budget process to function as intended and establishes whether, in the long haul, the forecasts facilitate fiscal sustainability. This chapter describes how the revenue forecast system in the state of Indiana develops that necessary trust and reports on the general forecasting accuracy of that system.

State revenue forecasts are frequently the source of controversy and political mischief because manipulation of the state budget constraint can be a tool for controlling the state spending plan. Both those interested in expanding the state government and those interested in constraining it have a stake in the forecast and that can create a conflict in producing a revenue baseline. A similar conflict produced the Indiana forecasting approach. The current system emerged in the mid-1970s to deal with the problem of competing and untrusted revenue forecasts designed to implement particular partisan fiscal objectives. Under the previous system (or lack of system), the governor and all parties in the state General Assembly developed their own revenue forecasts through a variety of unspecified and mysterious methods.† Each side produced forecasts that were driven as much by political agendas (a desire to spend more or to spend less, depending on the

* This chapter follows the standard distinction between revenue forecasts—the baseline under the existent set of tax laws and administrative practices—and revenue estimates (or fiscal impact estimates or revenue scores)—the estimated revenue consequences from a proposed change in the tax law. The process examined here deals only with the revenue forecasts. The Legislative Services Agency produces fiscal impact estimates for every bill.

† For preparation of the 1975 budget, the State Budget Agency (under control of the governor) prepared the official revenue forecast. The House of Representatives had a Democrat majority, the Senate had a Republican majority, and the governor was Republican. Many factions had their own revenue forecast and the legislative session focused about as much time debating the revenue forecast as it spent on appropriations.

political party or faction thereof) as by any realistic expectation that the forecast revenues would actually be collected. The forecast that fits the preferred political agenda and budgetary strategy would be the one brought forward by the particular process participant.

This environment of multiple forecasts meant that, effectively, there was no identifiable budget constraint for the state spending program. The governor had a forecast from the State Budget Agency (this office is now named the state Office of Management and Budget), and legislators used other revenue baselines of various pedigrees. Although some of the competing baselines certainly provided a better fiscal guide than others, that reliability was largely beside the point. Nobody knew which might be more reliable, and the lawmakers thus chose the one that best suited their own particular fiscal agenda. Multiple baselines effectively meant no baseline for budget development and no hard budget constraint to guide expenditure program deliberations. Baselines were ultimately produced through a process of negotiation among the competing parties, not through any definitive forecasting process.

Although the formal tools of forecasting are far from perfect, they are almost certain to be more reliable than the outcome of political negotiation. Economists, despite all the inaccuracy in their predictions, are likely to be more accurate forecasters than lawyers in politician clothes.

The Forecasting Process

The critical feature of the new forecasting process was to bring the political division in Indiana state government into a balancing act in a constrained way, to make the forecasting process as transparent as possible, and to drive the forecast on objective criteria as much as possible. The system also assigned clear responsibility for preparing the budget baseline. The reformers of the budget process created a single forecast that all parties in the budget process would use—governor and State Budget Agency from the executive branch and majority and minority parties in both houses of the General Assembly from the legislative branch—as they developed, deliberated, adopted, and executed the state budget.*

* Indiana is one of the few states with no legal requirement for a balanced state budget. The state constitution explicitly prohibits state debt (the state finances capital infrastructure with public authority debt), although allows debt for "temporary and casual deficits." The state did issue debt under that prohibition in the early part of the twentieth century, but that approach is no longer regarded as politically satisfactory. Although there is neither constitutional nor statutory balance requirement, the ethic of fiscal conservatism has been so strong in recent history that it is accepted that the governor will present, the legislature will pass, and the state will execute a budget that does not have a deficit. It will not borrow to cover operating expenditures.

The process establishes two distinct bodies: the Economic Forecast Committee (EFC) and the Revenue Forecast Technical Committee (RFTC). The two committees work independently and never meet, although in recent years there has been some preliminary and informal communication between the heads of the committees before either presents the final reports. The intention is to prevent one committee from influencing or biasing the work of the other in any direction. The reforms intended for the two committees to be professional, independent, and unbiased in performing their assigned tasks.

The two committees have distinct roles in the process:

1. The EFC is a somewhat informal group of private economists, some working for banks or other financial intermediaries, some from nonfinancial firms, and some from state universities. There are no state government economists in the group. All are volunteers. The EFC convenes late in the calendar year to provide calendar year, fiscal year, and quarterly forecasts for the remainder of the current fiscal year and the next two fiscal years. Their economic forecast currently includes U. S. personal income, Indiana nonfarm personal income, U.S. gross domestic product, and the implicit price deflator for gross domestic product.* The forecast is the consensus view of the members of the committee and is not produced from any state or national econometric model, although some members of the committee obviously have their own or have access to econometric models developed by others. Their forecasts usually work from forecasts of quarter-to-quarter rates of change, with those rates rolled together to create the annual forecasts. The EFC is structured to maintain objectivity and independence from any part of Indiana state government—and from the work of the RFTC.
2. The RFTC is responsible for translating the economic forecasts into forecasts for state taxes and miscellaneous revenues to the state general and property tax replacement funds. Its membership includes the governor's appointee (usually from the staff of the State Budget Agency) and four members appointed by the General Assembly, one each from majority and minority parties of House and Senate. Although the party of the governor always has sufficient members to win any vote, the committee functions by consensus and does not take votes (although it presumably could).† Meetings are open, formally announced, and members of the news media have attended them, although not in recent years. A number of former staff of legislative fiscal committees and the State Budget Agency also regularly attend the meetings, adding institutional history as economic conditions and tax structure changes.

* This is the data requested by the RFTC. At one time the EFC provided a forecast of Indiana personal income, but that has been replaced by nonfarm personal income. Presumably, the EFC would forecast other measures if requested by the RFTC.

† The author has been on the committee since 1976 and recalls no committee vote, except possibly to decide when to meet next.

> Because several of the committee members have served together for a number of years, a high degree of trust has developed within the committee and all have accepted the challenge of producing a forecast of state revenue that is as reliable as possible. Rather than having an agenda of high or low forecast to meet some legislative purposes, the common agenda has become one of forecast accuracy. The requirement of representation of both political parties insures a balanced focus and an absence of political agenda in the forecasts. Fortunately, politics has never shaped the discussions.

The forecasting work is scheduled to accommodate the Indiana state budget cycle. The initial revenue forecast is prepared in late November or early December, just as the General Assembly is organizing for its work during the spring months. The state is on a biennial budget cycle, with the legislature meeting annually in long (budget) or short (nonbudget or fixing-the-budget) sessions. The legislature adopts the biennial budget in the long sessions and may alter the adopted budget in the short sessions. The RFTC presents a revenue forecast that covers the current fiscal year plus the next two years when it delivers its forecast to the State Budget Committee (four members of the General Assembly plus the director of the state Office of Management and Budget). It is at this presentation that the forecasts of the EFC are added to the forecast methodology of the RFTC to produce the revenue forecast (although the head of the RFTC has actually received the economic forecasts a day or so earlier to insert the data into the methodology, with the possibility of reconvening the RFTC if the methodology produces strange results). The RFTC does not know what the economic forecasts will be while it is preparing its methodology.*

The formal logic is that the EFC presents the economic numbers to the Budget Committee and the RFTC tells the Budget Committee how to convert them into the revenue forecast, but of course the head of the RFTC has already done the math for them. The RFTC report to the Budget Committee analyzes the actual results for the recently completed fiscal year, reports the progress in the current year, presents the methodology proposed to translate the economic forecast into revenue for the current and two forthcoming years, and presents the forecast for those years.

This revenue forecast provides the context for General Assembly deliberations on the state budget and shapes the budget actually approved. It also provides the basis for the governor's budget recommendations. The governor's budget is developed within the constraint of a best guess of what the December forecast is going to be, based on a conservative rate of growth of revenue (somewhat more pessimistic in recession periods than otherwise). The governor's budget is delivered in early January, providing enough time to tweak budget requests to conform to the

* Some members of the RFTC do have graduate degrees in economics and can intelligently speculate on what the economic forecasts will be. But this is not a major concern of the committee.

official revenue forecast presented to the Budget Committee in early December. Thus, the forecast guides both the governor's budget and the legislative adoption of state spending programs.

The two-step forecasting process is critical, not only because it creates the aura of independence, expertise, and professionalism of the two committees, but also because it is consistent with a revenue logic that legislators understand: they accept the concept that there must be a linkage between economic conditions and revenue produced by the tax structure, and the two committees represent operations of the two parts of the system—the economy and the revenue generators. The structure avoids any "mysterious black box" in the forecasting system, thereby causing greater acceptance of the process and also providing a somewhat simpler approach to explaining errors at the end of the year. It is possible to dissect and report errors (economic forecast versus revenue generator), which is not possible with other forecasting techniques (univariate or error adjustment approaches, neural networks, etc.). The process helps establish the trust in the process that is needed if the baseline is to serve as a hard budget constraint.

On this cycle, revenue for each fiscal year is forecast in December, both one and two years before its start on July 1, as well as at midpoint. That gives the General Assembly a basis for building the biennial budget and for making adjustments along the way. There is also a forecast adjustment done in March or April, so the General Assembly has a last chance for adjustment before it adjourns for the year. These changes are usually modest and the forecast comes too late in the budget process to allow it to shape the budget policy in any significant fashion.*

In recent years, individual forecasts have been prepared for retail sales, individual income, corporate income, gaming, cigarette, alcoholic beverage, inheritance, and insurance taxes plus interest earned by the state and other miscellaneous receipts, the taxes that the general fund and the property tax replacement fund receive. Particular RFTC attention is given to retail sales, individual income, corporate income, and gaming tax revenue. These taxes amount to around 93 percent of revenue included in the forecast. In a few years of the history of the forecasting process, motor fuel taxes have also been forecast, but not recently (these are not general fund revenues).

Since the implementation of the process, it has produced the only revenue baseline used in development and adoption of the budget of the state of Indiana. Even without examining its accuracy, we can conclude that the process has achieved its principal objective. The budget deliberations are about policy, not negotiations over the revenue baseline.

* The head of the budget agency can summon the RFTC for special tasks. For instance, during a prolonged coal strike in 1978 that caused many Indiana businesses to shut down because of power shortages, the RFTC was convened to forecast the revenue impact of this economic shock. The committee determined that inventory buildup before the strike and likely business acceleration after the strike would leave no net impact, assuming the strike was not dramatically prolonged. This prognosis proved accurate.

Recent Forecasting Models

Forecasts have been done using simple annual regression models for the major taxes.* This is important because such an approach fits nicely into the logic of having the Budget Committee apply the methodology proposed by the RFTC to economic forecasts from the EFC to produce the revenue forecast. Ordinary least squares regression provides a straightforward scheme for doing this.†

The particular approaches for each tax are as follows:‡

1. Retail sales tax revenue is forecast from Indiana nonfarm personal income for the fiscal year and a dummy variable for 1996 through 2001 to account for the rapid creation and destruction of personal wealth in that period. That period was one of considerable difference in the income to sales tax revenue relationship and the RFTC lacked data to make allowance for the peculiarity any other way.
2. Individual income tax revenue is forecast from Indiana nonfarm personal income for the fiscal year.
3. Corporate income tax revenue is forecast from the calendar year real gross domestic product, the differential between corporate and individual income tax rates, and a dummy variable to remove atypical 2001 from the data series.§
4. Riverboat wagering tax revenue is forecast from Indiana nonfarm personal income, a dummy variable to account for periods in which dockside (non-cruise) gaming was permitted, and turnstile forecasts from the gaming industry. The revenue comes from two gaming excise taxes—admission count and gross receipts—that yield about 5 percent of state tax revenue.
5. Cigarette tax revenue is forecast from real Indiana nonfarm personal income, estimated cigarette prices in surrounding states, real Indiana cigarette prices, trend, and the real cigarette excise tax rate.
6. Alcoholic beverage tax revenue is forecast with separate equations for beer, wine, and liquor from Indiana nonfarm personal income, the real beverage price, and lagged beverage sales.

---

* For monitoring the forecast through the year, the annual forecasts are divided into monthly components generally on the basis of flows during the previous three years. On that basis, monthly year-to-date evaluations of the forecast are provided for the director of the Office of Management and Budget, the legislative leadership, and the news media.

† The committee has rejected simultaneous equation approaches because they would blur the distinct work assignments of the two committees and cause errors to compound in creating the revenue forecasts.

‡ The methodology, the forecast, and the monthly revenue flows are available on the Office of Management and Budget website: http://www.in.gov/sba/budget/revforecast05_07/rev_forecast_20051214_methodology.pdf.

§ Until recently, Indiana levied three separate corporate income taxes. Somewhat different methodologies were used for each and were combined to produce the total forecast.

The other categories of revenue are forecast by making judgmental adjustments to recent growth patterns, supplemented by information about administrative practices in the units responsible for their collection. Information from the departments responsible for collecting these revenues has proven extremely helpful in developing these forecasts. Forecasts for these other revenues are solely the work of the RFTC.

Forecasting equations are selected according to normal standards for estimating quality and goodness of fit, through out-of-sample forecasts done by omitting the recent year of data to see how a particular specification would have forecast that year, and by seeing how forecasts for the current year track against collections to date. Because the statistical performance of most specifications of the equations leaves little to choose from among the options, the choice of particular estimating equations usually involves a considerable degree of judgment as to which structural form and independent variables will move the forecast in the perceived right direction. When the RFTC feels that a particular equation seems likely to over- or underforecast, but still believes it to be the best of available options, it will partially compensate frequently when it selects the format employed for other parts of the forecast. The forecasting equations use nonfarm personal income rather than total personal income because, for Indiana, reported farm personal income does not seem to be a reasonable reflection of observed economic behavior.

Adjustments to the forecasts are made for changes in tax structure outside the model structure. These have recently included such things as changes in the statutory sales tax rate (a rate elasticity adjustment) and for significant revisions in the structure of the corporate income tax. Adjustments for changes in tax bases typically use fiscal note estimates from the Legislative Service Agency. These are increases or decreases to the result from applying the forecasting equation to EFC data and are shown in the methodology as adjustment factors.

Forecasting Results

The only meaningful test of a revenue forecasting process—beyond that of whether those building the budget accept its results—is the extent to which it produces forecasts that are reliable reflections of revenue available for the state to spend. Does the process yield an acceptable revenue baseline? Forecasts that are above actual collections will require the state to juggle its operations to accommodate a pace of operations consistent with those collections—and many of these choices in the middle of budget execution will be opportunistic and not good reflections of the choices that would have been made had an accurate resource constraint been known when the budget is being adopted. Forecasts that are below actual collections cause service provision to be below the amounts that taxpayers are paying for state services and create similar potential for misallocation of state resources. Hence, the forecasting process is testable according to the accuracy of its forecasts.

Tables 18.1 and 18.2 report the history of forecast accuracy for the four major Indiana state taxes since fiscal year 1989.* The tables focus on the forecast error in each year from forecasts done in December, one and two years before the start of each fiscal year.† These forecast points are important because they are before the legislative session begins, and thus, are most useful in shaping the fiscal discussions that occur in the session.

Some points are significant in the tables:

1. Two-year ahead forecast errors are generally higher than one-year ahead forecast errors. This is not unexpected because additional data are available in preparing the one-year ahead forecast and the horizon is not so distant.
2. Average error rates differ significantly across the taxes. The rates are lowest for the retail sales tax and highest for the corporate income tax. The corporate income tax error rates in some years are shockingly high. Not only are corporate profits volatile, but the state also has been changing its corporate tax structure in recent years and these shifts are difficult to account for in forecasts. Also, the traditional corporate form of business organization is being replaced by a variety of pass-through entities and this dynamic adds confusion to the forecasts.
3. Average absolute errors show similar variation, although they are higher than the simple averages because their calculation does not allow high negative errors to cancel high positive errors. One-year errors are smaller than two-year errors, sales tax and gaming tax errors are lowest, and corporate income tax errors are highest.

Table 18.3 provides a similar error report for total tax revenue, the significant forecast because it provides the baseline for the budget process:

1. The error two years ahead is often much larger than the error one-year ahead. This is both reasonable to expect and encouragingly shows the ability of the forecast process to learn from experience. The one-year ahead forecast has more data available and must stretch the forecast for a shorter period into the future.
2. Forecast accuracy is quite good for total tax revenue, the budget baseline. The two-year forecasts were within 4 percent of actual in nine of the eighteen years; the one-year forecasts were within 2 percent of actual in ten of the eighteen years. The absolute mean errors for two- and one-year forecasts were 4.2 and 1.7 percent, respectively. The median two-year absolute median error

* These data were graciously provided by Shah Towfighi, Indiana Department of Revenue. The gaming excise taxes have only been separately forecast since 2003.

† Errors are calculated according to the formula $(A/F_x) - 1$, where A = actual revenue, F = forecast revenue, and x = forecast dates one or two years before the start of the budget year.

Table 18.1 Actual, Forecast, and Errors for Indiana Sales and Individual Income Taxes, Fiscal Year 1989–2006

Fiscal Year	*Sales Tax, Actual*	*Sales Tax, Forecast, Two Years*	*Sales Tax, Forecast, One Year*	*Sales Tax Error, Two Years (Percent)*	*Sales Tax Error, One Year (Percent)*	*Individual Income, Actual*	*Individual Income, Forecast, Two Years*	*Individual Income Forecast, One Year*	*Individual Income Error, Two Years*	*Individual Income, Error, One Year*
1989	2065.9	2026.8	2040.5	−1.9	−1.2	1944.9	1851.0	1878.8	−4.8	−3.4
1990	2119.4	2188.6	2213.6	3.7	4.9	2089.5	2018.4	2074.0	−3.4	−0.7
1991	2183.7	2325.8	2236.3	6.5	2.4	2184.0	2204.4	2174.3	0.9	−0.4
1992	2245.9	2331.0	2309.7	3.8	2.8	2246.8	2260.1	2240.1	0.6	−0.3
1993	2368.7	2472.3	2396.3	4.4	1.2	2412.5	2386.8	2335.2	−1.1	−3.2
1994	2580.4	2483.5	2518.4	−3.8	−2.4	2541.9	2518.7	2511.1	−0.9	−1.2
1995	2786.1	2634.9	2727.2	−5.4	−2.1	276.8	2635.8	2653.9	−4.8	−4.1
1996	2942.6	2852.6	2924.4	−3.1	−0.6	2966.3	2806.5	2921.3	−5.4	−1.5
1997	3131.0	3036.4	2993.2	−2.5	−3.8	3196.5	3040.0	3055.5	−4.9	−4.4
1998	3209.1	3102.1	3263.2	−3.3	1.7	3476.6	3182.5	3361.8	−8.5	−3.3
1999	3396.0	3419.3	3435.9	0.7	1.2	3699.3	3501.9	3678.2	−5.3	−0.6
2000	3651.4	3554.6	3574.7	−2.7	−2.1	3753.3	3845.4	3823.3	2.5	1.9
2001	3686.8	3734.7	3700.0	1.3	0.4	3779.8	4085.1	4016.2	8.1	6.3
2002	3761.6	3904.0	3791.4	3.8	0.8	3540.8	4260.7	3731.6	20.3	5.4
2003	4172.6	3891.6	4302.9	−6.7	3.1	3698.0	3857.0	3697.9	4.3	0.0
2004	4721.0	4888.7	4716.1	3.6	−0.1	3808.0	3838.9	3780.4	0.8	−0.7
2005	4960.5	4937.5	4956.8	−0.5	−0.1	4213.2	3971.8	4102.1	−5.7	−2.6
2006	5226.3	5187.1	5174.1	−0.8	−1.0	4322.4	4308.8	4208.1	−0.3	−2.6
Mean error				−0.16	0.27				−0.42	−0.87
Median error				−0.61	0.14				−0.97	−0.98
Mean absolute error				3.23	1.77				4.59	2.37
Median absolute error				3.44	1.46				4.53	2.25

Source: Calculation from Indiana Department of Revenue (unpublished data).

Table 18.2 Actual, Forecast, and Errors for Indiana Corporate Income and Gaming Taxes, Fiscal Year 1989–2006

Fiscal Year	Corporate Income Tax, Actual	Corporate Income Tax, Forecast, Two Years	Corporate Income Tax, Forecast, One Year	Corporate Income Tax, Forecast Error, Two Years	Corporate Income Tax, Forecast Error, One Year	Gaming Tax, Actual	Gaming Tax, Forecast, Two Years	Gaming Tax, Forecast, One Year	Gaming Tax, Forecast Error, Two Years	Gaming Tax, Forecast Error, One Year
1989	758.5	722.2	734.2	−4.8	−3.2					
1990	753.3	774.1	758.7	2.8	0.7					
1991	647.2	810.2	653.0	25.2	0.9					
1992	672.1	677.4	669.4	0.8	−0.4					
1993	721.7	732.2	709.3	1.5	−1.7					
1994	798.6	761.2	772.6	−4.7	−3.3					
1995	950.6	805.0	868.7	−15.3	−8.6					
1996	982.1	910.2	1046.5	−7.3	6.6					
1997	999.3	1122.1	1062.5	12.3	6.3					
1998	1015.5	1081.6	1040.0	6.5	2.4					
1999	1044.4	1066.4	1044.4	2.1	0.0					
2000	985.3	1081.4	1057.9	9.8	7.4					
2001	855.3	1102.2	950.0	28.9	11.1					
2002	709.4	964.3	830.0	35.9	17.0					
2003	729.1	855.0	550.2	17.3	−24.5	430.8		427.6		−0.7
2004	644.7	560.5	608.3	−13.1	−5.6	601.5	550.7	593.9	−8.4	−1.3
2005	824.8	630.9	811.7	−23.5	−1.6	584.7	599.3	599.9	2.5	2.6
2006	925.4	754.6	810.7	−18.5	−12.4	589.9	641.0	596.7	8.7	1.2
Mean error				3.10	−0.50				0.91	−0.44
Median error				1.78	−0.20				2.50	0.21
Mean absolute error				12.78	6.32				6.54	1.44
Median absolute error				11.02	4.45				8.45	1.22

Source: Calculation from Indiana Department of Revenue (unpublished data).

Table 18.3 Indiana Revenue Forecasts, Fiscal Year 1989–2005: Actual, Forecasts, Error Rates, and Actual Growth

Fiscal Year	*Actual Revenue*	*Forecast, December, Two Years Earlier*	*Forecast, December, One Year Earlier*	*Error (Percent), Two Years Earlier*	*Error (Percent), One Year Earlier*	*Actual Revenue Growth (Percent)*
1989	5263.4	5027.9	5081.9	−4.47	−3.45	9.54
1990	5491.1	5397.3	5541.8	−1.71	0.92	4.33
1991	5536.0	5784.2	5521.4	4.48	−0.26	0.82
1992	5660.0	5703.0	5541.8	0.76	−2.09	2.24
1993	5970.1	5863.2	5906.1	−1.79	−1.07	5.48
1994	6432.2	6172.9	6246.6	−4.03	−2.89	7.74
1995	7067.1	6513.0	6793.3	−7.84	−3.87	9.87
1996	7513.5	7089.8	7469.4	−5.64	−0.59	6.32
1997	7970.4	7773.4	7789.6	−2.47	−2.27	6.08
1998	8421.3	8034.7	8334.5	−4.59	−1.03	5.66
1999	8883.2	8647.1	8882.8	−2.66	0.00	5.48
2000	9142.6	9209.2	9178.2	0.73	0.39	2.92
2001	9051.9	9641.7	9389.8	6.52	3.73	−0.99
2002	8708.9	9847.5	9005.5	13.07	3.41	−3.79
2003	9934.5	9249.5	9925.4	−6.90	−0.09	14.07
2004	10620.0	10739.6	10561.4	1.13	−0.55	6.90
2005	11436.2	11001.8	11312.4	−3.80	−1.08	7.69
2006	12060.6	11736.6	11712.7	−2.69	−2.88	5.46
Mean error rate				−1.22	−0.76	5.32
Median error rate				−2.56	−0.81	5.57
Mean absolute error rate				4.18	1.70	5.85
Median absolute error rate				3.91	1.08	5.57

Source: Calculation from Indiana Department of Revenue (unpublished data).

was 3.9 percent and the median one-year absolute median error was only 1.1 percent. Ordinary means and medians were, of course, even smaller because over- and underestimate amounts effectively cancel out; over time, the state would not have gotten into fiscal difficulty by accepting the forecasts completely in adopting its budgets.

3. The forecasts were below the actual more frequently than they were above—twelve times for the two-year and fourteen times for the one-year forecasts. Often, the overforecasts occurred in years of slow revenue growth, usually around a national recession.
4. The forecast process had problems in 2001 and 2002. The overestimates were large, absolutely and in comparison with prior experience. These years were recession-influenced and the forecasting process had difficulty dealing

with that. There were similar problems in the recession at the beginning of the 1990s.

5. Error rates are lower when revenue growth is higher. The correlation between annual revenue growth and the two-year forecast error is −0.9 and between annual revenue growth and the one-year forecast error is −0.7. Episodes of slow revenue growth create problems for getting the forecast right.
6. As expected, the error rates for total tax revenue are generally lower than for any of the individual tax forecasts. Only the sales tax forecasts show lower errors for certain statistics. Errors in specific taxes effectively cancel out in the total forecast.

Conclusion: Lessons from the Indiana System

The Indiana revenue forecasting system produces useful state revenue forecasts, which budget participants trust as their hard budget constraint for making fiscal decisions. The system is successful certainly not because of the high sophistication of the forecasting methodology because the methods themselves are quite simple, and certainly not because of the shockingly high degree of the accuracy of the forecasts. Those seeking sophisticated approaches as the answer to revenue forecasting in the budget process are looking in the wrong direction. *Trust and transparency* are far more important than other forecasting factors (although the general success of the Indiana system over the long term has made a major contribution in maintaining that trust).

Acceptance of the process and accuracy of results are interrelated. Early success in the 1970s helped establish the process and inaccuracy around the 2001 recession stressed the process. This concern shows in an editorial in the locally influential *Indianapolis Business Journal*:

> Indiana's method of anticipating tax revenue for building the state budget is superior to most others. It produces a generally accepted number lawmakers then use to determine their spending limits. This projection process does much to reduce the political gamesmanship inherent in other states where competing revenue estimates muddy the equation. It's just too bad Indiana's fiscal forecasters are wrong more often than television meteorologists. (Editorial staff, 2002)*

Recently, improvements in forecasting accuracy have dampened this criticism.

* At about this time, the auditor of state—historically, an office not involved in developing and approving the state budget—threatened to generate her own forecasts, a development that would have destroyed the consensus forecasting process and brought back the old era of negotiated budget baselines.

The important attributes of the system are as follows:

1. The process brings all interested parties into the forecasting process with attention to the need to have both Republican and Democrats present, regardless of political control of state instrumentalities at the moment.
2. The General Assembly and the governor agree to accept the forecast as the hard constraint in the budget process.
3. The process is completely transparent and open.
4. The process is stable and known to all participants in the budget process.
5. The process isolates economic forecasts from the revenue forecasts to preserve independence and further prevent political manipulations.

One former participant in the process writes, "The revenue forecast process has the support of the Budget Committee, the entire General Assembly and the executive branch because of the credibility that both the RFTC and the EFC have earned during years of service to the General Assembly and executive branch. The credibility has resulted from the independent, nonpartisan manner in which the committees operate and because the committees' forecasts over the years generally have been accurate. As a result, the General Assembly can devote all its energy to considering expenditure levels and expend none on disputes about expected state revenues" (Grew, 1997).

The technical modeling in the forecast process is not the critical element for service to the budget process, nor is it likely to be the critical element in other states as well. Most forecasting approaches, when competently done, will yield much the same outcome and all forecasts are subject to error.* What matters is that there are no political agendas shaping the forecast; that the process is open, transparent, and generally accepted; and that the participants in the budget process uniformly use the product of the process in deliberating the adopted budget. This is the great success of the Indiana forecasting process. Even more than the absolute accuracy of the revenue forecast to the budget process is that the forecast is accepted as the budget constraint for the development of the budget. Forecasts will be wrong. Hence, use of a reasonable number as the limit is more important than high accuracy and those seeking to improve budget process by finding a better technical forecasting model are simply looking in the wrong place.

So how good have the Indiana forecasts been in terms of their contribution to long-term fiscal sustainability? Of course the forecasts have been wrong. This is to be expected. However, from 1989 through 2006, if Indiana legislators had spent every dollar in the one-year ahead forecast, no more and no less, at the end of that period, they would have had an accumulated a surplus of $968.4 million or 0.7 percent of the tax revenue collected across those years. Not a bad record for

* In a conversation with the author a number of years ago, the distinguished economist Kenneth Boulding characterized economic forecasts in the following manner: "All forecasts are wrong. Including this one." Budgeteers expecting perfect forecasts will be disappointed.

creating a realistic budget constraint, certainly consistent with the objective of fiscal sustainability, probably better than could have been done with astrology and certainly better than would have been done by political negotiation. And maybe even better than Indiana television weather forecasters.

References

Editorial staff. 2002. Fiscal forecasters, legislators must sharpen skills. *Indianapolis Business Journal* 22 (Febuary 18–24): 16.

Grew, J. 1997. The fiscal perspective: Indiana's revenue forecasting process. *The Fiscal Letter* 19: 9.

Indiana Department of Revenue (unpublished data).

Chapter 19

Consensus Revenue Estimating in State Government: A Case of What Works in Kansas

John D. Wong and Carl D. Ekstrom

Contents

Introduction

According to Voorhees (2002, p. 175), "One of the most critical functions of a state government is the production of its revenue forecast." Unfortunately, Barry (2002, p. 3) points out that "The task of fiscal forecasters is as daunting as that of Sisyphus, the mythological characters cursed by Zeus to continually roll a large stone uphill, only to have it roll down again."

The National Conference of State Legislatures (1995) put forward a recommendation that states "establish a constitutional or statutory process to produce a revenue forecast that is binding upon the legislature and governor." Many states that followed this recommendation focused on a method of revenue forecasting known as consensus revenue forecasting. This technique employs a structured approach to enforce collaboration between the executive and legislative branches of government. Ten years later, the National Conference of State Legislatures (2006) conducted a study that indicated 22 state governments were using some form of consensus revenue forecasting (the rest of the states rely on more traditional executive or legislative branch projections or other techniques. In only 11 of these states does the official consensus forecast bind the budget. In 17 states (Alaska, Arkansas, California, Georgia, Idaho, Maine, Maryland, Minnesota, New Jersey, North Dakota, Oklahoma, Oregon, Pennsylvania, Texas, Virginia, West Virginia, and Wisconsin), the executive branch controls the revenue forecasts that are incorporated into the budget, while 11 states (Colorado, Connecticut, Hawaii, Illinois, Montana, Nevada, New Hampshire, Ohio, South Carolina, South Dakota, and Utah) use other techniques to arrive at official revenue estimates to include in the state annual budget adoption process.

Clearly, the act of forecasting revenues can be a contentious matter because revenues as a practical matter circumscribe expenditure decisions by establishing the limits on spending in the aggregate even when prudence, law, or politics may not require this. However, with the exception of the state of Vermont, all states have a requirement that mandates that budgeted expenditures do not exceed projected revenues plus accumulated reserves. If actual receipts turn out to be more than estimated, the opportunity for higher expenditures, which might otherwise have been budgeted, is foregone, at least for the short term. Even more contentious is the case when revenue is less than estimated, and budgeted expenditures must be reduced or other remedial action must be taken to remain within available resources. In recent years, this has been a common occurrence in many states.

This chapter presents an overview of the consensus revenue estimating process used in the state of Kansas where one of the coauthors has been a member of the six-member Consensus Revenue Estimating Group (CREG) since 1994. Past research has focused on assessing governmental revenue forecasting and has indicated that more attention has been paid to methodologies rather than institutional arrangements (Sun 2005). Thus, emphasis is placed on the specific techniques used in developing specific forecast rather than exclusively on the institutional aspects of this method.

Background

CREGs vary in size and scope among the states. Typically, membership is either drawn from elected and appointed officials in state government or may include outside consultants. Most frequently, this outside representation comes from state university or college faculty with identifiable expertise in public finance, macroeconomics, or forecasting. The size of the consensus group ranges from twenty-five in Delaware to two in several states. Typically, the smaller groups are balanced with an equal number of representatives from the executive and legislative branches. Most states include representation from outside of representative officials or staff from direct state government agencies, either executive branch or legislative. In none of the groups does the outside representation constitute a majority of the group.

The following sections provide a basic description of the budget process in Kansas and institutional arrangements for estimating state government revenues in the state. This discussion also includes consideration of the evolution of the system and ultimately a description of the current process.

Kansas Budget Process

In the executive branch, the budget process begins as soon as the legislative session ends. At that time, the budget staff prepares the comparison report. This report compares the budget recommended by the governor for the current and budget fiscal years (FYs) to the budget approved by the legislature. In June, budget instructions are distributed by the Division of the Budget to state agencies. On July 1, agencies use the budget instructions to submit a capital budget. Concurrent with the preparation of financial segments of the agency budget is the completion of agency strategic plans that are submitted with the budget in September. Agencies are requested to prepare one complete operating budget for submission on September 15. According to law, the governor cannot make a recommendation with respect to the budget request submitted by the judiciary. As a matter of policy, the governor treats the legislative budgets in the same way. Therefore, the governor includes these budgets as requested to present a complete state budget that accounts for all budget resources. Modification to the judiciary and legislative branch budgets, if any, is the responsibility of the legislature.

The individual budgets submitted by state agencies show program expenditures with appropriate funding sources for each program within the agency. Beginning on September 15, analysts in the Division of the Budget review agency budget requests. The Division of the Budget recommendations, based on these analyses, are provided to each state agency by November 10. The agencies then have ten days to determine whether to appeal these recommendations to the Secretary of Administration. Once the appeal process has been completed, the Division of the Budget staff prepares its presentations for the governor. The governor uses this information to make budget determinations for all agencies. The Division of the Budget then aggregates final recommendations and prepares the governor's budget report. During this same period, between September 15 and the commencement of the legislative session in January, the Legislative Research Department's fiscal staff is also analyzing agency budget requests. Following receipt of the governor's recommendations, legislative fiscal analysts begin updating their analysis for each agency to reflect the recommendations of the governor.*

The Revenue Estimating Task in Kansas

In all states, the general fund accounts for the general tax revenues, making this the focus of most revenue forecasting efforts. In fund accounting, earmarked taxes such as motor fuel excise taxes are deposited in special revenue funds and typically intergovernmental revenue as well as all enterprise revenue is accounted for in separate funds. Kansas is no exception because out of the approximately 1000 separate funds, the state general fund finances approximately half of all state expenditures. All functions of state government, except transportation, are supported in a major or significant way from the general fund, especially education, public welfare, general government health and hospitals, and public safety. Local units of government have a particularly heavy stake in general fund finances because approximately half of all expenditures made from that fund are in the form of state aid to various local units of government.

Revenues from most of the principal state taxes are credited to the general fund. This includes individual and corporation income taxes, retail sales and compensating use taxes, cigarette taxes, inheritance taxes, and insurance premium taxes. Interest earnings on idle funds are also deposited in the general fund. These tax and interest earning sources accounted for $5.1 billion or 93.9 percent of total general fund receipts in FY2006.

* Adapted from Kansas Division of the Budget (2007, pp. 237–248).

In every legislative session, estimated receipts and balances of the general fund are critical to the consideration of maintaining existing programs, financing new programs or expanding existing ones, and, on occasion, providing tax relief. The ultimate policy decisions affect all major functions of state government including, in recent sessions, transportation because there have been proposals to transfer money from the general fund to the highway fund and to shift the financing of the highway patrol from highway user taxes to the general fund.

The Revenue Estimating Process in Kansas before 1974

Immediately before the institution of the present revenue estimating procedure in 1974, the executive budget agency was responsible for the official or formal revenue estimates, which served as the basis for the governor's budget report. Frequently, however, the Legislative Research Department was asked to second guess these estimates, particularly when certain legislators thought that the executive's estimates might be too conservative and when these legislators advocated tax relief or financing of programs not recommended by the governor. This inevitably led to disputes between the governor and the legislature as well as among supporters and nonsupporters of the governor in the legislature. Following are three examples of such disputes:

1. In 1969, Governor Robert Docking vetoed the bill that established the Supplemental School Aid program and the appropriation of $26 million thereof. Both vetoes were overridden. He vetoed an additional $1 million for the School Foundation program, which was also overridden. These vetoes were made on the grounds that the legislature did not provide revenue to finance the expenditures, but a majority of the legislature apparently thought that existing resources were adequate or that the governor's revenue estimates probably were conservative.
2. In 1972, faced with declining balances in the general fund, Governor Docking recommended elimination of the federal income tax as a deduction on state corporation income tax and financial institutions' privilege tax returns. The legislature made disallowance applicable to only one tax year—partly because certain legislators disagreed philosophically with this means of raising additional revenue and partly because of some disagreement concerning general fund revenue estimates. (Disallowance of the federal tax deduction was made permanent in 1973 when the School District Equalization Act [SDEA] and other costly programs were enacted, e.g., state assumption of county welfare costs.)
3. In 1974, the basic budget controls under the SDEA were 105–115 percent. The legislature wanted to increase the "floor" 105 to 107, or at least to 106 percent, for FY1975, but there was disagreement with the governor and among some legislators about the sufficiency of revenues to do so.

> Consequently, a bill was enacted that provided that the "floor" would be 106 percent if general fund receipts in FY1974 were at least $523.5 million but less than $527 million, and would be 107 percent if receipts were $527 million or more. Actual receipts turned out to be $547 million; therefore, the floor was 107 percent in FY1975.

The preceding circumstances and other differences of opinion about revenue estimates resulted in the Legislative Budget Committee* in 1974, recommending that executive and legislative staff work together in the development of consensus estimates of receipts to the general fund to eliminate controversies between the two branches over the estimates. This procedure was started in the latter part of 1974 and in 1990; no law was formally enacted to codify the procedure; the clout of the Legislative Budget Committee was sufficient.[†,‡]

The Current Consensus Estimates: Participants and Procedures

Participants in the estimating process since its inception have been the Division of the Budget of the Department of Administration, two economists (one from Kansas State University and the other from the University of Kansas), the Department of Revenue, the Legislative Research Department, and two consultants who are staff members of the Department of Human Resources and the U.S. Crop and Livestock Reporting Service and who provide input on Kansas employment trends and the agricultural economy, respectively. This contrasts with states that have consensus groups composed of only direct appointees of the governor and the legislative leaders rather than defined staff members. Distinctive input from state university professionals is found in most consensus states despite an official absence in group membership and voting rights in decisions by the group. Their input in many states is limited to professional studies. In 1982, an economist

* The Legislative Budget Committee is a bipartisan committee of legislative leaders from both the House and Senate. Senators Robert Bennett, Ross Doyen, and Jack Steineger; and Representatives Pete McGill, Wendell Lady, Clyde Hill, and Pete Loux were members in 1974.

† K.S.A. 75-6701. Joint estimates of revenue to state general fund. (a) On or before each December 4 and on or before each April 20, the director of the budget and the director of the legislative research department shall prepare a joint estimate of revenue to the state general fund for the current and the ensuing FYs. (b) If before the final adjournment of any regular session of the legislature, any law is enacted providing for additional or less revenues to be deposited in the state treasury to the credit of the state general fund, the director of the budget and the director of the legislative research department shall prepare a joint estimate of such revenues. (c) In the event of a disagreement or failure to agree on a joint estimate of revenue pursuant to subsection (a) or (b), the legislature shall utilize the estimates of the director of the legislative research department and the governor shall utilize the estimates of the director of the budget.

‡ Adapted from Ryan (1983).

from Wichita State University was added to the group. There are then six voting members comprising the CREG. Because some of the organizations utilize more than one person in this effort, the typical CREG meeting involves between 12 and 15 individuals. Although there have been some changes in the group over the years, the group has remained rather stable for the years of its operation. CREG brings together professional economists with experience in taxation and economic forecasting, experienced researchers with expertise in statistics and economic analysis, and government administrators who provide perspective and experience. Although members come from quite different governmental units, the members have addressed their task in a professional capacity with little evidence that their organizational ties have influenced their positions.

Because of the diversity of training, experience, and orientation of the individuals who constitute CREG, differences naturally occur within the group in terms of forecasting approaches and methods. Examples of econometric, statistical, trend, and judgmental forecasts surface in the estimates of the individual forecasters. Although six separate estimates are initially developed, the group derives a consensus estimate from this, which represents the combined best estimate of the group.

CREG actually develops a consensus, although each forecaster comes to the meeting with independent estimates. The meetings are closed; only group members and their staffs attend and no official records of meetings are retained other than the final estimates and the supporting evidence behind these estimates. The meeting involves developing an agreed-on estimate for each revenue source. No votes are taken; each forecaster defends his or her forecasts and has an equal opportunity to present information to the group. However, an individual with superior or more detailed knowledge about a particular source may in some instances exercise more influence on the final estimate for that source. The give and take of discussion produces an agreement—a number that each member of CREG can "live with."

CREG makes revenue estimates twice a year. Table 19.1 outlines the annual CREG estimating cycle. The annual cycle of forecasting begins with a meeting in October of each year to discuss economic conditions and trends, actual receipts compared with the estimates for the preceding FY and for the current FY to date, recent changes in federal and state tax laws that will affect revenues, and any other matters that are germane to the estimating process. Factors considered include estimated changes in the gross national product, Kansas personal income, rate of inflation, employment and unemployment in Kansas, and short-term interest rates. The group meets again in November to review estimates that each participant (except the two consultants) has made independently for every source of general fund revenue, and it puts together the revised estimates for the current FY and the original estimates for the following FY.

The consensus estimates are not merely an average of the estimates made separately by the participants. The estimates for each source of revenue are examined and discussed. Many times the estimates for a particular source are not far apart; therefore, a consensus can be reached quickly. When there is a rather wide

Table 19.1 Annual CREG Cycle

Timing	*Action*
October	Review economic trends, year-to-date receipts, and impact of legislative changes
November	Revise estimate for the current year, and make an initial estimate for the budget year
April	Review economic trends, year-to-date receipts, fall estimates, and revise estimates for current and budget years
Postlegislative session	Conduct internal postlegislative session adjustments in light of legislative changes

Source: Kansas Division of the Budget, *The Governor's Budget Report, Volume 1: Descriptions and Budget Schedules, Fiscal Year 2008*, Kansas Division of the Budget, Topeka, KS, 2007, 248. With permission.

divergence among the independent estimates, there is a more extended discussion of the justification for the various estimates, especially the extremes, and the consensus is based on what seems to be a reasonable estimate in light of the economic assumptions made and other factors considered by the group.

In March or early April, while the legislature is still in session, the group meets once more to determine whether the estimates for either or both FYs should be adjusted in light of developments since it last met. The purpose of this second conference is to take advantage of five months of additional revenue collections and data. Any adjustments are reported promptly to the governor and legislative leaders along with the reasons for such adjustments.

In 1974, the participants agreed that if they could not reach a consensus for any FY, the executive and legislative staffs would report their estimates separately. This has not happened because the parties have reached a consensus every year. The governor, although not required by law, has consistently used the consensus estimates in the budget reports and the legislature has accepted them. In fact, within a day or two after the November meeting of the estimators, the consensus estimates are made available to the governor and legislative leaders of both parties so that they can use the estimates for fiscal and program planning before the next legislative session.

Traditionally, there is also a third revision of the forecasts made after the end of the legislative session. When legislation is considered, a fiscal note is prepared. The note quantifies the revenue impact of proposed legislation. These figures are typically prepared by the Division of the Budget in consultation with the Legislative Research Department and affected administrative agencies. The estimates provide data needed to revise the CREG revenue estimates as that year's legislation requires.

Also after the end of the legislative session, estimates are made for the FY that will begin more than a year later. These figures form the basis of the Division of the Budget instructions to state agencies regarding their funding requests for that FY. This session does not involve adjusting existing estimates for the current or subsequent FY. Its sole purpose is to provide guidance to the Division of the Budget.

Forecasting Techniques

This section provides a review of the specific techniques used by individual CREG members during the process of economic forecasting and then revenue forecasting. This includes consideration of alternative income concepts, adjusting receipts, elasticity, modifications, and timing.

National Economic Forecasts

A large number of national economic forecasts are available from private consulting firms, financial institutions, and federal and state governmental organizations and universities. Kansas subscribes to Moody's Economy.com forecasting services. In addition, various members of CREG have access to other services also. The group shares the information and provides the input for national economic forecasts prepared by CREG. They pay particular attention to those forecasters who have superior records of past accuracy and who provide detailed estimates for economic variables particularly significant for the economy of Kansas. These forecasts involve both yearly and quarterly predictions.

Kansas Economic Forecasts

Armed with a national economic forecast, the next step in revenue estimation is to develop a Kansas economic forecast involving the stepping down of national estimates to the state. This entails postulating and quantifying the historical relationship between the performance of the nation and the state, then projecting the state's economy from the national forecast.

Additionally, state forecasting entails examining the trends of important economic magnitudes in Kansas. By focusing on Kansas, the forecasters draw a somewhat different picture from the national or a step-down picture. The final step in Kansas economic forecasting then combines the two pictures into one view of Kansas' future.

They direct particular concern to Kansas employment; unemployment; agricultural prices, output, and income; the general price level; total personal income; and the components of personal income for the forecast period. They publish a summary of the state and national forecasts annually in the governor's economic report, and summarize the report on the revenue estimates that CREG provides to the Legislative Budget Committee and the governor.

Three Income Measures

Kansas personal income estimates are available from the U.S. Department of Commerce—quarterly, yearly, and by income type. This measure of the total income received by Kansans is an excellent measure for the objectives of that department, but it is not a good tool for estimating tax revenues. The fact is that, both conceptually and empirically, personal income is a rather poor predictor of individual income tax collections and of most sales or excise taxes. For example, personal income tends to be a somewhat imprecise predictor of individual income tax revenues because the definition of personal income does not match the definition of the individual income tax base. This incongruity contributes to the underestimation of individual income tax receipts during the late 1990s because the definition of personal income does not include capital gains that were a significant component of the robust economic expansion during that time.

To predict these revenues more accurately, forecasters developed two different income measures: income flow and money flow. Income flow measures the flow of dollars that, depending on a taxpayer's particular situation, could lead to an income tax obligation. Money flow measures spendable income before taxes and social security payments. Hence, it should be more closely related to purchases and, thus, retail sales tax collections.

The first step in the development of both of these flows is the elimination of the imputed income's portion of personal income. These imputations are properly a component of total income, but do not reflect income that is either taxable or spendable. The clearest example of what is eliminated is the estimated value of the housing services provided by owner-occupied dwellings—the figure is a part of the total income, but is neither taxable under the income tax nor spendable on items subject to the retail sales tax.

In the second step, forecasters remove certain nonwage and transfer incomes, such as employer-provided fringe benefits and transfer payments, from personal income to calculate income flow. Although these are a part of the income, they are not subject to the income tax. To the extent that individual Kansans receive money, these incomes are retained under the money flow measure. For example, compensation for injuries, welfare payments, and unemployment payments are included in money flow but not in income flow.

Finally, forecasters subtract social security taxes from the money flow (the individual neither receives this amount nor can he spend it), but they are retained when estimating income flow (the associated income is taxable under the individual income tax).

Adjusted Receipts

Although accurate data on historical receipts is available, this is flawed for the purpose of revenue estimation. Over the years, lawmakers made numerous changes to the Kansas tax structure: they added exemptions for some taxes, eliminated others; changed tax rates—both upward and downward; and changed the percentage of some of the tax collections that goes into the general fund. Thus, attempting to use historical data without adjustment in making future estimates is almost guaranteed to fail. For better estimates, forecasters must clean the tax data; hence, the need for adjusted receipts.

Forecasters take three steps when calculating a multiyear series of adjusted collections: (1) the tabulation of actual collections from each of the revenue sources of concern, (2) the adjustment of these collections for any changes in tax laws or administrative procedures that have occurred, and (3) the determination of the general fund contribution of each of these taxes in each year. In addition, the process of adjustment requires forecasters to select one year as the standard for all the three steps. This is accomplished by standardizing historic revenue collections based on current state tax laws, administrative procedures, and the allocated portion of each tax.

Each earlier year's collections are then recalculated to the current-year standard. In recent years, three types of legal and administrative changes occurred that necessitate adjustment: (1) changes in tax rates, such as the altering of tax brackets for the individual income tax; (2) changes in the tax base, such as the exemption of the purchase of some farm implements and residential utilities from the retail sales tax; and (3) changes in administrative procedures, such as the increased enforcement efforts by the Audit Services Bureau of the Revenue Department. Also some taxes, such as the bingo and tobacco products taxes, have only existed for a relatively short time. Nevertheless, forecasters must estimate what their tax receipts would have been had they existed.

Further, legal changes alter the portion of taxes that the law allocated to the general fund. For example, the motor and special fuel tax collections were once partially allocated to the general fund, although this is no longer the case. Also, the law changed the portion of the cigarette tax allocated to the general fund some years ago. The adjustment process eliminates any consequences of changes of this sort (Daicoff 1983, p. 18).

Elasticity

Having eliminated the revenue consequences of changing tax laws, administrative procedures and allocation portions, forecasters have produced a cleaned or adjusted revenue series, and economic analysis can begin. Economists have long employed the concept of elasticity to account for the relationship among prices, output, and receipts or expenditures. Because collections from a number of taxes, most notably the individual income tax, are dependent on income, the applicability of the elasticity measure is apparent.

Forecasters can calculate the income elasticity of each revenue source, thereby measuring the responsiveness of collections to income changes. Income elasticity is a measure of the responsiveness of a revenue source to changes in the level of personal income. An elasticity of less than one indicates that the revenue source is not highly responsive to changes in personal income. An elasticity of more than one indicates that the revenue source is highly responsive to changes in personal income. Forecasters can use two methods to compute income elasticities. The two-point method is computed by dividing the percentage change in receipts by the percentage change in income (Wong 2006, p. 14).

$$\text{Elasticity} = \left[\frac{\text{receipts in last year} - \text{receipts in first year}/\text{receipts in last year} + \text{receipts in first year}}{\text{income in last year} - \text{income in first year}/\text{income in last year} + \text{income in first year}}\right]$$

However, a problem with the two-point method is that its value is totally dependent on the values in the endpoint years. Therefore, if unusual circumstances exist in one or both of the endpoint years, the elasticity will be misleading.

With the trend method, forecasters use all values in the time period under consideration. The trend method is computed using a double-log regression of the natural logarithm of receipts as the dependent variable and the natural logarithm of personal income as the independent variable.

$$\text{In (receipts)} = \alpha + \beta \text{ In (personal income)} + \varepsilon$$

where

α = intercept term
β = slope term
ε = random error term

In a double-log linear regression, the coefficient of the slope variable is an estimate of the elasticity. Recently calculated personal income elasticities for the adjusted collections of Kansas general fund taxes are shown in Table 19.2.

Any tax that has an elasticity of greater than 1 has experienced a greater than proportional growth relative to income. For example, the income elasticity of the individual income tax is 1.21, implying a 1.21 percent collection growth if income grows at 1 percent. Total Kansas general fund tax collections, adjusted to current statutes and administrative procedures, exhibited an income elasticity of 0.97 for the period 1990–2006. Thus, a 1 percent increase in Kansas personal income produces a 0.97 percent increase in general fund tax receipts. If this relationship persists and lawmakers do not change the statutes and procedures, when personal income in Kansas increases, tax receipts for the general fund will increase at a slightly lower rate than that of the personal income.

Modifications

When forecasters consider revisions to estimates for FYs that are underway, collections to date are important. For example, if collections from the sales tax are running significantly behind what forecasters estimate, sales tax receipts for the

Table 19.2 Elasticities for Adjusted General Fund Tax Receipts

	FY1990–2006		*FY1997–2006*		*FY2003–2006*	
Tax Source	*Two-Point*	*Trend*	*Two-Point*	*Trend*	*Two-Point*	*Trend*
Property tax						
Motor carrier	1.04	1.09	0.75	0.70	2.45	2.07
Income and privilege taxes						
Individual	1.19	1.21	1.18	1.04	2.22	2.09
Corporation	1.08	0.46	0.86	0.12	7.88	8.91
Financial institutions	−0.43	−0.77	−0.39	−0.66	−0.01	−0.37
Estate tax	0.83	0.80	0.53	0.44	−0.09	0.34
Sales, use, and excise taxes						
Retail sales	0.92	0.91	0.82	0.73	0.67	0.62
Compensating use	1.15	1.22	1.14	1.07	1.18	1.57
Cigarette	−0.24	−0.21	−0.36	−0.38	−0.67	−0.53
Tobacco products	1.42	1.48	1.20	1.35	0.89	0.88
Cereal malt beverages	−0.56	−0.51	−0.40	−0.36	−0.61	−0.63
Liquor gallonage	0.45	0.42	0.65	0.62	0.87	0.60
Liquor enforcement	1.05	1.04	1.17	1.24	0.95	0.92
Private clubs	1.06	1.04	1.20	1.22	1.15	1.06
Corporate franchise	1.41	1.42	1.70	1.69	2.87	3.25
Severance	0.95	0.51	1.54	1.88	4.31	4.34
Gross receipts taxes						
Insurance premiums	1.21	1.13	1.39	1.40	1.26	0.93
Miscellaneous	0.96	0.98	0.73	0.68	1.06	0.80
Total	1.02	0.97	0.98	0.85	1.79	1.74

Source: Wong, J.D., *State of Kansas Adjusted General Fund Tax Receipts, Rates of Change, Elasticities, and Composition: Fiscal Years 1989 through 2006,* Division of the Budget, Topeka, KS, 2006. With permission.

current year would probably be reduced—unless there were good reasons to expect a greater than anticipated pickup in collections. Of course, any revision of current-year forecasts is likely to affect forecasts for future years.

Forecasters must make adjustments for tax changes within the FY. For example, if the Department of Revenue changes the withholding rates under the individual income tax on January 1 or the timing of collections, then the forecasters must modify the total collections for the year. Because major Kansas taxes depend on federal taxes, forecasters must be aware of changing federal tax statutes and procedures. This is particularly the case for the individual and corporation income taxes. CREG restricts itself to adjusting its estimates for federal changes that have been enacted although they have not become completely operative. However, they disregard federal tax law changes that are currently being contemplated. The group does not try to anticipate the federal legislative process.*

Forecast Results

Summarizing thus far, the formal meetings of CREG produce estimates of each of the revenue sources to the state general fund for the current and next FY, beginning on July 1. For some of the sources, such as agency earnings and interest earnings, they must rely on information obtained directly from the state agencies involved with these sources. They should prepare a public report to the governor and legislature shortly after the group completes its estimates. The next step is to develop the "spreads."

Spreads

The FY estimates are spread across the months by the Division of the Budget. Governing this activity is the historical relationship between monthly and yearly receipts. This automatically takes statutory and administrative payment requirements into account, such as April 15 for the individual income tax. Forecasters make further adjustment for deposit days at the end of the month because administrative procedures and the inability to deposit funds over weekends influence monthly collections. Finally, the proration method automatically takes any seasonality of receipts into account, such as retail sales tax collections from extraordinarily large December retail sales or auto sales in the spring.

Changing economic conditions should influence the yearly pattern of collections. However, because fiscal planning in Kansas concerns the ability of the state to finance its yearly expenditures, forecasters need to make only limited effort to estimate the monthly pattern of receipts and expenditures. The state's balances handle any monthly mismatch. The current and prospective low balances may require more concern with the spreads in the future.

Use

The estimated receipt numbers have obvious uses in fiscal planning. Because Kansas cannot budget a deficit, revenue estimates limit the noncapital expenditure proposals of the governor and enactments by the legislature. Budgeting in Kansas is restrictive in that planned expenditures cannot exceed beginning balances plus anticipated revenues—thus, the role of the receipts estimates. Because of this, the level of ending balances receives considerable public attention.

* Adapted from Daicoff (1983).

Track Record of the Consensus Estimating Group

An evaluation of the success (or failure) of the consensus estimating procedure can be made by examining the track record of the estimators. That is, how did actual receipts in a fiscal year compare with the estimates? Over the 32-year history of the Kansas CREG, the average difference from the original estimate has been $28 million or 1.1 percent. Statistically, the average difference between original estimate and actual receipts is zero ($t = 0.45$). The average difference from the final estimate has been $9.5 million or 0.3 percent. Statistically, the average difference between final estimate and actual receipts is zero ($t = 0.31$). This equates to a 5 percent mean absolute percentage error (MAPE) from the original estimate and a 1.2 percent MAPE from the final estimate. Agostini (1991) suggests that coming within 5 percent of actual receipts is a reasonable margin of error.

Since FY1976, original CREG estimates have been under actual receipts 19 times and over actual receipts 12 times. As might be expected, most of the overestimations occurred around and subsequent to a major economic downturn. The largest percentage departure occurred in FY1983 when actual receipts were 14.7 percent below the original estimate. The largest absolute departure occurred in FY2002 when actual receipts were $565.8 million below the original estimate. Since FY1975, final CREG estimates have been under actual receipts twenty-four times and over actual receipts eight times. The largest departure from the final estimate occurred in FY2002, when actual receipts were $211.9 million or 4.9 percent below the estimate. Table 19.3 shows the relationship between CREG estimates and actual receipts from FY1975 to FY2006. The adjusted original estimate is the estimate made in November or December before the start of the next FY in July and adjusted to account for legislation enacted, if any, which affected receipts to the State General Fund (SGF). The final estimate made in March, April, or June is the adjusted original estimate plus or minus changes subsequently made by CREG. It also includes the estimated impact of legislation on receipts.

Generally the original estimates, made some seven months before the start of the FY, are uniform but further from actual receipts than the revised estimates, which benefit from having been made four months into the year. Even in years when estimated total receipts proved to be quite accurate, considerably larger percentage "errors" were registered for some individual sources. Characteristically, one tax was overestimated and another was underestimated; the total benefited from the offsetting or compensating errors and was quite close.

Table 19.4 shows the average dollar departure of the estimate from the actual from FY1993 to 2006. The largest dollar overestimates were for individual income taxes, whereas the largest dollar underestimates were for retail sales taxes. Over this period, the preliminary estimates tended to understate actual revenues, whereas the session-year estimates tended to overstate actual revenues. On average, the preliminary presession estates were more accurate than the preliminary midsession estimates.

Table 19.5 shows the average percentage departure of the estimate from the actual from FY1993 to 2006. The largest percentage overestimates were for

Table 19.3 State General Fund Estimates

Fiscal Year	Adjusted Original Estimate	Adjusted Final Estimate	Actual Receipts	Difference from Original Estimate		Difference from Final Estimate		MAPE from	
				Amount	Percentage	Amount	Percentage	Original	Final
1975	—	614.9	627.6	—	—	12.7	2.1	—	—
1976	676.3	699.7	701.2	24.9	3.7	1.5	0.2	3.7	0.2
1977	760.2	760.7	776.5	16.3	2.1	15.8	2.1	2.1	2.1
1978	830.1	861.2	854.6	24.5	3.0	(6.6)	(0.8)	3.0	0.8
1979	945.2	1019.3	1006.8	61.6	6.5	(12.5)	(1.2)	6.5	1.2
1980	1019.3	1095.9	1097.8	78.5	7.7	1.9	0.2	7.7	0.2
1981	1197.1	1226.4	1226.5	29.4	2.5	0.1	0.0	2.5	0.0
1982	1351.3	1320.0	1273.0	(78.3)	(5.8)	(47.0)	(3.6)	5.8	3.6
1983	1599.2	1366.9	1363.6	(235.6)	(14.7)	(3.3)	(0.2)	14.7	0.2
1984	1596.7	1539.0	1546.9	(49.8)	(3.1)	7.9	0.5	3.1	0.5
1985	1697.7	1679.7	1658.5	(39.2)	(2.3)	(21.2)	(1.3)	2.3	1.3
1986	1731.2	1666.4	1641.4	(89.8)	(5.2)	(25.0)	(1.5)	5.2	1.5
1987	1903.1	1764.7	1778.5	(124.6)	(6.5)	13.8	0.8	6.5	0.8
1988	1960.0	2031.5	2113.1	153.1	7.8	81.6	4.0	7.8	4.0
1989	2007.8	2206.9	2228.3	220.5	11.0	21.4	1.0	11.0	1.0
1990	2241.2	2283.3	2300.5	59.3	2.6	17.2	0.8	2.6	0.8
1991	2338.8	2360.6	2382.3	43.5	1.9	21.7	0.9	1.9	0.9
1992	2478.7	2454.5	2465.8	(12.9)	(0.5)	11.3	0.5	0.5	0.5

1993	2913.4	2929.6	2932.0	18.6	0.6	2.4	0.1	0.6	0.1
1994	3040.1	3126.8	3175.7	135.6	4.5	48.9	1.6	4.5	1.6
1995	3174.4	3243.9	3218.8	44.4	1.4	(25.1)	(0.8)	1.4	0.8
1996	3428.0	3409.2	3448.3	20.3	0.6	39.1	1.1	0.6	1.1
1997	3524.8	3642.4	3683.8	159.0	4.5	41.4	1.1	4.5	1.1
1998	3714.4	3971.0	4023.7	309.3	8.3	52.7	1.3	8.3	1.3
1999	3844.7	4051.9	4113.4	268.7	7.0	61.5	1.5	7.0	1.5
2000	4204.1	4161.0	4203.1	(1.0)	(0.0)	42.1	1.0	0.0	1.0
2001	4420.7	4408.7	4415.0	(5.7)	(0.1)	6.3	0.1	0.1	0.1
2002	4674.5	4320.6	4108.7	(565.8)	(12.1)	(211.9)	(4.9)	12.1	4.9
2003	4641.0	4235.6	4245.6	(395.4)	(8.5)	10.0	0.2	8.5	0.2
2004	4605.5	4450.0	4518.7	(86.8)	(1.9)	68.7	1.5	1.9	1.5
2005	4490.5	4793.8	4844.3	353.8	7.9	50.5	1.1	7.9	1.1
2006	4834.0	5308.7	5394.4	560.4	11.6	85.7	1.6	11.6	1.6
2001–2006				(23.3)	(0.5)	1.5	(0.1)	7.0	1.6
1991–2000				98.6	2.8	29.6	0.8	2.9	1.0
1981–1990				(15.5)	(1.4)	4.5	0.0	6.2	1.4
Overall				(0.6)	0.5	7.6	0.3	4.7	1.2

Note: State general fund estimates are expressed in dollars (millions).

Source: Kansas Division of the Budget and Kansas Legislative Research Department, *State General Fund Receipts for FY 2007 (Revised) and FY 2008,* memorandum, Kansas Division of the Budget and Kansas Legislative Research Department, Topeka, KS, 2006. With permission.

Table 19.4 Average Dollar Departure of the Estimate from the Actual ($, Thousands) (FY1993–2006)

Tax Source	*Preliminary Presession*	*Preliminary Midsession*	*Presession Estimate*	*Midsession Estimate*
Property tax				
Motor carrier	687	562	504	570
Income and privilege taxes				
Individual	21,733	11,421	11,166	3,600
Corporation	7,245	(4,588)	6,912	(3,376)
Financial institutions	(567)	17	963	1,184
Estate tax	(7,538)	(6,538)	(6,850)	(2,871)
Sales, use, and excise taxes				
Retail sales	(11,829)	(17,439)	10,188	4,447
Compensating use	(1,331)	(665)	502	252
Cigarette	(4,228)	(4,787)	1,422	(53)
Tobacco products	(70)	(78)	(32)	(41)
Cereal malt beverages	36	16	32	(18)
Liquor gallonage	(74)	(224)	(7)	(149)
Liquor enforcement	(707)	(407)	(36)	101
Private clubs	(65)	(40)	(7)	26
Corporate franchise	(2,151)	(1,709)	(668)	(151)
Severance	(4,280)	(3,534)	(1,043)	(1,109)
Gross receipts taxes				
Insurance premiums	(242)	592	(1,363)	79
Miscellaneous	(132)	(16)	1	118
Total	(3,512)	(27,440)	21,663	2,444

Source: Wong, J.D., Paper presented at the Association for Budgeting and Financial Management annual meeting, October 7, Chicago, IL, 2004; original computations from Kansas Division of the Budget and Kansas Legislative Research Department, *State General Fund Receipts for FY 2007 (Revised) and FY 2008*, memorandum, Kansas Division of the Budget and Kansas Legislative Research Department, Topeka, KS, 2006. With permission.

corporation income taxes, whereas the largest percentage underestimates were for corporate franchise taxes. On a percentage basis, individual income taxes, retail sales taxes, and compensating use taxes on average tended to be estimated very accurately.

Table 19.6 shows the average percentage of total departure of the estimate from the actual from FY1993 to 2006. The largest average percentages of total departure were for the individual income tax and the retail sales tax. Although these taxes tend to be estimated very accurately on a percentage error basis, they comprise over 75 percent of the total forecasting error because they make up such a large proportion of overall tax revenues.

Table 19.5 Average Percentage Departure of the Estimate from the Actual (FY1993–2006)

Tax Source	*Preliminary Presession (Percent)*	*Preliminary Midsession (Percent)*	*Presession Estimate (Percent)*	*Midsession Estimate (Percent)*
Property tax				
Motor carrier	5.0	4.0	3.4	3.7
Income and privilege taxes				
Individual	0.7	0.2	0.5	0.1
Corporation	15.1	5.1	9.0	−1.4
Financial institutions	3.3	4.6	4.7	4.3
Estate tax	−5.7	−5.0	−5.5	−2.9
Sales, use, and excise taxes				
Retail sales	−1.4	−1.7	0.7	0.3
Compensating use	−1.7	−1.4	0.1	0.1
Cigarette	−2.7	−3.8	1.6	−0.2
Tobacco products	−1.9	−2.1	−0.9	−1.0
Cereal malt beverages	1.7	0.9	1.6	−0.6
Liquor gallonage	−0.4	−1.5	−0.1	−1.1
Liquor enforcement	−2.2	−1.3	−0.2	0.2
Private clubs	−1.4	−0.9	−0.3	0.3
Corporate franchise	−8.4	−7.0	−2.9	−1.1
Severance	−0.3	0.8	0.0	−1.2
Gross receipts taxes				
Insurance premiums	1.6	2.3	−1.1	0.5
Miscellaneous	−6.3	−1.7	1.2	5.9
Total	−0.6	−1.1	0.5	0.0

Source: Wong, J.D., Paper presented at the Association for Budgeting and Financial Management annual meeting, October 7, Chicago, IL, 2004; original computations from Kansas Division of the Budget and Kansas Legislative Research Department, *State General Fund Receipts for FY 2007 (Revised) and FY 2008*, memorandum, Kansas Division of the Budget and Kansas Legislative Research Department, Topeka, KS, 2006. With permission.

The FY2002 Estimates and the Revisions: The Off Year

FY2002 was definitely an off year for the consensus group. Actual receipts that year were \$565.8 million less than the original estimate and \$211.9 million below the last revised estimate. Although the estimating group anticipated the FY2002 receipts, an economic slowdown greatly affected their depth, breadth, and impact on Kansas much greater than the forecasters expected. The shortfall came despite the fact that the forecasters revised down the estimates in

Table 19.6 Average Percentage of Total Departure of the Estimate from the Actual (FY1993–2006)

Tax Source	*Preliminary Presession (Percent)*	*Preliminary Midsession (Percent)*	*Presession Estimate (Percent)*	*Midsession Estimate (Percent)*
Property tax				
Motor carrier	0.4	0.4	0.4	0.4
Income and privilege taxes				
Individual	43.3	43.3	42.8	42.8
Corporation	5.7	5.5	5.7	5.4
Financial institutions	0.8	0.9	0.9	0.9
Estate tax	1.6	1.7	1.6	1.7
Sales, use, and excise taxes				
Retail sales	35.4	35.5	35.8	35.8
Compensating use	4.8	4.9	4.9	4.9
Cigarette	1.6	1.6	1.7	1.7
Tobacco products	0.1	0.1	0.1	0.1
Cereal malt beverages	0.1	0.1	0.1	0.1
Liquor gallonage	0.4	0.4	0.4	0.4
Liquor enforcement	0.8	0.8	0.8	0.8
Private clubs	0.1	0.1	0.1	0.1
Corporate franchise	0.4	0.4	0.4	0.5
Severance	1.9	1.9	2.0	2.0
Gross receipts taxes				
Insurance premiums	2.3	2.4	2.3	2.3
Miscellaneous	0.1	0.1	0.1	0.1
Total	100.0	100.0	100.0	100.0

Source: Wong, J.D., Paper presented at the Association for Budgeting and Financial Management annual meeting, October 7, Chicago, IL, 2004; original computations from Kansas Division of the Budget and Kansas Legislative Research Department, *State General Fund Receipts for FY 2007 (Revised) and FY 2008,* memorandum, Kansas Division of the Budget and, Kansas Legislative Research Department, Topeka, KS, 2006. With permission.

April 2001 by $111.4 million, in November 2001 by $148.4 million, and in March 2002 by a total of $129.1 million.

The forecasters made the original estimates for FY2002 general fund receipts in November 2000. From a FY2001 increase of 6.7 percent (to a total of $4486.1 million), they anticipated receipts to grow to $4595.8 million (2.4 percent) in FY 2002. In April 2001, they lowered the estimate by $111.4 million. Subsequent legislative actions lowered this total slightly to $4449.4 million. CREG clearly anticipated a less robust economy by projecting a 0.9 percent growth in FY2002 receipts. Nonetheless, they anticipated normal growth in principal receipt sources—a growth of 5.5 percent for the compensating use taxes, 5.1 percent for the individual income tax, and 4.5 per cent for the retail sales tax.

In November 2001, the forecasters made a reduction in FY2002 estimates. The total reduction was $148.4 million; they decreased the general fund rate of change from 0.9 percent growth to a 1.8 percent decline from FY2001 receipts. Retail sales tax estimates were actually increased by $5 million, whereas they made decreases in individual income taxes ($25 million), corporation income taxes ($20 million), and compensating use taxes ($19 million).

They made a further reduction ($129.1 million) in March 2002; the reductions were concentrated in corporation income taxes ($95 million) and individual income taxes ($45 million). Again, they offered the record of collections and the sluggish economy as the main reasons for the reduction. Interestingly, the estimate for retail sales taxes ($10 million) was actually increased at this time.

Actual FY2002 Receipts

Despite these reductions, actual FY2002 receipts were still below the second revised estimates. The total collections were $4108.7 million, for a decline of 6.9 percent from FY2001. Receipts were then $565.8 million (12.1 percent) below the original estimate and $211.9 million (4.9 percent) below the second revised estimate. By this comparison, the major negative differences were recorded for the individual income tax ($180.4 million), compensating use taxes ($21.4 million), retail sales tax ($14.4 million), and corporation income tax ($6 million).

The directions of the revisions, in total and for most taxes, were generally correct; however, their magnitude was too small. The reason for the significant overestimation was an assumption that economic conditions, both nationally and in Kansas, would have a less significant impact on revenues and that conditions would improve more quickly than they actually did. As time passed, the impact of the economic downturn lingered. What actually happened was that the national economy remained sluggish and the recovery in Kansas lagged the national economy to a much greater extent than in other recent national recessions.

Timing of the FY2002 Shortfall

Through August 2001, state general fund receipts were actually running $8.6 million above the recent consensus estimate. However, after the terrorist attacks of September 11, state revenues finished the month $8.7 million below the last consensus estimate. By the end of October, state general fund receipts fell $29.7 million below the estimate. Despite a $148.4 million reduction in the consensus revenue estimate in November, state general fund receipts continued to lag behind the estimate. By the end of January, the revenue shortfall reached $97.6 million. Despite the CREG further reducing its estimate by $129.1 million at its March meeting, state general fund receipts still finished the fiscal year in June $211.7 million below the recent estimate. Individual income taxes finished the FY $180.4 million short of the March estimate, whereas compensating use taxes finished the year $21.4 million below the estimate, and retail sales taxes finished the year $14.4 million below the estimate.

Carryover to FY2003

The revisions to original FY2002 estimates and subsequent revenue shortfall carried over to the FY2003 estimates. In November 2001, forecasters estimated state general fund receipts at $4588.6 million; by March 2002, they reduced the estimate slightly to $4464.1 million; in November 2002 they further reduced it, this time significantly to $4152 million. The anticipated growth rates (from the estimated or actual FY2002 receipts) were 5.8, 6.1, and 1.1 percent, respectively. The first two figures are a comparison of estimated FY2002 receipts to estimated FY2003 receipts; the third figure compares actual FY2002 receipts to estimated FY2003 receipts. Again, the delay in the recovery from the national recession and the generally slow Kansas economy were the main reasons offered for these reductions.

Conclusions

This chapter presents an overview of the consensus revenue estimating process and the track record of the approach in Kansas. Procedures and methods of CREG are not uncommon from other states, but differences exist in this aspect of revenue estimation. In some states, a single formal econometric model is the focus of the estimating process. Private national economic consulting firms have often developed these state revenue forecasting models; in other instances, the models originate within the state, often with major inputs from state universities. Although these models may be more elegant than the CREG method, the formal models do not necessarily have a superior record of accuracy of estimation. According to Voorhees (2004, p. 668) "on the average the forecast has over 22.9 million dollars of error that can be attributed to the lack of consensual formulation." Furthermore, in rating a recent state of Kansas revenue bond issue, Moody's Investors Service (2006) concluded that a major strength of the state was "conservative financial management practices, such as binding consensus revenue forecasts."

As long as the national and state economies are experiencing regular growth and no major tax changes are made, most states are able to forecast revenues fairly accurately. A major change in the rate of national economic growth creates serious problems for state forecasting. There are two aspects of these problems: (1) determining how the state economy will respond to the national changes; and (2) how soon the national, and consequently the state, economy will return to its previous growth.

These aspects were particularly troublesome in anticipation and in the aftermath of the 2001 economic downturn. According to Dye (2004, p. 133),

> Fiscal year 2002 was the crisis year with a 7.3 percent decline in overall real per capita revenues and declines in 46 states. The problem continued into fiscal year 2003 with a 2.6 percent overall decline and 39 states with falling revenues after adjusting for price and population changes.

Estimation can be difficult if major tax changes are made. This is particularly the case when lawmakers adopt entirely new taxes. If only limited experience is available to draw upon in other states, major problems can emerge.

Some points that can be gleaned from consensus revenue estimating process in Kansas are as follows:

1. Bring to the table individuals with established credibility on technical forecasting and who are keen observers of state economic affairs.
2. Maintain reasonable stability in membership so that trust is maintained among them and institutional memory is broadly retained.
3. Provide sufficient transparency to the process, but afford opportunities for confidentiality in the sensitive issues to ensure the free flow of ideas.
4. Avoid the presence of high-profile political leaders with explicit policy agendas in the consensus sessions.

In 1992, Paul Posner, of the General Accounting Office, in a letter responding to Senator Bob Graham, provided evidence concerning a proposal to use a consensus forecasting process at the federal level that political volatility combined with economic volatility at the national level renders this process difficult, if not impossible, to apply (U.S. General Accounting Office 1992).

Other conclusions that can be drawn include the following:

1. The consensus revenue estimating approach is best linked to the state government and the general fund (the more volatile sources of revenue).
2. The institutional arrangement of consensus (characterized by professional dominance and transparency) does provide some improvement in the accuracy of forecasts and enabling "the decision making process of government to perform better and agencies to run more effectively, but more importantly, better forecasts will strengthen the confidence the public has in their government" (Voorhees 2004, p. 229). The evidence from Kansas indicates that aside from FY2002, the estimates generated by the consensus process have been remarkably accurate.
3. Given the institutional stability of the participants to this process at the state level, this process engenders considerable support and acceptance keeping the

major policy debates (other than tax policy and revenue enhancement) on the expenditure or outlays side of the budget.

4. There is considerable variation in the institutional composition of CREGs across the states. In some states, the process is more deeply embedded in the political process by the appointment of members by executive and legislative branch leaders. The existence of legislatively designated members from outside units such as state universities provides a degree of isolation from the direct partisan political influences as well as insuring greater stability of membership for the group.

What the consensus process brings to revenue forecasting is a stronger tradition for professionalism in the process and an acceptance of more rigorous analysis. This may have happened in many instances without the institution of consensus revenue forecasting, but it is clearly the case that this institution has embedded professional expertise on the revenue side of the budgeting process. The consensus process has done nothing to lessen the political aspects of allocation and may have served an additional beneficial role by shifting even more of the political debate to the expenditure side of the budget.

References

Agostini, S. J. 1991. Searching for a better forecast: San Francisco's revenue forecasting model. *Government Finance Review* 7(December): 13–16.

Barry, J. S. 2002. Fiscal forecasting: a perilous task. *Tax Foundation Special Report* 108(January): 1–12.

Daicoff, D. 1983. Kansas revenue estimating. In *Estimating Revenues of the State General Fund in Kansas.* Topeka, KS: University of Kansas, Capitol Complex Center, pp. 13–30.

Dye, R. F. 2004. State revenue cyclicality. *National Tax Journal* 57(March): 133–145.

Kansas Division of the Budget. 2007. *The Governor's Budget Report, Volume 1: Descriptions and Budget Schedules, Fiscal Year 2008.* Topeka, KS: Kansas Division of the Budget.

Kansas Division of the Budget and Kansas Legislative Research Department. 2006. *State General Fund Receipts for FY 2007 (Revised) and FY 2008*, memorandum. Topeka, KS: Kansas Division of the Budget and Kansas Legislative Research Department.

Moody's Investors Service. 2006. *Moody's Assigns Aa2 Rating to State of Kansas' Series 2006L Revenue Bonds (State of Kansas Projects) Issued through the Kansas Development Finance Authority.* New York: Moody's Investors Service.

National Conference of State Legislatures. 1995. *Fundamentals of Sound State Budgeting Practices.* Denver, CO: National Conference of State Legislatures, http://www.ncsl.org/programs/fiscal/fpfssbp.htm (accessed March 22, 2007).

National Conference of State Legislatures. 2006. *Legislative Budget Procedures: A Guide to Appropriations and Budget Process in the States, Commonwealths, and Territories.* Denver, CO: National Conference of State Legislatures, http://www.ncsl.org/programs/fiscal/ lbptabls/index.htm (accessed March 22, 2007).

Ryan, R. W. 1983. The purpose and history of the revenue estimating procedure. In *Estimating Revenues of the State General Fund in Kansas*. Topeka, KS: University of Kansas, Capitol Complex Center, pp. 3–11.

Sun, J. 2005. The dynamics of revenue forecasting from an organizational perspective: a review of the literature. *Journal of Public Budgeting, Accounting, & Financial Management* 17(Winter): 527–556.

U.S. General Accounting Office. 1992. *Consensus Revenue Forecasting*. Washington: U.S. General Accounting Office, GAO/AFMD-92-70R.

Voorhees, W. R. 2002. Institutional structures utilized in state revenue forecasting. *Journal of Public Budgeting, Accounting, & Financial Management* 14(Summer): 175–195.

Voorhees, W. R. 2004. More is better: consensual forecasting and state revenue forecast error. *International Journal of Public Administration* 27(8,9): 651–671.

Wong, J. D. 2004. Accuracy of Kansas revenue forecasting. Paper presented at the Association for Budgeting and Financial Management annual meeting, October 7, Chicago, IL.

Wong, J. D. 2006. *State of Kansas Adjusted General Fund Tax Receipts, Rates of Change, Elasticities, and Composition: Fiscal Years 1989 through 2006*. Topeka, KS: Division of the Budget.

3

UNCERTAINTY AND RISK ASSESSMENT IN BUDGET FORECASTING

Chapter 20

Forecast Errors: Balancing the Risks and Costs of Being Wrong

Qiang Xu, Hilke Kayser, and Lynn Holland

Contents

Introduction

In practice, there is no such thing as a perfect forecast. Forecast errors can arise from various sources, including an incorrect model specification; errors in the data; incorrect assumptions regarding the future values of explanatory variables; and shocks or events that, by nature, cannot be predicted at the time when the forecast was made. Thus, even under a correct model specification and correct assumptions, forecasts will differ from actual values. Forecast errors are typically assumed to be drawn from a zero-mean process, such as white noise. But theory tells us that the probability of a draw of zero from such a process is itself zero. Thus, errors having an expected value of zero are the best one can hope for because no model can presume to capture all of the factors that affect the variable under consideration.

Although the model specification may be correct, the analyst typically works with sample data rather than population data, making parameter estimates subject to sampling error. However, when a model is solved to produce a forecast, the model coefficient estimates are treated as fixed numbers when, in fact, they themselves are random variables. The forecaster can only hope to estimate the "true" model parameters within a statistically acceptable margin of error. For example, imagine two samples drawn from the same population that produce coefficient estimates of 0.85 and 0.75, respectively. The standard arsenal of tests indicates that both can be judged as statistically different from zero. Although estimates of 0.75 and 0.85 may not be different from one another from a statistical perspective, they could result in very different forecasts.

In light of many sources of risk, the forecaster must be prepared to make an assessment of the risks to the forecast, and evaluate the costs associated with those risks. After performing such an assessment, the forecaster may want to implement a feedback mechanism from the risk assessment back to the forecast. If the forecaster assesses the risk of being too high to be greater than the risk of being too low, then the forecast can be lowered to restore balance.

For example, it is unlikely that an econometric model can adequately capture the impact of geopolitical turmoil on oil prices. Consequently, when there is a war going on in the Middle East, the probability that actual oil prices will rise above the model forecast may be greater than the probability that oil prices will be below. In such cases, the analyst may not only want to make the asymmetric nature of the risks explicit, but also feel justified in making an upward adjustment to the model forecast.

Even when the forecast risks are balanced, the costs associated with forecast errors may not be. In many situations, the cost of an overestimate may outweigh the cost of an underestimate, and, in such cases, the analyst may feel justified in making a downward adjustment to the model forecast to balance the costs. In estimating budgetary revenues and spending, the cost of overestimating tax receipts may include the risk of a fiscal crisis, whereas no such risk is inherent in underestimation. These concerns lead to a discussion of the forecaster's "loss function" and an evaluation of the costs of being wrong.

The section Measures of Forecast Error introduces various measures of forecast error, including the notion of symmetric versus asymmetric error distribution. The section Risk Assessment: Monte Carlo Simulation and Fan Charts presents methods for assessing forecast risks (prediction intervals and density forecasts) and for presenting those risks to other interested parties. These methods include Monte Carlo simulation and the construction of fan charts. For simplicity of exposition, both the sections abstract from the forecaster's loss function, implicitly assuming that the forecaster's loss is simply proportional to the absolute value of the error itself. The section Generalizing the Forecaster's Loss Function introduces more general forms for the forecaster's loss function, and discusses the choice of an optimal forecast under a given loss function and a given distribution of risks. The section Statistical Comparison of Alternative Forecasts discusses methods for choosing forecasts from a list and combining them for a given particular loss function. The final section is the Conclusion.

Measures of Forecast Error

There are a number of statistics that are commonly used to measure forecast error. Suppose Y_t is an observed time series and one is interested in forecasting its future values h periods ahead. Define $e_{t+h,t}$ as the time $t + h$ forecast error for a forecast made at time t such that

$$e_{t+h,t} = Y_{t+h} - Y_{t+h,t}$$

where

Y_{t+h} = actual value of Y at time $t + h$
$Y_{t+h,t}$ = forecast for Y_{t+h} made at time t

Similarly, we define the percentage error as

$$p_{t+h,t} = \frac{Y_{t+h} - Y_{t+h,t}}{Y_{t+h}}$$

In addition, there are various statistics that summarize the model's overall fit. For a given value of h, these include the mean error (ME):

$$\mathrm{ME} = \frac{1}{T}\sum_{t=1}^{T} e_{t+h,t}$$

which can be interpreted as a measure of bias. An ME greater than zero indicates that the model has a tendency to underestimate. All else being equal, the smaller the ME, the better the model. We can also define the error variance (EV) as

$$\text{EV} = \frac{1}{T}\sum_{t=1}^{T}\left(e_{t+h,t} - \text{ME}\right)^2$$

which measures the dispersion of the forecast errors. Squaring the errors amplifies the penalty for large errors and does not permit positive and negative errors to cancel one another out. All else being equal, the smaller the EV, the better the model. Popular measures also include the mean squared error (MSE)

$$\text{MSE} = \frac{1}{T}\sum_{t=1}^{T} e_{t+h,t}^2$$

and the mean squared percent error (MSPE)

$$\text{MSPE} = \frac{1}{T}\sum_{t=1}^{T} p_{t+h,t}^2$$

The squared roots of these measures are often used to preserve units, which yield the root mean squared error (RMSE)

$$\text{RMSE} = \sqrt{\frac{1}{T}\sum_{t=1}^{T} e_{t+h,t}^2}$$

and the root mean squared percent error (RMSPE)

$$\text{RMSPE} = \sqrt{\frac{1}{T}\sum_{t=1}^{T} p_{t+h,t}^2}$$

Some less popular but nevertheless common accuracy measures include the mean absolute error (MAE)

$$\text{MAE} = \frac{1}{T}\sum_{t=1}^{T} |e_{t+h,t}|$$

and the mean absolute percent error (MAPE)

$$\text{MAPE} = \frac{1}{T}\sum_{t-1}^{T} |p_{t+h,t}|$$

It is clear that the length of the forecast horizon, *h*, is of crucial importance as longer-term forecasts tend to have larger errors when compared with shorter-term forecasts.

Risk Assessment: Monte Carlo Simulation and Fan Charts

Because no forecast can be expected to be 100 percent accurate, risk assessment involving measures of expected forecast accuracy has become increasingly popular. The construction of such measures is usually simulation-based and the availability of ample computing power has made these computations more widely feasible. The most common constructs for assessing risk are prediction intervals and density forecasts. A prediction interval supplements a point forecast with a range and a probability that the actual value will fall within that range. A density forecast goes one step further by assigning varying degrees of likelihood to particular values as one moves further from the point forecast. The basic tool for constructing these measures is Monte Carlo simulation.

Monte Carlo Simulation

Applications of Monte Carlo methods have increased manifold in the econometrics literature. In these studies, data are generated using computer-based pseudorandom number generators, that is, computer programs that generate sequences of values that "appear" to be strings of draws from a specified probability distribution. In fact, these sequences are deterministically generated, hence the term "pseudorandom" (Fishman 1996). A typical algorithm is based on a set of machine-specific constants and an initial "seed" value. A sequence of seed values is calculated recursively as a function of the constants, with each sequence uniquely determined by the initial value. The value of the pseudorandom number itself is calculated by dividing the current value of the seed by one of the constants commonly referred to as the modulus. If the desired distribution is something other than the standard uniform one, a distribution-specific transformation is performed.

A once widely used pseudorandom number generator, known as the linear congruential generator (LCG), generates a standard uniform variate, $x \sim U[0, 1]$, based on a set of constants $\{A, B, M\}$. Before generating a series, an analyst has to set the initial seed (i.e., an integer number) as seed_0 and then loop through the following steps until the desired number is reached:

1. Update the seed accordingly as $\text{seed}_j = \text{mod}(\text{seed}_{j-1} \times B, A)$
2. Calculate $x_j = \text{seed}_j/M$
3. Move x_j into memory
4. Return to step 1

The modulus function, mod(a, b), is the integer remainder after a is divided by b. For example, mod(11, 3) = 2. The larger is A, the longer is the "period" before the sequence begins to repeat itself. The seed sequence is essentially a difference equation, because given the initial seed, x_j is a function of x_{j-1}. Values for A and M are

Table 20.1 Output from a Simple Random Number Generator

Iteration	*Seed*	*x*
0	1234567	
1	1422014737	0.662177
2	456166167	0.212419
3	268145409	0.124865
4	1299195559	0.604985
5	2113510897	0.984180
6	250624311	0.116706
7	1027361249	0.478402
8	1091982023	0.508494
9	546604753	0.254533
10	1998521175	0.930634

Note: Authors' estimates.

typically chosen to avoid a draw of zero for $seed_j$. Dividing the current value of the seed by M (chosen to be greater than A) ensures a value for the random variate between zero and one. For example, suppose the seed is initialized at 1234567 and $\{A, B, M\} = \{2147483648, 16807, 2147483655\}$. The generator will produce millions of pseudorandom draws from $U[0, 1]$ before repeating. The first ten values produced by this random number generator are shown in Table 20.1.

The pseudorandom number generator is the engine behind Monte Carlo simulation. For a given model specification and a given set of exogenous inputs, Monte Carlo simulation can be used to evaluate the risk to the forecast due to variation in the dependent variable that cannot be explained by the model as well as the random variation in the model parameters. By assumption, the model errors are considered to be draws from a normally distributed random variable with a mean of zero. For the purpose of simulation, the model parameters are also considered to be random variables that are distributed as multivariate normal. The standard deviation of the regression errors and the means and standard deviations of the parameter distribution are derived from the regression analysis.

To simulate values for the dependent variable, a random number generator is used to generate a value for the model error and values for the parameters from each of the foregoing probability distributions. On the basis of these draws and values from the input dataset (which for purposes of the simulation is assumed to be fixed), the model is solved for the dependent variable. This "experiment" is typically repeated tens or even hundreds of thousands of times, yielding a similar number of simulated values for each observation of the dependent variable. The means and standard deviations of these simulated values can be used to construct a prediction interval and provide the starting point for creating a density forecast typically portrayed by a fan chart.

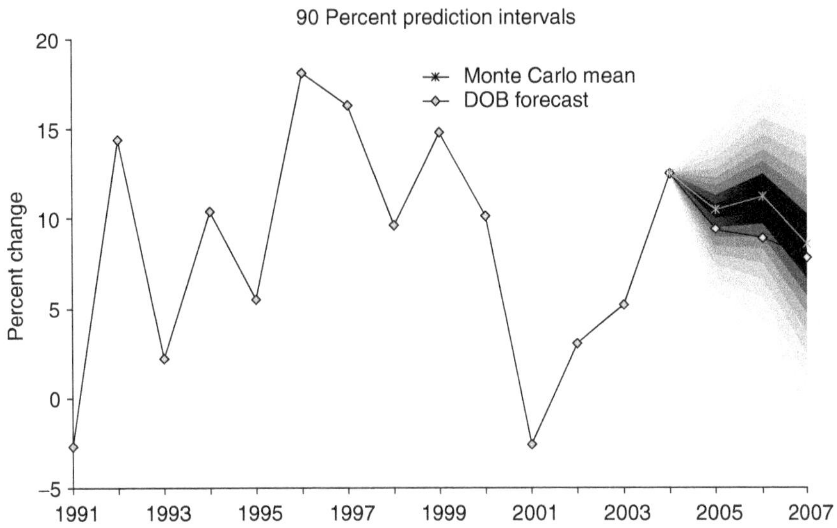

Figure 20.1 Fan chart for partnership(s) corporation income growth. With 90 percent probability, actual growth will fall into the shaded region. Bands represent 5 percent probability regions. (From NYS Department for Taxation and Finance; DOB Staff Estimates.)

Density Forecasts and Fan Charts

Fan charts display prediction intervals as shown in Figure 20.1. It is estimated that with 90 percent probability, future values will fall into the shaded area of the fan. Each band within the shaded area reflects 5 percent probability regions. The chart "fans out" over time to reflect the increasing uncertainty and growing risk as the forecast departs further from the base year, graphically depicting the risks associated with a point forecast as time progresses. Fan charts can exhibit skewness that reflects more down- or upside risk to the forecast, and the costs associated with erring on either side.

Theoretical Underpinnings of the Fan Chart

To capture the notion of asymmetric risk, the fan chart used by the New York State Division of the Budget (DOB) assumes a two-piece normal distribution for each of the forecast years following an approach inspired by Wallis (1999) and others. A two-piece normal distribution of the form

$$f(x) = \begin{cases} A \exp\left[\dfrac{-(x-\mu)^2}{2\sigma_1^2}\right] & x \leq \mu \\ A \exp\left[\dfrac{(x-\mu)^2}{2\sigma_2^2}\right] & x \geq \mu \end{cases}$$

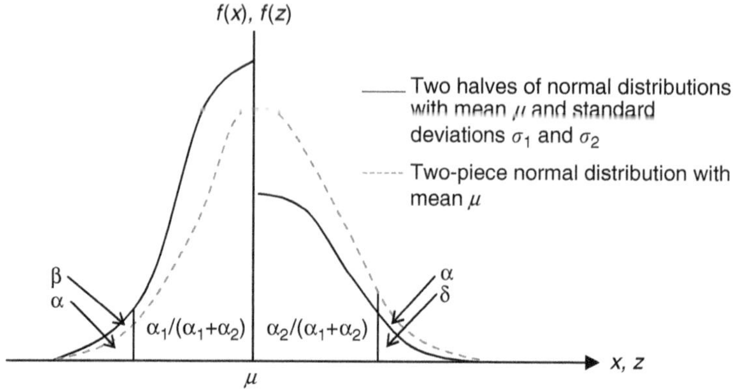

Figure 20.2 The two-piece normal distribution.

with A $= (\sqrt{2\pi}(\sigma_1 + \sigma_2)/2)^{-1}$ is formed by combining halves of two normal distributions having the same mean but different standard deviations, with parameters (μ, σ_1) and (μ, σ_2), and scaling them to give the common value $f(\mu)$. If $\sigma_1 < \sigma_2$, the two-piece normal has positive skewness with the mean and median exceeding the mode (see Figure 20.2). A smooth distribution $f(x)$ arises from scaling the discontinuous distribution $f(z)$ to the left of μ using $2\sigma_1/(\sigma_1 + \sigma_2)$ and the original distribution $f(z)$ to the right of μ using $2\sigma_2/(\sigma_1 + \sigma_2)$.

One can determine the cutoff values for the smooth probability density function $f(x)$ from the underlying standard normal cumulative distribution functions by recalling the scaling factors. For $\alpha < \sigma_1/(\sigma_1 + \sigma_2)$, that is, to the left of μ, the point of the two-piece normal distribution defined by $\text{Prob}(X \leq x_\alpha) = \alpha$ is the same as the point that is defined by $\text{Prob}(Z \leq z_\beta) = \beta$, with

$$\beta = \frac{\alpha(\sigma_1 + \sigma_2)}{2\sigma_1}$$

and

$$x_a = \sigma_1 z_\beta + \mu$$

Likewise, for $(1 - \alpha) < \sigma_2/(\sigma_1 + \sigma_2)$, that is, to the right of μ, the point of the two-piece normal distribution that is defined by $\text{Prob}(X \leq x_\alpha) = \alpha$ is the same as the point that is defined by $\text{Prob}(Z \leq z_\delta) = \delta$, with

$$\delta = \frac{\alpha(\sigma_1 + \sigma_2)}{2\sigma_2}$$

and

$$x_{1-\alpha} = \sigma_1 z_{1-\delta} + \mu$$

For the two-piece normal distribution, the mode remains at μ. The median of the distribution can be determined as the value defined by Prob($X < x_\alpha$) = 0.5. The mean of the two-piece normal distribution depends on the skewness of the distribution and can be calculated as

$$E(X) = \mu + \sqrt{\frac{2}{\pi}}(\sigma_2 - \sigma_1)$$

Choice of Parameters

In constructing its fan charts, DOB uses means from the Monte Carlo simulation study as the mean, μ, of the two underlying normal distributions. As mentioned earlier, if the two-piece normal distribution is skewed, the Monte Carlo mean becomes the mode or most likely the outcome of the distribution and will differ from the median and the mean. In the sample fan chart, the mode is displayed as the crossed line. Except in extremely skewed cases, the mode tends to fall close to the center of the central 10 percent prediction interval. As Britton et al. (1998) pointed out in their discussion of the inflation fan chart used by the Bank of England, the difference between the mean and the mode provides a measure of the skewness of the distribution. Given the skewness parameter, γ, DOB determines the two standard deviations, σ_1 and σ_2, as $\sigma_1 = (1 + \gamma)\sigma$ and $\sigma_2 = (1 - \gamma)\sigma$, where σ is the standard deviation from the Monte Carlo simulation study.

By definition, the mean of the distribution is the weighted average of the realizations of the variable under all possible scenarios, with the weights corresponding to the probability or likelihood of each scenario. In its forecasts, DOB aims to assess and incorporate the likely risks. Although no attempt is made to strictly calculate the probability-weighted average, the forecast will be considered a close approximation of the mean. Thus, the skewness parameter, γ, is determined as the difference between the DOB's forecast and the Monte Carlo mean. DOB's fan chart shows central prediction intervals with equal tail probabilities.

For example, the region in the darkest two slivers represents the 10 percent region in the center of the distribution. DOB adds regions with 5 percent probability on either side of the central interval to obtain the next prediction interval. If the distribution is skewed, the corresponding 5 percent prediction intervals will include different ranges of growth rates at the top and the bottom, thus leading to an asymmetric fan chart.

The 5 percent prediction regions encompass increasingly wider range of growth rates as one moves away from the center because the probability density of the two-piece normal distribution decreases as one moves further into the tails. Thus, the limiting probability for any single outcome to occur is higher for the central prediction regions than for intervals further out because a smaller range of outcomes shares the same cumulative probability. Over time, risks become cumulative and uncertainties grow. DOB uses its own forecast history to determine the degree to which σ_1 and σ_2 need to be adjusted upward to maintain the appropriate probability regions.

Generalizing the Forecaster's Loss Function

When the forecaster's loss function is more general than the simple one assumed for the earlier section, the forecaster's choice of an optimal forecast may deviate even further from the model forecast. Suppose a forecaster working for a manufacturing firm in the private sector is asked to provide guidance as to whether the firm should raise its level of inventories based on the outlook of demand for the company's product. If the demand is projected to be high, then the firm will proceed to build inventories; if low, then the firm will reduce inventories. There are costs to the firm of being wrong.

If the demand is unexpectedly low, the firm will have unplanned inventories, whereas if demand is higher than expected, the firm will lose market share. Tables 20.2 and 20.3 summarize the costs to the firm of bad planning under alternative loss structures, clearly illustrating that the loss structure will critically affect the firm's decision.

The construct for measuring the cost attached by the forecaster to an incorrect prediction is the loss function, $L(e_{t+h,t})$, where $e_{t+h,t}$ is as defined earlier. The cost associated with the forecast error is presumed to depend only on the size of the forecast error and to be positive unless the error is (in theory) zero. Typically, $L(e)$ is constructed to satisfy the following three requirements:

1. $L(0) = 0$
2. $L(e)$ is continuous, implying that two nearly identical forecast errors should produce nearly identical losses
3. $L(e)$ increases as the absolute value of e increases, implying that the bigger the size of the absolute value of the error, the bigger is the loss

Table 20.2 Under Symmetric Losses

Forecast/Actual	*High ($)*	*Low ($)*
High	0	10,000
Low	10,000	0

Table 20.3 Under Asymmetric Losses

Decision	*Demand High ($)*	*Demand Low ($)*
High forecast	0	10,000
Low forecast	20,000	0

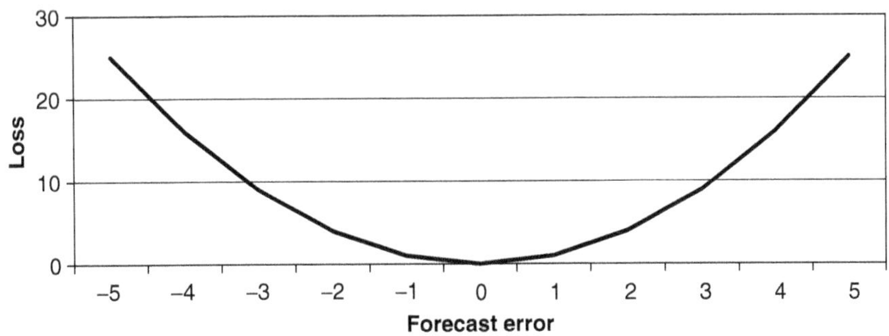

Figure 20.3 Quadratic loss function.

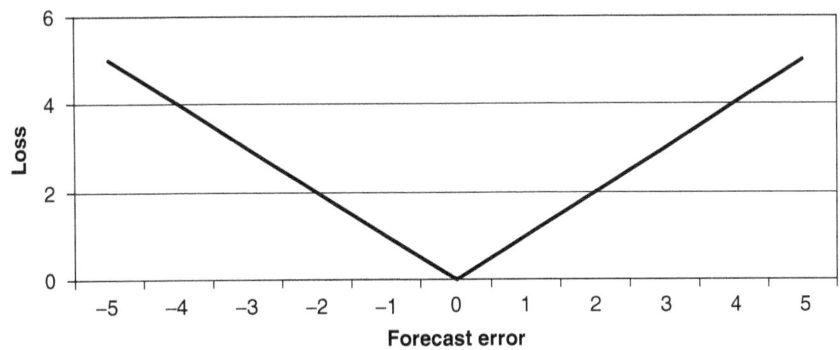

Figure 20.4 Absolute loss function.

Loss functions can be either symmetric or asymmetric. Depicted in Figure 20.3 is the quadratic loss function, where

$$L(e) = e^2$$

The squaring associated with quadratic loss makes large errors much more costly than small ones. In addition, the loss increases at an increasing rate on each side of the origin, implying symmetry. The absolute loss function is depicted in Figure 20.4, where

$$L(e) = |e|$$

This function is also symmetric, but the loss increases at a constant rate with the size of the error, producing a V-shape curve.

In reality, the costs associated with a wrong forecast may not always be symmetric. For example, if the costs associated with under- and overpredicting travel time

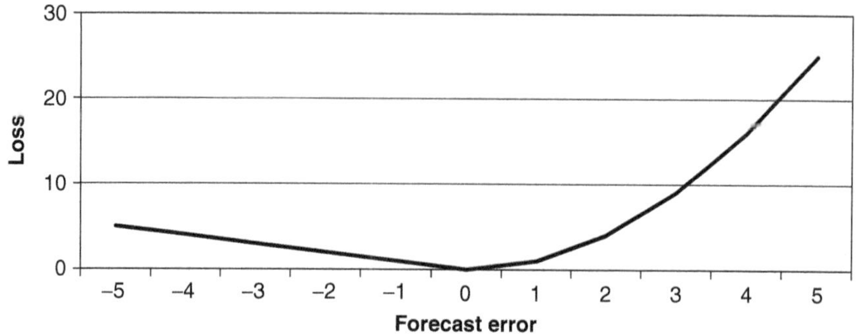

Figure 20.5 Linex loss function.

to the airport were symmetric, we would expect many more missed flights than we actually observe. The observance of few missed flights is an indication that the cost of a missed flight must outweigh the cost of arriving early and having to wait at the airport, implying that the loss function is not symmetric. As mentioned earlier, government budget analysts may also face asymmetric costs associated with over- versus underpredicting revenues. Indeed, the different branches of government may have asymmetric loss functions that are mirror images of one another. Industry analysts may also attach a higher cost to an overly pessimistic forecast than to an overly optimistic one.

Here we present the two asymmetric loss functions that are most popular in the literature. A more detailed presentation can be found in Christoffersen and Diebold (1997). The first is the "linex" function:

$$L(e) = b[\exp(ae) - ae - 1],\ a \in \mathbb{R} \setminus \{0\},\ b \in \mathbb{R}_+$$

The linex loss function is so named because for a greater than (less than) 0, it assigns a cost that is linear in the forecast error if the error is negative (positive), and exponential in the forecast error if it is positive (negative). Thus, negative forecast errors ($Y_{t+h} < Y_{t+h,t}$) are much less costly than positive errors. The linex loss function, which is depicted in Figure 20.5, may well pertain to forecasting the time it will take to get to the airport. A negative error implies a longer wait at the airport, whereas a large positive error could entail a missed flight.

Under the linex loss function, the optimal h-step-ahead forecast solves the following minimization problem:

$$\min_{Y_{t+h,t}} E_t\{b[\exp(a(Y_{t+h} - Y_{t+h,t})) - a(Y_{t+h} - Y_{t+h,t}) - 1]\}$$

Differentiating and using the conditional moment-generating function for a conditionally normally distributed random variate yields,

$$\hat{Y}_{t+h} = \mu_{t+h|t} + \frac{a}{2}\sigma^2_{t+h|t}$$

which assume conditional heteroskedasticity.* Thus, the optimal predictor is a simple function of the conditional mean and a bias term that depends on the conditional h-step-ahead prediction-error variance and the degree of loss function asymmetry, as measured by the parameter a. When a is positive (the greater is a), the greater is the bias toward negative errors (overprediction). In addition, when a is positive, the optimal predictor is also positive in the prediction-error variance.

A second commonly used asymmetric loss function is the "linlin" loss function, which can be expressed as follows:

$$L(e) = \begin{cases} a|e|, & \text{if } e > 0 \\ b|e|, & \text{if } e \leq 0 \end{cases}$$

The linlin loss function is so called because it is linear in the errors and is a generalization of the absolute loss function depicted earlier where the slopes are allowed to differ on either side of the origin. The optimal predictor solves the following minimization problem:

$$\min_{\hat{Y}_{t+h}} \left\{ a \int_{\hat{Y}_{t+h}}^{\infty} (Y_{t+h} - \hat{Y}_{t+h}) f(Y_{t+h} \mid \Omega_t) \mathrm{d}Y_{t+h} - b \int_{\hat{Y}_{t+h}}^{\infty} (Y_{t+h} - \hat{Y}_{t+h}) f(Y_{t+h} \mid \Omega_t) \mathrm{d}Y_{t+h} \right\}$$

The first-order condition implies the following result:

$$F(\hat{Y}_{t+h} \mid \Omega_t) = \frac{a}{a+b}$$

where Ω_t is the conditional cumulative distribution function (c.d.f.) of Y_{t+h}. If Y_{t+h} is normally distributed, then the optimal predictor is

$$\hat{Y}_{t+h} = \mu_{t+h|t} + \sigma_{t+h|t}\Phi^{-1}\left(\frac{a}{a+b}\right)$$

where $\Phi(z)$ is the standard normal c.d.f.

The foregoing results pertain to two fairly simple loss functions. However, Christoffersen and Diebold (1997) also show how an optimal predictor can be approximated when the loss function is more general using numerical simulation.

---

* Christoffersen and Diebold (1997) derive a "pseudo-optimal" estimator by replacing $\sigma^2_{t+h}|t$ with the unconditional h-step ahead prediction-error variance σ^2_h; the resulting estimator only being optimal under conditional homoskedasticity. However, under conditional heteroskedasticity, the "pseudo-optimal" estimator will fail to result in a lower conditionally expected loss than the conditional mean except during times of high volatility.

Although less restrictive, this approach may be less accessible to the average practitioner. Moreover, the literature does not mention anything about choosing values for parameters *a* and *b*. However, it is hoped that the preceding discussion has illustrated how the problem of asymmetric loss fits into the broader problem of forecasting and can provide a useful guideline on how to proceed and communicate the central issue.

Statistical Comparison of Alternative Forecasts

Choosing among Competing Models

Suppose one must choose between two competing models, A and B, for a given particular loss function. This can be couched as a hypothesis testing problem:

$$H_0 : E\left[L\left(e^A_{t+h,t}\right)\right] = E\left[L\left(e^B_{t+h,t}\right)\right]$$

$$H_A : E\left[L\left(e^A_{t+h,t}\right)\right] > E\left[L\left(e^B_{t+h,t}\right)\right] \text{ or } E\left[L\left(e^A_{t+h,t}\right)\right] < E\left[L\left(e^B_{t+h,t}\right)\right]$$

Equivalently, one might want to test the hypothesis so that the expected loss differential is zero

$$E[\mathrm{d}_t] = E\left[L\left(e^A_{t+h,t}\right)\right] - E\left[L\left(e^B_{t+h,t}\right)\right] = 0$$

If d_t is a stationary series, the large-sample distribution of the sample mean loss differential is

$$\sqrt{T}\,(\bar{\mathrm{d}} - \mu) \sim N(0, f)$$

where

$$\bar{\mathrm{d}} = \frac{1}{T}\sum_{t=1}^{T}\left[L\left(e^A_{t+h,t}\right) - L\left(e^B_{t+h,t}\right)\right]$$

is the sample mean loss differential, f the variance of the sample mean differential, and μ the population mean loss differential. Under the null hypothesis of a zero population mean loss differential, the standardized sample mean loss differential has a standard normal distribution.

$$B = \frac{\bar{\mathrm{d}}}{\sqrt{\hat{f}/T}} \sim N(0, 1)$$

where $\hat{f}$ is a consistent estimate of f.*

* Alternatively, the sophisticated practitioner might want to choose between competing density forecasts. This problem is treated rigorously by Tay and Wallis (2000), under loss functions of general form, but it is beyond the scope of this chapter.

Forecast Encompassing and Combination

Suppose one has two competing models, A and B, and statistical test results indicate that they are equally accurate. Should the models be combined?

Forecast Encompassing

Suppose models A and B produce forecasts $Y^A_{t+h,t}$ and $Y^B_{t+h,t}$, respectively. The following regression can be performed:

$$Y_{t+h} = \beta_A Y^A_{t+h,t} + \beta_B Y^B_{t+h,t} + \varepsilon_{t+h,t}$$

If $\beta_A = 1$ and $\beta_B = 0$, then model A forecast encompasses model B. If $\beta_A = 0$ and $\beta_B = 1$, then model B forecast encompasses model A. Otherwise, neither model encompasses the other and one may want to combine them (see Granger 1989).

Forecast Combination

The Blue Chip consensus forecast is a simple average of about 50 forecasts. However, under certain circumstances, equally weighting all of the participating forecasters may not be optimal. For example, suppose there are two forecasts, $Y^A_{t+h,t}$ and $Y^B_{t+h,t}$. One might combine them in a weighted average

$$Y^C_{t+h,t} = \omega \times Y^A_{t+h,t} + (1 - \omega) Y^B_{t+h,t}$$

where $Y^C_{t+h,t}$ is the combination forecast. Alternatively, one can write the problem in terms of forecast errors:

$$e^C_{t+h,t} = \omega \times e^A_{t+h,t} + (1 - \omega) \times e^B_{t+h,t}$$

with variance

$$\sigma^2_C = \omega^2\sigma^2_A + (1 - \omega)^2\sigma^2_B + 2\omega(1 - \omega)^2\sigma^2_{AB}$$

based on forecasters' past performances. The value of ω can be determined as the solution to an optimization problem where the objective is to minimize the weighted average forecast error. The first-order condition indicates that the simple Blue Chip weighting scheme is not necessarily optimal.

The foregoing methods abstract from consideration of the form of the forecaster's loss function. Elliott and Timmermann (2002) discussed, more rigorously, forecast combination under more general circumstances. The authors show that as long as the forecast error density is elliptically symmetric, the forecast combination weights are invariant over all loss functions, leaving only the constant term to capture the trade off between the bias in the loss function and the variance of the forecast error. As to the importance of the shape of the loss function to the choice of weights, the authors offer the intuitive conclusion that the larger the degree of loss function asymmetry, the larger the gains from optimally estimating of the combination weights compared to equally weighting the forecasts.

Following Elliott and Timmermann (2002), we generalize the problem of forecast combination by defining $\boldsymbol{Y}_{t+h,t}$ as a vector of forecasts and assume that $Y^C_{t+h,t}$ and $\boldsymbol{Y}_{t+h,t}$ are jointly distributed with the following first and second moments:

$$E\begin{pmatrix} Y^C_{t+h,t} \\ \boldsymbol{Y}_{t+h,t} \end{pmatrix} = \begin{pmatrix} \mu_Y \\ \boldsymbol{\mu} \end{pmatrix}$$

and

$$\text{Var}\begin{pmatrix} Y^C_{t+h,t} \\ \boldsymbol{Y}_{t+h,t} \end{pmatrix} = \begin{pmatrix} \sigma_Y^2 & \boldsymbol{\sigma}'_{21} \\ \boldsymbol{\sigma}_{21} & \Sigma_{22} \end{pmatrix}$$

Assume that the optimal combination forecast is a linear combination of the elements of $\boldsymbol{Y}_{t+h,t}$, giving rise to the forecast error defined as

$$e_{t+h,t} = Y^C_{t+h,t} - \omega^c - \boldsymbol{\omega}' Y_{t+h,t}$$

where $\boldsymbol{\omega}$ is a vector of combination weights and $\boldsymbol{\omega}^c$ a scalar constant, and e_t has the following first and second moments:

$$\mu_e = \mu_y - \omega^c - \boldsymbol{\omega}'\boldsymbol{\mu}$$
$$\sigma_e^2 = \sigma_y^2 + \boldsymbol{\omega}'\sum_{22}\omega - 2\omega'\sigma_{21}$$

Under a symmetric quadratic loss function, the first-order conditions of the minimization problem imply the optimal population values

$$\omega_0^c = \mu_y - \boldsymbol{\omega}'\boldsymbol{\mu}$$
$$\boldsymbol{\omega}_0 = \sum_{22}^{-1}\boldsymbol{\sigma}_{21}$$

Although Elliott and Timmermann (2002) present very general results, a common special class of cases is that of elliptically symmetric forecast errors, but asymmetric loss. The solution values for the optimal weights have the convenient property that only the constant term ω^c depends on the shape of the loss function. Thus, if

$$E[L(e_t)] = g(\mu_e, \sigma_e^2)$$

then ω_0^c is the solution to

$$\frac{\partial g(\mu_e^*, \sigma_e^2)}{\partial \mu_e} = 0$$

where μ_e^* is the optimal value for μ_e. Thus, under the assumption of normally distributed forecast errors and a linex loss function,

$$\omega_0^c = \mu_y - \boldsymbol{\omega}_0'\boldsymbol{\mu} + \frac{a}{2}\sigma_e^2$$

whereas under linlin loss,

$$\omega_0^c = \mu_y - \boldsymbol{\omega}_0'\boldsymbol{\mu} - \sigma_e \Phi^{-1}\left(\frac{a}{a+b}\right)$$

Conclusion

This chapter emphasizes the importance of assessing the risks to the forecast and evaluating the costs associated with those risks. In many settings, this exercise can be just as critical as the forecast itself. A proper risk assessment often requires the forecaster to consider the shape of his or her "loss function" and to possibly deviate from the traditional symmetric forms that tend to underlie conventional statistical procedures. The chapter presents the use of Monte Carlo simulation and the construction of fan charts as methods for both assessing forecast risk and presenting those risks to others. The chapter introduces both symmetric and asymmetric forms for the forecaster's loss function and discusses the choice of an optimal forecast under a given loss function and a given distribution of risks. Finally, the chapter discusses methods for both choosing from a menu of forecasts and combining forecasts where, again, the forecaster's loss function can be pivotal.

References

Britton, E., P. Fisher, and J. Whitley. 1998. The inflation report projections: understanding the fan chart. *Bank of England Quarterly Bulletin* 38: 30–37.

Christoffersen, P. and F. X. Diebold. 1997. Optimal prediction under asymmetrical loss. *Econometric Theory* 13: 806–817.

Elliott, G. and A. Timmermann. 2002. Optimal forecast combinations under general loss functions and forecast error distributions. Economics Working Paper Series 2002–2008, University of California, San Diego, CA.

Fishman, G. S. 1996. *Monte Carlo Concepts, Algorithms, and Applications.* Berlin: Springer.

Granger, C. 1989. *Forecasting in Business and Economics*, 2nd ed. San Diego, CA: Academic Press.

Tay, A. and K. Wallis. 2000. Density forecasting: a survey. *Journal of Forecasting* 19: 235–254.

Wallis, K. 1999. Asymmetric density forecasts of inflation and the Bank of England's fan chart. *National Institute Economic Review* 167(January): 106–112.

Chapter 21

State Fiscal Management: What Practitioners Can Learn from Risk Management Theory

Fred Thompson and Bruce L. Gates

Contents

In recent years, scholars have developed new analytical tools and financial instruments that could help governments cope more effectively with financial risk. In this chapter, we show how states can achieve structural fiscal balance and manage cyclical fiscal imbalance using analytical tools and financial instruments based on simple mean-variance analyses: Monte Carlo simulation, present value cash flow analysis, target budgeting, portfolio analysis, macroeconomic hedging, and optimal cash balance models. To illustrate the process through which mean-variance analysis can be used to identify the fiscal problems a state faces and to prescribe appropriate solutions, the reader is taken through the Oregon case. Although we use Oregon data for expository purposes, we make every effort to show where and how our home state is idiosyncratic.

Introduction

At some level of generality, all entities face the same fiscal problems: solvency, liquidity, and resource allocation. For governments, solvency is largely a matter of structural balance; liquidity a matter of cyclical imbalance; and resource allocation a matter of the intimate details of taxing, spending, and borrowing. Because state governments in America impose strict borrowing restrictions on themselves and cannot print money, their fiscal problems are almost *sui generis*. For state governments, the problem lies less in the details than in an inability to prevent or prepare adequately for imbalances resulting from the vicissitudes of the business cycle.

In recent years, scholars have developed new financial tools for the management of risk that could help state governments cope more effectively with the fiscal problems they face. In this chapter, we explain these tools and show how they fit together. Our analysis begins with the presumption that it makes sense to distinguish the problem of structural imbalance from the problem of cyclical imbalance. As will be seen, figuring out what to do about a structural deficit is conceptually easy, albeit often politically difficult—raise taxes or cut spending. What is difficult is diagnosing the problem. In contrast, it is easy to diagnose a cyclical deficit, but difficult to figure out what to do about it.

In the sections that follow, several analytically related instruments are described, which public officials could use to manage cyclical imbalance. Public budgeting and finance scholars have extensively discussed these instruments. Nevertheless, we believe we offer something new and potentially quite useful in showing how they fit together in terms of a common statistical and analytical framework. The basic notion that links these instruments is that they are all mechanisms for understanding and managing risk—where risk is understood in an actuarial sense, that is, we can predict its mean and distribution.

Depending on the situation, some mix of these instruments will represent the best response to the problem of cyclical volatility. Hence, the right mix will vary from state to state. In this chapter, the reader is taken through the process by which a prescription designed to meet the situation in one state is arrived at.

Business Cycles

An understanding of the problem of state fiscal balance begins with the dynamics of business cycles. Figure 21.1 illustrates the basic phases of business cycles: expansion, peak (or boom), contraction, and recessionary trough. In reality, the durations of business cycles are irregular and their magnitudes vary, as shown in Figure 21.2. A second reality is that, despite cyclical swings, real output has grown at a fairly

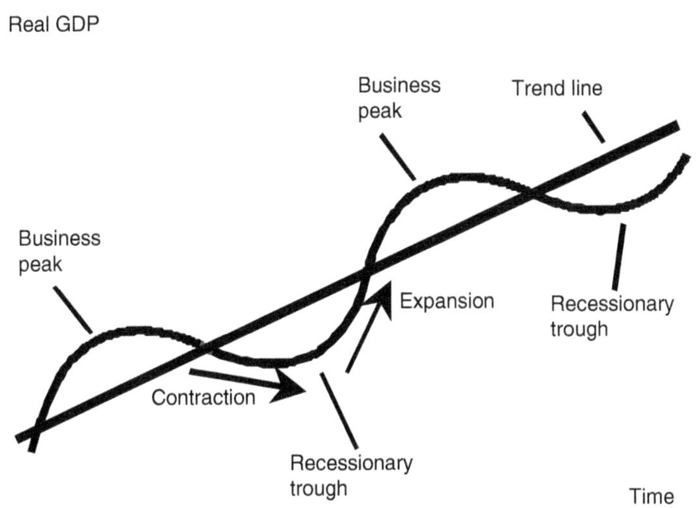

Figure 21.1 Hypothetical business cycle dynamics.

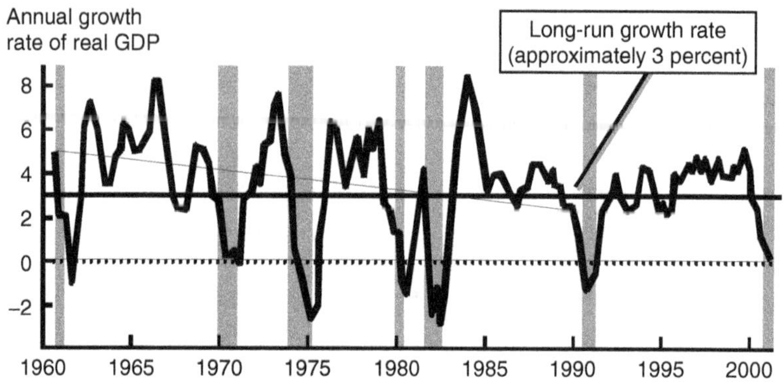

Figure 21.2 Real business cycles in the United States. (From Economic Report of the President, various issues. With permission.)

steady rate in the United States (as shown in Figure 21.2) and in most other industrial nations as well.

Cash deficits occur when outlays exceed revenues. They can have two components: a structural component and a cyclical component. The federal government defines a structural deficit as having insufficient revenues to meet current obligations when the economy is at full employment, which typically occurs during the expansionary phase of the business cycle. A cyclical deficit is a shortfall due to the business cycle, typically during the contraction phase of the cycle. This distinction is important because governments can compensate for cyclical revenue shortfalls in a variety of ways, but they can fix real structural deficits only by permanent reductions in outlays or permanent increases in taxes.

Unfortunately, the federal definition of structural deficits will not work for state governments, which must balance their budgets on an annual (or biennial) basis. Indeed, there is no generally accepted definition of the term for state governments. Regardless, there is a substantial body of literature purporting to show that this state or that one has a structural deficit. Of course, many of these works are little more than exercises in question begging. They implicitly define a structural deficit as not having enough money to meet current needs, often in the context of a plea for more taxes (Brown and Reading 2005). Others such as Hirsch and Mitchell (2002, 2003), Reshovsky (2002), and Watkins and Smith (2003) distinguish between structural deficits and cyclical deficits, more or less, as we do here, but compute the former in terms of a data series that run from trough to peak for obligations and from trough to trough or even peak to trough for revenue. In recent years, these extrapolations have usually produced substantial gaps and are often arguments for more taxes or for different ones. If the current expansion continues for a few more years, it is a safe bet that there will be a rash of extrapolations of this sort presented on behalf of tax cuts or spending increases.

For general purpose, the best definition of structural balance is "sufficient revenue to meet a state's fiscal obligations over the course of the business cycle"; under a structural deficit, revenue would be insufficient. This definition implies that state governments could achieve balance, at least in theory, by offsetting revenue shortfalls at the troughs of business cycles with revenue windfalls at their peaks, that is, they could offset cyclical deficits with cyclical surpluses. Much of this chapter is concerned with implementing this rather simple idea into practice and explaining the mechanisms that would make it feasible to do so.

Structural Balance

It is difficult to conclude whether or not a state has achieved structural balance by this definition. Every approach is flawed to a degree. The conventional approach is to measure revenues and expenditures peak to peak (or trough to trough) in constant dollars, subtracting one from the other. To do so, one needs data on revenues and outlays, a mechanism to date recessions, and a satisfactory price deflator. Forecasters can use job growth to time recessions, the national consumer price index (CPI) to convert nominal own-source revenues, and outlays to constant \$2000, although neither of these expedients is entirely satisfactory. Nevertheless, doing this tells us that in Oregon, for example, real tax revenues (before refunds) exceeded spending by \$1.4 billion, measured peak to peak and \$0.17 billion, measured trough to trough, which suggests that Oregon probably does not have a structural deficit.*

However, what we really want to know is whether revenue will grow as fast as or faster than spending. The conventional approach to measuring fiscal balance does not address that question. It tells us what happened, when we really want to know what will happen. We cannot just project revenues and spending into the future, because all the variables—gross state product (GSP), population, and inflation—that might be used to forecast revenue and spending are equally nonstationary. Moreover, as noted, one cannot predict the durations of business cycles or their magnitudes, which complicates matters, as does the fact that it is difficult to distinguish secular growth from cyclical expansion.

In financial economics, the future is typically assumed to be a random walk, albeit, perhaps, one with a long-term trend or drift. In a pure random walk, where you go next depends on where you are, but, from there, your path, either up or down, is completely random. Secular trends ought to be predictable (the estimated drift

* As a practical matter, Oregon has an expenditure limitation measure called the kicker, which requires the state to return unanticipated revenues (those not included in the biennial balanced budget enacted by the legislature) to taxpayers. Consequently, Oregon returned \$1.1 billion in \$2000 to taxpayers over the course of the last business cycle, leaving it nearly \$1.4 billion in the hole at the trough of the last recession (see Thompson and Green 2004).

in the walk—presumably, even drunks have some notion of destination in mind; more prosaically, the economy has a long-term drift), but in a random walk with drift, everything else is random, essentially noise. That includes the business cycle, which we can date after the fact, but cannot predict beforehand, and a whole lot more. (We will see later that this noise has two components: an unsystematic component, which can be diversified away, and a systematic component—the portion correlated with the business cycle, which can be hedged or insured against, but only at a cost.)

Mathematically, a random walk is an example of a Wiener process (also called Brownian motion), which is a continuous-time, continuous-state stochastic process with three distinguishing properties. First, it is a Markov process. This means that the probability distribution of future values of the process depends only on its present value.* Second, a Wiener process has independent increments. Third, the variance of the change in a Wiener process grows linearly with its time horizon.

In this instance, we would model state revenue and expenditure growth as Wiener processes with drift. The degree of drift or trend measures answers the question: Does Oregon have a structural deficit? If the drift of revenues is equal to or greater than the drift of spending, the state is in long-term balance or surplus; otherwise, it is not—it has a structural deficit. Of course, if the initial value of revenue is much below the initial value of spending, then it may take a long time for revenue to catch up. Implicitly, this approach assumes that the detrended process is essentially random noise. Clearly, that is not really the case. Public officials make all kinds of taxing and spending decisions. These decisions affect what we have called noise as well as drift. Nevertheless, the assumption that the detrended process is essentially random noise allows us to separate the problem of structural balance (drift) from the problem of cyclical imbalance (noise) operationally.

To estimate the drift coefficient, variance, and mean terminal value of a Wiener process, it is expedient to do some mathematical simulation (in this case a Monte Carlo simulation). Monte Carlo simulation is the easiest way for someone who is not a rocket scientist to estimate the results of a Wiener process. All we need is a spreadsheet and information on the mean and standard deviations of actual revenue and spending increments. The spreadsheet uses this information to randomly generate future values contingent on present values, which effectively simulates a Weiner process. (We subsequently used the detrended model produced by the simulation in the analysis described in the following sections of this chapter.)

To estimate the mean and standard deviations of revenue and spending increments, we used the year-on-year increases and decreases in Oregon revenue and spending for 1977–2003, scaled by the Bureau of Economic Analysis's recently released comprehensive revision of GSP estimates for 1977–2002 and its new

* More precisely, the distribution of future values conditional on present and past values is identical to the distribution of future values conditional on the present value alone.

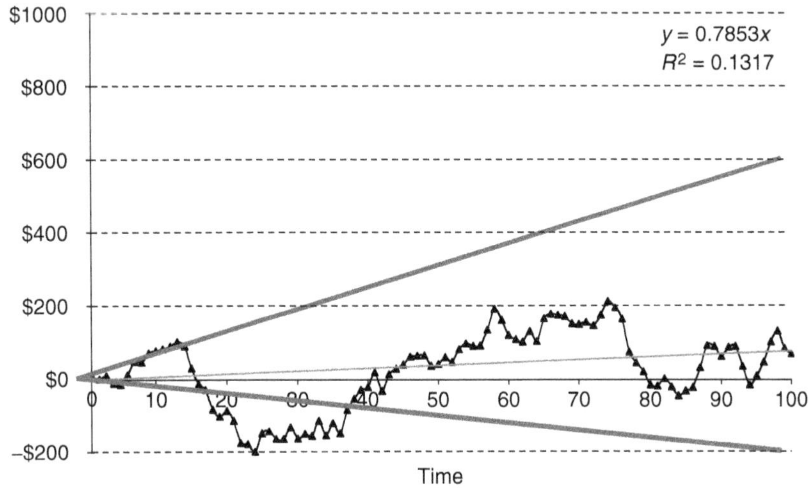

Figure 21.3 Monte Carlo simulation of Oregon's cumulative net revenues.

accelerated estimates for 2003.* Then we ran a series of simulations, setting both revenue and outlays initially equal to $5 billion, and computed the resulting patterns of surpluses and deficits. Typical results are shown in Figure 21.3. The intermediate line shows the average drift, which implies that, on average, revenues are growing 4 percent faster than outlays. The outside lines represent the standard deviation of the sum of the two processes. These values are calculated by running the simulation 225 times and computing the means and standard deviations from the resulting final values (the jagged line).†

This analysis shows that the state of Oregon almost certainly does not have a structural deficit. Actually, any other result would have been surprising. Oregon relies on progressive individual and corporate income taxes for 90 percent of its general-fund revenue. Both have high long-term income elasticities, especially the personal income tax (Bruce et al. 2004, Sobel and Holcombe 1996a). This means

* Although we have Oregon state revenue and spending data from 1950 onward, the data, especially the spending data, from earlier than 1977 is neither consistent nor very reliable. Unfortunately, the decision to use data from 1977 onward left us with a relatively small sample and an uncomfortably high estimation error. Before accepting the policy conclusions reported here, public officials in Oregon would be well advised to replicate our analysis using all the data available.

† The mathematically sophisticated reader will note that this is a roundabout way of estimating the drift coefficient, variance, and mean terminal value of a Wiener process. The values in this example can be calculated using Ito's Lemma and the Kolmogorov forward equation. However, we set out to describe a set of analytical tools that any analyst with a good understanding of Excel and basic statistics could use.

that Oregon's revenues should grow faster than the state product and, very likely, state spending as well. This is not necessarily the case in other states, which tend to rely more heavily on income-inelastic revenues (transactions, retail sales, state property taxes, or sin taxes).

The present value analysis is a second tool that is widely used in financial analysis. This tool can also be brought to bear on the question of structural balance. From a present value perspective, structural balance means that the present value of a state's projected revenues plus its net assets (assets minus liabilities) are equal to or greater than the present value of its projected operating outlays. Recently, Baker et al. (2002) used this method to assess the structural balance of all 50 states. They started with an average 1999 state tax payments and benefits received by citizens in each age and gender category, which they estimated from the Current Population Survey and the Consumer Expenditure Survey. They then projected these averages into the future using a labor-productivity growth rate of 1.5 percent per annum. Next, they multiplied year- and state-specific age–gender population estimates from the 2001 Social Security Administration's projection of the total U.S. population, by projected average revenues and expenditures by age and gender in that year to forecast total state revenues and expenditures for each future year. Finally, they calculated the present values of net cash flows using a 3 percent real discount rate. They found that imbalances ranged from a positive 48 percent of the present value of projected expenditures in Alaska to a negative 19 percent in Vermont.

We think that present-value analysis is a powerful tool for the assessment of structural balance. Moreover, we are highly impressed by the approach used by Baker et al. (2002) to estimate a state's future cash flows. Frankly, however, we are somewhat mystified by their reported results. They report that the present value of Oregon's projected net cash flows is negative by a very wide margin. We have tried to replicate their results, using their methodology, as we understand it. We find that Oregon's projected net cash flows are positive by an equally large margin. Moreover, our results are very robust to changes in assumptions about productivity and discount rates as well as changes in demographic assumptions. This means one of the two things. Either there is a large discrepancy between the spending and the tax data reported in the 1999 U.S. Census Bureau's State Government Finances survey of receipts, expenditures, and debt, which Baker et al. (2002) used to establish baseline state revenue, outlay, and net-asset positions for their projections, and the figures reported in Oregon's Consolidated Annual Financial Report, which we used; or one of us has made an error in transcription or calculation.*

* Note that neither they nor we used different discount rates for the revenue and expenditure streams. However, the expenditure stream is arguably subject to more state control than the revenue stream, and therefore the expenditure stream is less risky than the revenue stream (as we demonstrate empirically in the following section). This means we should probably use a higher discount rate for the revenue stream than for the expenditure stream. By making the two discount rates different enough, we could probably replicate their results.

Cyclical Imbalance

The toughest fiscal challenge state officials face is preventing or preparing for cyclical imbalance. Fortunately, researchers have learned a lot in the past decade about how to and how not to prevent cyclical imbalance and how to and how not to prepare for imbalance. In her magisterial review of the literature on state budgeting and finance, Rubin (2005, pp. 47–48, 65) wrote,

> Much of the literature on state-level budgeting follows the states' adaptation to and responses to cycles of boom and bust in the economy, including prevention (building up reserve funds that can be used in time of recession), temporizing (using delaying tactics to tide the state over until the economy improves), and balancing (increasing revenue and/or decreasing spending).... What would be useful here is an index of prevention of and perhaps a second and related one of preparation for recessions.

We think Rubin has it right, with one "caveat." Imbalances are not the result of recessions, but of cyclical and random changes in revenues and outlays. It is necessary to deal with expansions as well as contractions to achieve fiscal stability.

Schunk and Woodward (2005; see also Cornia et al. 2004) argue, for example, that the solution to the problem of cyclical imbalance at the state level lies in stabilizing spending growth through target budgeting. They imply that rapid and sustained revenue growth tends to encourage unsustainable tax cuts or spending increases. When recession strikes, state governments engage in a variety of expedients, many of them quite wasteful, to cope with the emergency. As long as the recession is fresh in the minds of public officials, their control of the purse strings remains tight (Thomas and Garber 2006). Gradually, however, funds accumulate and the need to spend becomes overriding (Reid 2005).

In some booms, state officials are swept away by the irrational exuberance of the times, funding massive infrastructure investments called forth by the elusive vista of permanent prosperity. Indeed, unsustainable state spending inspired by the length and magnitude of the Clinton era boom offers a neat, albeit probably specious, answer to how the relatively mild and short-lived 2001 recession could have led to such big fiscal problems for the states (Boyd 2002, Vasché and Williams 2005).

Schunk and Woodward (2005) propose a spending rule in which state spending is allowed to increase no faster than the sum of population growth plus inflation plus 1 percent real growth.* Revenue in excess of this amount would be partly diverted to a stabilization (or "rainy-day") fund, with the rest returned to the taxpayers.

* Schunk and Woodward's spending rule is arbitrary. Assuming, however, that we can model state spending and taxing as a Wiener process, it ought to be possible to calculate a spending rule using optimal control theory.

They then tested this model using aggregate spending and revenue data from the 50 states for the period 1992–2002. They found that, with a modest portion of surplus revenues partially invested in a rainy-day fund, their spending rule resulted in "stable growth of state budgets throughout the recession and sluggish recovery of the early 2000s" (p. 105).

Looking at California and South Carolina individually, they obtained similar results. California diverged from a sustainable path as early as 1996 or 1997, but would have been fine if it had merely practiced a little spending restraint over the next four or five years. South Carolina would have survived intact had it followed their rule, but it would have needed to put a higher portion of its surplus revenues into a rainy-day fund than California and that fund would have been almost completely depleted by 2004. Schunk and Woodward (2005, p. 119) conclude

> This spending rule has the effect of forcing fiscal discipline on state governments, not for the purpose of cutting the size of government but for the explicit goal of providing stability over the business cycle. This stability is a virtue because it provides a benchmark for state budget writers. It is a rule that governs how much money can be spent while still leaving it up to the discretion of lawmakers to decide how to allocate these funds.

Alas, when we applied Schunk and Woodward's spending rule to the Oregon case, it had no effect whatsoever on the consequent instability. Figure 21.4 shows that, during the first three biennia of the decade, actual spending tracked allowable expenditures under their stabilization rule almost perfectly. Then, actual spending

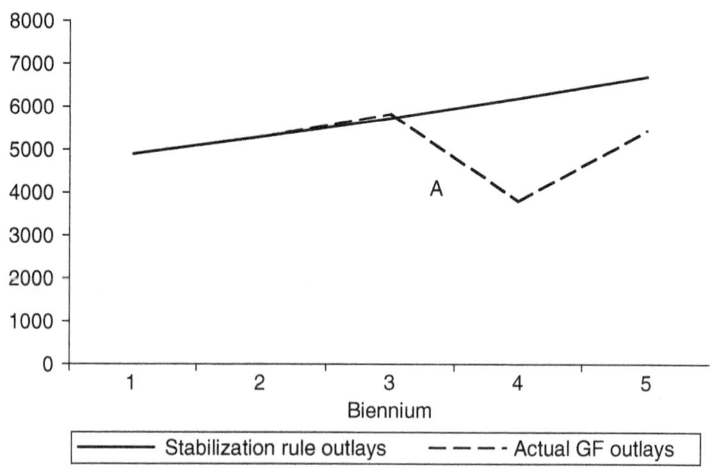

Figure 21.4 Oregon spending, actual, and stabilization rule.

general fund (GF) outlays fell below the stabilization rule—way below—and stayed there. Nevertheless, this result is perfectly consistent with their analysis. Oregon has long had a legislatively enacted expenditure limit that is almost identical to Schunk and Woodward's spending rule. The difference is that in Oregon we sent the entire surplus revenues back to the taxpayers—almost none was set aside for a rainy day. When the rainy day came, we had no money.

Reducing Revenue Volatility with Tax Portfolios

Even where state spending is on a stable, sustainable growth path, public officials must still deal with the problem of revenue volatility. Figure 21.5 starkly illustrates this problem. It shows year-on-year changes in real revenue growth in Oregon from 1950 to 2000. During this period, real revenue growth was between 3.5 and 4 percent per annum (nominal revenue growth rate for the whole period was almost 9 percent). Revenue volatility (the standard deviation or σ of year-on-year revenue increments) was a whopping 7.6 percent (13.4 percent for nominal revenues).

The state of Oregon is probably an extreme case. Earlier, tax specialists would have attributed its revenue volatility entirely to a high-growth, income-elastic tax base. The traditional view held that there was an inherent trade-off between revenue growth and stability (Groves and Kahn 1952). According to this perspective, income-elastic tax bases tended to grow faster than income, but fluctuations in income over the business cycle caused them to be unstable.

In the mean time, empirical analysis has demonstrated that this is not necessarily the case. Income taxes are not necessarily more volatile or faster growing than broad-based consumption taxes; corporate income taxes grow more slowly than personal income taxes and are more volatile; even some specific excises, such as motor fuel taxes, are fast growing and some are quite volatile (Bruce et al. 2004,

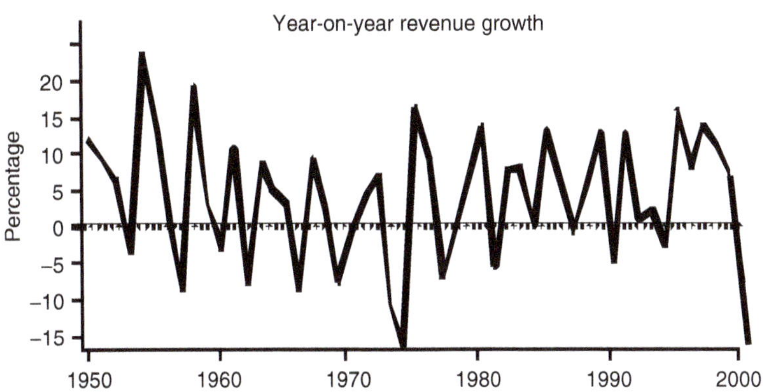

Figure 21.5 Real revenue growth, Oregon 1950–2000.

Table 21.1 An Illustrative, Two-Tax Portfolio

	Probability	*Income (Percent)*	*Alcohol (Percent)*	*Portfolio (Percent)*
Recession	0.10	−22.0	8.0	−7.0
Below average	0.20	−2.0	4.0	1.0
Average	0.40	10.0	0.0	5.0
Above average	0.20	18.0	−4	7.0
Boom	0.10	30.0	−8.0	11.0
Expected growth		8.0	0	4.0

Dye and Merriman 2004, Gentry and Ladd 1994, Otsuka and Braun 1999, Sobel and Holcombe 1996a). Indeed, Bruce et al. (2004; see also Fox 2003) show that the composition of the tax base, rate structures, and elements of administration can have bigger effects on growth and volatility than the tax type. For example, state policy makers can often significantly lower the volatility of revenue from broad-based taxes without adversely affecting revenue growth simply by eliminating exemptions or equalizing marginal rates.

So, if income taxes are not inherently more unstable than other tax types and if Oregon's income tax revenues are no more volatile than the average of state income tax revenues and less volatile than income taxes in many other states, what makes it exceptional, an extreme case? Here, the rather surprising answer is its heavy reliance on a single tax type—corporate and personal income taxes. Diversification of tax types can reduce revenue volatility and most states rely on a portfolio of tax types.

How does diversification of tax portfolios work? The answer is that portfolio volatility is a function of the covariance or correlation, ρ, of its component revenue sources (Gentry and Ladd 1994, White 1983).* Table 21.1, which shows two equally weighted revenue sources—the income tax and the alcohol tax— illustrates this basic idea.

Lacking further information about the economy in the coming year, we would assume that the likelihood of each of the five possible states that could occur was equal to its historical rate of occurrence or frequency. For each revenue source, these states are associated with an average year-on-year growth rate. With this information, we can calculate the expected growth and volatility, σ, of each of the revenue sources and of the portfolio as a whole. Expected growth is the weighted average of the growth rates (summed over the possible states of nature), or 4 percent. In contrast, the volatility of the portfolio, $\sigma_{\pi.} = 3.1$ percent, is much less than the volatility of either the income tax (13.4 percent) or the income and alcohol taxes

* This is, of course, merely a special application of ideas formulated in corporate finance having to do with risk and return (see Lintner 1965, Markowitz 1952, Sharpe 1964).

combined (8.9 percent). It is less than even the volatility of the alcohol tax alone (4.4 percent).*

Some of the remarkable implications of portfolio theory are as follows:

1. Average volatility will usually be reduced by adding tax sources, except where the two taxes are perfectly correlated, $\rho = +1.0$.
2. A two-tax portfolio could in theory be combined to eliminate revenue volatility completely, but only if $\rho = -1.0$ and the two taxes were weighted equally.
3. In general, tax sources have $\rho \approx 0.65$, and therefore, adding taxes to the portfolio tends to reduce but not eliminate volatility.
4. Only if we look at efficient tax portfolios is there a necessary trade-off between stability and growth. Moreover, it is possible to construct an efficient growth frontier, showing this trade-off (see Figure 21.6). All one needs is information on the covariance of the growth rates of each of the different tax types and designs that are obtained in the different states.
5. Moreover, it is theoretically possible to identify an efficient linear combination of growth rates and volatilities ranging from zero volatility to a state's optimal volatility at its current growth rate and beyond.

Figure 21.6 illustrates our efforts to apply these notions to Oregon. The point denoted as OR shows the growth and volatility of Oregon's actual tax portfolio. The other points denote various tax types as reported by Bruce et al. (2004), Dye and Merriman (2004), Gentry and Ladd (1994), Otsuka and Braun (1999), Sobel and Holcombe (1996b), and Holcombe and Sobel (1997). Then, by making some heroic assumptions, we identified all reasonable combinations of revenue sources and feasible weights that would give Oregon the same real rate of revenue growth that it currently enjoys—about 4 percent. Finally, we estimated the portfolio volatility (σ_p) for each combination and set of weights and located the minimum. According to our analysis, tax portfolio diversification could reduce Oregon's revenue volatility (σ) by more than 40 percent (from 7.6 to 4.4 percent), without substantially reducing revenue growth. This point is denoted as PE in Figure 21.6.

The problem with this solution is that, although it would significantly reduce revenue volatility, it would do so at the expense of tax fairness. Shifting from Oregon's existing tax portfolio to the efficient portfolio would reduce the cross-sectional income elasticity of Oregon's tax structure 25–35 percent, converting it from moderately

* In the illustrative example, the two tax types are equally weighted, that is, they produced the same revenue last year. Unequal weights complicate this calculation. Consequently, we use information about the covariance (ρ) of the components of the portfolio to calculate portfolio stand ard deviations. If, for example, the more stable tax source A had a weight of 0.3 and a σ of 0.2, the less stable tax source B a weight of 0.7 and a σ of 0.4, and their ρ was 0.4, then

$$\begin{aligned}\sigma_p &= \sqrt{W_A^2\sigma_A^2 + (1 - W_A)^2\,\sigma_B^2 + 2W_A(1 - W_A)\rho_{AB}\sigma_A\sigma_B} \\ &= \sqrt{0.3^2(0.2^2) + 0.7^2(0.4^2) + 2(0.3)(0.7)(0.4)(0.2)(0.4)} \\ &= 0.309\end{aligned}$$

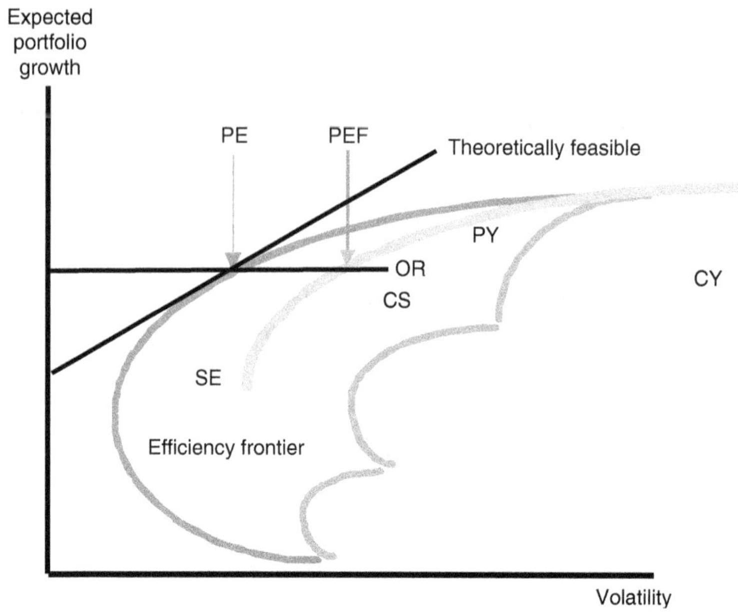

Figure 21.6 Feasible and efficient tax portfolios. PE = efficient portfolio, PEF = efficient and fair portfolio, OR = current tax portfolio, CY = corporate income tax, PY = personal income tax, CS = broad-based consumption tax, SE = selected excises.

progressive to slightly regressive. This result did not really catch us unaware because the efficient tax portfolio included sales taxes and greatly increased liquor and motor fuel taxes, but not corporate income taxes, and cut personal income tax rates in half.*

Following the approach formulated by Gentry and Ladd (1994), we replicated our search for efficient tax portfolios, this time constraining the weighted average of our synthetic portfolios to cross-sectional income elasticities equal to or greater than 1.25, the mean of Oregon's current tax portfolio, as well as its current rate of revenue growth. Unfortunately, a portfolio that would be both efficient and equally fair, would not significantly reduce tax volatility. This point is denoted as PEF in Figure 21.6.†

* This tax portfolio is nevertheless quite attractive on several dimensions. Because it would entail substantially lower marginal deadweight losses than Oregon's current tax portfolio, it would also be allocatively more efficient than Oregon's existing tax portfolio (see Diewert et al. 1998).

† It should be possible to design a broad-based consumption tax, for example, say a value-added tax with direct income-contingent rebates to taxpayers that would be as progressive as Oregon's personal income tax. This means that the theoretically feasible efficient frontier is probably much closer to the efficient frontier than shown in Figure 21.6. Figure 21.6 reflects only the tax types actually employed by the states and not what might be theoretically possible.

Using Futures and Options Contracts to Hedge against Revenue Volatility

There is a complementary approach based on this logic that could in theory be used to reduce revenue volatility: using financial derivatives to hedge financial risk (Swidler et al. 1999). What we have just mentioned, at least implicitly, is that portfolio strategies can effectively address the problem of unsystematic revenue volatility. Revenue volatility, however, has two components: an unsystematic component that can be diversified away through the construction of appropriate tax and revenue portfolios and a systematic component that varies directly with macroeconomic aggregates that cannot be diversified away. Hedging strategies are addressed primarily to systematic revenue volatility.*

Two kinds of financial derivatives can be used to hedge systematic revenue volatility: futures and options contracts. A futures contract is an exchange-traded obligation in which the payoff is the difference between the price of a financial asset—a commodity or an index—at the beginning (futures price) and the end of the contract (delivery price). When the price of the contract increases, the buyer is credited with the profit and the seller with the loss; when it decreases, the seller is credited with the profit and the buyer the loss. As Hinkelmann and Swidler (2005, p. 129) observe, "A futures contract is therefore a zero sum game in which the profits of one party equal the losses of the counterparty." Hence, using futures contracts to hedge revenue flows means sacrificing higher than expected revenue flows, and not just avoiding revenue shortfalls. Nevertheless, it follows that a state could fully stabilize revenue growth by "selling" futures contracts on financial assets—if the underlying asset values were sufficiently covariant with the state's revenue flows ($\rho = +1.0$).†

If, however, states want to only protect themselves against revenue shortfalls (keeping high revenue flows for themselves), they must purchase put options on the covariant financial asset. A "put" gives the buyer the right, but not the obligation, to sell the underlying financial asset for a fixed price, called the strike price. Of course, a state would exercise its option to sell the asset only if its spot price fell below its strike price. Unfortunately, options are not free. States would have to pay

* We are concerned here only with financial instruments. A proper discussion of state hedging would comprehend all state investments that reduce revenue risk, including physical investments in income-producing assets.

† This could be accomplished in theory by selling futures contracts on state revenue, but problems of moral hazard and, perhaps, adverse selection would probably make the design and operation of such markets prohibitively costly. In practice, Oregon's treasury refunded much of the state's debt a few years ago with variable rate bonds precisely because of the inverse correlation between interest rates and state revenue flows. In recent months, most new and refinance issues have been at fixed rates; however, as the treasury and the bond advisory council have been under considerable external pressure "to lock in low rates." Of course, all Oregon state debt issues feature a call provision (which gives the issuer the right but not the obligation to buy them back at a fixed price).

hefty premiums to purchase enough put options to provide meaningful insurance against unwanted revenue shortfalls.

The rub in using futures or options contracts to hedge state revenues lies in finding a financial asset that would be sufficiently covariant with state revenue to provide a good hedge. In one of the earliest explorations of this issue, Overdahl (1986) argued that commodity prices were likely to be highly correlated with state revenue flows and that existing derivatives traded on the New York Mercantile Exchange, or the Chicago Board of Trade could be used to hedge general revenue flows. For example, Iowa could sell corn futures and Texas oil futures to hedge revenues. Subsequent empirical analysis shows, however, that Overdahl was overly optimistic. Existing commodities futures markets provide few if any useful opportunities for states to hedge general revenues (Hinkelmann and Swidler 2004).

Thanks largely to Yale professor Shiller (2003), currently there is a movement afoot to create hedging instruments based on aggregate macroeconomic indicators. Goldman Sachs and Deutsche Bank already offer derivatives on nonfarm payroll and initial jobless claims. Futures and options based on indices such as gross national product or personal income will probably soon follow. None of these indices would represent a perfect hedge (a one-for-one offset for gains or losses). Nevertheless, according to Hinkelmann and Swidler, derivatives based on personal income (either futures or put options) could reduce revenue shortfalls by at least 60 percent in about 20 states, including New York, Ohio, Pennsylvania, and Massachusetts (Hinkelmann and Swidler 2004, 2005). Oregon is not one of the twenty, but it could still reduce year-on-year shortfalls by 40 percent or thereabout through macroeconomic hedging. The main drawback to this risk management strategy (besides the fact that these derivative instruments do not now exist) would be the size of the premiums Oregon would have to pay if it wished only to insure itself against revenue losses. These are conservatively estimated to cost between $180 and $240 million a year.

Self-Insurance against Revenue Volatility

Self-insurance is usually the best available alternative to buying insurance. Given the issue at hand, creating and maintaining state rainy-day funds is a kind of self-insurance. The problems here are, first, estimating the size of the rainy-day fund needed to avoid significant expenditure reductions or tax increases during future downturns and, second, formulating a contribution or savings rate rule to follow to achieve the desired fund size.*

Conceptually, assessing the adequacy of rainy-day funds of various sizes is an optimal cash balance or inventory problem (Archer 1966, Baumol 1952, Gates

* This portion of this chapter is based on Gates et al. (2005).

and Thompson 1988, Miller and Orr 1966).* One first estimates the mean and distribution of expected revenue shortfalls using the kind of Monte Carlo simulation described earlier. Then, to assess the relationship between the size of the cash balance and the probability of an unredressed revenue shortfall, one calculates the average probability of shortfall, given cash balances of various sizes. The probability of an unredressed revenue shortfall and the size of cash balances should be inversely correlated, with changes in the probability of revenue shortfalls decreasing at a decreasing rate as rainy-day funds are increased.

In an early, although quite sophisticated, study of this problem, Pollock and Suyderhoud (1986) estimated the minimum cash balance needed to achieve fiscal stability using quarterly Indiana data. They concluded that a beginning cash balance equal to 13 percent of 1983 outlays would have met the state's liquidity requirement 59 out of 60 quarters during the 1969–1983 period. They also found that withdrawals from the fund would have been required in 31 out of 59 quarters during this period. Navin and Navin (1997) used a similar method to estimate the optimal cash balance for Ohio using data for the period 1985–1995. They found that, to avoid disruptive expenditure reductions or tax increases, Ohio's fund needed to be about the same size. Sjoquist (1998) found that Georgia needed a rainy-day fund of over 27 percent to achieve fiscal stability. In what is easily the most comprehensive analysis of state rainy-day funds, although now somewhat dated, Holcombe and Sobel (1997) calculated the cash balance each state would have needed to weather the 1989–1992 recession (Sobel and Holcombe 1996a,b). They found that the average state needed a cash balance of 30 percent of 1988 expenditures; however, many could have made with 5 percent or less, whereas others needed more than 50 percent.

In a recent study, Wagner and Elder (2004) used a Markov-switching model to estimate real per capita personal income for each state during booms and busts, as well as the probability of switching from economic expansion to contraction and back again. Based on these results (together with the assumption that state revenues vary directly with personal income), they computed the savings rate needed during good times to buffer state governments against unrequited revenue shortfalls during bad ones. They found that, to provide a 90 percent buffer against cash shortfalls, the required contribution rate was 1.87 percent of revenue on average. Ten states needed contribution rates of less than 1 percent of revenues, with Kansas

* In their analysis of Utah's rainy-day fund, Cornia and Nelson (2003) utilize a value at risk (VAR) model rather than an inventory model. VAR identifies the worst loss over a target horizon, with a given level of confidence, and as such is widely used in the risk management literature. Cornia and Nelson used this approach because the software for it was readily available and because they wanted to develop a measure of risk over the business cycle for Utah's unique tax structure. Analytically speaking, however, what they did is not significantly different from what we describe here. But by decomposing the variance in Utah's cash flows into systematic and unsystematic components, their work more than any other inspired our attempt to show how a variety of risk management tools fit together to address the revenue volatility problem, and by analogy other public sector risk management problems as well.

requiring none. Eight states needed contribution rates of more than 3 percent of revenue, with Wyoming topping the list at 4.5 percent.

According to Wagner and Elder, Oregon is one of the states that must contribute more than 3 percent of general fund revenues (i.e., more than $150 million) each year to reduce the probability of a revenue shortfall to one in ten. To explore this relationship, we replicated their analysis using the data and Monte Carlo simulation described earlier (see Figure 21.3). In this instance, we assumed an annual contribution to a cash reserve of $\$X$, leaving the amount as a variable for user manipulation.* Each period, our model replenished the cash balance by a fixed amount, $\$X$, and depleted the cash balance to redress shortfalls when they occurred, until the reserve was exhausted. We then calculated the average probability of an unredressed revenue shortfall in 225 trials of 100 simulations given annual contributions to cash balances ranging from $0 to $0.5 billion, increased in $10 million increments.

As expected, we found that the probability of a revenue shortfall and the size of contributions were inversely correlated. With a zero contribution, the probability of a budget shortfall was 0.5. As the size of the annual contribution increased, the probability of a shortfall decreased. Over a range of contributions from $0 to $80 million, the relationship was approximately linear, and small incremental increases in the size of contributions generated relatively large decreases in the probability of a shortfall. However, diminishing returns set in as the size of the cash balance was further increased.† Consequently, these results suggest that Oregon would experience unredressed shortfalls only once every five years "on average," if it were to contribute $80 to $100 million (2000 dollars) each year to a rainy-day fund. Reducing the probability to one in ten would require contributions of more than $200 million and to one in twenty more than $400 million.

For Oregon, reducing the probability of a revenue shortfall to one in five using put options would have cost almost twice as much as self-insurance through contributions to a rainy-day fund, perhaps more. This represents big savings in terms of premiums avoided. Nevertheless, it might well be the case that some combination

---

* An earlier version of this analysis was reported in Gates et al. (2005). The analytic problems we reported in that study have been addressed in this analysis.

† For annual contributions to rainy-day funds over the range $80 million to $0.5 billion, the best-fit relationship between unredressed budget shortfalls and cash balances was

$$y = 0.3439e^{-0.0012x}$$

where

y = average probability of an unredressed budget shortfall
x = size of the contribution in millions

This formula accounts for 98.22 percent of the variance in the relationship. Solving for x yields the following estimation:

$$x = \frac{\ln(y/0.3439)}{-0.0012}$$

of derivatives and savings would be even better. We would also caution that the evidence is quite strong that rainy-day funds that are not governed by strict deposit and withdrawal rules, usually fail to deliver on their promised benefits (Wagner 2004).*

Participation in a Self-Insurance Pool as a Means of Insuring against Revenue Volatility

The recognition that most state legislatures failed to adopt contribution and withdrawal rules adequate to safeguard their rainy-day funds from themselves led Holcombe and Sobel (1997) to suggest that states establish a self-insurance pool that would operate independently of its members.† An arm's length relationship would reduce state pressure to spend cash reserves whenever they reached significant levels. Holcombe and Sobel further noted that clear rules governing contributions and withdrawals would improve state credit ratings, and thereby, reduce capital financing costs for states. Finally, they noted that by pooling their funds, the states could significantly reduce the amount of money each would have to contribute to achieve a given level of revenue stability. Based on their calculations, participation in a self-insurance pool would be 15 percent less costly than self-insurance.

This final conclusion follows from treating the determination of cash balances as an inventory problem. The standard formulation of this problem under uncertainty holds that the minimum inventory needed to avoid shortages a given percentage of the time is a function of the square root of the size of the cash pool. However, Holcombe and Sobel did not rest their argument on this formulation alone. Their conclusions reflected a careful analysis of the covariance of the revenue yields of various tax types with macroeconomic aggregates, which showed that the collective or pooled state variance was substantially less than the sum of the individual states.

Based on this finding, Mattoon (2004) of the Federal Reserve Bank of Chicago designed a national state rainy-day fund modeled on the unemployment compensation trust fund, a widely used countercyclical risk management tool. Mattoon proposed the creation of an experience ratings system that would trigger differential

* As one reader, Bill Conerly observed, absent these rules, "the use of a large cash balance to self-insure against a revenue shortage often leads future legislators to raid the balance, or at least feel comfortable starting programs that will have a substantial future cost."

† Mattoon (2004, p. 18) argues that "a quasi-governmental agency created by the states would be the logical organization to administer the fund. The agency would need to be autonomous enough to enforce rainy day fund rules and to have sufficient expertise to adjust rainy day fund structure to reflect emerging conditions. If specific experience ratings were created to reflect state revenue and expenditure volatility, the agency would need to have the staff expertise to calculate annual experience ratings. The agency would need to function as an independent third party administrator."

fund contributions for each state and permit borrowing from the national fund, with borrowing states charged interest for the use of their funds. Mattoon also simulated fund performance under differing rules governing contributions and withdrawals. Unfortunately, his simulations show that it would be much easier to devise rules for operating the fund once it was capitalized, than capitalizing it in the first place. Moreover, even if the self-insurance fund had been fully capitalized and operated according to his rules, Mattoon (2004, p. 19) concluded

> Twenty-two states would have exhausted their rainy day funds over this period with the state of California accounting for nearly 56% of the rainy day fund deficit. However, absent any other budget actions such as spending cuts or tax increases, the existence of the fund would have covered 74% of the cumulative deficit for the states. In addition, it should be remembered that rainy day funds should not cover structural state deficits. Recent state fiscal experience suggests that many states have experienced structural rather than cyclical deficits that will require revenue and expenditure actions in addition to tapping rainy day funds.

Conclusions

There are no free lunches in finance. Coping with a deficit, even a cyclical one can be painful. However, the risk management tools discussed here—Monte Carlo simulation, present value cash flow analysis, target budgeting, portfolio analysis, hedging, self-insurance, and self-insurance pools—are far less costly than are some of the expedients traditionally employed by states—shifting financial obligations to other jurisdictions, borrowing from enterprise and trust funds, deferring scheduled maintenance or the failure to replace worn-out or obsolete equipment, etc.* States should make use of them all. Moreover, they can be applied to a wide array of public sector problems, especially when making guarantees and mitigating risks remains a major function of government. They ought to be part of the standard repertoire of all public sector managers and not just financial managers.

If public officials were trusted to use these tools, it might make sense to go a little bit further. The pursuit of evermore stable revenues leads to exponentially increasing costs, regardless of the tool or tools used, although choosing the right mix of tools can slow the rate of increase. Assuming that public officials have achieved structural balance, stabilized expenditure growth, and taken appropriate steps to dampen revenue volatility, shouldn't they be allowed to borrow? Beyond some point, say, one in twenty years, or even one in ten years, borrowing is cheaper than the alternatives.

* Some of the costs of borrowing from trust funds are explored in Hansen and Thompson (2005).

Besides, from the citizens' perspective countercyclical borrowing is simply the other side of countercyclical savings. In both cases, the state would spend less or tax more in boom times to spend more or tax less during busts. The difference to taxpayers is largely a matter of timing, to save the state must take their money before it is needed (or keep it when it is not needed) and invest it until a shortfall occurs. Hence, taxpayers must either save less, borrow more, or defer consumption. In contrast, when the state borrows to meet cyclical needs, taxpayers do not have to reduce personal savings or increase personal debt until repayment of the state's debt is due. Arguably, borrowing is better for taxpayers because they can invest their savings more profitably than can the state and because the state can borrow more cheaply than they can. It is also a lot easier to figure out how much a state needs to borrow than it is to figure out how much to hedge or self-insure.

There is one further consideration, not all states have equally strict rules against borrowing. Most require the enactment of a balanced budget, but in many, if a shortfall subsequently occurs, public officials are free to borrow to redress the difference (Hou and Smith 2005). In Oregon, it has happened more than once that the legislature has balanced the budget by enacting tax increases that will be predictably rejected by the voters in the next scheduled election (Thompson and Green 2004).* The state then made up part of the difference through borrowing. One does not have to believe that this was the result of a cynical conspiracy to believe that it would have been better for all those concerned if state officials had honestly confronted the prospect of borrowing from the outset.

References

Archer, S. H. 1966. A model for the determination of firm cash balances. *The Journal of Financial and Quantitative Analysis* 1(1): 1–11.

Baker, B., D. Besendorfer, and L. J. Kotlikoff. 2002. Intertemporal state budgeting. NBER Working Paper No. W9067, July 2002. Available at SSRN: http://ssrn.com/abstract=319743_(accessed June 7, 2007).

Baumol, W. J. 1952. The transactions demand for cash: An inventory theoretic approach. *The Quarterly Journal of Economics* 66(4): 545–556.

Boyd, D. J. 2002. *State Fiscal Issues and Risks at the Start of a New Century.* Fiscal Studies Program, The Nelson A. Rockefeller Institute of Government, State University of New York at Albany.

Brown, J. and D. Reading. 2005. *Idaho's Structural Deficit: A Problem That Won't Go Away.* Moscow: Idaho Center on Budget and Tax Policy.

* This note will probably be of interest only to fellow Oregonians, but enacting new taxes, which are annulled by popular referenda, also has the effect of relaxing the kicker because only revenue collections in excess of the amounts budgeted (forecast) must be returned to taxpayers.

Bruce, D., W. F. Fox, and M. H. Tuttle. 2004. *Tax Base Elasticities: A Multi–State Analysis of Long Run and Short Run Dynamics*. TN: Knoxville Center for Business and Economic Research, University of Tennessee.

Cornia, G. C. and R. D. Nelson. 2003. Rainy day funds and value at risk. *State Tax Notes* 29(8): 563–567.

Cornia, G. C., R. D. Nelson, and A. Wilko. 2004. Fiscal planning, budgeting, and rebudgeting using revenue semaphores. *Public Administration Review* 64(2): 164–179.

Diewert, W. I., D. A. Lawrence, and F. Thompson. 1998. The marginal costs of taxation and regulation. In *Handbook of Public Finance*, eds. F. Thompson and M. Green. New York: Dekker, pp. 135–172.

Dye, R. F. and D. F. Merriman. 2004. *State Revenue Stability: Alternative Conceptualizations*. Institute of Government and Public Affairs, University of Illinois, December 13, Urbana, IL.

Fox, W. F. 2003. Three characteristics of tax structures have contributed to the current state fiscal crises. *State Tax Notes* (August 4): 375–383.

Gates, B., J. Brown, J. Page, F. Thompson, and R. Yoshida. 2005. Does Oregon need a rainy day fund? Like a fish needs a bicycle. *State Tax Notes* 36(2): 48–56.

Gates, B. L. and F. Thompson. 1988. Estimating the liquidity requirements of cash pools. *State and Local Government Review* 21(3): 105.

Gentry, W. F. and H. F. Ladd. 1994. State tax structure and multiple policy objectives. *National Tax Journal* 47(4): 747–772.

Groves, H. M. and C. H. Kahn. 1952. The stability of state and local tax yields. *American Economic Review* 42(1): 87–102.

Hansen, S. and F. Thompson. 2005. Appraising commitments, quasi-commitments, and guarantees. *Paper presented at the Association for Budgeting and Financial Management (ABFM) Annual Conference*, November 10–12, Washington.

Hinkelmann, C. and S. Swidler. 2004. Using futures contracts to hedge macroeconomic risks in the public sector. *Derivatives Use, Trading and Regulation* 10(1): 54–69.

Hinkelmann, C. and S. Swidler. 2005. State government hedging with financial derivatives. *State and Local Government Review* 37(2): 127–141.

Hirsch, W. Z. and D. J. B. Mitchell. 2002. Making California's state budget more user-friendly and transparent. *California Policy Options 2002*. UCLA School of Public Policy and Social Research, UCLA, CA: Westwood, pp. 20–46.

Hirsch, W. Z. and D. J. B. Mitchell. 2003. Making California's state budget more user-friendly and transparent: Further thoughts. *California Policy Options 2003*. UCLA School of Public Policy and Social Research, UCLA, CA: Westwood, pp. 23–49.

Holcombe, R. G. and R. S. Sobel. 1997. *Growth and Variability in State Tax Revenue: An Anatomy of State Fiscal Crises*. Westport, CT: Greenwood Press.

Hou, Y. and D. L. Smith. 2005. A framework for understanding state balanced budget requirement systems: Re-examining distinctive features and an operational definition. *Paper presented at the Association for Budgeting and Financial Management (ABFM) Annual Conference*, November 10–12, Washington.

Lintner, J. 1965. The valuation of risk assets and the selection of risky investments in stock portfolios and capital budgets. *The Review of Economics and Statistics* 47(1): 13–37.

Markowitz, H. M. 1952. Portfolio selection. *Journal of Finance* 7(1): 77–91.

Mattoon, R. 2004. Creating a national state rainy day fund: A modest proposal to improve future state fiscal performance. *State Tax Notes* 31(4): 271–288.

Miller, M. H. and D. Orr. 1966. A model of the demand for money by firms. *Quarterly Journal of Economics* 80(3): 413–435.
Navin, J. and L. Navin. 1997. The optimal size of countercyclical budget stabilization funds: A case study of Ohio. *Public Budgeting and Finance* 17(2): 114–127.
Otsuka, Y. P. and B. M. Braun. 1999. The random coefficient approach for estimating tax revenue stability and growth. *Public Finance Review* 27(6): 665–676.
Overdahl, J. A. 1986. *The Use of Crude Oil Futures by the Governments of Oil Producing States*. New York: Center for the Study of Futures Markets, Columbia Business School, Columbia University.
Pollock, R. and J. P. Suyderhoud. 1986. The role of rainy day funds in achieving fiscal stability. *National Tax Journal* 39(4): 485–497.
Reid, T. R. 2005. Revenue is starting to burn holes in states' pockets: Fiscal posture turns around. *Washington Post*, December 21.
Reshovsky, A. 2002. *Wisconsin's Structural Deficit: Our Fiscal Future at the Crossroads*. Madison, AL: Robert M. Lafollette School of Public Affairs, University of Wisconsin.
Rubin, I. S. 2005. The state of state budget research. *Public Budgeting and Finance* 25: 46–67 (special issue).
Schunk, D. and D. Woodward. 2005. Spending stabilization rules: A solution to recurring state budget crises? *Public Budgeting and Finance* 25(4): 105–124.
Sharpe, W. F. 1964. Capital asset prices: A theory of market equilibrium under conditions of risk. *Journal of Finance* 19(3): 425–442.
Shiller, R. J. 2003. *The New Financial Order: Risk in the 21st Century*. Princeton, NJ: Princeton University Press.
Sjoquist, D. L. 1998. *Georgia's Revenue Shortfall Reserve: An Analysis of Its Role, Size and Structure*. Fiscal Research Program, Andrew Young School of Policy Studies, Georgia State University. http://frp.aysps.gsu.edu/frp/frpreports/brief_reports/brief3.html.
Sobel, R. S. and R. D. Holcombe. 1996a. The impact of state rainy day funds in easing state fiscal crises during the 1990–1991 recession. *Public Budgeting and Finance* 16(3): 28–48.
Sobel, R. S. and R. G. Holcombe. 1996b. Measuring the growth and variability of tax bases over the business cycle. *National Tax Journal* 49(4): 535–552.
Swidler, S. M., R. J. Buttimer, and R. Shaw. 1999. Government hedging: Motivation, implementation, and evaluation. *Public Budgeting and Finance* 19(4): 75–90.
Thomas, R. and A. Garber. 2006. Gregoire: Let's stick to a budget. *Seattle Times*, January 11.
Thompson, F. and M. Green. 2004. *Vox Populi*: Tax and expenditure limitation initiatives in Oregon. *Public Budgeting and Finance* 24(4): 73–87.
Vasché, J. D. and B. Williams. 2005. Revenue volatility in California. *State Tax Notes* 36(1): 35–46.
Wagner, G. A. 2004. The bond market and fiscal institutions: Have budget stabilization funds reduced state borrowing costs? *National Tax Journal* 57(4): 785–804.
Wagner, G. A. and E. M. Elder. 2004. Recessions and rainy day funds in U.S. states: What are the odds your state is saving enough? Working paper, Duquesne University.
Watkins, M. P. and J. Smith. 2003. It's not just the recession: The budget crisis and Washington State's structural deficit. Seattle, Washington: Economic Opportunity Policy Institute.
White, F. C. 1983. Trade-off in growth and stability in state taxes. *National Tax Journal* 36(1): 103–114.

Chapter 22

State Tax Portfolios: An Integrated Methodology for Forecasting and Analysis

Ray D. Nelson

Contents

Introduction

In recent years, business cycle–related trends in tax revenues have complicated government budgets. During the boom of the late 1990s, revenues poured into public coffers at the federal, state, and local levels as growth in tax receipts financed rapid expenditure expansion. Subsequently, the mild 2001 recession caused revenues to plunge and forced state government officials to enact emergency spending cuts and tax increases to cope with deficits. Recently, the expanding economy has caused tax revenues to surge once again. In the future, the booms and busts of this business cycle pattern will continue to challenge tax revenue forecasters and public sector budget officials.

Because public finance shares much in common with its corporate counterpart, it seems reasonable that the well-developed applications of tested financial market models can aid public sector decision makers. Financial market portfolio managers face uncertainty from business cycles. They adjust their market positions to achieve their desired combination of expected return and risk. Similarly, state and local fiscal agents must also contend with the systematic risk inherent in the business cycle. Analogous to financial markets, their portfolios of taxes react differently to swings in the business cycle. Principles of financial portfolio management provide insights that aid forecasters as they anticipate tax receipts in conjunction with the budgeting process. Because forecasters are also often assigned to predict the impacts of tax reform, portfolio concepts can help in policy analysis.

The present research first reviews the public and corporate finance literature that outlines the accepted methodology applicable to the formulation of general portfolio models. Next, the discussion focuses on modeling the basic expected growth and uncertainty dimensions of the tax portfolio. Finally, the value of this model is demonstrated by considering forecasting and public policy examples.

Previous Tax Portfolio Research

Groves and Kahn (1952) lay the foundation for modeling tax portfolios by researching the trade-off between stability and growth. Building on the finance literature that considers the risk and return of equity portfolios, White (1983) adapts this methodology to tax problems and derives an efficiency frontier for the state of Georgia. Berg et al. (2000) make similar calculations for the city of New York. Misiolek and Perdue (1987) recalculate the efficiency frontier and emphasize the importance of considering real rather than nominal revenues. Dye and McGuire (1991) find that the specifications and structure of the individual income and general sales taxes affect their growth rates and variability. Suyderhoud (1994) researches diversification, balance, and fiscal performance of state revenue sources.

Public finance research also recognizes the importance of other goals in addition to stability and growth when formulating tax policy. Harmon and Mallick (1994) introduce vertical equity into the calculation of a three-goal efficiency frontier. Gentry and Ladd (1994) follow similar procedures to analyze four goals: revenue growth, stability, equity, and competitiveness with other states.

Rather than focusing on the calculation of a static efficiency frontier, the present analysis develops a framework that helps forecasters separate business cycle revenue growth from other possible causes. The framework also allows assessment and evaluation of proposals that add, rescind, or modify taxes in a state's revenue portfolio. The proposed framework uses a simplified approach similar to that employed by financial managers as they decide which equity and credit market securities to include in their portfolios.

Modeling Tax Revenues

States derive revenues from a variety of sources. Major revenue categories include property, sales, personal income, corporate franchise, motor fuels, severance, and other miscellaneous taxes, fees, and assessments. For many states, the three-legged stool of property, income, and sales taxes dominates in the revenue portfolio mix. Because of the heterogeneity among state economic conditions and tax codes, a generalized portfolio model must adapt to a variety of circumstances.

Revenue Growth

In a very simple model, next year's revenues R_1 can be calculated by applying the anticipated growth rate in revenues r_1 to the current or base year revenue R_0. Formally, this simply means

$$R_1 = R_0 \cdot (1 + r_1) \tag{22.1}$$

Forecasts for successive years can be calculated by multiplying the predicted growth rates for each additional year. This generalizes to the compounding product

$$R_s = R_0 \cdot \prod_t (1 + r_t) \qquad (22.2)$$

where R_s is the total revenue projected for any year s and depends on the growth rates r_t for each individual year t.

The forecasting challenge is to predict the rates of growth r_t over the forecasting horizon needed to plan expenditures and complete budgets. Braun (1988) lays the groundwork for quantitatively integrating the business cycle into the forecasting methodology. Holcombe and Sobel (1997) argue persuasively that forecasters should measure variability relative to the business cycle. They explain the differences between long- and short-run elasticities and propose estimating short-run elasticities using Equation 22.3.

$$r_{i,t} = \alpha_i + \beta_i y_t + \varepsilon_{i,t} \qquad (22.3)$$

where $r_{i,t}$ and y_t are continuously compounded percentage changes in the ith revenue and aggregate income in time period t. The variables $\varepsilon_{i,t}$ are the customary random error terms.

Growth Rate Analysis

Sharpe (1963) applies the regression concepts of explained and unexplained variance to decompose individual stock market returns into two components: systematic and unsystematic risk. The systematic risk is explainable by equity markets in general. The nonsystematic or idiosyncratic risk is specific to a given company. Brookings et al. (1989) cleverly apply this framework to state tax systems as they focus on alternative measures of growth and stability. Perdue (1992) further investigates the portfolio approach by comparing and contrasting absolute versus relative risk measures.

As in the case of equity portfolios, the multivariate nature of the tax problem complicates the modeling of uncertainty. Researchers such as Holcombe and Sobel (1997) establish that the business cycle imparts strong positive correlations among the growth rates for individual taxes, $r_{i,t}$. As in the case of equity market portfolios, tax system simulation is greatly simplified by the single index model. This approach significantly reduces the dimensionality of the simulation parameterization because only measures of systematic and unsystematic risk are required rather than an entire variance–covariance matrix.

The formulation in Equation 22.3 decomposes a given tax's growth rate into three components: noncyclical, cyclical, and idiosyncratic. The first is α_i or the noncyclical growth rate. This part of the overall growth occurs independent of aggregate economic activity. This constitutes regular factors other than those associated with the business cycle that cause tax revenues to increase or decrease.

The second or cyclical component meters the systematic sensitivity of each tax to the business cycle. Potential measures for the business cycle include such macroaggregates as gross state product, personal income, or total nonagricultural wages. Because β_i measures the percentage change in each revenue source relative to the state economy's growth rate, it is an elasticity. When $\beta_i > 1$, the tax is more volatile than the economy and when $\beta_i < 1$, the tax is more conservative than the economy.

The third growth component, the idiosyncratic $\varepsilon_{i,t}$ term, subsumes unpredictable events and reactions that affect tax revenues. This includes geopolitical events that impact state economies but which cannot be anticipated. Because they are not predictable, this factor has an expected value of zero. In a portfolio of equity market securities, it is hoped that because of the randomness of these factors, these terms tend to cancel one another within a portfolio because of the diversification effect.

As an illustration of these revenue components, consider the information for the major sources of revenue for the state of Utah listed in Table 22.1. The estimated parameters result from regressions performed on data that has been carefully adjusted for changes in the tax law. Because the legislative process naturally documents changes in the tax code, this provides a knowledge base that is useful for homogenizing annual revenue streams by adjusting for tax rate and tax base changes. This improves estimates of tax revenue elasticities.

In the Utah economy, for example, property taxes contribute approximately 30 percent of the tax revenue. Even when the economy has no growth, historically this tax has increased by an average of 3.8 percent per year. It has a β of 0.4, which means that this revenue source changes by a smaller percentage than the aggregate

Table 22.1 Major Components for Utah's Tax Portfolio

Tax	*Revenue Share (Percent)*	*Noncyclical (Percent)*	*Cyclical Volatility*	*Percentage Cyclical*
Property	30.30	3.80	0.4	9.90
Individual income	29.90	−1.40	1.4	78.30
Sales	27.30	−1.30	1.1	74.80
Motor fuel	3.50	1.60	0.0	0.10
Corporate franchise	2.20	−8.00	1.9	26.40
Special fuels	1.60	1.70	0.4	8.00
Insurance premium	1.10	3.00	0.6	5.90
Cigarette and tobacco	0.90	−5.00	0.6	12.70
Inheritance	0.20	4.40	0.6	0.10
Beer	0.10	0.20	0.2	1.30

Source: Estimated using data from Utah Governor's Office of Planning and Budget.

state economy. This is consistent with the finding that only approximately 10 percent of the variation in property tax revenue can be explained by total nonagricultural wages.

Tax Portfolios

By weighting each tax by its percentage of total revenue, the noncyclical, cyclical, and idiosyncratic components combine into a portfolio that generates revenue represented by

$$R_s = R_0 \cdot \prod_t (1 + \alpha + \beta y_t + \varepsilon_t) \tag{22.4}$$

This means that the total revenue has four components: the base amount R_0, the noncyclical growth rate α, the cyclical growth βy_i, and the random noise factor ε_t.

Tax Revenue Expected Growth and Uncertainty

The proposed tax portfolio methodology facilitates analysis of any modifications to a state's revenue portfolio. Such changes may arise from adding or deleting taxes in addition to changing the rate or base of an existing tax. Tax policy is sometimes determined only from the perspective of changes in R_0, the base amount. The proposed formulation expands this scope to include an assessment of revenue adequacy over a more expansive planning horizon. It also facilitates the determination of the risk and uncertainty that surrounds the expected growth path.

Expected Revenue Path

Changes in the R_0 initial amount occur whenever laws add or rescind taxes. Modifications in the tax base and rate also change the base amount. For example, adding a new tax increases the base amount from which revenues in future years will grow. Rescinding a tax does just the opposite. Broadening or narrowing a tax's base also causes vertical shifts in the initial amount. The same effect is true with changes in the tax rate as shown in Figure 22.1a.

Excluding the business cycle and random factors, a time series of expected revenues might look like the time path depicted in Figure 22.1b. The curve starts at R_0 and grows at the compounded rate of α. Increasing or decreasing the noncyclical growth rate alters the graph as shown in Figure 22.1b. Of course, the noncyclical influence of each tax on the portfolio depends on the percentage of initial revenue derived from the tax and the individual noncyclical growth rate α_i.

The second growth rate component meters the sensitivity of the portfolio with regard to the business cycle. Depending on its magnitude, the β value magnifies or

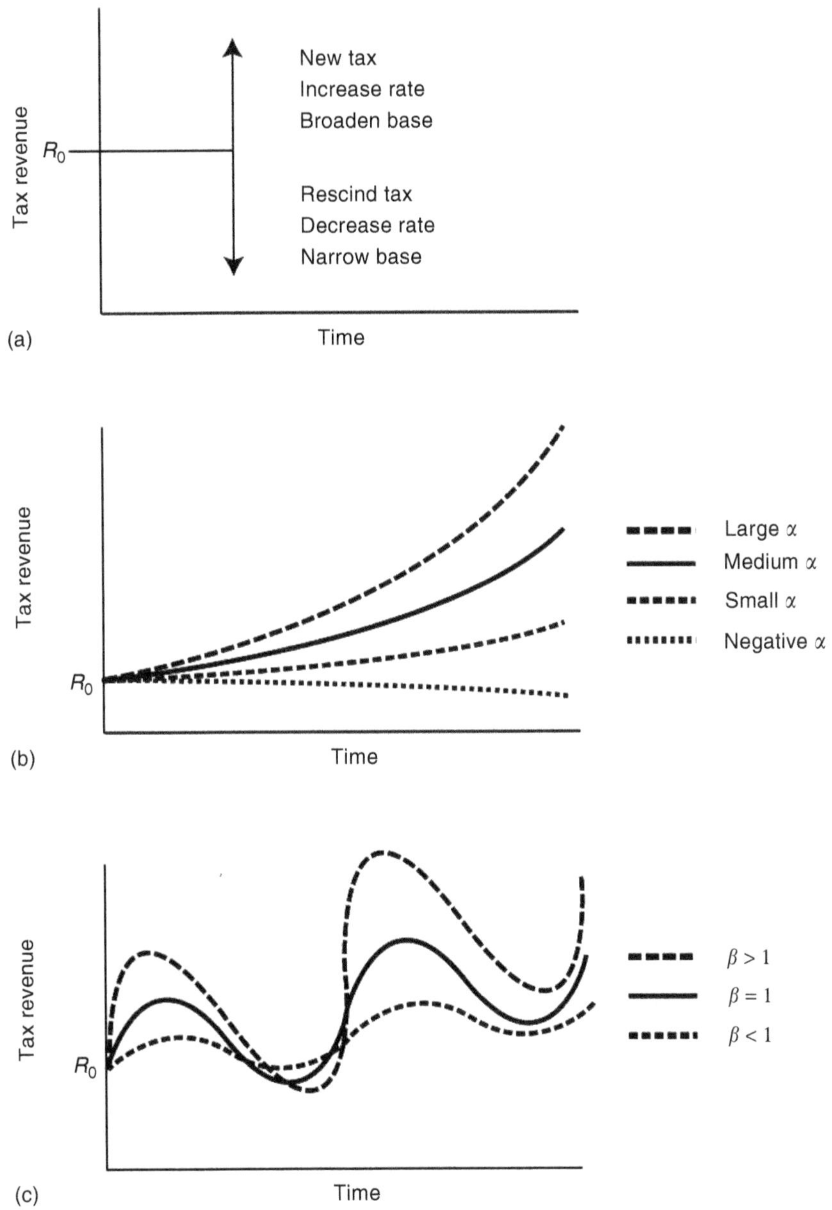

Figure 22.1 Potential effects of tax changes on expected future revenue paths. (a) Initial or base revenue, (b) noncyclical rate of change, and (c) cyclical rate of change.

attenuates the macroeconomic growth rate y_t. As shown in Figure 22.1c, larger values of β give steeper curves with more volatility, whereas smaller values of β result in flatter curves with less volatility. Because measures of aggregate economic activity such as total nonagricultural wages are influenced by population and inflation, it includes the potential effects of these variables on tax revenues. In a growing economy, a high volatility is advantageous because revenues grow faster than the economy. In the case of a macroeconomic decline, however, a high volatility means that tax revenues decrease by an even faster rate than the economy. This happens during a time when revenues are most needed to stimulate the economy and relieve social stress.

As an illustration of an expected revenue path, consider the portfolio of major tax revenues for the state of Utah shown in Figure 22.2. The base amount R_0 is the bottom gray rectangle in the graph. As also shown in Figure 22.2, if $\alpha = 2.0$ percent, then the part of the expected revenue attributable to noncyclical growth is represented by the middle or darker gray area in the center of the graph. Figure 22.2 shows that noncyclical growth is small relative to the cyclical growth that is shown as the top or darkest gray area in the upper part of the graph. Because the overall tax portfolio has $\beta = 1.1$ and assuming a growth rate of 4 percent for nonagricultural wages, the cyclical growth is 4.4 percent. Combining the noncyclical and cyclical statistics gives the 6.4 percent growth rate depicted as the total in Figure 22.2.

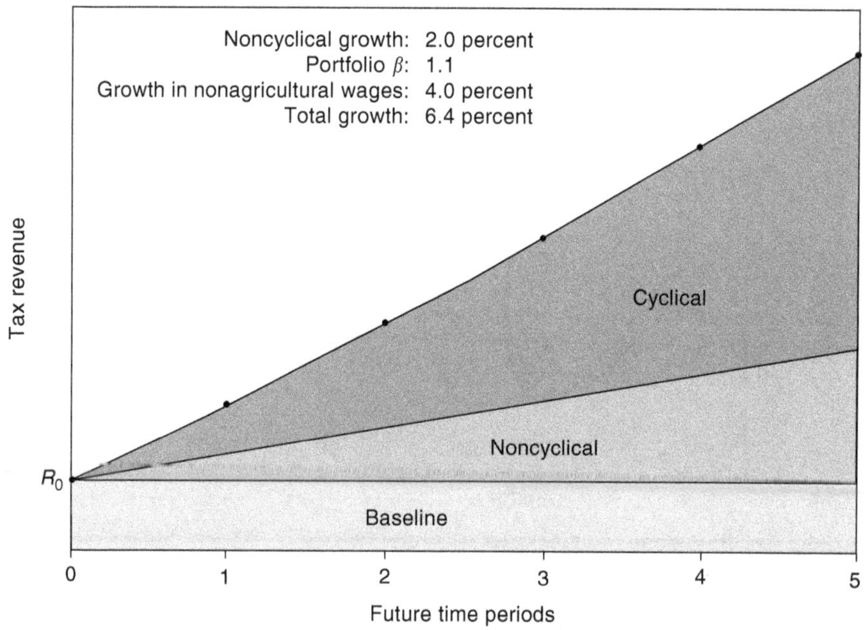

Figure 22.2 Expected growth rate for Utah's tax portfolio. (Graphed data from original Monte Carlo simulation.)

Revenue Risk and Uncertainty

Three sources of risk contribute to tax revenue uncertainty: systematic, unsystematic, and estimation. First, the systematic risk or that explainable by the business cycle arises because the future growth path of the economy is unknown. As shown in Equation 22.4, the business cycle imparts risk because the value of y_t is unknown and is itself a random variable. The second source of uncertainty is the unsystematic part that is unique to each tax source. The idiosyncratic nature of the random error terms, $\varepsilon_{i,t}$, imparts uncertainty to future revenue flows. Finally, because the values for α_i and β_i are estimated, they too are stochastic variables and must be included as the third source of risk.

Expanding Equation 22.4 reveals that a multitude of terms include the product of stochastic variables. Bohrnstedt and Goldberger (1969) establish the extreme analytical complexity that results when random variables are multiplied. This difficulty precludes mathematical derivations for the risk and uncertainty of revenue streams. For this reason, any assessment of the risk and uncertainty of tax portfolios requires Monte Carlo simulation.

The management science literature delivers a wide array of tested stimulation techniques and accepted methodologies that guide their application to the proposed tax portfolio model. Law and Kelton (2000) catalog Monte Carlo simulation methods. Vose (2000) details the simulation implementation of risk problems using readily available spreadsheet software such as @RISK® (Palisade 2002). These resources make the presently proposed analysis computationally accessible to state fiscal budgeting officials and analysts.

The Monte Carlo procedure simulates the random outcomes for the three different sources of uncertainty. Each of these sources of uncertainty must be represented by probability distribution functions (PDFs). A variety of distribution families as documented by Law and Kelton (2000) allow a multiplicity of distribution shapes, formulations, and estimation techniques.

For the systematic risk due to the business cycle, the shape of the probability distribution can be determined from either formal statistical estimation or subjective judgment. One could simply estimate the mean and standard deviation of past macroeconomic measures, and then model them with a well-known distribution such as the normal. Alternatively, following the methodology summarized by Morgan et al. (1990), the subjective probabilities of experts might more appropriately anticipate and therefore represent future events.

The regressions that estimate Equation 22.3 give the statistics needed to specify the uncertainty about the nonsystematic risk and estimated parameter values. Following the general linear regression, the nonsystematic risk, $\varepsilon_{i,t}$, has an expected value of zero. The standard error of regression gives an estimate of its standard deviation. An assumption of independence means that temporal and cross-tax correlations are zero. Similarly, standard regression output gives the expected values, variances, and covariances needed to specify the PDFs for the unknown parameters α_i and β_i.

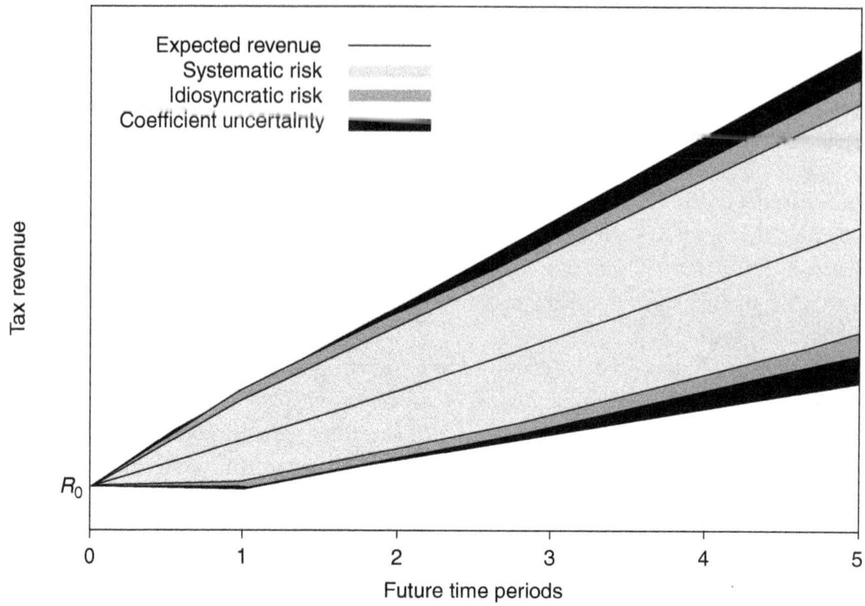

Figure 22.3 Sources of uncertainty for Utah's tax portfolio. (Graphed data from original Monte Carlo simulation.)

Forecasters can determine the relative importance of the three different sources of uncertainty by using a completed simulation. The graph in Figure 22.3 shows the size of each type of uncertainty. The total expectation line in the middle of the uncertainty interval is similar to the total expectation in Figure 22.2. The first band (lightest gray) surrounding the expected revenue depicts a range of possible outcomes caused by the systematic uncertainty attributable to the business cycle. The next tier of uncertainty depicted by the dark gray area shows the incremental uncertainty that comes from the combined nonsystematic risk from all of the different revenue sources. The black area shows that risk is caused by the uncertainty surrounding the values of the estimated noncyclical growth rates α_i and the tax elasticities β_i.

Simulation also fosters sensitivity analysis that allows the decision maker to assess the importance of the different sources of uncertainty on revenues. This is accomplished through regression analysis that relates the simulated revenue to the noncyclical, elasticity, aggregate macroeconomic, and idiosyncratic risk factors. The normalized regression coefficients are reported in the tornado chart shown in Figure 22.4. The statistics in the tornado chart reiterate the dominant importance of the total nonagricultural wage growth rate in determining revenue flows. The graph also gives a perspective about the importance of the cyclical and noncyclical growth rates, the idiosyncratic risk, and the coefficient risk. As would be expected,

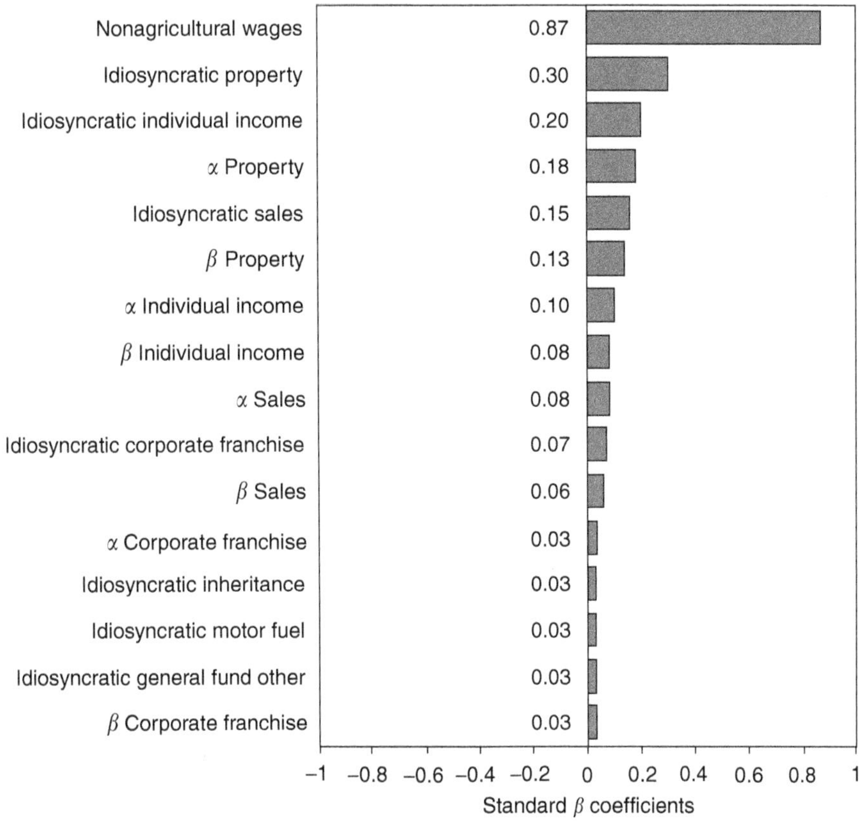

Figure 22.4 Tornado diagram of uncertainty sources for Utah's tax portfolio (Graphed data from original Monte Carlo simulation.)

the heavy weights in the tax portfolio for property, sales, and personal income taxes mean that these sources strongly influence total tax revenues.

Applications and Illustrations

Knowing the characteristics of different revenue sources aids forecasters in formulating and evaluating their projections. It also helps forecasters anticipate the possible future budgetary effects of tax code changes. As mentioned, the tax law often evolves to meet the exigencies of balancing state budgets. In the short run, this focuses code changes on the objective of matching the base amount R_0 with expected and hoped for budget expenditures. The proposed tax portfolio framework fosters a longer-run perspective by considering the effects on the noncyclical and cyclical growth potential that will affect budgeting for years to come. This framework finds useful application in evaluating current taxes, assessing code changes, and planning major public policy initiatives. Fiscal examples for the state of Utah serve to illustrate the application of the proposed framework.

Evaluating Current Tax Characteristics

As mentioned, states currently depend primarily on property, sales, and personal income taxes to fund their government activities. Although less significant in their importance, corporate franchise and motor fuel taxes are included in the current illustration because of their unique qualities. Consider how the proposed tax portfolio methodology measures important dimensions and characteristics for these five tax alternatives.

Property Taxes

Property taxes generate a reliable revenue stream as shown by the information in Table 22.1 and Figure 22.5. The graphs in Figure 22.5 are similar to those shown in Figures 22.2 and 22.3 for the overall state tax portfolio. The low β value means that property taxes are less volatile than the business cycle. The graphs in Figure 22.5 show the importance of both the noncyclical and cyclical growth components for property taxes. Because only approximately 10 percent of the variation in property tax collections is explainable by total nonagricultural wages, revenue growth in this tax is not as dependent on the business cycle as are some other taxes. The prominence of the noncyclical growth area in Figure 22.5a suggests that factors that are independent of the business cycle strongly affect the growth rate of property tax revenues. The cyclical growth shown in the graph in Figure 22.5a assumes a robust 6 percent growth rate for nonagricultural wages. Under this assumption, the business cycle does add significant growth to the time path. For lower values of expected nonagricultural wage growth, however, the noncyclical growth rate's dominance would be even more pronounced.

The importance of the noncyclical and unsystematic components is also obvious in the sources of uncertainty graph in Figure 22.5b. The simulations show that the uncertainty regarding revenues is dominated by the nonsystematic risk. Although the growth and elasticity coefficients α_i and β_i are measured imprecisely, their relative importance as a source of uncertainty is not large.

Sales and Use Tax

The second part of the three-legged revenue stool, the sales and use tax, has very different characteristics from property taxes. As reported in Table 22.1 and illustrated in Figure 22.6, after removing the very strong effect of the business cycle from tax

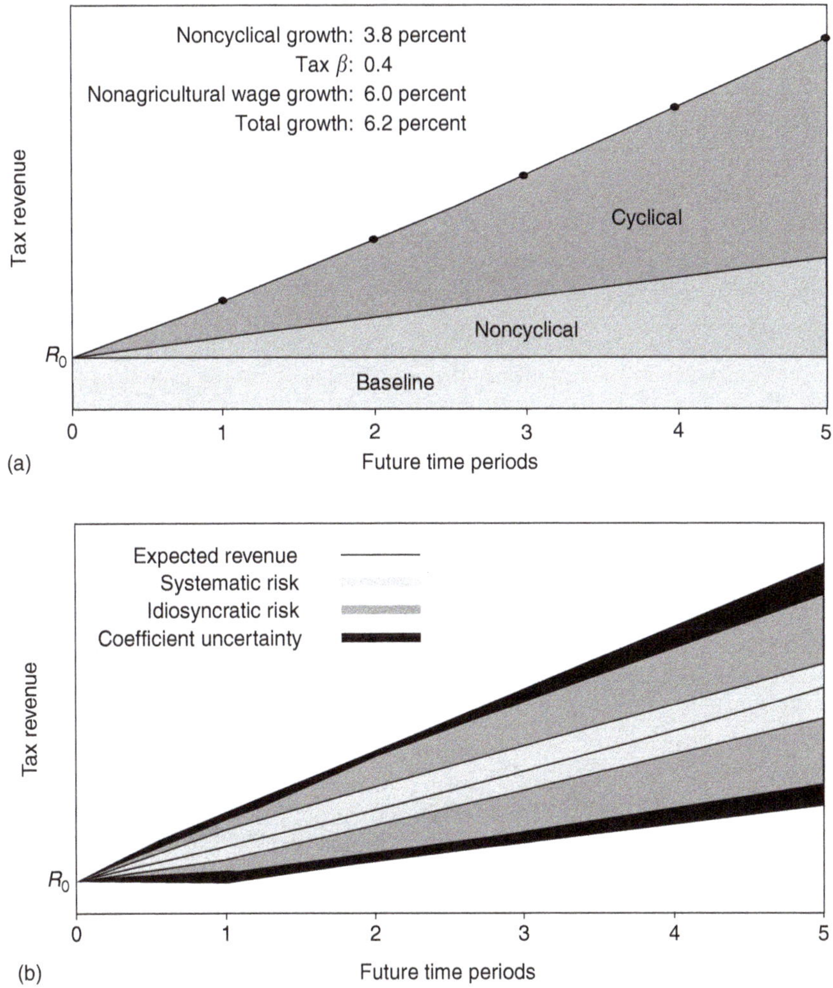

Figure 22.5 Potential growth and risk for Utah's property tax. (a) Expected growth rate (b) sources of uncertainty. (Graphed data from original Monte Carlo simulation.)

revenues, sales taxes have a tendency to decline. In other words, if nonagricultural wages were to stagnate at zero percent growth, sales and use tax revenues would actually decline as shown in Figure 22.6 because revenues decrease over time from their base value R_0. The cyclical I category of revenue growth is necessary to return to the baseline and represents the amount of revenue lost because of the secular decline. The cyclical II category of growth are the additional expected revenues due to the cyclical growth in addition to those in the cyclical I category.

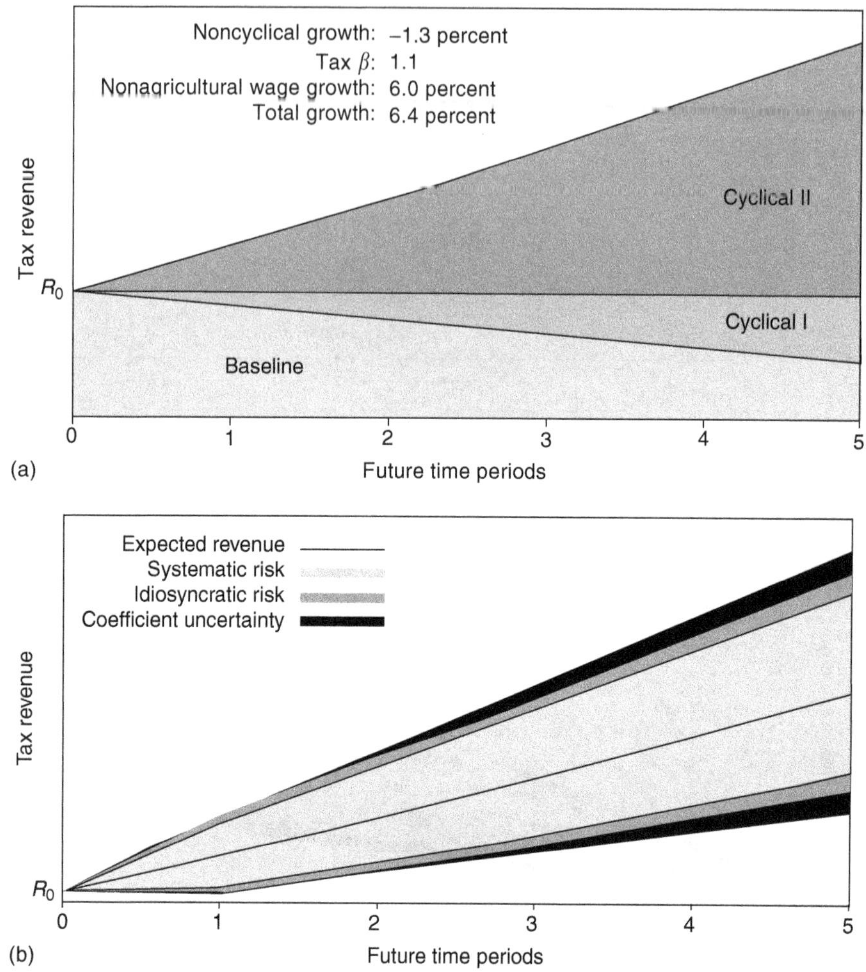

Figure 22.6 Potential growth and risk for Utah's sales tax. (a) Expected growth rate (b) sources of uncertainty. (Graphed data from original Monte Carlo simulation.)

With a β_i value of approximately 1, sales tax revenues move roughly in tandem with the aggregate state economy. In contrast to the property tax, the inherent risk of sales and use tax revenues comes from the business cycle. Approximately three-fourths of the variation in revenues is explainable by the rate of change in total nonagricultural wages. The high percentage of variation explained by the regression also means that α_i and β_i are more precisely estimated. The narrower bands shown in Figure 22.6b reflect the smaller standard deviations for the parameter estimates.

Individual Income Tax

In Utah, individual income taxes have been an extremely important revenue source that has fueled the growth in state government expenditures between 1995 and 2001. As expected and almost by definition, a very close relationship exists between income tax receipts and total nonagricultural wages. Table 22.1 and Figure 22.7 show that like sales taxes, this very significant revenue source exhibits a secular decline after the effects of the business cycle have been removed.

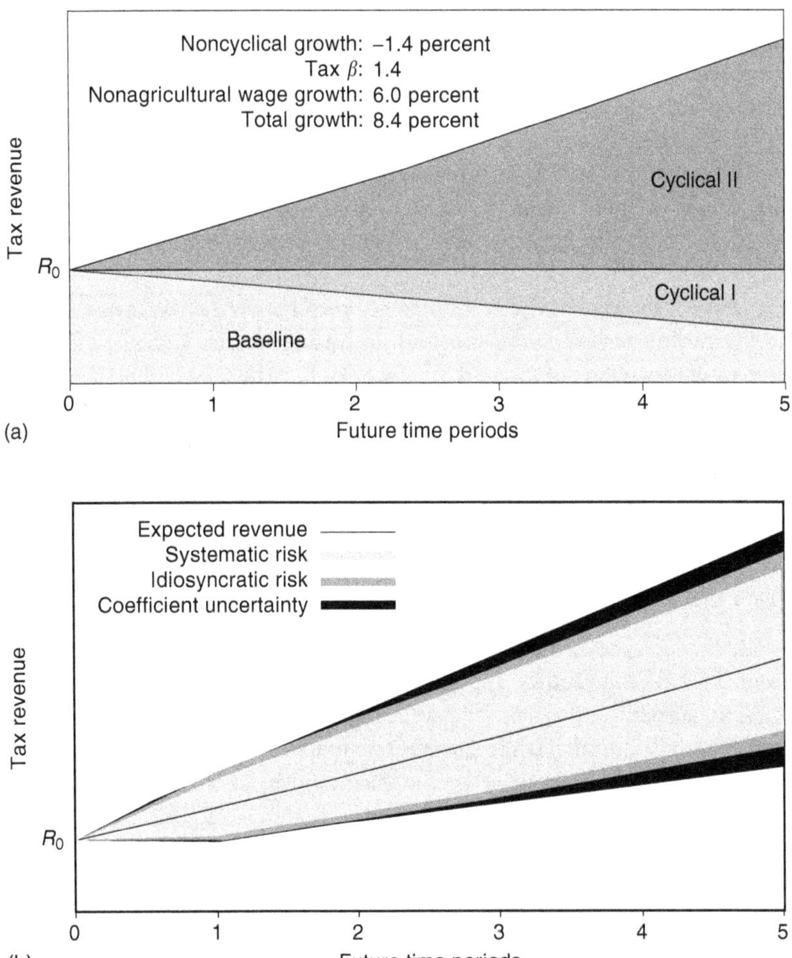

Figure 22.7 Potential growth and risk for Utah's personal income tax. (a) Expected growth rate (b) sources of uncertainty. (Graphed data from original Monte Carlo simulation.)

A $\beta_i = 1.4$ coefficient suggests that this tax is much more volatile than the sales and use tax. When the economy is growing, it delivers significant revenue that supports expenditure increases or that allows for tax cuts. However, during recessionary times, it strongly contributes to budget deficits. Because approximately 80 percent of the variation in this tax revenue is explained by the business cycle, it is not surprising that Figure 22.7 identifies most of the risk in individual income taxes as systematic. In a manner similar to sales taxes, the uncertainty attributable to the α_i and β_i estimated values is relatively unimportant.

Corporate Franchise Tax

The corporate franchise tax differs from the major three taxes because of its unique association with the business cycle. The β_i value of almost 2 means that although only approximately one-fourth of the variation in this tax is due to the business cycle, this revenue source contributes significantly to budgeting challenges. The small portfolio weight lessens the impact, but frequent and unexpected increases and decreases that sometimes exceed 50 percent present legislators and governors with interesting fiscal dilemmas.

Figure 22.8 shows that the growth rate of corporate franchise revenues declines precipitously after removing the effects of the business cycle. This matches national patterns where corporate taxes are decreasing. Unlike the sales and personal income taxes, the majority of the uncertainty of the corporate franchise tax comes from its unique, idiosyncratic characteristics. The uncertainty surrounding the estimated noncyclical growth rate α_i and the elasticity β_i is large enough to contribute consequentially to the risk found in budgeting.

Motor Fuel Tax

Figure 22.9 identifies an obvious distinguishing characteristic of motor fuel tax revenues. This revenue source appears to be independent from the business cycle and total nonagricultural wages. The cyclical growth rate is barely perceptible as the noncyclical factor dominates the growth rate graph. Almost none of the variation in motor fuel taxes is explainable by the business cycle. As shown in Figure 22.9, the preeminence of the idiosyncratic obscures any systematic risk. The uncertainty with regard to the noncyclical growth rate is an important source of uncertainty.

Tax Portfolio

Knowing characteristics of the individual taxes allows further insights to be drawn from the statistics in Table 22.1 and the graphs in Figures 22.2 and 22.3. Characteristically, the elements in the current tax portfolio tend to cancel one another. The expected growth graph in Figure 22.2 shows that secular declines in sales, income,

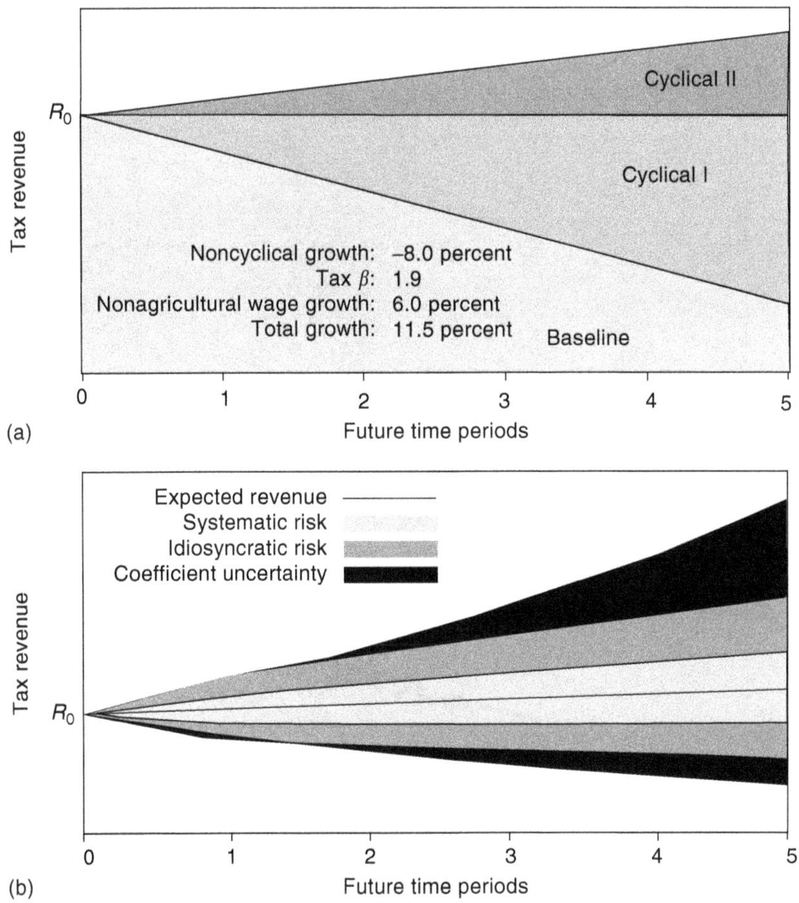

Figure 22.8 Potential growth and risk for Utah's corporate franchise tax. (a) Expected growth rate (b) sources of uncertainty. (Graphed data from original Monte Carlo simulation.)

and corporate taxes counterbalance the growth in property and minor taxes so that very little noncyclical growth exists in the portfolio. As would be expected and discussed previously, the tornado diagram from simulations identify the business cycle as the preeminent source of uncertainty. Given the predominance of sales and personal income taxes and their dependence on the business cycle, this is hardly surprising. Some diversification effects probably attenuate the idiosyncratic risks as one tax source cancels another. Because of the prominence of property, sales, and individual income taxes in Utah's portfolio, overall estimation risk is a relatively insignificant factor.

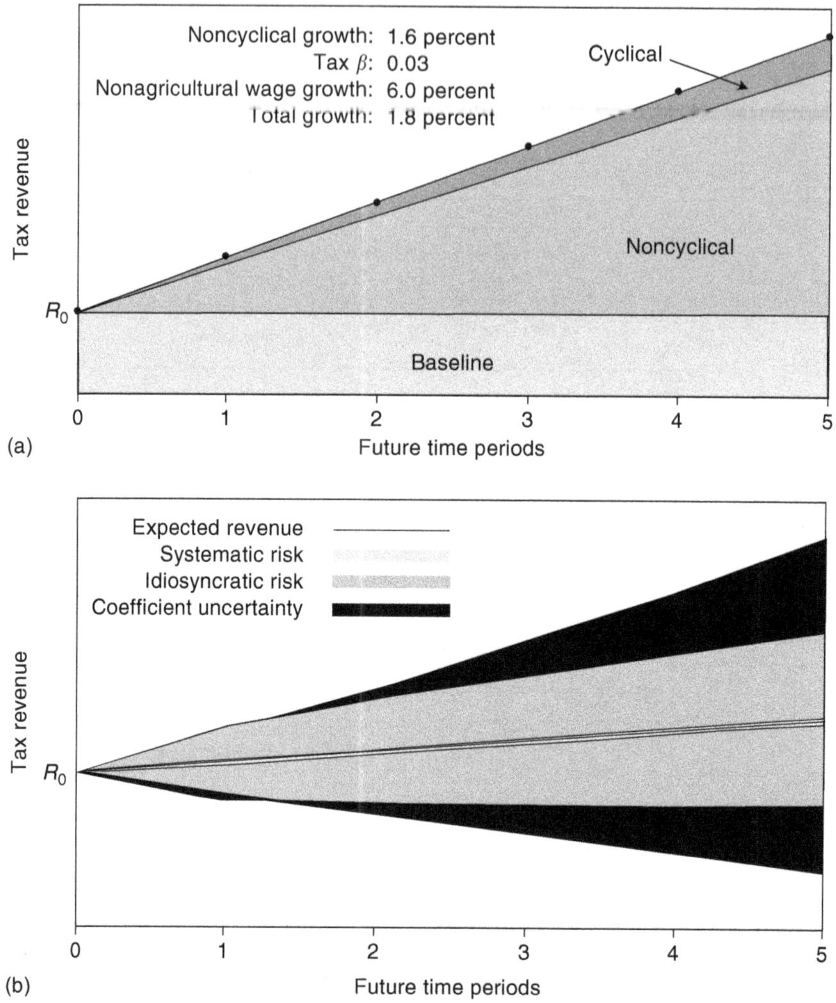

Figure 22.9 Potential growth and risk for Utah's motor fuel tax. (a) Expected growth rate (b) sources of uncertainty. (Graphed data from original Monte Carlo simulation.)

Tax Policy Changes

After the tax portfolio helps to identify and quantify a tax's characteristics, it can then help to design and anticipate changes that will give desirable growth and uncertainty characteristics. Sobel and Wagner (2003) propose avenues for achieving desirable characteristics relative to the business cycle. The tax portfolio organizes and adds to these ideas whenever policy makers consider creating new taxes, rescinding existing taxes, or changing either a tax's base or rate.

Creating and Rescinding Taxes

The portfolio methodology can contribute significant insights whenever state government officials consider proposals to add or repeal taxes. Often, the focus of analysis centers on the immediate effect of the tax on the initial or base revenue R_0. Depending on the relative size of the revenue generated by the tax and its characteristics, this approach may be adequate or may neglect important aspects that affect the tax portfolio's growth rates and uncertainty. A proposed minor tax might have such a small weight within the portfolio that it might not justify extensive analysis. A severance tax that augments revenues by harvesting low hanging fruit, for example, might not have any noticeable impact on revenues over time. In contrast, however, consider a proposal to replace sales or personal income tax with a value-added tax. This would radically alter the tax portfolio's noncyclical and cyclical growth rates and augment or attenuate its risk and uncertainty.

As a further example of tax changes, consider the possibility of eliminating a state's corporate franchise tax. Undesirable characteristics of this tax make it a high-profile candidate for removal. Government officials might hope, for example, that rescinding the corporate franchise tax would attract corporations to their state because of a more favorable business environment. Also, because similar business entities may pay very different levels of taxes, removing this tax would eliminate extensive horizontal equity problems. In addition to these dimensions of tax policy, analysts using the tax portfolio could consider the growth and uncertainty ramifications of such a decision. Of course, eliminating the corporate franchise tax would initially cause the base revenue R_0 to decline. Even though in most states corporate franchise tax does not provide a significant share of tax revenue, the tax has such unique and extreme characteristics that it does affects the portfolio. The tornado diagram for Utah's tax portfolio in Figure 22.4 identifies corporate franchise tax as having a discernable effect on the tax portfolio. This makes sense because $\beta_i = 1.9$ represents extreme volatility. The degree and magnitude of idiosyncratic risk similarly is very large. Eliminating the corporate franchise tax would decrease the base revenue, increase the noncyclical growth rate, decrease the tax portfolio β, and decrease the nonsystematic risk. It might even affect the growth rate, y_t, of the economy. All of these are important dimensions to consider in the policy decision.

Base Changes

Even without formal legislated changes in the tax code, tax bases naturally evolve. For example, as services claim a higher and higher portion of gross state product, the dominance of retail sales in the tax base causes it to narrow in scope. This might generate a secular decline in sales tax revenues such as the negative noncyclical growth for Utah sales taxes revenues reported in Table 22.1. One way to arrest this narrowing might be to broaden the sales tax base by initiating a tax on services. The broadening of the base would definitely cause the initial revenue R_0 to increase.

The portfolio model could frame the discussion about what would happen with the noncyclical and cyclical growth rates. This would include research and debate over whether taxing services would increase or decrease the elasticity β_i for sales taxes.

Another sales tax issue debates the inclusion of food in the base. Because of the regressive nature of sales taxes, vertical equity questions the fairness of a base that taxes food. Because food constitutes a necessity purchase, including it in the base probably increases the noncyclical growth rate of sales taxes and decreases the elasticity because food purchases do not fluctuate as much as other purchases when the state moves through different phases of the business cycle. The tax model identifies these as important discussion points in addition to vertical equity.

Rate Changes

Increasing and decreasing tax rates potentially alter the base amount, noncyclical growth, and cyclical growth rates. Because the federal tax code underpins much of the calculation of taxable income, much of the state individual income tax policy debate revolves around rates. This makes the income tax a good illustration of how the tax portfolio aids such a policy discussion.

Policy makers might question what would happen if tax rates were to become more or less progressive. A more progressive structure would result from either increasing the rates in the top income bracket or diminishing those of lower income. This would respectively raise or lower the base amount of revenue R_0. More progressive taxes would probably increase the volatility or β_i. Similarly, officials might analyze the outcome of widening or narrowing income tax brackets. Because of the traditionally large weight of income taxes in the portfolio, this could also significantly change the characteristics of the state's tax portfolio.

Conclusions and Extensions

The proposed methodology for evaluating portfolios eclectically draws from the extensive tax policy and risk management literatures. Significant and extensive research investigates the elasticities of tax revenues and volatilities of equity market securities. Because these two problems are conceptually identical, it allows a productive application of capital asset pricing model concepts to the public sector. Especially valuable is the ability to decompose revenue uncertainty into systematic and unsystematic risk components. Because the systematic risk corresponds to the correlated revenues observed every year due to the business cycle, this construct effectively models the observed high interrelatedness of individual tax sources within the state's revenue portfolio. The simplicity of the framework provides methodology that is computationally available to state fiscal and budget analysts using familiar spreadsheet software.

The portfolio methodology aids revenue forecasters in two principal ways. First, it allows forecasters to conceptualize tax growth rates as having noncyclical and cyclical components. This fosters better assessments and predictions for alternative business cycle scenarios. Second, it allows forecasters to better frame policy discussions about sufficiency, stability, and uncertainty. It provides foresight into revenue adequacy relative to societal spending goals. It accomplishes this by inviting policy makers to anticipate the impact of tax changes on the base revenue levels, noncyclical growth, and cyclical growth. It also formalizes and allows quantification of the levels of uncertainty due to the business cycle, specific taxes, or model parameter estimation.

The tax portfolio model promises potential for extension and further research. The illustrations in this chapter present the basics of the portfolio model without simulating the potential effects of duration and severity of business cyclical contractions. Such an addition would allow the portfolio framework to aid research and design of optimal rainy-day funds. The tax portfolio could also generate insights into the extent that diversification changes portfolio uncertainty.

Appendix

Revenue Calculations

The tax portfolio revenue R_s for any s years in the future simply compounds the growth rates r_t from an initial base amount R_0.

$$R_s = R_0 \cdot \prod_t (1 + r_t) \tag{A.1}$$

Because each state derives revenue from multiple tax sources, it makes sense to model the growth rates as a portfolio of taxes. The growth rate for all revenues for year t is simply the weighted sum of the growth rates from the individual taxes, $r_{i,t}$, or

$$r_t = \sum_i w_i r_{i,t} \tag{A.2}$$

where the weight w_i denotes the percentage of revenue derived from the ith tax.

Business Cycle

Holcombe and Sobel (1997) point out that the standard approach to elasticity estimation utilizes Equation A.3.

$$\ln(R_{i,t}) = \alpha_i + \beta_i \ln(Y_t) + \varepsilon_{i,t} \tag{A.3}$$

where

$R_{i,t}$ = level of the ith revenue source at time period t

Y_t = level of aggregate income during the same period

$\varepsilon_{i,t}$ = standard error term
β_i = income elasticity of the revenue

Following Groves and Kahn (1952), the income elasticity serves as a proxy for both the long-run growth and short-run variability of tax revenues.

Holcombe and Sobel (1997) outline and discuss the potential problems with this procedure. They explain the differences between long- and short-run elasticities. They propose estimating short-run elasticities using Equation A.4.

$$\Delta \ln(R_{i,t}) = \alpha_i + \beta_i \Delta \ln(Y_t) + \varepsilon_{i,t} \tag{A.4}$$

Because $\Delta\ln(R_{i,t})$ can be interpreted as the continuously compounded percentage change in revenue, hereafter denoted as $r_{i,t}$, and $\Delta\ln(Y_t)$ as the continuously compounded percentage change in aggregate income, y_t; then Equation A.4 can be rewritten, and β_i retains the elasticity interpretation

$$r_{i,t} = \alpha_i + \beta_i Y_t + \varepsilon_{i,t} \tag{A.5}$$

Using OLS with Equation A.5 gives asymptotically biased results with inconsistently estimated standard errors. Holcombe and Sobel (1997) find that dynamic ordinary least squares can give better estimates.

Tax Portfolios

Using Equation A.5 allows reexpression of Equation A.2 as

$$r_t = \sum_i w_i \alpha_i + \left(\sum_i w_i \beta_i \right) y_t + \sum_i w_i \varepsilon_{i,t} \tag{A.6}$$

The second term on the right-hand side of Equation A.6 gives the systematic component of total tax receipts. The third and last term in Equation A.6 represents the nonsystematic portion. Define the tax portfolio α as $\Sigma_i w_i \alpha_i$, the tax portfolio β as $\Sigma_i w_i \beta_i$, and the portfolio's random element ε_t as $\Sigma_i w_i \varepsilon_{i,t}$. Substituting these terms into Equation A.6 gives

$$r_t = \alpha + \beta y_t + \varepsilon_t \tag{A.7}$$

Substituting Equation A.7 into Equation A.1 gives

$$R_s = R_0 \cdot \prod_t (1 + \alpha + \beta y_t + \varepsilon_t) \tag{A.8}$$

References

Berg, J., J. T. Marlin, and F. Heydarpour. 2000. Local government tax policy: measuring the efficiency of New York City's tax mix, FYs 1984–1998. *Public Budgeting & Finance* 20(2): 1–14.

Bohrnstedt, G. W. and A. S. Goldberger. 1969. On the exact covariance of products of random variables. *Journal of the American Statistical Association* 64(328): 1439–1442.

Braun, B. M. 1988. Measuring tax revenue stability with implications for stabilization policy: a note. *National Tax Journal* 41(4): 595–598.

Brookings, C. G., W. S. Triplett, and S. C. Wells. 1989. Designing a state's portfolio of taxes: an application of financial theory. *Municipal Finance Journal* 10: 105–116.

Dye, R. F. and T. J. McGuire. 1991. Growth and variability of state individual income and general sales taxes. *National Tax Journal* 44(1): 55–66.

Gentry, W. M. and H. F. Ladd. 1994. State tax structure and multiple policy objectives. *National Tax Journal* 47(4): 747–772.

Groves, H. M. and C. H. Kahn. 1952. The stability of state and local tax yields. *American Economic Review* 42(1): 87–101.

Harmon, O. R. and R. Mallick. 1994. The optimal state tax portfolio model: an extension. *National Tax Journal* 47(2): 395–401.

Holcombe, R. G. and R. S. Sobel. 1997. *Growth and Variability in State Tax Revenue: An Anatomy of State Fiscal Crises.* Westport, CT: Greenwood Press.

Law, A. M. and W. D. Kelton. 2000. *Simulation Modeling and Analysis.* Boston, MA: McGraw-Hill.

Misiolek, W. S. and D. G. Perdue. 1987. The portfolio approach to state and local tax structures. *National Tax Journal* 40(1): 111–114.

Monte Carlo Simulations.

Morgan, M. G., M. Henrion, and M. Small. 1990. *Uncertainty: A Guide to Dealing with Uncertainty in Quantitative Risk and Policy Analysis.* Cambridge, NY: Cambridge University Press.

Office of Planning and Budget, State of Utah.

Palisade. 2002. *@RISK®: Risk Analysis and Simulation Add-In for Microsoft Excel®.* Newfield, NY: Palisade.

Perdue, D. G. 1992. Tax betas in state and local government tax structure analysis. *Public Budgeting and Financial Management* 4(2): 359–378.

Sharpe, W. F. 1963. A simplified model for portfolio analysis. *Management Science* 9(2): 277–293.

Sobel, R. S. and G. C. Wagner. 2003. Cyclical variability in state government revenue: can tax reform reduce it? *State Tax Notes* 29: 569–576.

Suyderhoud, J. P. 1994. State-local revenue diversification, balance, and fiscal performance. *Public Finance Quarterly* 22(2): 168–194.

Vose, D. 2000. *Risk Analysis: A Quantitative Guide.* Chichester: Wiley.

White, F. C. 1983. Trade-off in growth and stability in state taxes. *National Tax Journal* 36(1): 103–114.

4

OTHER TOPICS IN BUDGET FORECASTING

Chapter 23

Forecasting Revenues and Expenditures in the Public Sector: Guidance from a Code of Ethics

Robert W. Smith

Contents

Introduction

Scholars and practitioners have argued that there is no more empirical exercise in public financial management than the forecasting of revenues and expenditures (e.g., Zarnowitz 1985). At many levels this is an accurate observation, but perhaps these experts all too readily gloss over the normative dimensions of revenue and expenditure forecasting. Many other scholars quickly affirm the argument and cite a variety of econometric models used by federal, state, and local governments, and point to the professionalism of the forecasting function in the public sector (e.g., Feenberg et al. 1989). Others would emphatically rely on the sage wisdom of Wildavsky (1980) and other budget scholars, and question this proposition by saying that forecasting is more of an art than a science (Makridakis 1986). Still other scholars and participants in the budget process would agree with both positions, and would argue that budget forecasts of revenues and expenditures utilize very sophisticated econometric or other empirically driven approaches, but at the same time are tempered by the demands of a volatile political environment that many times impinge on the objective analysis offered by these budget prognosticators (e.g., Bunn and Wright 1991).

This chapter attempts to evaluate these positions by providing an overview of the state of the art and science of budget forecasting (both expenditures and revenues) by examining the value base for forecasting along a continuum from econometric or rational modeling on one end to a political or administrative perspective on the other. Specifically, this chapter identifies ethical dilemmas in the forecasting enterprise; examines their relationship to public sector ethics principles or values; and presents a code of ethics as guidance for both a positive and normative basis for forecasting in twenty-first-century budgeting.

Budget Forecasting in the Public Sector

Revenue and expenditure forecasting are important elements of the public budget process. In the budget process, the relevant budget actors prepare revenue and expenditure estimates (e.g., the executive and the legislature). To the degree that the budget being presented is first and foremost a political document, it becomes clear that each set of actors will have normative considerations that enter into the budget process. The executive wants to advance his or her policy agenda, the agency heads want the resources to pursue their programmatic initiatives, the legislature will want to cut executive budgets to maximize funding for legislative member projects and initiatives, interest groups will pursue increases in funding for their own policy initiatives, and taxpayers will seek to minimize budget increases that carry dramatic increases in taxes. Each of these budget actors carries an ethical compass that drives their budgetary prerogatives that they advance in the process.

Yet, forecasting is typically portrayed as a technical and professional exercise that is objective and nonpartisan, and is essentially a positivist view of public budgeting and finance. For revenue and expenditure forecasting, models are utilized that consider economic and demographic variables as well as underlying assumptions about future trends and how these variables might impact the forecasting model. In addition, on the revenue side, governments typically compartmentalize their approach and examine each revenue source independently to determine patterns or legislative or regulatory changes affecting the revenue source (Schroder 1982). What is central to understand about these models on either the revenue or expenditure side is that these models rely on various assumptions about economic conditions, demographic makeup, pending legislation, policy directions, and other political factors that might determine how the models are designed or what weight is assigned to certain variables. Hence, these otherwise-technical approaches involve normative considerations and varying degrees of ethical sensitivity.

Dimensions of Ethics in Budget Forecasting

Ethics in forecasting can be thought of along two dimensions: the technical and rational side and the political and administrative side (see Figure 23.1). On the

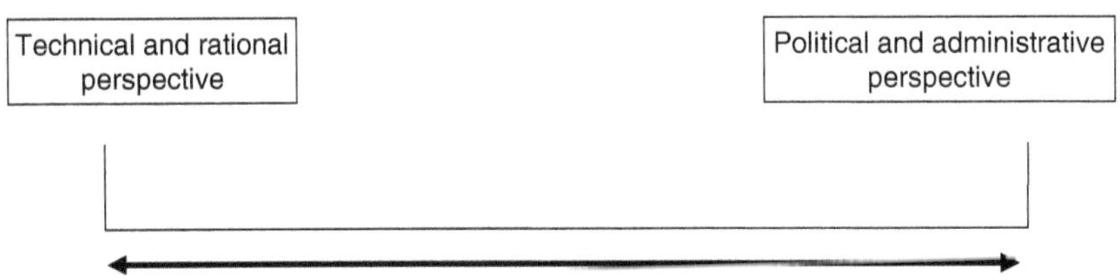

Figure 23.1 Value base for forecasting revenues and expenditures.

technical side, issues of process and how these factors make a difference constitute one set of ethical considerations related to modeling and demographic and economic variables that will affect the forecast. Often for statisticians or professional forecasters, the issue of ethics is not so much a matter of ethics as it is the appropriate amount of statistical bias that is built into the forecasting model being used. Bias in this context is not an ethical issue; it is a matter of technical proficiency or professionalism of the forecast itself (Ehrman and Shugan 1995, p. 126). This chapter takes the position that these factors are nonetheless ethical considerations. Indeed bias, and the degree of bias, carries with it a predisposition, preconception, or prejudice that can be the root of ethical dilemmas. How to overcome bias is an active topic of consideration in the applied ethics literature (Bostrom and Ord, 2006).

On the political and administrative side, considerations of how forecasts will affect the political environment and how administrative factors can influence the forecast are also crucial. Administrative issues arise when considering who will make the forecasts (central budget office, department or agency, legislative committee, or external consultants), issues concerning when the forecast will actually be pulled together are significant, and, of course, the expertise and disposition of those individuals responsible for the forecasts are also at play. The political issues at hand in forecasting have to do with considerations of political fallout and consequences from forecasting, considerations of the impact on various political stakeholders (unions, legislators, etc.) that are at hand, as are when and how to actually present the forecast to stakeholders or the public. The significance of reviewing some of the political and administrative sensitivities associated with forecasting are important in that no matter how the forecasting technique may be insulated from these types of political or administrative issues, they can never be totally isolated from the ethical imperatives behind these issues.

Strategic Misrepresentations in Budget Forecasting

In one of the clearest applications of ethical considerations in the budget process, Jones and Euske (1991) work on what they call "strategic misrepresentation" in budgeting, which is mostly concerned with the impact of misrepresentation in connection with forecasting in budgeting and how "ethical" the process may be, given the pressures of political and administrative controls. Jones and Euske sum up such efforts from their research by identifying 13 specific considerations that enhance misrepresentation in budgeting: uncertainty, information asymmetry, constraints on revenues or expenditures, rapid program growth or decline, political ideology, micromanagement, rigid control, inconsistent financial rules, audit pressures, multiple budget decision nodes, preexisting misrepresentations, accelerated decision windows, and short- versus long-term issues.

Table 23.1 Strategic Misrepresentations in Budgeting

Technical	*Political and Administrative*
Overall constraints	Uncertainty
Information asymmetry	Political ideology
Growth and decline	Micromanagement
Financial rules	Rigid controls
Preexisting conditions	Decision nodes
Short- versus long-term issues	Decision windows
	Audit pressures

Source: Adapted from Jones L. R. and Eukse K. J., *Journal of Public Administration Research and Theory*, 1(4), 437–460, 1991.

Table 23.2 Principles of Ethics

1. Rule of law and justice	7. Transparency
2. Evidence-based decisions	8. Efficiency and effectiveness
3. Accountability	9. Cooperation
4. Merit	10. Truthfulness
5. Equality (right and opportunity)	11. Trusteeship
6. Honesty and fairness	12. Inclusiveness

Source: Lewis, C., *Ethics or Corruption?* http://209.85.165.104/search?q=cache: bWVD_7Cd3qMJ:unpan1.un.org/intradoc/groups/public/docu-ments/ UNTC/UNPAN003965.pdf+ethics+principles+and+carol+lewis&hl=en&ct= clnk&cd=6&gl=us (accessed April 25, 2007), 1991.

In forecasting expenditures and revenues, these conditions may exist. These strategic misrepresentations are presented in Table 23.1. Yet, these specific misrepresentations in forecasting decisions are tied together under a broader umbrella of ethics. The precise delineation of ethical issues in forecasting can be divided into two components of strategic misrepresentation as shown in Table 23.1.

Before exploring how the identified strategic misrepresentations are evident in forecasting, this chapter must develop a linkage between these points of misrepresentation and their connection to principles of ethics. To do this, this chapter uses the 12 principles of ethics, applicable to the public sector, developed by Lewis (1991), and also demonstrates the connection to crucial considerations of ethics. These ethical principles are presented in Table 23.2. The actual approaches used in the technical and the political and administrative perspectives are explored in the following sections.

The Technical Perspective

Potential Misrepresentation and Ethics Principles

Although many strategic misrepresentations may be present in a technical perspective of forecasting, the chapter only examines three of the six misrepresentation scenarios most prevalent in forecasting: overall constraints, information asymmetry, and short- versus long-term issues.

Overall Constraints

Overall constraints can lead to ethical dilemmas because the forecaster is under pressure to reconcile the prevailing economic and political conditions even if there are absolute constraints on revenue-raising ability or new revenue sources. If there are automatic sequestrations or debt limitation ceilings, this will establish the parameters of the forecast. How these constraints are navigated represents potential ethical issues. One ethical issue to consider would be the "rule of law" in terms of respecting or acknowledging absolute limitations on revenue or expenditure. Also, issues of "honesty and fairness" in terms of societal conditions that require action beyond these constraints (e.g., a tax increase or program expansion) yet is closely aligned with ethical considerations of "efficiency and effectiveness." When projected revenues are insufficient to meet programmatic demands, is it efficient to simply adjust expenditure projections to match the tax or revenue constraints? Conversely, should a forecaster presume fewer clients in a social services program, which would lower expected expenditure projections? The ultimate ethical issue from a technical perspective is "evidence-based decisions" because it should be paramount that forecasters will only look at the evidence and guidance from their forecast models to establish the final predictive outcome. Ways to avoid this ethical issue might be to present multiple scenarios with a variety of assumptions built into the model that show varying degrees of revenue enhancement or expenditure projection, given overall constraints.

Information Asymmetry

Information asymmetry is a situation where one party in a negotiation has more or better information than another party in that negotiation. In the context of budgeting information, asymmetry is symptomatic of the process where the executive may have more information (about program operations and operating requirements) than the legislature. This gives an inherent advantage to the party in the negotiation or analysis of budgetary needs. The same is true in a forecasting environment where there may be more information or unilateral information supplied to one forecaster than another. This oftentimes results in incomplete information on which to base the forecast or an inaccurate basis on which to base the assumptions of the forecast.

The most obvious ethical principle confronted by forecasters is in the arena of "truthfulness." Is it truthful to obtain a more accurate or complete forecast by utilizing information exclusive to one forecaster? If forecasts are about presenting the most accurate and complete picture, and yet information access by one party over another allows a more complete forecast, is the profession of forecasting advanced or well served? Is telling the truth "always" an ethical imperative, given the imprecision of forecasting and fluctuating assumptions? If forecasting is a science, the answer is that all the known and unknown information must be somehow accommodated in a forecasting model. To simply not use complete information or to withhold information seems inconsistent with this professional norm.

"Transparency" is the other ethical principle to confront when dealing with a situation of incomplete or withheld information. Transparency requires complete disclosure of forecasting process, data, and assumptions that are shared with all parities responsible for the forecast. Should executive branch agencies be required to share all information with legislative forecasters? The inherent conflict between branches might argue "no," but the ethical imperative of transparency would argue "yes." To not be on the same page (via complete information requirements) means that one forecast will be different, wrong, or incomplete from a competing information-based forecast. Arriving at a consensus forecast will then be problematic because the basis of the consensus is flawed, probably advantaging one political or policy position. This seems inconsistent with a forecast process that requires complete information.

The final set of ethical principles to be considered is the principle of "cooperation and inclusiveness." The dynamic of conflicting forecasts (for advantage) is an implicit part of the forecasting process in the public sector, but does not foster an environment of cooperation and the viewpoint of everyone looking for a common denominator to start budget deliberations. Although consensus forecasting embraces this inclusiveness and fosters cooperation, the model of consensus forecasting typically happens only at a later stage or through the use of outside forecasters. Again, the misfit with ethics almost faults the process as being unethical.

Long- versus Short-Term Issues

Multiyear forecasting is a product of the budgeting process. The long-term consequences of budgeting for revenues and expenditures over a multiyear time horizon are what budgets are all about. Calculations of costs and benefits over the life of a capital project are crucial elements in deciding whether or not to advance projects. Expectations of future revenue streams (as taxes come online in out-years) or planned expenditures in the out-years (driven by growth projections) are central to issues of budgeting. At the same time, all of these long-term perspectives are based on a series of assumptions that carry some degree of ethical consideration.

In the short term, is it appropriate to count on using one time only nonrecurring revenues to fund an ongoing program? Is it appropriate in the long run to overobligate revenues with large capital-intensive projects? All of these considerations contain value and ethics elements.

Truthfulness is important in showing all the important variables that come together to present a forecast and not withholding information on a variable that might be crucial for a forecasting scenario. Transparency is probably the most significant ethical element in that if only some parties looking at or preparing forecasts have only partial information or are not privy to the actual models (and variables) used to develop the forecast. For ethical values of efficiency and effectiveness, forecasts are ethical to the extent they embody the professional and technical parameters of forecasting to be used as precision tools to achieve these outcomes. Also, evidence-based decision making lies at the heart of what the technical and professional mandates of forecasting require. Namely, that forecasts are based on proven and rigorous models and methodologies that can be followed in a logical sequence that produce the forecasts. Finally, "merit and trusteeship" are ethical principles in that forecasters must embrace the science and empiricism as the basis for forecasts that are presented by top decision makers for final disposition. Not adhering to meritorious work and serving their role as advisors to decision makers' forecasters do a disservice to these professional roots and training.

To be clear, this is not to suggest, as Jones and Euske (1991) do, that budgeting is a process that lies on the hinterlands of ethics in that some strategic misrepresentation (and perhaps ethical lapses) may be amenable to the enterprise of forecasting to achieve certain policy or programmatic goals. Yet, the conflict with a professional ethic seems clear. Each of these identified ethical values pertains to both the short- and long-run considerations and are consistent with misrepresentations in revenue and expenditure forecasting.

The Ethics of the Rational Forecast

What is surprising in a review of the relevant forecasting literature and in particular the *International Journal of Forecasting* is that there was only one article between 1985 and 2005, which identified with the issue of ethics in forecasting. Malinvaud (1987) articulates that the ethics of forecasting should be explicit and should center around two maxims: (1) forecasts should not be intentionally misleading (truthfulness in forecasting) and (2) forecasting should be produced in a competent manner (effectiveness and efficiency in technique). These two points highlight what is the prevalence of the technical approach to ethics in forecasting. It is in this vein that the most appropriate grounding in ethics for forecasters can be found in early work by the American Statistical Association (ASA) and the code of conduct advanced as "ethical guidance for statistical practice" (Ellenberg 1983). Discussions of such ethical concerns have been around for a long time and can be traced to 1949 and the development of a code of ethical practice for the profession. In most professional treatments of forecasting, these two ethical considerations are more appropriately examined as issues of bias or inconsistency that are portrayed as more technical issues than ethical considerations.

The Political and Administrative Perspective

Potential Misrepresentation and Ethics Principles

Similar to technical strategic misrepresentations, political and administrative misrepresentations can be equally insidious in the forecasting of expenditures and revenues in the public budgeting process. This section focuses on three misrepresentations: political ideology, micromanagement, and decision windows.

Political Ideology

In most respects, political ideology behind budget decision making is the most obvious basis for political and administrative misrepresentations in budget forecasting. Understanding that the political party that is in control of the purse strings or overall budget authority will likely advance its prevailing ideology articulated as either a "tax and spend" persuasion or the "no new taxes" mantra. These ideological mindsets will influence the forecasting assumptions that may point to the adequacy of current revenues to support programmatic goals or will drive the expenditure expectations of certain government programs or initiatives.

This chapter primarily considers ideological pressures within the context of the individual professional forecaster. An interesting question is how the internal political ideology may affect the individual forecaster's approach to forecasting assumptions. This presents a more tangible ethical dilemma concerning how far ideology should inform any forecasting decision. This question is examined in the following section.

One ethical issue or dilemma confronted in this perspective is the evidence-based principle, which stresses the imperative that decisions made in the public realm should be based on the objective analysis as presented by econometric modeling, given the set of prevailing economic, demographic, or programmatic assumptions. This evidentiary value base requires that regardless of the guiding ideological framework of the individual forecaster, the assumptions be grounded in the most realistic or high probability scenarios. Such assumptions can themselves be subject to a process of empirical analysis whereby consensus assumptions can be critically evaluated. For example, if there is an empirically relevant claim that future inflation rates on the following year's expenditures will fall somewhere between 3.5 and 5.5 percent, then an empirically derived (evidence-based) process can arrive at an inflation rate of 4.2 percent (either through a process of exponential smoothing or simple consensus forecasting models). Another example might be assumptions about the growth of the economy or size of populations served by certain government programs gleaned from widely available data sources. In the final analysis, such a consensus process occurs only at later stages of the forecasting exercise but could be incorporated much earlier in the process.

This evidence-based principle also leads directly to the next value basis that is implicit in a political ideological misrepresentation—honesty and fairness. What lies at the heart of this ethical dilemma in forecasting is that the imperative of political ideology often conflicts with the honest portrayal of expected fiscal conditions and ancillary budgetary impacts. A conservative ideology might lean toward the view that keeping taxes and revenue enhancements to a minimum and living within one's means is imperative for government and relevant policy makers. It is conceivable that these views would lead a like-minded forecaster or forecasting agent to subscribe to certain assumptions about the economy or demographic variables that could be utilized in an empirical forecasting model that could be expected to generate a forecast favorable to the conservative viewpoint that a tax increase is not likely given revenue or expenditure projections.

At the same time, a more liberal ideology would also probably influence one's views about the necessity for government programs and spending to help certain segments in society served by government. A sympathetic forecaster or forecasting agent might be expected to utilize assumptions about the economy and demographic factors that would support the liberal point of view that a revenue enhancement is necessary to support services at certain levels, given projected revenues or expenditures. At heart, these assumptions are inexorably linked to an ideology whether called liberal or conservative or Democratic versus Republican.

Honest disagreements over any set of assumptions are bound to occur in the forecasting world. In many cases, these assumptions may be both correct, given a certain frame of reference (e.g., time, definitions, valuation, and variable benefits or costs). What becomes more problematic is when the ideological imperative becomes a misrepresentation when the complete story or context is not presented. Oftentimes it becomes an issue of when not telling the complete truth, or telling only partial truth, constitutes a breach of honesty. This question is at the heart of the art and craft of policy formulation and analysis and is beyond the scope of this chapter. However, a focus on honesty in forecasting becomes of lynchpin for professionalism in forecasting. Knowing the boundaries of ideological imperative can be illuminated by considerations of honesty in forecasting methodology.

The final ethical principle or value confronted by an ideological misrepresentation is the value of "stewardship." Stewardship of the public interest can be the most illusive value to be confronted by forecasters, given any ideological framework. The liberal vision of stewardship can be vastly different from the conservative vision of stewardship. Liberals may see a positive role of government in the citizen's eyes and a vehicle to deliver equity and fairness. Conservatives may see government as an obstacle to free enterprise and an impediment to liberty. These views easily translate in terms of fiscal management and tax policies. A liberal perspective might argue for a more positive view of revenue growth to support programs from a view of growing expenditures demanded by citizens. A conservative point of view might see more restrictive revenue growth and a leveling off or decrease of expenditures as fiscally responsive to citizens. Both perspectives are legitimate roles in stewardship. In the case of government forecasters, each carries the value of stewardship of the public interest with an ideological disposition. Forecasters must exercise great care in understanding the multifaceted nature of stewardship—meeting the public interest of all citizens and not just citizens with a similar ideological perspective.

Micromanagement

Micromanagement becomes another potential misrepresentation in forecasting in public budgeting and financial management. The micromanagement can come in the form of legislative or executive demands translated into directives that are used in building forecasts at the organizational level, or it can come in the form of micromanagement of the individual forecaster or forecasting agent. This chapter focuses on the latter. At this level, outside manipulation or retooling of the forecasting model or fine-tuning of the assumptions become more important in the forecasting exercise than the running of the model itself to arrive at the forecast. When the temptation for excessive manipulation of a model or employing assumptions, which lie beyond the range of expected variances, these misrepresentations present ethical dilemmas.

For example, within a state transportation agency there has been growing impatience by members of the legislature about the success of a certain program for improving rural road safety. The program is supported by fees imposed on the transportation industry. In budget negotiations, the executive is placing certain pressures on the agency to demonstrate that the fee structure as it exists can support the program. But, the agency's senior managers are advancing the case that the fee structure is not sufficient to meet program needs for the next few fiscal years and want to offset legislative complaints about the program. They see boosting this fairly "hidden" fee increase as a way to get more funding more quickly into the program.

Agency budget staff initially conducts an analysis that shows a steadily growing revenue stream associated with these fees for the next five years, although for the first two years, the fee structure may be static or show only slight growth. Agency budget staffers conclude that they are able to adjust certain road usage numbers by transportation carriers that would result in lower revenue estimates from the fee in years one and two. The adjustment would involve using an older and less complete set of data for the projections than is commonly used. The state happens to have a more accurate database and could use these numbers to show higher projected revenue.

The agency's budget staff (forecasters) elect to use data elements and make some assumptions that result in lower revenue generation and press the case to the legislature for the need for increased fees. This micromanagement of the revenue projections hence misrepresents the forecast as part of a broader budgetary strategy. Many budgeters would see this misrepresentation more as a ploy or tool that is often used with little or no ethical baggage. They can take this position because "the ends justify the means." The agency can meet legislative demands, increase program resources, and also provide safer rural roadways in the state for citizens.

When these misrepresentations occur in the context of budget decision making (or the so-called budget gaming), the ethical propriety seems somewhat diminished. Budgeters oftentimes simply overlook or downplay ethical implications because misrepresentations are part of budget gamesmanship. Yet, does this scenario not precisely raise major ethical issues for forecasting when such misrepresentations are advanced to favor or benefit a certain position or set of decision makers? The most clear-cut ethical principle confronted in the preceding scenario is one of truthfulness. If there is a singular ethical imperative that applies to all levels of professional work, it is in knowing how far to micromanage elements of any operation. In many respects, this also involves broader management issues such as delegation and implementation. How much discretion should be given to subordinates for program operations or policy, and how much of the implementation of the program or policy should be given to experts or frontline employees in the operation? This is a difficult question and again beyond the scope of our current discussion, yet it seems evident that the ethical dimension of truthfulness is clearly at issue. Is it always prudent to tell the truth in budgeting or forecasting? What level of truth should be divulged? The scenario presented in this discussion reveals the problematic nature of "truth in forecasting." At issue is whose truth and how much truth, and whether truth should be always divulged when a superior asks or directs it not to be divulged.

The more pressing ethical dilemma or issue here is at the level of the individual forecaster. When should a forecaster withhold the truth or elements of truth? The question is further complicated because there is a fine line between the objective and subjective truths. A useful distinction in this regard can be found in the modernist versus postmodernist positions that have found application in the field of public administration (e.g., Miller and Fox 2006). Although it is not necessary to completely elaborate on the rich philosophical traditions that constitute the modernist versus postmodernist traditions in connection with objective versus subjective (or relative) truths, an overview may be appropriate. Postmodernists would likely point out that all truths are relative and that the foundation on which scientific or objective decisions are reached can be questioned and is constantly shifting. Thus, the role of objective data and modeling for purposes of forecasting may or may not reflect the reality of the budgetary or economic circumstances. To see the connection to ethics, Rasmussen (1993) argues that it is postmodern techniques of deconstruction (questioning) of reality (facts or data) that allows ethical claims to be exposed and contemplated. Therefore, it is imperative to proceed cautiously when grounding decisions in only objective truth. Postmodern deconstruction might ask: who provided the forecasting data; what data has been omitted or why this is the dataset we are interested in? In contrast, the modernist is firmly grounded in the strength of data and empiricism of the scientific method for guiding forecasting decisions. Modernists are interested in the metaphysical and the study of what reality is (Gustafson 2000). Therefore, forecasters taking a modernist point of view will dismiss that which can be known (epistemological stance) versus what is known (what science and rationality tell them). To be preoccupied, distracted, or misled by subjective claims have little meaning or use in forecasting. The modernist forecaster is driven by the data and the models grounded in reality. The point to emphasize is that the forecaster need not subscribe to one position or the other (modernist versus postmodernist), but clearly must acknowledge the distinction and implications of subjective versus objective truths in the forecasting enterprise.

If developing assumptions of a forecast carries with it different conceptions of truth (e.g., assuming growth in fees or a decrease in population served by programs), then the issue may be more a matter of objective-based truth. This means honest people with the same information can honestly disagree over the implications of certain data or projections. When subjective truth enters the picture, the forecaster must confront shaping the truth to a certain political or societal perspective beyond what the forecaster's professional judgment or modernist's orientation tells him or her. The ethical dilemma is more acute and needs to be somehow weighted or factored into the decision process of the forecast.

Another significant ethical dilemma confronted through misrepresentations of micromanagement lies in the area of transparency. This imperative is consistent with the notion of serving the public interest even in forecasting revenues or expenditures. Should a forecaster be bound to share all information relevant for developing the forecast? Shouldn't everyone at the forecasting table have the same information so that forecasting positions can be evaluated based upon open access to information? If only certain information is available to only certain parties, an ethical dilemma may arise in that inaccurate, misleading, or inappropriate data may lead to a certain forecasting scenario. If all parties have only partial information (similar to the quandary of information asymmetry), how can forecasts be ultimately held to a higher standard of scrutiny and analysis? Although, perhaps viewed as a technical point in forecasting, it is equally an ethical quandary that must be considered by all forecasters at the table.

Finally, in many respects principles of merit can also be compromised when micromanagement in forecasting is evident. Merit has a resounding application for the professional forecasters. No one wants to be accused of inappropriate or faulty methodology in arriving at a forecast. Indeed such accusations are the cause of the demise of careers and reputation for forecasters. Merit is something that cannot be decided in this chapter, and is the subject for professional guidance from the profession itself. Yet, the issue of merit is really not purely technical—it is an issue of ethics. Is merit the guiding principle or not? Is it something else (e.g., political or management pressures)? This ethical principle becomes one of implicit, rather than explicit, concern and is oftentimes beyond the parameters of guidance from the profession. It can only be resolved or decided at the level of the individual forecaster. Not to understand these influences as part of the process is really not embracing the view of the merit of the forecasting enterprise.

Decision Windows

The final political and administrative misrepresentation to be considered is decision windows or multiple or competing decision frames of reference. The forecasting considerations in this dimension concern offering multiple forecasts for multiple parties in the budgetary process. Jones and Euske (1991, p. 454) define one strategic misrepresentation in budgeting as "multiple and competing forums for budget decision making." This chapter presents this misrepresentation as a decision window.

In the development of this concept, the authors portray almost a "marketplace" where certain arguments, facts, and scenarios are presented depending on the audience involved (e.g., legislators and interest groups). In this scenario, certain themes or approaches "play" better than others. The scenario is no different when applied to revenue or expenditure forecasts. For example, legislators looking for holding the line on spending would likely prefer forecasts that reflect more restricted revenue growth. An advocacy group interested in expanding the same programs would like to see a rosy forecast that sees growth in revenues. Decisions about forecasts must take place under or within this backdrop. It does not necessarily mean that there will be four or five or more different forecasts—but it may. When forecasters advance their product before these audiences, certain assumptions of the forecast or modeling approaches may be used to highlight those forecast elements that will yield a forecast more consistent with those selected audiences. The issue is simply what assumptions we make (or weigh) as more significant, given the set of decisions that the varied parties in the budget process must make. One way forecasters may legitimately use such forecasts, within professional boundaries, has to do with the presentation of alternative forecast nodes that utilize different assumptions. Presenting the array of alternative forecasts can thus present decision makers (in any one decision window) the opportunity to weigh the merits of varied assumptions, given their decision preferences.

At face value, this type of "pick-and-choose" alternative forecast generation, or tailored forecasting, seems to conflict with ethical values. One ethical dilemma posed by this forecasting approach involves the value of "equity." Forecasting solely for the purpose of advancing one's decision window, audience, or constituency *de facto* implies an advantage for one party or group over another. This is precisely the reason why alternative forecast is being prepared or advanced. Although it may be possible to advance an argument that technically each alternative forecast is data driven and based on legitimate assumptions, the forecast is nonetheless a tool (or the means) to achieve a certain programmatic or policy end. This implies winners and losers.

A forecast presented in such a way prefers a designated winner to a loser or set of losers in the budgetary process.

The next quandary posed by multiple decision windows is trusteeship. Trusteeship is linked to notions of the public interest and the mantra of the greatest good for the greatest number, a median voter model or a Pareto efficiency model. The forecaster is no different from the primary policy maker in this ethical dilemma. Although the forecaster may not be in a position to choose the final forecast, program, or policy direction, he or she is in a position to present the tool or the rationale for the decision. In the classic public administration literature, the politics versus administration dichotomy shows public administrators (forecasters) as either (a) neutral competent providing information and forecasts to decision makers or (b) functioning with a political mindset advancing certain agendas in the public arena. The notion of trusteeship implies that forecasters find a balance between these positions. At either point of the politics–administration dichotomy it can be argued that the citizen is being better served. But the danger of residing at the political end of the dichotomy is that the imperative of politics may supersede the rational or neutral competent point such that an imbalance occurs. This tilt means certain political interests are valued over the others. It is in this sense that the dilemma of trusteeship arises. Who is the forecaster the trustee of: certain interest groups or the general citizenry? How does he or she know this?

The final ethical value to be confronted concerns inclusiveness. It becomes rather evident that tailored forecasts presented to audiences dependent on the decision nodes seem slippery at minimum, but explicitly mean leaving some parties to the process in the dark, with only partial information or with only the information they want to hear. This seems to directly confront with the rational basis in the profession of forecasting to include all the relevant data and allow open exchange to process the best possible forecast to the set of decision makers. This is clearly not the case when forecasts are presented based on a certain decision window. The ethical dilemma is that when inclusiveness is ignored, exclusiveness is advanced. Who decides who gets the information, what information, the accuracy of information, or versions of the information that clearly implies an exclusive basis for information sharing. Not to share information is one of those important budget anachronisms embraced by many parties in the budget process. However, if parties in the budget process start at different base points (forecasts), then some parties will always be disadvantaged if they do not have wide access to the information on which the forecast was based. The dilemma is that certain interests will be served, whereas others will be disadvantaged.

The Ethics of the Political and Administrative Forecast

Let there be no mistake that the budget is first and foremost a political document. The inherent politics in the budget process has been acknowledged and studied by seminal figures in public budgeting such as Rubin (1997) and Wildavsky (1992). The budget is an expression of interest and desires and priorities expressed through the political process and operationalized through the budget document and its processes. Therefore, it is no surprise that the political backdrop extends to the forecasting of revenues and expenditures as part of this process. Similar to the argument that professional standards and the professionalism of the process extend to the technical and rational process of forecasting, these standards apply to the political and administrative backdrop of forecasting. For some guidance in establishing the implications of this orientation to the political and administrative realm, it is appropriate to look at some related literature to understand the ethical implications of the forecasting enterprise.

Here the issues seem to resonate more with the ethical implications than do the technical aspects. If viewed from a rational and technical viewpoint, the ethical implications or dilemmas can be wrapped in the professional and neutral competent norms that all models, techniques, and assumptions are based on a nonbiased model where any variability falls within the professional acceptable norms or can be labeled as "technical advice," which can be accepted or not accepted by the decision makers. With respect to any bias in the modeling, it is merely a statistical bias that has little ethical relevance. And if within the boundaries of statistically significant bias, or error term, then there are really only different forecast outcomes not ethical issues.

In the political and administrative world everything is about the forecast as a political tool or administrative fiat. Conversely, there is an explicit weighing of political or administrative bias that is not easily dismissed as a statistical bias. It carries with it explicit ethical values that are built into the modeling, techniques, and assumptions.

The Forecasting Continuum: Positive to Normative

What this chapter has sought to do is to posit a continuum of ethical values that are consistent with the two main approaches used in revenue and expenditure forecasts in public budgeting. Professional forecasters may take issue with such a simplistic continuum to depict ethical dilemmas in the forecasting enterprise. Ethics scholars may take issue with the simplicity of the model that may mask a variety of shades of ethics or ethical values that are somehow not reflected in this continuum. But what this model offers is both a generic tool and conceptual device to better understand when, how, and if ethical issues are involved in forecasting revenues and expenditures. Even if some readers conclude that this states the obvious, then the utility of this conceptual continuum is one of assisting in the dialogue about just what the explicit or implicit ethical dilemmas in forecasting are, or should be.

However, this treatment of ethics in forecasting would not be complete without offering a normative model for the forecasting enterprise. The chapter, to this point, has avoided attaching weight to any normative perspective and in the preceding sections has only raised questions or possible implications. In an effort to provide a platform to examine the normative implications, this chapter concludes with a presentation of an idealized code of ethics for forecasting, which embraces the ethical and professional norms discussed to this point. The code is not an imposition of a select frame of conduct or definitive axioms. It is, however, a starting point for an explicit consideration of the ethical nuances that are imbedded in forecasting revenues and expenditure in the public sector.

Lens of Analysis: Codes of Ethics

Green and Tull (1978, p. 7) make an observation that "[e]very decision is based on a forecast." Moreover, Ehrman and Shugan (1995) place the forecast at the center of virtually all decision making. In this sense, most decisions have an ethical component or dimension. Forecasting is no different. Yet, it is evident that the professional and academic literature on forecasting has paid only limited attention to the impact or role of ethics in forecasting.

The clearest call for ethics in the forecasting enterprise has come from Gardner and Makridakis (1988) who offer a definitive call (or at minimum some standards of ethical comparability for the profession). Surprisingly, there is little guidance in this area and there is not a code of ethics for the forecasting profession. The International Institute of Forecasters (a cross-disciplinary professional association) is largely silent on the issue of ethics. The institute has promulgated best practices principles compiled as the *Principles of Forecasting*, but ethics is treated only as a piecemeal and in limited context (see http://www.forecastingprinciples.com/handbook.html). The Institute of Business Forecasting is also silent on a professional code of ethics.

Wachs (1990) offers the best discussion of the subject with a view toward responsibility for public policy with direct application to forecasting issues in public budgeting and finance. Wachs acknowledges the political implications of forecasts in the public sector and that forecasters in such roles balance their technical expertise in the field with the political implications. But in the public realm, the backdrop of laws and regulations require neutral and objective analysis whether in applying for grants or contracts or in implementing funding formulas that carry distinct political rewards for the respective department, agency or bureau. These political factors place the forecasts under explicit *de jure* and *de facto* ethical pressures.

Wachs traces a handful of such ethical dilemmas in forecasting public policy. One case involves forecasts for urban rail transits systems where a federal study determined that costs were higher in nine of the ten systems analyzed (e.g., the Miami metro system forecast cost per passenger served at $1.73, when the actual operating costs per passenger was $16.77). Pressures for optimistic forecasts on these projects were cited as one reason why forecasts were not on the mark. The actual instances of inaccurate, misleading, or incorrect forecast should not be the main argument advanced in this chapter. But it is the broader public interest at risk from inaccurate forecasts in the public decision-making process that is being illustrated here and advanced in Wachs's article.

Indeed, the contribution Wachs makes in his clear articulation of the reasons that forecasting in the public realm is wrought with potential ethical dilemmas: (1) forecasts cannot be verified until the actual action forecast is taken or completed, (2) forecasts are technically complex, and (3) forecasts always employ subjective assumptions. As discussed throughout this chapter, it is evident that forecasters on the political and administrative end of the continuum or the technical and rational end both use extensive databases, sophisticated techniques, and the latest computer modeling. Forecasters are indeed taught and trained in these approaches. These considerations often carry ethical dilemmas and in this regard help can be found in a code of ethics. As Wachs concludes in his work, one of the pillars of improvements in the realm of public forecasting would be the creation and articulation of a professional code of ethics. This chapter introduces a model code of ethics that might be considered by professional forecasters or their umbrella organizations.

The Code-Driven Forecast: Implications for Public Budgeting and Finance

The code being suggested in this chapter is best thought of as a cumulative or integrated model. It integrates the ethics codes promulgated by many professional organizations including Government Finance Officers Association (GFOA), Association of Government Accountants (AGA), International City/County Managers Association (ICMA), National Association of State Budget Officers (NASBO), and American Society for Public Administration (ASPA). As such, the model is neither exhaustive nor is it presented as a definitive work. It should be the purview of professional forecasters to devise such a code for their own profession. Yet, this code may offer a starting point for developing such a code and offering some rationale for how to use such a code as guidance when ethical pressures arise in the forecasting enterprise.

When we juxtapose the synopsis of applicable codes against the 13 possible strategic misrepresentations and ethical dilemmas introduced in this chapter, it is possible to synthesize approximately five core ethical mandates that serve as a basis for a code of forecasting.

1. *Honesty.* In the conduct of the individual forecaster consistent with the presentation of complete and accurate information in the process at all times.
2. *Public interest.* Analysis and judgments regardless of any prevailing point of view or favoritism to any one party or group.
3. *Merit.* The forecaster is bound to honor professional and technical standards of credible evidence, methodology, and assumptions in the forecasting process.

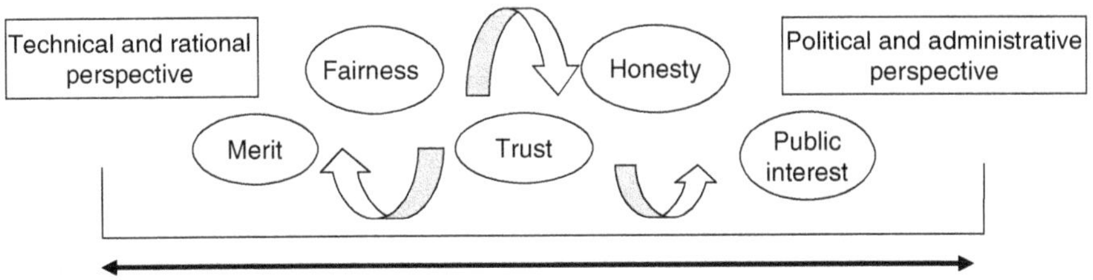

Figure 23.2 Five-point ethics code for forecasting revenues and expenditures.

4. *Trust.* Impartiality is the basis for loyalty to the organization, government, and citizen.
5. *Fairness.* Forecasters should embrace the viewpoint that all views in the public arena matter and inclusiveness in forecasting assumptions and methodology are to be incorporated.

These five principles are offered not because they are the definitive points forecasters must incorporate into all forecasting, but because they cover the strategic misrepresentations offered in this essay and embrace most if not all of Lewis's ethical principles. Figure 23.2 presents the five principles of forecasting as floating or residing along the continuum from technical and rational to political and administrative forecasts. One or more principles may be at play in any given forecast, but the key is that these value considerations must be addressed in any type of forecast advanced in public budgeting and finance. There may be some gaps, omissions, and imprecision in the articulation of what these ethical principles for forecasters embody. Yet, any forecaster who embraces these principles will likely have a framework for action when preparing, evaluating, or presenting a forecast. It seems appropriate that the profession of forecasting and its related professional associations embrace a movement to articulate a code of ethics that can, at minimum, give forecasters or members a pause to consider their actions in process, scope, and impact of their respective forecasts.

Conclusion

The overall implications of this five-point ethics code for forecasting or forecasting in public budgeting and finance remain unclear. This chapter has articulated one possible approach or guidance to avoid or navigate some of the ethical dilemmas that arise in the forecasting enterprise. But it is important to conclude with some thoughts and observations by a community of scholars known as futurists for guidance in this area (e.g., impact). Futurists engage in social forecasting (what society will and should look like in the future). Indeed, forecasting is a tool for the building of the future. Forecasts have and will continue to shape the future or at minimum the perception of what the future holds. This is a profound implication well beyond the instrumentality of the forecast for day-to-day budget and finance decision windows. A renowned futurist has commented that the "purpose of forecasting is to control the present" (Dublin 1989, p. 27). This lies at the heart of the ethical dilemma imposed by forecasting. If forecasts are determinants of the future, then the question that forecasters are duty bound to ask is whose future?

The proposed ethical principles for forecasting is an effort to advance some level of ethical thinking about this question in the context of public budgeting and finance decisions. The argument advanced in this chapter is that forecasters in the budget and finance arena have no less a charge and obligation. Their actions, decisions, methodology, assumptions, and views shape the future. There is no more noble a calling in many respects. It is a calling that requires and demands the highest standards of ethics to be applied in their work. Our future as taxpayers, citizens, and as a society demand it.

Appendix: Codes of Ethics in Professional Organizations

The following sections synthesize and summarize the codes, below focusing on those elements that are embodied in the 12 ethical principles advanced earlier. Certain principles or ethical tenets are highlighted because they specifically address points in the conduct of forecasting in the public sphere. What is not done is to synthesize all the codes into a singular code that is meant to provide guidelines. The framework of what is embodied or stressed by these codes is what is important for future forecasters to better integrate ethics into their work.

Government Finance Officers Association

The GFOA code calls for the highest ideals of honor and integrity, and personal relationships stressing respect, trust, and inspiring confidence. The code stresses responsibility to the public, the highest-quality counsel, and performance. Prudence and integrity are paramount. Upholding the constitution, legislation, and regulations are keys. More specifically, members are expected not to knowingly subscribe to or permit misstatements in any reports or omit material facts. All statements should be prepared consistent with law and generally acceptable practices. Members shall respect and protect privileged information. Members shall be loyal to the interest of their government body and not condone any illegal or improper actions. Members should respect rights of colleagues and shall avoid any conflict of interest or accrue personal or political gain (see Government Finance Officers Association 2007).

Association of Government Accountants

The AGA code explicitly promotes the public interest and the members are not bound exclusively to the needs of any one employer or client. Members place a premium on credible information and information systems, require the highest standards of performance, and must be straightforward and honest in delivering professional services. Members should be objective and fair, respect confidentiality of information, and follow technical and professional standards. Moreover, members should only render opinions that are based on the facts, disclose improprieties they may find, consider the public interest in the discharge of their duties, and always avoid an appearance of a conflict of interest (see Association of Government Accountants 2003).

International City/County Managers Association

Members are required to promote a sense of social responsibility, stress honor and integrity, serve the interests of all the people at all times, refrain from political activities, keep the community and public informed at all times, conduct oneself with merit, and seek no favor based on accidental information (see International City/County Managers Association 2004).

National Association of State Budget Officers

Members are encouraged to stress "being truthful, sincere, forthright, and candid where professional duties requiring confidentiality permit, so that persons are not misled or deceived." (National Association of State Budget Officers 1996, p. 173). Conduct should be consistent with core beliefs, fulfill commitments, make impartial decisions, seek all relevant information (including dissenting opinions), pursue open equitable and impartial processes to evaluate information, show respect for others, be responsible for personal actions, and demonstrate loyalty, but "refusing to subordinate other ethical obligations in the name of loyalty such as honesty, integrity and fairness. Members are obligated to make decisions on the merits, without favoritism, in the name of loyalty," offer independent objective judgment, and ensure that "government is conducted openly, efficiently, equitably, and honorably in a manner that permits the citizenry to make informed judgments and hold government officials accountable." (National Association of State Budget Officers 1996, p. 174).

American Society for Public Administration

Members must serve the public interest with compassion and fairness, stress citizen involvement and access, respect the constitution and laws, demonstrate truth and honesty and responsibility, promote merit and communication, and strive for professional excellence (see American Society for Public Administration 2007).

References

American Society for Public Administration. 2007. *ASPA's Code of Ethics*, http://www.aspanet.org/scriptcontent/index_codeofethics.cfm (accessed April 25, 2007).

Association of Government Accountants. 2003. *AGA Ethics Handbook*, http://www.agacgfm.org/about/2003EthicsHandbook.pdf (accessed March 11, 2007).

Bostrom, N. and T. Ord. 2006. The reversal test: eliminating status quo bias in applied ethics. *Ethics* 116(4): 656–679.

Bunn, D. and G. Wright. 1991. Interaction of judgmental and statistical forecasting methods: issues and analysis. *Management Science* 37(5): 501–518.

Dublin, M. 1989. *Futurehype: The Tyranny of Prophecy*. New York: Plume.

Ehrman, C. M. and S. M. Shugan. 1995. The forecaster's dilemma. *Marketing Science* 14(2): 123–147.

Ellenberg, J. H. 1983. Ethical guidelines for statistical practice: a historical perspective. *The American Statistician* 37(1): 1–4.

Feenberg, D. R., W. Gentry, D. Gilroy, and H. S. Rosen. 1989. Testing the rationality of state revenue forecasts. *The Review of Economics and Statistics* 71(2): 300–308.

Gardner, E. S. and S. Makridakis. 1988. The future of forecasting. *International Journal of Forecasting* 4(3): 1–6.

Government Finance Officers Association. 2007. *GFOA Code of Ethics*, http://www.gfoa.org/main/about.code.ethics.shtml (accessed April 15, 2007).

Green, P. E. and D. S. Tull. 1978. *Research for Marketing Decisions*, 4th ed. Englewood Cliffs, NJ: Prentice-Hall.

Gustafson, A. 2000. Making sense of postmodern business ethics. *Business Ethics Quarterly* 10(3): 645–658.

International City/County Managers Association. 2004. *ICMA Code of Ethics*, http://www.icma.org/main/bc.asp?bcid=40&hsid=1&ssid1=2530&ssid2=2531 (accessed March 12, 2007).

Jones, L. R. and K. J. Euske. 1991. Strategic misrepresentation in budgeting. *Journal of Public Administration Research and Theory* 1(4): 437–460.

Lewis, C. 1991. *Ethics or Corruption?* http://209.85.165.104/search?q=cache:bWVD_7Cd3qMJ:unpan1.un.org/intradoc/groups/public/documents/UNTC/UNPAN003965.pdf+ethics+principles+and+carol+lewis&hl=en&ct=clnk&cd=6&gl=us (accessed April 25, 2007).

Makridakis, S. 1986. The art and science of forecasting: an assessment and future direction. *International Journal of Forecasting* 2(1): 15–39.

Malinvaud, E. 1987. Analyse et prevision. *International Journal of Forecasting* 3(2): 187–194.

Miller, H. T. and C. J. Fox. 2006. *Postmodern Public Administration*. Armonk, NY: M. E. Sharpe.

National Association of State Budget Officers. 1996. *Budget Analyst Training Program. Module 12 Ethics and Standards of Professional Conduct*, http://www.nasbo.org/Publications/ PDFs/training_modules.pdf (accessed March 7, 2007).

Rasmussen, D. M. 1993. Business ethics and postmodernism: a response. *Business Ethics Quarterly* 3(3): 271–277.

Rubin, I. 1997. *The Politics of Public Budgeting: Getting and Spending, Borrowing and Balancing*, 3rd ed. Chatham, NJ: Chatham House Publishers.

Rubin, M. M. and N. Mantell. 2003. Revenue forecasting and revenue estimation. In J. Rabin (Ed.) *Encyclopedia of Public Administration and Policy*, New York: Marcel Dekker, pp. 1057–1065.

Schroder, L. 1982. Local government multi-year budgetary forecasting: some administrative and political issues. *Public Administration Review* 42(2): 121–127.

Smith, R. W. and T. D. Lynch. 2004. *Public Budgeting in America*, 5th ed. Upper Saddle River, NJ: Prentice-Hall.

Wachs, M. 1990. Ethics and advocacy in forecasting for public policy. *Business & Professional Ethics Journal* 9(1–2): 141–158.

Wildavsky, A. 1980. *Speaking Truth to Power: The Art and Craft of Policy Analysis*. London: Macmillan.

Wildavsky, A. 1992. Political implications of budget reform: a retrospective. *Public Administration Review* 52(6): 594–599.

Zarnowitz, V. 1985. Rational expectations and macroeconomic forecasts. *Journal of Business & Economic Statistics* 3(4): 293–311.

Chapter 24

Transparency in Government Revenue Forecasting

Charles Garofalo and Nandhini Rangarajan

Contents

Introduction

We live in a world of enormous uncertainty and most of us engage in forecasting to reduce or eliminate negative effects associated with such uncertainty. Forecasts provide important insights about the unclear future by using critical information from times past and present. A multitude of forecasts, made by the layperson and the expert alike, about the next killer tsunami, the next Super Bowl champion, future presidents elect, the next economic boom, imminent security threats, future fashion trends, and so on, emphasize the ubiquitous nature of forecasting. The expanding scope and significance of forecasting is further accentuated by its perceptible adoption over the years by a variety of domains such as sports, education, and business.

Revenue Forecasting in Government

The evolution of forecasting into an organizational activity with multidisciplinary influences is observable from the fact that it is no longer associated with just the quintessential number cruncher. Instead, as Sun (2005) observes, it incorporates elements of politics, human judgment, public expectations, and managerial considerations among others. For purposes of this chapter, we focus specifically on the use of revenue forecasting as an essential planning, policy, and decision-making tool in public sector organizational settings (Corder 2005, Jones et al. 1997, Makridakis 1996, Poister and Streib 1989, Sun 2005). The importance of revenue forecasting as a critical governmental organizational activity is emphasized by the fact that a "budget is first and foremost a public statement that reflects policies and priorities" (Sun 2005, p. 528). Budgets are public statements about who gets what, when, where, how, and why (Rodgers and Joyce 1996, p. 48). They are instrumental in elevating the social status of certain programs and policies through new or continued allocation of funds and lowering the status of others through budget cuts. Revenue forecasts typically play a crucial role in determining the ultimate creation, sustenance, and demise of new and existing programs and policies. As Shafritz et al. (2007, p. 483) observe, "the flow and management of funds is the lifeblood of our system of public administration." Revenue forecasts facilitate the smooth functioning of this system by making projections, predicting problems, and highlighting trends. Apart from serving essential policy functions, forecasts also facilitate efficient management by projecting spending patterns and revenue generation that can accommodate such spending plans (Schroeder 1982, p. 122).

Recognizing the importance of government revenue forecasting and its impact on individuals, organizations, and society at large, the scholarly literature on forecasting has focused on a variety of issues. Some prominent areas of research include forecasting methods (see, e.g., Auerbach 1996, Cirincione et al. 1999); forecasting processes (see, e.g., Shkurti 1990); internal and external forecasting environment of the organizations (see, e.g., Jones et al. 1997, Stinson 2002, Sun 2005); forecasting entities, errors and accuracy in revenue forecasting (see, e.g., Beckett-Camarata 2006, Mocan and Azad 1995, Plesko 1988, Rodgers and Joyce 1996, Stinson 2006); and general evaluation of forecasts (see, e.g., Jones et al. 1997).

The literature on errors in forecasting and evaluation of forecasts deserves special attention because it has the explicit aim of improving revenue forecasting. According to Armstrong (1988), forecasting, for the longest time, did not enjoy the intellectual attention or command the respect of academicians and practitioners as it does today. Stinson (2002) corroborates this point of view by observing that, despite the obvious advantages associated with government revenue forecasting, it is often criticized for problems such as overestimation and underestimation of surpluses or deficits. Shkurti (1990, p. 92) brings our attention to a phenomenon called "forecast trap" that makes forecasters withhold information to make their forecasts look good. The occurrence of such problems results in the loss of confidence in forecasts and respect for forecasters. It also raises questions about the ethical nature of forecasts. Therefore, one of the emerging streams of research relates to transparency in revenue forecasting, which is aimed at improving the quality of forecasts and securing public confidence in them (see, e.g., Bauer et al. 2006, Chortareas et al. 2002, Field 2004, Kopits 2000, Petrie 2003).

Objectives of the Chapter

Forecasting is an important organizational tool and activity. However, the ethical nature of forecasting can be questioned when its methods are not made transparent. Given this information, the two overarching objectives of this chapter are (1) to provide an in-depth understanding of the ethical environment of forecasting and the role of transparency in reinforcing the ethical nature of forecasting and (2) to understand the different types of resistance to change likely to be faced by the implementation of increased transparency as an ethical standard.

Organization of the Chapter

The chapter is organized into three main sections. In the section titled "Overview of Ethics and Transparency in Government Revenue Forecasting," the literature on ethics and transparency in government revenue forecasting is discussed. More specifically, arguments for and against transparency in government revenue forecasting are presented. In the next section, three proposals for achieving increased transparency in government revenue forecasting are provided. These proposals are specifically targeted toward changes at the individual, group, and other macrolevels of analysis. Then, different types of resistances that are likely to emerge as a result of the adoption and implementation of these proposals are examined. Finally, some conclusions are offered about how the juxtaposition of ethics, transparency, and change can have an impact on government revenue forecasting.

Overview of Ethics and Transparency in Government Revenue Forecasting

Our goals in this section are threefold: (1) to develop an ethical perspective on revenue forecasting; (2) to pave the way toward a more detailed exploration of transparency as a concept and as a component of revenue forecasting, in particular; and (3) to set the stage for our analysis of change strategies on both the organizational or cultural level and the level of forecasting practice itself.

In principle, government revenue forecasters, like all public administrators, are fiduciaries responsible to their principal agents—the citizenry—in service to the sovereign, trustees of the public interest. In practice, like all public administrators, they are members of bureaucracies and hierarchies, with multiple principals and stakeholders, as well as conflicting values and competing priorities. Nonetheless, finance administrators, like all public administrators, cannot avoid ethical issues or the requirements of decision making, accountability, and oversight that accompany them.

As in all specialties of public administration, the ethical and fiduciary nature of fiscal management is often overlooked or ignored, both in principle and practice, in favor of putative technical expertise and neutral competence. Although ethical reasoning and ethical responsibility are not displaced by rules or rewards and punishments, the inevitable wicked problems are purportedly tamed, as the moral content of fiscal management is drained away in deference to expediency and at least short-term consensus. In this connection, one of the major reforms recommended repeatedly is heightened transparency, and it is transparency and its complexities that are the focus of our treatment of revenue forecasting.

Transparency in Revenue Forecasting

Transparency, as an organizational principle and practice, is embraced in both the private and public sector. Like efficiency, it is an instrumental value intended to achieve certain purposes. But it is also a normative value intended to attain other purposes. The overriding aims of instrumental and normative transparency are to increase the information flow to shareholders or citizens, to facilitate more informed choices, and to insure greater accountability among organizational decision makers. Transparency is seen as essential to legitimate and effective governance because it may help to resolve the perennial principal-agent problem. Whether in private or public governance, a major challenge is controlling the information asymmetry that inevitably favors the interests of agents over those of principals (Florini 2002).

Although transparency is becoming a global norm in national security as well as economic, environmental, and regulatory policy, it would be naïve to think that the path toward transparency has been or will be smooth (Florini 2002, 2003, Stiglitz 1999). Despite its growing power and potential in governance, transparency, like other norms, does not implement or enforce itself. Resistance and objections to transparency, as well as the skills needed to interpret and apply information, and to discern the utility of transparency in specific circumstances, continue to pose important questions for twenty-first century governance.

In particular situations, the application of transparency often conflicts with other values or interests. Disclosure of information can jeopardize privacy, public safety, or proprietary data, and it may threaten reputations, markets, or political influence. Therefore, support for transparency must be nuanced, calibrated to the demands and details of particular circumstances, and must influence organizational performance toward a specified policy goal (Fenster 2006, Fung et al. 2002, 2004).

The emphasis placed on transparency, in general, parallels the concern for transparency in public sector fiscal affairs, including revenue forecasting. As Alt et al. (2005, pp. 2–3) note, "Fiscal transparency is now an integral part of public sector design ..." which "eases the task of forecasting future fiscal policy." On both the international and domestic levels, scholars and institutional analysts have probed the processes and prospects of fiscal transparency, in general, and revenue forecasting, in particular (Alt and Lassen 2006, Auerbach 1999, Bauer et al. 2006, Chortareas et al. 2002, Danninger et al. 2005, Heilemann 2002, Kopits 2000, Kyobe and Danninger 2005, Mensah et al. 2006, Petrie 2003). These inquiries have ranged from transparency in countries of the Organization for Economic Co-Operation and Development to the political economy of revenue forecasting in low-income countries to the roles of the International Monetary Fund, financial markets, and civil society to the performance and use of revenue forecasts. Therefore, in the past few years, a fairly sizable body of work has become available to academic and governmental specialists as well as members of the interested public. But, not surprisingly, many questions remain, especially relating to the meaning, interpretation, and application of transparency in revenue forecasting.

Field argues that revenue estimating is shrouded in secrecy. It means different things to different people. Therefore, like other policy or reform goals, we can infer that transparency is more likely to engender agreement in principle but to elicit disagreement in practice. The key in this regard is to identify our aims related to the level of transparency to be provided in any given situation.

Field also distinguishes between generalized and specific transparency. Generalized transparency consists of publishing explanations of how an agency prepares revenue estimates; sponsoring occasional conferences where revenue estimators describe their work; publishing source data such as the Internal Revenue Service's Statistics of Income or its "public-use file" that can be used by private organizations; and publishing retrospective analyses of the accuracy of prior revenue estimates. Specific transparency, in contrast, consists of publishing explanations of how a particular revenue estimate was prepared; releasing the assumptions made by an estimator in performing a specific revenue estimate; describing spreadsheets or simulation models used in doing a specific estimate; and releasing data used in making a specific revenue estimate without jeopardizing taxpayer privacy or business confidentiality. Again, which components are included depends on the goals and on the interests of those being served. Generalized transparency is enough for those whose primary concern may be the honesty and reliability of estimates, whereas for scholars, researchers, and tax professionals, at least some of the specific transparency components are essential.

Given these considerations, we can begin to appreciate the complexity of transparency as both a normative and an instrumental value. On the one hand, transparency can be seen as contributing to the enhancement of self-government, professional credibility, public knowledge, and accountability. Citizen access to information is believed to be fundamental in a democracy, and without it, self-government is impossible. Thus, if the basis of revenue forecasts is not publicly available, then claims of political manipulation are easy to make, and consistency and quality control are difficult to achieve.

But the arguments against complete or, perhaps, even increased transparency appear to be equally compelling. Field, for example, suggests that experience with tax-related matters under the Freedom of Information Act often leads tax agencies to stop producing documents that courts have ordered to be disclosed, especially when agencies lack staff or a mandate to promote disclosure. If assumptions and data sources are made public, the forecaster may stop preparing them and list only the most reliable assumptions and sources. Similar concerns have been expressed regarding the frequency and quality of meetings mandated by open government or sunshine laws (Fenster 2006).

An important objection to greater transparency in revenue forecasting is a reduced role for judgment in what is fundamentally an art rather than a science. Opponents of enhanced transparency fear that it will lessen estimators' independence in exercising their professional judgment, especially if their beliefs and assumptions cannot be easily documented. Whether required because of the lack of empirical data or because of ample empirical data that requires interpretation, judgment is vital in the forecasting and estimating process, and should not be sacrificed for purposes of disclosure (Field 2004).

We have, then, a set of assertions, assumptions, and objections associated with revenue forecasting in government that raise several important questions: What are the probable benefits and burdens of increased transparency? How can increased transparency be introduced into revenue forecasting at all levels of government? How can it be sustained? One possible response to these questions is consensus revenue estimating—a conflict-resolution process conducted before a legislative session to resolve disagreements over the revenue and expenditure figures to be included in the budget. This process, which has been adopted by half the states, involves legislative and executive branch participants as well as representatives of business and universities. It is public in nature, enabling interested citizens as well as the press to participate. In Field's (2004) judgment, as well as ours, consensus revenue estimation provides a sound object lesson for federal revenue estimators (Auerbach 1999). Although the need for greater transparency at the federal level in the United States is clear, the many calls for more transparency have not been heeded to any appreciable extent (Field 2004). Agency interests, incentives, and cultures simply have not led to the acceptance of increased transparency. Transparency is not a priority, and the payoffs are not there, particularly, if delayed estimates for the sake of transparency would lead to complaints and criticisms.

External pressure will be required to produce the change, but the source of such pressure is ambiguous at best (Field 2004). Congress, especially the tax-writing committees, may be the likeliest source, but it is not very interested in transparency issues. Accounting firms and their clients, other governmental organizations such as the Government Accountability Office, think tanks and research groups across the political spectrum, and universities may be other sources of change. But, again, the situation is murky.

Three Proposals for Increased Transparency

The practice of transparency in revenue forecasting requires a fresh perspective if the gap between theory and practice is to be narrowed and the transparency's normative and instrumental purposes are to be met. Transparency's effects on administrative costs, decision making, and open meetings, as well as the ambiguity associated with the sources of change, demand reframing if the moral and constitutional foundations of public administration are to be honored. Therefore, our aim at this point is to provide a model of moral agency and moral competence for revenue forecasters that can help to close the gap between transparency theory and practice, to contribute to the creation of a more nuanced approach to stakeholder demands for more or less transparency in revenue forecasting, and to suggest possible benchmarks and directions for practical organizational change. More specifically, we offer three provisional proposals that will guide our analysis of potential change strategies: (1) acknowledge the inherent moral agency of public administrators, including revenue forecasters; (2) encourage the creation of criteria for deciding what and how much information revenue forecasters should either disclose or withhold; and (3) adopt a revised consensus method as a pilot program to ascertain its applicability at all levels of government.

With regard to the first proposal, public administration is a fundamentally moral enterprise and the public administrator is a moral agent who has multiple principals with multiple priorities. Public administration exists to perform a morally justified task, namely, to serve the public good. Thus, when obligations to conflicting principles must be balanced, morality becomes the supreme principle for the public administrator, a condition consistent with the general tenor and tenets of the code of ethics of the American Society for Public Administration. As a result, given its inherent moral nature, public administration can claim moral legitimacy in governance.

Moral legitimacy, however, is not enough for effective public administration. Equally essential is moral competence, a key dimension of the professional skills required by good governance. Moral competence is nested in reciprocal commitments between citizens and public servants, an active understanding of the common good, recognition of the moral space for making choices, and the capacity to engage in ethical inquiry, manage competing claims, and tolerate moral ambiguity (Winston 2003). Public servants are moral actors whose discretion and decisions demand the application of moral judgment, rather than simple obedience to hierarchical directives. In light of the artistry associated with revenue forecasting, including the need for the exercise of judgment, revenue forecasters clearly qualify as moral agents. What may be required in some or many cases is heightened moral consciousness, as well as moral competence. Enhancing moral consciousness and moral competence in revenue forecasting, as in public service overall, requires intelligence, imagination, and initiative, as well as recognition of potential resistance to change, strategies designed to engender respect, reciprocity, and trust, and a professional commitment to what Gardner et al. (2001) call good work. Above all, it requires transformational or generative leadership that is willing to engage the incentive structure of the revenue-forecasting arena and of individual revenue forecasters, to shift from private- to public-regarding thought and behavior. This leads to our second proposal: the creation of criteria for deciding what and how much information to disclose or to withhold. These criteria should be formulated by a broad constellation of stakeholders, including representatives of the legislative and executive branches, the private sector, universities, the media, and other interested parties. Before formulating such criteria, however, these stakeholders must develop a consensus on the connection between their criteria and democratic governance. Their task is not to protect or privilege particular interests but to develop and advocate responsible transparency and, ultimately, citizen trust in the revenue-forecasting process. Again, shifting from parochial political or professional concerns to greater respect for citizens and the public space will require morally conscious and morally competent leadership.

Revenue forecasters, as moral agents, are obligated to justify the disclosure or withholding of information by specifying the aims, assumptions, and methods underlying their decisions. Revenue forecasting practices must be sufficiently transparent to determine whether they advance the values and goals embodied in ethical governance, or whether they are merely expedient stratagems to satisfy short-term political or professional considerations. In other words, in the exercise of their independent judgment, revenue forecasters must explain how and why privileging either disclosure or withholding of information contributes to more effective governance. If secrecy is warranted in a forecaster's judgment, then an explanation of the reasons for such secrecy is warranted as well. In either case—disclosing or withholding—"open government becomes a means to improve governance rather than an end in itself" (Fenster 2006, p. 941).

Finally, we turn to our third proposal—the adoption of a revised consensus method of forecasting at various levels of government. The adoption of such a method at the federal, state, and local levels depends on the institutional framework in which they operate. There is limited evidence for consensus forecasting at the federal level and we recommend serious federal consideration be given to implementing such a pilot program in the near future. At the state level, every state has its own guiding principles (Voorhees 1999, p. 652). The sheer fact that there are 50 different state governments and numerous local government units in the United States makes any homogenous consensus process possible. Even if state and local governments adopted some consensus forecasting process, it would render comparison difficult because there are a variety of consensus mechanisms from which to choose. According to data from the National Conference of State Legislatures website, there are 22 states that currently adopt a consensus approach for developing the official state revenue forecast. However, it is interesting to note that only in 11 of those 22 states does the official forecast prepared by a consensus process bind the budget. In 17 states, the official state revenue forecast is the responsibility of the executive branch and in the remaining 11 states some other entity such as the council on revenue or a board of independent economic advisors appointed by the governor takes responsibility for it. As Voorhees (1999, p. 654) observes, states can be categorized into three types based on how the official state revenue forecast is generated. In the first category of states, the official revenue forecast is the responsibility of a single agency. In the second category, it is the consensual responsibility of multiple state agencies. The third category consists of states where the official revenue forecast is the result of consensus among state agencies and external independent organizations. He also brings our attention to a variety of alternative consensual structures such as consensual multiple legislative agencies, consensual multiple executive agencies, consensual multiple legislative and executive agencies, and consensual independent conference. Voorhees (1999) demonstrates that states' use of consensual forecasting structures resulted in reduction of forecast errors. With the participation of members of the legislative and executive branches, as well as the private sector, universities, the media, and the interested public, the consensus process, modified to include morally informed reasoning, justification, and debate, is an appropriate venue for testing the viability of our proposals. In this setting, the aims, assumptions, and methods underlying revenue forecasts would be on display for all to see. We are proposing it as a possible improvement over present practice.

While making these three proposals for change, we have highlighted the obvious advantages associated with them. However, we acknowledge that public entities operate in a turbulent, ever-changing environment, experiencing external and internal turmoil in the form of institutional changes, political volatility, changing citizen demands, technological changes, shifting employee values, and so on. As a result, the adoption of change initiatives to move from a current state to a desired future state is an intricate process that is likely to evoke a variety of responses. We recognize that our proposals are likely to be embraced totally, embraced partially, or rejected totally depending on the circumstances and entities involved in the change process. As Van de Ven and Poole (1995, p. 521) observe, it is quite evident that "change and developmental processes go on at many levels, including the individual, group, organization, population, and even larger communities of organizations." The acknowledgment of the inherent moral agency of revenue forecasters is indicative of change that has to occur at the individual level. The creation of criteria for deciding what and how much information revenue forecasters should either disclose or withhold is likely to involve change at the individual and group levels. Finally, the adoption of consensus forecasting processes at the federal, state, and local levels is characteristic of a multilevel complex change strategy. In the context of transparency, public organizations engaged in revenue forecasting would ideally want to move from merely acknowledging transparency as a good normative or instrumental principle to putting it in practice. Therefore, it is essential to consider potential resistance dynamics related to our proposals and suggest ways to overcome them.

Acknowledgment of the Inherent Moral Agency and Moral Competence of Revenue Forecasters

Self- and external acknowledgment of revenue forecasters' inherent moral agency, moral legitimacy, and moral competence is an important step in achieving increased transparency. Revenue forecasters are likely to more readily acknowledge their role as moral agents and exercise moral competency when there is no moral ambiguity and no political or professional backlash associated with the exercise of moral competence and when their moral legitimacy and moral competence are reinforced by external acknowledgment in the form of legal statutes, public trust, and professional recognition. However, "transparency's status as a legal obligation for government entities in the U.S. and as an individual right for American citizens is remarkably vague" (Fenster 2006, p. 889). Therefore, determining the exact situations in which moral judgment and competence should take precedence over hierarchical directives can be a tedious exercise for revenue forecasters and can result in their resistance to disclosure. Even if they have made sense of the moral space in which they are operating, when a situation is morally ambiguous they are likely to withhold information if they perceive that privacy and secrecy are likely to be favored over disclosure given that they operate in a litigious world. Furthermore, revenue forecasters are most likely to resist disclosure as a result of situational predictors such as cost, workload, and legislation (Hoag et al. 2002), but are also likely to resist disclosure as a result of dispositional traits such as comfort in ingrained values, embedded routines, cynicism, negative emotional reaction to the reemphasis of their role as moral agents, their inability to think about the greater public good and cognitive rigidity (George and Jones 2001, Oreg 2003, Pardo Del Val and Fuentes 2003, Stanley et al. 2005). Other sources of resistance to change could be their loyalty to professional bodies that determine how revenue forecasting, as an activity with implications for academics and practice, should be carried out.

Situational impediments may be overcome by providing revenue forecasters more autonomy, and initiating mechanisms such as protection from political and professional counterattacks, that would intrinsically motivate them to exhibit moral competency. Dispositional impediments can be overcome by careful introspection and mechanisms targeted at unfreezing existing tendencies such as cognitive rigidity and cynicism through encouraging openness to new initiatives. Clearly, additional theoretical and empirical research is required in this area.

The Creation of Criteria for Deciding What and How Much Information to Disclose or Withhold

Creating criteria for deciding the type and extent of information to disclose or withhold, although an extremely important and necessary exercise, can be a difficult one to accomplish. The criteria for deciding what information to disclose and what to withhold may be guided by several factors such as the nature of the information requested, nature of the entity requesting the information, nature of the entity providing the information, purpose of request, timing of the request, laws relating to freedom of information and disclosure, and competition among organizations for scarce resources (Fenster 2006, p. 920). These factors are likely to impede disclosure under certain circumstances and encourage disclosure at other times. Emphatic citizen requests are likely to result in the disclosure of information in certain situations, whereas they could result in the withholding of information in other situations. In the context of increased transparency in revenue forecasting, citizens could potentially be opposed to the disclosure of tax information and any such documents that could jeopardize their privacy in the interest of increased transparency. Another aspect worth considering is ownership of information. As Fenster (2006, p. 919) observes, in times preceding the contracting-out phenomenon, government had monopolistic control over information because the empirical and scientific research on which government actions and regulations were based was done by government agencies. However, in recent times, there is a lot of debate about whether private firms should be subjected to the same rigors of transparency.

These problems may be overcome by a thorough examination and analysis of situations that warrant disclosure or withholding of information. The different variables associated with such procedures might provide insights on the timing, nature, and extent of information withholding or disclosure.

Adoption of a Consensus Method of Forecasting

According to Zarnowitz and Lambors (1987, p. 592), one way of achieving consensus forecasts is to use "averages from economic outlook surveys." In a similar vein, there are numerous studies that discuss the implications of achieving forecast accuracy by combining forecasts using different or similar methods as opposed to relying on just one randomly chosen individual forecast (see, e.g., Armstrong 1989,

Batchelor and Dua 1995). The Delphi technique based on the principles of anonymity, iteration, controlled feedback, and the statistical aggregation of group response (Rowe and Wright 1999, p. 354) has been a useful forecasting tool. As Rowe and Wright (1999, p. 354) observe, this technique is designed to achieve consensus among panelists by allowing for "human judgmental input." Despite its allowance for human judgmental input at various stages of the iterative process and its ubiquitous use in various fields, the Delphi technique is still evocative of the impersonal nature of pure statistical modeling. However, the consensus method of revenue forecasting that we propose is not just about arriving at agreement through an "average" of independently generated forecasts. Instead, it emphasizes moral reasoning, informed debate, and justification. Along the lines of deliberative democracy, it involves a "commitment to publicity, transparent reasoning and decision making by a representative body, enabling public discussion, unrestricted communication" (Fenster 2006, p. 897). There is an increasing need for the wider use of consensus revenue forecasting because the expertise and information relating to revenue forecasting rests in a select few, whereas the impact of such expertise and information through revenue forecasts has a much wider impact. Consensus revenue forecasting replaces decision making by a majority rule by taking into consideration the values, opinions, and interests of different stakeholders and is likely to result in high-quality agreements based on a variety of perspectives and different pieces of information (Innes and Booher 1999, pp. 412–413). Consensus techniques produce "tangible" products (such as revenue forecasts) and in addition they also provide "intangible" products such as mutual understanding of problems, shared intellectual capital, and so on (Innes and Booher 1999, pp. 414–415).

Despite such obvious advantages, consensus forecasting can result in suboptimal decision making because the emphasis on achieving consensus can compromise performance (see, e.g., Murrell et al. 1993). Because participants in the process arrive with competing priorities, some might perceive the process to be more effective when the emphasis is more on minimizing conflict rather than on choosing the rationally superior alternative (Reagan and Rohrbaugh 1990). Although this approach is ideal from an information perspective as different participants bring in a wealth of information and reduce forecasters' reliance on "outmoded assumptions" and their failure to update their methods (Voorhees 1999, p. 654), it could also lead to information overload, and thereby affect efficiency. This approach may face resistance at the individual level because the forecasting process, which was once the purview of the expert is now extending its boundaries to include the layperson. Consensus forecasting methods may be difficult to implement because trained revenue forecasters may fear dilution of expertise as a result of inclusion of members from a large cross section of people. Before a consensus revenue-forecasting approach can be used, there should be consensus about the nature of individuals, groups, and organizations that should be included in the process.

Conclusion

We recommended three proposals geared toward increased transparency in government revenue forecasting. Our analysis revealed obvious advantages associated with those proposals and some potential problems associated with their implementation. Overcoming such problems can be achieved only by acknowledging their existence. Our analysis of these three proposals for change and resistance to them from different levels has several important implications for the movement toward increased transparency in public revenue forecasting. As Field (2004) illustrates, there are a variety of arguments against increased transparency in the form of delays in revenue estimating because of the demand for more careful documentation, confusion of product and process, lack of staff resources, labor-intensive nature of revenue estimating, and so on. Such objections against increased transparency can potentially undermine the credibility and quality of revenue forecasts. However, such objections and resistance to increased transparency can have crucial information about the change process. As Piderit (2000, p. 785) observes, resistance to change can be conceived "as a cognitive state, as an emotional state, and as a behavior." Acknowledging the subtleties associated with resistance to increased transparency can result in a more nuanced approach. The study of resistance should be approached in such a way that it reflects the "complexity of individuals' responses to proposed organizational changes" (Piderit 2000, p. 783). Researchers (and by extension, practitioners) have ignored the "potentially positive intentions that may motivate negative responses" (Piderit 2000, p. 783). Reactions to change initiatives may not necessarily be manifested in a dichotomous manner (i.e., a clear yes or no). Instead certain entities might experience "ambivalence" about the proposed change initiative. Cognitive ambivalence is manifested where an employee simultaneously believes that a proposed change is necessary in the long run and that the organization is currently underprepared for such a change (Piderit 2000, p. 788). Intentional ambivalence is manifested when an individual expresses public support for change but engages in anonymous opposition to change through submission of views opposing the change (Piderit 2000, p. 788). Acknowledgment of the presence of such ambivalence, understanding the reasons for it, and predicting the variety of responses such ambivalence is likely to evoke is essential toward successful implementation of change initiatives (Piderit 2000).

The onus, therefore, is equally on supporters as well as resistors of increased transparency to facilitate a movement toward implementation of increased transparency. Successful implementation of increased transparency can be made only when supporters of increased transparency are able to gather employee support for the change rather than merely overcoming resistance to change. To accomplish this, supporters of increased transparency should delve deeper into the profound layers of information associated with resistance to increased transparency rather than dismissing it as a negative response. Similarly, those who resist implementation of increased transparency should provide qualitative reasons for why they dread change so that their concerns can be systematically addressed in moving toward the desired state of increased transparency.

As practitioners and scholars of public administration are well aware, reforms are daunting under any circumstances. Their putative benefits are speculative and long term. In contrast, their actual costs are real and immediate. Thus, reform requires continuity of leadership and investment of resources, which are both at a premium in most governmental organizations. Seasoned practitioners, bearing the scars of past political and bureaucratic battles, naturally tend to grow reluctant to take on one more struggle for change, thus lending credence to Field's (2004) uncertainty about the potential sources of increased transparency in revenue forecasting. Nevertheless, we maintain that our strategies for change may, under certain circumstances, lead to a modicum of effort toward greater transparency, accountability, and trust, at least between interested citizens, tax professionals, scholars, and their government. As advocates of open government, we should expect no less.

References

Alt, J. E. and D. D. Lassen. 2006. Transparency, political polarization, and political budget cycles in OECD countries. *American Journal of Political Science* 50: 530–550.

Alt, J. E., D. D. Lassen, and S. Rose. 2005. *The Causes of Fiscal Transparency: Evidence from the American States.* Sixth Jacques Polak Annual Research Conference, November 3–4. Washington: International Monetary Fund.

Armstrong, J. S. 1988. Research needs in forecasting. *International Journal of Forecasting* 4: 449–465.

Armstrong, J. S. 1989. Combining forecasts: the end of the beginning or the beginning of the end? *International Journal of Forecasting* 5: 585–588.

Auerbach, A. J. 1996. Dynamic revenue estimation. *Journal of Economic Perspectives* 10: 141–157.

Auerbach, A. J. 1999. On the performance and use of government revenue forecasts. *National Tax Journal* 52: 765–782.

Batchelor, R. and R. Dua. 1995. Forecaster diversity and the benefits of combining forecasts. *Management Science* 41: 68–75.

Bauer, R. A., A. Eisenbeis, D. F. Waggoner, and T. Zha. 2006. Transparency, expectations, and forecasts. *Economic Review-Federal Reserve Bank of Atlanta* 91: 1–25.

Beckett-Camarata, J. 2006. Revenue forecasting accuracy in Ohio local governments. *Journal of Public Budgeting, Accounting and Financial Management* 18: 77–99.

Chortareas, G., D. Stasavage, and G. Sterne. 2002. *Does It Pay to be Transparent? International Evidence from Central Bank Forecasts.* St. Louis, MO: Federal Reserve Bank of St. Louis Publication. July, pp. 99–117.

Cirincione, C., G. Gurrieri, and B. Van De Sande. 1999. Municipal government revenue forecasting: issues of method and data. *Public Budgeting and Finance* 19: 26–46.

Corder, K. 2005. Managing uncertainty: the bias and efficiency of federal macroeconomic forecasts. *Journal of Public Administration Research and Theory* 15: 55–70.

Danninger, S., M. Cangiano, and A. Kyobe. 2005. *The Political Economy of Revenue-Forecasting Experience in Low-Income Countries.* Washington: International Monetary Fund Working Paper Series.

Fenster, M. 2006. The opacity of transparency. *Iowa Law Review* 91: 885–949.

Field, T. F. 2004. Transparency in revenue estimating. http://www.heritage.org/Research/Taxes/cda04-15.cfm (accessed November 13, 2007).

Florini, A. 2002. Increasing transparency in government. *International Journal on World Peace* 19: 3–37.

Florini, A. 2003. *The Coming Democracy: New Rules for Running a New World.* Washington: Island Press.

Fung, A., M. Graham, and D. Weil. 2002. *The Political Economy of Transparency: What Makes Disclosure Policies Sustainable?* Cambridge, MA: John F. Kennedy School of Government, Harvard University.

Fung, A., D. Weil, M. Graham, and E. Fagotto. 2004. *The Political Economy of Transparency: What Makes Disclosure Policies Effective?* Cambridge, MA: John F. Kennedy School of Government, Harvard University.

Gardner, H., M. Csikszentmihalyi, and W. Damon. 2001. *Good Work: When Excellence and Ethics Meet.* New York: Basic Books.

George, J. M. and G. R. Jones. 2001. Towards a process model of change in organizations. *Human Relations* 54: 419–444.

Heilemann, U. 2002. Increasing the transparency of microeconomic forecasts: a report from the trenches. *International Journal of Forecasting* 18: 85–105.

Hoag, B. G., H. V. Ritschard, and C. L. Cooper. 2002. Obstacles to effective organizational change: the underlying reasons. *Leadership and Organizational Development* 23: 6–15.

Innes, J. E. and D. E. Booher. 1999. Consensus building and complex adaptive systems: a framework for collaborative planning. *Journal of the American Planning Association* 65(4): 412–423.

Jones, V. D., S. Brettschneider, and W. L. Gorr. 1997. Organizational pressures on forecast evaluation: managerial, political, and procedural influences. *Journal of Forecasting* 16: 241–254.

Kopits, G. 2000. *Transparency in Government Operations.* Presented at the Conference on Transparency and Development in Latin America, Washington, May.

Kyobe, A. and S. Danninger. 2005. *Revenue Forecasting—How Is It Done? Results from a Survey of Low-Income Countries.* Washington: International Monetary Fund Working Paper Series.

Makridakis, S. 1996. Forecasting: its role and value for planning and strategy. *International Journal of Forecasting* 12: 513–537.

Mensah, M. O., H. V. Nguyen, and S. N. Prattipati. 2006. Transparency in financial statements: a conceptual framework from a user perspective. *Journal of American Academy of Business* 9: 47–51.

Mocan, N. and S. Azad. 1995. Accuracy and rationality of state general fund revenue forecasts: evidence from panel data. *International Journal of Forecasting* 11: 417–427.

Murrell, A. J., A. C. Stewart, and B. T. Engel. 1993. Consensus versus devil's advocacy: the influence of decision process and task structure on strategic decision making. *Journal of Business Communication* 30: 399–414.

National Council for State legislatures. Legislative budget procedures: budget framework http://www.ncsl.org/programs/fiscal/lbptabls/lbpc2t4.htm (accessed March 20, 2007).

Oreg, S. 2003. Resistance to change: developing an individual differences measure. *Journal of Applied Psychology* 28: 680–693.

Pardo Del Val, M. and C. M. Fuentes. 2003. Resistance to change: a literature review and empirical study. *Management Decision* 41: 148–155.

Petrie, M. 2003. *Promoting Fiscal Transparency: The Complementary Roles of the IMF, Financial Markets, and Civil Society*. Washington: International Monetary Fund Working Paper No. 03/199.

Piderit, S. 2000. Rethinking resistance and recognizing ambivalence: a multidimensional view of attitudes toward an organizational change. *Academy of Management Review* 25: 783–794.

Plesko, G. A. 1988. The accuracy of government forecasts and budget projections. *National Tax Journal* 41: 483–501.

Poister, T. H. and G. Streib. 1989. Management tools in municipal government: trends over the past decade. *Public Administration Review* 49: 240–248.

Reagan, P. and J. Rohrbaugh. 1990. Group decision process effectiveness. *Group and Organization Management* 15: 20–43.

Rodgers, R. and P. Joyce. 1996. The effect of under forecasting on the accuracy of revenue forecasts by state governments. *Public Administration Review* 56: 48–56.

Rowe, G. and G. Wright. 1999. The Delphi technique as a forecasting tool: issues and analysis. *International Journal of Forecasting* 15: 353–375.

Schroeder, L. 1982. Local government multi-year budgetary forecasting: some administrative and political issues. *Public Administration Review* 42: 121–127.

Shafritz, J. M., E. W. Russell, and C. P. Borick. 2007. *Introducing Public Administration*. New York: Pearson Longman.

Shkurti, W. J. 1990. A user's guide to state revenue forecasting. *Public Budgeting and Finance* 10: 79–94.

Stanley, D. J., J. P. Meyer, and L. Topolnytsky. 2005. Employee cynicism and resistance to organizational change. *Journal of Business and Psychology* 19: 429–459.

Stiglitz, J. E. 1999. *On Liberty, The Right to Know, and Public Discourse: The Role of Transparency in Public Life*. Presented at the Oxford Amnesty Lecture, Oxford, United Kingdom.

Stinson, T. F. 2002. State revenue forecasting: an institutional framework. *Government Finance Review* 75: 12–15.

Stinson, T. F. 2006. Sources of error in state revenue forecasting or how can the forecast possibly be so far off. *Journal of Public Budgeting Accounting and Financial Management* 18: 100–126.

Sun, J. 2005. The dynamics of government revenue forecasting from an organizational perspective: a review of the literature. *Journal of Public Budgeting, Accounting and Financial Management* 17: 527–556.

Van de Ven, A. and M. S. Poole. 1995. Explaining development and change in organizations. *Academy of Management Review* 20: 510–540.

Voorhees, W. 1999. More is better: consensual forecasting and state revenue forecast error. *International Journal of Public Administration* 27: 651–672.

Winston, K. 1999. Moral competence in the practice of democratic governance. In J. D. Donahue and J. S. Nye Jr. (Eds.) *For the People: Can We Fix Public Service?* Washington: Brookings Institution Press. pp. 169–187.

Zarnowitz, V. and L. A. Lambros. 1987. Consensus and uncertainty in economic prediction. *Journal of Political Economy* 95: 591–612.

Chapter 25

Incorporating Fiscal Architecture into Budget Forecasting

Sally Wallace

Contents

Introduction

Changes in economic, demographic, and institutional characteristics are constantly occurring throughout the world. These changes imply opportunities and challenges for public expenditures and public revenues that differ depending on the type of economic and demographic change occurring. These forces define the "fiscal architecture" or the backbone of a country's expenditure needs and its revenue-producing potential. As such, they establish the framework for developing policies that make "fiscal sense" when defining practical options for policy design and implementation. The challenge of the fiscal architecture analysis is to systematically identify (on a spending category by spending category basis and then, in parallel, on a revenue type by revenue type basis) what factors affect past and future needs for public expenditures and revenue-generating capacity of a country or region. However, setting expenditure needs and revenue goals cannot occur in the absence of consideration of institutional constraints—be they the legal constraints regarding revenue authorization or administrative constraints such as the ability of tax administration to handle a new tax source—therefore, the fiscal architecture of a country includes the institutional parameters as well.

This chapter focuses on the development of a methodology to integrate the fiscal architecture concept into budget forecast analysis. In many developing countries, large changes in the economic base (e.g., reduction or expansion of the agricultural sector) and demographic factors (e.g., the migration of population or the aging of the population) have direct consequences on public sector budgets. However, in many developing countries, and in some developed economies, these factors are not regularly incorporated into budgeting and forecasting methodologies. The result is that, although governments could better prepare themselves for the impacts of these changes on budgets, they may need to resort to "emergency" measures to deal with budget shortfall pressures that could have been better planned for. This chapter presents the theory of fiscal architecture (the impact of these demographic and economic changes) in the context of expenditure need analysis and revenue forecasting, and applies the methodology to the case of India to show the impact of changes in the "architecture" on the realism of medium- to long-term (five to ten years) budget sufficiency in a developing country context.

Fiscal Architecture

Across the world, we witness demographic, economic, and institutional changes or trends that are largely beyond the control of any particular government (national or subnational). These trends include, among other things, labor supply, consumption behavior, investment, and migration of the population. Such factors may have strong impacts on the fiscal policies of governments. These economic and demographic trends define what may be called the "fiscal architecture" of a country, and help to shape the expenditure and revenue systems that public sector policymakers and practitioners need to consider and react to in their regular budgeting exercises as well as their medium- and long-term planning. Because these forces will vary not only nationally, but also by regions and other geographically smaller jurisdictions (e.g., municipalities), the fiscal architecture of regional and municipal expenditures and revenues will also differ within and across countries. Moreover, the increasing globalization of markets for products and services further magnifies the importance of recognizing these parameters and the opportunities they provide for (and the limitations they place on) policy makers.

Understanding how these economic and demographic trends may affect the choices for potential tax bases and spending needs of client populations will enable policy makers to design (and, as circumstances change, redesign) expenditure programs and revenue instruments to stabilize a country's long-term finances.

One might ask, what are the specific components of fiscal architecture and how do they interact with the structure of public finances? Here, the factors are broken down into three groups, and provide a set of examples for each group and some intuition regarding their implications for revenues and expenditures. A more detailed discussion can be found in Wallace (2001).

Demographics

There are numerous types of demographic changes that could impact public finances. Some of the changes that have proven to be the most important in terms of impacts on the public sector are as follows:

- *Population.* Population projections suggest that the developing world will continue to see the largest growth in population through the next half-century. Besides economies of scale, if a country wishes to maintain a given level of services, a large and growing population requires a higher level of public expenditure, which may or may not be commensurate with an expanded revenue base. With changes in population, there are also issues of migration (both in and out, each presenting different pressures on governments), changes in the urban–rural mix among the population, which affects both the demand for services as well as the delivery of services, will be influenced by the concentration of population in the country. As noted by Bahl and Linn (1992), migrants often settle in areas where land is cheap and services are lacking.
- *Age distribution.* Countries around the world are grappling with the consequences of an aging population. Currently, one out of every ten people are aged 60 years or above, by 2050, this will be nearly one out of every five people (see Figure 25.1) (U.S. Census Bureau). As seen in Figure 25.1, the percentage of the population aged 60 and above will increase from about 8 percent in 2000 to 19 percent by 2050. The working-age population

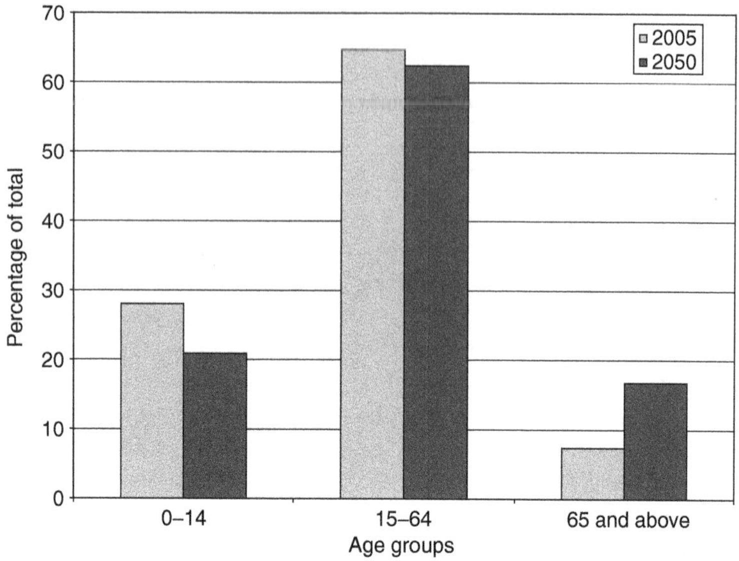

Figure 25.1 World distribution of population by age group. (From U.S. Census Bureau. Undated, world population information, http://www.census.gov/ipc/www/world.html. With permission.)

(middle bars) will shrink moderately in relative terms, whereas the youngest age group, zero to fourteen years, will fall from about 29 to 21 percent of the total population worldwide. Whatever the cause of an aging population, it requires a different mix of public services (more adapted housing and social services and less education) and a slowdown of the provision of other services (transit, etc.). Also, an aging population receives a greater part of its income as pensions rather than salaries, whereas its overall income is lower. This will reduce the yield from wage or income taxes to support general public services and government pension systems. Finally, an aging population may consume less of taxable goods and more of untaxed goods and services. In countries that are experiencing a surge in the percentage of younger people, the fiscal pressures will also be present, and will reflect increased demand for housing, education, and preventative types of healthcare.

- *Family size and composition.* The number of family members in a household and the composition (dual or single wage earner and dual or single care giver) are also important factors for the overall fiscal architecture of a country. Although directly related to the overall population and the age distribution issues discussed earlier, the average size of a family has its own implications for consumption and possibly income tax bases. Larger families consume more of certain goods such as basic foodstuffs, but not necessarily more on a per capita basis. Economies of scale can influence household consumption and larger (smaller) families could be equated to smaller (larger) levels of per capita consumption. This in turn could influence the overall level of consumption tax growth.

- *Health and education.* The demographic evolution of health and education standards will affect income distribution, labor supply, and overall population growth. Considered alone, however, we can identify factors in health and education that require significant public expenditure and may impinge on revenue potential. One of the most important factors in this arena is the level and growth of human immunodeficiency virus/acquired immunodeficiency syndrome (HIV/AIDS) cases in a number of countries. These changes will not only have direct impacts on the expenditure side of the budget, but also affect labor supply and consumption patterns and therefore revenue. Other health and education factors have a similar role in fiscal architecture.

Economic Factors

The underlying economic structure of a jurisdiction has direct implications for both revenue and expenditure structure. Although there are numerous types of economic factors that may be considered a part of the fiscal architecture of a country, the following three are highlighted in this section.

- *The output structure.* A country's revenue base is largely determined by the structure of industry and the output produced, and the composition of employment that goes along with production. Property taxes make more sense as a sustainable revenue source for nonservice-oriented economies; value-added taxes (VATs) may be more or less important depending on the importance of export in a country's economy. At the same time, industry structure and output have direct implications for expenditures, both short and long term. A country that is heavily invested in dying industries (such as manufacturing in many developed countries) will need to consider expenditures aimed at retraining and decommissioning of various parts of the country's infrastructure.
- *Distribution and composition of income.* The greater the importance of self-employment, the more difficult it is to tax labor income because tax laws make it easier to hide self-employment income than wage income (tax avoidance), whereas self-employment more easily accesses the informal untaxed economy (tax evasion) than wage employment (see Bird and Wallace 2004). In the same vein, an increase in real income or in marginal tax rates may tilt the compositions of labor income toward fringe benefits, which may not be included in the local income tax bases. Another difficult tax option is home employment. The trends in this distribution will impact the relative revenue alternatives of a country and hold implications for tax enforcement.

- *Resource endowment.* Some countries may be favored by a natural resource base that could give rise to a large revenue source. The ability to turn these resources into actual budget revenues depends on the structure of taxation in a country, the ability of the tax administration to collect such taxes, and the level of extraction of these resources. Some countries may need to expend significant public resources to be able to realize the revenue potential of these bases.

Institutional Factors

The economic and demographic changes discussed earlier do not occur in isolation. Each trend will be heavily influenced by past, present, and future policies and institutions of the individual nations and of those countries that are trading partners.

- *Property rights.* The clarity of property rights and the political and economic factors associated with establishing property rights will have significant impacts on both expenditures (off-loading of responsibilities of the government) and revenues (property and land tax bases).
- *The level of privatization.* Privatization will influence the resource flow of various revenues to central and subnational governments and between the levels of government. Privatization efforts could have a mixed effect on expenditures in the short run, but a positive longer-term effect, through higher efficiency and less of a burden on the public sector.
- *The intergovernmental arrangements.* The relationship among levels of government will have an impact on the policy options available to governments. In countries such as the United States, Denmark, Brazil, and South Africa with significant subnational government (noncentral government) autonomy, local governments can react to changing tax bases and expenditure pressures. In other countries such as Russia, Jamaica, and India, locals must wait for transfers and guidance from the center. It is not obvious which situation induces more fiscal stress.
- *The social safety nets.* Social safety nets are a response to the economic and social evolution of a country, but the structure of the safety net can be a self-fulfilling prophecy. If the welfare system is comprised largely of price controls, the efforts to reform will be quite different from market-based welfare systems. The level of the safety net is also important—it is quite difficult to transition away from high subsidy levels. In some countries such as the United States, Japan, Italy, Brazil, Singapore, and Thailand, the pressures from an increase in the elderly population relate directly to this issue.
- *The level of barter and the underground economy.* These factors, which have both institutional and economic dimensions, will directly influence revenue and expenditure reform. In countries such as Thailand, the Philippines, Zimbabwe, Bolivia, and Ukraine, in which the level of barter and underground activity is large, the resources expended at certain fiscal reforms will

likely be less productive without solving accounting and general tax compliance issues. These issues are closely tied, as well, with the overall level of corruption in a country. The World Bank (2007) provides an index of corruption tolerance and finds that countries such as Ivory Coast, Nepal, and the Central African Republic have a high tolerance for corruption, as opposed to those with very low tolerance such as Sweden, Denmark, and New Zealand.

- *Technological change.* The way in which production happens changes constantly. The ability to increase the welfare of individuals through new vaccines and treatments, more efficient modes of transportation, sound structural buildings, and more efficient communications and access to information occurs at differing rates. The rate of change in technology may very well be endogenous—government certainly influences education and development, which can affect technological change. However, some changes in technology are an outside force that leads to changes in demand for types of expenditures and may influence the way revenue is generated.
- *Voting rights and behavior.* With respect to the specific factors discussed earlier, the assumption is that the demands of the population will be heard. This could happen through social unrest or more peacefully, through voting for general levels of expenditures and types of taxes. If voting is an important component of the policy process, all these factors could impinge on public finances more quickly than in the cases in which the population has less opportunity to express their demands.
- *Shocks and other outside forces.* Every country has to deal with unexpected, unforecasted shocks to their system. We might consider the resiliency and robustness of an economy to shocks as a component of fiscal architecture. Consider a fiscal system such as India, Jamaica, Myanmar, Sudan, Brazil, and Honduras that may teeter on the edge of financial ruin with large budget deficits and large amounts of outstanding debt. Such countries would be hard-pressed to deal with a major shock such as a hurricane, a rapidly spreading new disease, major changes in prices of important exports, or war. The financial management, personnel, and flexibility of government policies are critical parts of the architecture that could significantly influence the ability of a country to react to shocks.

Table 25.1 provides a summary of the major trends in fiscal architecture and their implications for government budgets. These factors will have various impacts on revenue capacity and expenditure needs. If changes in the fiscal architecture of a jurisdiction are not considered in its budgeting, forecasting, and intergovernmental analyses, the complete fiscal potential of the jurisdiction may not be realized (putting pressure on budgets) and public resources may not be directed to areas that are conducive to progress and development. This issue is discussed in more detail in the following sections. Now, we turn to an analysis that connects the concept of fiscal architecture to budget forecasting.

Table 25.1 Illustrative Summary of Fiscal Architecture and Potential Fiscal Pressures

Variable	*Basic Trend*	*Effect on VAT*	*Import Duties*	*Corporate Income Tax (CIT)*	*Individual Income Tax (IIT)*	*Education*	*Social Safety Net*	*Primary Health*	*Roads and Transport*
Demographic factors									
Age distribution	Increase in the percentage of elderly	Increased consumption of nontaxable goods in some countries, reduce growth in VAT	Increased demand for imports	Reduced consumption of durable goods, reduce CIT	Reduced taxable income, reduce IIT	Reduced demand	Increase in the number of clients, increasing expenditures	Increase in the number of clients and intensity of care, increased costs	Ambiguous
Urbanization	Increased urbanization	May reduce due to the potential growth in the underground economy, depends on the formality of labor	Neutral	May reduce importance of corporate tax as tends to expand self-employed sector	May reduce importance of IIT as tends to expand self-employed sector	Increased demand, but potential economies of scale	Increased demand, but may be a longer-run issue	Increased demand	Increased demand for urban transport
Economic base factors									
Service sector growth (output composition)	Growth in sector as a share of GDP	More ambiguous than for CIT, IIT, evidence slightly for negative impact	Increase due to demand for more technology	Decrease due to decrease in tax handles	Decrease due to tax handles	Neutral	Neutral	Neutral	Demand for access will increase expenditures for telecommunications
Composition of income	Increase in transfer payments for the elderly	Ambiguous	Neutral	Neutral	Decrease due to exemptions for transfer income in most countries	Neutral	Increase in expenditures	Ambiguous	Neutral

Impact of Changes in Architecture on Public Budgets

Theoretically, public expenditures are made in an attempt to meet public wants. Governments neither always produce what is demanded by the public, nor do they always produce as much as the public demands. Central governments aim to meet the needs of a larger more heterogeneous population than local governments, whereas local governments concentrate on public goods that meet needs closer to home. In this way, public expenditures are determined by needs of the client population—be it the elderly, the young, or the growing industry.

Revenues, however, are collected to enable governments to produce public goods and in some cases to alter behavior. Taxes, fees, and charges are placed on various tax or transaction bases. The "clients" on the revenue side are taxpayers who are the subject of any particular revenue system (although few taxpayers see themselves as clients!). These basic relationships among clients, public resources, and expenditures provide us with a straightforward way to analyze the impact of changes in fiscal architecture on budget forecasts. The expenditure side is discussed first and then the revenue side.

Expenditures

Expenditures can be tied to client populations as follows:

$$\text{Exp}_i = \text{CPOP}_i * (\text{PXPS}_i) + \text{PXPS}_i * (\text{CPOP}_i) \tag{25.1}$$

where

Exp_i = total expenditure on the *i*th spending category
CPOP_i = client population of the *i*th spending category
PXPS_i = production expense of the *i*th spending category

Equation 25.1 simply states that the expenditure for any public good, *i*, is determined by the client population for the public good (CPOP) and the per unit cost of production of good *i*. Changes in expenditures can be expressed as

$$\Delta\text{Exp}_i = \Delta\text{CPOP}_i * (\text{PXPS}_i) + \Delta\text{PXPS}_i * (\text{CPOP}_i) \tag{25.2}$$

where Δ means "change." Therefore, changes in the client population can lead to changes in public expenditure, and changes in unit costs of production can also change expenditures.* Changes in client population include changes induced

* Changes in fiscal architecture can in fact affect the per unit cost of production, but this is not discussed in detail in this chapter. As an example, a reduction in the number of working-age population could drive up labor costs and affect the production cost of numerous types of public goods.

by demographic adjustments such as changes in age distribution (which affect pension, health, and educational expenditures) as well as changes in the economy (e.g., increased demand for infrastructure and technology, which may alter who is demanding services). If a government does not consider the impact of changes in the client population on expenditures, expenditures will lag in important areas and may be too large in other areas, leading to inefficient public goods provision. In such cases, it does not take long for the citizenry to react to the underprovision of certain goods.*

An example of the interaction between the changing age demographics and public expenditures can be found in the funding of basic education. The expenditure needs for education are a function of the per unit cost of production and the client population (assuming that the capital needs are considered separately). Because educational needs may differ by age group or other characteristics, the expenditures per student could be weighted to allocate funds among these different groups. The expression for calculating education expenditure need is therefore

$$\text{Expenditure need} = \sum_{i=1}^{n} (\text{CETE}_i * \alpha_i) * \text{pop}_i \tag{25.3}$$

where

i = particular program or subgroup (kindergarten, first to sixth grade, high school, special education, vocational programs, etc.)
CFTE = "cost per full-time equivalent student," which is often translated into the number of children in a jurisdiction
pop = population in the specific program
α = weight assigned to each individual program

The costs, or CFTE, are a function of a number of specific inputs, which can be expressed per full-time equivalent student (FTE):

- Staff salaries/FTE
- Operations expenses/FTE
- School administration expenses/FTE
- Staff development expenses/FTE
- Facility operation expenses/FTE

In developing countries, different levels of government may be assigned responsibility for some but not all of these expenditures. Accordingly, their cost function would be more limited. The formula can be an important indicator of the impact of changing age demographics on the basic education needs of the population because

* Admittedly, in some countries (such as Turkmenistan and Democratic Republic of Congo), the ability of citizens to voice their opinion may be limited based on the World Bank indicators of governance (The World Bank 2007).

the specific population group (as the client) enters into the needs calculation. The change in expenditure needs for a percent change in the school-aged population (by program) is the weighted value of the CFTE. If a country is experiencing growth in the school-aged population, it will face increased expenditure pressure as education needs increase (all others held equal for the moment).

As an example of the interaction between demographics and expenditure pressures, Table 25.2 provides detailed information on the distribution of school-aged children in three countries: Guatemala, Egypt, and Iraq. In Table 25.2, the first two banks of numbers are the actual number of children of three different school ages: five to nine, ten to fourteen, and fifteen to nineteen years. The third bank of numbers is the percent change in the population of each group. For example, Guatemala expects their youngest school-aged population to grow by 3.1 percent from 2005 to 2025, whereas in Egypt, the expectation is that the number of children in the youngest group will decline over the period and it will rise rapidly in Iraq. The fourth bank of numbers asserts a weight for each group—1.3 for the youngest children, 1.2 for the middle group, and 1 for the oldest children. In this example, the weights are simply for exposition—they are not actual policy weights used in these countries. We might expect, however, that if the cost per child were some average cost across all groups, then a government might want to prorate certain groups. If there is detailed, accurate information on each group, such weighting may not be necessary. However, in the case of developing countries, it is unlikely that such detailed information is available.

If unit costs (CFTE) are held constant, the growth in expenditure needs is simply the weighted increase in each particular population (this is noted as "minimum expenditures I"). In the case of Guatemala, it would be 1.25 × 3.08 for the youngest group, or 3.85 percent increase in expenditure needs. Looking across the three countries, we notice that Iraq is expected to experience the greatest increase in expenditure needs according to this method for estimating education expenditure needs, and Egypt the smallest increase. When we add an inflationary factor for unit costs (assumed to be 0.5 percent per year), we find that the total expenditure need increases substantially more in each country ("minimum expenditures II"). In Guatemala, all age groups experience a growth in need and the range is from 16.8 to 44.7 percent, in Egypt the growth in need ranges from 12.5 to 25.4 percent, and in Iraq it ranges from 36.0 to 55.8 percent. Because education is a major expenditure category in all countries, this example demonstrates the magnitude of the pressure on basic provision of services. If a budgeting exercise considers only the inflationary factor associated with the cost of provision, the government will miss the mark of expenditure need by a wide percentage. For example, in the case of the three countries in Table 25.2, the increase in expenditure needs would be estimated as 0.5 percent per year, which is equal to the increase in estimated unit cost price.

Across expenditure items, we expect changes in economics and demographics to imply changes in expenditure need. Although not an exhaustive list, the following provides an overview of major architecture–expenditure need links that are useful

Table 25.2 Example of Estimating Education Expenditure Need

	Country		
	Guatemala	*Egypt*	*Iraq*
	Age distribution (2005)		
Age groups			
5–9	1688	8736	3484
10–14	1565	8115	3066
15–19	1347	7827	2949
	Age distribution (2025)		
Age groups			
5–9	1740	8673	4182
10–14	1734	8671	4165
15–19	1721	8665	4057
	Total growth in population (percent) (2005–2025)		
Age groups			
5–9	3.08	−0.72	20.03
10–14	10.80	6.85	35.84
15–19	27.77	10.71	37.57
	Policy weights for educational programs		
Program groups			
Programs for children aged 5–9	1.25	1.25	1.25
Programs for children aged 10–14	1.15	1.15	1.15
Programs for children aged 15–19	1	1	1
	Minimum expenditures I: percent change (2005–2025)		
Expenditures for children aged 5–9	3.85	−0.90	25.04
Expenditures for children aged 10–14	12.42	7.88	41.22
Expenditures for children aged 15–19	27.77	10.71	37.57
	Minimum expenditures II: percent change (2005–2025)		
Expenditures for children aged 5–9	16.77	12.46	35.97
Expenditures for children aged 10–14	25.51	21.04	53.88
Expenditures for children aged 15–19	44.73	25.41	55.84

Source: Calculations using data from http://www.census.gov/ipc/www/idb/country/gtportal.html.

to consider in budget forecasting (all should be considered in a relative sense and not necessary as absolute increases or decreases in expenditures):

- *Aging population.* Increased expenditure growth for public pensions, healthcare, and public transportation; reduced expenditure growth for education

- *Urbanization.* Increased demand for all public goods in cities but may be accompanied by increased economies of scale in production; may increase income disparities between urban and rural and increase pressure for social safety net services in rural areas
- *Reduced family size, increase in single guardian-headed households.* Increased demand for social safety net expenditures and child care–related expenditures
- *Computerization of business.* Increased demand for infrastructure and technology
- *Service sector growth.* Increased demand for telecommunications development

These trends in fiscal architecture and their associated implications for expenditures provide us with a basis for estimating these relationships for budget forecasting. However, it is important to consider the revenue side implications as well and then, in turn, consider the net impact on budgetary revenues, which we do in the following section.

Revenue

On the revenue side, a similar analysis can be developed. A simplified expression for the relationship between public revenues and demographic and economic factors may also be expressed as follows:

$$\text{Rev}_i = \text{TXBASE}_i * (\text{TXRATE}_i) \tag{25.4}$$

where

Rev_i = revenue from source i
TXBASE_i = base for tax source i
TXRATE_i = tax rate for source i

The tax base and tax rate are unique to each revenue source, and the revenue sources of course vary by government. For personal income taxes or IITs, the base would be some measure of taxable income, which may or may not include wages, capital income, and transfers. For consumption taxes, the base would be a measure of taxable consumption. The fiscal architecture of the country will have far-reaching implications for the tax bases, whereas the tax rate is a function of the need for revenue and political economy of a country. Changes in each revenue source can be described by the following equation:

$$\Delta\text{Rev}_i = \Delta\text{TXBASE}_i * (\text{TXRATE}_i) + \Delta\text{TXRATE}_i * (\text{TXBASE}_i) \tag{25.5}$$

where Δ is the symbol for "change." Changes in the tax base can be attributed to changes in fiscal architecture including demographic changes as well as economic base changes. In fact, the level of tax compliance (thus influencing the tax base) could be affected by changes in the fiscal architecture as well. For example, studies of tax compliance and cultural norms suggest that older individuals are more likely to comply with tax administration than younger individuals (see, e.g., Clotfelter 1983, Cummings et al. 2005). Then we might expect that as a population ages, the natural rate of growth of certain tax revenues increases due to an increase in compliance. This impact is likely to be smaller than some other more direct tax base impacts as discussed in the following paragraphs.

A specific example of the impact of a change in fiscal architecture on revenue growth may help to clarify the concept. Consider the case of the personal income tax. In many countries, the base of the personal income tax comprises wage and salary income, capital income, and business income. Most countries (such as India, Russia, and the Philippines among others) do not tax all transfer payments. Many countries (such as Russia, Japan, China, and the United States) do not tax capital income and wage income at the same rate. To make things easy, we can consider an income tax system that taxes all income at a flat 13 percent rate (similar to that implied in the Russian Federation). Revenue forecasters are often given information regarding the forecasted growth in personal income (a reasonable proxy for the tax base). With this base information, it would appear that forecasting income tax revenue would be very easy.

In practice, the composition of income is going to be very important to provide an accurate revenue forecast. If personal income were expected to grow at an annual rate of 1.2 percent, then with a tax rate of 13 percent, we would expect revenue collections to grow by 1.2 percent per year. However, because personal income contains taxable and nontaxable income sources, it is important to decompose the components of personal income. Table 25.3 provides a detailed example of the issue. The first bank of numbers reports the baseline and forecasted income by type of personal income: wages, capital income, and transfer payments. This hypothetical distribution is expressed in millions of dollars and is roughly based on the current composition of personal income in the United States. In 2006 (base year), personal income contains $70.1 million in wages, $16.2 million in capital income, and $15.3 million in transfer payments. The second bank of numbers reports the forecasted composition of these three items. As seen in Table 25.3, the total personal income growth is 1.2 percent per year. But, the largest growing component in this example is the transfer payment component. As we noted earlier, this is not taxable in most countries. The final bank of numbers includes the forecasted personal income tax revenue assuming that all income items grow at 1.2 percent per year, and the revenue forecast using the "actual" distribution of income where transfer payments grow faster than other income sources. Figure 25.2 highlights this problem not considering this aspect of the fiscal architecture while forecasting revenue. Over a relatively short period of time, the divergence between the two forecasts reaches 3 percent of income tax revenues. This divergence could easily be the difference between a balanced and nonbalanced budget and is the likely result of

Table 25.3 Example of Revenue Forecast

	Year						
	2006	*2007*	*2008*	*2009*	*2010*	*2011*	*2012*
		Level of income (million dollars)					
Wages	70.1	70.8	71.5	72.2	72.9	73.6	74.3
Capital	16.2	16.2	16.2	16.2	16.2	16.3	16.3
Transfers	15.3	15.8	16.3	16.9	17.4	18.0	18.6
Total personal income	101.6	102.8	104.0	105.3	106.5	107.8	109.1
		Annual growth by type of income (percent)					
Wages		1.00	0.98	0.97	0.96	0.95	0.93
Capital		0.10	0.10	0.10	0.10	0.10	0.10
Transfers		3.30	3.30	3.30	3.30	3.30	3.30
Total personal income		1.20	1.20	1.20	1.20	1.20	1.20
		Revenue forecast (million dollars)					
Constant income growth of 1.2 percent		11.41	11.54	11.68	11.82	11.96	12.11
Differential income growth		11.31	11.40	11.49	11.59	11.68	11.77
Difference in revenue		−0.10	−0.14	−0.19	−0.24	−0.29	−0.34

Source: Calculations based on hypothetical data.

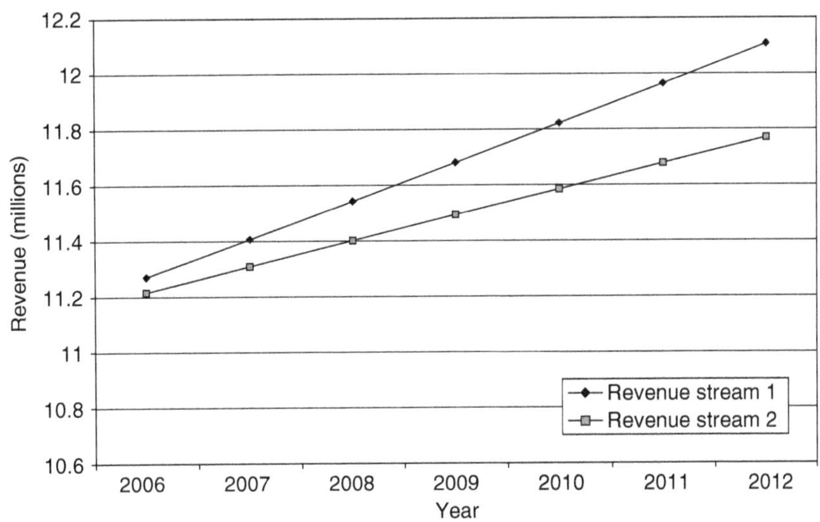

Figure 25.2 Revenue forecast, personal income tax (million dollars) (calculations based on hypothetical data).

ignoring the important changes in the economic base and demographics that give rise to a change in the composition of income.

There are a number of avenues for changes in fiscal architecture to impact revenue. Some of the major trends and their implications for important revenue sources are as follows:

- *Growing elderly population.* Increased consumption of nontaxable goods (medical goods and general services), which can reduce the growth in VAT; reduced consumption of durable goods, which may reduce CIT revenues; and reduced taxable income, which can reduce the growth of personal income tax and payroll taxes.
- *Urbanization.* Movement of individuals to the cities may lead to an increase in the growth of the underground economy making tax administration more difficult, thus we expect the growth of income taxes to fall.
- *Increase in service sector employment and self-employment.* Both of these changes in the economy make it more difficult for tax administrations to "find" taxpayers; therefore, we expect reduced revenue growth in all major categories but especially for income taxes.
- *Changes in the composition of income.* Capital income is more difficult to trace than wage and salary income; therefore, increased composition of capital income may reduce revenue growth. Also, as noted earlier, transfer payments are largely nontaxable; therefore, if an economy witnesses relatively large increases in transfer payments, revenue growth will be stymied.

Next, we layer on the final piece of the exercise—that of the institutional part of the architecture.

Institutional Factors and Policy Options

In some cases, a complete expenditure–revenue budget forecasting exercise that considers the fiscal architecture of a government will demonstrate a need to "change course" either in terms of the type of revenues used to support expenditures or in terms of making strategic choices with respect to the expenditures themselves. Institutions and other government policies may restrict these choices. As such, the institutions may not enter directly into the estimation of an expenditure or revenue forecast, but they do impact recommendations of how to adjust expenditures and revenue sources if the pressures from changes in fiscal architecture warrant adjustments.

In Table 25.4, some illustrative cases of pressures associated with changes in demographics and economic base and potential policy options are presented. In Table 25.4, institutional issues that will have a bearing on the efficacy of various options are also highlighted. For example, an aging population is expected to reduce revenue growth and increase the demand for health and pension expenditures.

Table 25.4 Illustrative Policy Matrix

	Direction of Trend	*Summary of Impact*	*Policy Options*
Demographic factors			
Age	Increasing percentage of elderly	Reduced tax base, reducing revenue growth, increased expenditure pressure from social services and housing (depends on what is covered in the tax base).	Adjust payroll tax system for pension payments, increase age for full benefits, means test benefits, and means test income tax exemptions. *Institutional issues.* Ability to means test benefits, importance of voter behavior (Do the elderly vote? Do they have a large impact?).
Economic factors			
Service sector growth	As a share of GDP, service sector is growing in most countries	As a share of GDP, could reduce the growth of tax revenues due to increased outlets for tax evasion.	Review of taxes for small business, institution of imputed taxes or taxes with thresholds to increase the revenue obtained from this hard to tax sector. *Institutional issues.* In countries with no history of using imputed or presumptive taxes, start-up costs to doing so can be prohibitive. Other options include more simple forms of business taxes such as licensing.
Computerization or Internet usage	Growing use of Internet for business throughout the world	There is an expected expenditure pressure related to telecommunications infrastructure. The revenue impact is less clear, although it is likely that domestic tax sources would decline due to the difficulty with taxing Internet transactions.	Long-term education and development of tax administration needs to take place to enable taxation of this form of commerce. *Institutional issues.* The strength of the tax administration is crucial to capturing the revenue potential associated with this expanding form of commerce. A weak administration will not be able to begin taxing such commerce and will increase the tax evasion problem associated with the Internet. Trade agreements and relations with other countries will increase or decrease the potential to tax this form of commerce. In some countries, this extends to subnational levels of government.

Targeted policy options include reducing pension benefits (directly or through an increased age of retirement) or increasing the payroll tax. Institutional constraints may prohibit means testing or may even prohibit increasing the age of retirement. In the case of service sector economic base growth, a policy option to deal with a potential increase in noncompliance would be to establish an imputed or presumptive tax system. However, in countries (e.g., Jamaica, Guatemala, and Ghana) with limited experience or severely limited resources for tax administration, such a tax may be impossible to implement. Instead, business licensing may be the optimal policy choice.

Creating an exhaustive list of the fiscal architecture and policy options for any one country is nearly impossible. In addition, these factors influence one another, making informed budget forecasting a very difficult business. However, consideration of the most important trends in fiscal architecture may improve the quality of budget forecasts in most countries and levels of government where such analysis is not typically considered. In many countries (Egypt, Sudan, Cote d'Ivoire, and many others), a lack of data is blamed for not incorporating fiscal architecture into budget forecasts. However, in cases where data is not readily available, experiences of other countries (for instance, those with recent focus on tax reform such as Columbia, Indonesia, and Poland) can be used to supplement data needs to develop a rich budget forecast. In the following section, we take up a case study in which we develop a budget forecast for a simplified budget containing two expenditure categories and two revenue categories.

Budget Forecasting Case Study

One could develop a systematic, econometric analysis of the impact of these demographic and economic changes on tax revenues (and expenditures) by source if the necessary detailed data was available. Such an analysis would estimate the growth in revenue by source as a function of tax rates and the economic and demographic infrastructure that affects the tax base and taxpaying population. This type of analysis would give us an objective, quantitative estimate of the impact of changes in the fiscal architecture of the country on its major revenue sources. Armed with this information, medium-term forecasts (five-year forecasts) could be made and decision making regarding needed future policy changes (and analysis of past reforms) would be enriched.

In many developing countries, we are hard-pressed to find comprehensive, consistent time series of expenditures, revenue, socioeconomic, economic activity, and demographic data. We can appeal to empirical findings in other countries such as Russia, Chile, or even in some cases, Organization for Economic Cooperation and Development (OECD) countries such as the United States of the links between these factors and revenue levels to assess the impacts of changes in any one particular country (such as our case of India). This case study is based on India. The actual forecasting that is done for the central government of India may or may not include aspects of the fiscal architecture of the country—there is not an obvious source of information on the specifics of the central government budget forecasting to make that determination.

Two expenditure items and two revenue items from the central government budget have been chosen as examples. The first part of the analytical work focuses on pension expenditures and the expenditures of one intergovernmental program, Sampoorna Grameen Rozgar Yojana (SGRY). On the revenue side of the budget, the focus is on the union excise duty and personal income tax.* The union excise duty is an indirect tax on all manufactured goods (broadly defined) (see Government of India 2005) up to the stage of the first wholesale dealer. The tax rate varies, with most goods taxed at a 16 percent rate. The personal income tax is on most forms of income and is subject to a progressive marginal tax rate structure. These expenditure and revenue categories were chosen based on their relative importance as reported in the budget of the Government of India as demonstrated in the information presented in Table 25.5. This data is used in the simulation exercise below. As seen in Table 25.5, the union excise tax revenues are the largest share of these items—comprising about 32 percent of revenue reported in the analysis. Over the time period studied in this analysis, the personal income tax grew by over three times, whereas on the expenditure side the growth in pensions is about 21/2 times over the ten-year period. These trends suggest that dynamic growth on both the revenue and expenditure sides of the budget provide a good case study for analysis.

As a federal country, the central government has expenditure and revenue-sharing arrangements with states and other subnational governments, which affect the final distribution of responsibilities between the levels of government. In this case study, I do not estimate the distribution of revenue between the central and subnational governments. Instead, I focus on the total reported level of collections of two of the central government taxes. In addition, this case study does not incorporate potentially important differences in the cost of expenditures by region of the country—the data necessary for such work is simply not available. I do, however, suggest how to expand the analysis to include such data as it becomes available.

General Framework

Within the budget forecasting framework, there are different ways to approach the integration of fiscal architecture. Currently, governments utilize various strategies in their forecasting. In terms of building up expenditure estimates, we might

* On the expenditure side, the budget for the country is broken down into plan and nonplan expenditures. Plan expenditures in the 2006–2007 budget are 65 percent of nonplan expenditures. The plan expenditures are developed by the Planning Commission, which is charged to develop five-year plans for the country. The plans may include very specific detail regarding expenditure determination (see, e.g., the 2006–2007 budget [Government of India 2006]).

Table 25.5 Selected Expenditures and Revenues, Government of India (Amounts in Crore)

Budget Item	*Year*										
	1995–1996	*1996–1997*	*1997–1998*	*1998–1999*	*1999–2000*	*2000–2001*	*2001–2002*	*2002–2003*	*2003–2004*	*2004–2005*	*2005–2006*
Pension	4,295	5,095	6,883	10,054	14,304	14,530	14,628	14,231	15,366	18,338	20,232
SGRY							1,710	8,642	9,640	4,490	NA
Personal income tax	15,100	19,010	28,750	21,430	26,684	35,271	34,438	37,300	40,269	50,929	66,239
Union excise	41,000	46,190	47,700	53,200	61,000	70,681	74,520	87,383	92,379	100,720	112,000
Total revenue receipts	100,787	130,783	138,514	157,665	179,504	206,166	212,572	236,936	263,027	300,904	348,474

Note: 1 Crore = 10 million, NA = not available.

Source: Government of India, Union budget and economic survey, http://indiabudget.nic.in/ub2006-07/glance.html. With permission.

differentiate between cost-reimbursement approaches and client-based (people-based) approaches. In the former case, expenditures are derived by calculating the cost of physical inputs—How many miles of roads? How far water has to travel? Etc. In the second case, expenditures are determined based on characteristics of the client population—How many and what is the distribution of school-aged children? What is the health of the elderly population? Etc.

The cost-based approach was often used in transition countries (Russia, Ukraine, and Kazakhstan) (The World Bank). The fiscal architecture methodology is more closely aligned with the client-based approach in that it shows how to meet the needs of the population. Capital expenditures should also be considered when integrating this methodology, however, they are not explicitly considered in this case study.*

A "bottoms-up" approach to expenditure forecasting will explicitly consider the important components of the fiscal architecture of any government. Although this approach is an intuitive one, many countries such as the Philippines, Ghana, and subnational governments in Russia use an incremental type of expenditure forecasting and adjust budgeted expenditures based on past expenditures adjusted by an inflation factor (Wallace 2001). There is no one way to estimate basic expenditures, but a general process follows Equation 25.1, expanded as follows by type of expenditures (see Alm [1999] for more details and an explanation of the uses of norms in various countries):

1. Estimate minimum required expenditures for different service categories on a per client basis. Options for calculating minimum expenditures:
   - *Education*. Teachers' wages, rental costs, percentage of students with physical disabilities, and percentage of children from low-income families
   - *Health*. Cost of healthcare professionals, infant mortality, life expectancy, and population density
   - *Transportation*. Wages, road grade, annual precipitation, and population density
   - *Police and fire*. Wages, crime rate, number of fires per capita, and population density
   - *Social welfare*. Minimum wage, distribution of age, distribution of income, and unemployment rate
   - *Public administration (costs associated with general running of the government including salaries, offices expenses, and so on) and others*. Population and average wage
2. Multiply the per client expenditure by the number of clients per service category

Data constraints often prevent governments from forecasting expenditures in such detail. When detailed data is not available, based on international experiences, we

* Capital expenditures should be analyzed with respect to the number of clients that need to be served, location of provision, and current capacity.

can at least offer some lessons on the direction of fiscal pressure associated with the important economic and demographic variables that form public demands for expenditures.

On the revenue side, the idea of incorporating fiscal architecture is to analyze the revenue capacity of a government—how much revenue can be obtained from a particular revenue source and how this changes as the base changes due to changes in economic and demographic structure. Revenue capacity estimates are often made in cross-country comparisons to judge how well countries do in attaining their revenue potential (see, e.g., Bahl and Wallace 2004, Bahl et al. 1996). These estimates typically use a general economic indicator (such as gross domestic product [GDP]) as a proxy for the tax base because a proxy such as GDP is available for most countries around the world. Comparative estimates of revenue capacity are useful for discovering where a country's tax collection is weak relative to peers. However, the differences may be due to policy instruments in the tax system (such as income tax thresholds, exemptions, and differential rates), and therefore, the capacity estimates must be combined with the specific tax laws and compliance rates to serve as a budget forecast.

A more disaggregated bottom-up approach to revenue forecasting that will explicitly include the fiscal architecture of the country decomposes the revenue as noted in Equations 25.4 and 25.5. The change in the tax base will be a function of the activity associated with the tax (employment and output in the case of income taxes, and consumption or manufacturing output in the case of VAT or sales taxes). Forecasts of the changes in the base may or may not be readily available. In cases where they are not, trends of recent change may be useful for short- to medium-term budgeting (through five years). In many countries including the Philippines and Jamaica and many other developing countries, the revenue forecast is driven off of elasticity estimates of the growth of particular revenues relative to a macroeconomic aggregate such as GDP or gross national product (GNP). Because elasticity is an estimate of the change in the revenue as GDP changes, it can pick up general trends in changes in the economy, but if there are important compositional changes as discussed earlier, the revenue–GDP elasticity will mask the specific changes that are occurring. This is exactly the case that was presented earlier when the impact of assuming that all income was growing at a constant rate versus knowing the growth in specific components was demonstrated. We now focus on the specific budget forecasting exercise for India.

Case Study

The two expenditures that I have considered for the India case, pensions and the SGRY program, serve different populations in the country. The central government pension system is aimed at central government employees. Similar to the U.S. Social Security system, the pension system has specified benefits, retirement ages, and provisions for family members, particularly spouses (for a detailed discussion of the system of benefits, see Government of India, undated). The pension outlays of the budget are therefore a function of the number of pensioners and their per person benefit. The number of pensioners is growing as India's population ages. The per person benefit is a function of the employee's enumeration in the past ten years of service. As wages and benefits rise over time, so also does the liability associated with the pension. Wages for public servants are set regularly by a Pay Commission, so there is some government control regarding the outlays for pensions, and one-year forecasts can be calculated based on the wage bill and the number of retirees.

A quick look at pension expenditures relative to GNP or revenue receipts (taxes, fees, and so on) shows a pattern of growth from 1995 to 2000, then a drop until 2004 where it picks up again (to about 0.7 percent of GNP). These fluctuations are due to the nature of wage setting in government. Over the medium to long run, however, budget forecasts may be done that incorporate the larger demographic shifts. This exercise incorporating the fiscal architecture can "warn" government about pending budgetary stresses in time for government to take thoughtful action.*

Because we cannot predict the wage policy in India, we will analyze the impact of the changing demographics of aging on a real wage—held constant at 2005 levels. In 2005, pensions were 0.7 percent of GNP and 6.1 percent of revenue receipts. If the real value of the benefits stayed constant and the growth in the number of government pensioners mirrored the overall growth in individuals aged 50 and above in India, by 2010, the expenditure outlay for pensions would increase by 18 percent. This implies that consistent with economic and revenue growth (similar to the growth from 2004 to 2005), pensions would use an additional 1.1 percent of revenue receipts and would equal 0.8 percent of GNP. In ten years, under the same scenario, pensions would claim an additional percentage of total revenue receipts (in real terms) and would be equivalent to 0.9 percent of total GNP. At this point, the increase in the value of the pension expenditure would equal 50 percent of the total food subsidy expenditure of the central government, or the entire social service expenditure of the central government plus the petroleum subsidy of the central government. The magnitude of the potential increase in pension expenditures due to the aging dimension of the population in India constrains the budget in ways that might be dealt with in the short run by adjusting the benefits through increased age of retirement or an adjustment in the benefit formula.

The SGRY program is another example where changes in the fiscal architecture of the country should be examined for medium- to long-run impacts on the budget.† SGRY is a social program that provides wage and food support for rural poor. The program is intergovernmental in nature in that the central government

---

* Medium- and long-term budget forecasts are not publicly available; therefore, we are not able to determine if such methods are in fact utilized.

† The SGRY program as it currently stands is being phased-out and another income support program for rural areas is being phased-in from 2006.

finances a large portion of the expenditure and distribution is done through subnational governments. The government sets the level of distribution (the expenditure need) based largely on the relative number of poor individuals in the rural areas of the country. Similar to the case with pensions, a one-year forecast may be relatively simple to estimate. Longer-term forecasts, however, need to consider the overall growth in population and the percentage of population living in poverty.

If we consider the percentage of people living in poverty as a constant, the population growth in India will quickly drive up the medium- to long-run forecast for this expenditure. Similarly considering the change in real terms, and assuming that the percentage of people in poverty remains constant, the percent increase in SGRY expenditure would increase to 8.3 percent over the period 2005 to 2010. This would increase the call on revenue receipts by about 0.3 percent. Over a ten-year period, the impact would be an additional 15 percent real increase in SGRY expenditures so that the claim on revenue receipts would increase by another 0.5 percent.

Together, when we consider the demographic changes in India over a ten-year period, these two expenditure categories alone would claim an additional 3 percent or more of revenue receipts—equal to about 12 percent of real income tax revenue. Changes in the fiscal architecture underlying other expenditure needs will put additional pressure on the budget. In addition, similar pressures will arise at the state and substate level. The pension scenario at the subnational government level will be very similar to that at the central government level because state governments tend to follow similar labor and wage policies.

There may be some expenditures for which future needs will naturally decline as a result of changes in demographics or the economy, but it is difficult to think of such a list, given the overall growth in India. Instead, the government will be faced with trade-offs related to the pressure of increased expenditure needs.

On the revenue side, I consider two taxes—the personal income tax and the union excise tax. The bases for these taxes are quite different. The personal income tax base comprises wage and salary income and also includes capital income and other enumerations (including, statutorily, many fringe benefits). The base of the union excise tax is manufacturing (state governments have jurisdiction over indirect taxation of services; therefore, this central government tax covers manufacturing).

Similar to the expenditure cases, these tax bases have some competition as India's economy moves forward. The income tax base is subject to potential erosion due to the increasing number of retirement-aged individuals, and, as services expand, the wage component itself may be difficult to capture. We are hard-pressed to find data on capital income in India, but with rising incomes, it is likely that capital income will become a more important component of overall income. Capital income is notoriously difficult to tax—therefore, again, we might expect some reduction in the growth of the income tax. Also, as the service sector expands, the union excise duty (the most important central government revenue source in 2006) may witness erosion of its growth.

One way to judge the impact of these changes on these two revenue sources is to track the collections of these taxes relative to total revenue receipts and relative to general movements in the economy (GNP) over time. Relative to total revenue receipts, both taxes appear to be leveling off since the economic recovery post-2001. The revenue growth that was seen in the mid-1990s appears to have hit a steady state by 2004, possibly reflective of the changes in demographics and economic base that are taking hold. Relative to GNP, the income tax has leveled off at about 1.6 percent of GNP from a high of 2.1 percent in 1998, whereas the union excise has hovered around 3.7 percent of GNP over the past three years. The previous high of the union excise tax against GNP was 3.9 percent in 1996.

If we calculate simple buoyancy estimates as percentage change in tax source/percentage change in GNP, the annual estimates of buoyancy for both taxes vary a lot from year to year due to changes in the tax law and changes in wage policies. In general, however, we notice a downward trend in the buoyancy estimates for the income tax and the union excise duty from 2001 to 2004–2005.

To analyze the impact of stabilizing or declining manufacturing on the growth of the union excise duty, we can estimate the productivity of the union excise duty per rupee of manufacturing GDP. Over the past several years, the productivity of the tax measured in this way has been around 0.2 rupee in tax per rupee of manufacturing output. Assuming no changes in tax administration productivity or compliance, we can use this as the effective tax rate on a rupee of manufacturing output. Manufacturing output growth was 6.3 percent in 2002–2003 and 6.6 percent in 2003–2004 (previous growth rates over the past decade ranged from 12.3 to 3.4). If manufacturing growth were to decline even as the overall economy grew and the service sector became larger, the base of the union excise would be eroded accordingly. Over a five-year period (through 2010), incorporating the "change in architecture" of a reduced annual growth rate of manufacturing to an annual rate of 5.0 percent in manufacturing versus 6.5 percent would reduce excise revenues by 1.5 percent. This is equivalent to about 25 percent of central government expenditures on social services.

The income tax erosion comes from slowing employment and wage growth. Public sector employment is about 22 percent of reported private sector employment. Approximately 1.9 million people are employed in the public sector and 8.4 million in the private sector in 2004. Public sector employment has fallen at an average rate of 3 percent per year over the past five years, whereas private sector employment has fallen at an average rate of 1 percent per year. If we assume constant compliance and real wages, then if the path of current employment growth continues, income tax revenue would fall nearly 3 percent over a five-year period. This is equivalent to 75 percent of the budgeted expenditure for intergovernmental aid for rural housing in 2005, or 50 percent of the cash component of SGRY for the same year.

These four examples highlight the usefulness of incorporating the changes in fiscal architecture into a country's budget forecast methodology. Analyzing four important budget items suggests that in the case of India, changes in demographics and economics will impinge quite substantially on budget flexibility over the next five years.

Conclusions

In this chapter, I investigated the role of incorporating fiscal architecture into the budget forecasting toolbox. Fiscal architecture describes the demographic, economic, and institutional backbone of a country. Changes in fiscal architecture will present countries with opportunities and challenges related to budget stability.

In the case of India, we saw that the major trends of the aging of their economy and the growth of nonmanufacturing output will reduce the natural growth of two major revenue sources over the next five years. At the same time, expenditure needs for pensions and intergovernmental aid programs will increase. By analyzing the impact of these trends early, governments are in a better position to develop reasonable policy alternatives within their institutional constraints. In fact, the government has some levers that it can use to adjust the pension expenditure pressure, namely, the definition of retirement age and benefits distribution. In the case of a program such as SGRY, the central government may simply not be able to fund the planned level of aid. Given the potential decline in income and excise tax, the central government may choose to rethink its excise tax policy so as to reduce to whatever extent possible the exemptions in the system.

These conclusions and recommendations are preliminary, and serious consideration to necessary changes can only occur after a complete analysis of all major budget items. However, even these preliminary results demonstrate the usefulness of incorporating fiscal architecture into budget forecast analysis. In addition, institutional issues such as corruption, accountability through the voting process, and relationships among levels of government may have additional implications for the efficacy of public budgeting. These are not incorporated directly into the budget analysis done here because I do not have good information on the likely changes in items such as corruption into the future. They are, however, important parts of a country's architecture, which could influence both revenues and expenditures.

References

Alm, J. 1999. International experience with expenditure norms. Working Paper, Andrew Young School of Policy Studies, Georgia State University, Atlanta, GA.

Bahl, R. and J. F. Linn. 1992. *Urban Public Finance in Developing Countries.* Washington: The World Bank.

Bahl, R., J. Martinez-Vazquez, and S. Wallace. 1996. *The Guatemala Tax Reform.* Boulder, CO: Westview Press.

Bahl, R. and S. Wallace. 2004. Comprehensive tax reform in Jamaica. Working Paper, Andrew Young School of Policy Studies, International Studies Program, Georgia State University, Atlanta, GA.

Bird, R. M. and S. Wallace. 2004. Is it really so hard to tax the hard-to-tax? The context and role of presumptive taxes. In *Taxing the Hard-to-Tax: Lessons for Theory and Practice*, J. Alm, J. Martinez-Vazquez, and S. Wallace (eds.). Amsterdam: Elsevier.

Clotfelter, C. 1983. Tax evasion and tax rates: an analysis of individual returns. *Review of Economics and Statistics* 65: 363–373.

Cummings, R. G., J. Martinez-Vazquez, M. McKee, and B. Torgler. 2005. Effects of tax morale on tax compliance: experimental and survey evidence. Working Paper 05–16, Andrew Young School of Policy Studies, International Studies Program, Georgia State University, Atlanta, GA.

Government of India. Ministry of Finance, Department of Revenue. 2005. http://www.cbec.gov.in (accessed September 1, 2006).

Government of India. Ministry of Personnel, Public Grievances, and Pensions, undated, http://persmin.nic.in/pension/index.html (accessed July 28, 2006).

Government of India. Union budget and economic survey. 2006. http://indiabudget.nic.in/ub2006-07/ubmain.html (accessed August 30, 2006).

The World Bank. 1996. *Fiscal Management in Russia*. Washington: The World Bank.

The World Bank. 2007. Worldwide governance indicators, http://info.worldbank.org/governance/kkz2005/ (accessed January 24, 2007).

U.S. Census Bureau. Undated. World population information, http://www.census.gov/ipc/www/world.html (accessed August 22, 2006).

Wallace, S. 2001. Fiscal architecture and the analysis of public expenditure needs and revenue capacity. Working Paper 01–11, Andrew Young School of Policy Studies, International Studies Program, Georgia State University, Atlanta, GA.

Chapter 26

Forecasting Practices in Emerging Countries: The Morocco Experience

Aziza Zemrani

Contents

Introduction

Revenue and expenditure forecasting practices are critical for budget preparation as well as other management practices such as planning. This is true in developed countries such as the United States and developing countries such as Morocco. This chapter approaches the subject of forecasting from a different perspective than the other chapters of this book as it focuses more on institutional concerns related to forecasting rather than techniques used in forecasting.

In many circumstances, revenue forecasting is a resource constraint and its adequacy influences the resource allocation decision of a nation. If integrated correctly in the budget preparation process, good forecasting can facilitate the allocation of expenditures across the government's programs. However, forecasting is more than a set of techniques of better guessing revenues and expenditures. For example, transparency in forecasting is critical for governments that wish to be democratic and accountable to elected political leadership. Elarafi (2006) argues that in addition to transparency in the forecasting process, there needs to be a systematic and scientific approach to both revenue and expenditure forecasting, as explained in other chapters of this book.

Forecasting is an even more important matter for developing countries, countries in transition, or countries that are emerging economically. For them, the problem of generating sufficient revenues for public expenditures is critical. Eltony (2002) notes that in some Arab countries, budget deficits and the inefficient and ineffective use of public expenditures impact the level of investment in human resources and basic infrastructure, which are the two major variables necessary to achieve sustainable economic growth.

During the past 20 years, many Arab countries embarked on a number of economic and financial reforms designed to raise tax revenues and to restructure tax systems, which have a hopeful positive trickle-down effect on the budgeting process including better forecasting of revenues and expenditures. This will become more evident as the reader proceeds through this chapter. In a survey of 16 Arab countries, Eltony (2002) discovered that tax revenue performance varied across them. The share of tax revenue in gross domestic product (GDP) was on average about 12.6 percent in 1994. Algeria was above 25 percent. Egypt, Jordan, Mauritania, Morocco, Tunisia, and Syria were between 15 and 25 percent. Bahrain, Lebanon, Yemen, and Oman were between 5 and 15 percent. Saudi Arabia, Kuwait, Sudan, Qatar, and United Arab Emirates were below 5 percent.

Penner (2001) points out that budgets are about the future and budget decisions must be based on forecasts. Thus, good or bad forecasting does have an impact on government resource allocations policy and management decisions. Often the impact on policy and management is directly related to the accuracy of forecasts and what processes are used to determine those forecasts. For developing countries especially, factors that significantly influence forecasts are often beyond the control of decision makers. Such reality must be appreciated. Nevertheless, some other factors, within the country, that could significantly improve budget forecasting also exist and are not being used. During 1985–1995, a sample of 34 low-income developing countries had tax revenues that were 77 percent of forecasts mostly due to political factors (Abed 1998). Lienert and Sarraf (2001) noted that weak institutional capacities are among the reasons for overstated forecasts in developing countries.

Some authors, such as Aaron (2000), believe that forecasting is unlikely to become much more accurate than it is today because of economic uncertainty. The pessimists argue that this is partially due to both the economic realities of their situation (Carlyle, cited in Primack et al. 1996) and "unscientific state of economic science" (Galbraith 1987). In addition, they point out that forecasting in other political and institutional organizations impinges on a developing nation's economic and budget forecasting (e.g., international conjecture and international organization donors).

Morocco is a typical example of an emerging country with significant forecasting challenges. Thus, not surprisingly, Moroccan forecasters are notoriously unreliable at predicting revenues and expenditures and other key factors that influence forecasts, which include the upcoming wave of technological change, the weather, earthquakes, and droughts. The latter is particularly important because the Moroccan economy is based on agricultural production.

This chapter consists of four sections apart from introduction. The first section Country Characteristics provides an overview of the Moroccan constitutional evolution and some detailed information on the organic legislation that informs government officials on how to go about budgeting and forecasting. The second section Forecasting Practices in Morocco compares ideal practices with problems in Morocco's actual forecasting practices. The third section Evaluation of Revenue Forecasting assesses the quality of forecasting used in Morocco by examining the identified institutional practices that exist in the country. The fourth section offers some conclusion and recommendations.

Country Characteristics

Budgeting in Morocco

This section discusses the specifics of budgeting in Morocco including its historical background that puts budgeting into its political context. This section is particularly important in understanding the factors that shape forecasting in an emerging country such as Morocco.

Morocco is a constitutional monarchy that has been in democratic transition. The first constitution was adopted in 1966 and subsequently replaced in 1972, 1980, 1992, and 1996. The first constitution introduced bicameralism into the parliament, which now consists of the House of Representatives and the House of Councilors or Advisors. The first house is elected by direct universal suffrage for a five-year term. The members of the second house are also elected but they represent local communities, professional organizations, and employees and serve a nine-year term that is renewable every three years (Cherkaoui 2002, Harakat 2006).

This process of democratization in Morocco has led to other changes such as opening access and opportunities to civil society for involvement in public affairs. Another by-product is greater transparency and accountability of government. These public administration reforms are major process changes that consolidate the rule of law and promote good governance in Morocco (Cherkaoui 2002). The constitution strengthened the legal status of the government's audit office (La Cour des comptes) that reflected the rising interest in establishing accountability in government. This period also was a time of rising interest in using a national development plan, which replaced the older national economic program. Many sections of the constitution of 1996 (Articles 45, 50, 51, 56, and 57) deal with voting conditions and potential amendments to the budget law.

The history of budgeting in Morocco started in 1913 with a system of financial organization known as *oumanas*, which means people with a fiduciary responsibility. It was established under the reign of Moulay Slimane in the nineteenth century and it marks the inception of public finance accounting practices (Marchal 1931). Despite its influence, the *oumanas* did not create a budget and did not make any estimate of expenditures. In the reign of Sultan Moulay Hassan (1873–1894), Amin El Oumanas took the title of Wazir El Malia. He was an equivalent of a Minister of Finance of a country like France. His organization had three divisions: the Amin of the Receipts, the Amin of Spending who paid the debts of the Makhzen, and the Amin of Accounts who controlled the accounts transmitted to the Makhzen by the *oumanas* (Bernoussi 1994, Cherkaoui 2002).

The starting point of a more organized and structured public finance and budgeting in Morocco was the inception of its democratic process in 1962, which occurred a few years after the end of the French protectorate. In this year, Morocco had its first constitution voted and adopted in 1966. Largely inspired by the French, Morocco's constitution affirms a number of democratic principles such as separation of powers, national representation, and multiple political parties. Four other constitutions followed in 1970, 1972, 1992, and 1996. Every constitution had a number of sections dealing with the finance or budget law (Elarafi 2006).

The parliament exercised its authority over public finance with specific legislation (called organic laws) that established the processes associated with public finance. This legislation created the process by which the parliament passes the finance laws and defines the two parts of the annual finance law, which are the "rectificative" finance law and the "reglement" law. Under the finance organic law, a decree of application defines the elaboration and execution of the budget law. Four finance organic laws have been in effect since independence: 1963, 1970, 1972, and 1998. The laws brought a new approach to budgeting in Morocco, that is, a budget oriented to results rather than focusing on the means of government (Abate 2004).

Forecasting Practices in Morocco

Ideal Practices

Given the complexity of financial phenomena and the influence augmented by extreme disturbances caused by the endogenous and exogenous factors as mentioned earlier, forecasting and the budget processes involve over more than a one-year timeframe. A management approach that is centered on performance requires strategic procedures that take several years to evolve even in developed countries. In theory, such an ideal approach to budgeting should guarantee the ability of the state to attain its desired results in a predictable timeframe. Such reforms involve more than the simple exercise of forecasting budgets, which traditionally consist of an extrapolation of past years and do not utilize analysts such as futurologists (Elarafi 2006). Ideally, such financial decisions should involve all the government decision-making units to ensure that the identification of desired performances should gain from the input of various different decision-making units within the government. Such integration is most likely to occur with a strategy designed to embrace all the management of finances within the state.

Budgeting decisions should be based on multiyear projections. First, analysts should view the budget in a macroeconomic framework that reflects financial equilibrium that is compatible with favorable macroeconomic objectives. Second, the analysts should use multiyear projections that include the likely impacts of current budget decisions associated with implementing the development policy of the state. This long-term approach requires well-developed technical involvements at all levels of government and should exceed the common procedures used in developing annual finance legislation. This approach to budgeting should be oriented toward achieving specific results through coordinating the government's planning, programming, and budgeting efforts. Thus, this ideal approach stresses the application of more rational and inclusive means of resource allocation (Elarafi 2006).

Forecasting Practices

The Moroccan political structure is a type of a centralized government with the ministry of finances as the major and key player in the budgeting process with all its components, that is, forecasting. The Ministry of Finance and Privatization is a key administrative structure, which illustrates the quality of the Moroccan administration's institutional capacity to fulfill its missions (African Development Bank 2004). This ministry with its top-level technical competences is capable of providing the necessary technical assistance in keeping with its missions to the various ministries. This is the case, for example, of the Commitment and Expenditure Control Department (CGED), which is mandated to (i) monitor the budgetary regularity of expenditure initiation proposals; (ii) inform the Ministry of Finance and Privatization about the conditions of budget implementation; and (iii) provide its support and assistance to management services, and contract services, in particular. The report previously cited assesses the budgeting practices in Morocco and acknowledges that the budget system is elaborate; has a legal framework; and a well-structured, reliable set of budget preparation and implementation procedures. However, all the documents referred for this chapter do not particularly specify the methods used and the well-defined econometric or any other method discussed in budgeting books procedures and theories.

The ministry organizational chart consists of different directorates and among them are the Directorate of Budget and the Directorate of Economic and Financial Forecasting. The investigation and exploration and examination of their job-related functions help to determine their contribution to the forecasting and budget process. However, the documents referred do not give accurate information on the process followed and the different methods used and applied. Despite these limitations, the information available through the years evaluated for this research provides the following remarks:

- The different finance acts (1999–2006) examined give an overview of the realizations in terms of revenues and expenditures (highlighted later in the Analysis section).
- The examination of the different reports cited earlier addresses the contextual framework for the previous and coming fiscal year including the national as well as the international environment and their implications on the fiscal status of the country.
- As of the fiscal year 2006, the ministry of finances improves its information accessibility through the Internet by providing quarterly reports on the realizations of the ministry. However, such information is not complete in terms of the methodologies used to process the predictions.
- The different reports do not specify or discuss the different methods or approaches to forecasting used in their previsions.
- The reports examined (available on the ministry Web site) describe at length about the international conjecture and its implications on the Moroccan performance, fiscal and financial, with no information on the econometric models used for such discussion.

As discussed in the following section, the Moroccan experience is unique in the sense that the information available sheds light on the inadequacy of the underlying methods required and approaches adopted so far. A more scientific approach along with more formality, transparency, and simplicity is necessary.

Morocco's Forecasting Experience

The Moroccan experience has resulted in poor forecasting, which is partially due to the fact that all key players are not clear about their role in the finance processes and the need for improved analytical and methods of planning. Like many countries, both planning and budgeting are significant and both involve forecasting. Ideally, the national plan serves as the foundation of forecasting, but the poor link between planning and budgeting makes accurate forecasting significantly more difficult. Planning should be a framework that provides a logical link between the nation's critical stakeholders in defining national objectives and resource allocation decisions. However, the existing process in Morocco has uncertain links between the plan and the budget including the articulation of planned objectives and their related desired government action (Elarafi 2006).

The inadequate links involve divergence in the perception of the plan among different stakeholders, incoherence that exists among plans, lack of measurability in the target specifications, and ineffectiveness of coherent procedures. Given the complexity of the forecasting process, which involves different key players and agencies, forecasting accuracy is made more difficult to achieve (Ansoff 1965, Porter 1980).

Inconsistency between Forecasting and Realization

This subsection addresses an inconsistency pertinent to forecasting and budgeting. The Moroccan state plans from 1956 to 2002 began in triumph and later diluted themselves or were replaced by other plans. Significant gaps existed between the budget data and the projected realizations of the plans largely due to financial uncertainties (Elarafi 2006). For example, the aggregation of the state expenditures during the last six finance laws (1996–2002) shows that the forecasting of the finance laws displayed a gap amounting to 20 percent, or 115 billion dirham. The first three executed years of the five-year program had an average growth of 3.5 percent per year. At the level of the budget aggregates, the report of the first two years of the plan mentions acceleration in the rate of increase of expenditures with an average growth of 7 percent during the years 2000 and 2001. This surpasses the plan threshold limit for such type of expenditure.

The Temporary Analysis of the Errors in Budgeting

The Moroccan temporary analysis examines the condition and movement of the national economy. It covers the past year, current year, and following two years. The purpose of the analysis is to identify the dynamic interactions that affect the national economy due to principal macroeconomic variable. This type of analysis often looks at the estimates used in the models, simultaneous equations, analysis of the temporal series, techniques used in financial anticipations, variations of the economical hypotheses, and uncertainty involved in estimating expenditure figures. The economical predictions and budget estimates are the backbone of the Organic Law of Finance (OLF).

This analysis permits the analyst to evaluate and even assess the reliability of the predicted results from the OLF. Some Moroccan scholars recommend that the presentation of the OLF should include statements about forecasting hazards specifically addressing the allocations of "unforeseen expenditures" (Elarafi 2006, Zemrani 1998). Hazards or uncertainties must be quantified appropriately. In addition, according to some International Monetary Fund (IMF; 2004, 2005) studies, these random errors or variations need to be extended over different categories. They include the variations in the principal hypotheses of the budget anticipations and their effect on the public finances under the macroeconomic assumptions (e.g., the effect on the budget deficit of an increase or decrease of 1 percent growth of the GDP, inflation, interest rate, or exchange rate as opposed to the rates used in the forecasting modeling). The uncertainty related to the amount of appropriations of specific expenditures needs to be highlighted in the budget. For example, a given activity may be conditional on unknown factors occurring outside. In such a case, the budget should note the probable cost and declare that it is subject to uncertainty and clarify the associated risk.

Underpinning Limitations

No official Moroccan documentation is available on the Web site of the Ministry of Finance concerning the use of econometric models. However, such information is available on the Web site of the French Ministry of Finance. The forecasting directorate of the French ministry provides an independent assessment of the models used that depicts the macroeconomic framework (Center on Budget and Policy Priorities [CBPP] 2005). The French ministry offer limited technical support under their cooperative arrangement with the Directorate of the General Economic Provisions.

Every year, during the exercise of its statistical functions, the Office of the High Commissioner for Planning prepares and publishes macroeconomic estimates that are independent of those prepared by the Ministry of Finance. This is in addition to the forecasting of the foregoing directorate. A World Bank Report (2003) notes that the Moroccans have significantly improved their data series that they use in forecasting and reporting their actual growth rates and their growth estimates.

The Moroccan Statistics Directorate of the Office of the High Commissioner for Planning has extensive *de facto* independence, but no legal insurance of its Directorate of Statistics and National Accounting (the Moroccan statistics agency) independence. Statistics as a tool of budgeting was increased in importance by the transfer of the former Ministry of Economic Forecasting and Planning to the

Office of the High Commissioner for Planning (High Commission of Planning, 2007, www.hcp.ma).

The existing government budget process does not cover the entire operations of the government. It is restricted to the operations of the central government agencies and does not cover the mandated social security system, local governments, and the public expenditures of the nonprofit institutions. The reality in Morocco is that those groups outside the government budget process are increasingly making more and more of the public expenditure decisions for the nation (Organic Law of Finances, Ministry of Finances). Ideally, the reporting and financial reporting process should be expanded to include all public expenditures and the quality of fiscal data should be improved as follows:

- The sources and methods used in the preparation of all fiscal data must be disclosed.
- Information on the monthly fiscal statistics should be provided.
- A publication schedule for the distribution of fiscal information should be issued (Ministry of Finances 1999, www.finances.gov.ma).

Full disclosure of government fiscal information, including information on budget forecasts, is important for a number of reasons including the fact that international research organizations have vested interest in accessing such information. Certainly, the most important reason is to ensure that the government remains accountable to its people and its stakeholders. Without such statistical accountability, the likelihood of corruption increases, likelihood of effective delivery of public services decreases, and community-led development becomes much more difficult (Center on Budget Policy and Priorities 2005). In addition there tends to be a greater likelihood of financial crisis without government transparency and financial accountability.

Evaluation of Revenue Forecasting

Analytical Approach Used

This section uses a critical approach to analysis developed by Kyobe and Danninger (2005) to assess the determinants of revenue and expenditure forecasting practices. They identified three key factors: formality, simplicity, and transparency. *Formality* concerns the forecasting process and it involves a series of questions such as what is the formality of the revenue forecasting process with all its components (i.e., formal definition, initiation, adjustment, revision, and finally documentation). They used an index that includes the formal forecasting methods employed. *Simplicity* concerns cohesiveness and centralization of the forecasting process. This variable includes the number of agencies involved in the production of forecasting revenues, which convey the idea of complexity or simplicity in the process.

Transparency is an index that quantifies the involvement of outside agencies, the publicity of macroeconomic assumptions made in the forecasting process, and the level of detail in the budget document. The ultimate objective in the development of this index is to assess forecasting credibility. Kyobe and Danninger (2005) hypothesize that there is a positive correlation between transparency and accuracy. In contrast, they also hypothesize that there is a negative correlation between transparency and any discretionary adjustments. Other factors remaining constant, one would expect that the higher the level of transparency, the higher the level of accuracy. And conversely, one would also expect that the lower the level of discretionary adjustments, the higher the level of accuracy.

The current practices in Morocco are examined here using the three index variables—index of formality, index of organizational simplicity, and index of forecasting process transparency. The analysis uses both quantitative and qualitative data. Although there are limitations to this approach of analysis, the findings of this approach shed useful light on Moroccan practices and are suggestive of what future research should be undertaken. The index of formality is the unweighted sum of four binary variables that check if the forecasting responsibility is formally (1) defined, (2) initiated, (3) revised, and (4) documented. This index is linearly additive and its scores can range between 0 and 4.

The index of organizational simplicity is the unweighted sum of three binary variables. They are whether (1) a single agency is responsible for the revenue forecast, (2) a single agency is responsible for the macroeconomic forecast, and (3) a forecast is produced. The index is linearly positive and the scores range between 0 and 3. This index examines the number of agencies involved in the revenue and macroeconomic forecast and the number of competing forecasts.

The index of forecasting process transparency is the weighted sum of eight binary variables. They are whether (1) the macroeconomic assumptions are published outside of the budget, (2) outside agencies participate in the revenue forecast, and (3–8) various types of revenue forecast–related information was published in the budget document. Variables 3–8 are given weights of one-sixth to aggregate information content in the budget document using the same weight as given to variables 1 and 2 (Kyobe and Danninger 2005).

Analysis

Table 26.1 presents the average sample, which includes Morocco, response for the three indexes. A formal definition of responsibilities exists only in 36 percent of the countries. About two-thirds of the countries formally (e.g., through budget circulars or budget manuals) initiate the annual budget revenue forecasting exercises. The forecasting process is formally documented in only half of the sample. Within a year, revisions of the revenue forecast occurred in 64 percent of sample and they are carried out on an "as needed" basis. Only one-half revised the budget forecasts one year ahead in the course of their budget preparation.

Table 26.1 Index Data from the Sample Countries

Variable Description	*Sample Mean (Percent)*	*Significant Regional Variation*	*Significant Variation by Per Capita Income*
General			
One agency responsible for forecast	91.1		
Macroeconomic forecasts by one agency	44.1		
Forecasting horizon for one year	64.7		
Budget forecast covering only central government	47.0		
Five or less people in charge of forecasting	23.5		
Methods			
Main forecasting methods (basic extrapolations)	83.9		
Use of econometric methods	12.9		
Use of disaggregate data	20.0		
Formality			
Forecasting responsibilities defined	36.6	Yes	
Forecasting formally initiated	68.7		
Formal revisions	64.7	Yes	
Formal documentation	51.6		
Organization			
Forecasting produced by one agency	47.1		
Only one uniform forecast produced	76.4		Positive
Macroforecast produced by single agency	44.1		
Transparency			
Nongovernment agencies participating in forecast	34.4		Positive
Information published outside budget document	36.3		
Information content in budget document			
Aggregate revenue forecast	82.3		
Breakdown of forecast into revenue types	85.3		
Data on past revenue outturns	58.8		
Analysis of past developments and forecasts	17.6		
Summary of macroassumptions	55.9		
Decomposition of forecast into various effects	20.6		
Interference			
Significant discretionary adjustment of technical forecast	36.3		

Source: Kyobe and Danninger 2005, 14. With permission.

How does this relate to Morocco? Morocco is among the worst. There is no formal process in publishing the forecasting results. The Ministry of Finance, through its Directorate of Budget, initiates the budget preparation using the macro- and microeconomic forecasts. However, for Morocco it is more than an internal process. The Ministry of Economics (called the Haut Commissariat au Plan) does the same thing but there is hardly any coordination between the two agencies.

In addition, Kyobe and Danninger (2005) report that approximately half (47.1 percent) of the countries put only one government agency in charge of the revenue forecast. This figure is slightly smaller for the macroeconomic forecast (44.1 percent). In most cases (76.5 percent), the government only produces one forecast and thus foregoes the option of competing forecasts. The authors report the average score of the simplicity index as low, and none of the sampled countries received a maximum score of three. Morocco did not score well on the simplicity index using its own information. A French document from the International Budget Office provides public information on the forecasting methodology used and the French technical assistance that is given to Morocco. Essentially, the assessment and evaluation of the econometric models are limited to the technical support provided by the French forecasting directorate due to a cooperative arrangement between the two countries.

About two-thirds of the sample meet only one factor and about 10 percent do not meet simplicity index factor at all. Scores of the indicator do not differ significantly across regions or country income levels.

About 82 percent of the sample had an aggregate breakdown for the revenue forecasts using revenue types. Fifty-nine percent published historical data using past revenues. A summary of macroeconomic assumptions was used in 60 percent of the sample. A few countries (18 percent) provided only some analytical work such as a summary of past forecasts and 20 percent decomposition the forecasts into their various effects. Interestingly, these countries are not high-income states and thus there is no significant income or regional variation for them. Because Morocco did not publish its forecasts, it scored low on this index.

Table 26.2 reports the agencies in the sample that used macroeconomic forecasts. Most (55.8 percent) used one agency. Including Morocco, 29.4 percent of the sample countries used two agencies and 14.8 percent used three or more agencies.

Table 26.2 Agencies Involved in Macroeconomic Forecasting

	Simple Agency	*Two Agencies*	*Three and More Agencies*
Survey (percent)	55.8	29.4	14.8
Ministry of finances	29.3		
Ministry of economy	20.5		
Others	10.5		

Source: Kyobe and Danninger 2005, 9. With permission.

Determinants of Forecasting Practices

Kyobe and Danninger's (2005) research points out the factors that influence revenue forecasting practices. Thus, by knowing these factors, one can make reasonable comment on the quality for revenue forecasting in particular countries. Kyobe and Danninger (2005) identified the following country characteristics that were essential for good revenue forecasting: the level of corruption in the country (using the [Kaufmann and Massimo, 2003] country corruption index); the size of government measured by expenditures related to GDP; per capita GDP; and population size. They used a linear and convex functional form of the independent variables or indices to run their linear regression. They argued that the change in the independent variables allowed for more robust significant findings.

Table 26.3 represents their findings. There is a negative relationship between country corruption and the level of transparency. Thus, corruption does have a negative effect on transparency that is consistent with an expected impact on accountability. In addition, there is a negative impact on formality and simplicity. The per capita income was positive, however, there was no significant relationship for all the three variables. The three factors looked at are the size of the central government, the position of fiscal and debt sustainability measured by central government, and the interest expenditure to GDP. Each was slightly negative but

Table 26.3 Characteristics of the Revenue Forecasting Process

	Formality	*Simplicity*	*Transparency*
Log population	0.279	−0.184	0.486
Log GDP	0.231	−0.004	0.135
Corrupt 1	−0.0287	−0.0327	−0.0673
Constant	−1.327	2.764	−2.911
Observations	28	33	31
R^2	0.06	0.09	0.36
Log population	0.052	−0.218	0.440
Log GDP/population	0.421	0.072	0.306
Expenditure/GDP	−0.069	0.003	0.000
Constant	0.549	2.240	−4.101
Observations	24	28	26
R^2	0.14	0.08	0.32
Log population	0.381	−0.230	0.409
Log GDP/population	0.437	0.053	0.296
IMF ten years	1.848	−0.078	0.077
Constant	−4.813	2.594	−3.837
Observations	29	34	32
R^2	0.21	0.06	0.32

Source: Kyobe and Danninger 2005, 11. With permission.

Table 26.4 GDP Growth Rate

Year	*GDP/Growth Rate*
2001	6.3
2002	3.2
2003	5.5
2004	4.2
2005	1.8
2006	5.4
Average	4.4

Source: Ministry of Finances, www.finances.gov.ma, 2007. With permission.

they were not statistically significant. Thus, larger governments do not mean that they are more accountable in the budget process. The three variables or indices used by the authors were regressed against per capita, corruption, the size of government to explore whether there is a correlation trying to detect the impact of such variables on forecasting practices.

Where does Morocco fit into this type of analysis? Table 26.4 shows the variation in GDP over a six-year period in Morocco. The fluctuation of growth is very unsteady. This confirms the forecasting challenge for a country like Morocco. Only better technical skills and the necessary expertise will improve forecasting under these circumstances.

International organizations such as the IMF have an impact on a country's forecasting practices. Systematic IMF involvement in a country does impact the design of revenue forecasting practices because technical assistance and structural fiscal reforms occur due to IMF actions (Center on Budget and Policy Priorities [CBPP] 2005). Thus, if conditions that influence revenues and expenditures program changes, then any related forecasts must also change. To gauge this IMF effect and determine other factors that might influence changes in forecasts, regressions were run on the three indexes. This is done by measuring the number of years a country has been under an IMF program during the past five and ten years, respectively. To do this, a series of ordinary least squares (OLS) regressions were applied to the three indexes (formality, simplicity, and transparency) while controlling the size of the population, GDP per capita, size of government, and level of corruption.

The results show some statistical evidence of the effect of the IMF involvement variable and formality. Thus, tentatively, countries with long IMF involvement have more formalized forecasting processes. Interestingly, neither transparency nor simplicity is affected by the IMF engagement. Although, one must exercise caution when applying and replicating these results to the situation in Morocco, the identified similarities between Morocco and the countries surveyed suggest that the generalization also applies to Morocco.

What is the revenue and expenditure situation in Morocco? Table 26.5 uses data from the Web site of the Moroccan Ministry of Finance for the years 2002–2007. Table 26.5 shows the difference from one year to another based on the discrepancies of finances reported by the government. Although the documents do not provide any information on procedures and econometric models, the figures do provide indirect indicators that can be used to compute the revenue and expenditure variations between the projected and observed data. The annual reports show the deficiencies of the projected figures. The percentages vary from both under- or overestimated revenues and expenditures. Because the Moroccan economy relies heavily on agricultural products, the reason for the differences only

Table 26.5 Trend of Statistical Data on Revenues and Expenditures

Year	*Sources*	*Revenues*	*Expenditures*	*Difference (Revenues)*
	Source 1			
2004	2002	95529	108055	
	2003	106158	114187	0.51
	2004	113047	123421	1.32
	2005:LF	118894	125769	2.75
	2005:LFA	122166	138985	
	2006:P	128573	135021	
	Source 2			
2005	2001	116044	110576	
	2002	95529	108055	
	2003	105613	114932	
	2004:LF	111550	116729	
	2004:LFA	109443	118880	
	2005:P	117562	126882	–1.12
	Source 3			
2006	2002	95529	108055	
	2003	106158	114187	
	2004	113047	123421	
	2005:LF	118894	125769	
	2005:LFA	122166	138985	
	2006:P	128573	135021	
	Source 4			
2007	2003	101583	118203	4.31
	2004	108647	126501	3.89
	2005	121641	146823	
	2006:LF	121876	138981	–5.49
	2006:LFA	128769	143320	
	2007:P	131896	149993	

Note: LF = Law of Finances; LFA = Adjusted LF; P = Projections

involves varying weather patterns. The reports also portray the international impact on the Moroccan economy.

Table 26.5 helps one understand the reasons behind the accuracy or inaccuracy in forecasting revenues and expenditures. The statistical data shows the discrepancies in the information. In addition, the data shows the differences between the projected budget, current budget, and adjusted budget.

Column two in Table 26.5 shows the year of the document from which the data was compiled. The differences in the last column concern only the revenues. The expenditures show that the forecasts reflect evidence of an unbalanced budget. Given the facts presented in Table 26.5, the case for more transparency and formality in budgeting exists for emerging countries in general and Morocco in particular.

Transparency

In 2006, the CBPP conducted a 122 multiple-choice survey of 59 countries, including Morocco, to assess the availability of the data that would allow government transparency and financial accountability to exist. Table 26.1 presents the key findings in succinct fashion. Essentially, the column on the left identifies the key indicators that need to exist if there is transparency and financial accountability. The column on the right represents how many of the 59 countries have these indicators. Note that 39 percent of the 59 countries provided either minimal or scant to none of the critical information that makes transparency and financial accountability possible. Of these, ten (Angola, Bolivia, Burkina, Faso, Chad, Egypt, Mongolia, Morocco, Nicaragua, Nigeria, and Vietnam) were at the very bottom. Four countries (Bolivia, Morocco, Nicaragua, and Nigeria) do make their proposed budget publicly available before adoption, but they provide only minimal information to the public (Center on Budget and Policy Priorities [CBPP] 2005).

In addition, the survey noted that the majority of countries, including Morocco, performed very poorly in terms of budget transparency. The level of transparency in a country is due to the willingness of the government to be accountable to its citizenry, and the lack of capacity to produce the data is not an overriding constraint. In other words, a lack of performance on open budget index is not a matter of capacity to gather or report the information. In addition, providing this information can be accomplished in a short period of time with a modest use of resources. Thus, these reforms can easily be done and they should lead to an increase in the accuracy of the revenue and expenditure forecasts.

The CBPP emphasized the importance of having an independent audit institution, which is often called the Auditor General Office or Court of Accounts. They noted that 17 countries do not issue audit reports to the public. Only 25 countries make partial information available to the public. Sixteen countries permit the chief executive of the country to fire the head of the audit agency without separation of power curbs by the legislature or judiciary. Thus, each has no independent audit agencies. Morocco is among this group.

Conclusion and Recommendations

This chapter explored the forecasting practices of Morocco. The assessment of forecasting practices helps to better understand the different limitations in the country's budget system. They are

- The macroeconomic models and the associated technical support are limited to only those provided by the French Ministry of Finance.
- There is a lack of harmony in the forecasting processes in the country.
- The fact that agriculture sector is key to forecasting means accurate growth in revenue is highly influenced by yearly weather variations.
- The World Bank suggests that there is room for improvement in forecasting and these improvements need to be addressed.
- A more rigorous and public forecasting methodology using clear models are needed, which include providing the public information on the econometric models used.
- Weak institutional capacities are among the reasons for overstating forecasts in developing countries, including Morocco.
- Morocco should be wise to improve the factors of formality, transparency, and simplicity.

This chapter examined Moroccan forecasting practices within the limitation of existing information. Clearly, forecasting, under the conditions of being an emerging nation, confounds forecasting practices. Although developing accurate forecasts are more difficult under these conditions, Morocco can improve forecasting by improving its budget transparency and strengthening its budget accountability. This can only happen when key players in the policy process—namely the government and the citizens—embrace the concepts of formality, simplicity, and transparency.

References

Aaron, H. J. 2000. Presidential Address: Seeing Through the Fog: Policymaking with Uncertain Forecasts. *Journal of policy Analysis and Management* 19(2): 193–206.

Abate, B. 2004. *The Budget Reform and the Expectations from the New Public Management.* Morocco: General Treasury Department, Ministry of Public Finances, September (1). www.finances.gov (09/16/2006).

Abed, G. T. 1998. Fiscal Reforms in Low Income Countries: Experience Under IMF Supported Programs, IMF Occasional Paper n° 160. Washington: IMF.

African Development Bank. 2004. Public Administration Reform Support Program Country. Operation Department North, East and South Regions. ONCB African Development Bank.

Ansoff, I. I. 1965. *Corporate Strategy*. City Published: McGraw-Hill, New York.

Bernoussi, M. 1994. *Moroccan Public Finance between Law and Edification of a Modern State*.

Center on Budget and Policy Priorities (CBPP). 2005. Open Budget Questionnaire. Washington. www.cbpp.org. (03/06/07).

Cherkaoui, M. 2002. *Institutional Reform and Efficiency of the Budget Process: The Case of Morocco*. Department of Economics, University Mohamed V, School of Judicial Sciences, Economics, and Social Sciences, Rabat, Agdal.

Danninger, S., A. Kyobe, and M. Cangiano. 2004. The Political Economy of Revenue-Forecasting Experience from Low-Income Countries, forthcoming IMF Working Paper (Washington: International Monetary Fund). Fiscal Affairs Department.

Elarafi, H. 2006. *State Public Finance Management: Budget, Accounting, and Treasury*. Morocco: Rejjes Edition.

Eltony, N. M. 2002. *Measuring Tax Effort in Arab Countries*. City Published: Arab Planning Institute, Kuwait.

Galbraith, J. K. 1987. *A History of Economics*. Harmondsworth: Penguin Books.

Harakat, M. 2006. Public Finances and Budget Law, 3rd Edition. In El. Maarif and Al. J. Rabat.

High Commission of Planning 2007. www.hcp.ma.

International Monetary Fund (IMF). 2004. Morocco Selected Issues. Country Report Number 04/164, International Monetary Fund, June.

International Monetary Fund (IMF). 2005. Morocco: Report on Observance of Standards and Codes IMF. Country Report Number 05/298, International Monetary Fund, July.

Kaufman, D., and M. Massimo. 2003. Governance Matters III: Governance Indicators for 1996–2002. World Bank Policy Research Paper 3106. Washington: World Bank.

Kyobe, A., and S. Danninger. 2005. Revenue Forecasting—How is it done? Results from a Survey of Low-Income Countries. IMF Working Paper (Washington: International Monetary Fund). Fiscal Affairs Department.

Lienert, I. C. and F. Sarraf. 2001. Systemic Weaknesses of Budget Management in Anglophone Africa. IMF Working Paper 01/211, Washington: International Monetary Fund.

Marchal, R. 1931. *Precis of Moroccan Legislation*. 5 La Somme Street: Edition chez l'auteur.

Ministry of Finances. 1999. Processes of Budget Preparation and Adoption of the Budget de document interne du Ministère des Finances. www.finances.gov.ma (07/08/2006).

Penner, R. 2001. *Errors in Budget Forecasting*. Washington: Urban Institute.

Porter, M. E. 1980. *Competitive Advantage: Creating and Sustaining Superior Performance*. New York: The Free Press.

Primack, M. L., J. F. Willis, and K. Choudhury. 1996. *Economics for Managers*. City Published: Cat Pub Co., California.

World Bank Report. 2003. *Appraisal of the Public Finance Management System*. City Published: The World Bank, Washington, June.

Zemrani, B. A. 1998. *Finances of the State in Morocco Volume I Financial Policy and Budgeting Law*. l'Harmattan, Paris.

Index

A

B

D

E

F

G

H

J

K

L

M

N

S

U

www.ingramcontent.com/pod-product-compliance
Lightning Source LLC
Chambersburg PA
CBHW071529300325
24315CB00003B/251
9781420045826